Truth on Trial

TRUTH ON TRIAL

The Lawsuit Motif in the Fourth Gospel

ANDREW T. LINCOLN

HENDRICKSON PUBLISHERS

Copyright © 2000 Hendrickson Publishers, Inc.
P.O. Box 3473
Peabody, Massachusetts 01961-3473

ISBN 1-56563-282-6

Printed in the United States of America

First printing — November 2000

Library of Congress Cataloging-in-Publication Data

Lincoln, Andrew T.
    Truth on trial: the lawsuit motif in John's Gospel / Andrew T. Lincoln.
        p. cm.
    Includes bibliographical references.
    ISBN 1-56563-282-6 (hardcover)
    1. Bible. N.T. John—Criticism, interpretation, etc. 2. Jesus Christ—
Trial. I. Title.

BS2615.2 .L49 2000
226.5'06—dc21
                                                                00-050536

To Carol

*In appreciation of all she has been and done
during the completion of this project*

TABLE OF CONTENTS

ABBREVIATIONS

General

C.E.	Common Era
ch.	chapter
ed(s).	edited by, editor(s)
lit.	literally
LXX	Septuagint
n(n).	note(s)
NAB	New American Bible
NIV	New International Version
NJB	New Jerusalem Bible
NRSV	New Revised Standard Version
NT	New Testament
OT	Old Testament
REB	Revised English Bible
RSV	Revised Standard Version
sec.	section
v(v).	verse(s)
vol(s).	volume(s)

Publications

BAGD	W. Bauer, W. F. Arndt, F. W. Gingrich, and F. W. Danker. *Greek-English Lexicon of the New Testament and Other Early Christian Literature.* 2d ed. Chicago, 1979
BibInt	*Biblical Interpretation*
BTB	*Biblical Theology Bulletin*
BZ	*Biblische Zeitschrift*

CBQ	*Catholic Biblical Quarterly*
ExpTim	*Expository Times*
HBT	*Horizons in Biblical Theology*
Int	*Interpretation*
JBL	*Journal of Biblical Literature*
JES	*Journal of Ecumenical Studies*
JR	*Journal of Religion*
JSNT	*Journal for the Study of the New Testament*
JTS	*Journal of Theological Studies*
NIB	*The New Interpreter's Bible*
SNTS	Society for New Testament Studies
TB	*Tyndale Bulletin*
VT	*Vetus Testamentum*
ZNW	*Zeitschrift für die neutestamentiche Wissenschaft und die Kunde der älteren Kirche*
ZThK	*Zeitschrift für Theologie und Kirche*

Hebrew Bible/Old Testament

Dan	Daniel
Deut	Deuteronomy
Exod	Exodus
Ezek	Ezekiel
Gen	Genesis
Hab	Habakkuk
Hos	Hosea
Isa	Isaiah
Jer	Jeremiah
Josh	Joshua
Lev	Leviticus
Mic	Micah
Neh	Nehemiah
Num	Numbers
Ps(s)	Psalm(s)
Zech	Zechariah
Judg	Judges
1 Sam	1 Samuel

New Testament

1 Tim	1 Timothy
Gal	Galatians
Matt	Matthew
Rev	Revelation

Rom	Romans
Eph	Ephesians
1 Cor	1 Corinthians
1, 2 Jn	1, 2 John

Apocrypha and Septuagint

1, 2 Esd	1–2 Esdras
1, 3 Macc	1, 3 Maccabees
Sir	Sirach/Ecclesiasticus
Wis	Wisdom of Solomon

Old Testament Pseudepigrapha

As. Mos.	*Assumption of Moses*
Jub.	*Jubilees*
T. Dan	*Testament of Dan*
T. Jud.	*Testament of Judah*
T. Levi	*Testament of Levi*
T. Mos.	*Testament of Moses*

Dead Sea Scrolls and Related Texts

CD	Cairo Genizah copy of the *Damascus Document*
1QS	*Rule of the Community*

Mishnah, Talmud, and Related Literature

b.	Babylonian version of Talmud
m.	tractate of the Mishnah
t.	tractate of the Tosefta
B. Meṣiᶜa	*Baba Meṣiᶜa*
Ber.	*Berakot*
Ḥul.	*Hullin*
Ketub.	*Ketubbot*
Qidd.	*Qiddušin*
Sanh.	*Sanhedrin*
Yebam.	*Yebamot*

Targumic Texts

Tg. Ps.-J.	*Targum Pseudo-Jonathan*

Other Rabbinic Works

Exod. Rab.	*Exodus Rabbah*
ʾAbot R. Nat.	*ʾAbot de Rabbi Nathan*
Num. Rab.	*Numbers Rabbah*

Apostolic Fathers

Barn.	*Barnabas*
1 Clem.	*1 Clement*

New Testament Apocrypha and Pseudepigrapha

Acts Pet.	*Acts of Peter*
Gos. Pet.	*Gospel of Peter*
Ps.-Clem.	*Pseudo-Clementines*

Early Christian Writers

Eusebius
Hier.	*Contra Hieroclem*
Hist. eccl.	*Historia ecclesiastica*

Jerome
Epist.	*Epistulae*
Pelag.	*Adversus Pelagianos*

Justin
1 Apol.	*Apologia i*
Dial.	*Dialogus cum Tryphone*

Lucian
Hist. conscr.	*Quomodo historia conscribenda sit*

Quintilian
Inst.	*Institutio oratoria*

Tertullian
Scorp.	*Scorpiace*

Philo

Mut.	*De mutatione nominum*
Spec.	*De specialibus legibus*

Josephus

Ant.	*Jewish Antiquities*

Other Ancient Writers

Aristotle
  Poet.   *Poetica*
  Rhet.   *Rhetorica*
Cicero
  De or.   *De oratore*
  Inv.   *De inventione rhetorica*
  Leg.   *De legibus*
Lucian
  Hist. conscr. *Quomodo historia conscribenda sit*
Pliny the Younger
  Ep. Tra.   *Epistulae ad Trajanum*
Suetonius
  Dom.   *Domitianus*
Thucydides
  Hist.   *History of the Peloponnesian War*

INTRODUCTION

Trials of Truth: Then and Now

Truth in matters of religion and meaning has always been in dispute. Yet there are some times and some places in which claims about truth are more intensely debated, are indeed put on trial. In the first century C.E. the rapid spread of the early Christians with their claims about Jesus produced considerable ferment, but of all the documents in the NT reflecting this missionary expansion and the tensions and disputes it generated between the Christian groups and their surrounding society, only one explicitly and consistently formulates such conflict in terms of a dispute about truth. Probably late in the first century and from a locality that it is impossible to determine with certainty, a Gospel was produced that depicts its protagonist, Jesus, claiming not only to witness to the truth but also to be the truth, that presents his conflict with his opponents in terms of fiercely polemical disputes about who is speaking the truth, and that has the Roman official at his trial asking, "What is truth?" For the author of the Gospel of John and the Christian community of which he was a part, belief in Jesus had resulted in a crisis of truth with profound religious, personal, and social consequences.

At the end of the twentieth century in the Western world, pluralism and postmodernism have radically called into question traditional notions of truth. Whether there is any such thing as truth outside the formal logical structure of propositions and whether, even if there is, humans can have any knowledge of such truth would be disputed by many. Christian truth claims, which already appear to be relativized by the competing claims of other world religions, are dismissed altogether by many who share the postmodern perspective on the collapse of confidence in either rationality or the imagination to gain access to truth and therefore its "incredulity toward metanarratives."[1] Truth is again on trial, with renewed intensity and critical consequences.[2]

To link reflection on contemporary issues of fundamental concern with a study of the Fourth Gospel may well seem to some not only an overly bold but also a foolish move, one that transgresses the proper boundaries of NT study and confuses categories by mixing historical, theological, and philosophical questions. Feminist and political readings of the NT have already and rightly called into question the validity of the conception of NT study as a purely historical enterprise, but it is still not common to find among the variety of reader responses those willing to concede they have explicit Christian theological interests at work in their reading.[3] In some circles, to admit such interests opens one to the charge of being "uncritical." To be critical is defined in terms of operating from outside the ideology of a text, and thus to be committed in any way to the claims of a sacred text is said to preclude one from the proper detachment required of critical scholarship. In this view, therefore, to study the Bible in a university or academic setting committed to critical ideals means a willingness to exclude from one's study any influence of prior confessional commitments.

Needless to say, this is a view that I do not share and that appears to me to be entangled in confusion. On the one hand, it appears still to be operating with the modern concept of the autonomy of critical reason, stemming from the Enlightenment, which many hold now to be discredited;[4] on the other, it frequently concedes in practice, with postmodernism, that criticism of texts cannot be in the business of discovering single meanings and that a plurality of meanings and approaches is inevitable. Marxist, feminist, and liberal humanist stances

---

[1] J.-F. Lyotard, *The Postmodern Condition: A Report on Knowledge* (trans. G. Bennington and B. Massumi; Minneapolis: University of Minnesota Press, 1984), xxiv.

[2] For an insightful Christian attempt to address this situation, see J. R. Middleton and B. J. Walsh, *Truth Is Stranger Than It Used to Be: Biblical Faith in a Postmodern Age* (Downers Grove, Ill.: InterVarsity, 1995).

[3] But see esp. F. Watson's major attempts to show the validity of an explicitly Christian theological approach as part of biblical studies in *Text, Church, and World* (Grand Rapids: Eerdmans, 1994); and *Text and Truth* (Grand Rapids: Eerdmans, 1997).

[4] Cf., e.g., A. MacIntyre, *Whose Justice? Which Rationality?* (Notre Dame: University of Notre Dame Press, 1988).

are acceptable contributors to this plurality because they operate from a standpoint outside the text, but the major approach this critical pluralism frequently cannot tolerate is a self-consciously Christian theological one. This view also tends to tar all Christian interest in the truth claims of the Bible with the brush of fundamentalism, recognizing neither the variety in Christian theological approaches to the Bible nor the fact that it is perfectly possible for Christians to distance themselves from some aspects of a text's ideology while affirming others, to wish to engage both in criticism and in appropriation. When insisted upon, this view would lead to the extremely strange situation that the one person to be excluded from critical study of the Bible in the academy is the person who still thinks the Bible is worth studying because it has something to say and who wishes to relate this conviction to his or her actual practice of criticism. Contemporary biblical scholarship may, then, provide one arena in which the trial of truth is being played out.

Even if one is not prepared to exclude theological reflection upon texts on these sorts of grounds, one might still think at least that the tasks of exegesis and theology are better kept separate. While these tasks might, in the traditional model of biblical interpretation, be distinguished—the former aimed at explaining, as best one can, the likely communication the text represented for its original readers, the latter aimed at interacting with the text's message for the sake of insight into God, the human condition, and life in the world—it is also clear that, even in this construal of their division, the two tasks are by no means totally separable. The methods employed, and therefore the results produced, in the attempt to treat the text as far as possible in its own terms still derive not simply from the text itself or its ancient context but from the very different and constantly changing world of present-day scholarship. They are not value-neutral but themselves influenced by a variety of worldviews with theological implications. Any attempted reading of an ancient text cannot be complete. Its selective focus and its mode of presentation reflect conscious and unconscious choices on the part of the interpreter, and not a few of these will be shaped by theological interests in the broadest sense of the term *theological*.

From within the discipline of NT studies, it may be thought that study of the Fourth Gospel is unpromising territory for relating the concerns of the text to much broader theological concerns. Although the latter may have been an earlier fashion in treatments of John's Gospel, more recent historical-critical treatments, it might be suggested, have rendered such an approach problematic. After all, although the text, on the surface, deals with issues of truth, it does so on its own terms, and these terms have increasingly been thought to be those of a sectarian group on the edges of developments in the early Christian movement.[5] In other words, it is held that the results of the attempt to read John in its original context have made it very difficult to see its message as transferable beyond that specific and limited context. This is indeed an important issue for any theological interpretation of John that also wishes to take seriously its historical setting and impact.[6] Whether it constitutes an insuperable obstacle is another matter and will be the subject of part of our later discussion.

So far I have mentioned a number of possible objections to the sort of study I propose. These have been primarily methodological, though involving deeper hermeneutical issues. A simpler objection to a study of the trial motif in the Fourth Gospel might be the impression on the part of some students of this Gospel that its forensic aspects have already been well worked over. So before sketching what I would like to explore, it is well to ask what exactly has already been undertaken in this area.

The Trial Motif in Scholarship on the Fourth Gospel

It has long been recognized that the themes of witness, judgment, and trial play a significant role in the Fourth Gospel. Commentaries on the Gospel frequently draw attention to these themes in passing, and from time to time articles have appeared that deal with particular passages in relation to one or other aspect. Interest in the themes seems to have been at its height in the sixties and early seventies and is reflected in the appearance of a number of monographs written largely independently of each other.

In "Justification in Johannine Thought," first published in French in 1946 and appearing in English in 1957, Théo Preiss drew attention to what he believed to be the strangely neglected juridical aspect of Johannine thought.[7] This neglect was soon remedied. In *Krisis,* published in 1964, the German scholar Josef Blank related the theme of

---

[5] An article by W. Meeks has been particularly influential in this regard: "The Man from Heaven in Johannine Sectarianism," *JBL* 91 (1972): 44–72; repr. in *The Interpretation of John* (ed. J. Ashton; London: SPCK, 1986), 141–73.

[6] D. Rensberger, *Johannine Faith and Liberating Community* (Philadelphia: Westminster, 1988), 135–52, grapples with this issue.

[7] T. Preiss, in *Hommage et reconnaissance à K. Barth* (Neuchâtel: Delachaux & Niestle, 1946), 100–118; ET "Justification in Johannine Thought," in T. Preiss, *Life in Christ* (London: SCM, 1957), 9–31.

judgment to the Gospel's eschatology and Christology.[8] James Montgomery Boice completed a doctoral dissertation in 1966 at the University of Basel on the idea of witness in John, relating the idea particularly to the Gospel's theology of revelation, and in 1970 a revised form of his study, which shows no awareness of Blank's work, appeared as *Witness and Revelation in the Gospel of John*.[9] The year 1972 saw the publication in Germany of *Martyria*, a tradition-historical investigation by Johannes Beutler of the witness theme in both the Gospel and the First Epistle of John.[10] Beutler interacts very briefly with both Blank and Boice.

Severino Pancaro's comprehensive study, *The Law in the Fourth Gospel*, published in 1975, acknowledges the work of Blank but deals with an aspect omitted by him, focusing on the law's role in the Jews' judgment of Jesus.[11] Anthony Harvey's monograph on the Fourth Gospel, *Jesus on Trial*, appeared in 1976 and, with the exception of a couple of passing mentions of Beutler's work, appears to have been written without reference to any previous studies of the topic.[12] In 1977 Allison Trites produced a broader work, the revision of an earlier doctoral dissertation completed in 1968 at the University of Oxford, *The New Testament Concept of Witness*, the longest chapter of which is "The Concept of Witness in the Fourth Gospel."[13] Not surprisingly, Trites was unaware of Pancaro's or Harvey's work, but he makes no mention of Blank and notes, significantly, that Beutler's study appeared too late for his consideration.[14] Seven years later came an interesting book by Paul Minear, *John: The Martyr's Gospel*, which reads a number of passages in the Gospel as messages from Jesus the victorious martyr through a prophet to potential martyrs among first the charismatic leaders and then the ordinary believers who constituted its original readers.[15] Although some of his main assumptions depend on the case to be made in this study, he does not make the case but rather intuits it,[16] and again shows no awareness of any of the scholarship on the theme of witness. Most recently,

---

[8] J. Blank, *Krisis: Untersuchungen zur johanneischen Christologie und Eschatologie* (Freiburg: Lambertus, 1964).

[9] J. M. Boice, *Witness and Revelation in the Gospel of John* (Grand Rapids: Zondervan, 1970).

[10] J. Beutler, *Martyria* (Frankfurt: J. Knecht, 1972).

[11] S. Pancaro, *The Law in the Fourth Gospel* (Leiden: E. J. Brill, 1975).

[12] A. E. Harvey, *Jesus on Trial* (London: SPCK, 1976).

[13] A. A. Trites, *The New Testament Concept of Witness* (Cambridge: Cambridge University Press, 1977).

[14] Ibid., 126, n. 2.

[15] P. Minear, *John: The Martyr's Gospel* (New York: Pilgrim, 1984).

[16] Ibid., xii–xiii.

Robert Maccini in the published version of a dissertation completed at the University of Aberdeen in 1994, *Her Testimony Is True*, reviews some of the material on the trial motif in his first main chapter, looking mainly at the forensic vocabulary, before pursuing in the bulk of his work an investigation of the primarily historical question of how the testimonies of women, as presented in the Fourth Gospel, would have been perceived by a first-century Jewish readership.[17]

Taking Another Look

With all these previous studies, not to mention the articles and essays listed in the bibliography, what is the justification for another monograph dealing with the trial motif? One answer is that these studies have, for the most part, dealt in a detailed fashion with only some aspects of the overall motif and from a particular angle of interest. Blank and Harvey, for example, have no discussion of Jesus' Roman trial, although Blank earlier wrote an article on this section of the Gospel.[18] Beutler's concern is more with the underlying tradition history of the language and concept of witness than with their function in the theology of the Gospel as we now have it. Blank and Boice, on the other hand, are mainly interested in how the concepts of judgment and witness serve what they consider to be the larger theological ideas of eschatology, Christology, and revelation. Pancaro's specific interest is the function of the law in the trial settings. Harvey recognizes that the motif is a literary one, but his primary interest is to exploit it for its potential illumination of the historical Jesus' setting within the Judaism of the time. Maccini is primarily interested in the role of women's testimony in the Gospel and the first century. There is certainly room, therefore, for a work that wishes to highlight and make accessible to general readers of the Fourth Gospel what is still for many a neglected major theme, and that attempts in the process to draw together and build on some of the findings of these earlier studies, done mostly in isolation from each other.

But a much more compelling justification, and one of the primary motivations for this monograph, is that since these earlier works (with the exception of Maccini's) were written, study of the NT, and therefore also of the Fourth Gospel, has undergone radical changes. In particular,

---

[17] R. G. Maccini, *Her Testimony Is True: Women as Witnesses according to John* (Sheffield: Sheffield Academic Press, 1996), esp. 32–62.

[18] J. Blank, "Die Verhandlung vor Pilatus: Joh 18,28–19,16 im Lichte johanneischer Theologie," *BZ* 3 (1959): 60–81.

literary and sociological investigations have come into their own and shed new light on the NT texts. In regard to John, Meeks in "The Man from Heaven in Johannine Sectarianism,"[19] Martyn in *History and Theology in the Fourth Gospel,*[20] and Brown in *The Community of the Beloved Disciple*[21] sparked new interest in what could be discovered about the history and social setting of the community from which the Gospel emerged, while studies such as Culpepper's *Anatomy of the Fourth Gospel*[22] and Stibbe's *John as Storyteller*[23] mark the more literary approach. I am convinced both that these recent approaches can be fruitfully brought to bear on the trial motif and that study of this motif can contribute to the issues surrounding the application of such approaches to the Fourth Gospel. If the three main types of investigation of the NT can be said to be the literary, the historical (including the sociological), and the ideological or theological, then in regard to the Fourth Gospel, the trial motif is peculiarly appropriate as a meeting place of all three. Indeed, the other major justification and motivation for a fresh study is the attempt to incorporate a critical appropriation of the trial motif for contemporary concerns, a project that does not constitute part of the earlier studies. The goal, then, is to produce a more wide-ranging exploration of the trial motif than has previously been undertaken and to employ a variety of perspectives. I am not claiming that this amounts to a more integrated approach. Such a position might suggest that there is some necessary unity among the perspectives. Instead I propose to look at the topic from a number of different angles and claim only that these are by no means incompatible and may indeed be mutually illuminating.

Although literary approaches to the Bible have moved beyond narrative and reader-response criticisms to poststructuralist, deconstructive, and ideological criticisms, the resources of these earlier approaches, which I shall be primarily employing, for illumination of the text have not yet been exhausted.[24] Of the literary, historical, and theological, the

---

[19] Meeks, "The Man from Heaven."

[20] J. L. Martyn, *History and Theology in the Fourth Gospel* (New York: Harper & Row, 1968; 2d ed. Nashville: Abingdon, 1979).

[21] R. E. Brown, *The Community of the Beloved Disciple* (New York: Paulist, 1979).

[22] R. A. Culpepper, *Anatomy of the Fourth Gospel* (Philadelphia: Fortress, 1983).

[23] M. W. G. Stibbe, *John as Storyteller* (Cambridge: Cambridge University Press, 1992).

[24] See, for a recent example of further exploration in this area, D. Tovey, *Narrative Art and Act in the Fourth Gospel* (Sheffield: Sheffield Academic Press, 1997).

literary task is primary, as the investigation of what the text says and how it works both within itself and in relation to its readers is essential for questions of the text's meaning. Only when conclusions have been formed at this level, however tentative they may be, is it possible to employ the text properly as a resource for enquiries into the world behind the text; then the text will provide historical evidence, first and foremost, for the time of its writer and readers, and conclusions are likely to be even more tentative.[25] The literary task is also crucial for entering what has become known as the world in front of the text, for engaging in critical theological appropriation of the text's message.

These observations set the agenda for the present study. Its initial focus, that of the first four chapters, will be on providing and explaining a literary reading of John in the light of the trial motif, employing mainly narrative critical and reader-response approaches and exploring the interplay between this text and previous texts of Scripture. After chapter 1's introduction to the overall narrative and to the lawsuit motif, chapter 2 tackles the broader literary question of the relation of this motif to the Jewish Scriptures. Some have taken to calling such a treatment "intertextuality," but this term, with its roots in poststructuralism, is not really appropriate for my interests. I look not just to exploit the interplay between texts regardless of their chronological relations or of whether the texts involved would have been known to first-century readers; rather, my aim is to take account also of genetic relationships and evidence of influence and dependence between the Gospel of John and earlier texts. It is insufficient simply to work with an overall analysis of the narrative and a discussion of isolated aspects of the lawsuit motif. So, after investigation of the scriptural background, chapter 3 provides some close readings of passages that reflect the main stages of the development of the motif in the light of this background. This gives a more detailed exegetical base from which to pursue further literary questions in chapter 4 and then to explore in chapter 5 the theological point of view that informs the trial motif. Although the various aspects of John's theology have been well worked over by others, viewing them through the lens of

---

[25] I disagree therefore with, e.g., Maccini, *Her Testimony Is True,* 17, who wishes to treat the Gospel's narrative as, first of all, a window onto the events in the life of Jesus. I do not hold that the Gospel cannot be treated in this way. But this is not the first historical setting for which the narrative provides evidence, and conclusions about the life of Jesus cannot be read off the surface of the narrative but can only be reached after rigorous historical analysis of the traditions that it incorporates.

the lawsuit motif not only provides a different angle of vision but also sheds fresh light and, particularly in some cases, makes an appreciable difference to the way in which one formulates the Gospel's theology.

Having come this far, we will now be in a better position to ask more directly historical and social questions about other catalysts for the evangelist's employment of the overarching trial motif. Chapter 6 therefore asks what factors, in the experience of the community from which the Gospel emerged, might shed light on why the trial metaphor was found appropriate; what social implications of such experience might help to explain, and be reflected in, the prominence (in addition to such notions as truth and judgment) of the value of glory or honor in the lawsuit; and which earlier Christian traditions relating to the trial motif may have been known, taken up, and reworked in the Fourth Gospel.

Any attempt to hold a conversation with this Gospel, in which our topic is appropriated for contemporary interests, raises a variety of issues. The final part of this volume addresses a number of these. Chapter 7 sketches how the trial as a metaphor for life still resonates in a number of ways in Western culture and literature, and points up the deeply disturbing irony that the major example of witness literature in our time comes from a group of twentieth-century Jews, survivors of the Holocaust and others, testifying to an event in which Christians and, in some measure, the history of Christians' interpretation of this Gospel are implicated. Given the way in which this Gospel's extensive reworking of traditions in order to tell the story of Jesus in terms of a cosmic lawsuit served the needs of the, at one time, marginalized group of Christians from which it emerged, and given that later, when the power ratio was reversed, the formulations of its truth claims were capable of serving as violent weapons against a marginalized Judaism, clearly a hermeneutic of suspicion, as well as one of retrieval, is required. This terminology derives from the work of Paul Ricoeur, who is also significant for this project because of his reflections on the biblical lawsuit motif in "The Hermeneutics of Testimony."[26] An exposition and critique of this essay, indicating its potential for facilitating contemporary appropriation of the lawsuit motif, forms the second part of chapter 7.

Chapter 8 raises some further matters that need to be addressed as part of this appropriation. First, there is a basic question: In the context of contemporary views of human freedom and knowledge, is it possible to repeat this Gospel's call for an acceptance of its perspective simply on

---

[26] Paul Ricoeur, "The Hermeneutics of Testimony," in P. Ricoeur, *Essays on Biblical Interpretation* (Philadelphia: Fortress, 1980), 119–54.

the basis of its own testimony? What is the relation between believing a testimony and exercising critical and indeed suspicious judgment? Three more specific questions are then explored: Having observed the evangelist's extensive reworking of the tradition in order to provide the emplotment of a cosmic trial, in what sense can one claim this sort of narrative to be true? What can be said about the truth of a narrative that can be charged with anti-Judaism in its depiction of the opposition in the trial? Finally, are this aspect of the cosmic trial and its history of interpretation consequences of the motif, with its grand claims to truth constituting a metanarrative that is inescapably marginalizing, oppressive, and violent; or are there elements in this narrative that are meant to subvert any such function?

Chapter 9 offers reflections on what it might mean to take seriously in our world just a few of the major elements of John's version of the cosmic trial, granted that those who wish to do so are shaped both by their religious texts and by their particular ecclesial and cultural locations. What might be the value of the theological retrieval of this metaphor about a trial that is meant to produce life and the conditions for human well-being, and in which the ultimate Judge undergoes judgment, and the authoritative Witness becomes the martyred victim, in order to accomplish this outcome? If Christian truth claims are inevitably disputed and therefore entail witness as advocacy, is there a role in a pluralistic academic context for biblical interpretation as a form of witness or advocacy? When the relation between truth and power depicted in the narrative is inserted into the networks of power in our worlds, what does it suggest about witness to the truth as service of the other and about witness as suffering? In the light of such considerations, what might it mean to bear faithful witness to the truth of this narrative, with all the perils associated with its notion of supersessionism in the context of dialogue with Judaism?

Although I have chosen to deal first with more literary issues, then to provide a description of the narrative's theological themes and raise historical questions before moving on to the issue of critical appropriation, this is not the only way to proceed, nor does it reflect exactly how my own reading has advanced. It has not been a matter of first coming at the narrative by means of an objective critical description, then moving on to the application of the findings. Rather, my experience as a reader was that of being caught up in the narrative and intuiting that the lawsuit motif made sense of its world as a whole and resonated with issues of truth and belief and uses of the trial metaphor in my own world. Literary and historical criticism then came into play in order to test and confirm this initial construal, and similarly, theological and hermeneutical reflection began to probe the experience of being addressed by such a construal of the narrative's world. My presentation is only one possible avenue into the fascinating and complex world of the Fourth Gospel. Clearly it is a reading shaped by my own particular interests and commitments, which will become apparent. Nevertheless, my hope is that what has proved exciting for one reader will also be sufficiently fruitful and suggestive to stimulate others in their engagement with the text of the Fourth Gospel.

I have attempted to integrate some of the results of earlier work on the trial theme into this new study. But besides interacting with the work of other scholars, I have tried to achieve the more difficult goal of writing at a level that can be appreciated by general students of the NT. My footnoting of others' work is therefore neither comprehensive nor exhaustive. A fuller listing can be found in the bibliography.

chapter one

THE LAWSUIT
and the NARRATIVE *of the* FOURTH GOSPEL

On reading the Fourth Gospel, one encounters again and again the two notions of testimony (or witness) and judgment. Their dominance and the distinctiveness they contribute to John's narrative can be highlighted by a statistical observation. The noun *witness* or *testimony* (μαρτυρία) occurs fourteen times in this Gospel in comparison with four times in the three Synoptics together, and the verb *to witness* or *to testify* (μαρτυρεῖν) thirty-three times in comparison with twice in the three Synoptics. Again, in connection with judgment, the verb *to judge* (κρίνειν) is employed nineteen times in the Fourth Gospel as compared with six times in Matthew and six times in Luke. Although the noun *judgment* (κρίσις) occurs eleven times in John as compared with four in Luke, its use is not as striking, since it is also a characteristic term in Matthew, where it appears twelve times.

It is not, however, just a matter of vocabulary. Both these concepts, which have, of course, strong juridical or legal connotations, form part of a larger motif, that of the lawsuit or trial, which shapes much of the narrative of the Fourth Gospel. The themes of this Gospel are intricately interwoven, and to isolate one carries the danger of the whole becoming unraveled; nevertheless, this major metaphor is arguably the most distinctive, pervasive, and comprehensive motif. It is from this motif that the issue of truth highlighted in the introduction takes its most distinctive features. Again the vocabulary statistics are striking. The noun ἀλήθεια occurs twenty-five times in this Gospel as compared with seven times in the three Synoptics together. The adjective ἀληθής, *true*, is found fourteen times in John as compared with once in Mark and once in Matthew. The related adjective ἀληθινός is featured nine times in John in comparison with once in Luke, and even the adverb ἀληθῶς, *truly*, occurs more frequently in this Gospel—seven times, as compared with three times each in Matthew and Luke and twice in Mark.

Under the umbrella of this lawsuit motif can be brought not only the concepts of witness, judgment, and truth but also, as we shall see, such obvious features as the Gospel's depiction of the public ministry of Jesus as a controversy with "the Jews"; its distinctive account of his trial before Pilate, which is the most extensive of all four Gospels; its treatment of the law; its use of Scripture and in particular its predominant relation to Isa 40–55; its view of the mission of the disciples; and its portrayal of the Spirit as Paraclete. To this motif are related also such significant themes as life, glory, the world, and belief; the Gospel's depiction of Christ as the one who is sent as God's agent and as employing "I am" sayings; and its perspective on eschatology, revelation, and monotheism. It is important not to get carried away and reduce the Gospel to this one dimension. Clearly our motif is related but subservient to the Fourth Gospel's message about Christ with its ascent-and-descent pattern and its emphasis on the oneness of the Son with the Father. But perhaps, second only to the narrative's unique Christology, this metaphor of a lawsuit on a cosmic scale is the most distinctive characteristic holding many of the elements of its plot and discourse together. Can this claim be maintained, and how exactly does the motif function?

The answer to these questions will unfold in three main stages. First, this chapter will set out the case in broad, general terms. Next, chapters 2 and 3 will attempt to support this by providing a discussion of this text's links with the Jewish Scriptures and then a more detailed sequential reading of the text in the light of this motif. Finally, chapter 4 will return to some of the broader literary issues that have been raised.

A. Orientation to the Narrative

Before we focus on our motif, this section describes some of the most significant features of the Gospel's narrative in order to provide the general reader with the necessary background and context.[1]

---

[1] For a fuller treatment of many of these points, including discussion of such categories as implied author, implied reader, and point of view, see the excellent discussion in Culpepper, *Anatomy.*

1. Overall Shape of the Narrative Discourse

It is widely recognized that the discourse shaping the final form of John's story has clear major sections. A prologue (1:1–18) and an epilogue (21:1–25) surround the main story, which itself has two main parts. The first of these (1:19–12:50) deals with Jesus' public ministry, the second (13:1–20:31) with his departure from this world. The second part itself has two clear subsections—13:1–17:26, in which the departure is interpreted by Jesus for "his own," the disciples, and 18:1–20:31, in which the departure takes place as the story line culminates in the passion and resurrection.

The prologue, which provides an extended introduction to the main character, Jesus, makes clear the implied author's point of view. The identity of the central figure is disclosed as that of the divine Logos (1:1, 14), and the implied reader is given clues about the significance of this figure's mission: it involves his glory (1:14), contrasts with Moses and the law (1:17), and entails making God known (1:18). There is also a preview of the outcome of this mission in 1:11–12: "He came to what was his own, and his own people did not accept him. But to all who received him, who believed in his name, he gave power to become children of God."

Not surprisingly, the public ministry is dominated by Jesus' deeds and words, both of which help to move the plot along. Jesus' deeds are predominantly depicted as signs, and there are seven of these (cf. 2:1–11; 4:46–54; 5:1–18; 6:1–15; 6:16–21; 9:1–41; 11:1–53). Some scholars have been so impressed by this feature that they have called this section of the Gospel "the Book of Signs."[2] But this is to make the signs more dominant than they in fact are, and not to do enough justice to the speech material. Nevertheless, their explicit association with the important concept of glory (cf. 2:11; 11:4) should be noted, since this certainly provides one major element of continuity with the second half of the Gospel's story. The words through which Jesus makes God known are primarily extended discourses.[3] These discourses do not necessarily

---

[2] Cf., e.g., C. H. Dodd, *The Interpretation of the Fourth Gospel* (Cambridge: Cambridge University Press, 1953), 290, 297; R. E. Brown, *The Gospel according to John* (2 vols.; New York: Doubleday, 1966–1970), 1:cxxxviii.

[3] This study uses the term *discourse* in two ways. The more general sense of the term, referring here to speech material, should not be confused with literary criticism's more technical use of the term for the rhetoric of the narrative as a whole, cf. S. Chatman, *Story and Discourse: Narrative Structure in Fiction and Film*

comprise a complete monologue from Jesus, and where extended speech material on the lips of Jesus is interrupted more than usual by debate or questions, dispute/discourse might be a better categorization. Given this, and granted some uncertainty because the discourses are far less clearly demarcated than the signs, it could be argued that there are seven major discourses in the public ministry as well as seven signs (cf. 3:1–21; 4:1–26; 5:19–47; 6:22–59; 7:14–39; 8:12–59; 10:1–18, with the fourth, fifth, and sixth of these passages being disputes/discourses).

Although much more remains to be said about how the encounter and the increasing conflict with significant features of Israel's religion and its representatives unfold during Jesus' public ministry, here attention will simply be drawn to episodes near the beginning and the end. The first major deed—changing water into wine at Cana (2:1–11)—both rounds off the initial response of the disciples to Jesus (cf. 2:11) and anticipates the significance of Jesus' mission, as the water of the Jewish rites of purification gives way to the wine and joy of the new life that Jesus provides. The next incident, in the temple in Jerusalem (2:13–22), further sets the tone for what is to follow. Its setting in this narrative shows Jesus confronting the Jewish authorities at the heart of their religious system, and the dialogue that follows and the narrator's comments make clear that the resurrected Christ is in fact to replace the old religious order represented by the temple. The last sign—the raising of Lazarus—precipitates the move towards Jesus' hour of death and glory (cf. esp. 11: 4, 8, 16, 49–53; 12:7, 23–36a). John 12:36b–50 forms the clear and appropriate conclusion to the public ministry; it deals with the response both to Jesus' signs and glory (12:36b–43) and to his words (12:44–50).

Brown, who calls the public ministry material "the Book of Signs," entitles the second half of the Gospel "the Book of Glory."[4] This does not sufficiently recognize that the signs themselves are signs of glory and that, for the Fourth Gospel, the whole of Jesus' life is a manifestation of his glory (cf. 1:14). It does highlight, however, that there is a sense in which the death and exaltation of Jesus are the particular moment of his glorification, his departure as glory. The section composed of John 13–17 begins, "Now before the festival of the Passover, Jesus knew that

---

(Ithaca, N.Y.: Cornell University Press, 1978), 15–42. In the latter sense, it is employed in distinction to *story*: the story is what the narrative is about (its events, characters, and setting), while the discourse of a narrative is how the story is told (its shape, sequence, juxtapositions, and persuasive strategy).

[4] Brown, *Gospel according to John*, 1:cxxxviii–cxxxix.

his hour had come to depart from this world and go to the Father," and the nature of the hour is made unmistakably clear when, after Judas has gone out in order to arrange for Jesus' arrest, Jesus asserts, "Now the Son of Man has been glorified, and God has been glorified in him. If God has been glorified in him, God will also glorify him in himself and will glorify him at once" (13: 31–32). In this section Jesus talks not only about his departure but also about what will happen after it. He will prepare a place for his disciples, return to remain with them, and send them the Paraclete. They will face both exclusion from the synagogue and persecution but will also experience joy and peace. Jesus' concluding prayer for himself and his followers again strikes the note of the hour of departure and its glory for both Jesus and God: "Father, the hour has come; glorify your Son so that the Son may glorify you. . . . I glorified you on earth by finishing the work that you gave me to do. So now, Father, glorify me in your own presence with the glory that I had in your presence before the world existed" (17:1, 4–5; cf. also 22, 24).

The events for which Jesus has been preparing his disciples unfold quickly in John 18 and 19. The Jewish authorities seize Jesus and hand him over to Pilate, and Pilate, after eventually coming to a verdict, hands Jesus over to be crucified. Yet even during his arrest, trial, and death, Jesus is portrayed as in control. While soldiers cast lots for his clothes, Jesus continues to care for his own from the cross by uniting his mother and the beloved disciple. Finally, he cries out in triumph, "It is finished," before he gives up his spirit (lit. "he handed over the spirit"—19:30). There follows in John 20 the episode of the discovery of the empty tomb, with the beloved disciple seeing and believing and Mary Magdalene meeting, but at first not recognizing, Jesus. The risen Jesus then authorizes and empowers the disciples for mission, and Thomas utters the climactic confession "My Lord and my God!" (20:28). The story comes to its first conclusion with a statement about why it has been written, highlighting the need for the response of belief in Jesus as the Christ and as the sort of Christ who is Son of God.

In the epilogue of John 21, the risen Jesus appears to his disciples in Galilee, enabling them to make an extraordinary catch of fish. The episode leads into a dialogue and comments from the narrator that tie up some loose ends from the preceding narrative about the relationship between Jesus and Peter and about that between Peter and the beloved disciple. Peter is to feed Jesus' sheep and to die a martyr's death, and the beloved disciple will also bear faithful witness through his involvement in the writing of the Gospel. In this way the epilogue helps to bridge the gap between the time of the story and the time of its Christian readers.

2. Discerning the Plot and the Characterization

Having selectively sketched some of the features of the narrative's overall discourse in order to enable us to appreciate something of its structure, we are now in a position to see the essential elements of its plot, which is, according to two widely quoted definitions, "the dynamic sequential element"[5] or "the structure of its actions, as these are ordered and rendered toward achieving particular emotional and artistic effects."[6] A further definition of plot as "the dynamic shaping force of the narrative discourse"[7] combines the emphases on movement and persuasion in the first two through its use of the terms *dynamic* and *discourse*.

One common way of setting out the basic aspects of a plot is according to the three-stage movement of setting or commission, complication or conflict, and then resolution. In the first stage the main character is given a commission or task. So Jesus in this Gospel is given a commission by God; there are a number of ways in which this is described—for example, to reveal or make God known (cf. 1:18; 17:6, 26), to display his glory (cf. 13:31, 32), to be lifted up (3:14; 8:28; 12:32–34), and thereby to give life (e.g., 3:16; 10:10). This is not the imposition of some alien schema on the text. The narrative discourse positively encourages this kind of reading. All the way through, Jesus makes clear that he has been commissioned. He repeatedly describes the Father as "the one who sent me," and in this connection the verb πέμπειν is used twenty-four times and ἀποστέλλειν seventeen times. In addition, Jesus talks of his mission as the task or work God has given him to do (e.g., 4:34; 9:4; 17:4). In the second stage, the complication, the protagonist faces obstacles and opposition that have to be overcome if the commission is to be carried out. Again in the Fourth Gospel, obvious opposition to Jesus' mission— in the shape of the chief priests and Pharisees (e.g., 7:32–52; 11:46–57), "the Jews,"[8] the world (e.g., 1:10c; 15:18), Judas (6:71; 13:2, 30; 18:2, 3), the devil or ruler of this world (e.g., 12:31; 13:2; 16:11), and Pilate— produces the conflict that runs through the story. The opposition is in fact involved in a counterplot within the plot, one that parodies the main

---

[5] R. Scholes and R. Kellogg, *The Nature of Narrative* (Oxford: Oxford University Press, 1966), 207.

[6] M. H. Abrams, *A Glossary of Literary Terms* (4th ed.; New York: Holt, Rhinehart & Winston, 1981), 127.

[7] P. Brooks, *Reading for the Plot* (Oxford: Clarendon, 1984), 13.

[8] Throughout this study the designation *the Jews* is to be understood as a reference to a corporate character within the narrative.

plot, since "the Jews" have as their task the destruction of Jesus and the originator of this commission can be seen to be the devil (cf. 8:44 in relation to "the Jews" and 13:2, 27 in relation to Judas). The irony of the opposition's counterplot is that, in its success in putting Jesus to death, it brings about the resolution of the main plot. This final stage—resolution—is the goal toward which the plot has been moving throughout. One indication of this is the constant reference to Jesus' hour, the decisive hour of glory (cf., e.g., 2:4; 7:6, 8; 12:23, 27; 13:1, 31, 32; 17:1). In the resolution the opposition is overcome and the commission completed. Again the language of the Fourth Gospel corresponds to such an analysis. Jesus can say to the disciples, "I have conquered the world!" (16:33), and the completion of his task is anticipated in his prayer "I glorified you on earth by finishing the work you gave me to do" (17:4). The key reference for the resolution is Jesus' cry from the cross in 19:30: "It is finished" (τετέλεσται, i.e., "the task is completed"). Jesus' mission culminates on the cross. Clearly, from the point of view of the implied author, against all appearances, in this "lifting up" God is most truly known. The death of the crucified Messiah is the supreme moment of his glorification and of God's glory.

The implied reader learns about the various characters in the Fourth Gospel primarily, though by no means exclusively, through discovering their role in the plot. Characterization emerges in the web of events and relationships that make up the plot. If the implied author reveals character by showing, on the one hand, and telling, on the other, then how the characters act and interact is the showing aspect. The telling aspect occurs in a number of ways. One is the comments of one character about another, including, in the Fourth Gospel, the titles for Jesus employed by other characters. Another is a person's direct speech, and in this Gospel the main character, Jesus, has much to say about himself, especially as the Son who is totally at one with the Father. A third way is the narrator's statements about a person. They are sometimes called "inside views" when the narrator tells what is going on inside a character's mind.[9] Those concerning Jesus nearly all underline Jesus' foreknowledge or, indeed, omniscience and are part of the characterization of him as sovereign and in control of events.

There is no real change or development in the character of the protagonist, Jesus, in the course of accomplishing his mission. Although the reader discovers more of what his identity entails, Jesus' identity basi-

---

[9] Culpepper, *Anatomy,* 22–25, provides a list of these in the Fourth Gospel.

cally remains the same as its portrayal in the prologue. What moves the plot along is how he achieves his goal and the responses to him as he does so. The other characters function as foils to his identity and as illustrations of the two contrasting types of response—belief or unbelief. The human opponents, whom we have already mentioned, are representatives of unbelief. This is particularly important to recognize when it comes to the Gospel's use of the term *the Jews*. Much has been written about this, but what needs to be made clear here is that the term is not purely an ethnic one. Sometimes it refers to the religious authorities, sometimes more generally to the crowds, but predominantly "the Jews" are the representatives of the unbelieving world; they are unbelieving Jews as opposed to believing Jews. This representative and not simply ethnic function can be seen on the surface of the narrative, as the following three examples demonstrate. In 9:22 the parents of the blind man, obviously Jews themselves, are said to fear "the Jews." This is as striking and strange as speaking of natives of London fearing the English. A similarly strange usage occurs in 13:33 when Jesus, a Jew, says to his disciples, themselves Jews, "as I said to the Jews so now I say to you." Then in 18:35 Pilate, the Roman governor, asks the ironic question "I am not a Jew, am I?"; he expects a negative answer, but the answer the implied readers are expected to supply is affirmative. In his response to Jesus, Pilate proves himself to be a Jew in the special sense of this narrative's discourse, namely, one who belongs to the unbelieving world. In a similar fashion, as the implied readers are introduced to the different characters who encounter Jesus in the narrative, they become conditioned to ask which group these characters represent. Will the characters recognize Jesus' true identity or not? Will they respond in belief and receive life, thereby becoming his followers who help his mission along? Or will they respond in unbelief, thereby becoming part of the opposition, the hostile world?

3. Irony and a Two-Storey Story

There is irony as the readers watch the characters' responses and frequent misunderstandings, because they have already been taken into the confidence of the implied author and know who Jesus is from the prologue.[10] This way of structuring the narrative coaxes its readers into sharing the implied author's point of view about Jesus as the incarnate Logos, the Son of God. Only if they are willing to accept this perspective,

---

[10] See esp. P. Duke, *Irony in the Fourth Gospel* (Atlanta: John Knox, 1985).

at least temporarily as they read the narrative, can they appreciate fully its ironies and double entendres. One example of this phenomenon is the questions that are posed by some of the characters out of ignorance or from a false assumption but that suggest the truth without their consciousness of it: "Can anything good come out of Nazareth?" (1:46); "Are you greater than our ancestor Jacob . . . ?" (4:12); "Surely we are not blind, are we?" (9:40); "I am not a Jew, am I?" (18:35). In each case the characters assume an answer the readers have been led to see as false in the light of the prologue and its development; for the readers, not to accept the implied author's view would be to surrender their superior understanding and privileged position vis-à-vis the characters in the narrative. This sort of irony—as also the dramatic irony, already noted, whereby the apparent success of the opposition in fact results in the resolution of the plot—works, as always, through the contrast of appearance and reality.

> Below is the appearance or apparent meaning. Above there is a meaning, perspective or belief that is contradictory, incongruous, or incompatible with the lower level. The victim, where there is one, is unaware of the higher level or blindly hostile to it. The reader is invited by the irony to leap to the higher level and share the perspective of the implied author.[11]

This two-storey phenomenon of irony reflects the two-storey nature of the ideological point of view of the narrative as a whole. Again and again its discourse conveys a vertical dimension in which the spatial categories "above" or "heaven" and "below" or "earth" are employed and in which Jesus and his followers are those who are from above (cf., e.g., 3:3, 31; 8:23). Not surprisingly, then, descent and ascent are key categories for interpreting the central character and his mission (cf., e.g., 3:13; 6:33, 62; 20:17); equivalent language is that of coming from the Father and going to the Father (cf., e.g., 8:42; 13:1; 14:12, 28; 16:28). For the implied author, implied readers can begin to appreciate the central character's full significance only when they are able to conceive of the central character and his task, which culminates in his death, in terms of the vertical dimension of the two-storey story.

There is a further and related sense in which this Gospel is a two-storey story. Its perspective from above is, from the temporal point of view, retrospective. The narrator is telling the story of Jesus from the vantage point of the group of followers who believe Jesus was indeed from above, and in both the prologue and the epilogue he uses "we" lan-

---

[11] Culpepper, *Anatomy,* 167.

guage in a confessional context (cf. 1:14, 16; 21:24). So within the narrative time there are the time of the story of Jesus and the time of the narrator and the implied readers. The relation of these two temporal perspectives is an interesting phenomenon that not only contributes to the implied readers' ability to recognize ironies but also sheds light on the nature of the narrative. Sometimes the two perspectives are clearly distinguished, and sometimes they are compressed. For instance, in 16:1–4 Jesus tells his disciples that there will come a time when they will be put out of the synagogue. Yet a situation that is here seen as distinct from the time of Jesus himself is elsewhere treated as integral to the time of Jesus' own story (cf. 9:22; 12:42). This juxtaposition of perspectives is one of a number of clues in the narrative itself that this story of Jesus is also, in large part, being narrated as the story of the implied readers' struggle and debate with the synagogue about their belief in Jesus. The literary analysis of the two-storey story thus dovetails with Martyn's discussion of the Gospel as a "two-level drama."[12]

B. The Trial Motif in the Narrative

Now that we have the bare bones of a narrative analysis that has carefully avoided any explicit discussion of our theme, the time has come to put flesh on it by demonstrating, in an initial way, just how far the extended metaphor of the trial or lawsuit is integral to and enhances such an analysis.

1. The Lawsuit and the Overall Shape of the Narrative Discourse

Not only does the motif occur in each of the five main sections of the narrative discussed above; it does so in highly significant ways. As often pointed out, but without its full force being appreciated, the poetic nature of the prologue's reflections on the Logos and his glory is disturbed primarily by the references to John the Baptist in 1:6–8, 15. What distinguishes these references to John is the totally dominating portrayal of his role as a witness. This also provides the link between the prologue and the public ministry. The very first words of the section on public ministry, in 1:19, are "This is the testimony given by John"; 1:19–28 contains John's testimony about himself, while 1:29–34 contains his testimony about Jesus. At the end of the public-ministry section, after the trial motif has been mentioned in 12:17, 31, the final pericope—

---

[12] Martyn, *History and Theology*, 60.

12:44–50—in its discussion of judgment highlights Jesus' word as judge. So there is an *inclusio* using our motif, and it provides an interpretative frame for the public ministry.

The trial motif is also explicit at the heart of the controversy with "the Jews" in the third discourse in 5:19–47 (cf. vv. 22, 24, 27, 29–39, 45) and the sixth discourse/dispute in 8:12–59 (cf. vv. 13–18, 26, 50). It has featured previously in 2:25; 3:11, 17–19, 26–28, 32, 33; and 4:39, 44 and occurs again in 7:7, and so it is now dominant enough to color the way in which the reader interprets the dispute and its aftermath in 7:14–52 (cf. v. 51) and the interrogation of the blind man in John 9 (cf. 9:39).

Central to the section constituted by John 13–17 are the two Farewell Discourses. In the first (13:31–14:31) the motif occurs in the references to the Paraclete, or Advocate, in 14:16, 26 and then again at the heart of the second (15:1–16:33) with reference to both the Paraclete and the disciples in 15:26, 27 and 16:7–11. In the fourth section the Roman trial of Jesus in 18:28–19:16a is in fact the central feature of the passion narrative, standing in the middle of three equal blocks of material, with the arrest and interrogation on one side (18:1–27) and the crucifixion and burial on the other (19:16b–42). While the trial before Pilate is central to the narrative of the passion, the death of Jesus is still its climax, and the theme is not absent from that climax. When the narrator inserts his own comments immediately after Jesus' death has been established, it is in terms of testimony in 19:35.

Finally, the epilogue itself closes on this note, with a twofold reference to the testimony of the beloved disciple in 21:24 as the narrator links his work to this testimony. In this way, not only does our theme provide the *inclusio* for the public ministry; with the references in the epilogue and the prologue, it also provides an overall *inclusio* for the complete narrative. In regard to actions within history, the Gospel begins with the witness of John the Baptist and concludes with the witness of the beloved disciple.

Both the pervasiveness and the positioning of the motif encourage readers to view the narrative, as a whole, from the perspective of a trial. In addition to introducing the theme of witness, the prologue provides both a cosmic backdrop for the trial and the implied author's point of view on its participants. Jesus is the unique representative of God, the incarnate Logos (1:1, 14), indeed the only God (μονογενὴς θεός), who is in the bosom of the Father (v. 18). His own people who did not receive him (v. 11) are representatives of the world that did not know him (v. 10). So ultimately the issues in the trial that follows are to be seen as not simply between Jesus and Israel but as between God and the world.

The notion of truth that is at stake also begins to be intimated through the references to the Logos as the true light (v. 9) and the one through whom grace and truth come into being (vv. 14, 17).

This narrative, unlike that of the Synoptics, has no account of a Jewish trial before the Sanhedrin. Instead, throughout his public ministry, Jesus can be viewed as on trial before Israel and its leaders. At one point he appeals to the law of evidence with its requirement of two witnesses: "In your law it is written that the testimony of two witnesses is valid" (8:17, 18). Deuteronomy 17:6 in fact talks of two or three witnesses being necessary before the death penalty can be carried out. But not surprisingly, in the narrative of the public ministry as a whole, which arguably has seven signs and seven discourses, the narrator explicitly designates seven witnesses. The first witness to be called is John the Baptist, who, as we have seen, has been introduced in this role in the prologue (cf. 1:7, 8, 15) and who now continues it in the public ministry (cf. 1:19, 32, 34; 3:26, 28). In 5:33 Jesus calls on John's witness with his claim "You sent messengers to John, and he testified to the truth." Then there is Jesus' own witness, of which he can say, "Even if I testify on my own behalf, my testimony is valid because I know where I have come from and where I am going" (8:14; cf. also 3:11, 32, 33; 7:7; 8:18). Jesus' works provide a further witness. "The works that the Father has given me to complete, the very works that I am doing, testify on my behalf that the Father has sent me" (5:36; cf. also 10:25). God has not only sent Jesus as the divine representative in the trial; God, too, is a witness: "the Father who sent me testifies on my behalf" (8:18; cf. also 5:32, 37). The fifth of the witnesses are the Scriptures. In a formulation that effectively sums up the use of the Scriptures in the narrative as a whole (cf., e.g., 2:17; 3:14; 6:31–33; 7:39), it is said that "they testify on my behalf" (5:39). The remaining witnesses in the public ministry are the Samaritan woman, on the basis of whose testimony many other Samaritans believed in Jesus (4:39), and the crowd who testify about Jesus' raising of Lazarus (12:17).

The various characters in the narrative, most notably the leaders of the Jewish people, have to decide whether they will believe Jesus' witness or the witness about him. It is noticeable that the deliberations provoked in the crowds by Jesus' mission revolve around the question of whether he is the true prophet, the Messiah, or whether he is a false prophet who deceives or leads the people astray (cf. 6:14; 7:12, 26, 27, 40–42). This takes up the issues and formulations of Deut 13:1–5 and 18:15–22, according to which a prophet who does signs and wonders but who leads the people astray is to be put to death. After the divisions within the crowd have been reported, the chief priests and the Pharisees rebuke the temple police and Nicodemus and reinforce the point made by some of the crowd by attempting to use the law or Scripture to show that Jesus is a false prophet. "Surely you have not been deceived too, have you? . . . Search and you will see that no prophet is to arise from Galilee" (7:47–52). "The Jews" have three other main charges against Jesus, arising from their understanding of the law. He is a violator of the Sabbath laws and therefore a sinner (cf. 5:16; 7:23; 9:16, 24). He is a blasphemer, attempting to make himself equal to God (cf. 5:17, 18; 10:30–39; cf. also 8:58, 59). And finally, he is an enemy of the Jewish nation. Belief in him will lead to the destruction of the nation by the Romans, and so, in accord with the law, the sinner or evildoer must be cut off, so that the nation as a whole will be saved (cf. 11:46–53).[13]

Because of his unique relationship to God, Jesus can function not only as the chief witness in the trial but also as judge. He can claim, "The Father judges no one but has given all judgment to the Son. . . . I can do nothing on my own. As I hear, I judge; and my judgment is just, because I seek not to do my own will but the will of him who sent me" (5:22, 30; cf. also 5:27–29; 9:39; 12:47, 48). Judgment has two aspects. Its positive aspect is the giving of life, while its negative connotation is condemnation. Receiving Jesus' witness is the equivalent of believing, and the result of both is eternal life. Not to receive his witness, that is, not to believe, is to pass judgment on oneself and to be condemned already.

> Indeed, God did not send the Son into the world to condemn the world, but in order that the world might be saved through him. Those who believe in him are not condemned; but those who do not believe are condemned already, because they have not believed in the name of the only Son of God. And this is the judgment, that the light has come into the world, and people loved darkness rather than light because their deeds were evil. (3:17–19; cf. also 3:33; 5:24)

So Jesus' mission inevitably involves judgment—both by people and on people. Those who see his signs and hear his words face a crisis (cf. κρίσις); they must decide who he is and whether to receive his witness. On this decision hangs life or death, although the narrative emphasizes that Jesus, in coming, is to bring the positive verdict of life (cf., e.g., 10:10). This present crisis, it is implied, is an anticipation of the final judgment (cf. 5:24–29) and its critical moment is when Jesus is lifted up from the earth (12:31, 32). In this light, it is not so much Jesus who is on trial as those to whom he has been sent, those who are acting as his judges. Since response to Jesus' witness entails making a judgment that

---

[13] For detailed discussion of these charges, see Pancaro, *The Law,* 9–125.

could be self-condemnation, it is incumbent on them to make the correct judgment, and so Jesus tells the crowd, "Do not judge by appearances, but judge with right judgment" (7:24). Those who judge falsely by attempting to use the law and Moses against Jesus will discover that Moses will in fact function not as their advocate but as their accuser: "Do not think that I will accuse you before the Father; your accuser is Moses, on whom you have set your hope. If you believed Moses, you would believe me, for he wrote about me" (5:45–46).

By the end of the public ministry, and independently of each other, the Sanhedrin has already reached its verdict about Jesus (11:47–53) and Jesus has already accepted this verdict of death (12:27–33). In terms of story time, the next significant episodes for our motif are the bringing together of prosecutors and witness in Jesus' interrogation and trial. In the interrogation before Annas, the issue of witness is again raised. In response to being struck on the face for his reply to the high priest, Jesus says, "If I have spoken wrongly, testify to the wrong" (18:23). In effect, he calls for a fair and proper trial. But the episode concludes with no testimony being produced. The climax of the motif is reached, however, in the formal trial before Pilate and its judgment of crucifixion (18:28–19:42). Only one or two of the key features of this Roman trial can be highlighted here in anticipation of the more detailed treatment in the next chapter. The stage settings, which for most of the trial have Jesus inside the praetorium and "the Jews" outside and Pilate scuttling back and forth between the two, contribute to the portrayal of Jesus as the central figure. He is on trial as king of the Jews, a royal Messiah (cf. 18:33ff.), and Son of God (cf.19:7ff.). Significantly, these are the two aspects of his identity that feature in the Gospel's statement of purpose in 20:31: "These are written so that you may come to believe that Jesus is the Messiah, [and the sort of Messiah who is] the Son of God." It is in the course of this trial that Jesus sums up his whole mission in terms of witness and truth: "For this I was born, and for this I came into the world, to testify to the truth" (18:37).

But the narrative is also interested in the would-be judges of Jesus—Pilate and "the Jews"—in order to show that they are the ones who turn out to be on trial. Pilate is portrayed initially as attempting to stay detached from this case and as using it to humiliate the Jewish leadership. In the end, despite his threefold avowal that he finds no case against Jesus (18:38; 19:4, 6), when faced with a choice between this alleged king of the Jews and the favor of Caesar, he decides against Jesus and proves himself culpable, even if this culpability is held not to be as great as that of the Jewish leaders, who have been clear from the start about the judgment they desire (cf. 19:11). The narrative allows three possible ways of reading the depiction of the actual moment of Pilate's verdict. Having made his final plea to have Jesus released but to no avail, Pilate brings Jesus out and then either sits himself or seats Jesus on the seat of judgment (ἤγαγεν ἔξω τὸν Ἰησοῦν, καὶ ἐκάθισεν ἐπὶ βήματος— 19:13). Is ἐκάθισεν, "he sat," to be taken as intransitive or transitive or as involving deliberate ambiguity? The next chapter will give reasons for opting for the transitive sense with its blatant irony. But even noting the issue underlines for readers the latent irony of the whole episode. The verdict is being pronounced on the one who is the real judge.

The trial exposes Pilate but also unmasks the Jewish leaders. Insisting on Jesus' death, they steadfastly resist Pilate's offer to have Jesus released, and in the process their comments become more and more revealing and incriminating. First, they choose Barabbas to be released instead of Jesus, and the narrator simply adds the comment "Now Barabbas was a bandit" (18:40). This comment recalls the narrative discourse both from the immediately preceding episode in the trial and from the public ministry. They choose a bandit rather than the good shepherd and thereby show that they do not belong to the flock that hears the shepherd's voice (cf. 18:37; 10:1–18). The last response of the Jewish leaders in 19:15 is particularly significant. "Pilate asked them, 'Shall I crucify your King?' The chief priests answered, 'We have no king but the emperor.'" At the time of Passover, when in particular the Jewish religious leaders would be expected to acknowledge their complete dependence on God and their hope for God's deliverance, they are portrayed as confessing their sole allegiance to Caesar. The full implications of the narrative's trial become apparent. In rejecting Jesus, the religious leaders reject their God. They, not Jesus, are the ones who are judged and condemned—and out of their own mouths.

It is only when the true witness and judge submits to the sentence of death that has been passed on him that he completes his task (cf. 19:30) and becomes the source of the positive verdict of life, as out of his pierced side come both blood and water (cf. 19:34). This picks up on the earlier water symbolism of the narrative's discourse, not least the scriptural citation in 7:38: "Out of his belly shall flow rivers of living water." The trial of Jesus has, after all, had a successful outcome. It is precisely at this point, however, that the narrator includes a reference to a witness to the outcome: "He who saw this has testified so that you also may believe. His testimony is true, and he knows that he tells the truth" (19:35). Why formulate the beloved disciple's confession in terms of witness when the trial of Jesus is over?

Readers know the answer to this question: there is another trial in progress that is in fact an extension of the same trial. And they know this because the announcement of the continuation of the trial into their own time has formed a significant part of the preparation Jesus has given his followers in John 13–17. Particularly in 15:18–16:15, Jesus tells the disciples that after he has returned to the Father, they will face the hatred of the world and expulsion from the synagogue but his cause must still be argued. This time there will be exactly the double witness required by the law to which Jesus referred in the public ministry (cf. 8:17). The disciples themselves are now to be witnesses: "You also are to testify because you have been with me from the beginning" (15:27). But they are not alone as they play their role in the lawsuit of history: "When the Advocate comes, whom I will send to you from the Father, the Spirit of truth who comes from the Father, he will testify on my behalf" (15:26). An advocate supports defendants at their trial. This Advocate will be with the disciples (14:16, 17). He will aid them in their witness to the truth because, as the Spirit of truth, he will guide them into all truth (16:13, 14; cf. also 14:26). But he will also have a prosecuting role, acting to convict the world that it has been wrong in its response to Jesus, wrong in its basic assumptions about sin, righteousness, and judgment (16:7–11). The role of the disciples and their relationship to the Spirit are underlined in the later commissioning of 20:21–22, which is to be read in the light of this earlier and fuller discussion: " 'As the Father has sent me, so I send you.' When he had said this, he breathed on them and said to them, 'Receive the Holy Spirit.' " Just as Jesus has been the Father's authorized agent as witness in the trial, so now the disciples are to be Jesus' authorized agents as they bear witness in the trial of truth that is still taking place: "As you have sent me into the world, so I have sent them into the world" (17:18; cf. also 13:20). Dahl has summarized this stage of the lawsuit well:

> The high court has already spoken its verdict, but its decision has still to be applied to individual cases. Trials are still going on; those who do not fulfill the conditions for acquittal are already judged by the sentence passed. Before local courts, who do not recognize the supremacy of the high court, the case must still be pleaded, but the final outcome is only the consequence of the legal victory already won.[14]

---

[14] N. A. Dahl, "The Johannine Church and History," in *Current Issues in New Testament Interpretation* (ed. W. Klassen and G. F. Snyder; London: SCM, 1962), 140.

Although I have discussed the last two sections in their chronological sequence in the Gospel's story, in their narrative sequence they are in
reverse order. The preparation of the disciples for witness comes before
the Roman trial of Jesus. This narrative sequence has its own effects.
One of these is to reinforce readers' privileged knowledge. Not only do
they know through the prologue who Jesus is and where he has come
from; now they are reminded of this, told where Jesus is going, and
given his own perspective on his departure and its consequences. In this
way the implied author ensures that the implied readers share his point
of view on the remaining narrative action and appreciate in particular
the significance and the ironies of the trial and crucifixion. What is of
special importance is that this narrative sequence enables readers to see
Jesus under interrogation and on trial as a paradigm for believers in
similar situations. They are encouraged to link Jesus' role with their own
by the fact that in his interrogation Jesus is questioned both about his
disciples and about his teaching (18:19). Indeed, the juxtaposition of
episodes, whereby Peter's failure under interrogation from a servant
woman (18:15–18) is followed by Jesus' steadfastness under interrogation by the high priest (18:19–24), which in turn is followed by two further denials on the part of Peter (18:25–27) before Jesus' faithful witness
in the trial before Pilate (18:28–19:16a) and in death (19:16b–30), poses
starkly the issues of witnessing with its two contrasting role models.

The epilogue of John 21 elaborates on our motif in two ways. The
beloved disciple is not only a model believer but, as we have seen, a special witness whose testimony in written form constitutes the narrative of
the Gospel and a call to a continued right response to Jesus the Messiah,
the Son of God, and who provides the bridge between the time of Jesus
and the time of the readers (21:24; cf. also 19:35; 20:31). Yet before the
narrative concludes with its reference to this witness, who apparently
dies a natural death (cf. 21:22, 23), it relates the rehabilitation of Peter
with his threefold affirmation of love and consequent commissioning,
corresponding to the earlier threefold denial. Earlier, too, Jesus had told
Peter, "Where I am going, you cannot follow me now; but you will follow afterward" (13:36). That time has now arrived, for not only is Peter
to feed Jesus' sheep; he is to follow him (21:19), to follow him all the
way by being the sort of witness (μάρτυς) who glorifies God in a martyr's death (21:18, 19). What happened to the good shepherd in the
laying down of his life will also happen to his undershepherd. Peter's
earlier aspiration to martyrdom, for which he proved himself totally un-
ready, can now be fulfilled (13:37, 38). For readers all too conscious of
their own frailties and inadequacies as witnesses and perhaps inclined to

think the models of Jesus or the beloved disciple beyond them, there is also the case of Peter on which to ponder—the failed witness who nevertheless is enabled to become a true witness.

2. The Lawsuit, Plot, and Characterization

A return to the earlier discussion of the plot will now indicate how illuminating the motif of the lawsuit between God and the world proves to be. In terms of the commission, Jesus' task can be seen to be that of witness and judge in the lawsuit. As we have seen, this is expressed in its clearest and most striking form in Jesus' assertion in the trial before Pilate. There is a double underlining of this saying's mission significance with the twofold introduction: "For this I was born, and for this I came into the world, to testify to the truth" (18:37). No other mission statement in the narrative receives this emphasis (cf., e.g., 6:38; 10:10; 12:46–47). This final mission statement comes in the context of the climax of the lawsuit motif, in the extended account of the trial before Pilate. It is not surprising, then, that this formulation is not simply one to set alongside the other depictions of Jesus' tasks, of making God known, displaying God's glory, being lifted up and thereby giving life, but can be seen as encompassing these other aspects. Witnessing to the truth about God entails making God known and manifesting God's glory. Witnessing faithfully to the end entails being lifted up so that the positive verdict of life becomes possible. Add to the description of Jesus' commission the element of judging, and the case becomes even more convincing. As we have observed, Jesus is to be the sort of witness who can also function as judge. Again there is a clear mission statement to this effect: "I came into this world for judgment so that those who do not see may see, and those who do see may become blind" (9:39; cf. also 5:22, 27, 30). Jesus' task of judging has both positive and negative consequences. The two elements—witnessing and judging—are spoken of together in key contexts (cf. 5:20–39; 8:13–18), are clearly part of a commission from God, and are linked to Jesus' being God's agent in the lawsuit.[15] The one who is sent is the authorized representative of the one who sends (cf. also 5:23; 12:44–45; 13:20). In regard to witness, Jesus claims, "the very works I am doing, testify on my behalf that the Father

---

[15] Cf. P. Borgen, "God's Agent in the Fourth Gospel," in *Religions in Antiquity* (ed. J. Neusner; Leiden: E. J. Brill, 1968), 140–41, who states that the "Johannine idea of the mission of Christ as God's agent is seen within the context of a lawsuit."

has sent me" (5:36; cf. also 3:32–34; 8:18). In regard to judgment, his claim is, "As I hear, I judge; and my judgment is just, because I seek to do not my own will but the will of him who sent me" (5:30; cf. also 8:16; 12:48–49).

If this is the commission, the complication can now be seen as follows. Jesus has come as the chief witness and judge in God's lawsuit with the world, but this results in conflict with the world, which will not receive his testimony. The opposition takes the form of countertrials, in which, both in the context of the Jewish trial of the public ministry and the Roman trial of the passion, accusations and charges are brought against Jesus and judgment is passed on him. The chief opponents, mentioned in the earlier discussion of plot, all function in the context of the countertrials. This is clear enough in the case of Pilate, of Judas, whose betrayal of Jesus leads to the interrogation before the high priest and the trial before Pilate, and of the chief priests and Pharisees and "the Jews," who have a role in both major trials. But it is worth pointing out that both the world and the devil, as opponents, are also explicitly linked to the judgment motif (12:31; 16:11).

Again the resolution is achieved by the counterplot being taken up into the main plot or, in terms of our motif, by the countertrials unwittingly achieving the purpose of the overall lawsuit. The world's verdict on Jesus is what enables him to complete his commission as witness and judge (19:30). For the implied author, witness to the truth about God and the world is most fully borne and finds its focus in the death of Jesus. His death is also the paradigm for faithful witness in the hostile world. At the same time, completion of Jesus' commission on the cross becomes the supreme moment of judgment (cf. the anticipatory "Now is the judgment of this world" in 12:31), the vehicle for the positive verdict of life for those who accept his testimony (symbolized in the water from his side) but also for the negative verdict of condemnation for those who do not.

The lawsuit motif plays its part in the characterization. To the prologue's portrayal of Jesus' identity are added these roles of witness and judge. In the role of witness, Jesus has a certainty about his origin and destiny that makes his testimony self-authenticating (8:14), and in his role as judge, he has a special authority (5:27). What is the relation between the two roles? Jesus appears as one among a number of witnesses in God's lawsuit, but he is the one whose witness is not only true but also self-authenticating, the one whose complete reliability as a witness and the solemnity of whose testimony are underlined by the double Amen formula ("Amen, amen" [NRSV "Very truly"]). This occurs twenty-five times as an introduction to his words, serves as a swearing ritual in this juridical context, and is unique to this Gospel.[16] This one, who in his witness speaks the words of God (3:32–34), cannot simply remain one voice among others. The truth of *this* witness becomes the standard by which to judge. This witness to the truth about God, by the very nature of his witness, must also become the judge.

We have already said that Jesus' identity basically remains the same, in the narrative as a whole, as its portrayal in the prologue. The characterization of him as both witness and judge reinforces this observation. The issues it raises throw us back to the issues of identity already raised in the prologue. On the one hand, Jesus' role as witness appears to support the human side of his identity, as he takes his place among other witnesses in the unfolding of the lawsuit in history and becomes a paradigm for his followers in their role as witnesses. On the other hand, the uniqueness associated with his witness, because of his origin and destiny and because of its self-authenticating character, makes it an attribute of the "stranger from heaven"[17] and places it on the side of the divine. One would think that his role as judge puts the emphasis even more clearly on this side. But this is not quite as straightforward as one might have anticipated. It is true that ultimate judgment and the ability to enact the positive verdict in giving life are divine prerogatives that are assigned to Jesus. Yet, whatever one makes of the specific force of the notion of forgiving and retaining sins in 20:23, it is inescapable that there Jesus also assigns an element of judgment to the mission of his followers. Just as Jesus' mission constituted a realized judgment of either salvation or condemnation, so the disciples' mission entails a realized judgment of either the forgiveness or the retention of sins, and this reflects God's judgment.[18] The Spirit's work of convicting that is carried out through the witness of the disciples also contains an element of judging (cf. 16:8–11). So Jesus' role as judge is not unique. But there does remain a significant distinction between Jesus and his followers in this respect. His judging activity shares the same qualities as his self-authenticating witness and has been delegated by God to him because of who he is: "For just as the Father has life in himself, so he has granted the Son also to have life in

---

[16] Cf. Trites, *Concept of Witness,* 22, 89–90.

[17] Cf. M. de Jonge, *Jesus: Stranger from Heaven and Son of God* (Missoula, Mont.: Scholars Press, 1977).

[18] The passive forms of the verbs ἀφέωνται ("they have been forgiven") and κεκράτηνται ("they have been retained") in the two main clauses of 20:23 are to be taken as divine passives (my translations).

himself; and he has given him authority to execute judgment, because he is the Son of Man" (5:26–27; cf. also 5:22–23). His followers' activity of judging is the result of a further delegation from Jesus and involves the declaration of a judgment that in principle has already been carried out in Jesus' own mission.

We can see, then, that as Jesus' character as witness and judge is elaborated through his narrative roles, there is the same tension between the human and the divine, the flesh and the glory, as in 1:14; the implied author holds the two together (although stressing the latter). This provokes a further question, which leads readers back to the prologue: if this witness and judge, participating as a human in the lawsuit of history, is on the divine side, what is the nature of his relationship to the divine? There is a oneness with God in the self-authenticating quality of his witness to truth and in his exercise of the role of judge, yet he remains the divine agent, the Son who has been sent by the Father to bear witness, the Son of Man to whom authority to judge has been delegated. Again this reflects the paradox of the identity of the main character set out at the very start of the prologue—the Logos who is one with God yet distinct from God (1:1).

The lawsuit helps in the characterization of the other figures in the narrative, for it highlights their roles in interaction with the protagonist. In discussing the shape of the narrative, we have already noted the positive roles of those who are witnesses to Jesus—John the Baptist, the Samaritan woman, the disciples, Peter, and the beloved disciple. "The crowd" is frequently portrayed as divided (cf., e.g., 7:43), although at one point it can be characterized more positively as witnessing to Jesus' works (12:17) and at others appears to be aligned with the unbelieving opposition as those who are unwilling to receive Jesus' testimony (cf., e.g., 6:24, 41, 52). Our earlier discussion has brought out the characterization of the chief opponents through their roles in the lawsuit. There is, however, an added dimension to the lawsuit's function in characterization. Up until now our emphasis has been on characterization occurring principally through the roles in the narrative. But through the extended discourses/disputes and the dialogue of the Roman trial, the framework of the lawsuit also enables the characters to be presented in a little more depth and portrayed with some shades and variations. Jesus' identity is elaborated as his convictions and certainties about his role and about the outcome and consequences of the lawsuit are repeated like variations on a theme. As we have observed, the shift in the characterization of Pilate as he comes to his verdict is also effectively conveyed. In this way, although the discourses/disputes prolong the action, at the same time they intensify the conflict by making the views of both sides clearer. The trial settings thereby become the vehicle for the exposure of the participants' motives and ultimate allegiances—those of Jesus and "the Jews" in both the public ministry and the Roman trial and those of Pilate in the latter. The encounter of other characters with Jesus, the witness and judge, is mutually revealing. This feature also reflects the cosmic dimension of the lawsuit motif as participating in the ongoing shining of the light into the darkness and in the light's exposure of those in darkness (cf. 3:20).

3. The Lawsuit, Irony, and a Two-Storey Story

Much of the narrative's irony is attached to the lawsuit motif, and one or two of the more prominent elements have already emerged, particularly in our discussion of the Roman trial with its dramatic ironies and the ironies on the lips of both Pilate and "the Jews." Again there is the overall irony of the plot resolution: the one who is on trial is at the same time the real judge, and the sentence of death passed on him is in fact both the moment the true verdict is pronounced and the vindication of his mission as witness. Inherent in this perspective is the further irony that the ruler of this world, who apparently pressed his case successfully against Jesus, has turned out not only to have lost this case but to have undergone judgment himself, forfeiting his hold over the world.

Our basic definition of the phenomenon of irony—as working with the contrast of appearance and reality—is itself reflected in the narrative discourse in terms of the lawsuit motif. "Do not judge by appearances, but judge with right judgment" (7:24). Sharing the implied author's privileged point of view, which can distinguish between appearance and reality, also entails sharing the evaluative point of view of the main character, who judges not by human but by divine standards (8:15, 16). To receive the testimony of the true witness, to acknowledge the verdict of the real judge, then, is also to comply with the implied author's norms and to share his evaluation of the verdicts of the various characters in the narrative.

The levels of appearance and reality, of human standards and divine standards, are the "above" and "below," the two storeys of the narrative. These are explicitly linked to the trial motif: "The one who comes from above is above all; the one who is of the earth belongs to the earth and speaks about earthly things. The one who comes from heaven is above all. He testifies to what he has seen and heard, yet no one accepts his testimony" (3:31–32; cf. also 8:14; 19:11). Knowing that Jesus is part of the lawsuit from above, God's lawsuit with the world, is what enables readers to see the trials of Jesus before Israel and before Pilate in their true light and to appreciate their ironies. Knowing the procedures and decision of the high court puts those of lesser earthly courts in perspective.

The two-storey story is also one in which the trial of Jesus and the trials of his followers can both remain distinct and yet merge, and the juxtaposition of temporal perspectives adds to the appreciation of the ironies. The two trials are held apart in 15:26–16:4, where Jesus talks about the future time in which the witness of the Advocate and of the disciples will be necessary and will have as possible consequences expulsion from the synagogue and death. But there are also clear signs of the linking of the two trials. The Spirit is called another Advocate whose work has significant continuities with Jesus' own task, and as we have seen, the witness of the beloved disciple provides the bridge between the time of Jesus' trial and that of believers. The links, however, are so close that they also lead to a compression of the two trials. It is highly significant, for instance, that the very first depiction of Jesus as a witness in 3:11 has him speak in the first person plural: "Very truly, I tell you, we speak of what we know and testify to what we have seen; yet you do not receive our testimony." The narrator and the readers who share his point of view are thus in solidarity with Jesus the witness par excellence. It is in this context of John 3 that a well-known phenomenon of the Fourth Gospel is particularly prominent, namely, that it is sometimes very difficult to distinguish between what is the witness of Jesus himself and what is the witness of the narrator. This colors the reading of the trials that follow. The issues about Jesus' identity and its implications are formulated in the light of what his witnessing followers have had to face in their own trials, and as is widely recognized, the narrative of the interrogation of the blind man in John 9 resonates particularly effectively with the experience of many of the readers. The perspectives can merge because, for the implied author, both the trial of Jesus and that of his followers are part of the overall lawsuit of God with the world.

What begins to emerge from this reading of the two-storey narrative is that Jesus' followers have faced a situation in which the synagogue holds that Jesus' condemnation by the law as a false prophet and his ignominious death by crucifixion give the lie to any claims that he was Messiah, Son of God. The narrative strategy of the Fourth Gospel with its lawsuit motif is to reverse this perspective. It tells the story of Jesus in such a way that it is precisely in his death that Jesus' witness is vindicated, it is precisely in the apparent ignominy of his crucifixion that the supreme manifestation of the truth of his cause is to be seen. The Gospel's point of view is that the truth of God's cause appears in and through what seems most ungodlike and that the crucified Jesus is in fact the embodiment of the truth about existence. And it tells this story in such a way that, by involving its implied readers in the narrative, it reinforces for them the right verdict they have made and, if they are experiencing the costs of such a verdict, gives them the resources of the perspective of the ongoing cosmic lawsuit so that they can continue their own witness.

chapter two

THE LAWSUIT, JEWISH SCRIPTURE, *and the* FOURTH GOSPEL

Why is this metaphor of the lawsuit so dominant in the narrative of the Fourth Gospel? Among the most likely answers to this question are the traditions and experiences the writer and many of his readers share. The traditions include both Scripture and traditions about Jesus in which his trial played a prominent part. Chapter 6 will have more to say about the Jesus traditions that may well lie behind the use of the motif in the narrative and about the experiences of the readers implied by the narrative. The focus of this chapter is on scriptural tradition. In Scripture it had already become natural to view through the lens of legal metaphor the attempt to arrive at religious truth and to secure religious commitment.[1] A concern with divine justice was prominent in Israel's religion, and inevitably the human legal process is reflected in this concern. It is evident in the writings of the early prophets, including the eighth-century prophet Amos. When Yahweh as divine judge condemns Israel's sins, at times the readers appear to be exhorted as those who stand accused in a court (cf. Amos 3:1), and Yahweh calls on witnesses to testify against them (cf. Amos 3:13).

---

[1] Cf. G. B. Caird, *The Language and Imagery of the Bible* (London: Duckworth, 1980), 157–58.

A. Appeals to the Law

The narrative of the Fourth Gospel portrays both Jesus and his opponents against the background of legal patterns found in the Jewish Scriptures. His opponents interpret Jesus and his followers in the light of Torah an judge him to be a false prophet who has led his followers astray. They take their lead in particular from Deut 13:1–11, where the appearance of a prophet who performs a sign or wonder and then calls people to follow after and worship other gods is seen as God testing the people to see whether they will follow the one true God. Such a prophet, who has "spoken treason . . . to turn you from the way in which the Lord your God commanded you to walk," is an evil to be purged from the midst of the people by being put to death. Indeed, even if the person who secretly entices people to worship other gods not known to the ancestors is a relative or intimate friend, that person is to be stoned to death. In Deut 18:20–22 the Torah also prescribes the death penalty for the false prophet who speaks in the name of the Lord but whose prophecy neither is fulfilled nor proves true. Elsewhere, in Lev 24:16, it is said that the whole congregation is to stone to death the one who blasphemes the name of the Lord.

The opposition to Jesus, therefore, sees its response to his signs and teaching as being in line with its understanding of Scripture and as part of its obedience to Torah. The charge that Jesus is leading the people astray surfaces in John 7:12, 47. Jesus' response under interrogation in 18:20—"I have spoken openly to the world; I have always taught in synagogues and in the temple, where all the Jews come together. I have said nothing in secret"—appears to reflect accusations of secret teaching of the kind condemned in Deut 13:6. His teaching is understood in terms of his making himself God or the Son of God and therefore as blasphemy that deserves to be punished by stoning or some other form of the death penalty (cf. John 5:17–18; 10:30–39; 19:7). In the last of these references, when "the Jews" say to Pilate, "We have a law, and according to that law he ought to die because he has claimed to be the Son of God," the law in view is Lev 24:16. This understanding of the law also accounts for the attempt to stone Jesus after he has used the divine self-predication "I am," in John 8:58–59. Both sides in the narrative's lawsuit refer to the laws about witnesses in Deut 17:6 and 19:15. These state that a single witness is not sufficient and that to sustain a charge or carry out the death penalty, two or three witnesses are necessary. The Pharisees complain that Jesus is witnessing on his own behalf and that therefore his testimony is not true (John 8:13); Jesus, on the one hand, recognizes this aspect of the law (5:31; 8:17) but, on the other, claims that it does not apply in his case (8:14) and distances himself from it by referring to it as "your law" (8:17).

B. The Lawsuits of Isaiah 40–55

It is significant that while the opponents want to judge Jesus from the law in terms of whether he is a true or false prophet, the narrator himself, though in places depicting Jesus as the prophet like Moses (cf., e.g., 12:49), does not always portray Jesus positively in terms of prophet.[2] He wants to move away from this limited perspective on the law and set it in a broader context. In order to do this, he brings to bear another legal model from Scripture, the covenant lawsuit (*rîb*). In this lawsuit pattern, God can have a controversy with the people and bring formal accusations against them (cf., e.g., Deut 32; Hos 4; 5; 12:2–14; Mic 6:1–8),[3] or on occasion humans can have a controversy with God and bring accusations against God (cf., e.g., Job 23:1–7; 40:1–9). Indeed, it has been claimed of Job as a whole that "formally it cannot be better understood than as the record of the proceedings of a *rîb* between Job and God Almighty in which Job is the plaintiff and prosecutor, the friends of Job are witnesses as well as co-defendants and judges, while God is the accused and defendant, but in the background and finally the ultimate judge of both Job and his friends."[4]

But it is Isa 40–55 in particular that provides the resources for the Fourth Gospel's narrative.[5] In it the lawsuit motif is especially dominant and colors much of the prophecy. It is widely agreed that Isa 42:18–25, 43:22–28, and 50:1–3 take the form of a lawsuit between Yahweh and Israel and, in an extension of the motif, Isa 41:1–5, 41:21–29, 43:8–13, 44:6–8, and 45:18–25 are in the form of a trial speech of Yahweh against the nations.[6] In other places there are disputations (e.g., 40:12–31;

---

[2] For an argument to this effect, see W. Bittner, *Jesu Zeichen im Johannesevangelium* (Tübingen: J. C. B. Mohr, 1987), 155–70.

[3] For discussion of the lawsuit form in the prophets, see esp. C. Westermann, *Basic Forms of Prophetic Speech* (London: Lutterworth, 1967).

[4] B. Gemser, "The Rib- or Controversy-Pattern in Hebrew Mentality," in *Wisdom in Israel and the Ancient Near East* (ed. M. Noth and D. Winton Thomas; Leiden: E. J. Brill, 1955), 134–35.

[5] Cf. Trites, *Concept of Witness*, 35–47.

[6] Cf. esp. C. Westermann, *Isaiah 40–66* (London: SCM, 1969), 15–18; A. Schoors, *I Am God Your Saviour: A Form-Critical Study of the Main Genres in Is. XL–LV* (Leiden: E. J. Brill, 1973), 239; R. F. Melugin, *The Formation of Isaiah 40–55* (Berlin: de Gruyter, 1976), 43–63.

44:24–28; 45:9–13; 46:5–11; 48:1–15; 49:14–26; 55:8–13), and both within the trial passages and elsewhere in 40–55, there are frequent references to judgment and witness. The basic elements in these ancient lawsuits were an introductory setting of the trial scene, which could often involve the calling of witnesses; an accusation leveled by the prosecutor, which might be introduced by a reminder of Yahweh's gracious deeds; a chance for the accused to provide a defense; and the case coming to a verdict.[7] For various purposes, some of the elements might be omitted in any particular occurrence of the device. In the case of a dispute between Yahweh and Israel, Yahweh can function as both prosecutor and judge, "since no one other than Yahweh can serve as guarantor of the covenant which has been broken. He must therefore both demand and preside at a trial. As a party to the action, he must additionally prosecute the accusations."[8]

1. Yahweh and the Nations

The trial speeches of Yahweh against the nations function as part of a cosmic lawsuit "in which Yahweh and his witnesses are placed on one side and the gods of the nations and their supporters on the other,"[9] and in these scenes also Yahweh is both prosecuting witness and judge. To the flagging faith of some of the hearers, it may well have seemed that their exile in Babylon meant the superiority of the Babylonian gods to Yahweh. But now in Isa 41:1–5 the nations are summoned to the proceedings of a court (LXX 41:1—"let them announce judgment," κρίσιν ἀναγγειλάτωσαν). Yahweh challenges them with a question about who has made possible the victorious career of Cyrus. When there is no reply, Yahweh asserts that Yahweh is "first, and will be with the last" (cf. LXX 41:4—"and for the coming times I am," καὶ εἰς τὰ ἐπερχόμενα ἐγώ εἰμι), a claim to be at work throughout history and therefore in the raising up of Cyrus. The nations have been challenged to make their case but, in the light of this claim, have no case to make and instead give way to fear and trembling. When the trial scene reemerges explicitly in 41:21–29 (cf. LXX 41:21—"your judgment draws near," ἐγγίζει ἡ κρίσις ὑμῶν), it is again clear that the purpose of the legal contest is to determine the identity of the true God and that the immediate issue is "whether or not Yahweh is the cause of Cyrus' advent and Babylon's

---

[7] Cf. also K. Nielsen, *Yahweh as Prosecutor and Judge* (Sheffield, JSOT Press, 1978), 25.

[8] Ibid., 40.

[9] Trites, *Concept of Witness*, 44.

downfall."[10] Deutero-Isaiah believes that this can be demonstrated by showing that Yahweh has predicted this course of events, since the one who is able in this way to predict future events must also be Lord of these events. The pagan gods themselves are asked to set forth their case, and when they fail to do so, Yahweh presents one, and it is Yahweh's ability to predict "the former things," to have made predictions that have subsequently been verified, that shows the gods to be worthless. The effective fulfillment of Yahweh's word is the deciding factor in the case, and this is reflected later in the closing section of Deutero-Isaiah in 55:10–11: "so shall my word be that goes out from my mouth; it shall not return to me empty, but it shall accomplish that which I purpose, and succeed in the thing for which I sent it."

This theme is repeated at the beginning of the next trial scene in 43:8–13, when the blind and deaf people of Yahweh (cf. 42:18–20) and all the nations assemble. The question is posed, "Who . . . foretold to us the former things?" and witnesses are required for verification. There is no reply to the question and no witnesses are produced, so again Yahweh's own case is stated. Here a new element emerges as Yahweh tells Israel, "You are my witnesses [LXX—μάρτυρες] . . . and my servant whom I have chosen" (43:10). The deaf and blind will nevertheless be witnesses because they will believe and understand "that I am he" (LXX—ὅτι ἐγώ εἰμι), a self-designation of Yahweh as the one true God that is characteristic of Deutero-Isaiah. The claim is made that, unlike other gods, Yahweh has existed from the beginning and is the only God and Savior Israel has known. Israel's calling to be God's witnesses (LXX—μάρτυρες) is then repeated in 43:12. It is significant that in both 43:10 and 43:12 the LXX adds that God is also a witness and thus its text has two witnesses. Although the trial is between Yahweh and the gods of the nations, the actual audience meant to be reassured by the proceedings is Israel. "The purpose of Deutero-Isaiah's proclamation, then, is to convince his people that Yahweh is right; it is to this end that he employs the language of the lawcourt, which is highly suited to apologetic."[11]

Thus, as the familiar themes are repeated in 44:6–8, Yahweh is introduced as the King of Israel, its Redeemer and Lord of hosts. Yahweh's uniqueness as the first and the last, besides whom there is no god, is asserted. Any challenger is invited to stand up in court (cf. LXX—στήτω) and state his case in terms of being able to announce ahead of time the things to come. Since no response is forthcoming, Yahweh turns to Israel,

---

[10] Nielsen, *Yahweh as Prosecutor and Judge*, 62.
[11] Ibid., 62.

reminding the people of their role as Yahweh's witnesses (LXX—μάρτυρες), who have no need to fear because they can testify to the reliable connection between Yahweh's word of proclamation and its fulfillment[12] and therefore to there being no other god besides Yahweh. In the final trial speech against the nations in 45:18–25, Yahweh is introduced as the Creator God who has not spoken in secret, as the "I am" (LXX 45:19— ἐγώ εἰμι ἐγώ εἰμι) who proclaims the truth. Now those called to assemble for trial and to present their case are the survivors of the nations, those who have survived after Cyrus's defeat of Babylon and his worldwide conquests.[13] Yahweh's claim to have told this long ago and to be the only God can now be seen to be verified by precisely the events that have made those called to trial the survivors. But at this point, instead of the condemnation of the nations that might have been expected at the end of the trial, there is an offer of salvation to those from the ends of the earth (LXX 45:22—οἱ ἀπ᾽ ἐσχάτου τῆς γῆς) if they will turn to the true God. An oath sworn by Yahweh confirms that it is the divine purpose that to Yahweh "every knee shall bow, every tongue shall swear." Since, in the nature of the case, there can be no greater authority by which to swear, Yahweh's witness to this promise of salvation is self-authenticating. The trial scene then ends with the prophet's comment that in the Lord all the seed of Israel shall glory (LXX 45:25—"shall be glorified," ἐνδοξασθήσονται).

2. Yahweh and Israel

"The very reason the case has come to court at all is Israel's lack of confidence that Yahweh is her defender."[14] This leads to the second lawsuit depicted by Deutero-Isaiah—that between Yahweh and the people of Israel. In the disputation of 42:18–25, the implicit charge against Yahweh is reflected in vv. 22, 24: Yahweh has left them to be robbed, plundered, and taken captive. Yahweh's reply is to turn the accusation back on Israel. Yahweh has not been blind to their fate or deaf to their cries (cf. 40:27). They are the ones who are deaf and blind, because of their failure to perceive why their plight has come upon them. Yahweh has been active in history. It is Yahweh who has brought about their plight as an expression of justified wrath at their disobedience. "The purpose of the trial is thus to convince Israel that the Exile was a just punishment for an actual sin."[15]

---

[12] Cf. Westermann, *Isaiah 40–66*, 141.
[13] Cf. R. N. Whybray, *Isaiah 40–66* (London: Oliphants, 1975), 111.
[14] Nielsen, *Yahweh as Prosecutor and Judge*, 68.
[15] Ibid., 70.

The situation is similar in 43:22–28, where Yahweh makes explicit who is the accused at the trial: "Accuse me, let us go to trial [LXX—'let us judge,' κριθῶμεν]; set forth your case, so that you may be proved right" (43:26). Again Yahweh's defense is conducted through an indictment of Israel. If Israel complains that its fate is undeserved because it served Yahweh by offering sacrifices, Yahweh asserts that, because of their sins, these sacrifices had not been offered to *Yahweh* and were not acceptable worship. Yet instead of condemnation, there is a surprising declaration of pardon. "I, I am He [LXX—ἐγώ εἰμι ἐγώ εἰμι] who blots out your transgressions for my own sake" (43:25). When Israel fails to set out its case, the scene is concluded with a further statement of Yahweh's defense. Yahweh's handing over of Israel to its present plight has been justified because of its consistent sin from the time of its ancestors through the period of its mediators or rulers. This point is driven home in 50:1–3. Yahweh is accused of having broken off the relationship with the people, like a husband who has divorced his wife or a father who has sold his family into slavery in order to pay his debts. Again the tables are turned, and Yahweh puts the blame for the situation of separation and slavery squarely on Israel: "because of your sins you were sold, and for your transgressions your mother was put away." Yahweh has done what is necessary in coming to the trial, but there is no response to Yahweh's defense (50:2a). It is not, as Israel is charging, that Yahweh is unable to rescue the people. All Yahweh has to do in reply is to remind the people of the divine power over nature already displayed at the time of their previous rescue in the exodus.

This emphasis on Yahweh's ability to rescue Israel provides the reminder that the lawsuits in Isa 40–55 are embedded within an overall promise of salvation. They are part of a message of comfort and assurance that is meant to remove fear and produce joy and praise. The prophet's insistence that the exile has not undermined or abolished Yahweh's faithfulness to the people comes as a word of comfort to Israel and, not surprisingly, "The Book of Consolation" has been the traditional title for this section of Isaiah. The prophecy begins and ends on this note: "Comfort, O comfort my people, says your God" (40:1), and "For you shall go out in joy, and be led back in peace; the mountains and the hills before you shall burst into song, and all the trees of the field shall clap their hands" (55:12). The assurance of Yahweh's comfort is offered throughout: "I, I am he who comforts you; why then are you afraid of a mere mortal who must die? . . . You fear continually all day long because of the fury of the oppressor, who is bent on destruction. But where is the fury of the oppressor?" (51:12–13; cf. also 49:13; 51:3;

52:9). Knowing such comfort means there is no need for fear: "do not fear, for I am with you, do not be afraid, for I am your God" (41:10; cf. also 40:9; 41:13–14; 43:1–2, 5; 44:2, 8; 54:4). Joy is to be the experience of this God's people: "So the ransomed of the LORD shall return, and come to Zion with singing; everlasting joy shall be upon their heads; they shall obtain joy and gladness, and sorrow and sighing shall flee away" (51:11; cf. also 41:16; 48:20; 49:13; 51:3). And praise and exultation accompany such joy: "Sing to the LORD a new song, his praise from the end of the earth!" (42:10–12; cf. also 43:21; 44:23; 45:25; 49:13; 51:3; 52:9; 54:1).

C. Further Influences from Isaiah 40–55

Three direct quotations from this Isaian prophecy appear in the Fourth Gospel—40:3 in John 1:23; 53:1 in John 12:38; and 54:13 in John 6:45. But in comparing John's use of Scripture with that of Matthew, Hengel makes the point that John "prefers the bare terse clue, the use of a metaphor or motif more than the full citation."[16] The next section will explore some of the ways in which the Fourth Gospel takes up Deutero-Isaiah's use of the lawsuit motif, but already it has become apparent that, along with this motif, other themes and language from the prophecy find echoes in the Fourth Gospel's narrative. At this point it is worth delineating more of these, without spelling out the specific links to the Gospel. This and the following chapter will point out most of these links later. Here their listing will simply enable a fuller appreciation of the extent of Deutero-Isaiah's apparent influence on the Fourth Gospel; these links will show that any of the latter's readers with knowledge of the Jewish Scriptures were expected to interpret the Gospel's narrative and especially its trial motif against this background.

Forensic language associated with our motif is found outside the trial passages that have been examined. In the LXX the noun κρίσις, *judgment,* occurs in 40:27; 42:1, 3, 4 (where the servant is appointed by Yahweh to carry out judgment); 49:4, 25; 50:8, 9; 51:4, 7; 53:8; and 54:17; the verb κρίνειν, *to judge,* appears in 49:25, 51:22; and the noun μαρτύριον is used of David's role as a testimony to the peoples in 55:4. In addition, the LXX in 41:11 uses for opponents οἱ ἀντίδικοι, the term for opponents in a lawsuit.[17]

---

[16] M. Hengel, "The Old Testament in the Fourth Gospel," *HBT* 12 (1990): 31–32.
[17] Cf. BAGD 74.

The issue of truth is at stake in the trial. Yahweh can be said to pro-claim the truth (45:19), and the function of witnesses is to experience and perceive the correspondence between Yahweh's word and Yahweh's deed so that they can confirm the truth of that word (41:26; 43:9). The servant will also bring forth judgment to truth (LXX 42:3—εἰς ἀλήθειαν ἐξοίσει κρίσιν). The LXX version of the trial speech of 41:21–29 stresses that the key question to ask of the gods of the nations is, "From where are you?" (πόθεν ἐστέ; 41:24, 28), and to this question they have no answer.[18] Throughout Isa 40–55, but particularly in the trial speeches against the nations, it is made clear that the true God is the only God: "I am the first and I am the last, and besides me there is no god" (44:6; cf. also 40:18, 23; 41:4; 43:10–11; 44:8; 45:5, 6, 14, 18, 21–22; 46:9; 48:12). This monotheistic emphasis is neither a statement of a numerical kind about God's being nor a statement about the uniqueness of this God's existence in relation to other gods; rather, it is a polemical assertion that Yahweh is the only God of the whole earth who can therefore act as lord of world history. The notion that the continuity between God's predic-tive word and its fulfillment provides the evidence for this assertion is found, as we have seen, in the trial speeches, but it also appears in 42:9 and 46:10. In this connection, the LXX version of Deutero-Isaiah fre-quently employs the ἐγώ εἰμι, "I am," formula for Yahweh's self-predi-cation as the one true God. It occurs four times in the trial speeches (cf. 41:4; 43:10, 25; 45:18), with 43:10 being particularly striking because of its reference to the people of Israel as witnesses who understand that "I am." But the formula in this absolute form is also found in 46:4 (twice), 48:12, and 51:12. Elsewhere ἐγώ εἰμι is used with a predicate—for ex-ample, "I am the Lord" (45:8, 19), "I am God" (45:22; 46:9), "I am your God" (48:17), "I am the first" (48:12), "I am he who comforts you" (51:12), and "I am he who speaks" (52:6). Not surprisingly, God's name also features prominently: "I am the Lord God, this is my name" (42:8) and "Therefore my people shall know my name in that day, for I am he who speaks" (52:6, cf. also 41:25; 42:10; 43:7; 47:4; 48:1, 9, 11; 51:15).

To talk of Yahweh as the true God, the "I am," and to talk of Yahweh's name are also to talk of Yahweh's glory. And in the contro-versy in which Yahweh, the gods of the nations, and Israel are involved, the glory of Yahweh is an issue. At the beginning of the prophecy, it is stated, "Then the glory of the Lord shall be revealed and all flesh shall see the salvation of God" (LXX 40:5). "What reveals Yahweh's glory is his

---

[18] In the Fourth Gospel, this is a key question about Jesus; cf. 7:27, 28; 8:14; 9:29, 30; 19:9.

action in history,"[19] and here it is the action of leading the people out of exile to salvation in their land, not just for Israel but for the whole world to see. Later Yahweh asserts, "my glory I give to no other" (42:8; 48:11; cf. also 40:26; 42:12; 43:7; 49:3). But Yahweh will also give glory to Israel, to the servant, and thereby Yahweh will be glorified: "You are my servant, Israel, in whom I will be glorified" (49:3; cf. 44:23; 45:25; 49:5; 55:5). In fact, the servant will be lifted up and glorified (LXX 52:13—ὑψωθήσεται καὶ δοξασθήσεται), and this will be with a glory not from humans (LXX 52:14).

Deutero-Isaiah and the Fourth Gospel also have major images in common. One of these is light. Yahweh has given the servant to be a light to the nations (cf. 42:6; 49:6), and Yahweh's judgment and salvation will be a light for the nations (LXX 51:4, 5). This image is sometimes combined with those of darkness and blindness: "I have given you as a . . . light to the nations, to open the eyes that are blind, to bring out . . . from the prison those who sit in darkness" (42:6, 7; cf. also 49:9) and "I will lead the blind by a road they do not know. . . . I will turn the darkness before them into light" (42:16). The nations and their gods are portrayed as blind (43:8; 44:18), as is also Israel as Yahweh's servant (42:18–20). The servant given as a light to the nations reflects Deutero-Isaiah's perspective, in which Yahweh's salvation extends beyond Israel (cf. LXX 40:5; LXX 42:4; LXX 45:22–23; LXX 49:6, 8; LXX 51:4–5; 52:10). Another image for the salvation Yahweh provides is that of water. Yahweh will do again for the people what Yahweh did when "he made water flow for them from the rock; he split open the rock and the water gushed out" (48:21). "For I give water in the wilderness, rivers in the desert, to give drink to my chosen people" (43:20; cf. 41:17–20; 44:3). In saving the people, Yahweh will be like a shepherd—"He will feed his flock like a shepherd; he will gather the lambs in his arms . . . and gently lead [LXX—'comfort'] the mother sheep" (40:11)—and later there is the assurance that no one can snatch out of Yahweh's hands (43:13).

D. The Fourth Gospel's Reworking of Deutero-Isaiah's Lawsuits

The implied reader who is also an informed reader and who not only has received Jesus' witness that the Scriptures testify on his behalf (5:39; cf. also, e.g., 2:17, 22; 7:39; 12:16) but has also picked up on the narrator's three direct citations from Isa 40–55 (40:3 in John 1:23; 53:1

---

[19] Westermann, *Isaiah 40–66*, 39.

in John 12:38; and 54:13 in John 6:45) will not fail to have heard re-sounding echoes from these chapters of Isaiah.[20] The placing of the first two of these explicit quotations, one right at the beginning of the public ministry, in John the Baptist's witness, and the other right at the end, in the narrator's summary, to form an *inclusio*, should give a major clue to the significance of this section of Scripture for the narrative. This scrip-tural depth enables the implied reader to discern clearly that, in the Fourth Gospel's narrative, the two lawsuits of Deutero-Isaiah have been brought together. The lawsuit between God and the nations becomes that between God and the world and provides the overarching frame-work within which Israel's controversy with God is now seen to be a part. In fact, Israel's lawsuit with God not only forms the counterplot within the main plot; Israel also now becomes the representative of the world in the main plot. In all this, as we have seen, God is now repre-sented by Jesus, God's authorized agent and chief witness. In the trial with the nations, Yahweh had a dual role as both accuser or prosecutor and judge, and in the trial with Israel he was also the accused. Jesus' role combines all these functions. As a witness, he is sometimes the accuser and sometimes the accused, and at the same time he is the judge. This in turn sheds further light on Israel's role. In Isaiah Israel had complaints against Yahweh, but in the process the accusers became the accused. This is replayed in the new lawsuit as the accusers of God's representa-tive, Jesus, again become the accused with not dissimilar charges laid against them.

Since, for the Fourth Gospel, Israel as a whole has now abdicated its place as the servant-witness in God's lawsuit with the world and become simply the accuser, a small group within Israel, Jesus first as the chief witness but then, too, his followers, takes over the role that the nation as a whole should have been playing in God's lawsuit with the world. In the case of both Jesus and his followers, as in Isaiah, the witness role is combined with that of the servant (cf. 13:15, 16; also 15:20). Israel's qualification to be a witness lay in the choice of this nation to believe and proclaim that Yahweh is the one true God, the "I am," the one whose word of prediction is realized in history. Jesus' relationship of depend-ence on, and oneness with, the Father is such that in his witness to the one true God he can use the "I am" designation of himself and, as the Logos who has become flesh, can embody the word that is realized in

---

[20] It is difficult, therefore, to understand Beutler, *Martyria,* 306, in his re-jection of any direct link between John's Gospel and the lawsuits of Isaiah. Blank, *Krisis,* 199–200, 311–12, had earlier recognized the link.

history. In the LXX, the term used most frequently for Yahweh's predictive word is ἀναγγέλλειν—*to announce or declare* (cf., e.g., 41:26; 42:9; 43:9, 12; 44:7; 46:10; 48:14). In the Fourth Gospel, the same verb is employed when Jesus, by implication, is the one who announces all things (cf. 4:25) and when the Paraclete continues his role (cf. 16:3, 15). It is clear from the lawsuit in Isaiah that, in Yahweh's dealings with the world, Israel as chief witness was meant to manifest Yahweh's name and be the bearer of Yahweh's glory. Now the same language is used in the Fourth Gospel for Jesus' role.

One key way of speaking about belief in Jesus in the Fourth Gospel is the language of believing in his name (cf. 1:12; 2:23; 3:18), and in the statement of purpose in 20:31, it becomes apparent that this is synonymous with believing that Jesus is the sort of Messiah who is Son of God. In delineating what it means for Jesus to be Son of God, the Gospel places special stress on the oneness of Jesus with God, which enables him to use of himself Yahweh's self-predication that functions as a name—ἐγώ εἰμι. It is natural, therefore, when Jesus speaks of having come in his Father's name (5:43) or having made his Father's name known to the disciples (17:6, 26), to think not only of the name "Father" but also particularly of "I am."[21] Most striking here is the way in which Jesus, particularly when on trial before Israel and at his arrest, employs the words ἐγώ εἰμι without any predicate (cf. 8:24, 28, 58; 18:5, 8). The narrator leaves no doubt about the significance of this formula on the lips of the main character because immediately after the third of these pronouncements in John 8 comes the attempt to stone Jesus for blasphemy. Similarly, the possibility of simply taking the saying in 18:5 as Jesus' straightforward identification of himself to the police and soldiers is removed by the narrator's depiction of the latter's response, "they stepped back and fell to the ground" (18:6)—the typical response to a theophany. Significantly also, the use of the predicateless ἐγώ εἰμι in 13:19 with the disciples appears, as in Isaiah, in the context of the ability to predict the future: "I tell you this now, before it occurs, so that when it does occur, you may believe that I am." And just as in Isaiah the one who declares, "I am" (LXX Isa 45:18), can also say, "I did not speak in secret" (Isa 45:19; cf. also 48:16), so in the Fourth Gospel Jesus can declare, "I am" at his arrest (18:5) and then also assert, at the interrogation that follows, "I have said nothing in secret" (18:20). The lawsuit of Isaiah contains a contrast between Yahweh's open declarations and the failure

---

[21] Cf. also F. W. Young, "A Study of the Relation of Isaiah to the Fourth Gospel," *ZNW* 46 (1955): 223–24.

of both the nations and Israel to respond when they are challenged to present a case. There is a similar note in Jesus' interrogation before Caiaphas. Jesus tells the high priest to check with those who have witnessed his teaching (18:21) and challenges the officer to testify to what he has said wrong (18:23), but in neither case do they produce witnesses or testimony against him. For the implied author, this simply underlines the rightness of Jesus' cause (cf. also 18:29, 38b; 19:4, 6).

In Isaiah the God whose glory is given to no other (Isa 42:8; 48:11) will be glorified in Israel—"You are my servant, Israel, in whom I will be glorified" (49:3; cf. also 44:23; 55:5)—and Israel will in fact be God's glory (46:13). Just as Israel, as the servant-witness, was meant to be the bearer of Yahweh's glory, so Jesus seeks the glory of the one who sent him (John 7:18), can ask his Father to glorify his name (12:28), and can then say of himself, "Now the Son of Man has been glorified, and God has been glorified in him. If God has been glorified in him, God will also glorify him in himself and will glorify him at once" (13:31–32). God's glory is bound up with Jesus' glory (8:54), and the implied author of the Fourth Gospel depicts Jesus as the bearer of God's glory throughout the narrative. The prologue sees the whole career of the Logos made flesh as one of glory (1:14). The signs in his public mission to Israel reveal his glory (cf. 2:11; 11:4), and the honor he deserves because of his relation to the Father is stressed (cf. 5:22, 23, 41). But Jesus' career moves towards a supreme hour of glory in his death and departure (12:23, 27, 28; 13:1; 17:1, 5). In a strange way, Israel's servant-witness was to combine a lifting up and glorification with suffering and death (Isa 52:13–53:12), and now in the Gospel's narrative the suffering and death of the witness are said to be the moment not only of his glorification but also of his lifting up (cf. 3:14; 8:28; 12:32–34). We have already referred to 8:28 in connection with the Fourth Gospel's taking up of the "I am" formulation. It can now be seen that it combines this in a creative fashion with the notion of the lifting up of the servant-witness, indicating that precisely in the exaltation, which is at the same time crucifixion, the unique divine identity of this witness as "I am" is disclosed.

Israel, as witness and as servant, was also meant to be a light to the nations, to open the eyes of the blind and to lead people out of darkness. The Fourth Gospel's presentation of Jesus as witness includes his claim to be the light of the world, and this is followed by the promise that whoever follows Jesus will not walk in darkness but will have the light of life (8:12; cf. also 1:4, 5, 9; 3:19–21; 12:35, 36). The following chapter of the Gospel establishes the claims of the witness in narrative form as the man born blind is led out of his darkness and enabled to see both literally and spiritually (9:1–41).

Again, the issues at stake in the foundational trial narrative and in its new version can be seen to be very similar. Israel's experience of exile and the events surrounding it had, for many, called into question Yahweh's claim to be the one true God, the Lord of history and in control of events. The prophet's response was, within the context of the cosmic lawsuit, to point to the correspondence between the word of Yahweh and the situation in the world and, on this basis, to provide consolation and encouragement instead of fear. Similarly, for the implied readers of the Fourth Gospel, the mission of Jesus had provoked dispute about the truth, resulting in conflicting claims about the true God and how God is known, and had raised questions about this God's sovereignty. The narrative frequently reinforces the idea that questions about belief in Jesus are at the same time questions about belief in God. Monotheism is again in view.[22] Jesus' opponents interpret his claims as a threat to monotheism, as blasphemy (cf. 5:17, 18; 8:58, 59; 10:30–39; 19:7). But the Gospel's discourse stresses oneness, not twoness, in speaking about Jesus' relation with God (cf. 10:30; 17:22) and makes clear that the Son is the Logos, the immanent expression of the one God. This is why, for the Fourth Gospel, to see Jesus is to see the Father (14:9), and Thomas' confession about Jesus—"My Lord and my God!" (20:28)—is totally appropriate, since to believe in Jesus is not to believe in a second God but in the one true God. This twoness in oneness is made clear in Jesus' prayer in 17:3: "This is eternal life, that they may know you, the only true God, and Jesus Christ whom you have sent."

The death by crucifixion of the Christ in whom the readers believe, together with what has happened to them because of this belief, raises the question of whether God has really been in control, just as Yahweh's sovereignty over history was an issue in Deutero-Isaiah. These concerns are reflected in the narrative's depiction of Jesus' mission as part of God's larger purposes in the divine lawsuit with the world and as comprising events that have been predicted in Scripture and are in accord with God's will and timetable. They are reflected also in the pains the narrator takes to show his main character, Jesus, in control throughout the narrative,

---

[22] Trites, *Concept of Witness,* 79, rightly draws attention to the parallel between Isa 40–55 and the Gospel but appears to miss the closeness of the connection. He writes, "In Isaiah 40–55 the debate is over the claims of Yahweh as the Creator, the only true God and the Lord of history . . . ; in John it is over the Messiahship and divine Sonship of Jesus." But the latter debate is also a replay, in a different setting, of the former—it is over claims about the only true God that are now embodied in claims about Jesus as the Messiah who is the divine Son.

especially in his arrest, trial before Pilate, and death, to indicate his omniscience, and to stress the reliable fulfillment of his words. The issue is also God's glory, now linked in the Fourth Gospel with Jesus' glory. Contrary to all appearances, proclaims this narrative, this glory is to be seen throughout Jesus' mission and particularly in the moment of his death. And as in Isaiah, the literary device of the cosmic lawsuit, which ties these concerns together, is meant to strengthen wavering faith and, by dealing with anxiety and fear, encourage the readers to play their own part as witnesses.

Both in Deutero-Isaiah and in the Fourth Gospel, the ultimate purpose of the lawsuit is the salvation of the world. Although it is not always apparent what form this salvation will take, it is clear in Deutero-Isaiah that Yahweh's purposes of salvation extend beyond Israel. The God who has brought the nations to trial is the only God of the whole earth, the Lord of world history, and the divine judgment includes not only an indictment of the nations but promises of salvation. The very fact that Israel is to be Yahweh's witness among the nations speaks of God's larger purposes. The servant is to bring justice or judgment to the nations (LXX Isa 42:1, 4), and in his name the Gentiles will trust or set their hope (LXX 42:4). The servant is to be a covenant to the nations (LXX 49:8) and a light to the nations (42:7; 49:6), and this light will be for salvation for the ends of the earth (LXX 49:6). What is said of the servant can also be said of Yahweh: "my judgment will be for a light to the nations," and "on my arm shall the Gentiles trust or set their hope" (LXX 51:4, 5). All flesh (LXX 40:5) or all the ends of the earth (52:10) shall see the salvation of God. And as we have noted, it is striking that the trial scene with the nations in 45:18–25 closes not with condemnation but with an offer to all the ends of the earth or to "those from the ends of the earth" (LXX) to turn and be saved (45:22, 23).

That (for the most part) unbelieving Jews take on the role of the world in the Fourth Gospel should not disguise the fact that the lawsuit remains a cosmic one and that its issues are for the whole world and not simply for Israel. The setting of the mission of the Logos is the world that came into being through him (John 1:3, 10), and the arena of his followers' mission and witness is to be the world (17:18; cf. also 17:23). Jesus' invitations are for anyone and everyone who will believe (cf., e.g., 3:15, 16). John the Baptist testifies to Jesus as the Lamb of God who takes away the sin of the world (1:29), and it is the Samaritans who confess that Jesus is the Savior of the world (4:42). Jesus is depicted as the light not just of Israel but of the world (8:12; 9:5; cf. 12:46). He gives life to the world (6:33, 51), and the universal scope of this gift of life is underlined in 17:2: "you have given him authority over all flesh, to give eternal life to all whom you have given him." And it is in the context of the visit of some Greeks to him that Jesus claims, "And I, when I am lifted up from the earth, will draw all people to myself" (12:32). Again, the primary purpose of the judgment in the Fourth Gospel's lawsuit is not condemnation but salvation. Jesus stresses that he has been sent not to condemn the world but in order that the world might be saved through him (3:17; 12:47).

E. The Lawsuit and Other Scriptural Links

The links with the lawsuit motif are not limited to chapters 40–55 within Isaiah. Isaiah 11:1–10 speaks of the future Davidic king as the bearer of the Spirit and as one who shall not judge by appearance or outward glory (οὐ κατὰ τὴν δόξαν κρινεῖ) or convict on the basis of report (οὐδὲ κατὰ τὴν λαλιὰν ἐλέγξει). The latter verb is used of the Spirit's role in the Fourth Gospel's lawsuit in 16:8, and elsewhere Jesus issues the warning not to judge by appearances but to judge with right judgment (7:24) and exemplifies this standard of judgment himself (cf. 8:15, 16). Interestingly, in this same context (cf. LXX Isa 11:12), the messianic king is also said to be a sign (σημεῖον) for the nations.

Deutero-Isaiah itself points back to exodus motifs, including that of the supply of water from the rock: "he made water flow for them from the rock; he split open the rock and the water gushed out" (Isa 48:21). One of the remarkable features of the account in Exod 17:1–7 is that this incident is set in the framework of a lawsuit. In Exod 17:2 the people are said to file a complaint or bring a suit against Moses. The NRSV translation "The people quarreled with Moses" does not capture the legal force of the Hebrew text's use of the root רִיב, *rîb*, which is reinforced in the name given to the place by Moses in 17:7—Meribah. As we noted earlier, *rîb* is the term used elsewhere for the covenant lawsuit, usually brought by Yahweh against Israel. Both verses (17:2, 7) see the incident also as a testing of Yahweh, hence the other place name—Massah (17:7; cf. also Deut 6:16). But to test Yahweh by bringing a suit against Moses is to put Yahweh on trial. So Meribah turns out to be Israel's suit against Yahweh.

Other details in the narrative confirm this interpretation. Despite having been fed with manna when they were hungry, the people now believe that the absence of water means that they are about to die of thirst. Their accusation against Moses is that he has betrayed them by bringing them to such a plight, and they are prepared to sentence him to death by stoning. Moses discerns that the real question at stake is not so much his leadership but "Is the LORD among us or not?" (17:7); it is the Lord whom they are testing and putting on trial. In this situation, Yahweh tells Moses to go on ahead of the people and to take with him a number of the elders of the people who will effectively serve as witnesses and judges in Moses' meeting with Yahweh. Moses is also to take with him the rod with which he struck the Nile. So Moses is to go in his role as judge (cf. also 18:13), bearing the rod of judgment. Because it represents the power of Yahweh's judgment (cf. also Isa 30:31, 32), this rod is also the symbol of Moses' power and authority. Now, instead of Moses having to stand before Yahweh to be judged, Yahweh promises to stand before Moses. Yahweh will stand trial and will stand on the rock. In this way, Yahweh becomes identified with the rock. It is significant that both in the Song of Moses in Deut 32:4, 15, 18, 31 and in Pss 78:35 and 95:1 (psalms that recall this incident in Pss 78:15–20 and 95:8, 9), God is in fact given the name "the rock." It may be even more significant that this title is used of God in the midst of the lawsuits in Isa 40–55, where Yahweh declares, "You are my witnesses! Is there any god besides me? There is no other rock; I know not one" (44:8), and where, as we have noted, the incident of water flowing from the rock is recounted (48:21). Paul's identification in 1 Cor 10:4 of the rock from which the people drank as Christ is a variation that provides evidence of the continuation of this type of interpretation into the first century C.E. So, when Moses is told to strike the rock on which Yahweh stands, in this legal setting Yahweh is receiving the sentence of judgment that the people wish to carry out on Moses. And when the true judge takes the penalty the rebellious people deserve, provision is made for them and a stream of life-giving water gushes out from the rock.

This is precisely the pattern in the narrative of the Fourth Gospel. At the Feast of Tabernacles, Jesus announces that he is the provision for those who are thirsty and that, in fulfillment of Scripture, out of his belly will flow rivers of living water. The narrator then explains that this is a reference to the Spirit that believers would receive when Jesus was glorified (7:37–39). Later, when Jesus is glorified through his death by crucifixion, blood and water flow from his side, and the reader is reminded of his earlier promise. In this way, when the true judge accepts the verdict of condemnation at the hands of those who deserve this verdict, once more the situation is reversed and the positive verdict of life is made available.

This description of the narrative pattern in the Fourth Gospel hides two interpretative problems associated with John 7:37–39. First, there is ambiguity about the punctuation. If a full stop is placed after πινέτω, "let [him] drink," then the water is said to flow from "the one who believes in me." But if the full stop is placed after the latter clause, then the subject of the Scripture citation is Christ rather than the believer. Both on internal grounds—of the relation posited between Christ or the believer and water and the Spirit elsewhere in the narrative—and on grounds of the likely sources of the citation, it makes better sense to place the full stop after "the one who believes in me" and therefore to see Christ as the one from whom the rivers of living water flow.[23]

The second problem of interpretation is the source of the citation. Most commentators agree that a composite citation is in view and that two types of scriptural material about living water have been combined. On the one hand, there is the exodus motif we have examined from Exod 17:6 (cf. also Num 20:8, 11; Deut 8:15), with its repetition in the Psalms (cf. Pss 78:15–20; 95:8, 9). On the other hand, there is eschatological material that speaks of the provision of living water in the future (cf. Zech 14:8, "On that day living waters shall flow out from Jerusalem"; Ezek 47:1–12, the vision in which water flows from the temple). The two types of material are linked in references in Deutero-Isaiah where the exodus motif is taken up to depict future salvation. In Isa 43:20 the new thing God will do will also include giving "water in the wilderness, rivers in the desert, to give drink to my chosen people," and in Isa 44:3 this giving of water is linked with the pouring out of God's Spirit. The Fourth Gospel depicts Jesus as the replacement of the Jerusalem temple. There is good reason to think, therefore, that it may well be associating the notion of the wilderness rock with that of the rock at the foundation of the Jerusalem temple, as in some Jewish traditions.[24] In any case, the sequence of the Fourth Gospel's narrative provides a strong warrant for seeing Exod 17 and the Meribah incident as a major ingredient in the composite quotation. In John 6 the miracle of the manna from Exod 16 is recalled and Jesus claims to be the bread of life. Now in John 7 the giving of water at Meribah from Exod 17 forms part of the scriptural reference as Jesus claims to be the source of living water.

But the significance of the Meribah tradition for the Gospel narrative goes further. When Jesus, as true witness and judge, undergoes the

---

[23] For a good discussion of these questions, see G. M. Burge, *The Anointed Community: The Holy Spirit in the Johannine Tradition* (Grand Rapids: Eerdmans, 1987), 88–93.

[24] E.g., *t. Sukkah* 3.3–18.

sentence of death and thereby is enabled to provide the positive verdict of life for believers, the beloved disciple witnesses both blood and water flowing from his side (John 19:34). Later Jewish traditions about the Meribah rock also hold that both blood and water came from the rock. The Palestinian Targum on Num 20:11 claims, "At the first time it dropped blood, but at the second time there came forth a multitude of waters" (*Tg. Ps.-J.* Num 20:11). Midrash *Exodus Rabbah,* which includes an interpretation of Ps 78:20, says, "Moses struck the rock twice, and first it gushed out blood and then water." It is highly likely, then, that the controversy of Exod 17 and its ongoing interpretation feed into the Fourth Gospel's cosmic controversy alongside the reworking of the lawsuit motifs from Deutero-Isaiah.

F. Scripture in the Lawsuit

The first part of this chapter noted that both parties in the Gospel's trial appeal to the law and therefore also to Scripture as witness for their case. From the implied author's point of view, the validity of the law lay in the past (cf. John 1:17), and in Jesus' confrontation with his opponents, he can refer to the law as "your law" (e.g., 8:17; 10:34). To judge simply on the basis of the law of Moses is unenlightened judgment (7:23–24). But even though the opposition also appeal to Scripture, Scripture does not receive the same negative evaluation nor does it become "your Scripture" in the implied author's perspective. In 7:41b–42 some of the crowd use Scripture to raise objections to Jesus' claims to messiahship: "Surely the Messiah does not come from Galilee, does he? Has not the scripture said that the Messiah is descended from David and comes from Bethlehem . . . ?" And in 7:50–52, when Nicodemus makes a more positive appeal to the law for a fair hearing for Jesus, his fellow Pharisees reply, "Search [the Scriptures] and you will see that no prophet is to arise from Galilee." In replying to the charge of blasphemy, Jesus appeals to Ps 82:6 as written in "your law" but then, in making positive use of the text, says, "and the scripture cannot be annulled" (10:34–36).

For the Fourth Gospel, Scripture, when viewed properly, witnesses to Jesus, and it does so in two main ways. The first is seen in the use of specific scriptural citations to show that what happened to Jesus was in fulfillment of Scripture and therefore according to the divine will. Scripture can be viewed as a prophetic document foretelling the identity of Jesus and significant aspects of his mission. Although the Fourth Gospel employs Scripture in this fashion, particularly in its passion narrative, in ways not found in the Synoptics, such use of Scripture appears substantially less in the narrative as a whole than its use in each of the Synoptics. It is more characteristic of the Fourth Gospel to employ the Jewish Scriptures to provide the background for the narrative's use of motifs, including that of the lawsuit, symbols, and types, which are all seen as summed up in Jesus.

Ultimately, however, in the implied author's perspective, Scripture is not there simply for people to search through it, looking for arguments to decide the truth of the claims about Jesus. The opponents search the Scriptures, but because they do not have the word of God abiding in them through believing in Jesus, they are unable to see the true role of the Scriptures in the lawsuit—that the Scriptures testify on Jesus' behalf (5:38, 39). Scripture needs interpretation in the light of God's new revelation in the incarnate Word, the one who now speaks the words of God (cf. 3:34). Jesus' discourse in John 6 about the bread of life serves as an example of this understanding of Scripture; here the commentary on the Scripture text of Exod 16:4, 15, cited in John 6:31, is interwoven with, yet made to serve, the commentary on the saying of Jesus himself in 6:27. Scripture has to be understood in the light of the word of Jesus, which supersedes it. It is his word, not that of Scripture, that provides life (6:63), that serves as the norm by which people will be judged (12:48), and that provides the commandment by which disciples are to orientate their lives (13:34). This understanding of Scripture is an eschatological gift. The promise of Isa 54:13 that "All your children shall be taught by the LORD" is cited in John 6:45, where it is explained that all who have learned from the Father come to Jesus. In 8:47 it is also made clear that, to hear the words of God truly, one needs to be "of God," that is, to share the perspective from above that comes from being born of God (1:13) or being born of the Spirit or from above (3:3, 5). In the narrative, the disciples exemplify such an understanding. They only remember and believe the word of Scripture in Ps 69:9 after the resurrection (cf. 2:17, 22), and they only remember and see the significance of Zech 9:9 after Jesus' glorification (cf. 12:16). This is so because it is only after Jesus' glorification that they receive the Spirit (7:39), who in glorifying Jesus teaches them all things and guides them into all the truth (cf. 14:26; 16:13, 14). Until they receive the Spirit, they do not understand the Scriptures (20:9). Being "taught by God" (6:45) is realized for them in being taught by the Spirit, and it is the Spirit who teaches them to understand Scripture as testifying to Jesus in the trial of truth.

Without such a Spirit-taught understanding, Scripture will function as a witness in a quite different sense. Within Scripture itself, this different sense of witness is foreshadowed. According to Deut 31:26 (cf. also 32:46), the written law, now part of Israel's Scripture, was to stand as a witness that could testify against disobedience on Israel's part. In the Fourth Gospel, it is claimed that those who do not believe that Moses wrote about and testified to Jesus will find that Moses' writings become instead the accusing witness referred to in Deuteronomy. Significantly, the Gospel's narrative's witness to Jesus, which incorporates Scripture's witness to Jesus, will itself become inscripturated (21:24, 25). And the purpose of this inscripturated witness is to contribute to faith in Jesus as Messiah, Son of God, so that, in the continuing cosmic lawsuit in which it plays its part, the Gospel's readers will not find themselves accused but instead experience the positive verdict of life (20:30, 31).

chapter three

SOME KEY STAGES
in the TRIAL PROCEEDINGS

Our depiction, to this point, of the trial motif in John's Gospel has been executed with a broad brush. Now that we have also seen the scriptural background that informs this motif, the time has come to fill in some of the details. We will not look at every reference relevant to the motif. Instead some key stages in the trial proceedings have been chosen for close reading.[1] The eight stages selected represent material where the cluster of notions associated with the motif are most evident. We could discuss Jesus' dialogue with the Samaritan woman, which leads to her testifying and the villagers accepting her testimony, but this forensic language occurs only at the end, in 4:39.[2] We could also include the dispute of 7:14–39, which mentions judgment (7:24), or the discussion in 10:22–39, which addresses the issue of testimony (10:25), since both entail an interrogation or mini-trial and the attempt to have Jesus arrested. But their inclusion would have made an already lengthy chapter intolerably long, and neither adds significantly to the picture that is developed from the other stages. The final stage, dealing with the testimony of the beloved disciple, is also omitted from this chapter and discussed instead

---

[1] No attempt has been made here to be comprehensive in the coverage of issues or in the interaction with secondary literature. Instead the main aim is to highlight the elements of the lawsuit motif and their function within the various passages.

[2] Maccini, *Her Testimony Is True,* 118–44, discusses at some length the encounter with the Samaritan woman and her testimony.

in the next chapter when we examine more fully the question of the narrative's closure.[3] Broader hermeneutical issues arising from the readings of these sections, such as the Gospel's apparent anti-Judaism and its treatment of the relation of truth and power, will be handled in later chapters.

A. The Testimony of John the Baptist (1:6–8, 15; 1:19–34; 3:25–30)

Apart from Jesus himself, the two most important human witnesses in the narrative of the Fourth Gospel are John the Baptist and the beloved disciple, and as we have seen, their testimonies frame the Gospel. There are also specific links between their testimonies. But of the two, the Gospel gives more space and emphasis to the witness of John the Baptist. Since he is the first witness called in the trial proceedings, it is not surprising that so much attention is given to his functioning in this role. This ensures that the reader will not be able to miss what will become the dominant motif in the narrative.

Its treatment twice in the prologue indicates just how significant John the Baptist's witness is for this Gospel. The instances occur, first, after the reference to the Logos as the light shining in the darkness and then in the midst of the community's confession about the Logos. There is much debate about the origin and composition of the prologue, but it has been argued with some plausibility that a hymnic piece about Christ as Logos has been taken up and adapted to form the introduction to the Gospel. There can be no denying that even in the prologue's final form the references to John the Baptist read very much like insertions into already structured material. If 1:6–8 were omitted, the motif of the Logos as the light would follow on quite naturally from v.5 to v. 9. Even more clearly, the assertion that "we have seen his glory" and that this glory of the Logos is full of grace and truth (v. 14) is continued in v. 16 with the confession that his followers have received grace from this fullness—in the same first-person plural language, so that the narrator's third-person singular account of John's testimony in v. 15 interrupts the flow quite abruptly. This grounds the prologue in the realm of history and indicates, just as did the early Christian preaching (cf. Acts 10:37; 13:24, 25) and the synoptic tradition, that the mission of Jesus had its starting point in connection with the mission of John the Baptist. But what is distinctive is the Fourth Gospel's al-

---

[3] See ch. 4, sec. D, below.

most exclusive conceptualization of the latter as a witness and of his message as a testimony.

John the Baptist is made a witness to crucial aspects of the Gospel's distinctive Christology. Witness has to be borne when claims about the truth, claims about the identity of Christ, are in dispute. As vv. 7–8 assert twice, John's mission is to testify to the one who is the light. Jesus will be depicted as the light again later in contexts employing aspects of the lawsuit motif—in 3:19–21; 12:35, 36; and 12:46 in connection with judgment, in 8:12 in connection with testimony, and in 9:5 in the narrative about the blind man and his interrogation. As our previous chapter noted, in the context of the lawsuit in Deutero-Isaiah, Yahweh declared that the servant was to be a light to the nations (Isa 42:6), and elsewhere in Isaiah the imagery of light is employed in messianic contexts (cf. Isa 11:2; 61:1, 2). The goal of John the Baptist's witness to the light is that through his testimony all might believe (John 1:7). This is the first use of a verb—πιστεύειν, *to believe*—that occurs ninety-eight times in the Gospel, and its occurrence here underlines that John the Baptist's testimony serves the same purpose as the lawsuit motif in the Gospel as a whole: it is to produce belief (cf. 20:30, 31). To believe through him is to receive his witness as true and thereby to accept as valid the claims about the one to whom he testifies. Throughout the narrative, belief is depicted as made possible through witness, and true reception of such witness—true belief—is shown to involve a person's total allegiance. The scope of John's witness in the formulation of v. 7 is also significant. The goal is that *all* might believe. This is appropriate in the cosmic setting of the prologue. It lifts John the Baptist's mission from one simply within Israel, as it is clearly portrayed in the Synoptics, onto the world stage. By being incorporated as witness in this narrative of the cosmic lawsuit, it now has a more universal audience.

The second reference to John the Baptist in the prologue again entails a witness to the Gospel's distinctive Christology, this time to Christ's preexistence. A literal translation of v. 15 would read, "John witnesses about him and has cried out, saying, 'This was he of whom I said, "He who comes after me has become before me because he was prior to me."'" The present and perfect tenses of the verbs employed for John's activity indicate its continuing significance, and his witness is in fact incorporated into the community's present witness to the Logos with its "we" language in vv. 14, 16. In the composition of the narrative, the testimony may well have been taken from the material in vv. 19–34, since it repeats almost verbatim the testimony of v. 30. But in the present narrative, this first instance has a significant change of tense—not "this is he," as in v. 30, but "this was he." John the Baptist's testimony here shares the same perspective as the rest of the prologue as it looks back on and witnesses to the career of Jesus the Logos as a whole.

The content of the testimony plays with the notion of being "before" and is to the effect that the one who comes after John in history is before him in rank because, in reality, he was also before him in time. In this way, John the Baptist is made to witness to the preexistence of Jesus, a view of Jesus that will color the narrative and be made explicit in a number of places (e.g., 8:58; 17:5, 24). This insight into Jesus' preexistence goes far beyond anything found in John the Baptist's message in the Synoptics and anything that the historical John the Baptist is likely to have been aware of in his relationship to Jesus. It shows how thoroughly the evangelist has incorporated tradition into his own narrative purposes, and is an instance of the way he has constructed the narrative as a whole by reading back the present beliefs of his community into his story of Jesus' mission. Witness to Jesus' preexistence is not, however, the main focus of John the Baptist's declaration. It is only the presupposition or warrant for the claim that the Logos is superior in rank to John himself. Some of the reasons for the necessity of such a claim become clearer in 1:19–34.

The dominance of the characterization of John the Baptist as witness can be seen from the *inclusio* that frames 1:19–34. The narrator now sets his narrative squarely within the arena of human history—during John's mission of baptizing—and on earthly terrain (cf. v. 28) and begins by describing the testimony (μαρτυρία) given by John (v. 19). This section ends with John himself talking about his activity of witnessing (μεμαρτύρηκα—v. 34). The passage falls into two parts—vv. 19–28 and vv. 29–34, the latter set on the following day. In the first, John's testimony is primarily about his own identity and mission and only secondarily about Jesus, while in the second, it is directly about Jesus and his identity and mission. Just as the lawsuit motif was carried forward in Deutero-Isaiah by means of trial scenes and disputations, so in the Fourth Gospel it is promoted by means of trial scenes and interrogations. In vv. 19–28 interrogation provokes John's testimony.[4] As will be the case throughout most of the narrative, the interrogators are the Jewish religious authorities. Priests and Levites have been sent from Jerusalem by "the Jews" (v.19) or the Pharisees (v. 24). The terminology of confession and denial used about John in 1:20 is closely associated with

---

[4] Cf. Blank, *Krisis,* 202: "Der Abschnitt 1,19–28 stellt ja in seiner Form ein juridisches Verhör dar."

that of witness and has clear forensic overtones.[5] Confession will be used in conjunction with the threat of excommunication from the synagogue (cf. 9:22; 12:42), while denial is used of Peter under interrogation (cf. 13:38; 18:25, 27). In regard to himself, John confesses and does not deny that he is neither the Messiah nor Elijah nor the prophet. This demonstrates beyond doubt his subordination to the one who will be the chief witness. But more is at stake. The strong emphasis of the formulation—"He confessed and did not deny it, but confessed"—and the triple-negative content of the confession about his identity cry out for further explanation. This phenomenon corresponds with the strictly superfluous negative statement of 1:8—"He himself was not the light"—and with the later repetition of the denial of messiahship in 3:28, the assertion by John that he must decrease while Jesus must increase in 3:30, and the declaration that John performed no signs in 10:41. From the perspective of the Fourth Gospel, and in contrast to the synoptic tradition, John is not to be thought of as Elijah (cf. Matt 11:14; 17:12; Mark 9:13; cf. also Luke 1:17) nor even as the prophet (cf. Luke 1:76). This begins to make sense when we read later in the narrative that some of John's disciples did not follow Jesus (cf. John 3:22–26) and when, on the basis of such evidence as Acts 18:24–19:7, Justin, *Trypho* 80, with its reference to the baptists, and the later Pseudo-Clementine *Recognitions* 1. 54, 60, we posit a continuing movement of followers of the Baptist who made high claims for their leader and with whom, at some stage, Johannine Christians came into dispute. John's testimony therefore has secondary apologetic force in relation to such a group. There is to be no doubt about his secondary status in comparison with Jesus. A similar apologetic appears to lie behind Matthew's redaction of the baptism of Jesus (cf. Matt 3:14) and the account in the *Gospel of the Hebrews*.[6]

John has a highly significant but nonetheless limited role as a preparatory witness. In order to identify himself positively, he quotes words from Isa 40:3: "I am the voice of one crying out in the wilderness, 'Make straight the way of the Lord.'" Whereas in the synoptic narratives these

---

[5] R. Bultmann, *The Gospel of John* (Oxford: Blackwell, 1971), 86–88, made the appropriate observations: "The cumbrous introduction to the Baptist's answer (v. 20) . . . has the full weight of the solemn testimony of a witness in a trial . . . . This, then, is the prelude to the struggle which runs throughout the whole of the life of Jesus: it is a struggle between Christian faith and the world, represented by Judaism, a struggle which is continually portrayed as a trial, in which the 'Jews' are under the illusion that they are the judges, whereas in fact they are the accused before the forum of God."

[6] Cf. Jerome, *Pelag.* 3.2.

words are part of the narrators' comments on the mission of John, here they constitute John's self-identification and add the authority of Scripture to his witness. When interrogated about his baptismal activity, John's response is that he simply baptizes in water (with an implied contrast that is not made explicit until John 1:33) and that there is one coming after him who is at present unrecognized but is so superior in status that John is not worthy to untie the thong of his sandal.

John's more direct testimony to Jesus in vv. 29–34 makes three major claims about him—he is the lamb of God (v. 29), he possesses the Spirit (vv. 32, 33), and he is the Son of God (v. 34). As has already been indicated, this Gospel's use of Scripture and its imagery is frequently hard to pin down. It often draws from a cluster of sources rather than a single identifiable one. This is the case in the identification of Jesus with the Lamb of God who takes away the sin of the world, which appears to combine the imagery of the servant-witness who bears the sin of many and is led as a lamb to the slaughter, from Deutero-Isaiah (Isa 53:4–12), with that of the Passover lamb, from the exodus tradition (Exod 12:1–11). The latter colors the depiction of Jesus' death, which, in this narrative, occurs at the same time as the slaughter of the Passover lambs (cf. John 19:14, 31) and is seen as that of an unblemished Passover lamb (19:36, citing Exod 12:46). After the repetition of the saying that Jesus' priority of rank is due to his priority through preexistence,[7] John makes clear that his baptizing with water had the purpose of revealing to Israel the one who was previously unknown (cf. 1:26). The one whom the narrative depicts as the revealer must himself first be revealed, and this takes place through the baptismal activity of John.

In contrast with the accounts in Matthew and Mark, Jesus' baptism, important as it was as the inauguration of his mission, is here not itself portrayed in the narrative but is recalled through John's testimony in vv. 32, 33. For the Fourth Gospel, the baptism of Jesus by John is subordinated to the dominant witness motif. In his testimony John claims that he, too, did not know Jesus until he received confirmation of what God had said about how he would recognize the baptizer with the Holy Spirit, and, accordingly, saw the Spirit descend and remain on Jesus. The verb μένειν, *to remain*, which can be used elsewhere in the narrative to indicate the permanence of the relationship between the Father and Jesus and of the relationship between Jesus and the disciples, is employed here for the permanence of the Spirit's relationship to Jesus. This

---

[7] John the Baptist's "This is he of whom I said . . ." is in fact, then, addressed to the reader, who is meant to recall the prologue's earlier version of the saying.

qualifies Jesus to baptize others with the Spirit, an event that takes place later at 20:22. It is highly significant that the passage of Isaiah that speaks of the Messiah as judge (11:3–5) also speaks of the Spirit of the Lord resting upon him (11:2).

But John's testimony to Jesus is more than that he is the Christ; it is that he is the Son of God, a key christological title in this Gospel, standing for everything unique in Jesus' relationship to God and for the oneness between the Father and the Son (cf. 10:30). In the synoptic tradition, at Jesus' baptism a voice from heaven declares Jesus to be the beloved Son, but in this narrative this declaration has become part of John the Baptist's testimony. It should be noted, however, that the reading "Son of God" in 1:34 is disputed. It has the better-attested external manuscript evidence, but it is possible, as a number of scholars hold, that the variant ὁ ἐκλεκτός τοῦ θεοῦ "God's elect [or 'chosen'] one"—should be accepted. The variant provides the more difficult reading, and it is easier to account for a scribe changing "chosen one" to "Son" than vice versa. If, on such grounds, this reading is preferred, it takes up the allusion to Isa 42:1 present in the synoptic accounts of the baptism but, in distinctive fashion, has ὁ ἐκλεκτός μου (LXX) in view. This would also underline the Isaianic background of the trial motif, since the elect one is the servant-witness and in 42:1 it is also said that Yahweh has put Yahweh's spirit on him and that he will execute judgment. The two perfect tenses in John 1:34—" And I myself have seen [ἑώρακα] and have testified [μεμαρτύρηκα] that this is the Son of God [or 'God's chosen one']"—again emphasize the continuing present significance of John's witness as a testimony that remains on record for the readers. The importance of the Baptist's testimony at the beginning of the narrative is not to be overlooked. The witness is to the superiority of Jesus over John, to the preexistence of Jesus, to the soteriological significance of his death, to his possession of, and ability to bestow, the Spirit, and to his divine sonship or elect status as the servant. All these are convictions dear to the evangelist's community but convictions that are in dispute. In this way, not only through the prologue but also through John's testimony, the point of view of the evangelist and his community dominates the narrative right from the start.[8]

---

[8] It is difficult to see, therefore, how Boice, *Witness and Revelation,* 80–81, can conclude that the content of the Baptist's witness is "lacking in themes peculiar to the Fourth Gospel" and that this indicates that "the evangelist desires to preserve John's testimony accurately and without alteration."

On the surface of the text, it appears from 1:34—"I myself have seen and have testified"—that John's testimony is to be understood as that of an eyewitness. But as will be discussed again later, matters are not quite so clear-cut. Even the testimony of 1:32–33—"I saw the Spirit descending from heaven like a dove"—is at best only a quasi-physical seeing. Whatever phenomenon the reader is meant to have in mind at this point (perhaps a vision), John hardly saw the actual Spirit. And "I myself have seen . . . that this is the Son of God [or 'God's chosen one']" clearly involves the insight of belief. The ordinary language associated with the stance of an eyewitness, just as much as the other everyday terminology from trial proceedings, can sometimes be employed with its plain sense in the narrative. But far more frequently it becomes subsumed under the overall metaphor of the lawsuit, which is dependent on the implied author's belief system for its meaning. In his believing, seeing, and testifying, John begins the chain of faithful witnessing that continues with the seeing and testifying of Jesus himself (cf. 3:32), of Jesus and the community (cf. 3:11), and of the beloved disciple (cf. 19:35). When John twice says, "I am not," under the threefold questioning, this is part of his confessing and not denying, but when Peter later twice says, "I am not," under his threefold interrogation (cf. 18:17, 25–27), this is clearly part of his denying and not confessing his relationship to Jesus. Depicting Peter's denial in this fashion shows up the failure of his witness not only in contrast to that of Jesus in the surrounding narrative but also in contrast to John here at the beginning.

In the prologue, the narrator made clear that the purpose of John the Baptist's testimony was to produce belief, and this is precisely the result when, after the extended witness in 1:29–34, he repeats his testimony about Jesus as the Lamb of God to two of his disciples, who promptly become followers of Jesus (1:35–37). Jesus will refer to John's testimony in 5:33–36, but the last appearance of John the Baptist himself in the narrative is in 3:22–30. The setting is in Judea, where Jesus' baptizing activity and his disciples are set alongside John's baptizing activity and his disciples.[9] This time the matters of John's identity and mission in relation to those of Jesus are raised by John's disciples, who recall his earlier witness to Jesus—"the one . . . to whom you testified" (3:26). In his reply in 3:28, John makes his followers witnesses to his own earlier witness, first, that he was not the Messiah (cf. 1:20) and, second, that he has been sent ahead of the Messiah (cf. 1:23, with John's citation from Isaiah

---

[9] Note, however, the rather strange parenthesis of 4:2, which is evidently anxious to distinguish between Jesus' activity and John's.

about making straight the way of the Lord). In this way, John's witness in his last appearance is shown to be consistent with that of his first appearance, and the following declarations about his role as friend of the bridegroom and about the necessity of his decrease and Jesus' increase only elaborate what his testimony has already made clear. Despite the narrative's strong underlining of Jesus' superior role, not least through John's own witness, it also suggests a clear continuity in the activity of witnessing. In a setting that juxtaposes Jesus and his disciples with John and his followers, the relation of the latter anticipates the pattern for the relation of the former. Just as John is a witness whose disciples bear witness to his witness, so Jesus is the chief witness whose disciples will also bear witness to his witness.

In numerous ways, then, the depiction of the first witness sets a pattern for the witness that follows—both that of Jesus and that of his followers. The narrator's aside in 3:24—"John . . . had not yet been thrown into prison"—reminds the readers of the outcome of his mission and thereby of the possible negative consequences of the activity of witnessing. And the very last reference to John the Baptist in the narrative, in 10:40–42, although it does not use witness terminology, conforms to what the reader now expects of the witness. When Jesus returns to the area where John had been baptizing, many confirm the validity of his testimony: "John performed no sign, but everything that John said about this man was true." And again John's witness achieves the intended effect: "Many believed in him [Jesus] there" (cf. 1:8). At this point, what is said of the first witness anticipates what will be said in 19:35 about the last witness in the narrative, the beloved disciple: "His testimony is true" and "He . . . has testified so that you also may believe."

B. The Testimony from Above and the Judgment of the Light (3:11–21; 3:31–36)

If the material on John the Baptist in 1:19–34 has introduced the first witness, it becomes clear in 3:11–21 and 3:31–36 that Jesus, as the protagonist, is to be the chief witness in the lawsuit. In the first of these passages, he uses this terminology of himself, and in the second, the narrator uses it about him (cf. vv. 11, 32, 33). In both passages it also becomes apparent that his witness is at the heart of the process of judgment that the lawsuit entails. Indeed, while vv. 11–21 functions, initially at least, as the continuation of Jesus' dialogue with Nicodemus, vv. 31–36 reads very much like the narrator's further reflections on the earlier discourse, picking up most of its themes.

But this description conceals the notorious problem in this chapter of where the words of the characters in the discourses cease and the reflections of the narrator begin. With most commentators and translations (but cf. NJB, NIV), I have assumed in the previous section that the discourse of John the Baptist extends from v. 27 to v. 30 and that vv. 31–36 are the comments of the narrator. The issue in vv. 11–21 is more difficult, and this is reflected in the indecision of English translations about where to put inverted commas. The NRSV, REB, NJB, and NIV have Jesus' discourse run through until v. 21, but the RSV and NAB complete it at v. 15. Others have suggested that the narrator's reflections in fact begin at v. 13, with its switch from first-person to third-person language. It is true that, until this point in the narrative, Jesus' discourse has been clearly marked by its first-person language and that third-person language about him has been confined to the narrator's prologue or to other characters, but soon Jesus talking about himself in the third person as the Son or the Son of Man in relation to God or the Father will be a clear feature within the framework of a first-person discourse (cf., e.g., 5:19–30). Certainly the other two usages of the distinctive lifting-up terminology in 3:14 are on the lips of Jesus himself (cf. 8:28; 12:32). A decision on this matter is not particularly significant for the exposition of the lawsuit motif. The issue simply shows how in this narrative the language of the main characters, particularly that of the protagonist, and the language of the narrator coincide, and it confirms that the witness of John the Baptist and of Jesus represents the confessional point of view of the narrator and his community. (Without going into argumentation here, I am inclined to see 3:11–15 as intended to be taken as the words of Jesus himself and 3:16–21 as the further commentary of the narrator about Jesus.)

In 3:11, at the point where Jesus' dialogue with Nicodemus takes up the language of witness and where Jesus for the first time uses this language of himself, there is a change from first-person singular to first-person plural: "Very truly [lit. 'Amen, amen'], I tell you, we speak of what we know and testify to what we have seen; yet you do not receive our testimony." This indicates that Jesus here represents the perspective of a wider group in their witness, that of Johannine Christians (cf. the similar plural language of witness in 1 John 1:2, 3) and, as we shall explore more fully later, suggests that the lawsuit motif played a significant part in the dialogue between the synagogue and the community with which Jesus is seen in solidarity. If Jesus is representative of the community's confession, it is equally clear that Nicodemus is a representative figure. The "you" of 3:11 is plural, and earlier Nicodemus, too, speaks this "we" language: "we know that you are a teacher who has come from God" (3:2). If the context of Jesus' first occasion for witness is to be understood, it is important to specify whom Nicodemus represents. As a Pharisee and ruler of the Jews, he clearly represents the Jewish religious authorities, but in particular he represents those who are sympathetic, to some degree, with Jesus' mission. He holds that Jesus is a teacher whose signs indicate that God is with him, that he has divine approval (v. 2). Despite the apparent promise of such a view of Jesus, the implied author leaves no doubt that it is insufficient, and he makes Nicodemus a representative of those Jews—including leading ones—who, though not hostile, have a gravely defective stance.

The preceding pericope, 2:23–25, includes the verb μαρτυρεῖν, *to witness,* and sheds light on such a group. It describes those who believe on the basis of Jesus' signs, but it makes clear from Jesus' response to them that their faith is defective. Although they trusted (ἐπίστευσαν) in his name, Jesus did not entrust (ἐπίστευεν) himself to them. The reason given for his response (in one of the narrator's "inside views") is his omniscience. He knew all people and what was in them; he could perceive therefore the depth and validity of their commitment and found it wanting. This pericope sets the scene not only for Nicodemus's assertion of a less than adequate allegiance but also for Jesus' role in the lawsuit. Because of his supernatural knowledge, Jesus is able to make a penetrating judgment about human responses. He is the judge who already embodies his own later exhortation not to judge by appearances but to judge with right judgment (cf. 7:24). The depiction of his role also recalls the messianic prediction of Isa 11:2–4: "the spirit of knowledge [shall rest on him]. . . . He shall not judge by what his eyes see." Because he is in possession of divine knowledge, Jesus needs no one to testify about anyone (John 2:25). Although this reference to Jesus needing the help of no other witnesses concerns judging the human condition and not specifically his own identity, it can be seen as anticipating one side of the paradox that characterizes the lawsuit as a whole (cf. the contrast between 5:31 and 8:14): although Jesus is the witness and judge who really needs no other witnesses because of his unique relationship to God, nevertheless, because in his incarnate form he participates in the conventions of the narrative's trial, he will be given the assistance of other witnesses.

Nicodemus's misunderstanding and incomprehension in the dialogue with Jesus show up the inadequacy of his initial confession. This exposure is brought to a climax in 3:10 with the parody of his confession in v. 2. There he claimed, "we *know* that you are *a teacher,*" but now Jesus turns the tables and asks, "Are you *a teacher* of Israel and yet you do *not understand* these things?" Then over against the inadequate christological confession of v. 2 is placed the true christological testimony of vv. 11–21. In contrast to Nicodemus's "we know" is set Jesus' "we speak of what we know and testify to what we have seen; yet you do not receive our testimony." The latter statement is introduced by the distinctive Johannine double Amen, which functions as a solemn oath underlining the truth of the testimony. Thus, although the first witness of Jesus is not made under hostile interrogation, its context is one of a clash of claims. One sort of claim about Jesus, though sympathetic to him, is ultimately not able to receive the true witness. In all probability, Nicodemus, as a ruler of the Jews who comes to Jesus secretly "by night," is meant to remind the readers of a group whom the narrator describes later, in 12:42–43: "many, even of the authorities, believed in him. But because of the Pharisees they did not confess it, for fear that they would be put out of the synagogue; for they loved human glory more than the glory that comes from God." And later still, in 19:38–40, Nicodemus is linked with Joseph of Arimathea, who is characterized as "a secret [disciple of Jesus] because of his fear of the Jews." The community's witness in 3:11–21, then, is made in the face of those who were crypto-believers but saw their place as remaining within the synagogue. From the narrator's perspective, they were unable to make the full confession about Jesus and to take its consequences and so have ended up on the wrong side in the trial of truth, which resulted in excommunication from the synagogue for those who did make the necessary confession.

In contrast to Nicodemus's inability to see (3:3), Jesus represents those who bear witness to what they have seen. Nicodemus is one of those who cannot see the kingdom of God, cannot see through the signs to the heavenly reality to which they point, because he has not been born from above (ἄνωθεν). This seeing of full belief has to be given from above, from heaven, from God. The community, on the other hand, claims to have seen the heavenly realities, and it bears witness to these and the community's link with them through the Son of Man, who has descended from heaven (3:13) and who is from above (ἄνωθεν, 3:31). The focus of the community's witness is thus on Jesus, who, as Son of Man, is in effect the sole eyewitness of that which is above, the heavenly world.[10] Jesus' words make clear the true sense in which he is "from God," in contrast to Nicodemus's insufficient testimony. He is from

---

[10] Cf. also the implications of 1:18.

God because he is a heavenly being, the descending and ascending Son of Man. In this narrative, the title "Son of Man," which, as in the synoptic narratives, is characteristically reserved for the lips of Jesus himself, is given a distinctive twist by its frequent association with the narrative's descent-ascent schema and its heaven-and-earth framework. True knowledge of the heavenly realm comes only from the Son of Man, who descended from heaven in the incarnation and has ascended to heaven in his exaltation. The verb employed for the motion of ascending is in the perfect tense, implying that the exaltation has already taken place and underlining that Jesus himself is giving the community's later christological witness. While no person who remains on the fleshly level, like Nicodemus, can make this confession about Jesus, the narrator's community can bear such a witness because, like Jesus, who has come from above, its members have been born from above.

In 3:14–15 a second distinctive element in the community's witness to the Son of Man is reflected in Jesus' words about being "lifted up," with this term's grim double entendre of exaltation through crucifixion. In ordinary usage, the Greek verb ὑψόω has no reference to crucifixion, but the narrator's comment after its use, in 12:33, makes clear that it includes this meaning for him. Perhaps the major catalyst in producing the double meaning originally was the Aramaic, where the verb אזדקּף does have both connotations—to crucify and to exalt. The Septuagint's Isa 52:13 may also have played a part, with its reference to the servant who will be lifted up and glorified, an estimate of the servant after his death. Its use here in John 3:14, 8:28, and 12:32–34 can be seen as this narrative's equivalent to the threefold passion prediction about the Son of Man in Mark 8:31, 9:31, and 10:33. The difference is that the double meaning of *lift up* is exploited in the Fourth Gospel because it encapsulates the witness that the Son of Man's suffering and humiliation is his glory. Instead of the synoptic pattern of suffering followed by glory, the lifting up of the Son of Man collapses suffering and glory, crucifixion and exaltation, into one. This lifting up is compared to Moses' lifting up of the serpent on a standard in the wilderness. In Num 21:8 it was said of the serpent, "everyone who is bitten shall look at it and shall live." Now, according to John 3:14–15, everyone who believes in the lifted-up Son of Man may have eternal life. In terms of the lawsuit motif, everyone who receives this witness about the Son of Man will also receive the positive verdict of life, the life of the age to come, which can be experienced already in the present.

The narrator's reflections in 3:16–21 continue the witness to the relationship between Jesus and God. In contrast to Nicodemus's view, not only is Jesus "from God" in the sense that he is the descending and ascending Son of Man who through his crucifixion/exaltation provides the link between heaven and earth; he is also "from God" in that he is the unique (μονογενής) Son whom God gave to the hostile world as the supreme demonstration of the divine love (v. 16). Furthermore, Jesus is "from God" since God sent this Son into the world as the fully authorized agent and representative in the lawsuit (v. 17). Here in vv. 17–19 we meet for the first time the language of judgment. The terms κρίνω, *to judge,* and κρίσις, *judgment,* can have either the more neutral connotation of putting on trial or the more negative connotation of condemning and punishing, depending on the context. In this instance, the latter connotation is in view. The purpose of the Son's mission in putting the hostile world on trial is not the negative one of condemnation, however much the world might deserve it (v. 17a). Rather, the trial process is meant to function as a rescue mission "in order that the world might be saved through him" (v. 17b). After all, the reason for sending the Son was that God loved the world. Whether the trial in fact functions in this way depends on the response of people to the unique Son and the witness about him: "Those who believe in him are not condemned" (v. 18a).

But if there is a positive realized eschatology of life, there is also a negative realized eschatology of judgment. Despite the primary intention of the Son's mission—to produce the positive verdict of eternal life—for those who do not believe in this unique Son of God, this negative response produces a negative verdict ahead of time in the lawsuit: "those who do not believe are condemned already" (v. 18b). For the implied author, people's response to Jesus constitutes their judgment; their judgment on him is at the same time a judgment on themselves. And because he is the light, he necessarily provokes judgment. In terms of the cosmic framework of the trial, Jesus' mission is seen as the focal point of the struggle between light and darkness, and the whole process of judgment results from Jesus as the light coming into the darkness of the world (v. 19).

If above and below, heaven and earth, provide the spatial coordinates for the lawsuit between God and the world, then light and darkness, determinative categories from the prologue (1:4–9), symbolize the moral and spiritual distinction that colors the spatial contrast and characterizes the relationship between the two parties. The coming of the light makes apparent people's ultimate allegiance, whether they love darkness or light, and in doing so puts their whole lives under scrutiny. According to 3:19–21, the light reveals not simply people's words but their deeds for what they really are. On the negative side, those who do evil attempt to evade the light lest their deeds should be exposed. The verb ἐλέγχω can mean *to expose* or *to convict*. The latter, juridical connotation is clearly to the fore later, in 8:46 and 16:8. Here the light-and-darkness imagery make *to expose* an obvious connotation. But the context is one in which the light judges the darkness, and so the notion of conviction about the guilt of evil deeds can hardly be absent. On the positive side, those who are willing to come to the light "do the truth" (my translation), and the judgment of the light reveals that their deeds have been done in God. This unusual expression reflects an underlying issue in the narrative, namely, that people's response to Jesus is indicative of their relation to God. The cosmic lawsuit exposes whether one's deeds are in conformity to its true judgment, and thus those who do the truth are revealed to be on the side of God rather than of the world that is opposed to the divine verdict.

John 3:1–21 provides its readers with a perspective on the community's relationship with the synagogue. Even the most sympathetic of the synagogue's leaders, by refusing to acknowledge Jesus openly and fully as the one whom the community believes him to be, are shown ultimately still to belong to the night and the darkness. The community's own witness to how Jesus is related to God may have led to its eventual judgment by the synagogue, but the community's judges have themselves been put on trial. In this cosmic trial, the criterion for judgment is precisely the issue that brought about the excommunication of members of the community: belief in Jesus as the descended and ascended (through crucifixion and exaltation) Son of Man and as the only Son of God.

In 3:16–21 the narrator's comments elaborate on the witness of Jesus as the representative of the community. Similarly in vv. 31–36, his comments elaborate on the witness of John the Baptist to Jesus' superiority in vv. 22–30. In so doing, they recapitulate themes from the earlier witness of Jesus and the community and the narrator's own ensuing comments in vv. 1–21. Jesus is not only superior to John; he is also above all because he has come from above, from heaven (v. 31; cf. vv. 3, 7, 13). In the superiority of his heavenly origin, he is contrasted with those who are of earthly origin and can speak only of earthly things (v. 31; cf. v. 6, "What is born of the flesh is flesh," and v.12, "earthly things"). Again Jesus' heavenly origin qualifies him to be the chief witness in the trial between God and the world: "He testifies to what he has seen and heard, yet no one accepts his testimony" (v. 32; cf. v. 11). The failure to receive Jesus' testimony has in view the world as a whole and "the

Jews" in general as the representatives of the world, as in 1:10–11, where "the world did not know him" and "his own people did not accept him." Just as, in the prologue, these statements are followed in 1:12 by "But to all who received him . . . ," so here the general failure to receive Jesus' testimony is followed in 3:33 by the assertion, "Whoever has accepted his testimony has set a seal to this, that God is true." Setting a seal means certifying one's approval and may well have had juridical connotations.[11]

What might have been expected here is a statement that to receive Jesus' testimony is to certify that his claims are true. Instead the narrator again underscores that a decision about Jesus is in fact a decision about God. For him, what has been at stake in the community's dispute with the synagogue and what is at stake in this lawsuit in the narrative is not just the truth of claims about Jesus but ultimately, as in the underlying lawsuit in Isaiah, the truth of conflicting claims about God. Is God, or is God not, the God who is known in Jesus? As 1 John 5:10 will put it, those who do not believe in the testimony concerning God's Son make God a liar. The connection between Jesus' testimony and God's truth is made explicit in John 3:34: "He whom God has sent [cf. the language of sending the Son in v. 17] speaks the words of God, for he gives the Spirit without measure." Jesus' words of witness in the lawsuit fully represent God. The prophets were given the Spirit by measure, but Jesus has been given the Spirit without measure, so that he speaks God's words continuously. The mention of the Spirit picks up on the earlier reference in the discussion with Nicodemus in vv. 5–8 but more particularly recalls John the Baptist's witness in 1:32, 33 about Jesus' permanent endowment with the Spirit. Jesus is the fully authorized agent of God in the lawsuit and the one on whom the Spirit remains, and so his words are God's words. In the Father's love for the Son, the Father has given him not only the Spirit but "all things" (v. 35), which include authority to judge (cf. 5:22, 27).

The narrator's closing reflection in v. 36 indicates that Jesus is not only the fully authorized witness but also the fully authorized agent in judgment, as in vv. 18–21. Again both positive and negative outcomes of the judgment are delineated. Belief in the Son results in the positive verdict of eternal life (cf. v. 16). On the negative side, the wrong response to Jesus is described this time not as unbelief but as disobedience, corresponding to the emphasis in vv. 19, 20 on people's evil deeds, and the consequence is not simply people's condemnation but the punishment

---

[11] Cf. Brown, *Gospel according to John*, 1:158: "The metaphor is one of setting a seal indicating approval on a legal document."

of God's wrath remaining on them. In this variation on the narrative's negative realized eschatology, the wrath that could be expected at the end-time judgment is seen as precipitated by Jesus' lawsuit mission and as remaining in effect.

C. Jesus as the Just Judge and the Testimonies to Jesus (5:19–47)

The setting for Jesus' extended witness in John 5 is one of increased hostility. His witness is given not to sympathetic synagogue leaders such as Nicodemus but to Jewish authorities who are described as persecuting Jesus (5:16) and as intent on killing him (5:18). This is the same sort of opposition that believers will themselves face (cf. 16:2, 33). Not surprisingly, both the community's later experience of trial and the earlier Isaianic lawsuit have left their marks on the narrative. The frequent occurrence, in this section of the narrative, of the key terms for our motif should be noted. The word κρίνω, *to judge,* occurs twice (5:22, 30); κρίσις, *judgment,* is found five times (vv. 22, 24, 27, 29, 30); μαρτυρέω, *to witness,* is employed seven times (vv. 31, 32, 33, 36, 37, 39); and μαρτυρία, *witness,* is used four times (vv. 31, 32, 34, 36).

It has been argued recently that two different forensic scenes— vv. 10–16, 30–47 and vv. 17–29—with different charges and defenses and coming from two different stages in the Gospel's composition, have been brought together here.[12] But in the narrative as it now stands, Jesus' discourse begins as a defense against a charge about claims concerning his relationship with God (vv. 16–18). In the first part (vv. 19–30), it is made clear that the one who is giving witness in his own defense is in fact the judge; in the second part (vv. 31–47), this witness is shown to conform to the laws of testimony, and then the tables are turned, so that the accusers become the accused.[13] This is very much the pattern we have seen in the lawsuits between Yahweh and Israel in Deutero-Isaiah, where Yahweh was both the accused and the judge and turned the accusations made against Yahweh back on Yahweh's accusers.

The charge against Jesus arises out of the sign he performs in which a lame man is healed. "The Jews" have accused the man of breaking the

---

[12] Cf. J. H. Neyrey, *An Ideology of Revolt: John's Christology in Social-Science Perspective* (Philadelphia: Fortress, 1988), 9–36.

[13] D. A. Lee, *The Symbolic Narratives of the Fourth Gospel* (Sheffield: JSOT Press, 1994), 107, also notes the role reversal whereby Jesus moves "from judge to accused to judge again."

Sabbath by carrying his mat (v. 10) and now bring the charge against Jesus that he is doing such healings on the Sabbath (v. 16). Jesus' answer to the implicit accusation that he is working on the Sabbath is a plain acknowledgment that this is so and that in this, as in all he does, he is only imitating his Father: "My Father is still working, and I also am working" (v. 17). This acknowledgment gives rise to a further charge, which is not explicitly made but is embedded in the reason given by the narrator that "the Jews" seek to kill Jesus: "because he was not only breaking the sabbath, but was also calling God his own Father, thereby making himself equal to God" (v. 18b). Such a formulation of the issue seems clearly to come from the Johannine community's christological dispute with the synagogue. It is also noteworthy that "the Jews" are portrayed as in fact having already determined the verdict in this trial at its outset: "For this reason the Jews were seeking all the more to kill him" (5:18a).

Jesus begins his self-defense in v. 19 with the words of solemn oath, "Very truly" ("Amen, amen"), and responds to the charge by spelling out his relationship with the Father. What the defense amounts to is that his activities show that he and his Father are one (and therefore, in the terms of the charge, equal), but that this relationship is not one that he has made for himself but, rather, one that he has been given by the Father. In fact, the formulation stresses Jesus' dependence on the Father, and this is in order to assert not so much his subordination to, but his oneness with, the Father. His dependence is so complete that what he does is totally at one with his Father's purposes. Verses 19–20 thus constitute an explanation of Jesus' earlier response in v. 17. He could say that his Father was working until now and that he was working, because, as the Son, he is simply doing what he sees his Father doing. It may well be, as Dodd suggests, that behind vv. 19–20a lies a proverb about an apprentice son that has been elevated into a christological statement.[14] Just as the apprentice son watches and then repeats the work of his father, a skilled artisan, so Jesus claims that in his works, such as the healing on the Sabbath, he is only imitating what he sees his Father doing. If his accusers have been surprised by the claims he has made in regard to such a work, they should, he asserts, be prepared for further astonishment because the Father, out of his love for the Son, has shown him greater works than such signs for imitation. The greater works are two in particular, of major significance for the lawsuit motif, since they are the giving of life and judgment (vv. 5:21–30). In other words, Jesus claims that

---

[14] C. H. Dodd, "A Hidden Parable in the Fourth Gospel" in *More New Testament Studies* (Manchester: Manchester University Press, 1968), 30–40.

the divine prerogative of delivering the final verdict in the cosmic lawsuit has been entrusted to him. This should indeed be a cause for astonishment (v. 20b), for those who have brought their charge against Jesus are being told that the accused is in fact the judge.

This claim begins to be spelled out in v. 21. Starting from the traditional expectation of God's end-time activity in the resurrection of the dead, which entails the giving of life, the claim asserts that this giving of eschatological life is also the Son's activity in imitation of his Father. This positive verdict of life is then seen as part of the whole process of judgment, so that in v. 22 κρίνω and κρίσις in all probability are neutral in force.[15] The Son's role in judgment is put in the strongest terms. It is no longer a case of copying what he sees the Father doing. Instead "the Father judges no one but has given all judgment to the Son" (v. 22). Jesus has in fact already been exercising this judgment in the preceding incident by telling the healed man that he is to sin no more (v. 14). The note of comparison with the Father returns in different form in the purpose clause of v. 23a. The Son has been given sole responsibility for judgment in order that all may honor him just as they honor the Father.

As Preiss observes, "Glory and honour have a strong juridico-social nuance in John."[16] What is at stake for the community in the trial is the reputation of its founder, and this is seen as vindicated by his relationship with God, which makes Jesus the judge rather than the accused or condemned one, with the shame that accompanies the latter status. Indeed, the role of the Son as the fully authorized representative in the lawsuit of the one who has sent him means that not honoring the Son is the same as not honoring the Father (v. 23b). Since giving honor and/or glory to God is equivalent to recognizing God as God (cf., e.g., Rom 1:21; 1 Tim 1:17; Rev 4:9, 11), this amounts to a very strong claim on Jesus' behalf about his oneness with God. This oneness is underlined in 5:24 as the Son's judging activity is given a present focus. John 3:16–19 has already asserted that the verdict of either life or condemnation depends on one's response to the Son and that this verdict is experienced already in this life. But in the repetition of the notion here, the proper response is formulated not simply as believing in the Son but as hearing his word and believing the one who sent him. Again, therefore, Jesus' word is so completely at one with God's that to accept the witness of the former is

---

[15] *Pace* Lee, *Symbolic Narratives,* 116.

[16] Preiss, "Justification in Johannine Thought," 16, n. 1.

also to accept the witness of the latter. The result of such belief is described as having eternal life, not coming to judgment (this time in the sense of negative judgment), and therefore passing from the condemnation of death to the experience of the positive verdict of life.

John 5:25–27 develops this realized eschatology of judgment, centering on the activity of the Son (cf. "the hour is coming, and is now here" (v. 25a) and what follows, which emphasizes the latter clause). These verses indicate that whatever the different nuances of meaning they convey, the titles "Son of God," "Son," and "Son of Man" function as virtual equivalents in the narrative. The dead hear the voice of *the Son of God* and live (v. 25). The Father possesses life in himself and has granted *the Son* also to have life in himself and at the same time has given him authority to judge because he is *Son of Man* (vv. 26–27). One of the three main contexts of Son of Man sayings in the synoptic tradition is that of final judgment, and so it is not surprising to find this designation employed here for Jesus as the one with authority to exercise judgment. The emphasis that the Father has given (ἔδωκεν) Jesus to have life in himself and has given (ἔδωκεν) him authority to judge can be seen as a further response to the charge of v. 18 that he was making himself (ἑαυτὸν ποιῶν) equal to God. The hearers should not be surprised that Jesus' claim to exercise the divine prerogative not only is made in regard to the present stage of the lawsuit but holds for its final stage also (vv. 28–29). Despite the narrative's stress on the realized aspect of judgment, it retains the future, final aspect of traditional expectations about the judgment, associated with the resurrection of the dead. This time, "the hour is coming" (v. 28) stands alone without the accompanying "and is now here" of v. 25. At that hour it will be the voice of the Son of God (cf. v. 25), or the Son of Man (cf. v. 27), that the physically dead will hear, and their resurrection will be either to a verdict of life or to a verdict of condemnation. The mention of Jesus' voice as the agent of resurrection anticipates, in the narrative sequence, his cry "with a loud voice" outside Lazarus's tomb, resulting in the appearance of Lazarus still wrapped in his graveclothes (11:43–44), and this in turn anticipates the eschatological judgment of which this discourse speaks.

Just as in 3:19–21 the judgment provoked in the present by the coming of Christ exposed people's deeds in their true light, so this final judgment will again be on the basis of people's deeds—whether they have done good or evil. The first part of Jesus' defense speech ends on an *inclusio* that, in exactly the same way in which he had begun speaking (5:19), stresses his dependence on his Father: "I can do nothing on my own" (5:30). This time the notion of dependence supports what has become the main claim in his defense, namely, that he is in fact his accusers' judge. Just as his perspective on the deeds that provoked the charge was that they were done in imitation of what he saw the Father doing, now his view of his judging is that it is in imitation of what he hears the Father saying. His judgment can therefore be said to be just (cf. 7:24), because in it he is not seeking any interest of his own but is simply carrying out his commission. His will is so fully dependent on, and therefore identified with, the will of the one who has sent him that his judgment is bound to be just—it is God's judgment. In this way, the community's claim about the relationship of Jesus to God, which caused so much dispute with the synagogue, is framed in terms of the lawsuit, in which Jesus is at one with and fully represents God the judge; in addition, the dispute itself is given a narrative setting through the device of the charge and the defense speech, in which the implied author allows the defendant to emerge as the judge.

On the basis of the first part of the trial scene, it could be alleged that Jesus was appearing as the sole witness in his own defense. In terms of Jewish legal conventions, this would make his testimony invalid (5:31). As we have noted, Deut 19:15 holds that three, or at least two, witnesses are needed for valid testimony. So in John 5:32–40 Jesus appeals to a series of further witnesses. At first sight, it appears that five witnesses are adduced to provide proof for Jesus' case—an unspecified other (v. 32), John the Baptist (vv. 33–35), Jesus' works (v. 36), the Father himself (vv. 37–38), and the Scriptures (vv. 39–40). But the five do not constitute a straightforward list where each is distinct and has the same status as witness, as commentators frequently suggest.

The first reference is deliberately ambiguous. It could simply mean that Jesus is claiming the required other witness, the truth and validity of whose testimony he has no reason to doubt. It does not become clear until v. 37 that this other is in all probability the Father (cf. also 8:17, 18, where the two witnesses required are Jesus and the Father).[17] Jesus' works, which are given him by the Father, and the Scriptures, which are the Father's word, can, then, both be seen as the visible aspects of the Father's testimony. This testimony is contrasted to that of the Baptist.[18] To be sure, the first witness mentioned by Jesus, just as it is the first witness in the narrative as a whole, is that of John the Baptist, and it appears at first that John might even be the other to whom Jesus has just referred. But interestingly, he does not directly appeal to John's testimony,

---

[17] Cf. Blank, *Krisis,* 203; Beutler, *Martyria,* 257.

[18] Contra Boice, *Witness and Revelation,* 80, who includes John the Baptist's testimony as part of the Father's testimony in this argument.

and then virtually discounts it in favor of the "[greater] testimony" (5:36) provided by the Father. Instead John's testimony is introduced so that Jesus can toy with his accusers by reminding them that they themselves provided him with another witness by instigating the interrogation of John, at which he testified to the truth (v. 33; cf. 1:19–28). In imagery reminiscent of the prologue's "He himself was not the light, but he came to testify to the light" (1:8), John's witness is described not as the light itself but as a derivative brightness, a "burning and shining lamp" that disseminates the light (5:35). Yet having recalled the witness that his accusers have already heard, Jesus can then make clear that this is not the other witness to which he has referred. Indeed, he does not accept this testimony because it is human (v. 34a). He has mentioned it by way of concession, to accommodate to the need for human salvation: "I say these things so that you may be saved" (v. 34b).[19] Here the interplay or indeed tension between Jesus' divine nature and his role on the human scene becomes explicit. Another obvious example of this phenomenon in the narrative is his prayer of thanksgiving for the resurrection of Lazarus in 11:42, where no sooner has he uttered it than he immediately makes clear that he has no need for such a prayer; he has made it in order that the crowd might believe that he has been sent by the Father. Here in John 5, the thought is that Jesus' relationship with the Father is such that his testimony is really self-authenticating, but the narrative has mentioned human witnesses in order to accommodate to the conventions of a human trial and thereby enable people to receive his witness and be saved.

The other testimony to which Jesus is willing to appeal is greater than that of John. It is the testimony of the Father himself (5:36–40). In the first instance, this witness consists of the works the Father has given Jesus to complete, works such as the healing of vv. 1–9, which has provoked this controversy. Although the term σημεῖον, *sign*, is not directly connected with the theme of witness, its meaning overlaps with that of ἔργον, *work* (cf. 6:30; 7:31; 9:3–4, 16), and the signs are clearly meant to be included in the testimony of Jesus' works.[20] The narrative's point of view is that such works are viewed in their true perspective when they are seen as bearing witness to the divine origin of Jesus' mission, to his commissioning as the Father's representative in the lawsuit: "the very works that I am doing, testify on my behalf that the Father has sent me"

---

[19] Cf. Beutler, *Martyria*, 258.

[20] For a discussion of signs and works in this narrative, see esp. de Jonge, *Jesus: Stranger from Heaven and Son of God*, 31–36.

(5:36). In 10:25 the same point will be made—"The works that I do in my Father's name testify to me"—and in 15:24 Jesus will also make clear that such works have a condemnatory function in the lawsuit for those who do not believe.

The second aspect of the Father's witness is introduced by the clear statement that Jesus' commissioning Father has himself testified on Jesus' behalf. The perfect tense of the verb *to witness* is employed, indicating that this witness has taken place in the past but has continuing significance. To what does this witness refer? The answer becomes clear via the charges against "the Jews" that follow. They would claim that, if anywhere, God testified and left such testimony when God revealed God's self in Torah and its inscripturation. This was when Israel heard God's voice (cf., e.g., Exod 19:9; Deut 4:33; Sir 17:13) and saw God (cf., e.g., Exod 19:11; Deut 5:4; Sir 17:13), and Torah was God's word that remained in their hearts (cf., e.g., Deut 6:6; 30:14; Ps 119:11, 34). But whatever their claims about this revelation, Jesus asserts that none of them are true. His accusation in 5:37b echoes that of Yahweh against Israel in Isa 48: 8 ("You have never heard"). And the reason given for the denial of their claims is that those who make them do not believe him, the one whom God has sent and who is now the repository of God's self-revelation. As the Gospel as a whole makes clear, hearing God's voice, seeing God, and having God's word abide in one are all now associated with Jesus (cf., e.g., 3:34; 14:9; 15:7). The Scriptures do indeed constitute the Father's continuing witness in the lawsuit, but because they refuse to come to Jesus, that is, to believe in him, the Jewish opposition fail to see that the Scriptures witness to Jesus. They search the Scriptures in the hope of gaining eternal life, but they refuse the hermeneutical key provided by God's present revelation in Jesus and thereby miss out on the verdict of life that he as judge now renders (cf. 5:21, 24).

Although the importance of the issues of glory and honor for the community behind the Gospel will become apparent,[21] it is not immediately clear how the discussion of glory in 5:41–44 furthers the argument at this point. What is clear is that the clash between Jesus and his accusers is presented as a clash of perspectives about glory and that he is not prepared to submit to usual human evaluations of where honor lies, particularly since such evaluations have just dishonored him by considering him a lawbreaker and blasphemer (v. 18).[22] The clue to the connection with

---

[21] See ch. 6, sec. A.3, below.

[22] Since human honor is one's reputation in the eyes of others, it should be clear that Jesus "is rejecting a core value of Mediterranean societies," as B. J.

what has preceded is provided by the similarity between Jesus' statements in v. 34 and v. 41.[23] In the former statement, Jesus said that he
does not accept human testimony, while in the latter he says he does not
accept glory from human beings. To accept the testimony of another
about oneself is to depend on the opinion of another for one's reputation or honor. This normally would be part of defending one's honor in
a court of law. But because of who he is, Jesus' case is viewed as unique.
Just as, because of his relationship with the Father, the only testimony
other than his own that he will accept is that of the Father, so also the
only glory he will accept is that which the Father gives him in vindicating his claims (v. 44; cf. also 7:18; 8:50; 17:1, 5, 24).

Thus, the charge Jesus lays against his accusers is that they do not
have a true love for the God they profess (5:42), for, if they did, they, too,
would seek God's glory above all else (v. 44b). They have not realized that
what is at stake in their trial of Jesus is God's glory. Instead they remain on
the merely human level of concern about their honor and reputation in
the eyes of each other: "you accept glory from one another" (v. 44a). Jesus
charges that because they are caught up in the human system of assessing
reputation, they are quite prepared to accept someone who comes in his
own name, because such a person depends on human testimony and
thereby colludes with the system (v. 43b), but they are prevented from accepting the one who comes in the name of the Father (v. 43a), who will
most certainly act to protect the honor and glory of his name (cf. 12:28).
As the tables begin to be turned here and the defendant becomes the
prosecutor, the whole criterion for his accusers' judgment is indicted.
They claim to be accusing Jesus out of a concern for the reputation of the
only God, which they see threatened by Jesus' assertions, and they interpret these assertions as an attempt by Jesus to make himself equal with
the one God. But the counterclaim questions their deepest motivations and
loyalty. If they were truly concerned about "the glory that comes from the
one who alone is God" (5:44b), they would believe in the one whose total
dependence on the Father demonstrates that he seeks only the Father's
glory; they would acknowledge the one in whom the Father's honor is
now invested, as Jesus has claimed in the first part of his defense (v. 23).

The turning of the tables is taken further in vv. 45–47. There is
really no need for Jesus to accuse his opponents. Ultimately, their accuser before the Father will be Moses. Moses, the one on whom they

---

Malina and R. Rohrbaugh, *Social-Science Commentary on the Gospel of John* (Minneapolis: Fortress, 1998), 122, emphasize.

[23] Cf. Bultmann, *Gospel of John*, 262–63.

have set their hope (v. 45b), as demonstrated in their observance of the law, the one whose disciples they will later claim to be (cf. 9:28), turns out to be the accusing rather than the defending counsel—ὁ κατηγορῶν instead of ὁ παράκλητος, both technical legal terms in Greek that became loanwords in Hebrew juridical usage. The irony of this indictment is enormous, as traditional expectations about Moses are completely reversed. Moses was viewed as Israel's great defender, intercessor, and advocate (cf. *Jub.* 1.20, 21; *T. Mos.* 11.17; *As. Mos.* 12.6). But here, as part of the role reversal in the irony of the cosmic trial, not only do Jesus, the accused, become the judge and "the Jews," his accusers, become the accused; in addition, Moses, the counsel for the defense, becomes the counsel for the prosecution. In the lawsuits against Israel in Deutero-Isaiah, Yahweh defended himself by indicting Israel, by turning the accusations against Yahweh back on Israel. It was not Yahweh who was deaf and blind but Yahweh's accusers. Here Jesus is doing the same. The controversy began with "the Jews" using Moses to accuse Jesus, charging that Jesus had broken the Sabbath laws. It finishes with Jesus using Moses to accuse unbelieving Jews. And the presupposition for the accusation is that Moses wrote about Jesus. This is the point of view that pervades the narrative—that Jesus is the fulfillment of everything in the law—a view that shades over into the idea that Jesus is the replacement of everything in the law. The reason for the unbelief of Jesus' opponents can now be portrayed as a lack of true belief in Moses, despite their own avowals: "If you believed Moses, you would believe me, for he wrote about me" (5:46).

This formulation, in terms of Moses' writings, links the final element of Jesus' defense with the main thrust of its second part—the Father's witness to Jesus in Scripture. The writings of Moses, like the rest of the Scriptures (cf. v. 39), testify about Jesus. A magnificent illustration of how they do so will appear in the narrative's next chapter with its discourse on the bread of life, a discourse that is at the same time a midrash on Exod 16 (cf. John 6:25–59). But here, at the end of the trial scene, the depiction of Moses' writings as a positive witness to Jesus not only removes them as a court of appeal for "the Jews" but also makes the writings a negative witness against them. The latter function of their witness is precisely a role that, according to Deuteronomy, Moses himself had envisaged for the law: "Take this book of the law and put it beside the ark of the covenant of the LORD your God; let it remain there as a witness against you" (Deut 31:26; cf. also 32:46).

D. The Truth of Jesus' Testimony and Judgment (8:12–59)

Jesus' discourse/dispute in John 8:12–59 has the same narrative setting as that of 7:14–52—at the time of the Feast of Tabernacles and in the environs of the temple. The earlier discourse/dispute has its own legal overtones: the language of judging (7:24; cf. v. 51), the appeals to the law (vv. 19, 23; cf. also v. 51), disputes about Jesus' origins and destiny (vv. 27–29, 33–36), references to the truth of his claims (v. 18) and the truth of the one who has sent him (v. 28), various verdicts about his claims (vv. 40–52), and reminders of the death sentence that has already been determined by the Jewish authorities and their attempts to arrest him in order to proceed with their intentions (vv. 19, 20, 25, 30, 32, 44, 45). The forensic aspects of Jesus' encounter with opponents, however, become more concentrated in 8:12–59, which develops a number of the issues already raised in 7:14–39. Many of the features of Jesus' defense speech in the trial scene of 5:19:47, including its ironies, also recur here in John 8.

The different sets of accusers act as markers for the main divisions of the defense. In 8:12–30 the opponents are designated first as "the Pharisees" (v. 13) and then as "the Jews" (v. 22). The different designations here also indicate that this material falls into two parts—vv. 12–20, which is rounded off by the narrator's comments about the setting, and vv. 21–30, which again concludes with the narrator's remarks about the response of belief on the part of many. In vv. 31–47 there is apparently a change, as the audience becomes the Jews who had believed in Jesus (cf. v. 31), while in vv. 48–59 the opposition is again simply "the Jews" (vv. 48, 57).

The differing designations of these groups may well mean that different controversies from various stages in the community's history have been brought together in this trial scene. As the material now stands, various common themes link them together, but there is considerable debate among scholars about whether, in this final form, the reader is meant to take "the Jews" in vv. 48–59 as the same group described as "the Jews who had believed in him" in v. 31. Some deal with the difficulty by ignoring v. 31 as a gloss that was introduced to make a transition from v. 30, so that throughout the chapter the disputants with Jesus can be seen as disbelieving Jews.[24] Others wish to see the material in vv. 31–59 as designed both to encourage believers and to refute typical Jewish objections to belief in Jesus.[25]

---

[24] E.g., Dodd, Brown, and Lindars.
[25] E.g., Schnackenburg and Beasley-Murray.

Both of these suggestions, however, solve the problem by creating excessively awkward readings. I prefer to take the indications of audience as straightforwardly as possible, since the final form of the narrative seems designed to be read as a continuous debate. The best way to do so is to take seriously the description of v. 31 and to read the dispute of vv. 31–47 as one with Jews who have believed but whose belief is so deficient that by the time v. 47 is reached, it has become exposed as hostile unbelief. The dispute continues with this same group, but because, in the narrator's view, they have now been shown to be in reality unbelievers, they simply fall back into the category of those designated as "the Jews." This reading is supported by the fact that the material in vv. 48–59 has much in common with that in vv. 12–30—the themes of judging and knowing God and the use of the "I am" formulation. At the same time, v. 55—"I would be a liar like you"—makes clear that the same group is in view in vv. 48–59 as in vv. 31–47, since the implicit accusation that Jesus' opponents are liars has been made in v. 44.

Despite the difference it makes to our reading, the changing shape of the opposition is not as important as the consistent character of the overall dispute, which again has the features of a lawsuit.[26] As we have seen, the various strands of Jewish opposition are the accusers who interrogate Jesus and bring charges against him. At the beginning, his accusers are also his judges, but as in 5:17–49, although Jesus starts as a witness in his own defense, the roles become reversed; attack is seen as the best form of defense as he becomes prosecutor and judge of the opponents, leveling counteraccusations and charges against them. Again at issue are the claims Jesus makes about his identity, and—typical of Jewish legal process—crucial for the outcome is the establishment of the veracity and character of the witnesses on either side. These features will become clear as we highlight the main elements in the four stages of the trial scene that are suggested by the differing designations of the opposition.

(i) 8:12–20

Jesus' self-identification as the light of the world (8:12a) is part of the motif whereby he replaces the significance of the Feast of Tabernacles,

---

[26] Cf. J. H. Neyrey, "Jesus the Judge: Forensic Process in John 8,21–59," *Biblica* 68 (1987): 509–42, although, as S. Motyer, *Your Father the Devil? A New Approach to John and "the Jews"* (Carlisle, England: Paternoster, 1997), 144–45, points out, this should not be taken to mean that this passage follows some typical form of report of legal proceedings.

with its water and light imagery (cf. also 7:37–39). He employs the "I am" formulation, which, with the formulation in 8:58, forms an *inclusio* for the trial scene as a whole and signals clearly that the question of Jesus' identity will be the focus of the dispute throughout. The saying will be taken up again in the following chapter in connection with the healing of the blind man (cf. 9:5). But readers have already been shown that light is also intimately associated with the motif of judgment (cf. 3:19–21), and will be reminded of this association here by Jesus' further claim that whoever follows him "will never walk in darkness but will have the light of life" (8:12b). In the judgment provoked by the coming of the light, there is the negative effect of revealing and condemning what belongs to the darkness; there is also the positive effect (which is in view in Jesus' claim here) that the illumination produces life—the salvific verdict in the cosmic trial. Thus, Jesus' claim to be the light functions both as an evocation of the theme of judgment and as a foil for the discussion of testimony that follows.

The Pharisees respond to Jesus' extraordinary assertion by claiming that it cannot be true, since it is testimony about himself and therefore invalid according to the laws of testimony.[27] In 5:31, as already noted, Jesus himself conceded this point and immediately appealed to his Father's testimony on his behalf as a second witness. Here he delays before making such a concession to the law (cf. 8:17, 18). This time he first wants to make quite clear that the exceptional identity of the one who is testifying about himself makes his witness valid anyway (cf. also 7:17, 18). His statement about his identity is in terms of knowing where he has come from and where he is going. His origin and destiny are key notions, in the narrative, in the depiction of Jesus' distinctive identity. He has come from and is going to God, the Father, heaven, above, glory— these terms are all functional equivalents in underlining his divine origin and destiny. So the narrative has it both ways in its portrayal of Jesus. On the one hand, in 5:31, 32, Jesus as a human being is totally depend-

---

[27] Harvey, *Jesus on Trial,* 47–48, 56–57, claims that Jewish law did allow for cases where there might be only one witness, appealing to *m. Ketub.* 2 as an example, and argues therefore that Jesus was quite in line with Jewish legal procedures at this point. If this is so, it undermines Harvey's claim that the Fourth Gospel is concerned to replay the trial of Jesus according to all the normal legal procedures, because the implied author shows no knowledge of such a law. Instead the implied author, in both 5:31 and 8:17-18, has Jesus explicitly acknowledge the Deuteronomic ruling about the need for more than one witness and, in 8:14-16, gives a quite different justification for Jesus witnessing on his own behalf.

ent on his Father and in need of the Father's validating testimony. On the other hand, here in 8:14, he is so at one with God that his witness is self-authenticating, for by definition God needs no one to validate God's testimony. This is the same paradox—the distinctiveness and yet the oneness of the relationship between the Logos and God— that is set out in the very first words of the prologue (1:1).

By their failure to allow that, in Jesus' case, testimony about himself would be valid—a failure that in turn rests on the failure to recognize his divine origin and destiny—the Pharisees lay themselves open to the charge Jesus now levels against them in 8:15a: "You judge according to the flesh." This indictment means more than that they are simply following the human conventions of Jewish forensic process or judging according to appearances (cf. 7:24). As has become clear from its earlier usage (cf. 1:12; 3:6; 6:63), *flesh* can have the negative connotations of the sphere that is opposed to God and the Spirit. It is equivalent to the world, earth, or below, in contrast to God, heaven, or above. So the claim is that the Pharisees, in pursuing their judgment against Jesus, are doing so in a manner that demonstrates their captivity to the realm of hostile unbelief and its values.

Jesus then asserts, in stark contrast, that he judges no one (8:15b). The assertion raises difficulties for interpretation because it also stands in contrast to Jesus' clear earlier statement about his judging (5:30) and to the declaration later in this context (8:26). But those who take the contrast as a straightforward aporia[28] ignore the fact that, in its immediate context, the assertion of 8:15b is qualified both by what precedes, in 8:15a, and by what follows, in 8:16. It may well be, then, that it should not be taken as an outright denial of any judging activity on Jesus' part; nor should it be harmonized by interpreting judging as condemning, to make it in line with the statement about the primary purpose of Jesus' mission in 3:17. Rather, Jesus is pointing out that "by human standards his judgement is no judgement"[29] because it is not according to worldly values and is not exercised as an independent human judgment.

The immediate qualification of 8:16, by removing Jesus' judging activity from the whole sphere of the flesh, sets it in the context of the cosmic trial and on a different plane—that of the above—which has just been invoked to explain his origin and destiny; it explicitly makes his judgment

---

[28] E.g., Neyrey, "Jesus the Judge," 509, 512.
[29] Bultmann, *Gospel of John*, 281.

a divine activity. What is said about Jesus' judging activity in v. 16 ("Even if I do judge, my judgment is valid") parallels what has been said about his witness in v. 14 ("Even if I testify on my own behalf, my testimony is valid"). In both cases, Jesus claims that his breaking of the expectations and conventions of the human forensic process are justified by his participation in the greater cosmic trial and his unique relationship to its instigator. Jesus' judging had been depicted in two ways in John 5. On the one hand, Jesus could say, "The Father judges no one but has given all judgment to the Son" (5:22; cf. also 5:27); on the other, he could assert that he does not carry out this activity on his own but in dependence on his Father and in imitation of what he hears his Father saying (cf. 5:30). Here in 8:16 the two emphases are simply brought together: Jesus asserts that his judgment is true because it is not he alone who is executing it; it is a joint enterprise involving him and the Father who sent him.

In 8:17 Jesus reverts to the topic of testimony. The shifts back and forth between Jesus as witness and Jesus as judge would appear sudden and awkward were it not for two points: first, the fact that the trial scene of John 5 has already prepared us for the irony of Jesus' dual role, and, second, our knowledge of the cosmic trial in Isaiah, where Yahweh also has the roles of both witness and judge. Having stressed his self-authenticating witness from the perspective of this cosmic trial, Jesus can now return to the Jewish conventions of the earthly trial and (as he did in 5:31–37) accommodate himself to its requirements by stating that there are the necessary two witnesses—himself and his Father (8:18). The distance between the two levels is underlined by the formulation in 8:17: "In *your* law it is written that the testimony of two witnesses is valid." This is part of the broader device of the narrative as a whole that distances Jesus and his followers from their unbelieving compatriots, designated "the Jews." Here Jesus makes a concession to the opposition's standard of judgment—their law (cf. Deut 19:15)—by claiming two witnesses in his defense. But the concession is ironic. The law required two witnesses, not including the accused person, and an appeal to God is not envisaged as one of these. The force of the appeal to the law appears to be that if the law demands two human witnesses, then Jesus will supply two divine witnesses—himself and the Father.[30] In the end, however, Jesus' witness to himself and his and the Father's joint witness amount to the same thing because of the unity between the Son and the Father who sent him. The gulf between Jesus' and his opponents' perspectives is again immediately made plain through the narrative's typical device of misunder-

---

[30] Cf. Pancaro, *The Law*, 277.

standing. Jesus has referred to his Father, and now the Pharisees ask, "Where is your Father?" (8:19a), as if they want him to produce his physical father as a witness on the spot. This enables Jesus to declare that such a question is evidence that they know neither him nor his Father. From his perspective, the unity between himself and his Father is such that to know him is also to know his Father (8:19b). So, as in 5:22b, 37, 38, 42, the accusation is a radical one. For all their zeal to carry out the law in prosecuting Jesus, his opponents do not really know the one who gave them that law in the first place. Failure to recognize that Jesus is one with the Father as his fully authorized representative in the cosmic lawsuit is failure to know the one who has sent him.

This setting of the cosmic lawsuit may be recalled even in the way Jesus speaks of his fulfilling the requirement of the law in 8:18. Instead of simply stating, perhaps with an emphatic ἐγώ, "I testify on my own behalf, and the Father who sent me testifies on my behalf" (NRSV), Jesus uses a periphrastic construction with ἐγώ εἰμι—"I am the one who testifies on my behalf"—underlining his identification with the role of the witness. Two factors suggest that LXX Isa 43:10 may well be in view here. First, the verse speaks of two witnesses, Yahweh and Israel, the servant. Second, the servant has just been portrayed as a light to the nations in Isa 42:6, and it is Jesus' declaration that he is the light of the world that has sparked off the dispute in John 8 in the first place. Through the claims to be both the light and the one who bears witness, the narrative depicts Jesus as taking on the role envisaged for the servant in God's lawsuit with the world.

(ii) 8:21–30

The second stage of the dispute develops two themes already found in the first. In 8:14 Jesus spoke of his origin and destiny: "where I have come from and where I am going." Now the focus is on the latter as he speaks of his going away. In both v. 12 and v. 18, Jesus identified himself by using the ἐγώ εἰμι formulation with a predicate. Here the question of his identity is raised particularly by means of two absolute ἐγώ εἰμι statements (vv. 24, 28). Once again the device of misunderstanding is employed to illustrate the great divide between the perspective of Jesus and that of "the Jews." When Jesus says that where he is going, they cannot come, they take him to be talking about suicide, and Jesus uses this gross incomprehension as evidence of the totally opposite origins of himself and his opponents. Whereas he is not from this world but from above, they are from below and from this world (vv. 21–23). Jesus also says in v. 21, "you will search for me, but you will die in your sin."

Those who belong to the below will inevitably experience the death that characterizes this realm of unbelief. As we have seen, only those who, like Jesus, are from above can experience the life of that realm, and it is belief in Jesus and his testimony that enables a person to be born from above, not to perish, and to have eternal life (cf. 3:3–16). In 8:24 the means to escape perishing in one's sins is to "believe that I am." As the object of the belief that can rescue from death, ἐγώ εἰμι is of supreme importance, yet it is ambiguous for the hearers in the narrative, as the Jews' question, "Who are you?" (v. 25), underlines.

It is possible that "from above" in v. 23 is the antecedent that is meant to supply an implied predicate, but it is much more likely that the cosmic lawsuit of Isaiah provides the background enabling the reader to take the "I am" as it stands, absolutely, and to understand it adequately. The very same words of v. 24 are found in LXX Isa 43:10: πιστεύσητε . . . ὅτι ἐγώ εἰμι. There Israel is called to witness in order to believe that "I am," where the phrase stands for Yahweh's claim to be the only God and the only Savior of Israel (cf. 43:10c–13). Here, in an astounding move, Jesus is depicted as using of himself Yahweh's words of self-identification and, in so doing, calling the representatives of Israel of his day to believe that their one God is now to be identified with himself. The background of Isa 43:10–13 also sheds light on why Jesus has talked of people dying in their sins unless they "believe that I am." These words, which conveyed Yahweh's claim to be Israel's exclusive Savior, now, on Jesus' lips, indicate that his identification with such a claim is the sole means for Israel to be rescued from its sins.

At this point, such claims appear to be lost on Jesus' narrative audience. Their question "Who are you?" allows the implied reader to appreciate the irony of their response to the "I am" statement and provokes frustration on the part of Jesus, who (on the most likely construction of a difficult sentence) asks why he is speaking to them at all. Nevertheless, their incomprehension is not permitted to frustrate his mission more than temporarily. Jesus still has much to say about his listeners, and what he has to say is in his role as judge (8:26a). The truth of that judgment must be heard and must prevail, and this is reinforced by the reminder of his role as the fully authorized representative of the one who is true: he therefore simply speaks to the world in the lawsuit against it what he has heard from the source of its true judgment (v. 26b, cf. v. 16). The narrator then underlines the audience's incomprehension with the observation that it did not understand that the one to whom Jesus has been referring was the Father (v. 27). In the face of such a response, Jesus announces to his hearers that there will come a time when they will understand the intimate relationship he has with the Father: the Father is with him, and he is so in harmony with the Father's will that he always does what pleases the Father and says precisely what the Father wants him to say (vv. 28b–29). That crucial time is when they have lifted up the Son of Man, which, as we have noted in regard to 3:14 (cf. also 12:32–34), is the time of Jesus' exaltation to glory by means of his death by crucifixion. Of the three references to lifting up in the narrative, this is the one that lays stress on the human agents. The appropriate response to this event—realizing what it reveals of Jesus' relationship to the Father—is again formulated in terms of "I am": "then you will realize that I am." Although it is possible but somewhat awkward that the implied predicate is the Son of Man,[31] it is more likely, in the light of 8:24 and the Isaiah background, that we have once more an absolute use of the expression. The wording is paralleled in LXX Isa 43:10, which has γνῶτε . . . ὅτι ἐγώ εἰμι; John 8:28a has γνώσεσθε ὅτι ἐγώ εἰμι. To the objection that such an understanding of the "I am" statements is inconsistent with the emphasis that follows both statements, in vv. 26 and 28–29, on Jesus' dependence on the Father,[32] it need only be replied that Jesus' identity with God, and yet his distinctiveness from God as the Son dependent on the Father, is the paradox that is characteristic of the whole Gospel, beginning with its prologue.

Several distinctive aspects of this narrative's point of view coalesce at this point in the trial scene. Jesus' unique relation to God, in which he can take up the divine means of self-identification, is highlighted by his use of "I am." The key moment of the divine verdict in the trial, the vindication of Jesus' claim, is to be the same moment at which the opposition appears to have had its way, namely, its crucifixion of Jesus, which, from the divine perspective, is his glorification. Far from being Jesus' humiliation, such a death is to be seen as his exaltation. Far from involving his abandonment by the Father, it is to be seen as confirmation that the Father has not left him alone. Response to the divine verdict on Jesus will be determinative in the divine verdict on humans. In elaborating this theme in v. 28, the narrative discourse has brought together two elements from Isa 40–55—not only the "I am" formula but also the language of lifting up (cf. Isa 52:13)—to indicate, in striking fashion, that the lifting up on the cross will be the means by which the divine identity and glory of Jesus as the servant-witness will be revealed. Understanding

---

[31] Cf., e.g., Bultmann, *Gospel of John,* 349.

[32] E.g., G. C. Nicholson, *Death as Departure: The Johannine Descent-Ascent Schema* (Chico, Calif.: Scholars Press, 1983), 113.

that, in the crucifixion/exaltation, Jesus is supremely revealed as the one who can identify himself by "I am" will mean, as in Isa 43:10–13, that Israel can experience salvific rather than condemnatory judgment and fulfill its role as witness to the "I am."

Somewhat surprisingly in the light of the previous comments about the audience's incomprehension, the narrator now indicates that many believed in Jesus (8:30). The combination of incomprehension about Jesus' relationship with the Father and belief in Jesus may, however, prepare the reader for the discovery (which follows in the rest of the chapter) of the grave deficiencies of such a belief. The response of Jewish believers, which, from the narrator's perspective, is to be seen as pseudo-belief, may also serve to point the reader away from the straightforward story line to the wider narrative world, in which the experience of the community has been merged with that of Jesus. Those who initially believed but who were not able, when the time of testing from the synagogue came, to confess openly the community's distinctive belief about Jesus' unique relationship as Son of God to his Father became a major cause for disappointment and then disapprobation as apostates. This conflict is reflected in the remainder of the trial scene.

(iii) 8:31–47

The vocabulary of witness and judging has by now largely receded, but that the overall trial scene continues is clear from the accusations and counteraccusations that follow. They revolve around Jesus' identity and his opponents' inability to accept his claims about himself. In 8:31–47 what is at stake in the trial is formulated primarily in terms of the truth, while in vv. 48–59 the issue will focus more on Jesus' glory or honor.

The question whether the Jews who have believed in Jesus have exercised true faith is immediately raised by the way in which Jesus addresses them. They will show themselves to be truly his disciples if they continue in his word (v. 31). The test of true discipleship is knowing the truth that is able to liberate them (v. 32). As will be clear from the parallel statement in v. 36—"If the Son makes you free, you will be free indeed"—the truth is God's revelation embodied in Jesus. The Jewish believers immediately cast doubt on the nature of their belief by the incomprehension they reveal in their response. They show more concern about being descendants of Abraham than about being followers of Jesus and deny the need for liberation with the claim that they have never been slaves to anyone. There is obvious irony on the political level that such a claim is made by those under Roman occupation, but presumably they intend it more as an expression of their internal religious freedom—including freedom from idolatry (cf. also 5:41) and sin—on the basis of their relation to God through the covenant with Abraham. Jesus does not allow them to get away with their claim even on this level, pointing out that all who sin thereby show themselves to be slaves to sin. He then contrasts the slave who does not remain in the house with the son who remains forever. On the one hand, this is an immediate reminder of the opening of this section of the argument. The condition for being a true disciple was to remain in Jesus' word. The one who commits sin is the slave who does not remain in the house and, by extension, does not remain in Jesus' word. On the other hand, in the light of the audience's claim to be Abraham's descendants, there is also a reminder of the Genesis narrative, in which there are two sorts of descendant from Abraham—a slave son and a free son, Ishmael and Isaac. Paul exploited this aspect of the Genesis narrative in his polemic against Judaizing opposition in Gal 4:21–31.[33] Here, however, while "the Jews" are the slave descendants, it is Jesus himself who is primarily in view as the free son who is able to liberate others (John 8:36).

As scriptural background, Isaiah is again not remote from this discussion. The message of its trial scenes and their surrounding context comes to those in exile, those in Babylonian captivity, and Yahweh's self-announcement as "I am" also announces Yahweh as Israel's sole Savior and Redeemer (e.g., Isa 41:14; 43:14; 44:22–24; 47:4; 48:17, 20; 52:3; 59:20). The notion of redemption includes liberation from slavery and oppression. Yahweh recalls the people to their Abrahamic descent (cf. 41:8; 51:2) and promises to free and restore them (cf. 45:13; 49:6, 25; 51:11, 14; 61:1–4). What is required of them is an acknowledgment of their internal condition of sinful rebellion, which has led to their external condition of slavery (cf. 42:24; 50:1; 53:4–6; 55:6, 7; 59:1–16, 20). The motifs are replayed here as Jesus, after revealing himself in terms of "I am" and as the one who delivers Israel from death in its sins, now presses for an acknowledgment by these particular Jews that they are indeed in a sinful condition and in need of his liberation.

In his role as prosecutor and judge, Jesus goes further and, while acknowledging his hearers' physical descent from Abraham, charges them with seeking to kill him (John 8:37, 40); this charge is, of course, confirmed by their action at the end of the trial scene (cf. v. 59). The charge indicates that the issue goes deeper than claims about who is a son of

---

[33] Cf. C. K. Barrett, *The Gospel according to St. John* (2d ed.; Philadelphia: Westminster, 1978), 346; Neyrey, "Jesus the Judge," 521–23.

Abraham. It concerns whether ultimate spiritual paternity can be traced to God or to the devil. The test for such paternity is what a person says and does. On the one side, Jesus claims to speak the truth that he has heard from his Father (vv. 38, 40). On the other side, he denounces his hearers for not doing what Abraham did (presumably his hospitality to, and reception of, God's messengers is in view; cf. Gen 18:1–8); instead, by their refusal to accept the truth and their intent to kill him, they reveal their descent from the father of lies and the murderer from the beginning, that is, the devil (John 8:39–45). In the course of this denunciation, the hearers interject that they were not born illegitimately (ἐκ πορνείας) but have one father, God (v. 41). This appears to be a claim that they are not unfaithful idolaters (cf. LXX Hos 1:2; 2:4) but are faithful to the one God of the Shema (Deut 6:4). Jesus' response is that if God were truly their Father, they would love Jesus, since he has been sent from God (8:42), and they would hear the words of God, which he speaks (v. 47).

This section, which began by emphasizing that real belief entails knowing the truth that Jesus reveals about himself (vv. 31–32), concludes with his condemnation that his hearers do not believe the truth he is telling them (vv. 45–46). By now it has been made perfectly plain that the supposed Jewish believers in Jesus are bereft of genuine belief. Indeed, the fiercest polemic in the narrative has been reserved for them. Not only are they not true followers of Jesus; they are not true sons of Abraham, they are not even sons of God, but their paternity has to be traced to the devil. All this underlines in the most radical way that, from the narrator's point of view, in this lawsuit a verdict about Jesus is at the same time a verdict about God. In the perspective arising out of the conflict between the community and the synagogue, to have an initially positive attitude to Jesus but then not progress to recognizing the truth that behind the "I am" of Jesus lies the "I am" of Israel's one God is not simply to apostasize or to remain in the synagogue. It is to place oneself among those whom Isaiah had earlier indicted, those "who are called by the name of Israel . . . and invoke the God of Israel, but not in truth or right" (Isa 48:1).

(iv) 8:48–59

The counteraccusation of the hearers, who are now no longer called the Jews who had believed but simply "the Jews," is equally fierce. If Jesus charges them with having the devil as their father, they now confirm such alienation from God by alleging that Jesus is a Samaritan and thus the one who is a heretic, an apostate from Israel, and that he has a demon and so is the one who is possessed by the devil (8:48; cf. v. 52). Of course, to be a Samaritan or possessed by the devil would also make the witness Jesus has given inadmissible in terms of Jewish law.[34] From the narrator's point of view, these accusations are seen as lies (cf. v. 55) and thus as substantiating Jesus' prior accusation about his hearers' relationship to the liar and the father of lies (v. 44). In the context of the lawsuit, lies can in turn be seen as the equivalent to bearing false witness about Jesus. The Jewish trial narratives in the synoptic account contain the motif of false witness against Jesus; since, in the Fourth Gospel's narrative there is no formal Jewish trial but the public ministry, which takes the shape of a trial before "the Jews," is its functional equivalent, these false accusations can perhaps be seen as part of that same equivalent. As Ricoeur has rightly noted, "False testimony cannot at all be reduced to an error in the account of things seen: false testimony is a lie in the heart of the witness."[35]

In denying that he has a demon, Jesus maintains instead that he is honoring his Father. His claims cannot therefore fall into the category of demonic blasphemy, which would dishonor God. He is also concerned about the dishonor such accusations do to his own person (v. 49; cf. also 5:23). This does not mean, however, that he is simply concerned about his own glory. The one whom his opponents claim as their God, but without knowing this God, glorifies Jesus (8:50, 54, 55). In v. 50c these accusations and counteraccusations are all explicitly placed in the context of the cosmic lawsuit, as Jesus asserts that his own honor and glory will be upheld and vindicated by the ultimate judge, God. This explicit reminder of the overall trial motif also underlines that the opponents are being judged, their accusations exposing their unbelief. Despite this, Jesus under solemn oath continues to offer the positive verdict of life: "Very truly ['Amen, amen'], I tell you, whoever keeps my word will never see death" (v. 51). Those who evidence true belief by holding on to Jesus' word come what may (the equivalent to remaining in his word in v. 31) will escape condemnation by having passed from death to life (cf. 5:24). This offer provokes repetition of the accusation that he has a demon and of the charge that, in offering life, Jesus is making himself equal to God in God's prerogative as life giver: "Who do you claim to be?" (lit. "Whom are you making yourself?" cf. 5:18; 10:33; 19:7).

The questioning of Jesus' identity includes what will turn out for the reader, in the light of 8:58, to be an ironic question: "Are you greater than our father Abraham, who died?" (v. 53a). Jesus takes up the reference to

---

[34] Cf. Harvey, *Jesus on Trial,* 94.

[35] Ricoeur, "Hermeneutics of Testimony," 128.

Abraham in v. 56, claiming, "Your ancestor Abraham rejoiced that he would see my day; he saw it and was glad." Abraham functions here like Moses in John 5. He is raised as a witness for the opposition against Jesus, but then the tables are turned and he becomes a witness for Jesus in his prosecution of the opposition. Jewish tradition held that Abraham had been shown the end times by God (2 Esd 3:14), and his laughter in Gen 17:17 was interpreted as rejoicing (Philo, *Mut.* 154; cf. also *Jub.* 15.17; *T. Levi* 18.14); these elements are now combined in a christological application. Typically, "the Jews" are portrayed as totally misunderstanding Jesus by remaining on the earthly level. They can only mock at the difference between Jesus' relatively short life span and the age he would have to be in order to have encountered Abraham (John 8:57). Their incomprehension provides the foil for Jesus' climactic statement about himself.

With the astounding claim "before Abraham was, I am," Jesus rounds off the discussion of Abraham and, more significantly, brings to a conclusion the dispute about his identity, which had begun with the "I am" saying with a predicate in v. 12 and intensified with the absolute "I am" sayings of vv. 24, 28. This final saying clearly contains an absolute use of "I am." Its present tense, which contrasts with the aorist infinitive (γενέσθαι) that expresses Abraham's coming into existence, indicates that more than a claim to preexistence is being made. As with the earlier absolute uses of "I am" in vv. 24, 28, a reference to LXX Isa 43:10, with its lawsuit context, again appears to be in view. Significantly, there Yahweh's self-revelation in terms of ἐγώ εἰμι is also contrasted with the temporal existence of another being, of whom the aorist tense of γίνομαι is employed: ἔμπροσθέν μου οὐκ ἐγένετο ἄλλος θεός, "Before me no other god came into existence." There is a possibility (problems of dating mean that it can be no more) that not only Isa 43:10 but the Targum on this passage may be reflected at this point in the dispute in the Fourth Gospel, since the Targum on Isaiah contains a striking reference to Abraham that corresponds with the reference in John 8:56: "I, even I, am the Lord; and beside me there is no saviour. I declared to Abraham your father what was about to come; I delivered you from Egypt . . . ."[36]

In any case, Jesus' claim to be the self-revelation of the one true God is now unmistakable. Any ambiguities that remained after the claims of vv. 24, 28 have been removed, and even Jesus' Jewish hearers now recognize his meaning. The narrator's comment is, "So they picked up stones to throw at him" (v. 59a), which leaves the reader to assume that

---

[36] Cf. D. M. Ball, *"I Am" in John's Gospel* (Sheffield: Sheffield Academic Press, 1996), 195–97.

they have interpreted his words as a blasphemous identification with God (cf. 10:33). This audience has reached its verdict and ironically, in the attempt to carry it through, has proved the charge that Jesus had leveled against them (cf. 8:40). But the time for the final human verdict that will coincide with the decisive announcement of the divine verdict has not yet arrived, and so the closing words of the narrator are, "but Jesus hid himself and went out of the temple" (v. 59b).

We have noted the significance of the links with Deutero-Isaiah's lawsuit for the interchangeability of Jesus' roles as witness, defendant, prosecutor, and judge and for his claims to be the "I am" who can rescue his people from death in sin and redeem and liberate them from slavery to sin. The lawsuit in Isaiah also prepares the reader for the issue being formulated in terms of both truth (John 8:31–47) and glory (vv. 48–59). The truth of Yahweh's word and deeds had been at stake (cf. Isa 41:26; 42:3; 43:9; 45:19), as had Yahweh's glory, a glory that is Yahweh's alone (cf. esp. Isa 42:8; 48:11) but that Yahweh will also give to Israel, the servant, and thereby glorify Yahweh's own self (cf. Isa 49:3; also 44:23; 45:25; 49:5; 55:5).

In addition, this scriptural background illuminates the role of the Jewish hearers in John 8 in two ways. First, they are seen as like Israel in Isaiah, bringing accusations against God, here in the person of God's representative, Jesus, and in the process becoming the accused. It is worth noting the similarity between the charges Jesus brings against his hearers and the accusations Yahweh turns on Israel in the lawsuits and disputations.[37] Jesus indicts their lack of knowledge (John 8:14, 19, 55; cf. Isa 48:8). They judge according to the flesh (John 8:15), and while he is from above, they are from below (v. 23). This recalls Yahweh's indictment in Isa 55:9: "For as the heavens are higher than the earth, so are my ways higher than your ways and my thoughts than your thoughts." Jesus' hearers are said to be slaves because of their sin (8:33, 34); Yahweh told Israel that, because of its sins, it had been sold into slavery (Isa 50:1). The audience are those who in fact do not hear (8:43, 47), just as Israel, according to Yahweh's charge, did not hear (Isa 42:18, 20). Jesus accuses them of dishonoring him (8:49), just as Israel was accused of not honoring Yahweh (Isa 43:23). Paternity is mentioned in both sets of accusations. Yahweh told Israel that its ancestor was a transgressor (Isa 43:27) and that from birth it, too, had been a rebel (Isa 48:8); now Jesus says that his hearers' ancestor is the devil (8:44).

---

[37] Motyer, *Your Father the Devil?* 146–47, finds significant parallels in Hosea's prophetic polemic against Israel.

Second, instead of being the witnesses who understand and believe that "I am," the status of unbelieving Israel as the accused now in fact associates it with the role of the nations and their gods from Isaiah. They are no longer true children of Abraham, and despite their claim not to be children of fornication (8:41), this is what, by their refusal to acknowledge the one true God as revealed in Jesus, they demonstrate themselves to be—unfaithful idolaters. In Isa 44:9 it is said of those who make idols that "their witnesses neither see nor know. And so they will be put to shame" (cf. also Isa 44:18; 45:20); throughout John 8 Jesus' opponents are said to know neither him nor God (8:14, 19, 55; cf. also vv. 27, 43). Like the nations, Jesus' hearers are deaf to God's word (8:47; cf. Isa 42:8). They accuse Jesus of having a demon after he has depicted them as children of the devil. Again in Isaiah, it is the nations as idolaters who are linked with enchantments and sorcery (cf. Isa 44:25; 47:12, 13). Later in Isaiah, Israel itself is indicted for its idolatry, and such idolatry is seen as participation in the demonic (cf. LXX Isa 65:11—"you are those who have left me, and forget my holy mountain, and prepare a table for the devil [τῷ δαίμονι]"; cf. also Deut 32:17). Clearly, in the narrative of the Fourth Gospel, unbelieving Israel has abandoned the role it was intended to have by God; it is now to be seen as part of the world and the world's idolatry in its refusal to recognize the claims of the one true God.[38] In a suggestive discussion, Stibbe claims that, "by using the forensic motifs of Isaiah's trial scenes, John is able to satirize the Jews who had believed in Jesus in John 8.31–59"; he cites definitions of satire as judgment and the satirist as witness, judge, and executioner; and he provides the important reminder that in this passage it is not Jews in general at whom such fierce invective is directed but Jews who had once believed.[39] Chapter 6 of this study will explore some of the possible reasons lying behind this portrayal of former believers.

E. The Interrogation of the Man Born Blind (9:1–41)

The trial of Jesus in John 8 is followed in John 9 by the trial of the man who had been blind. Jesus had been on trial for claims about his

---

[38] Motyer, ibid., 146, refuses to allow the Gospel's depiction of "the Jews" as representatives of the world to inform the allusions to Scripture and therefore disputes the links between the audience and the nations in Isaiah.

[39] M. W. G. Stibbe, *John's Gospel* (London: Routledge, 1994), 107–31, esp. 123.

identity, particularly the claim (repeated here immediately before the miracle in 9:5) to be the light of the world. Part of the earlier claim was, "Whoever follows me will never walk in darkness but will have the light of life" (8:12). Now Jesus' verification of the claim through the giving of sight to the blind man leads to this man's interrogation. The imagery of light and darkness ensures that the framework of the cosmic trial, with which the reader is now familiar, will not be forgotten. And the force of the narrative is clear. If the one who is the light is subjected to opposition, trial, and rejection by the forces of darkness, it will be no different for his followers who have experienced the light of life.

Although 9:1–41 is treated separately here, it should also be seen as part of a more extended unit that is completed in John 10, which not only refers back to the episode with the blind man (cf. 10:21) but continues the themes of interrogation and judgment.[40] In this first section of the more extended unit, however, in which we see "Johannine dramatic skill at its best,"[41] the author's fondness for groups of seven is evident in the structuring of the episode into seven scenes (vv. 1–7, 8–12, 13–17, 18–23, 24–34, 35–38, 39–41).

The central scene, vv. 18–23, suggests the perspective from which the episode is to be viewed, and if those who see chiastic features in the arrangement of the discourse are correct,[42] these simply underline the significance of this scene. Toward the end of the dialogue between the blind man's parents and "the Jews," the narrator provides his only extended comment as part of an "inside view" of the parents' fear: "for the Jews had already agreed that anyone who confessed Jesus to be the Messiah would be put out of the synagogue" (v. 22). All the elements of this assertion reflect a time later than that of the mission of the earthly Jesus—a situation in which people could be expected to make a formal confession of Jesus as the Christ, in which Jewish religious authorities would have formally agreed about what to do in response to such confessions, and in which this response took the form of excommunication from the synagogue. As a result particularly of the work of Martyn,[43] the anachronistic nature of the narrator's comment has been seen as the clue to reading this narrative, and by extension the Gospel

---

[40] Cf., e.g., Dodd, *Interpretation of the Fourth Gospel*, 354–62.

[41] Brown, *Gospel according to John*, 1:376.

[42] E.g., Duke, *Irony*, 118; M. W. G. Stibbe, *John* (Sheffield: JSOT Press, 1993), 105.

[43] Martyn, *History and Theology*, 24–62. Among others, Dodd, *Interpretation of the Fourth Gospel*, 357, n. 1, had already noted this: "The beggar on trial suggests

as a whole, as a two-level drama: the blind man is not only someone healed by Jesus but also the representative of those Jewish Christian readers who have been expelled from the synagogue because of their confession about Jesus. Chapter 6 of our study will discuss the historical referent of the narrator's comment. Our interest here is simply to reinforce the special significance, for the readers, of what happens to the blind man as a consequence of gaining his sight. His role as a model for the readers is further facilitated by two factors: he becomes the central character in place of Jesus in vv. 8–34, which "comprise the longest absence of Jesus in John's Gospel,"[44] and his character undergoes greater development than that of any other figure in the Gospel.

The blind man begins as a representative of all humanity because there is a sense in which all are born blind and in darkness. As Jesus asserts later in 12:46, belief in Jesus is necessary if people are not to remain in darkness, and as we have already noted, he has claimed earlier that birth from above is required if people are to *see* the kingdom of God (3:3, cf. also 3:19–21). Once he has received his sight from Jesus and Jesus has moved offstage, the man becomes increasingly representative of Jesus' followers. First he undergoes interrogation from his neighbors and others who had observed him begging (9:8–12). Their questioning initially focuses on his identity, on whether this can be the same person they had known, and then on how the change took place. The man witnesses to Jesus' initiating activity in his reception of sight but then, when asked about Jesus' whereabouts, has to confess his ignorance. The questioners may appear at first simply motivated by natural curiosity, but something more negative in their attitude seems to be involved when we are told at the beginning of the next scene that "they brought to the Pharisees the man who had formerly been blind" (v. 13). Ominous overtones are also suggested, especially in the light of 5:1–18, when the narrator only now reveals that it was a Sabbath day when Jesus opened the man's eyes (9:14). The indications are, therefore, that the man has been taken to the Pharisees because others suspect something is amiss. This reaction might well be familiar to many of the original readers, who would have known what it was like to be reported to or hauled before the religious authorities because of their witness to the life-changing experience of believing in Jesus.

---

to the Christian reader his own situation in the world-enlightened in baptism and called on to confess Christ before men."

[44] Duke, *Irony,* 119.

In John 9 "the theme is clearly trial and judgment."[45] And the elements of a trial emerge from v. 13 onwards.[46] In the scene of vv. 13–17, the absent Jesus is the subject of the Pharisees' interrogation, and the man who was blind functions as a witness who is cross-examined. It is Jesus' activity and its significance that are contested, as the division of opinion in v. 16 indicates. Thus, a verdict needs to be reached about Jesus' healing, which is viewed as involving a double violation of laws governing the Sabbath—not only the healing itself but also his making clay in the process. In the next scene, the healed man's parents are called as witnesses (vv. 19–23). By the time the man himself is called back for a second interrogation (vv. 24–34), the verdict on Jesus has been reached (cf. v. 24). Now gradually the man's own witness to Jesus becomes the focus of the trial, and a negative verdict is pronounced on the man (v. 34). After the short scene in which Jesus and the blind man are reunited and that functions as the latter's vindication (vv. 35–38), the concluding scene—in a final dramatic and ironic reversal—has a verdict of judgment pronounced this time not by the Pharisees on Jesus but by Jesus on the Pharisees (vv. 39–41).

In the first interrogation, the Pharisees concentrate on how the man received his sight. In a brief reply, the man concludes by testifying, "now I see" (v. 15)—the sixth reference, up to now, to the fact of his sight (cf. vv. 7, 10, 11, 13, 14). His account produces a divided judgment on the key issue of Jesus' relationship to God. In contrast to Jesus' own witness (cf. 6:46; 7:29), some of the Pharisees are quite sure Jesus is not "from God" (v. 16: παρὰ θεοῦ) because he has violated the Sabbath. Others focus on the sign and cannot understand how one who can do such signs could be a sinner. The divided judgment underlines the centrality of what is at stake. Is Jesus to be viewed as a sinner or from God? Those who stress the law and Jesus' violation of the Sabbath come to the former conclusion. But those who are open to the witness of Jesus' works by seeing the sign are also open to a different conclusion.[47] The division over Jesus makes them turn to the man for his evaluation of his healer's identity. Prodded into witness, he replies that Jesus is a prophet.

The following scene introduces a change in the designation of the authorities. Any sympathetic Pharisees disappear, and instead the antagonists are called "the Jews"—those hardened in opposition and unbelief. The authorities also adopt a change of tactics. Convinced that the man

---

[45] Ibid., 126.

[46] Cf. also Blank, *Krisis*, 255.

[47] Cf. Pancaro, *The Law*, 20.

can see, they now question whether he was ever blind in the first place. They call his parents and ask, "Is this your son, who you say was born blind?" (v. 19). The parents confirm the central fact that he was born blind but are evasive about the significance of his present sight, professing ignorance about how this has happened and who did it. It is significant that the parents have not in fact been asked who performed the healing and yet they realize that this is the underlying issue in the interrogation. Their equivocation and unwillingness to identify Jesus as the healer, explains the narrator, derives from their fear of the authorities and of the consequences of confessing Jesus as Messiah, and this fear overrides any responsibility for, and solidarity with, their son. As Staley suggests, the narrator's explanation "turns an unnecessary and rude conversation into a courtroom drama."[48] Just as Jesus' mission produced division within his family (cf. 7:3–8), so witnessing to him in the context of the conflict with the synagogue could produce alienation within the families of his followers, as some of the original readers would have been well aware. So the parents put their son back in the dock, "knowing full well that he will be subject to the very sentence that they themselves are afraid to face."[49] Their fear of "the Jews" and reluctance to risk what could be construed as a public confession become the foil for the action of the man himself in the next scene, where he fearlessly and boldly confronts the authorities.[50]

In this long fifth scene (vv. 24–34), the man who had been blind comes into his own as a character. The authorities have reached a definite verdict about Jesus—"We know that this man is a sinner"—and enjoin the man to give glory to God. This language functions as a call to confess or admit the truth,[51] putting the witness under solemn oath. The REB captures the force of the injunction: "Speak the truth before God." At the same time, there is an irony in the formulation, since readers know that the way to give glory to God in this Gospel's narrative is to believe that Jesus in his signs is the revealer of God's glory. The man's witness begins in a low-key fashion. He claims not to know whether Jesus is a sinner (but cf. v. 31), and concentrates on what he is absolutely sure

---

[48] J. L. Staley, "Stumbling in the Dark, Reaching for the Light: Reading Character in John 5 and 9," *Semeia* 53 (1991): 68.

[49] D. Rensberger, *Johannine Faith,* 47.

[50] Cf. J. L. Resseguie, "John 9: A Literary-Critical Analysis," in *Literary Interpretations of Biblical Narratives* (2 vols.; ed. K. R. Gros Louis; Nashville: Abingdon, 1982), 2:299.

[51] Cf. Josh 7:19; 1 Esd 9:8; *m. Sanh.* 6.2.

of—his own experience: "One thing I do know, that though I was blind, now I see" (v. 25). When the authorities cast doubt on the credibility of his witness by asking, for a third time, how this has happened, the man grows more confident in the face of this stubborn refusal to believe his account. The one born blind can now accuse his interrogators of being deaf: "I have told you already, and you would not listen" (v. 27).This echoes Jesus' own counteraccusations in the preceding trial (cf. 8:43, 47). Emboldened, the man turns to wit and sarcasm—"Why do you want to hear it again? Do you also want to become his disciples?"—and in the process reveals his own commitment: he is one of Jesus' disciples.

The authorities take the bait and respond by reviling him and revealing their own allegiance. The contrast of v. 28—a disciple of Jesus over against disciples of Moses—goes to the heart of the conflicting claims in the trial, already anticipated in the contrast of the prologue between Jesus and Moses (cf. 1:17). The religious authorities link Moses and God through their assertion that God has spoken to Moses. The rival claim, as we have seen, holds not only that God has spoken to Jesus (cf. 8:26, 28) but also that Jesus speaks God's words (cf. 3:34; 7:16; 12:49, 50) and that in fact he embodies God's word as the Logos (cf 1:1, 2, 14). The opposition, however, does not know where Jesus has come from—πόθεν, a significant term in the debate about Jesus' identity, focusing on his origins (cf. 7:27, 28; 8:14; 19:9). The authorities have failed to perceive the amazing nature of the sign, and the man finds this failure itself amazing, exclaiming ironically, "Here is an astonishing thing! You do not know where he comes from, and yet he opened my eyes" (9:30). He then provides theological reflection on his experience. He starts with an agreed premise ("We know" that God does not listen to sinners but to those who do God's will), reminds them that it is totally unprecedented for someone to heal a person born blind, and concludes that, for someone to have done this, he has to have been from God. The authorities earlier asked the man for his view of Jesus. Now they have been given a fuller version of what they asked for, but do not like what they get. They are reduced to abusing the man in terms of their theology that his blindness was caused by sin (cf. v. 2), rebuking him for daring to try to teach them his theological insights, and then casting him out. The excommunication his parents had feared (cf. v. 22) is precisely the outcome of his witness.

But at this point Jesus reappears on the scene. He finds the one who has been driven out. The contrast between rejection by the synagogue and acceptance by Jesus would have resonated with the readers, who might well also recall Jesus' earlier promise: "anyone who comes to me I will never drive away (or cast out)" (6:37). In the company of Jesus, the man quickly develops his christological insight. Jesus draws out his faith; his question to the man about belief in the Son of Man results eventually in the man's full-blown Johannine confession of faith— "Lord, I believe [that you are the Son of Man]"—and his worshiping of Jesus. The latter act, whose appropriate object is God, makes his confession equivalent to that of Thomas later in 20:28: "My Lord and my God!" The title "Son of Man," which can sometimes be virtually synonymous in this Gospel with "Son" and "Son of God," appears to be chosen here for two reasons. First, as in John 3 and the discussion with Nicodemus, it underlines the issue of Jesus' identity as "from God" because, as 3:13 put it, the Son of Man is the one who descended from heaven, from God. And second, "Son of Man" has close links with judgment, the theme taken up in the following verse. As Son of Man, Jesus is the one who has been given authority to judge with the verdict of either life or death (cf. 5:25–29, esp. 5:27: "and he has given him authority to execute judgment, because he is the Son of Man"). After his earthly trial, the man confesses his faith in the one who is the ultimate judge. The Son of Man, with authority to judge, is outside the synagogue in the company of the one judged and condemned by human religious authorities.

The actual term *judgment* (κρίμα) is withheld until the final scene (9:39–41), which opens with Jesus' solemn pronouncement: "I came into this world for judgment so that those who do not see may see, and those who do see may become blind."[52] Again Jesus' mission as judge has both positive and negative outcomes. The positive aspect has been clearly demonstrated in the blind man's reception of sight, and now the negative aspect will be underlined regarding the religious authorities. The whole incident is in fact a narrative embodiment of Jesus' earlier words about the judgment produced by the light coming into the world (3:19–21).

Some of the Pharisees who hear Jesus' pronouncement ask the ironic question "Surely we are not blind, are we?" (9:40). The form of the question anticipates a negative response, and readers are set up either to expect Jesus to tell these Pharisees instead that they are blind or simply to be left to savor the irony. But the irony is prolonged and deepened, as Jesus agrees with them that they are not blind: "If you were blind, you would not have sin. But now that you say, 'We see,' your sin remains" (v. 41). The blindness Jesus refers to is the kind of blindness

---

[52] Cf. Duke, *Irony*, 126.

that knows it is blindness—the blindness of the blind man who was ready to obey in order to receive sight. What the Pharisees are suffering from is in fact an illusion of sight, and this has caused a far deeper darkness than they are aware of, in which they refuse to acknowledge their blindness and therefore are unable to accept the light when it is offered.[53] Bultmann expresses this well: "'Blindness' is no longer simply a wandering in the dark, which can always become aware that it is lost, and so have the possibility of receiving sight; for now it has forfeited this possibility. He who does not believe is judged (3.18) and judgement is carried out on him precisely in his holding on to the delusion that he can see."[54] The Pharisees linked the man's blindness with sin (9:34), as had the disciples earlier (v. 2), but now sin is said to be truly the cause of the Pharisees' deeper spiritual blindness, an illusion of sight. The trial is completed and the tables turned with the final judgment of condemnation: "your sin remains." *To remain or abide* (μένειν) is part of the Gospel's distinctive vocabulary and generally has a favorable connotation, but the force here is reminiscent of its negative usage in 3:36, where again in a pronouncement of judgment it is asserted that "whoever disobeys the Son will not see life, but the wrath of God remains on him" (NAB).

If trial and judgment provide the theme, the development of two sorts of judgment about Jesus as the bringer of light provides the movement and irony of the narrative.[55] The judgment of the man born blind, with its progressive knowledge and bold confession of who Jesus is, has increasing clarity of sight. This man judges Jesus on the basis of his experience of receiving sight. He begins by perceiving Jesus as the man who healed him (v. 11), moves to acknowledging him as a prophet (v. 17), then confesses that he is Jesus' disciple (v. 27), that Jesus is from God (v. 33), that he is Lord and Son of Man (v. 38a); finally, he worships Jesus (v. 38b). The Pharisees judge Jesus on the basis of their interpretation of the law (cf. esp. v. 28—"we are disciples of Moses") and are unable to see that if they believed Moses, they would believe Jesus (cf. 5:46). This contrasting judgment of the religious authorities develops into deeper and deeper blindness. It starts with a divided verdict about Jesus' act of healing (9:16) and an apparent willingness to hear the healed man's judgment (v.17), but then turns into an unbelieving attempt to discredit the healing (vv. 18, 19), a verdict that Jesus is a sinner (v. 24), a

---

[53] Cf. ibid., 124.
[54] Bultmann, *Gospel of John,* 341.
[55] Cf. Resseguie, "John 9," 302.

reviling of the man born blind for his confession (vv. 28, 34a), and a casting of him out of the synagogue (v. 34b). Finally, their claim not to be blind exposes the desperate darkness of the sin in which they remain (vv. 39–41).

Significantly, both the developing christological insight and the hardening of the opposition take place through the clash of claims. The blind man's understanding of Jesus' identity grows through the process of witness, conflict, interrogation, trial, and rejection. At the same time, the religious authorities increasingly define themselves in opposition to the claims that emerge. Again this appears to mirror the experience of Johannine Christians in their conflict with the synagogue authorities, in which claims about the significance of Jesus would not only have sparked off conflict in the first place but would have been elaborated and refined in the continuation of the conflict, provoking further counter-claims. As Rensberger suggests, "For the Johannine community, the truth about Jesus came, not at the beginning, nor even simply at the end, but out of the midst of this process of confession, rebuke, and stub-bornly continued confession itself."[56] In the narrative's trial of truth, the truth about Jesus not only is the subject matter of the trial but is itself shaped and formed by means of the trial.

As indicated a number of times in our discussion, this narrative echoes 3:1–21 in several ways: the issue of Jesus being "from God"; the theme that the judgment is produced by the light, with its dual effect of coming to the light and seeing or remaining in the darkness; and the use of "Son of Man." In John 3 Jesus teaches the teacher of Israel who does not understand; in John 9 the man born blind teaches the teachers who do not know (cf. vv. 30, 34). In addition, in 3:11 Jesus asserted, "we speak of what we know and testify to what we have seen"; in John 9 the man not only uses the "we know" terminology (cf. v. 31) but is the witness par excellence to what he knows and sees: "One thing I do know, that though I was blind, now I see" (v. 25). There is no mistaking that this disciple is portrayed as identified with the witness, trial, rejection, and vindication of Jesus.

There are also echoes yet again of the trial scenes and their context in Isa 40–55. In Isaiah the servant-witness is given as "a light to the nations, to open the eyes that are blind, to bring out . . . from the prison those who sit in darkness" (42:6–7; cf. also 49:6–7, 9). It is the nations assembled for the lawsuit who are blind and deaf (43:8), and these wor-

---

[56] Rensberger, *Johannine Faith,* 46.

shippers of idols "do not know, nor do they comprehend; for their eyes are shut, so that they cannot see" (44:18), and "their witnesses neither see nor know" (44:9). In John 9 these characteristics are transferred to Israel in the persons of the religious authorities (cf. 9:27, 29, 39). In Isaiah, Israel, as God's witness, is told again and again not to fear or be afraid (cf., e.g., 44:8; 41:10, 13, 14; 43:1, 5); in the trial of John 9, this is the test that the parents fail (v. 22), but their son passes it with a display of boldness laced with humor and irony.

F. Jesus and the Judgment of the World (12:37–50)

The narrative of the public ministry, which began with the witness of John the Baptist, closes on the note of judgment (cf. 12:47–48). The conclusion is in two parts. In vv. 37–43 the narrator summarizes the response to Jesus' signs, and in vv. 44–50 the protagonist himself summarizes what has been at stake in the response to his words. The two sections sum up the trial of the public ministry. In the first, the narrator acts as counsel for the defense as he provides an apology for the response to Jesus' deeds; in the second, the person who is on trial is allowed to give a final statement about his teaching and its significance.

Just before the summing up, the trial motif has emerged in two passages, vv. 17–18 and 30–33. In the former, the crowd who were with Jesus when he raised Lazarus continue to testify about this sign. This reference raises again the issue—which will also come to the fore in the concluding section of the chapter—of whether Jesus' signs are those of the true prophet (cf. 6:14) or those of a false prophet who leads the people astray (cf. 7:12). One might have thought, according to the law of evidence (cf. Deut 17:6), that because so many people are witnessing to this sign, its legitimacy would be considered proven. The Pharisees' response as they say to one another, "You see, you can do nothing. Look, the world has gone after him" (ὀπίσω αὐτοῦ ἀπῆλθεν—John 12:19), not only expresses their failure to cope with the impact Jesus has made. It also recalls Deut. 13:1–11 and its discussion of the false prophet who leads the people astray from the command to go after the Lord their God (ὀπίσω κυρίου τοῦ θεοῦ ὑμῶν πορεύεσθε—LXX Deut 13:5). The Pharisees still see this as a sign of the false prophet, in line with the Sanhedrin's verdict, already reached earlier in response to the signs, to put Jesus to death and thereby purge the nation (John 11:47–50, cf. Deut 13:5, 9, 10).

Later in John 12, the arrival of the Greeks to see Jesus precipitates his announcement that the hour of his glory has now arrived (vv. 24, 27).

His appeal to the Father, "glorify your name," is met with the pronouncement of the voice from heaven, "I have glorified it, and I will glorify it again" (v. 28). Jesus sees God's own glory and honor at stake in the trial, and the voice confirms that God's reputation is inextricably bound up with that of God's authorized agent. Jesus' mission, including the signs, has already demonstrated God's glory, and it will be demonstrated again in the event of Jesus' crucifixion/glorification, which is about to unfold. The voice, recalling the *bat qol* in rabbinic stories, functions to confirm the truth of Jesus' cause to the crowd (cf. v. 30). Jesus earlier claimed the Father as his key witness (cf. 5:32, 37), and now this witness appears to be given a direct say. But far from clinching the case, the voice is not perceived for what it really is (12:29, cf. also 5:37). Jesus then explains the significance of the voice's pronouncement: "Now is the judgment of this world; now the ruler of this world will be driven out. And I, when I am lifted up from the earth, will draw all people to myself" (12:31–32). The acceptance by Jesus of his "hour" is a crucial part of a decisive cosmic event. In the trial taking place between God and the hostile world, Jesus' hour, in which the human court judges and rejects him, becomes the very point in history at which God reverses this decision and gives the divine verdict of judgment on the world. A similar note will be sounded in Jesus' declaration in 16:33—"I have conquered the world," where the verb can have the connotation of emerging triumphant and justified from a debate.[57] As Bultmann explains, "The world has already lost its case; it is condemned."[58] Not only is the world judged; so also is its ruler (cf. 14:30; 16:11), designated in 8:44 and 13:2 as the devil and in 13:27 as Satan. Here again there is a reversal. The one behind the world's casting out of Jesus and the synagogue's casting out of Jesus' followers (cf. 9:34) is himself cast out. The hour of the Son of Man's glorification in death, when the great reversal occurs, is then described as the time when he is lifted up (12:32–33); again one recalls that the servant-witness in Isa 40–55 is to be lifted up and glorified (cf. LXX Isa 52:13).

The narrator's summary in 12:37–43, seeking to provide an explanation for the negative outcome of the trial in Israel as a whole, depicts two kinds of negative judgment about Jesus that had resulted—that of outright unbelief in the face of the evidence provided by Jesus' signs, and that of inadequate belief, the response of crypto-Christians. Scripture, in

---

[57] Cf. Bultmann, *Gospel of John*, 594, n. 8; also 564, n. 2; cf. also Trites, *Concept of Witness*, 112, n. 3.

[58] Bultmann, *Gospel of John*, 593.

particular Isaiah, is introduced as a witness (cf. 5:39) to demonstrate authoritatively that the negative response of unbelief does not mean that the trial is now out of God's control. The citation from Isa 40–55 in John 12:38 (LXX Isa 53:1) is part of the *inclusio* at the end and the beginning of the public ministry. At the beginning, John the Baptist quoted LXX Isa 40:3 in the course of his witness. Here in the conclusion, the words from Isa 53 indicate that the response to Jesus is the same as the unbelieving response to the words ("our report") and actions of God ("the arm of the Lord") through the servant-witness. What has happened can thus be viewed as the fulfillment of what was predicted in Scripture. Since this was predicted, there is a sense in which the majority of Israel could not believe (John 12:39). This is reinforced by a further citation from earlier in Isaiah, reworked so that now God is said to have blinded the eyes of the people and hardened their hearts so that they might not turn and be healed (cf. Isa 6:10).[59] Thus here, as in the narrative as a whole, God's sovereignty and human responsibility are held together. Unbelieving blindness to the signs is willful and culpable but also part of God's overall purposes. The reader is also reminded of the significance of blindness in the narrative of John 9 and particularly of the negative side in Jesus' statement of the dual purpose of his mission: "I came into this world for judgment so that those who do not see may see, and those who do see may become blind" (9:39). The context of the citation from Isa 6 enables Isaiah to be produced as a witness now in a more positive sense. Isaiah said these things because he had in fact been able to see Christ's glory ahead of time, and in such passages he spoke of Christ and his mission (John 12:41). The allusion is to Isaiah seeing the Lord (Isa 6:1, 5), the one whose glory filled the whole earth (Isa 6:3). *Targum Isaiah* conflates this to speak of Isaiah seeing "the glory of the Lord" (6.1) and asserts that he saw "the glory of the shekinah of the King of the ages" (6.5). Just as in John 8:56 Abraham's seeing of the end times could be given a christological application, so too can Isaiah's seeing of the Lord and the glory of the Lord.

It appears that John 12:42a will introduce the positive response to Jesus' mission: "Nevertheless many, even of the authorities, believed in him." But it becomes clear that, from the narrator's perspective, it is a

---

[59] The LXX simply puts what has happened to the people in the passive, while the Masoretic text attributes this to the prophet's message. Although the subject of the verbs "blinded" and "hardened" is not stated here in 12:40, it is unlikely to be anyone other than God, contra Blank, *Krisis,* 301–5, who argues that the devil is in view.

pseudo-belief, a belief that does not come to expression in public witness because these people fear that the Pharisees will put them out of the synagogue (v. 42b). Those in view are in all probability the crypto-Christians, similar to Nicodemus and the parents of the blind man, whom the Johannine community viewed as ultimately no different from unbelievers. Here the narrator indicts them, imputing their fear to loving glory from humans more than the glory that comes from God (v. 43). They should not only have seen but have been willing to confess openly the glory of God that came to expression in Jesus' signs. Like the Jews accused in 5:44, they have not fully realized that what is at stake in the lawsuit in the person of Jesus is the glory of God. Here lies the cause of their ultimate unbelief: "How can you believe when you accept glory from one another and do not seek the glory that comes from the one who alone is God?" (5:44). How important are their reputation and honor in the synagogue and in Jewish society in the light of the reputation and honor that God bestows? In contrast to the servant-witness of Isaiah, whose glory is not from humans but who is content to be glorified by God (LXX Isa 52:13, 14), and in contrast to the witness, Jesus, who does not seek glory from humans (John 5:41) but relies on God the judge to seek his glory (8:50) and on his Father to glorify him (8:54), their belief is judged as failing to come to genuine confession or testimony because they put a higher premium on glory or honor from humans than on glory from God.

Jesus' last speech on his own behalf in the trial of the public ministry summarizes his role in the trial. His first words underline that God and the divine glory are the real issue. The response of belief in Jesus is ultimately a response of belief in God. Seeing Jesus is seeing God, because Jesus is the one whom God has sent, God's fully authorized agent in this lawsuit with the world (12:44, 45). As in earlier passages, Jesus identifies his mission as the coming of light into the world, and as elsewhere (cf., e.g., 3:19), this image conveys connotations of judgment. But initially the positive effects of the light are in view: "so that everyone who believes in me should not remain in the darkness" (12:46). Indeed, Jesus can go on to say that he does not judge those who fail to keep his words, because the purpose of his mission is not to judge the world in the sense of condemning it but to save it. Here the assertion of 3:17 is repeated: the lawsuit with the world is primarily a rescue mission in which the verdict of life is to be given (cf. 12:50). Nevertheless, for those who reject Jesus and his word, there will be a judgment. Whereas in 3:18 this judgment is seen as a self-condemnation that is taking place already, here in 12:48 it is a judgment on the last day, when precisely the word that Jesus has spoken will function as the judge. Jesus' word can function as judge because it is none other than the word of judgment God would pronounce (cf. 5:27, 30). Jesus claims to have spoken only what the Father has commanded him to speak (12:49–50). Because of his relationship to the Father, his words not only are the witness to the truth at issue in the trial but also serve as the judge, the final criterion of that truth.

The formulation of the last two verses also recalls the dispute about whether Jesus is the true prophet or a false prophet. Jesus' words contain unmistakable allusions to Deut 18:18–19.[60] He is claiming to be the true prophet, the prophet to come, the prophet like Moses, of whom God says, "I will put my words in the mouth of the prophet, who shall speak to them everything that I command. Anyone who does not heed the words that the prophet shall speak in my name, I myself will hold accountable." As the one who speaks the words that God has commanded and to which all will be held accountable, Jesus' defense is that, far from being a false prophet, he fulfills all the criteria for the true prophet like Moses. What is more, he knows that the words his Father has commanded are eternal life (12:50). This saying recalls Jesus' earlier assertions, "anyone who hears my word and believes him who sent me has eternal life" (5:24) and "The words that I have spoken to you are spirit and life" (6:63), and also Peter's response, "You have the words of eternal life" (6:68). The commandments given to Moses were the means of life—long life in the land (Deut 32:45–47; cf. also 8:3)—but now the commandments given to the prophet like Moses are the means of eternal life. The authorities in the trial are still judging on the basis of their interpretation of Moses' commandments and have failed to realize that the commandments given to Jesus have replaced the old commandments as the criterion for judgment and as the means of life. This is part of their failure to see that Moses wrote about Jesus (5:46). The saying "I know that his commandment is eternal life" (12:50a) enables the trial framework for the ministry to end on a positive note. The witness of Jesus' words as an expression of God's commandment are meant to provide the judgment of life, life that has the quality of the age to come (cf. v. 47b). The final assertion—"What I speak, therefore, I speak just as the Father has told me" (v. 50b)—underlines that the witness of Jesus' word expresses precisely God's word. But it also indicates that the conclusion of the public ministry forms an *inclusio* not only with its beginning but

---

[60] Cf. Harvey, *Jesus on Trial,* 86–87.

also with the prologue: not only is the dual outcome of the ministry anticipated in 1:10–12; Jesus' word as the complete expression of the Father's word also recalls the Logos of 1:1, 14, in whom are life and light and glory (cf. 1:4, 5, 14).

With the one exception of the citations from Isaiah, the first of which simply brings to the surface the scriptural trial scenes underlying the whole narrative of the ministry, all the themes in 12:37–50 have been sounded before in the ministry. Now they are brought together as a summation of Jesus' case. Particularly significant is that the theme of judgment dominates the formulation of the summation on Jesus' lips. In line with the earlier treatment of the trial motif, light and darkness provide the cosmic backdrop for the lawsuit between God and the world, and the witness, this time of Jesus' word in particular, turns out to be the judge. As the section in its entirety makes plain, if the response is unbelief, the judgment will be negative, but Jesus' mission is salvific and its intended outcome is the positive verdict of eternal life.

G. The Preparation of the Disciples for Testifying and the Role of the Paraclete (15:26–16:15, cf. also 14:16–17, 26)

After the completion of the public ministry, in 13:1–17:25 Jesus is depicted with his own (cf. 13:1), with the disciples who have received him (cf. 1:12). The foot washing at the supper (13:1–30), the two Farewell Discourses (13:31–14:31; 15:1–16:33), and Jesus' prayer (17:1–26) are all designed to prepare the disciples for Jesus' departure and for understanding its significance for them. The various sections of this material may well have been shaped at different stages of the community's history before being brought together in their present form.[61] The farewell discourse, in which a leader or another figure on the point of death attempted to console those left behind and make provision for the future, was a well-known literary form in both Jewish and Greco-Roman literature.[62] Typically, one of its major features was the discussion of successors for the hero or leader and their future role. Within the overall framework of the cosmic lawsuit, the Farewell Discourses in this narrative become the appropriate place for treating Jesus' successors in the lawsuit as it continues in history after his departure. Both the disciples

---

[61] See F. F. Segovia, *The Farewell of the Word: The Johannine Call to Abide* (Minneapolis: Fortress, 1991), 320–28, for suggestions about the three stages that may well lie behind 13:31–16:33.

[62] See ibid., 5–20, for a review of this genre's motifs.

and the Paraclete are to assume such a role, and the discourses suggest what this will entail. Our focus will be on the section of the second discourse that deals with the witness of the disciples and the function of the Paraclete. The briefer earlier discussion of the first discourse in 14:16–17, 26 prepares for what is said about the Paraclete; it reflects general opposition between believers and "the Jews" or the world (cf. 13:33; 14:17, 19, 22, 27). The fuller treatment in the second discourse appears to reflect a period of bitter hostility between the Johannine Christians and the synagogue (cf. 16:2).

Two elements in the earlier mention of the Paraclete are not explicitly brought out later; it is therefore worthwhile to underline them. The first is that the Holy Spirit (cf. 14:26) is *another* Paraclete (v. 16), whom the Father sends in Jesus' name (v. 26). As we shall see, the term *Paraclete* has primarily, though not exclusively, forensic connotations, though not one clear-cut forensic role. A major role is that of one called alongside to help in a law court—an advocate. Since the Spirit of truth is described as another Paraclete, this underscores the narrative's presentation of Jesus. Both his earlier witness in the public ministry and his later witness before Pilate are that of a Paraclete, advocating his own case, which is also the case of God, in the trial of truth with the world. Conversely, the Spirit is continuing this forensic role of Jesus in the continuing lawsuit after the glorification of Jesus. This is emphasized through the description of this other Paraclete as the one "whom the Father will send in my name." Just as Jesus' mission has been in his Father's name (cf. 5:43; 10:25), so the Spirit's mission will be in Jesus' name, as his fully authorized representative, taking his place in the continuation of the trial.

The second element that is not made explicit but is implied later in 16:13–15 is that the Paraclete will "remind you of all that I have said to you" (14:26). This bringing to remembrance is not simply a reproduction of Jesus' words but an unfolding of their significance for the new situation in which the disciples find themselves. As many commentators have observed, this sort of remembering, which combines historical tradition and interpretation in the light of the community's needs, informs the distinctive point of view of this narrative's witness to Jesus and his words. "The Johannine mode of vision and the work of the Paraclete belong inseparably together."[63] There may well be parallels between what is said about the Paraclete's relationship to the Jesus tradition and the midrashic way of treating Scripture in the synagogue, particularly through

---

[63] F. Mussner, *The Historical Jesus in the Gospel of St. John* (trans. W. J. O'Hara; London: Burns & Oates, 1967), 44.

the figure who later came to be known as the Methurgeman.[64] In terms of the lawsuit, the Spirit's witness as that of another Paraclete links the witness of Jesus with the witness of the disciples, with the result that the narrative's drama can be played out simultaneously on two levels.[65] By linking Jesus and the disciples in this way, the Paraclete also, in the later setting of the disciples, "recreates and perpetuates the situation of judgment and decision that marked the ministry of Jesus."[66]

In 15:26–16:15 the forensic context of the Paraclete's work is explicit. Just as Jesus' role in the world has been seen in terms of the cosmic lawsuit, so now the disciples' role in the world is placed within the same framework. The elaboration of the latter falls into two sections—one of warning (15:26–16:4a) and one of consolation (16:4b–15). These in turn each have two sections. There has already been warning about the hatred of the world (15:18–25). The warning continues by first stressing the need for witness to endure (15:26–27) and then indicating more specifically the situation of hostility in which this witness will be necessary (16:1–4a). The consolation emphasizes the advantages of the Paraclete's presence with the disciples, first in specifically forensic terms (16:4b–11) and then more generally, in relation to the truth (16:12–15).

Although Jesus' own witness will have been completed and the verdict in the trial pronounced, the lawsuit continues after his departure, and in his absence there will continue to be a witness to the verdict. The witness is twofold, that of the Paraclete and that of the disciples (15:26–27), thereby fulfilling the Deuteronomic injunction about the need for two witnesses (cf. Deut 17:6). The witness of Jesus is replaced by, and continues through, that of the Paraclete, who will witness to Jesus. Earlier, as we have seen, the Paraclete's link with Jesus was stressed by Jesus' being designated as another Paraclete (cf. John 14:16). Here the links are underlined in a different fashion. Just as Jesus has been sent by the Father, so he now sends the Paraclete from the Father. According to *b. Qidd.* 41a, an agent can appoint an agent,[67] and here the Paraclete is the authorized agent of the authorized agent in the lawsuit. At the same time, it is made clear that the Paraclete is intimately related to God. Jesus sends him from the Father, and he is also described as the Spirit of truth (cf. 14:17) who

---

[64] For an argument to this effect, see E. Franck, *Revelation Taught: The Paraclete in the Gospel of John* (Lund, Sweden: Gleerup, 1985), 105–16, 132–44.

[65] See Martyn, *History and Theology,* 148–51, for his distinctive elaboration of this link.

[66] Barrett, *Gospel according to St. John,* 467.

[67] Cf. Borgen, "God's Agent," 143; Harvey, *Jesus on Trial,* 106.

comes from the Father. In both cases the formulation is παρὰ τοῦ πατρός, the same terminology used for Jesus' relation to the Father in 16:28 (cf. also 17:8). Thus, the Paraclete is both the Spirit of Jesus and the Spirit of God. The Paraclete's function as witness in the lawsuit between God and the world is explicit. Just as Jesus bore witness to the truth before the world and this had a dual impact—there were those who received his witness and those who rejected it and for whom it became judgment—so the Paraclete's witness about Jesus is both for those who receive it, the disciples, even though they are themselves witnesses (cf. 16:13–15), and for the still unbelieving world, for whom it becomes judgment (cf. 16:8–11).[68] In addition, the designations "Paraclete" and "Spirit of truth" themselves reinforce the trial motif.

Something more therefore needs to be said about the meaning of *Paraclete*.[69] It is significant that παράκλητος has a clear primary meaning in Greek—*advocate* in a legal context—and that it became a loanword in Hebrew and Aramaic with precisely this meaning. This need not be taken to imply that Paraclete was the designation for a professional legal office. Instead a person of influence, a patron or sponsor, could be called into a court to speak in favor of a person or a person's cause, thereby providing advocacy. This well-known meaning should govern the way the term is interpreted in the Fourth Gospel. Its most likely background is in the Jewish Scriptures and Second Temple Judaism, with their interest in intercessory figures who functioned as advocates, sometimes in the heavenly court, and whose advocacy could sometimes take the form of counteraccusation.[70] Some commentators dismiss this meaning on the grounds that the Paraclete is a prosecuting rather than a defending counsel in this Gospel. But this is to ignore that the Paraclete does have the forensic role of speaking in favor of a person or cause—Jesus and his cause. He witnesses about and glorifies Jesus (15:26; 16:14). The Paraclete also has an advocacy role in relation to the disciples, aiding the disciples in their witness, since his witness takes place through theirs. This objection also ignores the fluid and paradoxical characteristics in the presentation of the protagonists in both the Fourth Gospel's and the Jewish Scriptures' lawsuits, in which the witness for the defense can also be the prosecutor and indeed the judge. Those who prefer to interpret the title "Paraclete" in terms of the use of παρακαλεῖν and παράκλησις, found

---

[68] Cf. Franck, *Revelation Taught,* 54–56.

[69] For a good overview and critique of scholarly discussion on the Paraclete, see Burge, *Anointed Community,* 3–45.

[70] Cf. Harvey, *Jesus on Trial,* 109–11; Burge, *Anointed Community,* 13–23.

elsewhere in the NT but not in this Gospel, ignore the fact that precisely this appellation—and not the verb *to exhort* or the noun *exhortation*—is used of the Spirit and his role in this narrative.[71] To be sure, the contexts in the Fourth Gospel qualify and add to this primary meaning, *advocate*, so that helper and teacher are functions that provide a further dimension to this forensic one. But the use of παράκλητος indicates that advocate in a lawsuit is the core referent from which the reader is meant to start. "This context of juridical trial and persecution presents us with the most likely catalyst for John's introduction of ὁ παράκλητος. In fact, it is the comprehensive activity of the Spirit as a forensic witness that best explains the varied tasks of the Paraclete in the Farewell Discourses."[72]

Why is the synonym for the Paraclete *Spirit of truth* (cf. 14:17; 15:26; cf. also 16:13)? Language about the spirit of truth, in contrast to the spirit of deceit or wickedness, may well have contributed to this formulation (cf. *T. Jud.* 20.1–5; 1QS III, 18, 19; IV, 23). Still, in these traditions the two spirits are the equivalent to the good and evil inclinations within humanity, whereas in this narrative the Spirit is clearly the Spirit of God, who is not conceived of as already within human beings. In the Fourth Gospel, truth is the true judgment, embodied in Jesus, about God and God's relation to the world, and in the context of the lawsuit motif, it is what is at stake in the trial. So the "specific characterization as 'the Spirit of truth' involves the Paraclete directly, like Jesus himself, in the meaning, disclosure, and proclamation of truth."[73] Just as Jesus is the witness to this truth (18:37) as he reveals or embodies it (14:6), so the Spirit is the revealer of this same truth as he witnesses to Jesus.

Parallel to, and linked with, the witness of the Paraclete, the disciples also continue the witness of Jesus in and to the world: "You also are to testify" (15:27). Just as witness was at the heart of Jesus' mission, so it defines the role of his followers, and the entire context makes plain that just as Jesus met persecution and rejection because of his witness, so too will they. The sending of Jesus as witness functions as the paradigm for the sending of his followers (cf. 17:18; 20:21). Like the Paraclete,

---

[71] Contra, e.g., Barrett, *Gospel according to St. John*, 462.

[72] Burge, *Anointed Community*, 205, following I. de la Potterie, *La vérité dans S. Jean* (2 vols.; Rome: Biblical Institute Press, 1977), 1:468; and F. Porsch, *Pneuma und Wort: Ein exegetischer Beitrag zur Pneumatologie des Johannesevangeliums* (Frankfurt: Knecht, 1974), 222–27. Cf. also Boice, *Witness and Revelation*, 153–58; and Franck, *Revelation Taught*, 20–23, who, however, in the rest of his work downplays the forensic context too much.

[73] Segovia, *Farewell of the Word*, 96.

"they are to be the agent's appointed agents."[74] The qualification for this role is their association with Jesus "from the beginning" of his mission (15:27). This puts them in a position to provide witness to the significance of Jesus' mission as a whole. Thus, their knowledge of Jesus' mission, interpreted for their new situations under the guidance of the Spirit, will continue to play an important role in the disciples' future witness. This is later reinforced by the stress in 20:30 that Jesus' signs were done "in the presence of his disciples." Later, too, just as Jesus has asserted that he has sent the Spirit for the role of witness, he declares that he has sent the disciples for their role in the continuing lawsuit—"As the Father has sent me, so I send you" (cf. also 17:18)—and the link between the Spirit's witness and theirs becomes clear as Jesus breathes on them and says, "Receive the Holy Spirit" (20:21–22). The Spirit's witness is to be primarily in and through that of the disciples, and the witness of the disciples is to receive its impetus and sustaining power from that of the Spirit. Already in 15:26–27 it is clear that this is the relationship between the two witnesses, that of the Paraclete and that of the disciples, because in 15:26a the disciples are identified as the recipients of the Paraclete, "whom I will send to you."[75]

In 16:1–4a the consequences of the disciples' witness in the world are set out, and an *inclusio* ("I have said these things to you . . ." [vv.1, 4]) stresses the purposes of the warnings both in the preceding part of the discourse and in their elaboration in this section. In between, vv. 2–3 predict the extreme circumstances Jesus' disciples will face in their confrontation with the world, and provide an explanation for this state of affairs. Earlier, in 9:22 and 12:42, it is the narrator who has mentioned exclusion from the synagogue; now Jesus himself prophesies, "They will put you out of the synagogues." As chapter 6 of this study will explore more fully, such an experience is likely to have involved Jesus' followers in both informal and formal interrogations and trials. The disciples will have to experience what the man who was blind experienced in John 9. Clearly, this envisages that the synagogue leaders would have enough support from other members of the synagogue to enforce their ban. To be driven out from what had been their religious community and to be cut off from links with those amongst whom they had previously lived and worshiped would therefore have been extremely traumatic. But this is not all that Jesus' followers will have to face. Jesus

---

[74] Harvey, *Jesus on Trial*, 106.

[75] Cf. Blank, *Krisis*, 215–16; Bultmann, *Gospel of John*, 554; Beutler, *Martyria*, 275; Segovia, *Farewell of the Word*, 198, 201, n. 51.

also predicts that for some "an hour is coming when" witness will become martyrdom (16:2). Just as Jesus faces his hour, so his witnesses will face theirs. The context—the clash of religious commitments—indicates that those who will carry out the killings are from the same groups who will exclude from the synagogues, namely Jews: "those who kill you will think that by doing so they are offering worship to God." In other words, those who carry out the persecution and killing see this as part of their devotion to God in rooting out apostasy (cf. the later *Num. Rab.* 21—"everyone who sheds the blood of the godless is like one who offers a sacrifice"). As in John 15:21, this zealous persecution is ascribed to its perpetrators' not truly knowing either the one whom they claim to serve or Jesus, whom God has sent (cf. also, e.g., 8:19, 54–55). The conviction that the service of God requires the killing of Jesus' followers throws into sharp relief the ultimate issue of the trial—who is the true God and how is this God known? From the implied author's perspective, the persecution and death of Jesus' followers underline that their persecutors have failed to acknowledge the God who, as the Father, had sent Jesus and who was most fully revealed in his death.

Two major purposes are served by the portrayal of Jesus here as prophesying about these persecutions. First, Jesus' words ahead of time are meant to prevent his followers from falling away from the faith (the NRSV's "stumbling" does not capture the force of σκανδαλίζειν in 16:1). To be forewarned is to be forearmed when the test actually comes. By recalling Jesus' words, his disciples will be enabled to overcome their fear of possible death and to see such an eventuality as a form of the witness they have been asked to bear. Second, when the persecutions come, the disciples will remember that Jesus predicted them (v. 4a), and this in itself will reassure them of the truthfulness of his words. They will be able to see that, in terms of his earthly trial, he was truly the prophet like Moses and, in terms of the cosmic trial, is the divine revealer whose word is confirmed.[76] This in turn will reinforce for them his sovereign control of events, enabling them to see their own trials as part of God's purposes in history. It is worth pondering the context in which the trial metaphor is employed here. Normally underlying the use of the language of witness, advocacy, and trial would be a basic confidence in the due processes of human law and justice. But we have here a reminder that, for many who are minorities, the legal system fails to function in this way. It is a setting of increasing hostility, aggression, and

---

[76] Cf. Trites, *Concept of Witness*, 88; A. Reinhartz, "Jesus as Prophet: Predictive Prolepses in the Fourth Gospel," *JSNT* 36 (1989): 3–16.

violence, where they can expect their witness not to be accepted and justice, as they see it, not to be done, that the metaphor functions for these followers of Jesus, who find themselves in a minority in their social world. The overarching framework of an ultimate cosmic trial is meant to enable them to stay true to their convictions with some sense of calm despite the perceived injustice and persecution of this world's legal processes.

In the consolation that begins in 16:4b–11, our attention will be on the advantages that are said to accrue for the disciples because of Jesus' departure and the coming of the Paraclete whom Jesus will send: "And when he comes, he will prove the world wrong about [or 'convict the world of'] sin and righteousness and judgment: about sin, because they do not believe in me; about righteousness, because I am going to the Father and you will see me no longer; about judgment, because the ruler of this world has been condemned" (vv. 8–11). Here the Paraclete clearly has a prosecuting role in the trial between God and the world. He is the defending counsel for the disciples but the prosecutor or accuser in regard to the world.[77] *Testament of Judah* 20.5, talking of the spirit of truth and the spirit of error, asserts, "The spirit of truth testifies to all things and brings all accusations. He who has sinned is consumed in his heart and cannot raise his head to face the judge." But again the Paraclete is not seen as carrying out this activity independently of the disciples, for, as John 16:7b makes plain, the activity will only commence when he comes to the disciples, and the implication must be that the prosecuting will take place primarily through them and their witness. In the continuation of the lawsuit in history after the time of Jesus' mission, the Paraclete will make clear its consequences, bring accusations, and obtain convictions on three counts. The three issues—sin, righteousness, and judgment—and the reasons for the world's conviction on these issues are set out.

Scholars, however, highly dispute the interpretation of these cryptic verses. In a penetrating discussion of their difficulties, Carson urged interpreters to be consistent in their treatment of all three instances, particularly in the force they give to "convict" in each case; in their construal of ὅτι as causal or explicative; and in the way they relate the three terms—sin, righteousness, and judgment—to the world.[78] The

---

[77] Bultmann, *Gospel of John*, 561–62, captures the passage's significance well: "The image that comes before the eyes is that of a lawsuit of cosmic dimensions, taking place before the court of God. The world is accused, and the Paraclete is the prosecutor."

[78] D. A. Carson, "The Function of the Paraclete in John 16:7–11," *JBL* 98 (1979): 547–66.

reasonableness of his advice in the first two areas is apparent, if we hold that the passage was to be intelligible to its original readers. But Carson's desire for strict consistency has too high a price, especially in the third area, where it requires that righteousness be taken in an ironic sense, as the world's pseudo-righteousness, and demands that a note of eschatological urgency be read into the causal explanation for convicting the world about its false judgment. Precisely the cryptic reference to the three issues of sin, righteousness, and judgment and the absence of any possessive adjective allow flexibility about how each is related to the world.

Still, clarity, if not total consistency, is incumbent on interpreters in these matters. To this end, here is a brief explanation of the assumptions underlying the reading that will follow. The verb ἐλέγχειν with the preposition περί is taken to mean *to convict of,* in the sense here of exposing the true situation of each issue in such a way as to confront the world with, and prove, its guilt.[79] Whether those in the world are subjectively convinced of their guilt does not appear to be in view here.[80] They may or they may not be.[81] Although this part of the narrative later expresses the goal that the world come to believe as a result of the disciples' unity (17:21, 23), the dominant characterization of the world is in terms of being unable to receive the Spirit of truth (14:17) and of hating the disciples and their witness (15:18–22; 17:14). The primary point is that whether the world recognizes it or not, the Paraclete convicts it of its guilt in the context of the cosmic lawsuit.

What is the relationship of sin, righteousness, and judgment to the world? Sin is clearly the world's sin. Righteousness, or justice, is not the righteousness that belongs to the world but the rightness of Jesus' case in the trial between God and the world: convicted of the righteousness of Jesus' cause, the world is at the same time convicted of its own guilt in his unlawful condemnation. And judgment is not the judgment the world makes but the judgment on the world in the lawsuit: it is convicted of the justice and inevitability of its condemnation by the judge. The subordinate clauses beginning with ὅτι are construed not as explicative, providing the content of sin, righteousness, and judgment, but as causal.[82] They are

---

[79] The verb frequently has this force in the LXX in contexts of judgment; cf., e.g., LXX Ps 49:8, 21; Wis 1:8; 4:20.

[80] *Pace* Carson, "Function of the Paraclete," 558.

[81] Cf. Franck, *Revelation Taught,* 60–61.

[82] *Pace,* e.g., Harvey, *Jesus on Trial,* 113–14. Although Segovia, *Farewell of the Word,* 230–31, construes each clause as laying down "a correct definition of each term," he claims that his interpretation is not explicative.

causal, however, not in the sense of providing reasons why the Paraclete proves the world is wrong but in the sense of providing reasons why the world is convicted.[83] Carson disputes whether on this latter reading the clauses still modify the verb. An English example should, however, illustrate that this objection is not justified. In the sentences "The teacher punished the boy because she believed that rules should be kept" and "The teacher punished the boy because he had broken the rules," both subordinate clauses modify the verb and both are causal; they simply give different causal explanations—one explaining the teacher's reason for carrying out the punishment, the other explaining the grounds of the punishment. The same holds for ὅτι clauses in Greek. Here the clauses could explain the Paraclete's reason for convicting the world or explain the grounds for the world's conviction. It is the latter type of causal explanation that informs our discussion.[84]

The world will be convicted of sin because those who belong to it do not believe in Jesus. Throughout the narrative, failure to believe has been the primary characteristic of sin and the grounds for condemnation (cf., e.g., 3:18; 5:45–47; 8:24; 9:41; 12:48; 15:22). Earlier the world, as represented by "the Jews," tried to convict Jesus of sin (cf. 8:46; 9:24; 10:33) and Jesus attempted to turn the accusation back on his accusers. Indeed, his witness had a prosecuting dimension, as he testified against the world that its works were evil (7:7). Now the tables will continue to be turned through the work of the Paraclete as Jesus' alter ego.

The righteousness at issue is that of Jesus. Righteousness (δικαιοσύνη) here has clear forensic connotations, as in Paul's thought. The noun is not used elsewhere in the Gospel, but the adjective δίκαιος appears twice in the context of right or just judgment (cf. 5:30; 7:24). The Paraclete will convict the world of the righteousness of the one it has condemned to death and of the justice of his case. He has been vindicated by the divine judge in the trial, and the Paraclete can drive home this verdict because Jesus' departure to a realm where he is no longer visible to his disciples constitutes his glorification, the divine seal of approval on his death. In 16:14 the Spirit's task of glorifying Jesus is for the sake of the disciples, but it is in pointing to Jesus' glory that the Spirit also convicts the world of righteousness. Inseparable from the world's confrontation with the justice of Jesus' cause is its conviction for the injustice of its own part in his trial and condemnation and therefore for its guilt.

---

[83] *Pace* Carson, "Function of the Paraclete," 553.
[84] Cf. Blank, *Krisis,* 335–36.

Finally, the Paraclete convicts the world of its judgment. The negative outcome of the trial's verdict is in view; here the grounds for the world's condemnation are that its ruler has been condemned. In line with 12:31–32, Jesus' lifting up in his death and exaltation is seen as the point at which the ruler of the world receives his judgment of being cast out (ἐκβάλλειν). This makes certain the condemnatory judgment of the world under his rule: because its ruler has been judged, the world itself must fall under the same judgment. As prosecuting counsel, the Paraclete carries out his task in the light of the verdict in the main trial about Jesus' mission (cf. 19:30). This is also indicated through the convictions about sin and judgment being positioned on either side of, and thus highlighting, the conviction of the world in regard to the central issue of the rightness or righteousness of Jesus' cause.

The prosecuting work of the Paraclete through the witness of the disciples amounts to the establishment of a total reversal of values in the light of the cosmic trial and its verdict. "Given the fundamental difference between the values of the world and those of God as already revealed by Jesus . . . it is those who claim to be on the side of God and to represent the values of God who will be convicted by the true values of God as revealed by Jesus and proclaimed by the Spirit-Paraclete after Jesus."[85] What is said here about the Paraclete is part of this Gospel's realized eschatology. In traditional Jewish eschatology, these issues of sin, righteousness, and judgment were expected to be dealt with at the judgment of the end times. But by convicting the world on these matters in the present, "the Spirit . . . places the world in the position which it will occupy at the last judgment."[86] Although this occurs through the witness of the disciples, they do not here become judges. They proclaim the verdict that has already been reached and press home its implications. "Whereas Jesus is said 'to condemn' the world, functioning in the role of judge, those who continue Jesus' mission are said 'to convict' the world, acting in the role of prosecutor."[87]

The next part of Jesus' reassurance of the disciples (16:12–15) takes up "the Spirit of truth" designation for the Paraclete (cf. 15:26), and they are promised that this Spirit of truth will lead them "into all the truth,"[88] that is, into the whole of the revelation embodied in Jesus in all its impli-

---

[85] Segovia, *Farewell of the Word,* 233 and n. 25.

[86] Barrett, *Gospel according to St. John,* 90

[87] Segovia, *Farewell of the Word,* 235.

[88] NRSV. Although "in all the truth" is the better-attested reading, there is little distinction in meaning.

cations. In this way the Spirit continues where Jesus left off ("I still have many things to say to you"—16:12) and makes a vital contribution to the witness of Jesus' followers to the truth that is at issue in the trial. The Spirit is able to do this because what was said about Jesus' witness to, and revelation of, the truth of God is true also of the Spirit: "he will not speak on his own, but will speak whatever he hears" (16:13; cf. 5:30; 8:28; 12:49; 14:10). Just as Jesus was in such intimate dependence on his Father that his words were to be considered God's words, now the Spirit has a similarly intimate and dependent relationship with Jesus, so that he is able to "take what is mine and declare it to you" (16:14, 15). And since "all that the Father has is mine" (16:15), in declaring what belongs to Jesus, the Spirit also declares what belongs to God. Again this underlines the Spirit's role as a continuation of that begun by Jesus in his declaration of the things of God. Through his declarations, Jesus claimed to bring glory to God (cf. 7:18; 17:1, 4). Now, as the Spirit takes the teaching, mission, and person of Jesus and declares their significance to the disciples, he glorifies Jesus (16:14). In other words, through the mediation of the Spirit, Jesus' "unity with the Father, the divine character of his mission and revelation will become evident."[89] Operating in this way, the Spirit also enables the disciples to bear witness to Jesus. Among the matters the Spirit will declare to the disciples are "the things that are to come" (16:13). Just as Jesus predicts the future, not least in this section of the narrative, so the Spirit will also continue this predictive activity, giving insight into the future the disciples will have to face and into the course of the cosmic lawsuit that has already become operative in history. As the Spirit continues the mission of Jesus, there is a parallelism in their roles. This is also the reason for the clear temporal differentiation between the witness of Jesus and that of the Spirit in this narrative (cf. 7:39; 16:7; 20:22).

It is worth underlining the connection between what is said about the Paraclete's activity among the disciples in 16:12–15 and what is said about his activity in the world in 16:8–11. If indeed it is through the disciples' witness that the Paraclete carries out his prosecution of the world in regard to the truth of the cause of Jesus, then it is imperative that the disciples have as comprehensive an insight into this truth as possible and that the Paraclete therefore continually direct them in the whole truth that it is his role to disclose as the Spirit of truth. Thus, "in the course of their mission and proclamation of this 'truth' in and to the world,

---

[89] Franck, *Revelation Taught*, 74.

guided and informed by the Spirit-Paraclete as Jesus' successor in their midst, the disciples will indeed be able to convict an unbelieving and hostile world."[90]

Deutero-Isaiah and its lawsuits again prove illuminating for our passage. Earlier we have seen that Jesus takes over Israel's role as a witness in the trial between Yahweh and the nations. But now, in the continuation of the trial after his departure, his disciples take up this role. In LXX Isa 43, both v. 10 and v. 12, which speak of Israel as Yahweh's witness, add the assertion that Yahweh is also a witness, thus preserving the law's requirement of double witness. Here in the Fourth Gospel, the dual witness is also retained, and this time the divine witness is supplied by the Paraclete. In Isa 44:6–8 (cf. also 42:9; 46:10) Israel is to testify to the reliable connection between Yahweh's declarations and their fulfillment in history, which show Yahweh to be the true God. Jesus' predictions about what will befall the disciples are to be seen in this light. His followers and the readers of this narrative would be able to recognize the truth of his declarations about such future events as the coming of the Paraclete and their exclusion from the synagogue and to see this as confirming his divine identity, to which they bear witness.[91] Significantly, one of the formulations used in Isaiah about Yahweh's predictions of the future is *declaring the things to come* (cf. Isa 41:22, 23; 44:7); in the Gospel's narrative, it is the Spirit who declares the things to come. Since "declaring of things to come is a privilege of Yahweh that false gods do not possess,"[92] this underlines that the Spirit comes from the Father (John 15:26) and is the divine Spirit. In addition, just as Yahweh declares the truth (Isa 45:19), so the Spirit is the Spirit of truth who in his declaratory activity will guide in all truth (John 15:26; 16:13). In the cosmic lawsuit, Yahweh not only was judge but also acted as prosecuting witness or counsel. Here the Paraclete is not only defense counsel but also clearly, in 16:8–11, takes on a prosecuting role.

Of the issues on which the Paraclete will convict the world, that of righteousness also plays a significant part in Isa 40–55. In the LXX the verb δικαιόω is employed in the sense of *to prove right* or *to vindicate* in the trial (43:26), Yahweh is said to vindicate the servant-witness (50:8), and as the judge, Yahweh declares or brings near righteousness or justice (cf. 45:19, 23, 24; 46:13; 51:5, where the noun δικαιοσύνη is used). In regard to judgment (κρίσις), in Isaiah it is Yahweh's Spirit who enables

---

[90] Segovia, *Farewell of the Word,* 244–45.

[91] Cf. Reinhartz, "Jesus as Prophet," 10–11.

[92] Brown, *Gospel according to John,* 2:708.

the servant to bring forth judgment on the nations (42:1, 3). In John 16:8–11 it makes sense, then, to see righteousness as entailing the divine vindication of Jesus' witness and judgment as the verdict of judgment on the world, brought home to it by the Spirit-Paraclete.

Above all, it is striking that Jesus' words about the disciples and the Paraclete as his successors function in the Fourth Gospel's narrative as consolation to the disciples in the face of his imminent departure, for comfort is precisely the function of the lawsuit motif for Israel in the context of Isa 40–55. The first words of Deutero-Isaiah are, "Comfort, O comfort my people, says your God" (40:1), and the last are a promise of joy and peace (cf. 55:12, 13). In between are exhortations not to fear— "Do not fear, or be afraid . . . You are my witnesses!" (44:8, cf. 40:9b; 41:10, 13, 14; 43:1, 5; 44:2b; 51:7; 54:4)—including not to fear those who persecute and oppress (51:12, 13); further promises of future rejoicing, joy, and gladness (41:16; 51:3, 11; 52:8); and declarations of God's comfort (49:13; 51:3, 12; 52:9b). As features of the trial motif are taken up in the Gospel's Farewell Discourse, not only do they themselves function as encouragement for the time after Jesus' departure; their context, from beginning to end, drives this purpose home. The disciples are exhorted not to be troubled or afraid and to take courage (John 14:1, 27b; 16:33b), they are given promises of peace (14:27a; 16:33a), and they are told that the provisions made for them are a cause for joy and rejoicing (14:28b; 15:11; 16:20b–24).

H. The Trial before Pilate (18:28–19:16a)

A number of recent scholarly treatments, outside the commentaries, of the Roman trial in the Fourth Gospel have appeared, but this section of narrative is so significant for our motif that a further fresh rehearsal of its contribution is indispensable.[93] Again our focus is on the presentation of the trial in the narrative, as the lawsuit motif builds to a climax, rather than on the historical issues raised. It is appropriate to the cosmic aspect

---

[93] Cf., e.g., C. H. Giblin, "John's Narration of the Hearing before Pilate (John 18,28–19,16a)," *Biblica* 67 (1986): 221–39; Duke, *Irony,* 126–37; Rensberger, *Johannine Faith,* 87–106; Stibbe, *John as Storyteller,* 105–13; R. E. Brown, *The Death of the Messiah* (New York: Doubleday, 1994), 723–877, containing treatment of the Johannine account of the Roman trial interspersed with that of the Synoptic accounts; T. Söding, "Die Macht der Wahrheit und das Reich der Freiheit: Zur johanneischen Deutung des Pilatus-Prozesses (Joh 18,28–19,16)" *ZThK* 93 (1996): 35–58; H. K. Bond, *Pontius Pilate in History and Interpretation* (Cambridge: Cambridge University Press, 1998), 163–93.

of the motif that this climactic trial takes place before Pilate, the representative of the Roman Empire. The issues in the lawsuit have a Jewish context, but as this episode indicates, they also have universal significance.[94] As observed earlier, the Roman trial stands in the middle of the three equally long sections of the Passion Narrative, with Jesus' arrest and interrogation on one side (18:1–27) and his crucifixion and burial on the other (19:16b–42); it thus constitutes its central feature. It is another of the Gospel's episodes that have seven scenes (cf. 9:1–41); here they follow the movement of Pilate back and forth between the praetorium and "the Jews."[95] "The Jews" are gathered in the outside court of the praetorium, while Jesus is held in the inside room, and Pilate's constant passing from one setting to the other reflects the pull of two different poles operative in his struggle to come to a judgment.

1. 18:28–32

This first scene takes place in the outside court (cf. 18:28–29) of the procurator's or prefect's official residence in Jerusalem, where Pilate demands to know what "the Jews'" accusation against Jesus is, but receives no clear answer. The narrator supplies a reason for "the Jews" remaining outside, namely, "to avoid ritual defilement and to be able to eat the Passover." The ritual defilement to be avoided could be contact with a corpse, which carried a seven-day contamination. Laws in view could be those, found later in the Mishnah, declaring Gentile houses unclean because Gentiles sometimes buried corpses in or underneath them, particularly premature babies or fetuses.[96] The narrator's point in supplying this reason, however, is surely both theological and ironic. He indicates right at the start of the trial what has been apparent throughout the narrative: it is their stance toward the law that defines the opponents of Jesus and that is the source of their determination to see him sentenced to death (cf. 19:7).[97] At the same time, this enables him to depict "the Jews" as scrupulously concerned with ceremonial purity but lacking moral scruples. They will not enter the Gentile house, but they are eager to make use of its Gentile occupant in order to do away with Jesus. They fear that impurity will prevent them from eating the Passover lamb, but

---

[94] Cf. Söding, "Die Macht der Wahrheit," 37.

[95] See esp. Brown, *Gospel according to John*, 2:858.

[96] On the complexities of the discussion, see ibid., 845–46; Barrett, *Gospel according to St. John*, 532–33.

[97] Cf. Söding, "Die Macht der Wahrheit," 39.

from the narrator's perspective, they are implicated in the death of the true Passover lamb (cf. 19:14, 31, 36).

The exchange between Pilate and "the Jews" in 18:29–32 serves a number of purposes. First, "the Jews" are shown not to have a clear accusation or charge to bring against Jesus (vv. 29, 30), although in fact v. 33 will soon presuppose that the charge was that Jesus claimed to be king of the Jews, that he was a political subversive with royal pretensions. Because this does not, however, emerge in the reply of v. 30, Pilate can tell "the Jews" to take Jesus and judge him according to their law. This, of course, is what they have already been doing in the public ministry, and the Sanhedrin's verdict was that Jesus should die (11:47–53). Pilate's comment leads to the response that expresses their frustration and exposes their real intention: "We are not permitted to put anyone to death" (v. 31b). The historical accuracy of this assertion has been widely debated, but in all probability, even if there are some instances of the Sanhedrin executing a person by Jewish methods, it could not claim the right to do so and would not have attempted to do so while Pilate was in the city to prevent disturbances. If this is correct, it also puts a different slant on the attempts of Jesus' opponents earlier in the narrative to stone him. This would have been illegal under Roman jurisdiction. But the implied author's point is a theological one, about the impotence of the law to do what "the Jews" want it to do.[98] From his perspective, the law, by which they are judging Jesus, has not been able itself to lead to his condemnation and death, as they claim it should. On three occasions in the earlier narrative, they claimed that the law convicts Jesus of blasphemy and sought to kill him (cf. 5:18; 8:59; 10:30–31). Jesus, however, claimed that Moses had written about him and was accusing *them* (5:45–46) and that the law permitted him to call himself Son of God (10:34–36).

These earlier attempts to carry out a death sentence on Jesus on the basis of a religious charge under the law were thwarted, and so his opponents have now been forced to bring a political charge and involve the Romans in order to convict Jesus of a capital offense. Pilate's response to "the Jews," then, serves as a reminder of who has the political power and the legal ability to execute.[99] The narrator's comment in v. 32, however, is that all this only brings about the fulfillment of Jesus' own words and thereby, we might add, establishes the truth of his testimony, because he had indicated the kind of death he was to die. In the very first reference

---

[98] Cf. Pancaro, *The Law,* 314.
[99] Cf. Bond, *Pontius Pilate,* 176–77.

to his witness (3:11–15), Jesus had talked of the Son of Man being lifted up, and the third use of the lifting-up terminology in 12:32–33 (cf. also 8:28) had made explicit that this was a reference to the nature of his death: " 'I, when I am lifted up from the earth, will draw all people to myself.' He said this to indicate the kind of death he was to die." Jesus, as master over his own life and death (cf. 10:17–18), had already determined that being lifted up on a Roman cross was the way he would die. So "the Jews' " transference of his case to Pilate is simply the means of enabling his words to be fulfilled. But those lifting-up words also indicated clearly that elevation on a Roman cross is not a cause for shame but the movement of exaltation to the glory of the Father, and they hinted that, in the process, Jesus will also be fulfilling the role of the servant-witness, who was also to be lifted up and glorified (cf. LXX Isa 52:13).

2. 18:33–38a

The second scene moves inside the praetorium (cf. 18:33) and provides dialogue between Pilate and Jesus about the fact and nature of Jesus' kingship. To Pilate's question "Are you the King of the Jews?" Jesus responds with his own question, asking about the origin of Pilate's question. In the by-now familiar pattern, the accused becomes the accuser, the one on trial becomes the judge, and from the first words of Jesus, Pilate is put on the defensive, put on trial. For the reader, Pilate's reply is highly ironic and immediately indicts him. At one level his response, "I am not a Jew, am I?" (v. 35a), is meant to distance himself from any personal interest in his earlier question, but at another level this later question epitomizes the entire issue of the narrative's lawsuit. It has become abundantly clear that, in the discourse of this narrative, "the Jews" represent the world that is being put on trial, the unbelieving world hostile to God's authorized agent and witness. So the question is also to be understood as, "I do not belong to the world that rejects you, do I?" As with the discourse's other ironic questions, this one grammatically expects a negative answer, but the reader is meant to supply a positive one. And in this case, the development of the trial soon confirms that positive answer.[100] Pilate will not be allowed to distance himself from the issues in some neutral role; in the context of the larger lawsuit, he is himself judged as he ultimately places himself at the disposal of "the Jews" and fails to recognize Jesus' witness to the truth.

---

[100] Cf. W. A. Meeks, *The Prophet-King: Moses Traditions and the Johannine Christology* (Leiden: E. J. Brill, 1967), 67; Bond, *Pontius Pilate*, 179.

The distinctive use of the term *the Jews* in this Gospel's narrative is underlined by the play on its ethnic and symbolic senses in vv. 35–36. Pilate intends to dissociate himself ethnically from "the Jews" but ironically is aligned with them symbolically because they represent the world in the dispute between God and the world. The former dissociation is furthered by his telling Jesus that it is "your own nation" and its religious leaders, the chief priests, who are "the Jews" disputing Jesus' kingship over them. But Jesus the Jew then also dissociates himself from "the Jews" symbolically when he declares, "If my kingdom were from this world, my followers would be fighting to keep me from being handed over to the Jews."

The question of the nature of Jesus' kingship is taken up in vv. 36–37. For the implied author, "King" is an appropriate title for Jesus, provided it is understood in the right way. In 1:49 and 12:13 "King of Israel" is a positive acclamation, but in 6:15 those who wish to make Jesus king are evaluated negatively. Jesus' assertions here are crucial to a right understanding. In 18:36 he defines his kingdom and thus his kingship negatively and in v. 37 defines this kingship positively. Negatively, his kingdom is not of this world. As Jesus declared about himself in 8:23, its origin does not lie in this world, and as in that earlier declaration, that means that it is from above, that is, from God. For this reason Jesus would have nothing to do with those who wanted to make him king earlier, in 6:15; his kingship can only be established by God, not by human means. And so Jesus makes clear here to Pilate, who is used to thinking in terms of political power, that he is not planning an uprising to bring about his kingdom by this-worldly means. Otherwise his followers would be armed and would have fought to prevent his arrest. Indeed, in the narrative of the arrest, the one follower who did use the sword, Peter, was severely rebuked (cf. 18:10–11). This does not mean that Jesus' kingdom is totally otherworldly.[101] Its origin is not from this world, but it manifests itself in this world wherever people listen to his voice, as v. 37 will make clear. And although it will not be achieved by political means, it will have political implications, as this trial itself reveals. Religious and political dimensions of the kingdom are inextricably interwoven, since, for both "the Jews" and Pilate, acknowledgment of Jesus' kingship is shown to clash with loyalty to Caesar's rule.

When Pilate asks again, "So you are a king?" Jesus does not give unequivocal confirmation. Presumably this would still be open to

---

[101] See esp. Rensberger, *Johannine Faith*, 97.

misunderstanding despite his explanation of the nature of his kingdom, and it is not clear that Pilate has appreciated the all-important qualification Jesus has provided. Jesus therefore puts some distance between himself and the title: *"You* say that I am a king." He does not categorically refuse to be known as king but this time—and most significantly—redefines the nature of such kingship positively in the light of his mission to be a witness to the truth: "For this I was born [ἐγὼ εἰς τοῦτο γεγέννημαι], and for this I came into the world [καὶ εἰς τοῦτο ἐλήλυθα εἰς τόν κόσμον], to testify to the truth [ἵνα μαρτυρήσω τῇ ἀληθείᾳ]" (18:37). The twofold introduction gives this statement of Jesus' mission special weight. Its distinctiveness is shown in the fact that no other mission statement in the narrative is given such emphasis (cf., e.g., 6:38; 10:10; 12:46).

From what we have seen in the narrative to this point, it is not surprising that Jesus' entire task in this world can be summed up in terms of witness and truth. "He has come in order to . . . make God's reality effective over against the world in the great trial between God and the world."[102] Jesus' kingship is subsumed under, and reinterpreted by, his witness to the truth.[103] Although the issue of Jesus' kingship will continue to play a dominant role in the trial and crucifixion, because it provides the political dimensions that enable "the Jews" to present Jesus as a threat to Roman occupation (cf. 19:12), it should be remembered that kingship is not the protagonist's own characterization of his role. Instead kingship is subordinated to the overarching motif of the lawsuit and the role of witness; thus, as later chapters of this study will examine further, the issue of power is subordinated to that of truth. Jesus does not so much have subjects over whom he rules as followers who accept his witness and who hear his voice as truth. And although his kingdom is not of this world, he and his followers clearly have a mission in and to this world, that of witnessing to the truth.

As elsewhere in the narrative, the witness to truth is at the same time a judgment that exposes people's basic loyalty and commitment, their attitude to the truth: "Everyone who belongs to the truth listens to my voice" (18:37c). In the trial in John 8, "the Jews" are accused of not hearing the word of Jesus when he speaks the truth, and the reason given for their failure to hear is that they are not "from God" (8:45–47). There is another earlier parallel in the narrative to the thought of 18:37c, in the

---

[102] Bultmann, *Gospel of John*, 655.

[103] Cf. also Bittner, *Jesu Zeichen*, 161–62; Rensberger, *Johannine Faith*, 97: "Jesus is king as the witness who asserts the claim of God on the world."

Good Shepherd discourse, in which the sheep are those who hear the shepherd's voice: "you do not believe, because you do not belong to my sheep. My sheep hear my voice" (10:26–27a, cf. also 10:3–4, 16). Jesus' assertion to Pilate, then, puts his judge on trial regarding the truth. The reader can perceive it as a challenge to Pilate to show himself belonging either to "the Jews" of John 8 or to Jesus' sheep of John 10. Pilate's response with the famous question of 18:38a—"What is truth?"—is probably best taken neither as sneeringly sarcastic nor as profoundly philosophical, but simply as an attempt to evade Jesus' witness and a sign of his failure to hear. "The dramatic irony of the question lies in our knowledge that the one to whom the question about truth is asked is himself the Truth."[104] As if to demonstrate the superficial nature of his question, Pilate apparently does not stay for an answer (cf. v. 38b), but with his question and subsequent action, he has now clearly answered his own earlier question from v. 35—"I am not a Jew, am I?"—and aligned himself with "the Jews" of 8:43–47, who do not hear Jesus' witness to the truth.

3. 18:38b–40

In the third scene, Pilate, having retreated outside (cf. v. 38b) immediately after his dialogue with Jesus, announces that he finds Jesus not guilty and appeals to the custom of releasing a prisoner at Passover. His declaration of Jesus' innocence (v. 38b) means that, from this point, the trial is a travesty of justice, being carried out with the judge explicitly aware that the accused is innocent, but this declaration is made subordinate to the offer to release Jesus (v. 39). Since "the Jews" have already made plain to Pilate what they wish to do with Jesus (v. 31), it is difficult for the reader to give him credit for making a genuine offer. He knows that the Jews do not want Jesus released, and calling him "King of the Jews" is not calculated to achieve his release. The sincerity of his pronouncement of Jesus' innocence is also undermined by Pilate's action at the beginning of the next scene, where he has Jesus scourged; it suggests that Jesus' innocence is not a matter of much consequence for Pilate.[105] He appears to be more interested in toying with Jewish nationalistic and messianic hopes. Whatever his motives, his failure to act decisively on his own announcement of Jesus' innocence, like his attempt to evade the issue of the truth, is itself a decision.

---

[104] Duke, *Irony,* 130.

[105] Cf. Rensberger, *Johannine Faith,* 93. Bond, *Pontius Pilate,* 181, also argues that Pilate's actions should not be taken as a serious attempt to release Jesus.

To increase the dramatic effect and heighten the irony, the narrator leaves to the end of the scene his comment about the identity of Barabbas: "Now Barabbas was a bandit" (v. 40b). The term employed— λῃστής—was used by Josephus for bandits and insurrectionists. Pilate's declaration of Jesus' innocence can now be seen to have served as a foil for exposing the hypocrisy of "the Jews." They had presented Jesus to Pilate as a political subversive who deserved death. But even though Jesus has been declared innocent, they prefer to have released to them someone who is undeniably an insurrectionist. There is further irony in the narrator's comment. In rejecting "the King of the Jews" for a robber-bandit, "the Jews" show again that they do not belong to the flock of the good shepherd and are unable to hear his voice, because in the only other uses of λῃστής in the narrative, in 10:1, 8, bandits are contrasted with the good shepherd. And what is more, Barabbas's name (lit. *son of the father*) contains its own irony. In this narrative, where the claim of Jesus to be the Son of the Father has brought about his trial, "the Jews" now choose instead of Jesus not only an insurrectionist but one whose name reflects Jesus' claim.

4. 19:1–3

Pilate's move inside for this central fourth scene is implied in 19:1. He has Jesus scourged, and the Roman soldiers mock Jesus by investing him with the insignia of royalty. The crown of thorns and the purple robe compose the two mock insignia, and the theme of royalty is at the heart of the physical abuse endured by Jesus. The soldiers come up to him as if to swear allegiance with the words "Hail, King of the Jews!" but then suddenly hit him in the face instead. Only in this Gospel's narrative do the scourging and mocking occur *before* Pilate has given Jesus over to be crucified. The different sequence has the effect of displaying the blatant dramatic irony that the one who is on trial is robed as king throughout the rest of the proceedings.

5. 19:4–7

Returning outside (cf. vv. 4–5), Pilate again announces that he finds Jesus not guilty and employs the mockery of Jesus to mock the crowd, but they demand Jesus' crucifixion on the ground that he has made himself the Son of God. This synopsis of the scene conveys nothing of its sense of theater. Pilate emerges from the praetorium to announce that he is about to bring out Jesus and confirm his innocence. But then, when Jesus appears, he is in fact dressed as the king "the Jews" have accused him of wanting to be. Pilate underlines his mockery both of Jesus and of the whole business of Jewish royalty and taunts "the Jews" by pointing to this "caricature of a king"[106] with the words "Here is the man!" (v. 5b). And instead of acclamation, the hostile Jews, who are now specified as the chief priests and their temple police, yell out, "Crucify him! Crucify him!" In v. 6b Pilate is provoked to reply in effect, "Crucify him yourselves! I don't think you've got a case against him." With this third declaration of Jesus' innocence (cf. also 18:38b; 19:4), Pilate again indicates both that he finds Jesus poses no real threat to Roman power and that he is contemptuous of "the Jews," because he knows very well that they have no authority to do what he says and they have reminded him explicitly of this in 18:31. He is simply rubbing salt in the wound of their lack of sovereignty as a nation. It is enough, however, to force "the Jews" to come clean about their real reason for wanting Jesus' death and to express the religious accusation behind the political charge: "We have a law, and according to that law he ought to die because he made himself Son of God" (19:7; NAB). The law in view is presumably Lev 24:16—"One who blasphemes the name of the LORD shall be put to death." This statement of "the Jews" encapsulates the main issue in the continuing conflict and trial between the synagogue, with its Torah, and Johannine Christians, with their Christology, and is a charge already known to the readers from the previous narrative (cf. esp. 5:18; 10:33–35). Readers also know by now that, yes, Jesus has claimed to be Son of God but, no, he has not *made* himself Son of God. On the contrary, his claim has always been that he says and does nothing on his own and that his identity and functions as the Son have been granted him by the Father (cf., e.g., 5:19, 20, 26).

6. 19:8–11

Inside again in the sixth scene (cf. 19:9), Pilate now questions Jesus about his origins and engages in dialogue about power or authority. It is fear that causes him to move back into the praetorium so that he can question Jesus inside; it is the accusation about Jesus being Son of God that has reduced the representative of Roman power to fear before a man accused on a capital charge, who would normally be expected to fear him. Since this is the first mention of fear on Pilate's part, the comparative form of the expression that can be translated "he was more afraid" (NRSV) is probably better taken as "he was greatly afraid."[107] Despite his

---

[106] Cf. Bultmann, *Gospel of John,* 659.

[107] Cf. Barrett, *Gospel according to St. John,* 542.

earlier arrogance, Pilate is now depicted as realizing that he has become embroiled in an issue that goes beyond the political, one in which his decision might well have greater consequences than he had previously imagined. The mention of the title "Son of God" prompts Pilate to ask the question that has been raised about Jesus throughout his ministry— "Where are you from?" This has been one of the ironically ambiguous themes in the narrative (cf. the use of πόθεν in 7:27–28; 8:14; 9:29–30), and readers know by now the appropriate answer: from heaven, from above, from God. They need to supply this answer because Jesus does not give one. The time when Pilate could have heard the answer and listened to Jesus' witness to the truth has passed, as has been seen in 18:38. If readers needed help in supplying the answer, the use of the term ἄνωθεν, *from above*, in the ensuing dialogue in 19:11 would jog their memory.

When Pilate receives no reply, he resorts to reminding the accused of his plight and of his own authority to release or execute him. "Ironically, he boasts of his power to release, when it is clear that before the pressures of the world outside he has no such power. Soon he will explicitly try to release Jesus and will miserably fail (v. 12)."[108] When Jesus does reply, his point about power is a different one: "You would have no power over me unless it had been given you from above" (v. 11a). Pilate's authority over Jesus comes from the same place as Jesus himself.[109] This authority does not derive from himself or from the emperor; it comes from above, from God. The Roman trial is here put in cosmic perspective. Pilate has power as judge in this trial only because God has assigned him this role in the lawsuit of history. His power and responsibility are qualified in a further way: "therefore the one who handed me over to you is guilty of a greater sin" (v. 11b). But to whom does this refer? Given the force of the preceding clause, one might have thought of God, but assigning ultimate cause to God is one thing, imputing sin to God is quite another, and so this possibility must be ruled out. The verb *to hand over* is used to characterize Judas' role in a number of earlier references (cf. 6:64, 71; 12:4; 13:2, 11, 21; 18:2, 5). The consistency of this characterization makes it conceivable that Judas is in view. On the other hand, once Judas's act of betrayal is over, the narrative depicts the chief priests and "the Jews" as responsible for the handing over to Pilate (cf. 18:30, 35). The formulation in the singular is capable of having a general referent, and so it may be best to see "the greater sin" as lying

---

[108] Duke, *Irony*, 133.
[109] Cf. Rensberger, *Johannine Faith*, 98.

with "the Jews," as represented particularly by the chief priests. Thus the witness who has been put on trial not only points to the one with ultimate authority in this trial but also again becomes judge himself as he hands down his own verdict of guilty on those who have brought him to trial.

7. 19:12–16a

This last scene returns to the outside (cf. 19:13), where the trial reaches its conclusion as "the Jews" interject the insinuation of Pilate's treason against Caesar, the judge's seat is occupied, and the chief priests persuade Pilate to crucify Jesus by declaring their own loyalty to Caesar. Jesus' statement about the limits of Pilate's power prompts Pilate's first truly serious attempt to release him (ἐζήτει ἀπολῦσαι αὐτόν, "tried to release him"). But the Jews now drop the religious charge and revert to the political issue in forceful terms: "If you release this man, you are no friend of the emperor [or 'Caesar']." There are questions about the historical referent here—whether "friend of Caesar" has in view the particular title *amicus Caesaris,* which belonged to all senators but was also granted to other exceptional citizens, or whether it is simply a general reference to someone in the emperor's favor. If the former is meant, it has been suggested that Pilate may have gained this distinction because he was a favorite of Sejanus, who had had great influence with Tiberius. In any case, "the Jews" are depicted as playing on Pilate's political relationship with a suspicious Tiberius, who was known to act swiftly and brutally in response to any hint of treason. They present Jesus' kingship as a rival to Caesar's power: "Everyone who claims to be a king sets himself against the emperor" (v. 12b). In this interpretation of the situation, for Pilate to release Jesus would be tantamount to taking sides against Caesar. The dilemma of Pilate's own situation of trial now becomes even clearer. He is faced not simply with a decision between Jesus and "the Jews" but also with a decision between Jesus and Caesar.

Although Pilate will succumb to their pressure, he is determined first to attempt to humiliate "the Jews" a little more. In a repetition of the action of the central scene, he leads out Jesus, who is still attired in the crown of thorns and the purple robe, and this time makes his mockery of "the Jews" more explicit by declaring not, "Here is the man!" but, "Here is your King!" But there is a further difference in this scene, a difference that has caused much debate and that was mentioned in passing in chapter 1 of this study. Pilate sits, or seats Jesus, on the judgment seat (v. 13b). The question is whether the verb ἐκάθισεν is to be interpreted as transitive or intransitive in force. Does the narrator's dramatic and theological irony so color his account that he depicts Pilate as seating

Jesus on the judgment seat, or does he simply depict Pilate as sitting on the judgment seat in readiness to make his verdict? Grammatically, the argument is inconclusive. On the one hand, the only other use of the verb in this Gospel (cf. 12:14) is intransitive. On the other hand, the object does not need to be repeated after ἐκάθισεν if it is already there with a previous verb, and where Jesus is the object of two verbs elsewhere in the Gospel, the object is positioned between the two (cf., e.g., 19:1, 6). This point is clear also from Eph 1:20, where ἐκάθισεν is used transitively with Christ as the object but without the pronoun being repeated. It has been suggested that the narrator is being deliberately ambiguous and allowing for both interpretative possibilities.[110] But this is the least satisfactory solution, since, although the narrative is characterized by various double meanings, nowhere else do these depend on a grammatical ambiguity. There are parallels in other narratives for both interpretations. In Matt 27:19 it is clearly Pilate who sits on the judgment seat, but in Justin, *1 Apol.* 35, and in *Gos. Pet.* 5.7, both apparently independent of the Fourth Gospel, Jesus is mocked by setting him on the judgment seat and calling on him to judge ("Give righteous judgment, O King of Israel"—*Gospel of Peter*).

In the Fourth Gospel's Roman trial, if Pilate is the one on the judgment seat, two items seem strange: not only has he not been depicted as sitting there before; there is also no formal pronouncement by him of a verdict (unlike Matt 27:24). But if Jesus is seated on the judgment seat, this reads more naturally as an additional part of Pilate's humiliation of Jesus, which he employs to mock "the Jews." Jesus has already been dressed up as king; now the judge's bench serves as his throne in this mock coronation. In either interpretation, there is the irony that the one on trial is the real judge while the judge is himself put on trial. The question is whether the irony of judging is blatant at this point and thus whether the narrator's perspective has shaped the account in a direction similar to that of Justin and the *Gospel of Peter*. The blatant irony of kingship and the mention of the judgment seat in the context of the mocking of Jesus as king tilts the balance toward seeing the irony of judging as blatant and therefore taking the verb as transitive.[111] To dismiss this in-

---

[110] Cf., e.g., Barrett, *Gospel according to St. John,* 544; J. Ashton, *Understanding the Fourth Gospel* (Oxford: Clarendon, 1991), 227–28 and n. 41; Bond, *Pontius Pilate,* 190, n. 105.

[111] Cf. I. de la Potterie, "Jésus roi et juge d'après Jn 19, 13, Ἐκάθισεν ἐπὶ βήματος," *Biblica* 41 (1960): 217–47; Meeks, *Prophet-King,* 73–76; Beutler, *Martyria,* 319; G. R. O'Day, "The Gospel of John," *NIB* 9:822.

terpretation on the ground that Jesus functions exclusively as king and not as judge in the Roman trial is to ignore the points that "king" as a title has been subordinated to witness (cf. 18:37) and that the reader has already been introduced to the paradox of the witness acting as judge.[112] It is also to ignore the close links between king and judge in Isa 11:1–10, which, as suggested in chapter 2 of this study, lies behind this Gospel's depiction of Jesus as—like the future Davidic king—one who does not judge according to appearances. What is more, the divine judge who calls the lawsuit in Isa 41:21 is named the King of Jacob, the God who calls the people of Israel to be witnesses in Isa 44:6–8 is King of Israel, and elsewhere in the Jewish Scriptures Yahweh the king is also Yahweh the judge, active to intervene in justice (cf., e.g., Ps 10:16–18; Dan 4:37). Here, then, to mock Jesus as king is already to mock him as judge. But most important, throughout the narrative Jesus the witness has also been seen to be Jesus the judge, and so the readers have been prepared for the climactic trial scene now to make this paradoxical point in the most graphic way. Within this trial scene itself, readers have also already been prepared by the discourse to view both Pilate and "the Jews" as those who stand exposed and judged before Jesus. Now, in the final scene, this irony becomes explicit and takes on narrative form.

In the midst of this scene of mockery, the narrator inserts a chronological note (19:14a). This seems a strange point at which to remind readers that this action is taking place at about midday on the day of Preparation for the Passover. It fills out the hint given in the explanation of "the Jews'" behavior in the first scene (cf. v. 28b) and will be exploited more fully in the narrative of the crucifixion (cf. 19:31, 36). Here, in the final scene, it adds to the surrounding irony in perhaps two ways. It prepares for what can be taken as "the Jews'" faithlessness in their renunciation of their Passover confession in the next verse, at the very time they are about to commemorate God's faithfulness to them. It also anticipates the outcome of the trial for any reader who has kept in mind the witness of John the Baptist from 1:29.

Pilate's second attempt to humiliate "the Jews" by presenting Jesus as their king is followed by a similar response to that of 19:6. This time,

---

[112] *Pace*, e.g., C. H. Talbert, *Reading John: A Literary and Theological Commentary on the Fourth Gospel and Johannine Epistles* (New York: Crossroad, 1992), 241. Brown, *Death of the Messiah*, 1388–93, also argues against the transitive view but does not sufficiently take into account the pervasiveness of the trial motif and its ironies in the Fourth Gospel as a whole nor that such an act would be a mockery not only of Jesus but also of the Jews whom Pilate next addresses.

however, those who cry out are simply designated "the Jews" (cf. v. 14b), and the response is more vehement. There are three imperatives instead of the two in 19:6: "Away with him!" is repeated before "Crucify him!" Pilate does not give up on his sarcastic jest, and what he says next provokes and enrages "the Jews" still further: "Shall I crucify *your King?*" (the word order in Greek suggests this emphasis). This produces the final and shocking words of the chief priests, "We have no king but the emperor" (v. 15c). For implied author and readers, the irony is immense. Not only is Jesus cast aside as messianic king; so also apparently are all expectations of a royal Messiah who would deliver Israel from foreign oppression. Instead "the Jews" proclaim their loyalty to the oppressor. What is more, they demonstrate one of the themes of the narrative—to reject Jesus is to reject God. By proclaiming their loyalty to Caesar as a way of securing Jesus' death, they end up renouncing their God. Israel had always claimed Yahweh as its king (cf., e.g., Judg 8:23; 1 Sam 8:7). Indeed, "We have no king but the emperor" turns out to be a parody on Israel's profession to have no king but God. The eleventh of the Eighteen Benedictions contains the prayer "May you be our King, you alone!" and certainly by the second century C.E., the Passover liturgy included the Nishmat hymn with the lines "From everlasting to everlasting you are God; Beside you we have no king, redeemer or saviour, No liberator, deliverer, provider, None who takes pity in every time of distress and trouble. We have no king but you."[113] If the latter already existed when the Gospel was written, the irony is increased by the renunciation of any such confession just as the observance of Passover begins (cf. 19:14). Through the chief priests' words, this narrative portrays "the Jews" as judging and condemning themselves. They have accused Jesus of blasphemy, but now they are shown to be guilty of apostasy by accepting Caesar's exclusive claim to kingship instead of God's. Again the assertion of 3:18—"those who do not believe are condemned already"—takes on narrative form.

If "the Jews" complete their condemnation in 19:15c, Pilate completes his in v. 16a. Having gained from "the Jews" a declaration of their loyal subjection to Rome, he now hands Jesus over to be crucified, despite his threefold avowal of Jesus' innocence. Pilate hands Jesus over "to them." But to whom? The natural referent, given the antecedents in vv. 14–15, would be "the Jews," represented by the chief priests. This would certainly complete the account neatly. "The Jews" brought Jesus

---

[113] Cf. Meeks, *Prophet-King,* 76–78.

to Pilate at the beginning, and now he hands Jesus back to them at the end, underlining that the major responsibility for the death of Jesus lies with "the Jews" (cf. v. 11). But since the "they" who crucify Jesus (cf. vv. 18, 23) are the Roman soldiers, these are surely the referents in v. 16b—"So they took Jesus"—and thus those to whom Jesus is handed over in the first place in v. 16a.[114]

Whatever traditions lie behind this narrative, they have been elaborated and woven into an account that provides a worthy climax for the overall lawsuit motif and its ironies.[115] In his witness to the truth, Jesus becomes the judge, and both "the Jews" and Pilate are judged by their response to Jesus. Thus the Roman trial becomes the vehicle for the irony that the apparent judge and the apparent accusers are in reality being judged by the apparent accused. Indeed, one could just as easily entitle the episode "The Trial of Pilate and the Jews before Jesus" as "The Trial of Jesus before Pilate."[116] "The trial before Pilate spins this irony into a fine and intricate tapestry."[117] Part of the irony is that Pilate, as the judge who is judged, also acts as a witness to Jesus despite himself through his threefold declaration of Jesus' innocence, his announcement "Here is your King!" and his refusal, subsequent to the trial, to alter the wording of the superscription on the cross from "The King of the Jews" (cf. vv. 21–22).[118] The characterization of Pilate in particular makes the point that, despite his mockery of this Jewish affair, he too is faced with an unavoidable decision about the truth embodied in Jesus and his witness. His failure to decide in favor of Jesus means that he ends up aligned with "the Jews" as part of the unbelieving hostile world in this cosmic trial.

Again, for those with ears to hear, there are echoes from the cosmic lawsuit of Isa 40–55. There the issue at stake was the claim of Yahweh to exclusive lordship: "I, I am the LORD, and besides me there is no savior"

---

[114] Perhaps the ambiguity is to be explained by the awkward incorporation of traditional material into the narrative; cf. Barrett, *Gospel according to St. John,* 546.

[115] O'Day, "Gospel of John," 826, sees this clearly: "In the trial before Pilate, then, the juridical metaphors and imagery about Jesus are brought to their dramatic conclusion. Story line and theology completely coalesce, because the 'trial' becomes both metaphorical and actual."

[116] Cf. Blank, "Die Verhandlung vor Pilatus," 63.

[117] Culpepper, *Anatomy,* 172.

[118] *Contra* Trites, *Concept of Witness,* 85–86, who misses the irony. Such elements in the narrative are hardly to be taken as straightforward confessions of Pilate's belief in Jesus' claims.

(43:11); "There is no other god besides me, a righteous God and a Savior; there is no one besides me" (45:21c). In John, instead of being witnesses to the truth of this claim, as they should have been, "the Jews" reject the authorized representative of their God and, in so doing, abjectly reject their God's exclusive claim, putting themselves on the side of the nations and their gods. In effect, the chief priests' final words mean that they cease to be the special people of God and become just one of the nations subject to Caesar. Caesar's representative in the narrative, Pilate, despite the political power he can employ to toy with "the Jews," is ultimately shown by his actions to be like the gods of the nations in Isaiah—impotent (cf. Isa 44:10; 45:20; 46:7). As for Jesus, he takes on Israel's role as the servant-witness: "By a perversion of justice he was taken away" (53:8a). And the imagery used of his suffering combines with the Fourth Gospel's Passover imagery: he is "like a lamb that is led to the slaughter" (53:7). Because he is confident of God's vindication in the trial with his adversaries (50:8), however, he is enabled to give his back to be struck and not to hide his face from insult and spitting (50:6, cf. John 19:1, 3). Indeed, he can be seen as confuting every tongue that rises against him in judgment (cf. 54:17) and, even though on trial, as the judge who executes justice (cf. Isa 42:1, 2, 4).

chapter four

THE LAWSUIT
and LITERARY ISSUES
REVISITED

Now that we have looked at the shaping of the narrative as a whole in terms of the cosmic lawsuit, set this motif against a scriptural background, and examined some of its key passages in greater detail, in this chapter we will reflect further on some of the main aspects of a primarily literary approach to our topic.

A. Story, Discourse, and Persuasion

The pervasiveness of the lawsuit motif—with its major themes of witness, interrogation, trial, and judgment—in the narrative of the Fourth Gospel provokes a question. How far are the story events determined by the discourse, in which the lawsuit motif is so dominant? Later chapters will explore this question from other angles. Here we shall simply underline that indeed the discourse is determinative. After all, in the traditions about Jesus, there were stories of controversy between Jesus and the religious authorities, of a trial before the Sanhedrin and a trial before Pilate, but it is only this narrator who chooses to omit an actual trial before the Sanhedrin, to depict instead Jesus' public ministry as a trial, and to give the trial before Pilate such prominence in his narration of the passion. It is only this narrator who portrays the roles of John the Baptist and Jesus in terms of witness, who describes the Spirit as Paraclete, and who has a beloved disciple whose primary function is as a witness. Clearly, the characters, events, and relationships in the tradition are only the material for a potential story. It is the discourse that has determined this narrative, and there is no story of Jesus in the Fourth Gospel independent of its narrative discourse.[1] And within this narrative discourse, the pervasive lawsuit motif colors both the actions and the words. It not only figures as part of the events in the plot and their setting; it also appears prominently in the speeches of the characters and the narration of the narrator.

Most readers look for something more in a narrative than simply the action of the plot or the interaction of the characters. One of the main additional factors is "the thematic development that seems to have some bearing on their own situations."[2] It is this that the motif of the lawsuit provides in the Fourth Gospel. The use of its cluster of themes reinforces the effectiveness of the narration, giving it coherence and unity. Indeed, it has been claimed that in the Fourth Gospel an overriding theme such as this may be a more predominant unifying factor than structure, plot, or logical consistency.[3] Preiss, who did so much to rehabilitate the themes of judgment and witness, has written,

> The thought of John has something elusive about it. In a style of grandiose monotony, it develops a few unchanging themes: Father, Son, love, life and death, light and darkness, truth and falsehood, judgment, witness. Looked at closely, its poverty is extreme, like those melodies of only three or four notes. And yet on this reduced keyboard we hear a music of infinitely varied harmonies, each note evoking so many reverberations that even the most attentive ear cannot capture them all at once.

He continues, "All these themes are curiously interwoven with each other: none of them is capable of being analysed and explained in isolation."[4] Chapter 1 of our study claims that if any of these themes predominates and is able to take in the others, then it is the combination of witness and judgment, seen as part of an overall trial where truth is the issue at stake and life and death are the verdicts. Chapter 5 will attempt to demonstrate this regarding the theological point of view that emerges from the narrative.

For the sake of convenience, we have talked about the "lawsuit motif." *Motif* here stands for the cluster of interrelated themes that recur

---

[1] Cf. T. Todorov, *The Poetics of Prose* (Ithaca, N.Y.: Cornell University Press, 1977), 55: "Narrative is a discourse, not a series of events."

[2] T. M. Leitch, *What Stories Are* (London: Pennsylvania State University Press, 1986), 108.

[3] Cf. J. Dewey, "*Paroimiai* in the Gospel of John," *Semeia* 17 (1980): 90.

[4] Preiss, "Justification in Johannine Thought," 10.

in a variety of forms and connections. The themes, such as judgment, truth, witness, and advocacy, function as leitmotifs within the overall motif of the lawsuit. They provide repeated but varied signs that enable readers to orientate themselves and that give unity by pointing to a major overarching idea. The key words and themes and actual interrogation or trial scenes recur throughout the narrative and set up an echo effect. The echoes encourage the making of connections and emphasize the overall motif, but the differences in context and the variations on the theme also produce a richness and diversity within the unifying motif. Many of the key words and themes appear in the discourses or dialogues, which often slow down the development of the plot but at the same time allow readers to appreciate the thematic development of the narrative. The pattern of recurrence enables the dominant motif to expand and grow in significance. This underlines that the words and themes also function as more than leitmotifs. The conceptual network of the cosmic trial forms a coherent metaphorical system that structures the narrative discourse. Isolated expressions, such as bearing witness to the truth, judging, and acting as advocate, turn out to be part of a whole metaphorical system.[5]

The conceptual metaphor embedded in the narrative is that human existence under God, and therefore Christian existence, is a trial. But the metaphor is indispensable to the truth it conveys. The medium of the narrative shaped by this dominant metaphor is the message of the Gospel. Its impact is to open up a perspective on life in a way that goes beyond what simply discursive description is able to effect. After all, what makes a narrative different from a summary of its plot is that it verbally displays a state of affairs and does not merely report it.[6] The lawsuit motif in this narrative discourse provides the interpretative framework through which the narrator assigns meaning and value to the Jesus story for himself and his readers. It thus enables the mission of Jesus and its implications to be displayed in such a way as to invite the readers' involvement. It does not so much supply new information as a new way of seeing that is designed to evoke particular responses. The narrative's

---

[5] One of the contributions of Ricoeur to the discussion of metaphor has been to move from a theory that revolved around particular words to one that took into account metaphorical discourse and then the expansion of this in narrative. Cf. esp. P. Ricoeur, *The Rule of Metaphor* (Toronto: University of Toronto Press, 1977); and *Time and Narrative* (3 vols.; Chicago: University of Chicago Press, 1984–1988).

[6] Cf. Leitch, *What Stories Are,* 18–41. For some reflections on the Fourth Gospel as a display text, see Tovey, *Narrative Art and Act,* 193–201.

metaphorical discourse has the power to give its readers the experience of the cosmic trial and to affect how they perceive and live in the world. It creates the possibility of participation in the metaphor's referent because it draws readers into the trial and confronts them with the necessity of their verdict and of living with its consequences. In generating and evoking an alternative perspective on reality, it becomes a metaphor to live by.[7]

As it integrates the plot and the narrative discourse as a whole, the lawsuit motif also performs several functions in the narrative's strategy of persuasion. Narrative does not fall easily into the ancient rhetorical categories of deliberative, judicial, or epideictic rhetoric. Yet this narrative is clearly aimed at persuading, and so a brief consideration of some of the aspects of rhetoric is still likely to prove illuminating. Before asking about the rhetorical goals of this narrative discourse, it would be well to focus on the rhetorical situation and its *stasis*, that is, the question at issue, even though these matters anticipate our later discussion of readers. In this narrative a "we," representing a community of belief that is in turn represented by the witness of the beloved disciple, addresses a "you" (plural) whom it calls to believe this witness. The main issue about which belief is solicited is the identity of Jesus as the Christ, the Son of God.[8] Because of the nature of the claim made about Jesus as Son of God, the issue also includes a claim about God.

The lawsuit is clearly a highly appropriate vehicle for displaying this issue, since it is a primary means of settling disputed claims and since there is already a scriptural tradition of dealing with claims about God in such a context. Given all that we have seen, it might seem clear that the rhetorical strategy of this narrative falls into the judicial category. Such a conclusion would, however, be misleading, since judicial rhetoric aims at eliciting a judgment about a past state of affairs. Although the narrative deals with the past, it does so in order to support a claim that is under dispute in the present. For this reason, it would be more accurate to suggest that, like epideictic rhetoric, it aims at instilling and enhancing certain beliefs and values in the present. The narrative presents itself as testimony in a trial, but it is only partially calling for a judgment about a past state of affairs—what happened to Jesus—and even then is concerned to establish not what the past events were but what their meaning

---

[7] Cf. G. Lakoff and M. Johnson, *Metaphors We Live By* (Chicago: University of Chicago Press, 1980).

[8] For fuller discussion of the statement of purpose in 20:31, see sec. G, below.

is. It is primarily calling for a judgment about the present validity of beliefs about Jesus, based on its presentation of his mission, a mission it regards as already adjudicated. This testimony in a continuing trial is needed in order to convince people about the verdict that is already in and that has present significance for them. Obviously, in order to be persuaded by the narrative's stance on the present significance of Jesus and the verdict of life he has made available, its readers also need to share the narrative's perspective on the past.

In order to be persuasive in its testimony, the narrative also needs to deal with the counterclaims to the convictions of the community it represents. They include the allegation of blasphemy relating to the community's beliefs about Jesus' relationship to God; the objection that someone who died in disgrace, executed by the Romans, could not possibly be the Christ, the Son of God; accusations that he was a false prophet who attempted to lead the people astray; and citations of the law and Scripture to buttress these points and rule out the validity of the community's claims. By means of the lawsuit motif, the narrative makes its response. It has Jesus himself under interrogation and on trial, responding to such counterclaims and voicing the community's present convictions. It narrates the lawsuit in such a way as to show that the divine verdict has already quashed the counterclaims and that, far from being his moment of disgrace, Jesus' Roman-style execution was the culmination of a career characterized by the aura of the divine glory and reputation. The narrative employs the law and Scripture as witnesses for Jesus and against his opponents. It makes a point of presenting Jesus as quite the reverse of a false prophet, as one whose predictions are fulfilled to the letter and are part of the reliability of his witness.

By dealing with the counterclaims its readers will confront, the narrative serves as an apologetic. But this is not an apology addressed to outsiders as much as one intended to help those already sympathetic to the cause and who already know the issues at stake. This evaluation is reinforced by considering two other elements of rhetoric. All persuasive discourse employs not only *logos*, argumentation found here in Jesus' speeches and in the presentation of the narrative discourse as a whole, but also *ethos*, the persuasive power of the speaker's character, and *pathos*, the arousal of the appropriate emotions in the audience.

The *ethos* of this narrative testimony is tied particularly to the character and quality of the narrator as a witness. The community endorses his witness, and it is presented as that of the beloved disciple (21:24). The designation "the disciple whom Jesus loved" is itself a recommendation of his character. But this is only effective in the persuasion of those who are inclined already to evaluate Jesus highly and therefore to be impressed by someone who was in an intimate relationship with him. Respect for this narrator is enhanced by his presence and insight at key stages of the last part of Jesus' mission. But the *ethos* of the narrator is also linked to that of the protagonist of his narrative, who is his chief mouthpiece. As already noted, the language and style of the narrator is indistinguishable from that of Jesus, and this obviously reinforces the connection. The good character of Jesus is questioned by the opposition, who accuse him of being a sinner (9:24) and having a demon (8:48). Such accusations are dealt with by exposing the opposition's prejudices. Since, for the narrator, the goodness of Jesus is not in doubt because of who Jesus is, it does not need to be demonstrated at any length. His good works of healing and restoring life should have been evidence enough (10:32). The *ethos* of the narrator's Jesus is displayed chiefly through the presentation of Jesus' relationship with God; of his omniscience; of the reliability of his predictions; of his role as the witness who also functions as judge when under interrogation and on trial; of the way he faces death; of his love for, and preparation of, his disciples; and of the divine vindication in both his death and his resurrection.

For the *pathos*, too, of the narrative's lawsuit to be effective, a basic identification by the readers with Jesus and his cause needs to be presupposed, since the main emotions the narrative is designed to arouse are admiration and sympathy for Jesus and his views and antipathy toward his opponents. Any readers inclined to share the opposition's perspective are not likely to be persuaded to change their minds, given the disdain that is evoked by the presentation of their views. The dominant feeling toward Jesus that the narrative aims to produce is admiration that also includes awe and worship. There is admiration for the way he handles his interrogations and trials; for the way he confronts and outwits his opponents; for his supernatural knowledge, his control of his destiny, and his eluding of attempts to kill him; and for the certainty of his witness to his relationship with God. Admiration becomes awe when his powerful signs display the life-giving verdict of the lawsuit and when the members of the arresting party prostrate themselves as he identifies himself as "I am." And awe becomes worship when readers are drawn into Thomas's confession, "My Lord and my God!" At other, rarer times, admiration is mixed with sympathy as the intended response—when Jesus shows his humanity in weeping and being angry at Lazarus's death, when he washes his disciples' feet, when he is frustrated by their lack of understanding, and when he is victimized, mocked, sentenced to death, and crucified.

There is another set of emotions aroused in connection with the lawsuit motif, however, and again these pertain to those who have already identified with Jesus' cause. Indeed, they are emotions that would be evoked in those who are feeling the cost of such an identification. Particularly the Farewell Discourses and Jesus' prayer in John 17 are meant to produce reassurance and encouragement for such readers. While their situation of conflict, persecution, trial, and possible death is acknowledged, the lawsuit motif provides the context for producing consolation and confidence. They are reminded that the decisive stage of the cosmic trial has already been completed, that they have the powerful and enlightening presence of the Paraclete to assist them in their witness, that they have access to God their Father in Jesus' name, and that, as a consequence, joy and peace are to be experienced instead of fear, since in their witness they are part of God's continuing purposes in the lawsuit. The testimony of the narrative as a whole is likely, then, to be most persuasive for readers who have already accepted the truth of this testimony but need to be strengthened in their acceptance.

In exploring the narrative discourse in relation to the lawsuit motif, attention needs to be paid to the discourse's three key elements—its beginning, its middle, and its end. To these we now turn.

B. Narrative Opening

The prologue opens with a reference to the Logos, and the Logos is then identified with both life and light: "in him was life, and the light was the light of all people" (1:4). In the context of the preexistent Logos's activity in creation and with the allusions to the Genesis narrative, this first reference to life and light surely signifies primarily the qualities of the Logos necessary for his role in creating, sustaining, and illuminating humanity. But clearly, both life and light will later take on further connotations in the context of the incarnate Logos's mission. These further connotations do not simply await the narrative proper but are already suggested in the prologue itself. Verse 9 speaks of the coming of the true light into the world. And when we ask what is involved in the coming of the light into the world, the answer of the rest of the narrative is clear. In coming into the world, the light functions to judge humanity. The first reference to light after the prologue makes this explicit: "And this is the judgment, that the light has come into the world, and people loved darkness rather than light" (3:19). The last does also: at the end of his public mission in Israel, Jesus summarizes this mission in terms of his coming as light into the world and connects this with the judgment of both condemnation and salvation (12:46–48); the incarnate Logos as the light is the agent of judgment (cf. also 9:4, 39). The concept of life undergoes a similar development. In the prologue it is said that those who receive the light when it is in the world also receive new life—they are born of God (1:12–13). Again, the first time this terminology is taken up in the narrative proper is in 3:1–21, where those who believe have eternal life (3:15–16), the result of a birth from above or of the Spirit (3:3, 5–6); and in the summary at the end of the mission, eternal life is said to be the content of Jesus' salvific judgment (12:50).

The two terms from the prologue come together again in Jesus' witness that provokes the trial scene in 8:12–59: "I am the light of the world. Whoever follows me will never walk in darkness but will have the light of life" (8:12). Life is the positive verdict produced by the judgment of the light. The prologue has put these symbols of the lawsuit in their cosmic context and intimated the course of the lawsuit in history. When the symbols take on the clear connotations of the later narrative, the reader is able to perceive that the cosmic lawsuit is not simply one feature of the later discourse but has already been introduced as a dominant motif right from the start.

This perception is reinforced, as we have seen, by the fact that the first reference to a human character in the narrative is to John the Baptist and that immediately this character is described as a witness (1:7). It soon becomes apparent to readers how important this motif of witness is for the structuring of the narrative, and by the end they are able to recognize in the reference to the witness of the beloved disciple an *inclusio* on the motif. It is clear also that the references to John the Baptist's testimony in 1:6–8 and 1:15 do not simply interrupt the prologue with this motif; rather, there is an integral relationship between this aspect of the lawsuit and the main content of the prologue. After all, John is described as a witness to the light, and the light is the Logos who becomes incarnate to bring God's judgment to the world. John is a witness in this cosmic lawsuit.

But for informed readers who return to the narrative opening in the light of their reading of the narrative as a whole and in the light of the scriptural foundation that informs the lawsuit imagery, there are further intimations of the lawsuit theme. The opening of the Fourth Gospel establishes the lawsuit as the narrative frame. It not only provides the cosmic setting that the trial had in Isaiah (God in relation to the world, and light in relation to darkness) but also introduces two of the major witnesses in the trial (John the Baptist, who bears witness to Jesus, and Jesus himself, who is to be the main witness). Jesus the incarnate Logos is not described as a witness here. Yet when we ask how the Logos, as God's self-expression in the world, carries out this function, the dominant answer we find in the narrative proper is that the Logos comes to expression through the words and deeds of Jesus as the witness and judge who fully represents God. Similarly, when the end of the prologue describes the mission of the incarnate Logos as making God known and we ask how, in the narrative as a whole, he has made God known, the same answer is required—primarily as witness and judge in the lawsuit. In the light of the rest of the Gospel and its presentation of the stance of the opposition, the antithetical parallelism of 1:17, which sets Jesus in contrast to the Mosaic law, can be seen to establish from the start the criterion of judgment in this cosmic trial.

But we are not yet done. The opening of the narrative also introduces two other crucial concerns for the trial—truth and glory. In the trial scenes of Isa 40–55, the key feature of Yahweh's defense, the evidence adduced for Yahweh's being the one true God, is the correspondence, the fit between Yahweh's predictive word and what happens in history. And it is to this truth that Israel is to bear witness in its belief in, and understanding of, Yahweh as "I am." In the prologue of the Fourth Gospel, the protagonist is described as the Logos who has become flesh (1:14). Whatever the other connotations attached to the incarnate Logos from its background in the Jewish wisdom tradition, in view of the links with the scriptural lawsuit, the reader can see highlighted the same key issue of the relation between God's word and the world. The Logos become flesh provides the instance par excellence of the reliable connection, the precise correspondence, between God's word and its realization in history. Whatever the prehistory of the prologue, its notions of witness and the Logos are not awkwardly juxtaposed but integrally connected in its final form, signaling that, in this narrative shaped by the trial motif, the same ultimate concerns are at stake as in the scriptural trial scenes—how is the one true God to be known, and how is the truth of conflicting claims about this God to be judged? To these questions the same reply will be given: the God who is the sovereign God of history is known, and claims about this God are decided through the correspondence between God's word and its fulfillment in God's deed. But the difference is that this time the correspondence is embodied in a person, Jesus. Again a witness to the correspondence is needed. A double witness can be found in the prologue, just as in the epilogue. The witness of John the Baptist in 1:15 is included within that of the narrator and his community (1:14–18). And the community's witness is precisely to this correspondence: "And the Word [Logos] became flesh and lived among us, and we have seen his glory." The point of view of the ensuing narrative is that the truth about God that is in dispute is to be identified with Jesus as the incarnate Logos. Not only is it his task to bear witness to the truth (18:37); he also claims to embody this truth (14:6). Just as in the prologue the incarnation provides the point of correspondence between God's word and God's deed in the world, so in the narrative as a whole the fit between word and deed in Jesus' mission is made clear, particularly through the striking correspondences between discourses and signs and between predictions and their fulfillment. The prologue's witness already intimates that the truth on trial is summed up in Jesus. The Logos is "full of grace and truth" (1:14), and grace and truth have come into being through him (1:17). It should not be surprising, then, that the Logos's embodiment of the relation of God's word to the world and his making God known can be identified with Jesus' witness to the truth that dominates the rest of the narrative. The narrator underscores the point later in 3:33, in his comment on Jesus' testimony. A decision about Jesus' witness is not simply a decision about the truth of *his* claims. Rather, "whoever has accepted his testimony has set a seal to this, that *God* is true."

In the lawsuits of Isa 40–55, Yahweh's glory is of paramount concern. In establishing Yahweh as the one true God, they also establish Yahweh's sovereign reputation and entitlement to honor. The same holds for Jesus in the Fourth Gospel's lawsuit. In the prologue, the narrator and his community supply this witness about the incarnate Logos: "we have seen his glory" (1:14b). It is an acknowledgment that the whole mission of the incarnate Logos established his reputation and honor, but the reader also knows from the rest of the narrative that this especially includes what would, by conventional assessments of honor, seem totally to undermine it—his ignominious death. In this narrative discourse, this death is at the center of his climactic hour of glory. Again, in all this, the glory of the incarnate Logos as God's self-expression is identified with the glory of God's own self: "Now the Son of Man has been glorified, and God has been glorified in him" (13:31). The prologue already indicates that, in the mission of Jesus in the cosmic lawsuit, his entitlement to honor is secured and that this honor reflects on God's honor. It is "the glory as of a father's only son" (1:14c).

Admittedly, some of this significance of the prologue for our motif can only be appreciated in retrospect by the informed reader. But this is only to take account of the dynamics of both reading and writing. Reading frequently leads to an informed rereading because only in the light of the ending and the whole can the implications of the opening of a narrative be more fully understood. In terms of writing, the advice frequently given to students to write the introductions to their essays or dissertations last is pertinent here. And to draw on a historical-critical point, it is generally held that the prologue in fact was part of the last stage in the evangelist's composition of this Gospel and was therefore produced in the light of what follows in the rest of the narrative. It should not be surprising, therefore, if readers' experience of the opening of the Fourth Gospel, not least in regard to the significance of the Logos designation for the trial motif, is in line with the words of T. S. Eliot:

> We shall not cease from exploration
> And the end of all our exploring
> Will be to arrive where we started
> And know the place for the first time.[9]

C. Narrative Middle

Does this narrative have a middle? In terms of the plot, one distinctive episode provides the link between the first part of the Gospel, with its public mission, and the second half, with its farewell material, trial, and passion. The raising of Lazarus is this pivot. It constitutes the seventh and climactic sign but is also, in contrast to the Synoptics, where the temple incident performs this function, the event that provokes the protagonist's arrest and condemnation. The Lazarus episode is an extensive unit, running from 11:1 to 12:11. Many see it as extending only as far as 11:44, but this is to cut it off too abruptly and miss the close connections and development established in the material in 11:45–12:11.[10] John 11:45–57 contains the response to the miracle, including the division caused by it. The anointing of Jesus for burial by Mary in 12:1–8 is explicitly set in the home of Lazarus with Lazarus himself present (cf. 12:1–2), and the whole section is rounded off in 12:9–11 by an account of Lazarus becoming the focus of attention for the crowd and for the chief priests who plan to kill him. Part of the reason many discussions stop at 11:44 is that the actual miracle is so delayed in this sign story that when it happens, interpreters think the story has finally reached its conclusion, forgetting that, as in other miracle stories, the response is an integral part of the account.

---

[9] These oft-quoted lines are from *Little Gidding* V.
[10] Cf. esp. Lee, *Symbolic Narratives*, 191–97, who sees a chiastic arrangement in 11:1–12:11.

How is this event related to our description of the plot in terms of the lawsuit motif? The raising of Lazarus (not related until 11:43–44) produces reverberations into the closing part of Jesus' public ministry, narrated in the last part of the episode (cf. 11:45–53; 12:9–10) and then in the context of Jesus' entry into Jerusalem (cf. 12:17–19). Each reference points to the division of allegiance, an indication of the judgment in progress, caused by Jesus' final sign. Many Jews believe in him, but others are hardened in their hostile opposition. The final reference in 12:17–19 is particularly significant, since the narrator employs the language of witness regarding the positive response: "The crowd that had been with him when he called Lazarus out of the tomb and raised him from the dead continued to testify." The Pharisees, on the other hand, continue to be frustrated by what appears to be Jesus' universal appeal. The immediate aftermath of Lazarus's resurrection has already indicated the action the opposition intends to take to remedy this. The Sanhedrin has met in response to the dismayed reaction of some Jews to the raising of Lazarus, and in the absence of Jesus, the defendant, and without any formal legal procedures, it has already reached its verdict on his fate: "From that day on they planned to put him to death" (11:53); "The chief priests and the Pharisees had given orders that anyone who knew where Jesus was should let them know, so that they might arrest him" (11:57). So, as a result of the Lazarus episode, there is the negative verdict of the authorities, prompted by some Jews who had been present, but there is also the continuing witness of others.

These links are on the surface of the narrative. But it is not only in its consequences that the episode is connected with the lawsuit. The event itself is integrally related to the overall motif. Just as it provokes the main anticipation of the final negative verdict on Jesus, so the raising of Lazarus is itself the main anticipation of the trial's positive verdict of life. Earlier Jesus has made clear that, as the Son of Man, he is the agent of judgment for eternal life or death, for a resurrection of life or a resurrection of condemnation (cf. 5:19–29). Now, in the conversation with Martha, he offers this assurance: "I am the resurrection and the life. Those who believe in me, even though they die, will live, and everyone who lives and believes in me will never die" (11:25–26). Jesus claims here to be not simply the embodiment of eternal life but the embodiment of Israel's hopes for the physical resurrection of the dead. Martha makes a positive response but does not appear to realize the implications, for her brother, of Jesus' claim to embody the resurrection (cf. 11:39–40). In this striking and elaborate account, we are then shown a weeping and angry, yet authoritative, Jesus confronting and defeating death's hold over Lazarus.

The prolepsis here is twofold. Lazarus's resurrection anticipates the final resurrection, with its salvific judgment (cf. 11:24–25). It also anticipates the verdict that is already made in the resurrection of Jesus. The one who claims to embody the resurrection will make good this claim as he takes up his own life after laying it down. Both the similarities and the differences between the two accounts confirm this anticipation of Jesus' resurrection. In both cases there is a tomb and a stone that has to be removed. In both cases the focus is on the grief and faith of women disciples—Mary and Martha, and Mary Magdalene. And in both accounts the graveclothes and particularly the facecloth (σουδάριον) are mentioned (11:44; 20:7). But the difference is vital. Lazarus, raised by Jesus, came out of the tomb bound hand and foot and with his face wrapped in a cloth. Jesus, taking up his own life, has left these wrappings in the tomb and will need them no more because his is a resurrection to eternal life, not simply a temporary restoration to earthly life.

At this stage in the plot, however, life for Lazarus means death for Jesus; in terms of our motif, the anticipation of the verdict of life for those who believe is what brings about the negative denouement of the verdict of death on Jesus. This, too, is anticipated within the account itself. In 11:4 Jesus' first words on hearing of Lazarus's illness make this point—"This illness does not lead to death [for Lazarus]; rather it is for God's glory, so that the Son of God may be glorified through it"—and the reader knows that the moment of God's and the Son of God's glory is Jesus' death. Then, through the ensuing dialogue between Jesus and the disciples in 11:7–16, the narrator underlines the expectation that, in going to Judea to deal with Lazarus's death, Jesus is going to his own death. The remarkable ending of 12:9–10, where the one who has just been raised is himself shortly afterward the object of a plot to murder him, is designed to ensure that the reader will not miss the force of this account of Lazarus's raising. It has not been told simply for the sake of this miracle, which can so easily be reversed. It is a sign, but only a sign. By associating the plot to kill Lazarus with that to kill Jesus, this ending serves to underline the point made from the very beginning of the episode—that, in this sign involving Lazarus, life and death are inextricably linked, not only because Lazarus himself moves from death to life and back to possible death but also, and more especially, because it foreshadows Jesus' move from life to death and back to life. What happens to Lazarus both entails the death of the one who has given him life and anticipates the decisive restoration to life of the life giver himself. As a result of the initial overcoming of death for Lazarus, the one who embodies the verdict of resurrection and life is himself put under the sentence of death and then is anointed for burial ahead of time. Thus this all-important episode at the middle of the story is told from a perspective that sees both Jesus' death and his resurrection as the culmination of his mission in the lawsuit. In this death and resurrection to life, to both of which the resurrection of Lazarus points, the decisive verdict that rescues humanity from the great enemy, death, will take place.

D. Narrative Closure

Endings of narratives are vital for the retrospective analysis of the direction of their plots and for their readers' perception of their coherence and unity. Readers need a satisfactory sense of closure that helps them to relate the parts of the narrative to the whole. In this regard the Fourth Gospel presents an interesting case. In traditional interpretations of the Gospel, because the crucifixion is so clearly the theological climax, the accounts of the empty tomb and the resurrection appearances are frequently viewed as problematic. Does the Gospel really need a resurrection account if Jesus' glorification takes place in his death? The inclusion of the burial and resurrection stories is usually accounted for by reference to the pressure exerted on the evangelist's composition by the traditions he has inherited. And because some scholars have held that the Gospel comes to an end at 20:30–31 and that John 21 is a later addition, they have treated the latter as even more of an anticlimactic appendix to the Gospel's theology.[11] Is the issue of closure any different for an analysis that attempts to do justice to the final form of the narrative? Similar questions confront the reader, but they are posed in different terms. There is no mistaking that Jesus' final words as he is dying, "It is finished" (19:30), mark the climax and resolution of the plot as far as the protagonist's earthly life is concerned. Yet the narrative is not completed until two chapters later, in 21:24–25. What, then, is the relation between the completion of the main plot and the end of the narrative as a whole? And what is the relation between the statement of purpose in 20:30–31 and the end of the narrative?

In talking of narrative closure, then, our focus is on the very end rather than John 21 as a whole.[12] What is the end of the narrative in its

---

[11] For further discussion of such a view, see ch. 5, sec. B, below, and its exploration of the role of the resurrection in the Gospel's presentation of Jesus.

[12] In a recent essay, B. R. Gaventa, "The Archive of Excess: John 21 and the Problem of Narrative Closure," in *Exploring the Gospel of John* (ed. R. A.

final form takes up and develops what has been the significance of the beloved disciple's role—that of the ideal witness who has been responsible for the written testimony constituted by the narrative. In 21:24 a distinction is made between the beloved disciple and his witness and the narratorial "we" who are confirming this witness as true. The narrator, who again invokes the community of faith with which he is aligned (cf. the "we" in 1:14, 16; cf. also 3:11), is not himself the beloved disciple. This also indicates that γράψαι is best taken as "has caused to be written" rather than as "has written" (NRSV). In 19:19, 22 the verb is also employed in this way to describe Pilate's role in writing the inscription on the cross. Clearly, this narrative closure is formulated in terms highly significant for the lawsuit motif, for, while acknowledging that many more books could be written about what Jesus did, the narrator chooses to describe his own account as being linked to the testimony of the beloved disciple and to make a claim to that testimony's truth. In terms of the role of the lawsuit in the narrative discourse, 21:24 clearly offers a satisfactory closure. It provides an *inclusio* on this motif, linking the beloved disciple's witness in the writing of the Gospel back to John the Baptist's witness, which is featured twice in the prologue. It thereby reinforces for the reader that the lawsuit motif is a key feature for interpreting the narrative as a whole and discerning its coherence. Now even the writing down of the narrative itself is presented as playing an integral role in the continuation of the lawsuit in history.

The mention of the writing of an account provides the most explicit link between 20:30–31, where γράφειν, *to write*, occurs twice, and the ending in 21:24–25. The statement of purpose talks of writing about the signs done by Jesus in order to produce belief that he is the Messiah, the sort of Messiah who is Son of God, and in order that, in turn, belief may result in experiencing the positive verdict of life. It should be remembered that this emphasis on the readers' belief follows on naturally from the appearance that singles out Thomas in 20:26–29 and that concludes with Jesus' words "Have you believed because you have seen me? Blessed are those who have not seen and yet have come to believe." The account is written down in order that others may be able to believe without

---

Culpepper and C. C. Black; Louisville: Westminster John Knox, 1996), 240–52, deals with the whole of John 21 and sees John 20 and 21 as two relatively independent endings that are in parallel. While this approach generates some helpful insights, it is difficult to see how the reader of the Gospel as it now stands could be expected not to treat John 21 as building on John 20, despite one or two awkwardnesses that this causes.

seeing, and this will take place on the basis of the witness of the disciples who, like Thomas, have seen and believed. The narrator stresses in 20:30 that Jesus' signs, which formed part of the witness to him in the lawsuit of the public ministry, were done "in the presence of his disciples." This is in order to show that the disciples are the vital link in the chain between these signs and those who will come to believe without having seen them. Part of the disciples' task as witnesses in the ongoing lawsuit is to provide reliable testimony to what Jesus has done.[13] Further support for this interpretation and for the link it provides between the task of the disciples in general and that of the beloved disciple in particular in writing the narrative (21:24) is found in the fact that the beloved disciple himself is described earlier as one who "saw and believed" (20:8).

It is the notion of a continuation of the lawsuit that also makes sense of the distance between the resolution of the main plot and the end of the narrative and enables the closure to be experienced as satisfactory. The narrative itself has made amply clear that, in the narrative world beyond the story of Jesus' earthly mission, the lawsuit will continue. Immediately before his own mission is about to be completed, Jesus has instructed his followers that they are to continue this mission as witnesses with the aid of the Paraclete. Although, at the end of this instruction, the disciples acknowledge that Jesus knows all things and declare their belief that he has come from God (16:29–30), the reader suspects that they are not yet up to the task they have been given. The suspicion is reinforced by Jesus' immediate prediction that they will be scattered and will leave him alone (16:32), by Peter's threefold denial (18:15–18, 25–27), and by the absence of all but the beloved disciple and the three women at the crucifixion. If the necessity of the resurrection appearances has been questioned in terms of the completion of Jesus' own task in the plot, certainly they are vital if the reader is to have any sense that his followers have undergone the necessary change and come to a belief adequate for them to be able to carry out their own task. Indeed, it is in the context of a resurrection appearance that Jesus now commissions the disciples as a group for their task—"As the Father has sent me, so I send you"—and fulfills his promise to give them the Paraclete as co-witness by breathing on them and saying, "Receive the Holy Spirit" (20:21–22). And it is in the empty tomb (cf. 20:8–9) that the beloved disciple himself comes to the belief that qualifies him to be "the perceptive witness" to the significance of the events of the narrative.[14] It is also in the

---

[13] Cf. Bittner, *Jesu Zeichen*, 221–24.
[14] Cf. R. Bauckham, "The Beloved Disciple as Ideal Author," *JSNT* 49 (1993): 36–39.

context of a resurrection appearance that the rehabilitation of Peter in particular is completed, in readiness for his witness, which will take him to a martyr's death (21:15–19). Significantly, Peter's question about the fate of the beloved disciple (v. 20) links these two witnesses and leaders. One is the shepherd who becomes a martyr, the other a witness who does not meet martyrdom but dies a natural death (v. 23). To prevent odious comparisons and to underline the validity of both types of witness, the narrative stresses that what counts is not the actual outcome of the witness but the will of Jesus, which determines the outcome (v. 22). In this light, the following reference, at the end of the narrative, to the role of the witness of the beloved disciple in the writing of the Gospel can be more clearly seen as a specific task within the more general assignment of witnessing that he shares with all the disciples as they continue the mission of Jesus.

But there is a further way in which the reader is helped to see the link between the resolution of the main plot and the end of the narrative: through the beloved disciple, who was present at the moment of resolution and whose presence is related by the narrator to his role as witness (19:35). But while most commentators agree that "he who saw" in 19:35 is the beloved disciple, the figure is not explicitly identified. A good case can be made for this figure in fact being the soldier who pierced Jesus' side. This soldier is the direct antecedent in the narrative for the clause "he who saw this has testified"; such an identification could then be said to be John's equivalent to the confession of the centurion in the synoptic accounts. It can also be argued that the Scripture cited by the narrator in v. 37 points in this direction, since in that text the same group who have done the piercing look on the one they have pierced. In this interpretation, the clause "so that you also may believe" (v. 35) is then taken as indicating that the testimony of the soldier has been passed on by the narrator to produce or enhance the readers' faith. In support of this reading, it is also claimed that the reader would expect from v. 27b—"And from that hour the disciple took her into his own home"—that the beloved disciple has left the scene.[15]

This view is attractive, but I am still inclined to think that, in the context of the narrative as a whole, the best candidate for this role is the beloved disciple. It is in keeping with his function as a key witness to

---

[15] For advocacy of this view, see, e.g., Minear, *John: The Martyr's Gospel,* 70–73; H. Thyen, "Johannes und die Synoptiker," in *John and the Synoptics* (ed. A. Denaux; Leuven: Leuven University Press, 1992), 103–4.

significant moments in the last part of Jesus' ministry—the announcement of the identity of the betrayer (13:23–26), the significance of the death here, the significance of the empty tomb (20:8), and the recognition of the risen Lord (21:7). "From that hour" in 19:27b cannot be held to rule this out as a possibility. The use of the term *hour* is not only highly significant but also very elastic in this narrative discourse. The hour of glorification is depicted as having already arrived as early as 12:27 (cf. also 13:1). It is likely that the same hour is in view here, and in fact the glorification that characterizes the crucifixion is displayed as the blood and water come from Jesus' side, recalling the prediction of 8:38 and the narrator's comment that this awaited fulfillment until Jesus' glorification (8:39). So "from that hour" may well be meant to be taken as "after Jesus' death and glorification." Two other factors support the identification of the figure in 19:35 with the beloved disciple. First, just as the narrative's ending will endorse the truth of the beloved disciple's witness, so the truth of the witness in 19:35 is endorsed. Second, 20:31 states the purpose of the beloved disciple's witness, which constitutes the Gospel, in terms of an address to the readers ("so that you may come to believe"); 19:35 is the only other place where the readers are addressed directly, and there, too, the figure's testimony is "so that you may believe."[16]

If, then, we take the beloved disciple to be the witness in 19:35, the links with 20:31 and 21:24 mean that this disciple can be seen as the bridge between the lawsuit in which Jesus himself was involved and the lawsuit in which his followers continue to be involved. By focusing on the witness of the beloved disciple in its closure, the narrative links two key moments in the cosmic lawsuit—the decisive moment when the principal lawsuit is completed (in the pronouncement of God's verdict in the death of Jesus) and the highly significant moment for the continuing lawsuit when the written witness to that verdict is completed (in the composition of this narrative). Why are his witness and its truth stressed so much in 19:35? If, as we have argued, the cosmic lawsuit motif is dominant in the narrative, then the decisive moment has to be God's verdict in the death of Jesus, and this verdict requires a witness. The verdict is expressed symbolically through the blood and water flowing from Jesus' side. The beloved disciple supplies the witness, and this is the one point in his entire telling of the story where the narrator as the beloved

---

16 Cf. Bauckham, "Beloved Disciple," 40, who holds, however, that, in the light of these connections, "there can be no doubt that the witness of 19:35 is indeed the beloved disciple."

disciple stops and explicitly addresses the readers to make sure they have understood the significance of what he has just told them.

The function of the beloved disciple's witness to the positive verdict of life resulting from Jesus' death is the same as that of his written witness in the Gospel as a whole. It is in order that the readers might believe. The role of witness to the truth about God in Scripture's cosmic lawsuit has moved from Israel as a whole to Jesus and to his followers accompanied by the Spirit, and it can now also take on a new, written form. As we have seen, in 19:35, just as he will do in the closure, the narrator makes a claim about the truth of the beloved disciple's witness. Only regarding three characters does the narrative underline the truth of the witness—God the Father in 5:32 (cf. also 8:17), Jesus in 8:13–18, and now the beloved disciple in 19:35 and 21:24. And in 21:24 the narrator adds his own and his community's endorsement of the beloved disciple's witness: "and we know that his testimony is true." Just as, in the prologue, an analogous endorsement was added to that of John the Baptist, so here the formulation is added to that of the beloved disciple as another form of the required dual witness.

If we inquire into the ending's claim about the truth of the beloved disciple's witness encapsulated in the Gospel, the scriptural foundation and its notion of correspondence between word and deed may again offer a clue. Just as the prologue makes the incarnation of the Logos the point of correspondence between God's word and God's deed in the world, so the testimony of the narrative as a whole has been at pains to demonstrate the fit between word and deed. Again we should recall that, besides depicting the mission of Jesus as involving events predicted in Scripture, the narrative has also frequently set out the correspondence between Jesus' own predictions and their fulfillment. In addition, it has presented the striking correspondence between discourse and sign: the one who claims to be the light of the world gives sight to the blind man, and the one who claims to be the resurrection and the life raises Lazarus from the dead. There is also, in the context of the Gospel's story world, a match between the predictions of Jesus in the Farewell Discourses about his departure and its consequences and what the readers know to have happened. The ending of the narrative itself strives to make clear that there has been no mismatch between what Jesus predicted about the beloved disciple and his actual fate (21:22–23). The narrator and the community also confirm the truth of the beloved disciple's narrative because, in turn, they have experienced the correspondence between its words and what has taken place in their own history: "It is not what the disciples knew or even what Jesus knew that stands at the end of the Gospel, but what the community in the present knows."[17]

The mention of the death of the beloved disciple serves, as death often does, to signal the replacement of generations. Not only has the narrative portrayed Jesus' death and his replacement by another Advocate who works through Jesus' immediate witnessing followers; it now also suggests the death of two of these leading followers by the mention of Peter's martyrdom and the question about the beloved disciple's death. The latter is, of course, of more significance for the Gospel's community. The "we" of the present generation who endorse his testimony will have to carry on from the beloved disciple. His testimony acts as a bridge between the past and the present generation of witnesses, becoming part of their collective memory. There is a final irony attached to the beloved disciple's testimony. Even though the readers have now been told that Jesus did not predict that this disciple would remain until Jesus came, the writing down of his witness provides for this form of his witness to remain until the coming of Christ.[18] Despite his death, his witness will have a continuing role in the further playing out of the cosmic lawsuit within history. His written witness can play this role even though it is not a final or exhaustive witness. Following typically extravagant rhetorical conventions, the narrator, this time speaking in the first-person singular, comments not only that Jesus did many other things (cf. 20:30—"many other signs . . . which are not written in this book"), but also that if they were all written down, the world itself could not contain the books that would have to be written. Nevertheless, partial, provisional, and incomplete as it is, he can still claim that the witness of this book is true.

Thus, the narrative ending provides a closure to the lawsuit in which Jesus is witness and judge and in which he also embodies the truth to which witness is to be given and by which judgment is to be made. And because the beloved disciple is also the model disciple and because his witness plays its own distinctive role in the ongoing lawsuit, this is a closure that also opens out into the time of the readers. In its reference to the written form of the beloved disciple's witness, the narrative meets readers' demand for a sense of an ending, but it also fulfills their wish for the narrative to continue indefinitely, providing their own lives with a sense of meaning. From now on, this very testimony will play a major role in providing this sense of meaning and in equipping them for their own task of witness.

---

[17] Gaventa, "Archive of Excess," 244.
[18] Cf. Bauckham, "Beloved Disciple," 42.

E. Plot and Characterization Revisited

The relation of the plot and the narrative world in the Fourth Gospel is a complementary one. The discourse of the narrative world is in terms of a cosmic lawsuit, and the plot involves the protagonist in interrogations and trial scenes that result in judgment. In other words, the narrative world implies a system of values that is unfolded in the plot. In particular, the action of the plot reveals the real nature and significance of Jesus' mission, reinforcing in the process his identity and relation to the world set out at the beginning of the narrative.

Our earlier discussion of plot concentrated largely on showing how the lawsuit motif informed each of the major elements of plot, viewed as a causal dynamic sequence whose key moments are commission, conflict, and resolution. Our closer look at key passages and our examination of the opening, middle, and closure of the narrative have reinforced how extensively the cosmic-lawsuit aspect of the narrative discourse informs the development of the plot. Some recent analyses of the plot of the Fourth Gospel have focused on other aspects of the narrative, such as its genre and its literary structure or pattern.[19] While scholars disagree about how exactly plot is to be defined, the working definitions I have used earlier appear to me to be right in stressing the dynamic sequential element and the affect this is designed to produce. Whatever else is distinctive about the plot, it is surely the element of movement or progression that needs to be highlighted, and this will involve causal sequence and conflict and have an affective dimension. The movement of the narrative embraces the characters in it, and so plot and characterization, though distinguishable for some purposes, are also interrelated.[20] Genre and literary structure or pattern may have an indirect bearing on the progression of the action, but a depiction of these is not, on the view advanced here, the same as a depiction of the plot. What drives the action of the Fourth Gospel's narrative forward is Jesus' mission, which produces a divided response involving him in increasing controversy and conflict with the representatives of official Judaism, who plot his death. This death turns out to be the means by which he completes his mission, and together with his resurrection and the giving of the Spirit, the

---

[19] Cf., e.g., F. F. Segovia, "The Journey(s) of the Word of God: A Reading of the Plot of the Fourth Gospel," *Semeia* 53 (1991): 23–54; R. A. Culpepper, "The Plot of John's Story of Jesus," *Int* 49 (1995): 347–58.

[20] See J. Phelan, *Reading People, Reading Plots* (Chicago: University of Chicago Press, 1989).

successful completion of his role enables those who respond positively to his mission to be his successors in a mission that extends beyond the world of the story line. Put all too briefly and abstractly, this expresses some of the major elements of the narrative's progression.

As soon as flesh is put on this skeleton through the narrative's discourse, then Jesus' mission is seen as making God known, and this is characteristically shown through his depiction as a witness. Witness is part of the process of judgment that leads to a divided response, and the increasing conflict takes the shape of interrogations and trials leading to the final trial before Pilate. The sentence of death turns out to be the means of the salvific judgment of life. The resurrection of Jesus to life makes clear that this verdict has been passed on him, and his resurrection brings his followers to the necessary level of belief to be commissioned as witnesses and to receive the promised Spirit, who will also act as an Advocate in the continuing trial that constitutes their mission in the world. The beginning of the narrative also highlights the plot in terms of such themes—life, light, witness, truth, and glory. The middle, with its episode absolutely pivotal for the plot, is formulated in terms of life and death as the positive and negative verdicts in the lawsuit. The closure makes the narrative itself a witness in the continuing lawsuit in which Jesus' followers now have their part to play, and through the witness of the beloved disciple, the closure is tied to the earlier resolution of the plot, with its divine verdict on Jesus' death. Other episodes in the narrative that have not been explicitly treated can be described in relation to these main aspects of the plot. Thus, for example, the gathering of a group of core disciples in 1:39–51 follows causally from the initial witness of John the Baptist and is an essential presupposition for this group's later role; and the first sign and the temple incident in John 2, by showing Jesus' claims about his relationship to key aspects of Jewish religion, provide the context necessary for understanding the disputes that will follow.

This is not to make absolutely everything in the narrative fit this analysis or to make exclusive claims for this reading of the plot. But if an analysis of the plot is concerned with causal sequence and the movement of the action but fails to reckon with the narrative discourse's treatment of it in terms of this dominant motif, it is likely to be deficient. For example, Segovia's treatment of the plot in terms of the journey of the Word from God into the world and then back to God helpfully highlights the motif of this cosmic journey and the geographical journeys of Jesus within his mission. This journey also takes in the element of movement, and descent and ascent are key elements in the narrative discourse. But this reading of the plot is nevertheless in danger of giving the journey itself too great a prominence. It is what this cosmic journey is for, its purpose, that makes the difference to the major actions in the plot; I have argued that this purpose is to inaugurate the judgment of the cosmic lawsuit. Similarly, it is not so much the geographical movement of Jesus to and from Jerusalem, however important this may be to the structuring of the discourse, but what happens in the various locations that provides the causal factors for the plot's progression. Only in passing does Segovia mention the purpose of Jesus' mission—"revealing the Father."[21] And it is significant that when, near the end of his analysis, he depicts how the death of Jesus brings the plot to an effective end, the journey motif disappears and he, too, talks of conflict, of condemnation, of victory and vindication, and brings back into play the notion of the mission of revelation entrusted to Jesus by the Father.[22] Part of the difference between the two discussions is, as suggested earlier, about how much emphasis should be given to the dynamics of action in the definition of plot. Another difference is about how much weight should be given to internal thematic criteria. How should one balance form and content? Clearly a discussion of plot in terms of the cosmic-lawsuit motif stresses thematic content. But, it can be argued, this is entirely appropriate for a work that has such a clear confessional or didactic purpose.[23] The problem of overstressing the thematic is that it can lead to reducing all the elements of the plot to functions in the cosmic lawsuit. The problem of overstressing the formal elements is that it can equally lead to an abstraction that fails to convey the distinctives of the emplotment of this particular narrative.

Culpepper's earlier and later analyses of plot[24] do give weight to the purpose of Jesus' mission, to conflict, and to thematization. He rightly stresses the importance of the varying responses to Jesus for the

---

[21] Segovia, "Journey(s) of the Word of God," 36.

[22] Cf. ibid., 46. A. Reinhartz, *The Word in the World: The Cosmological Tale in the Fourth Gospel* (Atlanta: Scholars Press, 1992), esp.16–28, makes effective use of this cosmic-journey motif, which she describes as the cosmological tale, in depicting the plot of the Fourth Gospel. She integrates the purpose of Jesus' mission, including its aspect of judgment, and the conflict the mission provoked more fully into this cosmological framework.

[23] Phelan, *Reading People, Reading Plots,* argues for giving an appropriate place to thematization in analysis of both plot and characterization and claims that, the more didactic a work, the more significant will be the thematic functions.

[24] Culpepper, *Anatomy,* and "Plot of John's Story."

development of the plot. In the earlier work he discussed the notion of anagnorisis, discovery or recognition,[25] one of the categories in Aristotle's analysis of the plots of tragedies, and in the later study he takes this further, showing how various episodes in the narrative are scenes of attempted, failed, and occasionally successful recognition.[26] Both studies describe Jesus' mission in the plot in terms of revealing the Father, taking away the sin of the world, and empowering the children of God.[27] These observations provide some illumination but also raise questions. What Culpepper calls "recognition scenes" have lost much of their resemblance to Aristotle's category. In Aristotle's analysis, the recognition scene, which most frequently is one major event and happens to the protagonist, comes after the complication of the plot, entails something previously unknown coming to light that changes the whole situation, and is most effective if it is combined with the peripeteia, the reversal of the protagonist's fortunes.[28] But applied to the Fourth Gospel, this category now describes the reactions of all the other characters to the protagonist and is no longer a major turning point but a whole series of lesser progressions, most of which have to be categorized as *failed* recognition scenes. One might, therefore, ask how much is gained by this analysis that could not have been achieved by staying with the narrative's own categories (often expressed in terms of seeing and knowing) of believing and unbelieving responses, or acceptance or rejection of the protagonist's witness in word and deed, as descriptions of what moves the plot along. Again, without wishing to push our own proposal too hard: while Culpepper's three-part description of Jesus' mission has the advantage of employing terminology from the prologue and the latter part of John 1, it has the disadvantage that this terminology is hardly to the fore again in the narrative discourse, where particularly the first description— in terms of making God known—is far more characteristically expressed in the terminology of the lawsuit motif.

Our earlier analysis of the plot was basic, employing the categories of commission, complication, and resolution, but there are other, more intricate variations on such plot description where the focus is on the action in the narrative. Of these, one of the better-known models is the actantial analysis of structuralism, based on the work of A. J. Greimas.[29]

---

[25] Culpepper, *Anatomy,* 81–84.
[26] Culpepper, "Plot of John's Story," 353–56.
[27] Culpepper, *Anatomy,* 88; and "Plot of John's Story," 357.
[28] Cf. Aristotle, *Poet.* 11.4–8.
[29] A. J. Greimas, *Sémantique structurale* (Paris: Larousse, 1966).

In this analysis there are six actants—Sender, Object, Receiver, Helper, Subject, and Opponent—which are related along three axes, those of communication, volition, and power. On the axis of communication, the Sender initiates an action meant to communicate to the Receiver an Object of which the Receiver is in need. This mandate or commission is given by the Sender to a personage who assumes the role of the Subject. Thus, the Subject is the one sent by the Sender to transmit the Object to the Receiver. The axis of volition emphasizes the role of the Subject in fulfilling this commission and dealing with obstacles that might hinder it. On the axis of power, the Subject is viewed in terms of the power needed to move from volition to the completion of the commission. The power is provided in the form of the Helper, and the forces that hinder the completion of the action are seen as the Opponent.

When we apply this model to the Fourth Gospel seen as a lawsuit, the Sender is clearly God the Father. *Father* is used of God 120 times in the narrative; but on only three occasions is the designation accompanied by a descriptive adjective, and one of these (17:25) is δίκαιος, "just" or "righteous" (NRSV). Similarly, if we do not include the use in the title "Son of God," *God* occurs 72 times in the narrative and is only twice accompanied by a descriptive adjective—once ἀληθής (3:33) and once ἀληθινός (17:3; cf. also 7:28). The Object is the trial constituted by Jesus' mission, with its witness issuing in the judgment of either life or death. The Receiver is the world (with Israel as its primary representative), which is put on trial. There are numerous references in the narrative to the world as the Receiver of some aspect of the Object as defined in terms of the trial. The key verse for Jesus' mission makes this clear: "for this I came into the world, to testify to the truth" (18:37; cf. also 8:26; 18:20). Jesus' mission is not only described in general terms, as coming or being sent into the world (cf. 10:36; 11:27; 16:28; 17:18). There is also frequent talk of the light coming into the world; this coming entails judging the world, as the light exposes the darkness (cf. 1:9–10; 3:17–19; 8:12; 9:5, 39; 11:9; 12:31, 46–47), but it is a coming and judgment that are meant to result in life for the world (cf. 6:33, 51). Jesus as the one who is sent, God's authorized representative, is equally clearly the Subject, who carries out the commission in his roles as both chief witness and judge in the lawsuit. Both the Helper and the Opponent take on a variety of forms in the narrative. The Helper primarily includes the other witnesses we have listed in the public ministry—John the Baptist, God, Jesus' works, the Scriptures, the Samaritan woman, and the crowd. These witnesses also include those who are to function as the witnesses in the ongoing lawsuit after Jesus' departure—the disciples, the Paraclete, and the beloved disciple. And it is noteworthy that the language of sending is explicitly employed regarding both the first witness, John the Baptist (cf. 1:6), and the first two continuing witnesses, the disciples and the Paraclete: "As the Father has sent me, so I send you" (20:21; cf. also 17:18); "The Advocate [or 'Helper'], the Holy Spirit, whom the Father will send in my name" (14:26; cf. also 15:26; 16:7). The Opponent includes those who do not receive Jesus' witness, primarily the world (ὁ κόσμος in its negative Johannine sense of the world in opposition to God); "the Jews," sometimes more specifically the chief priests and Pharisees; Pilate; and the ruler of this world, the devil. In the context of the lawsuit, it is no accident that the Opponent includes the devil, who in Jewish and early Christian thought was also known as Satan, the arch-accuser of the people of God (cf. 13:27).

This study's earlier discussions of plot referred to the trials of Jesus, which constitute the counterplot. This counterplot can be described through an actantial model with inverse values. Here the Receiver is Jesus, and the Object is to put him on trial and pass judgment on him. The trial of the public ministry, with its attempts to stone him, and the trial before Pilate, with the judgment of crucifixion, reveal this structure. The ultimate initiator of this action is the devil as Sender. This is the axis of communication. On the axis of volition, the Subject is now those who were meant to be the Receiver in the main plot, that is, the world represented primarily by the "Jews," his own who did not receive him and thereby unwittingly received the countercommission. Along the axis of power in the counterplot, Helper and Opponent are reversed. The Helper includes the law, Judas, and Pilate, while the Opponent is not only Jesus but also those who witness with him in the trial.

Stibbe has also subjected the Fourth Gospel to a creative and illuminating structuralist analysis, employing Greimas's actantial model.[30] He points out that the language of sending appears tailor-made for this Gospel, with its frequent use of πέμπω and ἀποστέλλω, sees the Object in general terms as life, and looks at the counterplot, with its potential for parody, and also micro-plots within the main plot. He appears, however, to have confused in the actantial model the Receiver, to whom the Object comes, with the Subject, who receives the mandate for action, and therefore makes Jesus both the Receiver (instead of the world) and the

---

[30] M. W. G. Stibbe, "'Return to Sender': A Structuralist Approach to John's Gospel," *BibInt* 1 (1993): 189–206; cf. also the version of this material in his *John's Gospel*, 38–53.

Subject.[31] In what Stibbe sees as the central plot statement, John 3:16,[32] it should be observed that it is the world and believers within it who are the Receiver of the Object. In addition, it should be noted that it is not only the language of sending but also that of receiving that makes the Fourth Gospel so appropriate for an actantial analysis. Recognition of this provides confirmation for the identification of the Receiver as the world, represented primarily by Israel. The verb λαμβάνειν is used nineteen times and παραλαμβάνειν once for receiving some aspect of the Object, such as Jesus himself, his words, or the Spirit, and on each of these occasions, it is the world or Israel and those within them who constitute the Receiver. Only once, in 10:18, is λαμβάνειν employed for the mandate or command Jesus receives from the Father. The dominant pattern is set by the language of the prologue, where the true light comes into the world, comes to what was his own, and his own people do not receive him (1:9–11). Yet there are those who do receive him, who in fact receive from his fullness, grace upon grace (1:12, 16). Other passages that illustrate clearly this pattern are 13:20, with its fourfold use of λαμβάνειν—"Very truly, I tell you, whoever receives one whom I send receives me; and whoever receives me receives him who sent me"—and 14:17, with its talk of "the Spirit of truth, whom the world cannot receive." Particularly significant for the prominence of the lawsuit motif in the plot are the four occasions on which testimony or witness is the Object to be received: "Very truly, I tell you, we speak of what we know and testify to what we have seen; yet you do not receive our testimony" (3:11; cf. 3:32–33; 5:34).

There are advantages to defining the Object in the way suggested here. It allows the Object to be more comprehensive in its scope. It takes in life, but it also does more justice to the dark side of the Fourth Gospel's narrative, to the clear indication that God's dealings with the world have a twofold outcome. By seeing the Object simply as life, Stibbe is able to argue that John portrays Jesus as a superhuman, solitary hero without helpers.[33] But when the Object is seen as the trial that God is carrying out with the world and as including the witness that results in a judgment of either life or death, a rather different emphasis emerges. The other witnesses in the trial of the public ministry must now be seen

---

[31] See D. F. Tolmie, *Jesus' Farewell to the Disciples: John 13:1–17:26 in Narratological Perspective* (Leiden: E. J. Brill, 1995), 141, n. 140, for the same criticism.

[32] Cf. Stibbe, "Return to Sender," 193.

[33] Ibid., 194–96.

as helpers, as must the disciples, the beloved disciple, and the Paraclete in the ongoing trial. This does not detract from Jesus' distinctive role as the chief witness and the judge; and certainly, as the plot reaches its climax in the trial before Pilate and the carrying out of its verdict, the focus is almost entirely on Jesus and the sovereign authority with which he fulfills his commission, It does, however, redress the balance somewhat in the continuing debate about how human or superhuman the narrative's characterization of Jesus is. In line with this, it also means that there is more of a parallel between Jesus' role in the cosmic trial and that of the disciples than Stibbe allows.[34] Both are given helpers in their tasks of witnessing. But the difference and uniqueness of Jesus' witness still remain and are captured in the paradoxical assertions of 5:31 and 8:14. On the one hand, Jesus can say that if he testifies about himself, his testimony is not true; thus, for the sake of the conventions of the trial, he appeals to the other witnesses, who constitute the Helper. On the other hand, he can say that even if he testifies on his own behalf, his testimony is true because he knows where he has come from and where he is going. So, strictly speaking, although he is given helpers, there is a sense in which Jesus does not in fact need them because, for the implied author, Jesus' origin and destiny make his witness self-authenticating.

Our comments on characterization will be briefer than what has been said about plot. An analysis of the characterization of any of the figures illuminates the narrative less than a consideration of its main themes. This suggests clearly that their function is ideological. What is ultimately significant about them is whether they are witnesses to the truth or opponents of it, whether they receive the witness of Jesus or refuse it. Characters are defined by their allegiances, and having to make a verdict in the trial makes these allegiances clear. This also indicates that the characters are subordinated to the plot. This does not, however, mean that all characters are merely embodiments of belief or unbelief, or plot functions. The narrative does display characters such as the Samaritan woman, the blind man, and Pilate as distinctive individuals and allows for development in their response to Jesus.

Not surprisingly, the matter of characterization is particularly linked to this Gospel's theme of witness. Indeed, in the conventions of Jewish legal disputes, what was crucial was not so much the facts that were attested by the witness as the nature and character of the witness. "A Jewish court was not so much concerned (and indeed was not equipped) to investigate *facts:* the main question it had to decide was the admissibility

---

[34] Ibid., 204.

and competence of the witnesses."[35] But this narrative's overall trial is metaphorical. To be sure, within this framework it takes up some elements of the Jewish understanding of law, such as the need for two or more witnesses, but it exhibits no signs of needing to be thoroughly consistent in adherence to Jewish legal standards of the day, as would an actual brief. For Christian readers, the narrative, at most, simply needs to be plausible about the aspects of the legal code that it appeals to in developing its larger portrayal of the cosmic lawsuit. It does not attempt to be an actual legal document that would convince those who are unpersuaded by employing all the correct legal conventions and establishing the authority of its witnesses according to these conventions.

These comments provide a reminder that, in reflecting on how the characterization contributes to the credibility of the witnesses, the nature of the intended audience becomes a vital factor. To whom would the witnesses need to be made credible? If, as argued later in this chapter, the implied readers are believers who already know the story of Jesus and are acquainted with the Jewish Scriptures, then the characterization of the witnesses as credible for such readers will be a different matter than for outsiders who need to be convinced of the basic facts of the story. This has relevance also for the characterization of "the Jews." If the audience were unbelieving Jews who needed to be convinced, it might provide shock tactics, but it would not be the most persuasive strategy to characterize them in the predominantly negative way this Gospel does, as representatives of the world hostile to God. Normally, unless an audience is already extremely eager to have its opinions changed, it is unlikely that it wishes to listen to the viewpoint of someone who treats these opinions negatively.

Because it can assume a basic knowledge of the Gospel story, the narrative can treat most of its positive characters who serve as witnesses as already credible through their association with the story. It does not have to go out of its way to establish their integrity or competence.[36] To call on John the Baptist and the beloved disciple as key witnesses, for example, is to be able to rely on the readers' knowledge of such characters—in the case of the former, from the gospel tradition, and in the case of the latter, from their acquaintance with the community and its history.

---

[35] Harvey, *Jesus on Trial*, 47.

[36] If the implied readers are believers, then for all its historical interest, the project of Maccini, *Her Testimony Is True*, to establish whether a first-century Jewish audience would have found the witness of the women in the narrative

Jesus' witness will be treated more extensively in the next chapter.[37] Only a few comments need be made here. First, Jesus' characterization as a witness illuminates the whole of his mission. His words and his deeds (his works, including signs) are part of the witness, but so is his death. The characterization of Jesus as a witness allows this death to be seen as of a piece with his life—indeed, to be the appropriate outcome of that life—since witness entails such a commitment of one's life that one is willing to surrender it, in fidelity to the truth to which one bears witness. In the case of Jesus, the double meaning of μάρτυς is fully displayed. In addition, it is through his witness that the reader discovers who Jesus is, since his testimony is what uncovers his identity. Particularly in cases where there is only one witness and therefore one testimony, everything depends on the reliability and credibility of this one witness, and judges have to make up their mind on this basis. For Jesus' claim that he had come from God, had been sent by the Father, and had seen heavenly things, no other witnesses were available. It is little wonder, then, that the characterization of this witness concentrates on his unique relationship to God, which allows him to be a credible witness. But again, for whom would this characterization be credible? For unbelievers, precisely this aspect of Jesus' portrayal would have been in dispute in the first place. Only if someone is already inclined to grant Jesus some special status would characterizing him in this fashion be likely to enhance his credibility.

Equally important for the effectiveness of the narrative as a whole is the credibility of the narrator, which is linked to the witness of the beloved disciple. In this way the beloved disciple is the disguise through which the real author becomes the implied author. Section D, above, has already discussed elements of the witness of the beloved disciple; what is being claimed by his depiction will be treated later.[38] Here it is worth noting that his intimate relationship with Jesus, which is reinforced with every mention of him, establishes the credibility of this key witness. Not only is he "the disciple whom Jesus loved"; as is often noted, his relationship with Jesus is also portrayed at one point, when he is reclining in Jesus' lap, as indeed paralleling the intimate relationship of Jesus with God (cf. the use of κόλπος in 1:18 and 13:23). In addition,

---

credible according to their legal system, may well be beside the point in terms of the narrative's own presentation

[37] See ch. 5, sec. B; for the roles of the disciples and the Spirit as witnesses, see ch. 5, sec. F.

[38] See ch. 8, sec. B.

he is characterized as a credible witness because he is present at the decisive moments in the plot—Jesus' prediction of his betrayal, Jesus' death with its constituting of a new community and its provision of life, and the discovery of the empty tomb. If the anonymous disciple in 1:35 is also to be taken as the beloved disciple, then he is also present throughout the mission of Jesus. His stature is further enhanced when he becomes a replacement for Jesus in relation to Jesus' mother (cf. 19:26–27). The portrayal of his unique personal knowledge and experience thus builds up the *ethos* of the implied author's witness through the beloved disciple. As Bauckham has emphasized, this characterization of the beloved disciple as a perceptive witness makes him the ideal author.[39]

The anonymity of this disciple may have two major functions.[40] On the one hand, for later readers, the lack of a specific name to distinguish sharply his identity from theirs encourages their identification with this unnamed character and invites them to share in his perceptive witness and therefore also the implied author's point of view.[41] On the other hand, for the earliest readers, too, making the beloved disciple an anonymous character may well have contributed to the characterization of him as ideal author. Bauckham argues that this disciple would not have been unknown by name to the original readers, so for them his anonymity would not have been meant to have the effect of concealing his identity. It would, rather, have had the effect of distinguishing him from the named characters in the narrative and preparing for the disclosure at the end that this character is indeed distinctive—he is the one to whom authorship is attributed.[42]

F. The Lawsuit and Genre

The effectiveness and impact of the narrative of the Fourth Gospel are due to the match between its content and its form. It is a narrative that asserts that the truth about God, Christ, and life is to be seen in terms of the metaphor of a cosmic lawsuit, and it displays this assertion by making its discourse and plot have Jesus on trial, a trial in which the

---

[39] Bauckham, "Beloved Disciple," 35–42.

[40] Tovey, *Narrative Art and Act,* 143–47, lists five possible functions of this anonymity, including the two featured here. His other three have too many problematic aspects to be convincing.

[41] Cf. D. R. Beck, "The Narrative Function of Anonymity in Fourth Gospel Characterization," *Semeia* 63 (1993): 143–58, although Beck formulates the function of the anonymity in terms of enhancing the beloved disciple's role as the paradigm of true discipleship.

[42] Bauckham, "Beloved Disciple," 43–44.

other characters (and, by extension, the readers) have to come to a verdict and are invited to become witnesses. In this way it not only makes a truth claim but also enables its readers to experience this claim. To put it the other way around, it not only narrates a story that involves its readers; it does so in such a way that they cannot escape its truth claim. One of the main ways in which it achieves this is the presentation of itself as a testimony, a written narrative testimony, in the trial.

The Fourth Gospel is not simply about a trial; it is itself a testimony in the trial. In 21:24 μαρτυρία refers to the Gospel's written account. In everyday usage of the term, testimony always takes the form of a narrative about what has been witnessed. This testimony about the life, death, and resurrection of Jesus also takes the form of a narrative. And here the narrative's extended trial metaphor is what brings together its historical and theological aspects. The juridical ties together "testimony as confession (of faith) and testimony as narration (of facts)."[43]

Given the extent to which the lawsuit motif shapes this Gospel, one might be tempted to suggest that the genre of the Gospel is that of a testimony or defense speech in a trial. This would, however, be to jump to a wrong conclusion. The Fourth Gospel does describe itself as witness, but it is a category mistake to see this as a description of its genre.[44] All testimony involves narration, but this narration could be within a variety of forms or genres. Narrative can indeed be seen as a subdivision of forensic rhetoric. One element of a witness's speech was the exposition of the facts of the case in the form of a narrative—the *narratio*—and Lucian could say that "the body of a work of history is simply an extended *narratio*."[45] Testimony is the mode or function of this Gospel's narrative, the perlocutionary effect that the narrative itself makes explicit. But when genre is defined in terms of both form and content, then the actual genre of this narrative about Jesus is ancient biography. All the canonical Gospels belong to a subgenre of the *bíos*.[46] The form that the Fourth

---

[43] Ricoeur, "Hermeneutics of Testimony," 142. In Ricoeur's terms, the quasi-juridical dimension of testimony mediates between the quasi-empirical and the religious dimensions.

[44] Cf. E. Arens, *Christopraxis: A Theology of Action* (Minneapolis: Fortress, 1995), 97: "Different types of texts can function as testimonies; that is, they can be produced, used, interpreted and received as testimonies. . . . Testimony does not form its own literary genre."

[45] Lucian, *Hist. conscr.* 5.

[46] See R. A. Burridge, *What Are the Gospels? A Comparison with Graeco-Roman Biography* (Cambridge: Cambridge University Press, 1992), esp. 41–42 on the distinction between mode and genre, and 220–39 on the Fourth Gospel.

Evangelist's witness takes and the content of this witness are a life of Jesus. It is simply that the emplotment of this ancient biography is dominated by the motif of the trial. This signals that this biography has, like other ancient biographies, an apologetic and polemical function.

> Biography was from its inception a genre that found its home in controversy. Biographers . . . were self-conscious mediators of specific traditions, and their works had both apologetic and polemical aims, apologetic in defending, affirming, and sometimes correcting opinion about a hero; polemical in suggesting by the strength of the defense, and sometimes by outright attack, the unworthiness of other traditions by comparison.[47]

Clearly, John's biography draws out the significance of Jesus' career in a context where this significance is under dispute.

This biography's function as testimony is integral here, since testimony is given by one who has direct knowledge or experience of some person or event and is therefore in a position to speak about these when they are in dispute. In a lawsuit this ability enables the witness to speak for or against an accused person.[48] Testimony is the speech act produced in such a setting. When the dispute is philosophical or religious, testimony represents the truth of the convictions held by witnesses. Since these are frequently in the face of opposing views, testimony can include speaking against such views as false. All this underlines that narrative as testimony is not simply a recalling of history but a reinterpreting of history that transforms it by investing it with a particular significance as it bears on contested claims. The Fourth Gospel, then, is a subgenre of ancient biography;[49] its narrative testimony recalls traditions about the mission of Jesus in the light of the disputes that have arisen in the setting of its author and in the light of this author's convictions about where the truth lies in the disputes.

G. The Lawsuit and the Reader

The narrative discourse does not itself explicitly draw together all the elements in the lawsuit motif to make a coherent synthesis in the way chapter 1 of this study attempts to do. But such features as the positioning of the motif at the beginning and the end of the narrative, the context and shape given to the public ministry, the dominance of the

---

[47] P. Cox, *Biography in Late Antiquity: A Quest for the Holy Man* (Berkeley: University of California Press, 1983), 135.

[48] Cf. Trites, *Concept of Witness,* 9.

[49] For a fuller discussion of ancient biography in relation to the truth of the Fourth Gospel's narrative, see ch. 8, below.

Roman trial, and the motif's major contribution to the depiction of the roles of Jesus and the disciples encourage the reader to make precisely such a coherent synthesis. In particular, the narrative frame has the function of helping the reader to arrive at a synthesis. The witness motif at the beginning of the Gospel in 1:7–8, 15—however extensively one believes this is related to the rest of the prologue—and at the end of the Gospel in 21:24 means that the lawsuit frames the narrative. The similar *inclusio* on the lawsuit motif at the beginning and end of the public ministry of Jesus (cf. 1:19; 12:47–49) serves as a frame within a frame. The overall frame of a narrative establishes its dominant evaluative or ideological perspective on the world it describes. The world of the Fourth Gospel is clearly to be seen in terms of a trial on a cosmic scale that determines the function of its plot and characters. But the frame of a narrative has a further significance. It provides the transition from the world of the reader to the world of the narrative and vice-versa.

> The importance of the problem of the frame, that is, of the borders of the artistic work, is evident. In a work of art, whether it be a work of literature, a painting, or a work of some other art form, there is presented to us a special world, with its own space and time, its own ideological system and its own standards of behavior. In relation to that world, we assume (at least in our first perceptions of it) the position of an alien spectator, which is necessarily external. Gradually, we enter into it, becoming more familiar with its standards, accustoming ourselves to it, until we begin to perceive this world as if from within, rather than from without. We, as readers or observers, now assume a point of view internal to the particular work. Then we are faced with the necessity of leaving that world and returning to our own point of view, the point of view from which we had to a large extent disengaged ourselves while we were experiencing (reading, seeing, and so forth) the artistic work.[50]

In this way the frame helps the reader to enter into and to exit from the narrative world. In the Fourth Gospel, crossing the threshold into the world of the lawsuit and moving from an external to an internal perspective are aided by the narrator's use of the first-person plural in the prologue (1:14, 16). Readers are in this way included as among those who have true insight into the main character in the trial: "and we have seen his glory. . . . From his fullness we have all received, grace upon grace." The transition back into the world of the reader is achieved in a similar fashion. The readers have had their verdict about Jesus' witness reinforced, have seen the need to become witnesses themselves by their immersion in the world of the narrative, and have been prepared for the

---

[50] B. Uspensky, *A Poetics of Composition* (trans. C. Zavarin and S. Wittig; Berkeley: University of California Press, 1973), 137.

return to an external point of view by the death of the two dominant representatives of the authorial point of view in the story—Jesus and the beloved disciple.[51] Now they are again included in the narrator's community through the use of the first-person plural as they leave the narrative: "and we know that his testimony is true" (21:24).[52] The frame, therefore, both highlights the symbolic world of the narrative as that of God's lawsuit and, by its use of "we" language, invites readers to share the perspective and values of such a world and then take these back into their own world.

The framing, then, plays an integral part in the reader's construal of the text. "A fiction is presented to us in the form of a narration . . . that guides us as our own active narrativity seeks to complete the process that will achieve a story."[53] What Scholes calls the reader's narrativity entails the ability to make connections and to see significant relations between the various elements in a narrative. In this regard, the Fourth Gospel can be considered a successful narrative, avoiding the extremes of either underspecification or overspecification.[54] On the one hand, the reader does not have to invent any details to construct a coherent story in terms of the trial. The frame and cues are all there. On the other hand, the narrative is not so explicit that it supplies all the connections and leaves the reader with no work to do. This activity required of the reader compensates for the coercion exercised by the narrative regarding its ideological point of view and allows the reader the freedom to add connections and draw implications that the story does not make fully explicit. The narrative also encourages the reader to make the connections necessary to view the whole in terms of a lawsuit the resonances it evokes with the reader's knowledge of Scripture and, as we shall see, with the experiences of the community from which it emerged.

All persuasive discourse, including that in narrative form, makes its audience judges. The ancient rhetoricians understood this. Aristotle believed that the point of rhetoric was to bring people to make a decision: "The object of rhetoric is judgment [κρίσις]," and "he who has to be persuaded is a judge."[55]

He also held that the goal of persuasion was belief, that people believe what they see or think they see, and that the speaker enables his audience

---

[51] Cf. ibid., 148.
[52] Cf. Culpepper, *Anatomy*, 46–47, on the ending as part of the frame.
[53] R. Scholes, *Semiotics and Interpretation* (New Haven: Yale University Press, 1982), 60.
[54] Leitch, *What Stories Are*, 35–41.
[55] Aristotle, *Rhet.* 2.1.2; 2.18.1.

to "see" by establishing or appearing to establish the truth through the various means of persuasion.[56] But ultimately the audience determines the success of a speaker's efforts at persuasion. It functions as judge, with the speaker always, in an important sense, the one on trial. Cicero spelled out the latter aspect: "Judgment is passing upon us as often as we speak."[57] This is literally the case in forensic discourse. But Cicero also recognized that in successful persuasion there comes the point at which the audience has been won over and no longer criticizes or judges because it has already given the speaker its verdict.[58]

If all persuasive discourse, including its narrative form, makes its readers jurors, then a narrative that is itself a testimony in the trial it presents highlights this process. Particularly in the case of the Fourth Gospel, the implied readers as jurors are not detached, neutral observers.[59] As they experience the events of the narrative unfolding, they are drawn into its world and its clash of values and forced to take a stance in relation to its chief character and his claims. The injunction of 7:24—"Do not judge by appearances, but judge with right judgment"—is, in effect, addressed also to readers. In context this refers to judging Jesus not simply by the outward regulation of the law—in this case, the Sabbath law, which, by the same criterion, "the Jews" break anyway by circumcising on the Sabbath—but by seeing in his work the realization of God's eschatological activity (cf. 5:17). Judging with right judgment will mean that a person recognizes that Jesus' teaching is not his own but God's (7:16–17) and that he is true or reliable because he seeks God's honor or glory rather than his own (7:18). Resolving to do the will of God, which in John means having faith, will enable such a right judgment (7:17).[60] Thus, the call to judge rightly is a call to believe—in line with the purpose of the Gospel as a whole.

But the role of readers as jurors is not a simple one. They are judges who assess the attitudes and actions of all the characters, under the guidance, to be sure, of the implied author's viewpoint in the discourse. They are judges who are expected to be familiar with the basic facts of this case and to be in sympathy with the stance and witness of its main character. They are therefore judges who have already come to a basic conviction, and the process of judging, as the issues with which they are

---

[56] Cf. Aristotle, *Rhet.* 1.2.6.
[57] Cicero, *De or.* 1.123–25.
[58] Cf. *Or. Brut.* 210.
[59] Cf. Culpepper, *Anatomy*, 105, n. 19. Harvey, *Jesus on Trial*, 17, speaks of the readers being challenged "to reach their own verdict."
[60] Cf. esp. Pancaro, *The Law*, 368–79.

familiar are retried in their presence, confirms that initial conviction. This is a reminder that the reader's judgment does not take place in isolation or in the abstract.

> Judgment requires a community: no judge can operate outside a legal system; no just weighing can take place on scales not calibrated with other scales; and nobody would trust a real estate agent who lacked experience in comparing appraisals with other agents. Perhaps the legal metaphor is least misleading, because it reminds us that all judgment is pointless unless it can be shared with other judges who rely in turn on their past experiences.[61]

Hence, the reader as judge is expected to be able to share the judgment of the community represented by the narrator and declare about the narrative testimony of the beloved disciple, *"we know that his testimony is true"* (21:24b).

But the jurors are also the accused, the judges who are judged. Since their basic conviction is still in the process of formation, the narrative's exploration of God's claim on the world, with its deep sifting of all allegiances and its reversal of the usual criteria of judgment, puts their own attitudes and commitments on trial. After all, the implied author depicts various types of faith and seeks to bring his implied readers to what he considers to be authentic faith. There is a further aspect to the jurors' role. As their judgment is reinforced and their faith refined, they are expected to identify with the characters in the narrative who undergo a similar experience. Like the disciples, they are being prepared to be effective witnesses. Because of the nature of his witness, Jesus also becomes judge. Because of the nature of their judgment, readers can become witnesses. The process of evaluation and assessment is molding them to be advocates in what they know to be an ongoing case.

The implied readers of the Fourth Gospel, then, are like a jury. For the most part, however, the implied author assumes that they will have been convinced by the rightness of his case. By being shown the story of Jesus from the perspective of this narrative, they can be strengthened in their own verdicts about Jesus, have any defective judgments set straight, and be better equipped for their own role as witnesses as the cosmic lawsuit continues to unfold in history. But how does this construal of the nature of the Fourth Gospel's jury fit with the Gospel's own statement of purpose? In considering the intended effect of the narrative on the implied reader, clearly 20:30–31 should come into play, since these verses spell out the persuasive aim of this presentation,

---

[61] W. C. Booth, *The Company We Keep: An Ethics of Fiction* (Berkeley: University of California Press, 1988), 72.

shaped by the lawsuit, and directly address the readers in doing so. Up to this point, our discussion has assumed a particular reading of this key passage. But because this is disputed territory, my reading of the passage and my reasons for this reading should be made explicit. The following discussion will treat four main issues—the scope of this statement of purpose, the nature of the belief it is hoped to elicit, the way in which the content of this belief should be construed, and the relationship between this statement of purpose and the narrative discourse in which it is embedded.

"Now Jesus did many other signs in the presence of his disciples, which are not written in this book. But these are written . . ." "These" (ταῦτα) refers to the signs that have been written, in contrast to those too numerous to record. The contrast to the term "other" in this verse is in the context of the accounts of the resurrected Jesus' appearances to his disciples, and Jesus' response to Thomas, "Have you believed because you have seen me? Blessed are those who have not seen and yet have come to believe" (20:29), suggests that the signs that have been written to enable belief have as their primary referent the empty-tomb story and the resurrection appearances, from earlier in John 20, that brought about the belief of the beloved disciple, Mary Magdalene, the disciples, and Thomas. But the "in this book" formulation of v. 30 indicates that, by extension, the signs that have been written would naturally also include the signs from the public ministry in the earlier part of the narrative.

So, are only the miraculous events that have been recorded in the book designed to produce belief? This would be very difficult to maintain, since clearly Jesus' words are also meant to be believed and to result in life (cf., e.g., 5:24; 6:63, 68). It is more likely that, in this summary statement of purpose about the book as a whole, σημεῖον, *sign*, has the further connotation of being able to represent Jesus' mission as a whole. This mission is depicted in terms of words and deeds, discourses/disputes and signs, and either of the two is able to stand for the whole. This view gains support from the fact that in 12:37–38 Jesus' performance of signs that did not result in belief is explained in terms of Isa 53:1, which speaks of believing "our message [ἀκοή]" or report.[62] Further, both ways of viewing Jesus' mission can be linked to the one term *works* (ἔργα). The signs are seen as works in 5:36; 7:3; 9:3–4; 10:25, 32, 37–38; 14:10–11; and 15:24, while the words of Jesus are closely associated with

---

[62] Cf. T. Söding, "Die Schrift als Medium des Glaubens: Zur hermeneutischen Bedeutung von Joh 20,30f," in *Schrift und Tradition. FS J. Ernst* (ed. K. Backhaus and F. G. Untergassmair; Paderborn: F. Schöningh, 1996), 362.

such works in 10:25–27, 14:10, and 15:22–24. In two places—4:34 and 17:3—the whole of Jesus' mission, both his signs and discourses, can be categorized under the one term *work*. There are good reasons, then, for thinking that when the term *signs* is used in a summary of the purpose of what is written in this book, it too can draw in the whole revelatory aspect of Jesus' mission.

The witness of this book to the revelatory activity of Jesus in the context of a cosmic lawsuit is meant to produce belief. But is this initial belief, and so is the purpose evangelistic? Or is it meant to produce continuance in belief, and so are the implied readers already Christians? A textual issue plays a large part in this discussion. Does the original text of 20:31 have πιστεύητε,[63] a present subjunctive, or πιστεύσητε,[64] an aorist subjunctive? The former would suggest continuation in belief, while the latter would more strongly indicate an initial coming to belief. The textual evidence for the former is stronger.[65] Whether tense alone is sufficient to decide the purpose of the Gospel may be another matter, but at least the resolution of the textual question allows believers to be seen as among the implied readers. The other two issues also bear on the implied readership and must be dealt with before we reach a firm conclusion.

What is it that the readers are meant to believe? Is it that "Jesus is the Christ, the Son of God" or that "the Christ, the Son of God, is Jesus"? One might at first wonder whether there is any significant difference, but Carson has argued that if Jesus is the predicate rather than the subject of the clause, then the Gospel is not answering the question "Who is Jesus?" but "Who is the Messiah?" and such a question would be asked by unconverted Jews, proselytes, and God-fearers, for whom the category "Messiah" would be of interest and importance.[66] While this reading is syntactically possible, it is much more likely and in line with the pattern elsewhere in the Gospel that Jesus is the subject of the clause.[67] Certainly, the Gospel as a whole does not read as if it addresses those who already know what the titles "Christ" and "Son of God" entail and

---

[63] So 𝔓66vid ℵ* B Θ.

[64] So A C D L W ℵ2.

[65] See esp. G. D. Fee, "On the Text and Meaning of John 20,30–31," in *The Four Gospels, 1992* (3 vols.; ed. F. van Segbroek et al.; Leuven: Leuven University Press, 1992), 3:2193–2205.

[66] D. A. Carson, "The Purpose of the Fourth Gospel: John 20:31 Reconsidered," *JBL* 106 (1987): 639–51. He is followed by Maccini, *Her Testimony Is True*, 32; and Tovey, *Narrative Art and Act*, 88.

[67] Cf. Fee, "Text and Meaning of John 20, 30–31," 3:2205.

who simply need to be persuaded that Jesus is a worthy candidate for such titles. Rather, again and again, what appears to be at issue is the identity of Jesus, and the implied author is at pains to make clear what it means to claim that Jesus is the sort of Messiah who is Son of God, with all the connotations of a unique relationship to God that the latter designation bears in the discourse.[68] The narrative presupposes that the mission of Jesus has provoked different judgments about who exactly he is. Its literary retrial both narrates these divisions of opinion and attempts to reinforce its point of view about his identity—a point of view that is made explicit from the start, in the prologue. The implied reader is expected to share this point of view from the outset in order to appreciate the ironies of the unfolding story and to be confirmed in this perspective by the time the narrative reaches its conclusion. It is from this perspective also that implied readers are expected to identify in particular with the role of Jesus' followers in the narrative.

It could still be replied that this stance is only necessary for readers to adopt temporarily while entering the narrative and that they might therefore not necessarily accept the implied author's point of view before they begin reading. But now we are talking about possible real readers. The implied reader, on the other hand, is expected to share the dominant point of view. If the implied reader were envisaged primarily as someone who needed to be converted, we can easily think of quite different rhetorical strategies that would have taken into account his or her initial stance and therefore have been more likely to be effective. In constructing the implied reader, the way in which arguments have been selected and deployed in the narrative discourse is, after all, most telling. Here the implied reader is far better seen as someone who knows of the original outcome of Jesus' mission and trial but now needs to be given a perspective on this that will support an allegiance at odds with the verdict of official Judaism both on Jesus' identity and on the claims of his followers about this. The amount of space that the narrative in John 13–17 gives to addressing explicitly the concerns of Jesus' followers reinforces this view.[69]

---

[68] This is to agree with de Jonge, *Jesus: Stranger from Heaven and Son of God,* 84, that "Son of God" is an interpretative comment on "Christ," a title that is inadequate by itself for this Gospel.

[69] Fuller discussions of the implied reader reach a similar conclusion. Cf. Culpepper, *Anatomy,* 205–27: "Analysis of the gospel's indications of its intended audience confirms, or at least complements, much of the recent research which has concluded that John was written for a particular community of believers"

Too many scholars who have noted the trial motif have then jumped to the conclusion that the writer who employed it must have been anxious to prove a case about Jesus to unbelievers and to convince them by the sort of evidence produced in the Gospel.[70] Several observations can be made about such a reading. It may at first sight appear that the account of the public ministry lends itself to such an interpretation. But even if this were the case, this would be to confuse the narrative of the public ministry with the Gospel as a whole. But, as our readings of the disputes in the public ministry have suggested, they are scarcely formulated to make a straightforward case to unbelievers. They are more for the sake of believers, so that they can be confirmed in their belief by seeing the issues they have faced in their time about Jesus' identity replayed in the time of Jesus. Even some of those who recognize that the narrative is in some sense a literary retrial still tend to read the account of the public ministry without doing justice to the two-level nature of the narrative. To appreciate the issues in the disputes, readers need already to have some idea of what it is to hold that Jesus is Son of God in the Johannine sense. The disputes hardly set out to introduce and prove this case about Jesus' identity to those who know little about him. They assume it, know it is disputed, and defend it in the face of objections and misunderstandings. Jesus announces his identity, and then this is supported by his appeal to the variety of witnesses. The influence of Isa 40–55 on the narrative is also evident here. Just as in Deutero-Isaiah the lawsuit with the nations was played out for the sake of its Jewish audience, not to convince the nations but to reassure Israel, so in the Fourth Gospel the controversy with "the Jews" is rehearsed for the sake of its Christian audience, not to convince Jewish unbelievers but to reassure believers and to give them perspective in the face of opposition to their confession about Jesus.

Such a conclusion is compatible with the history of reception of this Gospel, which has often proved effective as an evangelistic document. A written testimony that was produced for one purpose could also prove to be useful for other purposes. Once the document became detached

---

(p. 225). Also M. Davies, *Rhetoric and Reference in the Fourth Gospel* (Sheffield: JSOT Press, 1992), 349–75: "The readers implied by the text of the Fourth Gospel, therefore, were Christians who already knew the basic story of Jesus" (358).

[70] Cf., e.g., Harvey, *Jesus on Trial*, 17; Trites, *Concept of Witness*, 78; Maccini, *Her Testimony Is True*, 19, 31, although he is not prepared to limit the readership entirely to unbelievers (cf. 32).

from its original setting, inevitably there would be occasions when its witness came to those who were unbelievers or were encountering the claims about Jesus for the first time. Although, like the lawsuit motif in Isaiah, the trial motif in John was intended primarily to give assurance to insiders, clearly the Gospel's overall story and elements in it, such as its accounts of individuals encountering Jesus and being challenged to respond in belief, have turned out to be persuasive for those who encountered its testimony as outsiders.

Nevertheless, the implied readers of the Gospel are believers. The Fourth Gospel sets out its convictions about Jesus in the prologue and then illustrates, confirms, and reinforces these convictions in the narrative as they are being contested. Implied readers are invited to make the same journey and to have belief strengthened in the process. This conclusion should not, however, mean that we envisage these readers to be of only one sort. There is evidence in the text that such readers could have been Jewish or Samaritan or Greek, that they might have been well informed about Judaism or needed from the narrator explanations of some basic terms and aspects of Judaism.[71] The cosmic aspect of the lawsuit particularly lends itself to the universalization of the scope of the implied readership, and it has enabled a variety of real readers to feel themselves addressed by the "you" to whom the narrative speaks. If, as the prologue underlines, the narrative is about a process of judgment involving God and the world, then its issues transcend their settings in both the mission of Jesus and in the experience of the community represented by the narrator. The necessity of accepting the witness of Jesus and aligning one's life with God's verdict in the trial remains for those who encounter the narrative's testimony, wherever and whenever they are situated in space and time.[72]

The narrative also leaves room for readers to enter its world at various points on its faith continuum—as those whose verdict needs more appropriate formulation, as those whose verdict needs to be reinforced, as those who have made their verdict and become witnesses, and as

---

[71] On the heterogeneous nature of the readership implied by the text, see Culpepper, *Anatomy*, 225; C. R. Koester, "The Spectrum of Johannine Readers," in *"What Is John?": Readers and Readings of the Fourth Gospel* (ed. F. F. Segovia; Atlanta: Scholars Press, 1996), 5–19.

[72] Reinhartz, *Word in the World*, 38, makes a similar point about the "cosmological tale" of the Fourth Gospel: "It is . . . by universalizing the specific temporal and spatial boundaries of the historical and ecclesiological tales that the cosmological tale allows and encourages readers to situate themselves within the gospel and to see themselves as its addressees."

those who fall into more than one of these categories. Readers can therefore identify with characters in the narrative who have to pass their verdict, with the disciples who are commissioned to become witnesses, but also—contrary to expectations that might be raised by the discourse's emphases on Jesus as a unique divine figure—with Jesus himself. As we have seen, the importance of Jesus' role as witness in the climactic Roman trial narrative and the significant fact that the Gospel depicts it after setting out the disciples' task as witnesses in the Farewell Discourse mean that Jesus on trial is to be seen as a model for the disciples on trial.

The discussion of framing that opened this section suggested that the relation between text and reader was a movement from the world of the reader into the world of the text (where the reader takes on temporarily the role of the implied reader) and then back from the text's world to the reader's world (which is now seen in the light of, and shaped by, the text's world). Does this mean that since the narrative claims to be reliable, such a reader has to accept all its evaluations? As testimony, the narrative still has to submit to judgment. But is the only judgment the reader is allowed to make a completely positive one? As soon as we take into account, as we must, that the implied reader is always concretized in a real reader, our notion of the movement between text and reader has to be more complex. The real reader, "in actualizing the role of the reader prestructured in and through the text, transforms it."[73] Such a reader is not simply a victim of the narrative discourse and the implied author's persuasive strategy. Real readers have the opportunity for multiple readings of the narrative, can become aware of the ways in which they are drawn into the world of the text, can distance themselves, and can ask questions about the validity of that world and its values. They can set up a continuing conversation between their own convictions and those in the text. They can become resistant readers, reading against the grain of the text and its values in order to retain their own independent identity and values. The judgments of the jury of real readers can be as varied as the jurors themselves, ranging from full acceptance to critical acceptance to outright rejection of the narrative's witness.[74] At this point all that needs to be underlined is that whether the readers we have in mind are implied or real readers, they are put in the position

---

[73] Ricoeur, *Time and Narrative,* 3:171.

[74] For reflections on the absence of real readers from reader-response approaches to John and for an attempt to fill the gap, see J. L. Staley, *Reading with a Passion* (New York: Continuum, 1995).

of judges by the Gospel's witness and, from the perspective of this witness, are also being judged as they reveal their basic allegiances by the nature of their readings. We will later examine more fully to what extent one can be both accepting and critical of the Gospel's witness and thereby reveal more of the basic stance entailed in our own reading.[75]

---

[75] See ch. 8, sec. A.

chapter five

THE LAWSUIT
and the THEOLOGY *of the*
FOURTH GOSPEL

The move from literary issues in the previous chapter to theological concerns in this need not be seen as an abrupt jump. In many ways it takes up and extends a key category within narrative criticism, namely, point of view. This is a term that we have already employed from time to time to indicate the perspective of the implied author, which the implied readers are expected to adopt toward the main character and the values this character embodies and toward the events of the story. Literary critics enumerate a variety of aspects of point of view; this study has been referring to the ideological, or evaluative, point of view. For example, the sentence of death carried out on Jesus is, from the implied author's point of view, to be evaluated not as humiliation or shame but as the supreme moment of Jesus and of God's honor or glory. Characterization, irony, symbols, and motifs all communicate the implied author's evaluative point of view. Clearly, what God and Scripture say will also have a vital function, since by definition they establish norms and standards for judgment. And if the main character is presented as one with God and as fulfilling Scripture, then obviously this underlines that his perspective is normative within the Gospel's narrative world. What this chapter is inquiring into, then, in a more sustained way is the evaluative point of view of the implied author in certain areas of theological concern. To put it another way, we are attempting to explore the witness of this narrative testimony to essential theological components of its lawsuit motif. The key areas for investigation turn out to be a conveniently Johannine seven, matching the more conventional categories of theology; Christology; eschatology and soteriology; revelation; pneumatology and Christian existence; the relation to Israel, the law, and the Scriptures; and the stance toward the world.

Describing John's theology systematically is notoriously difficult to do because its themes are so intricately interwoven. Nevertheless, the attempt is worth making for the sake of clarity in our discussion. This is not meant to be in any way a comprehensive description of Johannine thought but a means both of bringing together our findings so far and of reflecting further on their implications in order to show how the lawsuit motif affects all the main areas of this Gospel's theology. One danger is, of course, that this could still all too easily develop into a comprehensive analysis. For reasons of length, therefore, much of what follows will need to remain suggestive rather than comprehensive. Another danger is that the beliefs and perspectives that have been woven so creatively into a dramatic narrative will be distorted by being artificially isolated from this narrative and therefore from each other. A related danger is to assume that stating a set of ideas deduced from the narrative is the same as penetrating to its essential content or that its message defined in this way can somehow substitute for the narrative itself. These hazards remain constant. They may be an inevitable consequence of such an analysis.

Three factors may help prevent these hazards from obscuring the impact of the lawsuit motif as a whole in its narrative setting. The first is simply to remain aware of the dangers. The second is to keep in mind throughout this discussion the findings of our earlier chapters about the shaping of the whole narrative and its discourse by this motif. The third is to appreciate the overlap and links with other areas of thought that will become apparent in the examination of any one. But I do not want to be too apologetic about an analysis of the Gospel in terms of its theological themes. Just as a historical and sociological investigation can be valid in its own right and at the same time shed light on the narrative as we now have it, so asking about the theological perspective that informs the narrative and its message has its own legitimacy.

One other factor needs underlining, even at the risk of stating the obvious. The theological world of thought presupposed by the narrative's leading motif is that of the Jewish Scriptures. In particular, Deutero-Isaiah's lawsuits or trial speeches between Yahweh and Israel and between Yahweh and the nations inform much of this narrative's discourse. As we have seen, this does not mean that this world of thought is simply taken over wholesale. It does mean, however, that, whatever the modifications playing themselves out in the narrative, we should assume that the primary framework for understanding them remains the perspective of the beliefs underpinning the Scriptures and their development within Second Temple Judaism. In these Scriptures the lawsuit is part of a covenant relationship between Yahweh and Israel, in which both parties in the covenant call each other to account. In Isa 40–55 Yahweh takes the initiative and calls Israel—and, in an extension of this relationship, the nations—to trial, but in the process Yahweh is willing also to be put on trial. For both Yahweh and Israel, the lawsuit is a vehicle for contesting whether the other party has kept its part of the covenant, has remained faithful to its covenantal pledges. Especially in regard to the role of the law and the temple in this relationship, the witness of Jesus in the Fourth Gospel effects a decisive disruption in what had previously been thought about the covenant. But such innovations can only be understood if we keep in mind the covenantal arrangement within which they originated.

A. The God of the Trial

The reminder of the previous paragraph is particularly relevant when it comes to the narrative's testimony to God. If what dominates the use of the cosmic lawsuit in Isaiah is the monotheistic claim that Yahweh is the only true God, it is scarcely likely that, in taking up the perspective of this material, the Fourth Gospel would abandon the claim that is at its heart. In other words, from the implied author's point of view, the claims for the identity of Jesus made in his narrative are unlikely to have been considered any threat to, or undermining of, Israel's fundamental confession of belief in one God. One of the distinctives of this Gospel is that its testimony about God is so intricately linked to its testimony about Christ and vice versa.[1] The talk about a cosmic lawsuit provides a reminder that, for all the focus on Christ in this narrative, it is by no means christomonist (i.e., employing Christ as a regulative principle to the exclusion of other aspects of theology). An investigation from this angle has to start, at least formally, with God because a cosmic lawsuit is all about the relationship between God and the world.

---

[1] See, e.g., Barrett, *Gospel according to St. John,* 97–98: "The gospel is about Jesus, but Jesus (if one may put it so) is about God. The gospel is in the fullest sense of the term a *theological* work. . . . John . . . was writing about Jesus in terms of God, and, correspondingly, about God in terms of Jesus."

Furthermore, there would be no talk about the world—and Israel as part of it—being brought to trial if the implied author did not share the belief that God had the right to do so. The presupposition is clearly that, as its Creator, God has sovereign rights over this world and that all humanity, especially Israel, with whom God has entered into a special covenantal relationship, owe God acknowledgment and allegiance. The entire motif of trial and judgment is based on such a notion of God, and there is no dispute between Jesus and the opposition on this. The dispute is, rather, about whether this trial is now taking place with Jesus as its divine agent. The language of the prologue, however, makes the assumptions of the lawsuit explicit. God's Logos, who was God (1:1c), is the one through whom all things, or the world, came into being (vv. 3, 10). Taking up the mission to pursue the divine lawsuit, the Logos "came to what was his own" and to "his own people" (v. 11). The prologue establishes the rightful claim, but it also makes clear that its subsequent narrative's focus on the incarnate Logos's pursuit of the claim is the pursuit of God's claim. The prologue's *inclusio* ensures that this will remain the dominant perspective. Not only does its first verse both distinguish the Logos from God and identify the Logos with God; by asserting (in what is probably the best-attested reading of v. 18, though not given in the NRSV) that one who is "only God" makes God known, it also underscores that the incarnate Logos is God's self-expression. In this trial it is through the Logos that God comes to expression as witness and judge: "He whom God has sent speaks the words of God" (3:34a). This perspective is also reinforced at the end of the public trial before Israel, in Jesus' summation of its issues. His claim is that, in what has taken place, he has not spoken on his own but has spoken just as the Father has told him (12:49–50). His word as witness and judge has been God's word. This public phase of the trial before Israel has been about God.

Another way in which the narrative discourse makes this point is its insistence that, as the initiator of the lawsuit, God has sent Jesus to make God's case. We have already noted the frequency of the sending language regarding Jesus' mission in the trial; such formulations are also connected with the witnessing, judging, and verdict in the trial. In the dispute of John 5, for example, Jesus claims that his works testify that the Father has sent him (v. 36), that his judgment is just because he seeks the will of the one who sent him (v. 30), and that anyone who hears his word and believes the one who sent him has eternal life and does not come under judgment (v. 24). And in his summary, he asserts that his word will serve as judge because "the Father who sent me has himself given me a commandment about what to say and what to speak" (12:49).

Thus, Jesus is God's authorized agent or representative in the lawsuit, and the relation between the authorizer and the agent is so close that a person's response to, and treatment of, the latter are considered to be a response to, and treatment of, the former. This is spelled out explicitly on a number of occasions. In 5:23 Jesus says, "Anyone who does not honor the Son does not honor the Father who sent him" (5:23). His summary makes the same point: "Whoever believes in me believes not in me but in him who sent me. And whoever sees me sees him who sent me" (12:44–45; cf. also 14:9). And in warning his followers later about the world's hostility, he can say, "Whoever hates me hates my Father also" (15:23).

In line with the Fourth Gospel's articulation of God's relationship to Jesus in terms of both unity and distinctness, God's witnessing and judging is sometimes seen as taking place in Jesus and sometimes as being carried out alongside the activity of Jesus. In order to comply with the Deuteronomic law about the need for more than one witness, in 5:32, 37–38 and 8:17–18 God's witness is treated as an independent witness. In 5:36–40 it is made clear that the Father's witness to Jesus is twofold. It consists both in the works that the Father has given him to complete and in God's word of witness in Scripture. In this light, witnessing in the lawsuit becomes a joint enterprise of Father and Son: "I testify on my own behalf, and the Father who sent me testifies on my behalf" (8:18). Later in the same trial scene, Jesus says of his witnessing activity, "I do nothing on my own, but I speak these things as the Father instructed me. And the one who sent me is with me; he has not left me alone" (8:28–29). The same is true of judging. God is the ultimate judge (8:50) but has given the activity of judgment to Jesus in his capacity as the Son or the Son of Man (5:22, 27). Thus, judging also is viewed as a joint enterprise: "it is not I alone who judge, but I and the Father who sent me" (8:16). In the earlier dispute also, this activity is seen as one that Jesus does not carry out on his own but in cooperation with the God who is instructing him: "I can do nothing on my own. As I hear, I judge" (5:30). God, then, both gives divine backing to Jesus' activity in the lawsuit and identifies the divine self with that activity. Not surprisingly, therefore, in the interrogation of 10:22–39, which also leads to the attempt to stone him, Jesus can say that, in giving eternal life, the trial's positive verdict, "the Father and I are one" (v. 30) and that, in his relationship to the Father, which is at issue in his mission, "the Father is in me and I am in the Father" (v. 38). God and Jesus are one in their task of bringing suit against the world.

But why has God initiated this lawsuit in the first place? And if God has done this as Judge, what does divine judgment entail? Again we need to bear in mind the scriptural assumptions that inform this narrative. In taking up the cosmic-lawsuit motif from Deutero-Isaiah, the implied author is likely to share its perspective that the lawsuit is not primarily about judging humans for their deeds and punishing them for not performing rightly. Rather, in that lawsuit and elsewhere in the Jewish Scriptures, what Yahweh is asking for is recognition of Yahweh's own self as the only true God and the sort of relationship of trust that arises out of this recognition. Israel's performance (and, for that matter, Yahweh's performance) then becomes an issue, but only within the context of fidelity to the covenant relationship. In the Scriptures, to appeal to Yahweh as Judge, to ask Yahweh for judgment, is not to ask to be punished but to ask for divine assistance in gaining justice. It is a request by those who feel themselves wronged, oppressed, or persecuted that expects Yahweh to come to their aid—if need be, in an act of rescue or salvation—and secure the conditions that are necessary for life and well-being. All this holds true for the Fourth Gospel. Its lawsuit is about both the sovereign God's self-vindication and this God's concern for a justice in the world that will secure life for God's representative, for God's people, and for the world.

Clearly, in this trial there is sovereign self-regard on God's part. God wants recognition as God. God's name, God's reputation, and God's truth, the reliability of the divine word, are at stake, and God is determined to secure these. Jesus recognizes that God's name is at issue in his mission. In 12:28 he asks, "Father, glorify your name." The voice from heaven, which is meant to be a public pronouncement for the sake of the crowd, although the narrator gives no grounds for thinking they have understood it (cf. vv. 29–30), responds, "I have glorified it, and I will glorify it again." The reader, if not the narrative audience, is meant to recognize that this lawsuit is about God's name and reputation and that God has been active and will continue to be active, even in the imminent condemnation to death of his authorized representative, to ensure that the divine name is honored. Throughout the narrative the point is made that, in Jesus' witness, God's name is on the line. Jesus states, "I have come in my Father's name" (5:43), claims that his works are in the Father's name (10:25), is acclaimed as "the one who comes in the name of the Lord" as he enters Jerusalem for the final time (12:13), and summarizes his accomplished mission as having made the Father's name known (17:6). As noted earlier, this concern about the divine name is not unrelated to the fact that Yahweh's self-designation in Deutero-Isaiah—

"I am"—is at the heart of the trial scene in John 8:24, 28, 58 and leads to the charge that Jesus is making himself equal to God, a charge that results in the authorities' determination to secure his death. If Jesus not only claims to come in God's name but even uses the divine name for himself, then clearly, in the implied author's view, in this trial, like the scriptural trials of Isa 40–55, God has not only chosen to risk the divine reputation but will be jealous to preserve it.

The prominence of the notion of glory throughout the trial reinforces this emphasis on God's sovereign self-regard. The irony of "the Jews'" injunction, in their interrogation of the man born blind, to give glory to God has been noted (cf. 9:24). Unwittingly, they have pinpointed the ultimate issue in the trial of Jesus and his followers—God's glory. In Deutero-Isaiah and in the Jewish Scriptures as a whole, "the glory of Yahweh refers to the claim and aura of power, authority and sovereignty that must be established in struggle, exercised in authority, and conceded either by willing adherents or defeated resisters."[2] In the Fourth Gospel also, God's glory concerns God's entitlement to be honored and esteemed as the one sovereign God. And if humans do not give God the glory that is God's due, then God has to secure it. God does this in the lawsuit by glorifying Jesus; in ensuring that honor is brought to Jesus, God brings honor to God's self. Because the Son of Man has been glorified in the coming of his hour, "God has been glorified in him" (13:31). Since Jesus, unlike his opponents (cf. 5:44), honors the Father and does not seek his own glory, God the Judge will seek Jesus' glory (8:49–50) and will therefore secure God's own honor. These explicit explanations of the relationship between Jesus' glory and God's glory indicate that when elsewhere the emphasis is on Jesus' glory, whether in his signs or in his death, it is not Jesus' glory alone that is in view. The glorification of Jesus remains the vehicle for God achieving the recognition that is God's rightful due.

In the lawsuits of Deutero-Isaiah, aspersions had been cast on Yahweh's sovereignty and glory through questioning whether Yahweh really was in control of the events of history. Did not Israel's exile show that Babylon and its power were what really counted? The Fourth Gospel's lawsuit reflects similar concerns. Do not the death of the Messiah and the fate of his followers as recipients of the world's hostility and persecution give the lie to the sovereignty of their God in history? The narrative's portrayal of Jesus' own sovereign foreknowledge, its perspective

---

[2] W. Brueggemann, *Theology of the Old Testament* (Minneapolis: Fortress, 1997), 283.

on Jesus' death as exaltation, its underlining of his vindication through his resurrection to life, and its presentation of his followers' experience of eternal life in the present address such concerns. And God is shown to be in control in other ways. From the implied author's perspective, Caiaphas's decision, on behalf of the Sanhedrin, that Jesus is to die rather than have the nation destroyed by the Romans (11:48–50) is in fact not uttered on his own but is a prophecy (v. 51). It is a vehicle for the divine prediction of the outcome of the trial. In particular, God's previous witness in Scripture indicates that this trial and its outcome were known in advance. The allusions to the servant-witness from Isa 40–55 and the indications that the events of the passion have taken place in order that the Scriptures might be fulfilled (cf. John 19:24, 28, 36–37) all promote this perspective. Not even the unbelief of the majority of the Jewish people catches God unawares. God has already foreseen this in Scripture in the unbelieving response to the servant-witness, related in Isa 53:1, and in the unbelieving response to Isaiah himself, which Isaiah is told to proclaim in Isa 6:10 (cf. John 12:37–40).

Finally, in terms of God's sovereign interest in the lawsuit, God's truthfulness and reliability are at stake. This overlaps with the previous issue of God's sovereignty in history. We have already considered how the truth of Yahweh's word was a central topic in Deutero-Isaiah, highlighted both at the beginning and at the end of this section of Scripture. In the midst of, and in contrast to, human inconstancy, God's word endures as faithful: "The grass withers, the flower fades; but the word of our God stands forever" (Isa 40:8). And the effective activity of this word is stressed: "so shall my word be that goes out from my mouth; it shall not return to me empty, but it shall accomplish that which I purpose, and succeed in the thing for which I sent it" (55:11). In between these references, it is the correspondence between Yahweh's word and the events of history, particularly the raising up of Cyrus, that has been crucial to Yahweh's case. In the Fourth Gospel, the truthfulness of God's word and God's fidelity to this word also play their role in the lawsuit. This becomes clear immediately in the prologue (1:1), where God's word is hypostasized as the Logos who is with God and is eternal. But this Word is also effective in history; indeed it takes on a particular historical form, it is enfleshed (1:14). When the history of the enfleshed Word is narrated, it above all takes the form of witness. The incarnate Logos characterizes himself in this fashion and, like Yahweh's word in Isa 55:11, sees himself as sent—sent to succeed in the task of witnessing. So the correspondence between God's word and historical events is embodied in the mission and person of Jesus. The truth and reliability of

God's word, like God's reputation in God's name and glory, are tied to the role of Jesus in this lawsuit. Jesus' witness is depicted as true and reliable because he is convinced that the one who sent him is true and he is simply declaring in his witness to the world what he has heard from this one (John 8:26). Since Jesus speaks the words of God, "whoever has accepted his testimony has certified this, that God is true" (3:33–34). It could not be clearer that, in the mission of Jesus in the trial, God's truth and reliability are at stake.

The sovereign God is not only concerned, however, for the divine reputation in this trial. As in the scriptural lawsuits, God is also passionately concerned to make judgment for God's people and for the created world. And as in Scripture, this faithful and loving Judge is prepared to intervene to rescue those in need, to restore them to well-being and thereby reassure them that justice is maintained in the world. The purpose for which God has instigated the trial is precisely to bring about life, that quality of life which is in fact a share in the life of the Logos (cf. 1:4). God has sent the Son on a rescue mission: "Indeed, God did not send the Son into the world to condemn the world, but in order that the world might be saved through him" (3:17). The motivation for the bringing of judgment, that is, justice, is God's love for the world, and the salvation the divine judgment effects is a reversal of humankind's condition of perishing and the accomplishment of eternal life (cf. 3:16). Not only is this made clear in the narrator's continuation of the discourse with Nicodemus; it is also part of Jesus' summary of the trial before Israel in 12:44–50. There Jesus states that his word will serve as the judge because he has spoken under the command of the Father who sent him and the Father's "commandment is eternal life" (12:49–50). Despite this divine purpose in the trial, and again in line with the portrayal of Yahweh in Scripture, when the divine commandment is disregarded or disobeyed, a severe side to God's judgment emerges. Not only do humans condemn themselves by rejecting the offer of life; they provoke God's righteous indignation: "whoever disobeys the Son will not see life, but must endure God's wrath" (3:36b).

God's involvement in the lawsuit does not cease with the death and resurrection of Jesus. Jesus is replaced with another divine agent, the Spirit. This new Advocate is also said to be sent by the Father (14:26) and to come from the Father (15:26). The Spirit will carry on God's concern with judgment and righteousness (16:8–11), will establish God's truth as the Spirit of truth (14:17; 15:13), and will be the means of accomplishing God's purpose in the trial's positive verdict of life (cf. 7:39). The risen Jesus' breathing of the Spirit on the disciples in 20:22

recalls Gen 2:7, where God breathes on the man and he becomes a living being. The God who endowed humanity with life now endows its representatives with new life through Jesus' breathing on the disciples. God's involvement extends to the role of these disciples in the lawsuit. Their witness will have divine backing not only through the accompanying divine Spirit but also through God's standing behind their announcement of the divine verdict as they pronounce forgiveness for those who receive their witness, and the retention of sins of those who reject it. The passive forms of the verbs in the two main clauses of 20:23 are to be taken as divine passives. Remarkably, God's reputation is also now tied up with the role of Jesus' followers in the world. Jesus prays that God will protect in the divine name those to whom this name has been made known (17:6, 11, 26), and he asserts that the divine glory given him has been passed on to them (17:22). The unity of the witness of Jesus' followers is in view in connection with both the divine name and the divine glory. And if their witness leads to death, this will enhance the divine reputation, as in the case of Peter's martyrdom, by which he glorifies God (21:19).

Clearly, the God who has instigated the lawsuit is not simply a spectator as it unfolds, but is intensely involved. The extent of this involvement is encapsulated supremely in the notion that God's immanent presence in the world, the Logos, becomes incarnate (1:14) and in this incarnate form receives the world's sentence of death. As in Deutero-Isaiah, God is willing to be subjected to trial. The account of the Meribah incident, as discussed in chapter 2 of this study, went further: Yahweh the Judge stands on the rock receiving the sentence of judgment from Moses' rod. But in the Fourth Gospel, through identification with the incarnate Logos in the outworkings of human history, this God takes the final consequences of a willingness to be tried and judged. This is not simply a sovereign judge who remains aloof but a judge who is judged and undergoes the sentence of death. This narrative's discourse justifies speaking of a God so involved as to become "the crucified God." If the Logos language stresses the identity between God and Jesus in the trial, the Father-Son language reminds the reader of their distinctness. In terms of the latter categories, God's passionate commitment to the lawsuit with the world is expressed as a love for the world that extends to God's giving the only Son in order to achieve the positive verdict of life (3:16). Either way, God's committed involvement is expressed in Jesus and is a commitment to the death. Israel's God goes all the way in staking the divine reputation on Jesus: the central issue of the lawsuit is whether this God will now be acknowledged as the God who is known in Jesus. It should be clear now why, in the Fourth Gospel, theology is also Christology and Christology is also theology. In this narrative's trial of truth, the *logos* about *theos* is the witness embodied in the incarnate Logos, Jesus.

B. The Witness of Jesus

As mentioned, a key description of Jesus' role in this Gospel's narrative is that found on Jesus' own lips in the climactic trial before Pilate, with the double underlining of the trial's mission significance: "For this I was born, and for this I came into the world, to testify to the truth" (18:37). The truth at issue in the trial concerns God and how God is known. It concerns God's reputation and reliability, including God's truthfulness. The truth to which Jesus' mission is directed, then, is primarily the truth about this God, particularly this God's disclosure in Jesus. In witnessing to God, Jesus also witnesses to the truth about himself and to the truth about God's purposes for humanity and the world. And in precipitating the need for a decision or judgment, his witness becomes a witness to the truth about humanity's present relation to God. How does Jesus testify to this truth? In his deeds and words—the signs and discourses—and supremely in his death, which signifies that witnessing is an activity for which one will literally give one's life. The witness of Jesus' "works," which include his signs, is highlighted in 5:36: "The works that the Father has given me to complete . . . testify on my behalf" (cf. also 10:25). The signs that Yahweh performed in bringing Israel out of Egypt were also seen as part of a great series of trials to which Yahweh submitted in a contest with Pharaoh (Deut 4:34; 7:19; 29:3).[3] Jesus' signs are part of his representation of God in this new cosmic trial. It would be expected in the context of a lawsuit that Jesus' words constitute his witness, but this is underlined by the parallelism of the formulation with which Jesus himself first mentions the notion of witness: "we *speak* of what we know and *testify* to what we have seen" (3:11). That Jesus' death is of a piece with his witness—indeed forms its culmination—is indicated by the key mission statement's location (18:37) in the context of the trial whose outcome Jesus already knows will be the sentence of death. But it is also signaled from the start, since the first words of Jesus explicitly designated as witness include the assertion that the Son of Man must "be lifted up" (3:14).

While 18:37 formulates witness as the purpose of Jesus' own life and of his own mission in the world, as noted in the previous section,

---

[3] Cf. also Boice, *Witness and Revelation*, 96.

the same mission of witness can also be formulated in terms of Jesus' relationship to God and of what he has been sent by God to accomplish. Thus in 3:33–34 Jesus' testimony can be characterized as a speaking of the words of God, because he is the one "whom God has sent." His witness is that of the authorized agent who fully represents God in the lawsuit. Jesus also makes this clear elsewhere: "My teaching is not mine but his who sent me" (7:16). As this authorized witness, Jesus is seen as fulfilling the predictions about two scriptural figures. The formulation in 12:48–50—that Jesus speaks everything he has been commanded to speak and that people therefore are held accountable to his word—recalls Deut 18:18–19 and what is said about the prophet like Moses. And John 12:38, in the earlier part of the summary of the trial before Israel, cites Isa 53:1 about the servant-witness. Jesus will continue this role as he washes his disciples' feet and then goes to suffering and to a death that, like that of Isaiah's servant-witness, is at the same time a lifting up and exaltation (cf. Isa 52:13–53:12).

The Gospel emphasizes in a further way the relationship between Jesus and God entailed in Jesus' witness. Like all human witnesses, Jesus speaks of what he has seen and heard, but with a striking difference: what Jesus has seen and heard and what becomes the content of his witness are heavenly things (3:12). He is uniquely qualified to witness to these realities because he has descended from heaven (v. 13), or come from above (vv. 31–32). As Jesus puts it in the trial scene of 8:12–58: "the one who sent me is true, and I declare to the world what I have heard from him" (v. 26) and "I declare what I have seen in the Father's presence" (v. 38). He is a particular type of agent and a special kind of Son, who has previously been in heaven in the presence of God. Here the prologue's designation of Jesus as the incarnate Word needs to be recalled, for these descriptions are entirely fitting for the Logos, who was with God (1:1) and who, as only God, is in the bosom of the Father (v. 18). This last reference is particularly significant for Jesus' role as witness because the notion of a witness as someone who reports what he or she has seen is to the fore. A witness to God therefore should be someone who has seen God. But as v. 18a underlines, "no one has ever seen God." The only exception is the Logos, who was with God and was God (v. 1). Only one with this status as God can be qualified to witness and to make God known (v. 18b), because only such a one can be said to have seen God and indeed to continue to see God (cf. 5:19). As the witness who declares what he has seen and heard above with God, Jesus is the incarnate Logos, the immanent and articulate presence of the one God on the earthly stage of the cosmic lawsuit.[4]

That Jesus is portrayed as both human and divine affects the way his witness is depicted. As a human witness, he accedes, at least formally, to the demands in both John 5 and John 8 that there be more than one witness in his case, in conformity to the legislation in Deuteronomy. And in the trial as a whole, the implied author explicitly names other humans, such as John the Baptist, the Samaritan woman, the crowd, Jesus' disciples in general, and the beloved disciple in particular, as witnesses. But even when Jesus lists more than one witness and talks of the Father as the second witness, whose testimony is provided through Jesus' works and through Scripture, these are not the sort of witnesses that the Deuteronomic law had in view or that would have been accepted in the legal conventions to which his opponents appeal. They only serve to highlight that in the end Jesus is essentially testifying about himself. Despite the law, such testimony is to be deemed true because of Jesus' unique identity (8:14). Because of his divine origin and destiny, his witness is self-authenticating. In the nature of the case, only God could confirm such testimony, and from the perspective of the implied author, Jesus is one with God. Even where the categories used for Jesus' relation to God are those expressing a distinction between them as Son in relation to Father, the end effect is still to maintain that the Son's witness is the Father's witness and vice versa.[5] Thus, regarding the witness of his works, such as his healing on the Sabbath, Jesus can say, "the Son can do nothing on his own, but only what he sees the Father doing; for whatever the Father does, the Son does likewise" (5:19). The complete dependence of the Son as agent on the Father as authorizer underlines the total unity of their collaborative witness in the cosmic trial: "I testify on my own behalf, and the Father who sent me testifies on my behalf" (8:18; cf. also vv. 28–29). There has been much discussion about whether, with the emphasis on his relation to God, enough remains of Jesus' humanity for the portrayal of that humanity in the Fourth Gospel to be plausible.[6] At any rate, regarding his witness, this narrative depicts a Jesus whose humanity is not thinkable apart from his union with God.

---

[4] On the connection between Jesus as witness and Jesus as Logos, see ibid., 65–72.

[5] Cf. Blank, *Krisis,* 216–24.

[6] See, e.g., E. Käsemann, *The Testament of Jesus* (Philadelphia: Fortress, 1968); and M. M. Thompson, *The Humanity of Jesus in the Fourth Gospel* (Philadelphia: Fortress, 1988).

Just as in Isa 40–55 Yahweh appeared as witness, accused, accuser or prosecutor, and judge, so, in this new version of the cosmic lawsuit, Jesus as God's representative has all these roles. In the disputation of John 5, the trial scene of John 8, and the account of the trial before Pilate, such roles are strikingly juxtaposed. In each, Jesus is the accused. In 5:16–18 Jesus stands accused of breaking the Sabbath and making himself equal to God. In 8:12–13 the accusation is that, in calling himself the light of the world, Jesus is witnessing to himself. As this scene unfolds, the further accusation arises that he is a Samaritan and has a demon (8:48). Clearly, Jesus is the accused in the Roman trial. The charge at first is that he claims to be the king of the Jews. Only later does the real accusation surface, that he has claimed to be the Son of God (19:7). The accused gives witness, and soon this witness becomes prosecuting witness as Jesus goes on the offensive and mounts his own accusations. The counteraccusations build up in 5:37b–47. Jesus' opponents are charged with never having heard the Father's voice or seen his form, not having his word abiding in them, refusing to come to Jesus for life, not having the love of God in them, accepting glory from one another instead of seeking the glory that comes from God, and not believing Moses. The accusations Jesus levels in 8:12–59, too many to list, begin with the charge that his opponents judge by human standards (v. 15), move through the charge that they are of their father, the devil (v. 44), and end with the charge that they do not know the God they profess (vv. 54–55). Jesus' accusing role is inevitably much more muted at the final trial. Nevertheless, his first words are a counterquestion that puts Pilate on the defensive, implying that he is conspiring with the Jewish religious authorities (18:34). Later Jesus' very silence has an accusing force (19:9b), and when he does respond a final time, it is to remind Pilate of where any power Pilate has ultimately comes from and to accuse the Jewish leaders of the greater sin in his indictment (19:11).

Jesus' prosecuting role already shades over into a judging one. And witness becomes judgment when it is witness against evil: "The world . . . hates me because I testify against it that its works are evil" (7:7). Indeed, the very content of Jesus' witness as truth and its nature as self-authenticating mean that his witness has to be the criterion of judgment and he has to be at the same time judge. In the three sections we have singled out for observing Jesus as witness, accused, and accuser, he is also the judge. In the forensic scene of 5:19–47, the accused who gives witness soon claims to be also judge (v. 22), one whose judgment is exercised in both the present and the future (vv. 24–29) and is just (v. 30). The claim that leads to the trial scene of John 8 is, "I am the light of the world" (8:12). The activity of the light entails judgment, either enabling those in the dark to see or exposing the deeds of those who choose to remain in darkness (cf. 3:19–21; 12:46). This testimony quickly turns to actual judgment as Jesus claims his judgment is true because he is accompanied in his judging by the Father (8:16), pronounces the judgment that his interrogators will die in their sin (v. 21), and adds that he has much about which to make a negative judgment (v. 26). By the time of the Roman trial in 18:28–19:16a, Jesus' activity as judge has been so clearly depicted that here it can be established primarily by irony that the accused whose mission is to witness to the truth is also the judge. He holds center stage between Pilate and "the Jews," whose words and actions expose both to judgment. He is mocked as king of the Jews, with all the associations of that messianic title with just judgment, and in all probability he is even seated, as part of the mockery, on the judge's bench.

Yet connecting accusation and condemnation with judgment in some of the above references could give a distorted picture of Jesus as judge in the Fourth Gospel. Those who oppose the divine purpose of the lawsuit receive negative judgment, but the overall purpose of the lawsuit's judgment remains for Jesus, as we have seen it was for God, to reverse alienation and death and produce life. Jesus' mission statement in 10:10 ("I came that they may have life, and have it abundantly") is in complete harmony with the mission statements about witnessing to the truth in the lawsuit and about judging ("I came into this world for judgment so that those who do not see may see, and those who do see may become blind" [9:39]), because the goal of the witness and the judging is the positive verdict of life. Only where there is willful refusal to receive this life and its light does the secondary outcome of a judgment of death and blindness follow. Because some of the Pharisees refuse to admit any blindness and are adamant that they see, they receive the negative judgment—"your sin remains" (9:41). This perspective on the purpose of Jesus' role as judge is reinforced at the end of the public ministry to Israel in 12:47b–48, where he says, on the one hand, "I came not to judge the world, but to save the world," but, on the other, adds, "The one who rejects me and does not receive my word has a judge; on the last day the word that I have spoken will serve as judge."

Whereas others judge by appearances (cf. 7:24) or judge according to the flesh (cf. 8:15), Jesus does not. Instead his judgment is in line with that of the messianic king of Isa 11:2–5, who "shall not judge by what his eyes see, or decide by what his ears hear; but with righteousness he shall judge the poor." This judge was to be one on whom the Spirit of the

Lord rests, and John the Baptist had testified to seeing the Spirit remain on Jesus (John 1:32–33). That Jesus' judging is not ordinary human judging is clear from the narrator's comments in 2:23–25: Jesus did not entrust himself to those who believed on the basis of his signs, "because he knew all people and needed no one to testify about anyone; for he himself knew what was in everyone." Jesus' omniscience about humans means that he can dispense with the need for witnesses in making his own judgments. He judges from the divine standpoint.

Regarding the relationship between Jesus and God, the patterns at work in the narrative's portrayal of Jesus as judge are similar to those in its depiction of him as witness. Responsibility for judging appears to be handed back and forth between Jesus and God. Jesus can say that the Father judges no one but has given all judgment to the Son (5:22), or has given him authority to judge because he is the Son of Man (5:27), and yet state in 8:15 that he himself judges no one. This suggests that, for the implied author, it makes little difference which of the two is judge because of the unity of their relationship. Indeed Jesus himself is made immediately to qualify the assertion of 8:15 in terms of this relationship: "Even if I do judge, . . . it is not I alone who judge, but I and the Father who sent me" (8:16; cf. also v. 26). Here again, within the unity of the work of judgment, Jesus functions as God's authorized agent. In the summing up of the trial before Israel, Jesus also asserts that his word of witness will serve as judge because "the Father who sent me has himself given me a commandment about what to say and what to speak" (12:48–49). Earlier, another of Jesus' statements of complete dependence referred to judgment, and again its force is to stress the total unity of Jesus' will and God's will in this activity: "I can do nothing on my own. As I hear, I judge; and my judgment is just, because I seek not to do my own will but the will of him who sent me" (5:30).

We have seen that, just as in the scriptural lawsuit Yahweh's name, glory, and truth were at issue, so the same holds for God in the Fourth Gospel's trial. Since Jesus represents God in the trial, Jesus' name, truth, and glory are also key concerns in the presentation of his witnessing and judging. Jesus has not only come in his Father's name (cf., e.g., 5:43); his own name is central to the lawsuit's process. Indeed, to accept Jesus' witness is to believe in his name, to acknowledge his identity, to commit oneself to who he is. Both the prologue and the Gospel's statement of purpose make the point that the positive outcome of the trial depends on one's attitude to Jesus' name. In 1:12, to receive the Logos is the same as believing in his name, and the result is to receive the life of God as children of God; in 20:31, the purpose of this narrative testimony about the lawsuit is that "through believing you may have life in his name." This is formulated in terms of the negative aspect of judgment in 3:18, where believing in the name of the only Son of God is what enables people to escape the verdict of condemnation. And in the dispute that centers around this name, Jesus argues from Scripture that it is not blasphemy to call himself God's Son (10:33–36). Jesus' name will also be crucial for his followers in their witness. As he prepares them for this future role, Jesus reminds them three times of their access to God through his name for whatever they need for their mission (cf. 14:13–14; 15:16; 16:23–24). In this mission the Spirit will come to them in Jesus' name to continue the cause associated with his identity (14:26); but this identity will also remain hotly contested, and hostile response to their witness will be on account of his name (15:21).

Twice in the prayer of John 17, Jesus asserts that the Father's name has been given to him (17:11–12). The clearest reference for this in the narrative is Jesus' remarkable use of the divine self-identification, "I am." The use of this name, which, as noted, is so pervasive in terms of Yahweh's identity in the lawsuits of Isa 40–55, underscores the self-authenticating nature of Jesus' witness. It is significant that seven of the eight times that the "I am" formulation without a predicate is found on Jesus' lips occur in parts of the narrative closely associated with the trial.[7] Three times "I am" is an important part of Jesus' witness in the trial scene of John 8. Then it is employed in connection with his betrayal and three times in the account of his arrest. Jesus asserts that belief that "I am" is essential if his hearers are to avoid the negative outcome of the judgment and are not to die in their sins (8:24). In 8:28 he links recognition of his identity as "I am" to the event of his being lifted up; Jesus' identification with God through his use of the divine name is here tied to his death and exaltation. Most significantly, his witness as "I am" finds its culmination in the crucifixion, which will be at the same time his elevation in glory. But the claim to have existed before Abraham as "I am" in v. 58 brings the trial scene to an end and underlines that witness is always contested. This particular witness in this context can only be controversial, and Jesus' narrative audience attempt to stone him for the blasphemy they perceive in such a claim.

---

[7] The other is 6:20, in the episode of walking on the water. I take the use in 4:26 to have an implied predicate (the messiah) and that in 8:18 to have the rest of the sentence as its predicate ("I am the one who witnesses about myself").

In Isa 43:10 Yahweh had chosen Israel to be witness and servant so that it might know and believe that "I am." Israel would witness to Yahweh as "I am" on the basis of the reliability of Yahweh's word. In the preparation of his disciples for witness, Jesus tells them that they are chosen (13:18) and servants (13:16) and then, through the words of Scripture in Ps 41:9, predicts his betrayal by one of them, "so that when it does occur, you may believe that I am" (13:19). The disciples are to be witnesses to Jesus' sovereign control of the events of the lawsuit, confirmed by his ability, like that of Yahweh, to predict the future, even the event that will lead to his trial and death. And the function of Jesus' witness as "I am" at his arrest in 18:5–6, 8 is to underline his divine sovereignty in this and the following scenes, which appear to contradict his claims. The narrator's first comment after Jesus' "I am" is to point out that "Judas, who betrayed him, was standing with them," reminding the reader of the fulfillment of the earlier prediction, which was meant to result in belief in Jesus as "I am." The depiction of the reaction of the arresting group, which steps back and falls to the ground, is clearly meant to ensure that the reader will not miss the force of Jesus' self-identification, since such a reaction would have been expected in an encounter with a theophany. There is to be no mistaking that the witness who goes to trial and judgment is one who bears the divine name "I am."[8]

The fulfillment of the prediction about Jesus' betrayal (cf. 13:19) is, as noted earlier in this study, only one of a number of such fulfillments of Jesus' words that underline their truthfulness (cf. also e.g., 2:22; 14:29; 16:4; 18:32; 21:23), and fulfillment of predictions is itself only one of the means that the narrative employs to reinforce the reliability or truth of his witness. On the basis of the Samaritan woman's testimony that Jesus' words correspond to the reality of her life and have proved true ("He told me everything I have ever done"), other Samaritans also believe (4:39). The mission statement about his witness claims that it is a witness to the truth (18:37). The repeated double Amen formula to introduce Jesus' sayings functions as his vouching for the truth of his testimony. There are explicit statements in John 8 that both his testimony and his judgment are true or valid (8:14, 16), and another asserting that to be committed to his word of witness is to know the truth (vv. 31–32). He accuses the opposition of "trying to kill me, a man who has told you the truth that I heard from God" (v. 40), and later in the same discourse insists that he is telling the truth (cf. vv. 45–46). Indeed, he himself as

---

[8] For a detailed examination of the "I am" sayings from a similar perspective, see Ball, *"I Am" in John's Gospel.*

the witness is said to be true and to have nothing false in him (7:18). What is more, in his witness Jesus constitutes the way to the Father, a way that is reliable, and so, as the way, he is also the truth (14:6).

In the prologue the glory of the incarnate Logos is said to be "full of grace and truth" (1:14). The community claims to have witnessed this glory, including the steadfast love and utter reliability that have been evidence of his entitlement to honor. In the lawsuit as a whole, Jesus' reputation is at stake; the perspective of the implied author is that the aura of the honor to which Jesus was rightly entitled is to be seen throughout his mission as a witness and—the point of greatest controversy for the claims of his followers—supremely in his death. Israel as the servant-witness in Deutero-Isaiah was meant to be the bearer of Yahweh's glory, and now Jesus asserts that it is the Father who seeks his glory and indeed glorifies him (John 8:50, 54). The reason Jesus as the Son has been given the role of judge by the Father is "that all may honor the Son just as they honor the Father" (5:22–23a). Jesus' reputation is not simply parallel to that of the Father. The two are so bound up together that in fact "anyone who does not honor the Son does not honor the Father" (5:23b). In Jesus' public mission to Israel, the signs that constitute the witness of his works reveal his glory (cf. 2:11; 11:4), but this mission moves toward his supreme hour of glory in his death and departure (cf. 7:39; 12:23; 17:1, 5). As the hour arrives and Judas goes off to betray him, Jesus says of himself, "Now the Son of Man has been glorified, and God has been glorified in him. If God has been glorified in him, God will also glorify him in himself and will glorify him at once" (13:31–32). Jesus' reputation and honor, and therefore the divine reputation and honor in this lawsuit, are maintained, and they are maintained above all precisely in the moment that appears to normal judgment to be one of humiliation and shame—the sentence of death by crucifixion. As we have seen, the threefold prediction of Jesus' being lifted up has reinforced this paradoxical evaluation of his death. Israel's servant-witness was to combine a lifting up and glorification with suffering and death (Isa 52:13–53:12); in the Gospel's narrative, the death of the witness is not only a lifting up on the cross but an exaltation, a lifting up in glory (cf. 3:14; 8:28; 12:32–34).

Thus, at the heart of the cosmic lawsuit is the death of Jesus as the witness and the judge. If all humans are mortal, then Jesus' mortality at least makes this witness fully human. Even one who is incarnate as the Logos is susceptible to death, because he is incarnate. But the death of a witness is a particular kind of death. The implied author leaves no doubt that Jesus' death is the culmination of the witness of his life. We simply need to remind ourselves of the narrative's plot.[9] If Jesus' mission or task is to testify to the truth, then the mission is completed on the cross. "It is finished," asserts Jesus in 19:30. His earlier prayer to the Father looked back on his successful mission: "I glorified you on earth by finishing the work that you gave me to do" (17:4). Jesus' witness in the trial has enhanced the divine reputation because it is a witness that culminates in death. It is inevitable that, in thinking of the narrative's portrayal of the death of the witness, we are drawn to the double meaning of the Greek term μάρτυς—both witness and martyr. In carrying through his witness to the point of death, Jesus as martyr submits this witness to the verdict not simply of Pilate but of the one from whom Pilate derives his power (cf. 19:11a), the ultimate Judge in the lawsuit. His final act of witness lays bare what is entailed in this trial of truth—it is a contest of claims that is literally a matter of life and death. To be a witness to the truth is to stake one's life on the truth. The suffering and death of *the* witness thus become the paradigm for his witnessing followers. As we have seen, the narrative sequence is deliberate. Jesus first prepares his disciples for witness in John 13–17, including warnings about persecution and death in 15:18–16:4, and then, with Peter's failure under interrogation as a foil (18:15–18, 25–27), demonstrates what it is to be a faithful witness in such circumstances.

Jesus' crucifixion is also the death of the judge. The one who was ready to pronounce the verdict of life or death on others is himself sentenced to death. The one to whom has been delegated all judgment submits himself to the world's judgment in the conviction that he is also submitting himself to the Father's judgment in the cosmic lawsuit. If dying on the cross is the completion of his witness, then it is appropriate that this be also the time at which judgment is rendered. Although Jesus' fate appears to give the lie to those earlier claims about judgment, the entire burden of the narrative is to persuade its readers that the one who is sentenced in the Roman trial is nevertheless still the judge in the cosmic trial. Its point of view is that the world's judgment of him is in reality his judgment of the world and its ruler (cf. 12:31; 16:11, 33). In his death Jesus remains judge just as he remains witness. Indeed, his witness to the truth, in its refusal to concede to the violence of this world's deathly power struggles (cf. 18:36), is itself a judgment on such a world. The profound ironies of mocking the royal judge at the Roman trial and the

---

[9] By ignoring the role of witness in the plot, Boice, *Witness and Revelation*, 31, ends up denying that in the Fourth Gospel the witness of Jesus is centered in the cross.

superscription on the cross—"Jesus of Nazareth, the King of the Jews"—reinforce the notion that, in the cosmic perspective, the power of the judge is exhibited in the weakness of suffering and death. Jesus remains judge while transforming the criteria normally associated with judgment.

Jesus' death, then, is that of the judge who is judged. Many interpreters have suggested that there is little notion of Jesus' atoning death in this Gospel. It is difficult to avoid the conclusion that they have concentrated on individual references and missed the larger pattern of thought in the narrative.[10] It seems clear that Jesus the judge is judged on behalf of, indeed instead of, those who deserved this judgment. The negative verdict on humanity in this Gospel's trial is the death entailed by sin—" you will die in your sin" (8:21, 24). But it is the one who pronounced such a verdict of death who himself undergoes it. He absorbs the destructive judgment of humans in this world and, instead of passing on its deathly consequences, he opens up the possibilities of new life. It is no accident that the narrative discourse contains clear reminders that the trial and judgment of the judge take place on the day of Preparation for the Passover, the day on which the Passover lambs were slaughtered. Indeed, this secondary Passover motif forms an *inclusio* for the account of the Roman trial, occurring at the beginning (18:28) and at the end (19:14). The crucifixion scene also contains a reminder of the day of Preparation (19:31). The soldiers' not breaking Jesus' legs is taken as the fulfillment of Scripture—"None of his bones shall be broken" (19:36). One likely source for such a citation is the regulation about the Passover sacrifice in Exod 12:10 and Num 9:12. Both the judgment theme and the Passover theme are brought to bear on the significance of Jesus' death, and both are necessary to appreciate the implied author's perspective. Unless the cosmic lawsuit reverses the situation, humanity will remain in its condition of death due to sin. But the judge takes the sentence of death on himself and thereby deals with its cause. The two motifs merge when we recall the testimony of John the Baptist: the judge who is judged is at the same time the Lamb of God who takes away the sin of the world (cf. 1:29).

Now that this theme of atonement has been introduced in terms of Jesus as judge, we can return to the presentation of his role as witness, in

---

[10] Bultmann's pronouncement has been influential: "The thought of Jesus' death as an atonement for sin has no place in John, and if it should turn out that he took it over from the tradition of that Church, it would still be a foreign element in his work" (*Theology of the New Testament* [2 vols.; New York: Scribners, 1955], 2:54).

which the theme is not spelled out so clearly. Earlier I simply suggested that in his death Jesus submits his witness to the verdict of the ultimate Judge. Yet the dominant influence of the scriptural lawsuit from Isaiah cannot be forgotten. Again and again, in what is said of Jesus, the implied author makes clear allusions to Isaiah's depiction of the servant-witness, and regarding Jesus' death he explicitly develops the formulation about the suffering servant being glorified and lifted up (cf. LXX Isa 52:13). In the well-known passage that follows the mention of his being lifted up, the servant-witness is also seen as a lamb led to the slaughter (Isa 53:7). This witness dies in a perversion of justice (v. 8), yet at the same time his death is a judgment by God (v. 4b; cf. v. 10a). In this judgment the witness takes the sentence of "punishment that made us whole" (v. 5b), because "the LORD has laid on him the iniquity of us all" (v. 6b). In this way, when the servant-witness "poured out himself to death, . . . he bore the sin of many" (v. 12b). In the light of what we have seen of the convergence of the judgment and Passover sacrifice themes in Jesus' crucifixion, it requires no great stretch of the imagination to suspect that this portrayal from the lawsuit, also utilized frequently in early Christian traditions that would be known to the readers, was expected to inform implicitly their understanding of the death of the witness.

Although the following observation has already been made in the previous section, it is worth reiterating here in the context of the notion of atonement, because some traditional views of this matter have played off a sacrificing Jesus against an angry God who demands appeasement. The relationship between Jesus and God in this narrative means that its perspective is quite different. Jesus as witness and judge is both fully representative of and at one with God, and this holds for his roles as the witness who dies for his testimony and the judge who is judged. Jesus dies as the incarnate Logos, and the Logos is God's own immanent expression and presence in the world. In Jesus' death as witness and judge, God has become vulnerable to the cycle of human alienation and violence that is death in sin. Just as God is identified with Jesus in judging, so God is identified with Jesus in being judged. The human alienation from God that is death is taken into the life of this God in an act of divine self-giving in love (cf. John 3:16). Jesus' taking of death and sin on himself is to be seen, then, as the death of the "Christlike God."

The death of Jesus as witness and judge is the point at which judgment is given. The negative verdict of death is absorbed, and from Jesus' side flow blood and water, the symbol of the positive verdict of life (cf. 19:34). This judgment reveals how both God and Jesus want their reputation to be known—death is the hour of glory, lifting up in crucifixion is exaltation. As many scholars have suggested, one might have expected that Jesus' role in the trial would now be over. Has he not been exalted on the cross? Is not the cross the point of his return in glory to the Father?[11] But the narrative's story line about Jesus continues with the accounts of the empty tomb and the resurrection appearances. Given the centrality of Jesus' death for the trial motif, are these accounts superfluous for the Gospel's dominant perspective on Jesus, forced on the evangelist by their prominence in the traditions he has inherited?[12] To take such a view would be to miss the significance of the lawsuit motif for this narrative's portrayal of Jesus. We should start by remembering the prologue's perspective, that this witness and judge is the *incarnate* Logos, in whom was life (1:4) and whose mission in the world now entails mediating divine life to those who will believe in him (vv. 12–13). In terms of the lawsuit motif, his mission is to accomplish the judgment that results in the verdict of life. This already raises the question whether, in accomplishing this mission of putting the world back into relationship with the source of life, the Logos will retain the new identity of the incarnate Logos or will leave the flesh behind in returning to God.

The question is quickly put to rest by Jesus' witness. In 2:19 he asserts, "Destroy this temple, and in three days I will raise it up." Later he claims the sovereign power both to lay down his life and to take it up again (10:11, 15, 17, 18). Preparing his disciples for his absence and for their future witness, he promises that they will see him in "a little while" (14:18–19; 16:16–24). Given the importance of establishing the reliability of Jesus' witness, it would be unthinkable for there not to be an account of the fulfillment of such major predictions. What is more, it is also now out of the question that the future glorification of the witness will mean the abandonment of his incarnate form. What becomes apparent from Jesus' witness is just as clear from the presentation of him as judge. In 5:19–29 Jesus claims that the two aspects of divine judgment— the giving of life and condemnation—have been delegated to him. The earlier depiction of the Logos in 1:4 is echoed as he declares, "For just as

---

[11] Again the pronouncement of Bultmann, ibid., 56 has been influential: "If Jesus' death on the cross is already his exaltation and glorification, *his resurrection* cannot be an event of special significance. No resurrection is needed to destroy the triumph which death might be supposed to have gained in the crucifixion."

[12] For a fuller discussion of this issue, see A. T. Lincoln, " 'I Am the Resurrection and the Life': The Resurrection Message of the Fourth Gospel," in *Life in the Face of Death: The Resurrection Message of the New Testament* (ed. R. N. Longenecker; Grand Rapids: Eerdmans, 1998), 122–44.

the Father has life in himself, so he has granted the Son also to have life in himself" (5:26). As the living Logos/Son, Jesus has the power in both the present and the future to pronounce the verdict of life. At the end of history, it will be his voice that inaugurates the bodily resurrection of the dead for a judgment of either life or condemnation. In the bread-of-life discourse of 6:25–59, Jesus also claims the power to give eternal life in the present to those who come to him and then to raise them up at the last day (cf. vv. 39–40, 44, 54). Given that the verdict of the over-all trial includes the body in eternal life, it would be very strange if, when its incarnate mediator died, the verdict on him failed to include life for his body.

The passage on the raising of Lazarus has already been discussed as the narrative middle. Its pivotal place in the narrative and its themes surely clinch the case being made here. It is this incident that leads to the decision of the Sanhedrin to kill Jesus (cf. 11:46–53, 57) and therefore to his final interrogation, trial, and death. In enacting the judgment of giving life to Lazarus, Jesus seals the death sentence of his own judgment by the Jewish authorities. This final sign in the witness of works before Israel, in its temporary restoration of Lazarus to human bodily life, not only points to the verdict in the overall trial, to the eschatological life provided by the judge; in so doing, it also indicates that this life will embrace the body. At the heart of the account is the "I am" saying of 11:25—"I am the resurrection and the life"—in which Jesus claims to be the embodiment of eschatological expectations about the resurrection of the dead and the source of the verdict of life. The claim is substantiated in the other event of which the raising of Lazarus is an anticipation, namely, Jesus' own resurrection. Indeed, without the more decisive defeat of death in his own resurrection, where Jesus, unlike Lazarus, needs no one to unbind him and has left the graveclothes behind (compare 11:44 with 20:7), this claim would not ring fully true.

The resurrection of Jesus, then, is integral to the lawsuit and its concerns. The account of the empty tomb demonstrates the reliability of his earlier witness about what would happen to his body, and together with the account of the appearances, it completes the vindication of the judgment concerning Jesus. The negative aspect of this judgment, his death, can be seen as the hour of glory, but this evaluation does not obviate the need for the positive aspect, the verdict of life, to be demonstrated in his resurrection. The death and the resurrection of the witness and judge are not in competition or conflict in the story line but are complementary. It is significant that the message the risen Jesus tells Mary to pass on is not that he is risen but that he is ascending (20:17). This links the resurrection accounts with the earlier discourse about Jesus' ascent (cf. 3:13; 6:62) and his return to the Father who sent him (cf., e.g., 7:33; 14:28; 16:28). Now both the death and the resurrection can be seen as vital stages of the ascent in glory. For the implied author, the climax of Jesus' story is not the death itself nor the resurrection itself but the return of the crucified Jesus in a resurrected body to the Father. The decisive stage of the lawsuit is over as the incarnate Logos returns to God. The form in which the Logos returns now bears the marks of the trial's sentence of death (cf. 20:20) in addition to embodying its verdict of life.

C. The Trial's Outcome—Life or Condemnation?

We have just seen how the verdict in the cosmic lawsuit—life or the condemnation of death—is a key element in the narrative's depiction of the mission of Jesus as witness and judge, particularly its presentation of his death and resurrection. But the purpose and outcome of the trial will repay further investigation and will take us into the areas traditionally described as the soteriology and eschatology of the Fourth Gospel.

An initial question might well be, If the dominant motif is a trial, how appropriate is it to think of salvation in such a context? But to raise such a question is to forget the scriptural background of our motif. It has already been pointed out in reference to God as Judge that Yahweh's judgment entailed acting to establish justice and restore conditions of well-being. This notion dominates Deutero-Isaiah, where it is frequently formulated in terms of salvation or redemption or their equivalents. After all, the lawsuits there come into play precisely because Israel was in a situation that required intervention by Yahweh. Israel was in exile, and the issue is whether its God is the sort of God who is able to do anything about this and rescue Israel from its plight. If Yahweh really is God, then this means that Yahweh has the power to save. So again and again, while Israel is depicted as having "become a prey with no one to rescue" (Isa 42:22) or as having "no one to save you" (47:15), in Yahweh's speeches Yahweh is described as "your Redeemer" (cf., e.g., 41:14; 44:6, 24; 47:11; 48:17; 49:7; 54:5, 8) and as acting to redeem Israel (cf. 43:1; 44:22–23; 48:20; 52:3, 9). Neither the gods of the nations (44:17) nor their sorcerers and astrologers (47:13) can save, but Yahweh is "your Savior" (cf. 43:3; 45:15, 21). Indeed, in Isa 43:11–13 Yahweh asserts that because Yahweh is "I am," "besides me there is no savior. I declared and saved and proclaimed, . . . and you are my witnesses. . . . there is no one who can deliver from my hand." Yahweh also asks, "Is my hand shortened, that it cannot redeem [or 'save']? Or have I no power to deliver?" (50:2) and promises, "I . . . will save" (46:4) and "my salvation will not tarry; I will put salvation in Zion, for Israel my glory" (46:13). This salvation will be eternal (45:17; 51:6; cf. also 51:8). The term for salvation is often paralleled by צֶדֶק (LXX—δικαιοσύνη), *righteousness* or *righteous judgment* (cf., e.g., 46:13; 51:5–6, 8). To judge righteously is to save, and the goal of the lawsuit is that "all flesh shall know that I am the LORD your Savior, and your Redeemer" (49:26) and that "all the ends of the earth shall see the salvation of our God" (52:10). Thus, "when God saves, God does justice; when God does justice, God saves—unless one refuses to be saved."[13] If we summarize the various images for such salvation within these chapters of Deutero-Isaiah, we find it consists in light for those in darkness, release for those held captive, food and water for the hungry and thirsty, justice for the oppressed, love for the abandoned, blotting out of transgressions for sinners, comfort instead of fear, glory instead of shame, power instead of weakness, joy instead of mourning, and life instead of death.

In the Fourth Gospel, too, the judgment of the cosmic lawsuit entails salvation. The terminology is explicit in a number of places. The purpose of the lawsuit's judgment is stated as clearly as possible in 3:17: "God did not send the Son into the world to condemn the world, but in order that the world might be saved through him." Here it is formulated in terms of the relationship of agency, but at the conclusion of the public mission, in 12:47b, Jesus makes the same point equally clearly in terms of his own initiative in the trial—"I came not to judge the world, but to save the world," where "judge" in the first clause again has the negative connotation of "condemn." As one whose witness is self-authenticating, Jesus does not strictly need other witnesses, but he goes along with legal convention and mentions John the Baptist's testimony "so that you may be saved" (5:34). He also claims to be the point of entry into salvation (cf. 10:9). And after Jesus has testified to the Samaritan woman that "salvation is from the Jews" (4:22), other Samaritans later believe the witness of this Jewish Messiah and confess, "this is truly the Savior of the world" (4:42).

The narrative also depicts this salvific judgment as justice operative for Jesus and his persecuted followers. For those who accept the testimony of Jesus, this judgment is the light that enables them to see; freedom from slavery to sin; the bread and the water of life; comfort, assurance, and peace to replace fear; glory to replace shame; the power or authority to become children of God, to ask anything in Jesus' name,

---

[13] M. Volf, *Exclusion and Embrace* (Nashville: Abingdon, 1996), 221.

and to do greater works than his; joy to replace weeping and mourning; and life instead of death. But the dominant imagery for salvation in this narrative's discourse is the last; the everlasting salvation of Deutero-Isaiah becomes eternal life in the Gospel.

If the purpose of God's sovereign and faithful judgment for the world is an act of rescue that provides the world with life, this means that its present plight is death. The prologue suggests that this is the case. Although all things were created through the Logos, in whom was life (1:3–4), when his mission in the world is summarized in vv. 10–13, it is seen to entail putting created life back into relationship with its source, enabling humans to receive new life from the same origin as the Logos, to be "born . . . of God." The assumption has to be that the Logos comes into a world that has in some sense become separated from the divine life that created it. And to be alienated from the life of the Creator is to be given over to the power of death, the force at work in the world to subvert the Creator's purposes for life. This is the reason the narrative recounts a fresh initiative by the Creator, a new judgment on behalf of the world, that will provide the possibility of rescue from death's destructive hold.[14]

The plight of humanity as death is not an implication that needs to be drawn from the discourse; it is explicit in it.[15] Humans can simply be depicted as those who in their present existence are dead (5:25), while to accept the witness of Jesus is to have "passed from death to life" (5:24). The purpose of Jesus' coming is that people may "not die" (6:50), and the promise that is held out to those who believe is that they will not see or taste death (8:51–52), they will never die (11:26). But the negative judgment that falls on those who refuse to believe Jesus' witness that "I am" is that they will die in their sin or sins (8:21, 24). The connection of death with sin is, of course, highly significant. As elsewhere in the biblical tradition, the hold of death over humanity is not seen as a condition that has been brought about without human compliance. It is the result of the refusal of the relationship to the Creator, evidenced in disobedience to, or disregard of, the Creator's revealed will for human life. It is true that in this Gospel the primary sin is not to accept the witness of Jesus (cf., e.g., 15:22, 24; 16:9), but it is also clear that this new disregard

---

[14] Rensberger, *Johannine Faith*, 142, explains that saving the world in John's Gospel "meant to recall it from its self-absorption to its stance as creature before its Creator, yielding an obedience to God that could undo the structures that maintained it apart from God in the darkness of its hatred."

[15] On the concept of death and dying in John, see Blank, *Krisis*, 143–58.

for God's claims is at the same time a perpetuation and exposure of an already existing attitude toward God. The sin of the world that the Lamb of God has come to take away (1:29) is not simply the refusal to believe in Jesus. People can be characterized by Jesus as already slaves to sin by the very act of committing sin (8:34). The condemnation resulting from refusal to see when encountered by the light and refusal to admit the need for seeing is that "your sin remains" (9:41), and since sin remains, death remains.

Another way of referring to this destructive force is the use of the verb ἀπόλλυμι, *to perish* or *to suffer destruction*. God gave the only Son out of love for the world, "so that everyone who believes in him may not perish" (3:16; cf. also 10:28). In these references, perishing is contrasted with having eternal life, as also in the juxtaposition of food that perishes and food for eternal life in 6:27. In 17:12, where the cognate noun is employed, Judas is characterized as a "son of destruction," someone destined for the perdition that is death.

Thus, the death and destruction caused by sin are the plight from which humanity needs to be rescued, but they are also the condition to which those who refuse the rescuing judgment are condemned. Condemnation is the negative aspect of judgment. The one who believes does not come under such judgment or condemnation (5:24); but it can be pronounced in the present (cf. 8:26), and there will also be a future judgment at the final resurrection that involves condemnation (5:29). This negative verdict falls also upon the ruler of this world (16:11). This verdict can be described in two ways. On the one hand, it is rendered by God or Jesus, and in it God exercises righteous anger or wrath: "whoever disobeys the Son will not see life, but must endure God's wrath" (3:36). On the other hand, humans condemn themselves by rejecting the witness they have been given: "those who do not believe are condemned already, because they have not believed in the name of the only Son of God" (3:18). One of the bitter ironies of the Roman trial is the narrative enactment of the latter aspect, as both Pilate and "the Jews" condemn themselves by their words and deeds.

Salvation in the Fourth Gospel's trial comes through the positive verdict of life. Ironically, it may be necessary for modern readers to keep reminding themselves that life is a positive verdict in this narrative, since in trials today being sentenced to life means something quite different—imprisonment for life, normally as a substitute for the death penalty, and as the result of being found guilty. Here the term *life* occurs thirty-six times and on seventeen of these occasions is accompanied by the adjective *eternal*. Eternal life in this narrative discourse does not simply signify the duration of such life but takes up the notion of the life of the age to come, denoting the quality of life appropriate to that age. Clearly this life is not the same as present creaturely existence because such existence is caught up in the cycle of death. But neither can it be viewed as divorced from created physical life or as existing on some separate "spiritual" level. At present in the midst of existence still subject to death, the experience of life has its source and content in the relationship to Jesus and God that comes through believing and affects all of human living. But it is also made clear that this positive verdict includes resurrection and therefore that created bodily life is embraced by eternal life.

That life is the intended outcome of the lawsuit is apparent at every stage. The preview of the Logos's mission in the prologue has already been mentioned (cf. 1:4, 12–13), and the dialogue with Nicodemus takes up the notion of experiencing new life by being born of God, in its talk of being born from above or of the Spirit (3:3, 5–7). The latter leads into the first mention of eternal life in 3:15, where it is the result of believing in the lifted up Son of Man, and the repetition of the terminology in 3:16, where it is the result of believing in the Son whom God has given out of love for the world. Both of these references also indicate that eternal life is intimately tied to the death of Jesus. All of Jesus' signs bear witness to this life, whether it is through the supply of the wine and joy of the new order, the restoration of people to health and sight, the provision of bread that points to the bread of life, the mastery of the chaos waters through walking on the sea, or, in particular, the raising of Lazarus from the dead. Not only the witness of his works but also that of Jesus' words conveys life (cf. 6:63, 68).

Many of the symbols in the discourses have life as a primary referent—bread, water, light. Indeed, regarding the last, Jesus declares, "Whoever follows me will never walk in darkness but will have the light of life" (8:12). Light can thus serve to elucidate the entire judging function of Jesus' mission (cf. 3:19–21), but because, for those who come to the light, it means the receiving of sight (9:39a) and no longer remaining in darkness (12:35–36, 45), it is also particularly appropriate as a reference to the positive outcome of the judgment as life. The narrative contains a number of other key statements that highlight this outcome. A mission statement of Jesus indicates that this positive verdict is its goal: "I came that they may have life, and have it abundantly" (10:10). The summary of the trial before Israel states that the witness of Jesus' words that will also serve as the judge on the last day has been the Father's commandment and "his commandment is eternal life" (12:50). Eternal life in 17:3 is the believing recognition of the verdict on what is at issue in the trial—the identities of God and Jesus: "And this is eternal life, that they may know you, the only true God, and Jesus Christ whom you have sent." And the purpose statement for the narrative as a whole is, "that you may come to believe that Jesus is the Messiah, the Son of God, and that through believing you may have life in his name" (20:31).

The theme of eternal life is particularly prominent in Jesus' defense speech in 5:19–47 and in the pivotal episode of the raising of Lazarus. Both passages draw out the eschatological significance of the term and connect it with resurrection. In the former, Jesus claims the divine prerogatives of judging in general and of giving life in particular and asserts that the one who believes on the basis of his word of witness has eternal life now. To make this absolutely clear, it is spelled out that this means that such a person does not come under condemnation but has already passed from death to life. Jesus' word of witness "operates as a power to beget life. . . . The speech line is nothing less than a lifeline."[16] Indeed, "the hour is coming, and is now here, when the dead will hear the voice of the Son of God, and those who hear will live" (5:21–25). What is more, at a future hour at the end of history, this same voice will inaugurate the physical resurrection of the dead for a judgment of either life or condemnation (5:28–29). This brings clearly into play the eschatological expectations already inherent in the notion of the life of the age to come. Jesus' claims hold together both the present ("the hour is coming, and is now here" [5:25]) and the future ("the hour is coming" [5:28]) aspects of judgment. The positive verdict is already in operation, but there also remains a future verdict. The future element is in line with the sequence of Jewish expectations—resurrection is followed by judgment with its possible twofold outcome. But the "realized" element in Jesus' claim requires a reversal in sequence—the judgment is already taking place in response to Jesus' witness, and the dead hearing the voice of the Son of God and living is a consequence of the verdict in this judgment. In what follows in this passage, the emphasis returns to the present. Jesus says that his Jewish opponents search the Scriptures in the hope of finding in them the life of the age to come. Yet they fail to see that the Scriptures are not an end in themselves but witness to him, and so they refuse to come to him for life (5:39–40).

In the Lazarus episode, the theological issues emerge most clearly in Jesus' dialogue with Martha. When Jesus tells her that her brother will live again, she understands this to be a reference to the end-time resurrection (11:24). Her incomprehension serves as the foil for Jesus' self-

---

[16] Minear, *John: The Martyr's Gospel*, 95.

identification: "I am the resurrection and the life" (11:25). Jesus claims to be the fulfillment of traditional Jewish eschatological hopes, embodying both the power to raise the dead and the positive verdict of the final judgment as life. This underlines that the verdict in the trial, like the witness, is not simply a word or pronouncement but is embodied in the person of Jesus. The significance of this striking "I am" declaration is elaborated in the parallel clauses of 11:25b–26a: "Those who believe in me, even though they die, will live, and everyone who lives and believes in me will never die." Their force hangs on the different meanings of *to live* and *to die*. Believers in Jesus may undergo physical death; but this cannot affect the eschatological life they already have in him, and they will continue to live beyond death. The point is then underlined almost tautologically. To have such life through believing in Jesus means that believers will never experience the spiritual death of alienation from God because the quality of life they enjoy is eternal. Death cannot disrupt the life Jesus gives. Instead believers in him who die will continue to live, and at the last day this life will take on new bodily form, as the temporary raising of Lazarus that follows this conversation signifies. Elsewhere Jesus also makes the promise that believers will both have eternal life and be raised up at the last day (6:39–40, 44, 54).

It is frequently stated that the realized aspects of the judgment of both life and condemnation in the Fourth Gospel are quite distinct from the Jewish conceptual world that forms the backdrop for its thought. It is also stated that the intense focus on Christology in this Gospel has produced this distinctive emphasis. But even if we limit our area of comparison to Jewish eschatological expectations, this is only partially true, since we also find in Jewish apocalyptic writings various notions of anticipation of the end-time events.[17] The eschatological dimension of judgment in the Fourth Gospel, however, is played out not only within Jewish ideas of the judgment of the end time but also within the framework of the lawsuit from the Jewish Scriptures. In the latter, judgment takes place in the present, in the context of the covenant relationship in which both parties can be put on trial. In itself the notion of judgment with both positive and negative verdicts in the present is by no means completely new or distinctive. What is distinctive is that God is now represented in the trial by Jesus. The realized aspects of the judgment have certainly been informed by the conviction that the implied author shares

---

[17] For substantiation of this point, see A. T. Lincoln, *Paradise Now and Not Yet* (Cambridge: Cambridge University Press, 1981), esp. 169–80, on the links between Pauline realized eschatology and apocalyptic writings.

with most early Christians that God has acted ahead of time in history in Christ to inaugurate the age to come. But this christological conviction has been combined with the guiding motif of a present lawsuit from Isa 40–55. The vehicle for the narrative elaboration of a primarily realized eschatology was therefore already in place in the scriptural depiction—in terms of a trial—of this present relationship between Yahweh and Israel and between Yahweh and the nations. The eschatological emphasis that now also informs the notion of judgment in the Fourth Gospel serves to heighten the seriousness of the issues that are at stake. It also accounts for the depiction of this lawsuit as working itself out in two stages. The present realization of the eschatological perspective is the lawsuit of Jesus' mission culminating in the decisive verdict of his death and resurrection and the experiences of either life or judgment that this verdict has made available. But there remains a future aspect in both parts of the verdict, and so a second stage of the lawsuit continues even though the judge has already pronounced on the central issues.

Another observation often made about realized eschatology, such as that found in the Fourth Gospel, is that it leads to a shift from the dominance of temporal categories to that of spatial categories. Thus, it is said, in this narrative the focus on the present aspect of salvation helps to explain the emphasis on heaven and earth, above and below, with Jesus, the descending and ascending Son of Man, the link between them. This is also the reason eternal life has its source in the above, so that people need to be born from above, the reason Jesus' kingdom is not of this world, and the reason those who refuse his witness are from below. While there is some truth to these observations, they do not provide a fully adequate explanation of this aspect of the Fourth Gospel's discourse. The very fact that the lawsuit of Deutero-Isaiah is a cosmic lawsuit means that the spatial categories of heaven and earth are already found in the motif that has been taken over by this Gospel. The scriptural lawsuit is cosmic not only in the sense that it includes both Israel and the nations but also in the sense that the created cosmos is the setting in which it unfolds. There are frequent references to this setting, which also points to Yahweh's creative sovereignty (cf., e.g., Isa 40:22–23; 42:5; 44:24; 45:12, 18; 48:13; 51:16). In 45:8 the heavens are called on to shower down righteous judgment from above (LXX—ἄνωθεν), and the earth is called on to open up so that both salvation and righteous judgment spring forth. In 51:6 salvation and righteous judgment have as a backdrop the heavens and the earth below; the permanence of the former is contrasted with the transience of the latter. Finally, Isa 55:9–11 is particularly significant because the difference between heaven and earth stands here for the difference between Yahweh's ways and thoughts and those of humans; Yahweh's word that accomplishes Yahweh's purposes in the world is likened to the rain and snow that come down from heaven and do not return there until they have accomplished their task of watering the earth. Scripture, then, clearly provides the conceptual means for depicting the coming or descent of the Logos from heaven and his return or ascent there after accomplishing the purposes of a salvific judgment that itself has this spatial or cosmic setting.

But when does the verdict that is made ahead of time, the verdict of the heavenly judge, take place in this narrative? Jesus offers life and judges throughout his mission, but this is within a plot that progresses toward his death as the critical hour of judgment. His death is both the world's judgment on him and God's judgment of both him and the world. As noted, by absorbing the negative verdict of death, Jesus also becomes the source of the positive verdict of life. Blood and water flow from his side (19:34). That this is the key moment of the lawsuit, not to be missed by the reader, is signaled in four different ways. First, a witness is supplied—in all probability the beloved disciple who is depicted at the cross in vv. 26–27.[18] Second, the narrator, who appears to be identified at this point with this witness, the beloved disciple, quite unusually stops and addresses the readers, telling them that this witness is given so that they may believe (v. 35a). Third, there is a double underlining of the truth of this witness: "His testimony is true, and he [best understood as the witness himself] knows that he tells the truth" (v. 35b). Fourth, the narrator indicates that this event is the fulfillment of not just one but two Scriptures. The piercing of Jesus' side is a substitute for the usual practice of breaking the victims' legs. This is seen as the fulfillment of "None of his bones shall be broken." As already discussed, the texts about the Passover lamb from the exodus tradition are significant as a source, but like a number of others in this Gospel, this scriptural citation serves to recall more than one tradition. The other tradition alluded to here is that of the suffering righteous one. In Ps 34:19–22, as the sign that the Lord rescues the righteous and redeems their life so that none of them will be *condemned,* "he keeps all their bones; not one of them will be broken." So the piercing of Jesus' side, in place of the breaking of his legs, is a sign of God's verdict. Against all appearances, Jesus has not been condemned but approved as righteous. The source of the second citation is clear. "They will look on

---

[18] See the discussion of the witness's identity in ch. 4, sec. D.

the one whom they have pierced" is taken from Zech 12:10. It is in a passage about the death of the good shepherd that goes on to talk of mourning for him as for an only child and says, "On that day a fountain shall be opened for the house of David and the inhabitants of Jerusalem, to cleanse them from sin and impurity" (Zech 13:1).

This scriptural reference to the one who has been pierced sees a fountain for cleansing resulting from the piercing; this takes us back to the depiction that has occasioned these scriptural citations in the first place: "one of the soldiers pierced his side with a spear, and at once blood and water came out" (John 19:34). Within the Gospel's own frame of reference, the significance of the blood and water is not difficult to discover and fits the connotations suggested by the scriptural citation and its context. The significance of the blood is set out in John 6, and that of the water in John 7. In 6:52–59 there are clear eucharistic overtones, but the basic reference is to the necessity of believing in the effectiveness of Jesus' death in order to have life: "unless you eat the flesh of the Son of Man and drink his blood, you have no life in you. Those who eat my flesh and drink my blood have eternal life" (6:53–54). Chapter 2 of this study has already discussed 7:38. With its talk of rivers of living water flowing from Christ's belly, it provides the key to the meaning of the water that comes from Jesus' side, namely, the life of the Spirit that comes from Jesus' glorification. Both the blood and the water, then, point unmistakably to the positive verdict of life for others that comes from God's verdict of approval rather than condemnation on the death of the witness and judge.

Despite the narrator's stress on what happens in Jesus' death, we have also seen that the positive verdict is completed in Jesus' resurrection and ascension. The resurrection underlines that life for Jesus, just as he has promised for those who believe in him, takes in the body. Indeed, the life his followers will enjoy appears to depend on his own resurrection life. In the Farewell Discourse, Jesus promises to return to them: "In a little while . . . you will see me; because I live, you also will live" (14:19). Earlier, too, there has been an indication that believers' experience of the living water that flows from Jesus awaits a future point in the narrative: "He said this about the Spirit, which believers in him were to receive; for as yet there was no Spirit, because Jesus was not yet glorified" (7:40). It looks, then, as if the explanation for this phenomenon—that the verdict is offered during Jesus' mission as witness and judge but only decisively takes place in his death and resurrection—lies in the dual temporal perspective that characterizes the narrative discourse. What only becomes apparent after the verdict of the death and resurrection is retrojected into the earlier stage of the trial, in a collapsing of temporal perspectives. This appears also to be the best explanation of the formulation in 6:27c, where, after Jesus declares that the Son of Man will give eternal life, he also asserts, "For it is on him that God the Father has set his seal." If, as in 3:33, the notion of setting a seal has reference to ratifying a legal testimony or judgment, then the thought here is that God is confirming the divine verdict of approval on Jesus as the dispenser of the positive verdict of life. There is no need to look back to the baptism or incarnation as the time when this confirmation was given. Rather, this is a proleptic confirmation of the verdict that is yet to be given in the cross and resurrection.

The narrative's temporal perspective is, however, more subtle than the talk of collapsing or overlapping temporal perspectives alone allows. The retrojection reaches back to the time before the earthly stage of the trial, so that the life and, for that matter, the glory of Jesus are already experienced by him as the Logos, who is with God from the beginning of time. From this perspective, the life that Jesus offers during his mission can be seen as the divine life of the Logos. Sometimes the statements connecting Jesus and the ability to give life appear to reflect his divine origin as the Logos. "Just as the Father has life in himself, so he has granted the Son also to have life in himself" (5:26) and "Whoever follows me . . . will have the light of life" (8:12) echo the prologue's formulation about the Logos, "in him was life, and the life was the light of all people" (1:4). On the other hand, the assertion that "those who eat my flesh and drink my blood have eternal life, and I will raise them up at the last day" (6:54) makes such life dependent on the verdict that takes place in the death of Jesus. And the saying "I am the resurrection and the life" (11:25) makes his resurrection also essential to the positive outcome of the trial.

Ultimately, these two perspectives are not at odds in the narrative discourse. As the Logos, Jesus brings the life of the Creator to an alienated world. But to be effective in such a world, this life has to take on its alienation and death. So eternal life in the Gospel begins with the creative life of God in the Logos and ends with the resurrection life of Jesus that empowers his followers. Resurrection life is the restoration of humanity's links to the divine life that were imparted in creation. The two perspectives come together in a formulation such as that of 6:51: "I am the living bread that came down from heaven. Whoever eats of this bread will live forever; and the bread that I will give for the life of the world is my flesh." Jesus brings the divine life into the world as the Logos, but human experience of this eternal life depends on what happens in the giving of Jesus' flesh. We may still wish to press our questions. Why is it necessary for Jesus to die to open up the life of God to others? Do not God and the Logos have the power simply to bestow life on whom they will? The response implicit in this narrative's discourse is still that indicated briefly above: the latter course of action would not do justice to the nature of the relationship that has been established between God and humanity nor to the fact that the seriousness of humanity's plight is of its own making. It was necessary for the life of the world to go through death for the same reason that the Logos became flesh. If death's destructive hold is to be broken, humanity needs the life of God to be opened up for humanity—to be manifest in human form and to overcome death—from within the human situation of death. The cosmic lawsuit between God and the world is about God's willingness to identify God's own self with the plight of humanity, about God's loving accommodation to the needs of humanity ("God so loved the world"). God risks the divine life by being put on trial and sentenced to death ("he gave his only Son"). As the divine life absorbs the sentence of death on humanity in Jesus' death and embodies the verdict of life in his resurrection, this opens the way for humans, through believing, to be united with the life that overcomes death ("so that everyone who believes in him may not perish but may have eternal life" [3:16]).

Thus, believers can experience the positive verdict of the lawsuit in the present. It is difficult not to see here an equivalent of the Pauline notion of justification[19] when the entire pattern of the Fourth Gospel's narrative is taken into account. After all, because Jesus submits to the sentence of death in the cosmic lawsuit, those who believe can receive the verdict of no condemnation. The sentence of death is reversed and instead becomes the positive verdict of life, the life of the age to come. In Paul, too, Jesus' death meets the requirements of God's just judgment (cf. Rom 3:25, 26), reversing the situation of condemnation and enabling the verdict of justification and life (cf. Rom 5:18).

Just as in Paul there is a tension between the verdict of justification ahead of time and the necessity of a last judgment, so in the Fourth Gospel there is a question—in the case of both life and condemnation—

---

[19] I am assuming here, unlike some recent interpreters of Paul, that his notions of righteousness and being justified have major forensic connotations. See A. T. Lincoln, "From Wrath to Justification: Tradition, Gospel, and Audience in the Theology of Romans 1:18–4:25," in *Romans,* vol. 3 of *Pauline Theology* (ed. D. M. Hay and E. E. Johnson; Minneapolis: Fortress, 1995), 130–59, esp. 135–49.

about the relationship between the present verdict and the future judgment of which Jesus continues to speak. On the one hand, "the coming of the Last Day is not thought to bring a new and independent act of judgment; rather it will reveal the final outcome of the lawsuit that has been in progress over the claims of Jesus Christ."[20] On the other hand, if there were no room for any real difference between the state of affairs at present in the trial and the final verdict, then the latter would appear to be superfluous except as a public demonstration of the present verdict. But we should not minimize the importance of this public and open demonstration for Jewish thought. Justice must be seen to have been done. Hence, the notion of a resurrection even for condemnation.

There does appear to be a difference of emphasis in how the tension between the present and the future affects those who have rejected the witness at present and those who have received it. Clearly, as we have seen, for the believer the full experience of the positive verdict as it affects physical life awaits the future. But in the meantime, regarding belief, the narrative indicates the possibility not so much of the verdict itself being reversed as of the relation of believers to this verdict undergoing a reversal. Some characters move from initial belief to unbelief (cf. 6:66; 8:31–59), and there are exhortations about the necessity of continuing in Jesus' word if one is to be truly a disciple (8:31) and warnings about the fate of those who fail to abide in him (15:6). "For the disciples, therefore, present experience of eternal life calls for validation 'on the last day': faith in Jesus' word is the work not of a moment but of a lifetime. . . . The abundant life (10:10) that Jesus has opened up for his disciples is a life in which they must continue."[21] The eschatological judgment will at least then reveal what remains ambiguous in the present—who has genuinely believed and has eternal life.

As already noted, the final judgment will add on the negative side the dimension of a visible and open display of the condemnation that has been incurred. But there are no real clues about any change in a negative response to the present encounter with the testimony to Jesus. If, on the positive side, what appears now to be belief may, in some cases, turn out to be unbelief, then it is possible that, in some cases, what appears now to be unbelief may be revealed as belief. Besides portraying clear-cut responses to Jesus' witness from most of its characters, the narrative also has some room for different shades of response, for progressive

---

[20] Trites, *Concept of Witness,* 123–24.
[21] J. T. Carroll, "Present and Future in Fourth Gospel 'Eschatology,'" *BTB* 19 (1989): 67.

belief and for progressive unbelief. But since the narrative is designed to reinforce the validity and necessity of the belief that receives the positive verdict, it has no interest in whether those who presently condemn themselves by refusing to accept the witness will have a chance at the end to review their refusal. All the emphasis is on the seriousness of the consequences of the judgments that are made at present. Jesus' assertion that the one who rejects his witness now will have a judge on the last day and that the judge will be precisely the witness he has already given (12:48) makes plain that the criterion for judgment remains the same between the present and the future. It does not address the issue of whether there is room for a change in the response to this criterion. We are left only with questions. Does the nature of the divine verdict that has already been given offer hope about its final ratification? Since that verdict was only reached by a love that went through death to offer life, when confronted with the full reality of that intended positive judicial outcome at the end, will those who have declined to accept the witness only confirm their decision? It would be strange if the offer no longer held. It would be even stranger if it were still declined. On the other hand, given the extent of the divine love that offers life through undergoing death and the once-for-all quality that the narrative depiction attaches to it, is there anything further that can be added to the offer? And what more would it take to encourage a free acceptance of it?

The background of the scriptural lawsuit and Yahweh's judgment may offer a partial answer to such questions. A common pattern, reflected in Isa 40–55, is that first Yahweh judges the people in wrath, in this case handing them over to Babylon: "I was angry with my people, I profaned my heritage; I gave them into your hand, you showed them no mercy" (Isa 47:6). But then Yahweh determines, for the sake of Yahweh's own reputation as much as out of fidelity to the covenant that Israel has in any case broken, to reverse the situation and to bring home the exiles: "For my name's sake I defer my anger, for the sake of my praise I restrain it for you, so that I may not cut you off" (48:9).[22] Thus, what appeared to be Yahweh's complete judicial condemnation and abandonment of Israel turns out to have been "for a brief moment" (54:7–8). The lawsuit in Deutero-Isaiah means that Yahweh did not give up on the relationship with Israel, and it emphasizes Yahweh's salvific purposes. The portrayal of Yahweh as judge signifies not only Yahweh's ability to pronounce the right verdict but also Yahweh's acting to uphold

---

[22] See Brueggemann, *Theology of the Old Testament*, 296–310, on Yahweh's resilient relatedness and this two-stage sequence.

Israel's rights, particularly those of the needier among the people. As Nielsen emphasizes, the dual function of Yahweh as prosecutor and judge within the lawsuit signifies, on the one hand, that Yahweh's punishment of the people "was not merely an expression of arbitrary anger . . . in this sense, the lawsuit contributes to an understanding of Yahweh's righteousness," and, on the other, that Yahweh desired the people to be led to repentance and to return to Yahweh for forgiveness.[23] "He is at one and the same time the prosecutor who exposes the people's guilt, and the judge whose task it is to secure the rights of the downtrodden."[24] The lawsuit expresses the tension within Israel's understanding of Yahweh, an understanding both "of Yahweh's will to punish, which is grounded in his righteousness; and of Yahweh's will to save, which is grounded in his love."[25]

The reader of the Fourth Gospel might well expect some variation of this pattern to hold even after God became most fully involved in the life of God's people, after the Logos came to his own and the majority of his own people did not accept him (John 1:11). The matter is complicated by the fact that in John unbelieving Israel now takes the place of the nations in Deutero-Isaiah's lawsuits. But even there Yahweh is able to surprise. In the final trial speech against the nations, instead of the pronouncement of condemnation that might have been expected, there is the offer of salvation for all who are willing to turn to Yahweh: "Turn to me and be saved, all the ends of the earth!" (Isa 45:22). Given this Gospel's setting, which chapter 6, below, will look at more closely, it is not surprising that the Gospel shows no explicit interest in this question and instead concentrates its attention on the role of the new community that becomes Jesus' own (John 13:1). Yet this role has, as a major feature, the mission to the world, and there is certainly no indication that the unbelieving world (or hostile Jews, as its main representatives) has been completely written off. The aim of the mission is still to convince people of the verdict.

Perhaps the best that can be said is that the narrative depicts what has happened in Jesus as definitively anticipating the end, and therefore the response to him as also a definitive anticipation of the end. Yet it also allows that responses can change. Statements about the consequences of a less than appropriate present response can also serve as exhortations to a change of heart. So, present decisions in the trial really anticipate the

---

[23] Nielsen, *Yahweh as Prosecutor and Judge,* 75–77.
[24] Ibid., 82.
[25] Ibid., 83.

end, but they *only anticipate* the end. The final verdict remains until then, and remains where it belongs—with God.

D. The Truth at Issue

Discussion of the Fourth Gospel's notion of truth takes on a distinctive shape when it is set, as it surely should be, within the context of the lawsuit. It is instructive, therefore, to begin by recalling that this notion also plays a role in the scriptural lawsuit of Isa 40–55. It appears in two types of setting. The first setting is associated with righteous judgment or justice. Thus in 42:3 (LXX) the task of the servant is "to bring forth righteous judgment to truth." In 45:19 Yahweh is the "I am" (cf. LXX) who speaks the truth and declares righteous judgment. In contrast, in 48:1 Israel is depicted as invoking its God but not in truth or right judgment. The second setting is connected with the fulfillment of the divine word. In the trial speeches of Yahweh against the nations in 41:21–29 and 43:8–13, it is Yahweh's ability to predict "the former things" that clinches Yahweh's case. Such ability is meant to produce the response "He is true [NRSV: 'right']" (41:26). The same point is made in 43:9, where the response of Israel in particular as witness to the fulfillment of the foretelling of "the former things" is to be, "It is true." This is how Israel is to "know and believe me and understand that I am [NRSV: 'I am he']" (43:10). Thus, in the scriptural lawsuit, truth is the equivalent of right or just judgment. It therefore stands for the entire process of judgment, culminating in the verdict. Truth is what emerges in and through the lawsuit. For Yahweh, to judge justly is to determine, declare, and demonstrate the truth. But a further implication is that what the truth as judgment and verdict is will depend on the issue at stake in any particular trial. In Deutero-Isaiah the issue is whether Yahweh is the one true God who is able to save, and so this becomes the truth that is determined, declared, and demonstrated. But truth is not only inextricably connected with judgment; it is also bound up with witness. Since Yahweh stakes the truth of Yahweh's claim on the effectiveness of the divine word in history and since, as always in a trial, the truth is contested, witnesses are needed who can vouch for the correspondence between Yahweh's word and Yahweh's deed that fulfills such a word. The clear implication here is that when Yahweh submits to trial before humans, Yahweh's truth is made dependent on the witness of particular humans to it. How are people to know that Yahweh's judgment is true and that Yahweh is "I am"? Through witnesses who declare that Yahweh and Yahweh's word are true.

It is within this complex of ideas that we must see what truth entails for the Fourth Gospel. Truth concerns the disclosure or revelation of the divine reality, as many studies point out.[26] But this notion is not in the abstract; it functions in the context of judgment and witness in the narrative's lawsuit. This narrative amply demonstrates what we have seen in the Scripture that was formative for it—that truth is the judgment in the lawsuit, that it is always disputed, part of a contest of claims, and that it depends on witness. It also presupposes, as does the scriptural lawsuit, that truth can indeed be established because there is a divine judge. But the Fourth Gospel now gives all these elements of truth a new twist.

If truth is the judgment and verdict about an issue at stake and its content is determined by that issue, what is the issue here? It should not be surprising if we turn to the statement of purpose for one formulation of the issue. In the light of 20:31, it is apparent that at its heart is whether the crucified Jesus is the Messiah, the Son of God, and—from the rest of the narrative discourse we can add—therefore one with God. We have already seen that, from the rest of the discourse's depiction of the relation between Jesus and God, we are also justified in putting the issue the other way around. As it concerns God, it is also whether God is the God who is now known in the crucified Jesus. Truth is the affirmative judgment on the interrelated issues as this judgment develops in the narrative into a culminating verdict. Because the issue revolves around the identities of God and Jesus and because, in the nature of the case, both bear witness to their own identities, their witness becomes both part of the judgment and part of the issue to be judged, part of the truth claim that is the cause of the lawsuit.

Naturally, the implied author stresses both the truth of their witness and the truth of their persons. The circularity of the proceedings is apparent in 5:32, where Jesus makes the concession to the legal conventions by admitting that, according to them, his testimony on his own behalf is not valid. He invokes God as a further witness, but even here God's testimony is made to depend on Jesus' own testimony about its truth: "There is another who testifies on my behalf, and I know that his

---

[26] On truth in John, see esp. Bultmann, *Theology of the New Testament,* 2:18–19; J. Blank, "Der johanneische Wahrheitsbegriff," *BZ* 7 (1963): 163–73; Y. Ibuki, *Die Wahrheit im Johannesevangelium* (Bonn: Peter Hanstein, 1972); de la Potterie, *La vérité dans S. Jean;* R. Schnackenburg, *The Gospel according to Saint John* (3 vols.; vols. 1–2: New York: Seabury, 1980; vol. 3: New York: Crossroad, 1982), 2:225–37.

testimony to me is true." Elsewhere, when the sending language is to the fore, there is, as we would expect, more of a distinction: "The one who sent me is true" (7:28; 8:26), and Jesus describes the Father who sent him as "the only true God" (17:3). Later in the same prayer, Jesus declares that God's word is truth (17:17), but again, since Jesus himself is the present form of God's word in this narrative discourse, this also entails a declaration about himself.[27] Perhaps the integral relation between the two issues in connection with truth is most clearly stated in 3:33, where the narrator explains, "Whoever has accepted his [Jesus'] testimony has set a seal to this, that God is true." The truth of God and God's cause depends on the truth of Jesus' witness and his cause.

Jesus' words, as already noted, employ the distinctive double Amen introductory formula twenty-five times to emphasize the truth of what follows. It is as if Jesus as witness swears an oath to the veracity of his testimony. Jesus also claims that his teaching is from God, with the obvious implication that it is therefore true, and then asserts explicitly that, as one who seeks not his own glory but God's, he "is true, and there is nothing false in him" (7:17–18). This assertion provides a strong response to the charge that he is a false teacher who is deceiving the people (cf. v. 12b).[28] Not surprisingly, it is in the heated contest of claims in 8:12–59 that the issue of truth is most to the fore. In response to accusations about the singleness of his witness, Jesus declares that this witness is nevertheless true because of his divine origin and destiny (v. 14). Not only is his witness true for this reason; so also is his judgment in the lawsuit (v. 16). Again, a little later, Jesus bases his witness and his negative judgment of condemnation of his opponents on what he has heard from the Father, claiming that the one who has sent him is true (v. 26). An initial belief in the truth of his cause is not enough. It is continuing belief in his word that enables people to know the truth of the issue at stake in the trial and to experience the salvific effect of its true judgment in liberation from sin (vv. 31–32). When Jesus' witness becomes accusatory, he charges these Jews who have revealed themselves to be unbelieving with "trying to kill me, a man who has told you the truth that I heard from God," again identifying his own witness and judgment with God's (v. 40). Their murderous intent and refusal to accept the truth of his word, he says, stem from the fact that they have as their father one who

---

[27] Given the preceding request that the disciples be sanctified in the truth, it is unlikely that the Jewish Scriptures are in view in this reference to God's word, *contra* Boice, *Witness and Revelation*, 64–65.

[28] Cf. Pancaro, *The Law*, 92–101.

is a murderer and liar, the devil, who "does not stand in the truth, because there is no truth in him" (v. 44). If true judgment in the trial is about providing the positive verdict of life in a world where death has its hold, then this statement makes abundantly clear that the devil, as the ruler of this world, incorporates most fully all the values of the opposite side in the lawsuit. As befits his names, he is the slandering accuser, representing the destruction and violence of death. Here we see the issues in their starkest contrast—either true judgment and life or the false judgment of the lie and death. Jesus can then only return to his insistence that he speaks the truth, and to his question "If I tell the truth, why do you not believe me?" supplies his own answer, that it is because his opponents "are not from God" (vv. 45–47). He thus underlines the inevitable circularity entailed by the narrative's notion of truth. Bultmann has captured this aspect of Jesus' witness well: "The paradox is that the word of Jesus does not find its substantiation by a backward movement from the attesting word to the thing attested—as it might if the thing itself were confirmable irrespective of the word—but finds it only in the faith-prompted acceptance of the word."[29]

Because Jesus' witness is to his own cause and is self-authenticating, the truth of his witness thereby becomes the criterion of true judgment (cf. 12:48). In the nature of the case, there can be no criterion drawn from elsewhere by which to adjudicate Jesus' witness. This witness also embodies the truth of the issue about which judgment is being made. The insistence that he is the true light (1:9), the true bread (6:32), the true food and drink (6:55), and the true vine (15:1) underscores that the salvific judgment that brings sight, life, and fruitfulness into a dark, dead, and barren world is embodied in his own person. The claim that, as the only way to the Father, Jesus is also the truth (14:6) makes it explicit that the issues of the trial are summed up in him.

But if truth is true judgment culminating in a verdict that establishes the truth at issue, then Jesus' embodiment of this truth culminates in his death and resurrection. What decisively shapes Jesus' witness also decisively shapes the narrative's perspective on truth. The placement of the strongest statement about Jesus' mission—that he is to testify to the truth (18:37)—is highly significant.[30] It comes in the trial before Pilate, when, as he knows, Jesus is about to be sentenced to death. More specifically, it comes in the midst of a dialogue about power and in a setting that involves a struggle for power between Pilate and the Jewish religious

---

[29] Bultmann, *Theology of the New Testament*, 2:68.
[30] Cf. also Söding, "Die Macht der Wahrheit," 54.

leaders.[31] Jesus is the object of the action, the one without power. He has been taken (v. 28) and handed over to Pilate by the Jewish authorities (vv. 30, 35), and at the end will be handed over by Pilate (19:6a) and taken (19:6b). Between these events Jesus is summoned and interrogated by Pilate, taken and flogged, dressed up as king, mocked and struck in the face, and twice led outside by Pilate to face his accusers. The Jewish religious leaders have used their power to arrest Jesus and to hand him over to Pilate (18:35). They are impotent to carry out by themselves the death sentence that they believe Jesus merits under the law (cf. 18:31; 19:7), but expect to use their influence to persuade Pilate to carry out the sentence on a different charge, that of being a politically subversive claimant to messianic power. Pilate, the representative of Roman power, is not anxious to be manipulated, but Jesus' first words in reply to Pilate's question, "Are you the King of the Jews?" are also a question that reminds Pilate of the power struggle in which he has become embroiled: "Do you ask this on your own, or did others tell you about me?" (18:34).

Pilate will later remind Jesus that he, Pilate, has the power in this situation, and Jesus will respond that any authority Pilate possesses has in fact been delegated to him from above (19:10–11). In the power struggle between Pilate and the Jewish religious leaders, honors eventually appear to be divided fairly evenly. The latter get their way by using intimidation and reminding Pilate that, by releasing Jesus, he could well be seen as disloyal to the emperor (v. 12). But Pilate gets his way by not handing over Jesus to be crucified until he has extracted from the religious leaders a confession of complete allegiance to the emperor and his powers, which amounts to a betrayal of their supposed allegiance to God as their one King (v. 15). This is such a major concession, however, that, at the level of the play for power, the narrative has Pilate keeping the upper hand.[32] Another element in the contemporary political power struggle is brought to our attention by the Roman trial episode. Besides Pilate, the representative of Roman imperial power, and the Jewish religious leaders, those willing to accommodate to this power, there is Barabbas, the brigand and insurrectionist, representing an alternative response to Roman imperialism. The narrative presents a choice between Jesus and Barabbas just as it presents one between Jesus and Caesar.

Jesus' declaration that his mission is to testify to the truth is set in this context and itself addresses the issue of power. To the question of

---

31 Building on the work of Söding and Rensberger, Volf, *Exclusion and Embrace*, 264–71, has an illuminating discussion of the passage from this angle.
32 Cf. also Rensberger, *Johannine Faith*, 92.

whether he is the king of the Jews and therefore, from Pilate's perspective, whether he is staking out some claim to political power, Jesus' delayed reply is that his royal power, his kingdom, does not have its origin in this world. It is a power that is not caught up in the destructive forces of this world's cycle of deadly violence. If it were, Jesus' followers would have participated in this cycle by fighting for him (19:36). Jesus thus clearly distances his notion of power from the revolutionary option represented by Barabbas. Then he subordinates the entire question of royal power to that of truth: "You say that I am a king. For this I was born, and for this I came into the world, to testify to the truth" (18:37a). The truth of the cause to which Jesus witnesses—that of his and God's identity in the world—subverts normal human assumptions about power and also thereby subverts human assumptions about truth that see truth as simply a form of power. Jesus adds, "Everyone who belongs to the truth listens to my voice" (18:37b). Again, the power of his cause is not effected by force. It gathers adherents as they accept his witness, and in the process this witness continues its judging function of sifting and exposing humans' basic allegiances in the cosmic trial. Accepting Jesus' witness in all its apparent powerlessness indicates that one is aligned with the true judgment that is taking place.

The irony of the narrative reinforces the subversion because, as already discussed, the accused witness, who is at the mercy of the competing powers, is depicted as in fact the royal judge and even seated on the judge's seat. Jesus' witness to the truth is ironically established as the true judgment in this trial. The one who, on the human level, should have been exercising true judgment is left asking, "What is truth?" (18:38). In the light of what truth in the lawsuit entails, we can read this question now not simply as a failure to understand but also as an expression of both bafflement and lack of concern about true judgment in the case. His question puts this judge on the wrong side in the overall trial. It is all the more ironic since the one who embodies true judgment in the cosmic lawsuit is standing before him.

That Jesus' testifying to the truth is completed by his dying cry, "It is finished" (19:30), underscores that true judgment, with its culminating verdict on the issues of Jesus' and God's identities, is reached precisely in the death of the witness and judge. The determinative perspective on truth locates this truth in the utter weakness of the cross. The truth of this narrative is the truth of the victim. The identity or "godness" of God is disclosed in the crucified Jesus. The glory of this truth—and the prologue describes the glory of the incarnate Logos as full of grace and truth (1:14)—does not lie in its ability to impose itself by force or even in its power to convince and confound but is revealed in the humiliation and powerlessness of Jesus' death.

Since the resurrection completes the verdict, it cannot be left out of our account of true judgment in the trial. If this judgment means that the destructive power of death has been absorbed in the death of the judge so that life can be restored, then the resurrection of Jesus is the embodiment of this truth and of its verdict that life for humans is not a negation of creation but its eventual fulfillment in a resurrection body. It means that truth is life-giving. No wonder, then, that, as the unique means of access to God, Jesus can say both "I am . . . the truth" and "I am . . . the life" (14:6) and that the truth of his witness, "I am the resurrection and the life" (11:25), is confirmed. Thus, the weakness of the truth at the same time involves power, the power of life over death. The narrative does not allow us to forget that its truth includes both elements and that they remain in a dialectical relationship, whereby the power of life is only possible in and through the powerlessness of death. It does this in two ways. First, the verdict of life is signaled precisely at Jesus' death in the blood and water that flows from his side, and the truth of the beloved disciple's witness to this significance of Jesus' death is stressed (19:34–35). Second, the narrative makes clear that the resurrection does not triumphalistically supersede the crucifixion, because the marks of the victim's woundedness remain in the hands and side of the risen Jesus (20:20).

Truth as true judgment in the lawsuit is embodied in Jesus. But truth as the judgment and the cause that is judged continues to feature in the ongoing lawsuit after Jesus' death and resurrection. The Advocate is the Spirit of truth, contributing to true judgment of the issues at stake by testifying concerning Jesus (15:26; cf. 14:17; 16:13), driving home the verdict to the world (cf. 16:8–11), and giving the disciples fuller insight into the trial's issues (16:13). Jesus prays that these disciples will be set apart by God in the truth, that their mission in the world therefore will be one distinguished by the issues endorsed in the trial of Jesus' witness (17:17).

The second major aspect of truth in the scriptural lawsuit involved the correspondence between Yahweh's word and deed and the need for witnesses to this truth. Jesus is the witness to God and God's truth, and he claims to be in such dependence on God that everything he says and does on earth indeed corresponds to what the Father is saying and doing (cf., e.g., 5:19–20; 8:26, 28; 12:49–50). But if truth is the reliable connection between the word of God and its fulfillment, then the witness to truth is essentially witness to Jesus, since Jesus is that word, the Logos.

And it is the fit between word and world and word and deed in Jesus' mission to which witness is borne. This occurs in a number of ways. The Samaritan woman's testimony is to the match between Jesus' word and her own life (4:39). The royal official believes when he perceives the match between the time when Jesus told him his son would live and the time when the recovery began (4:53). What Jesus claims in the discourses is frequently shown to correspond with what he does in the signs. The one who has fed five thousand people with five loaves and two fish has truth in his cause when he also claims to be the bread of life. The one who claims to be the light of the world gives evidence for the truth of the claim in giving sight to the man born blind. The one who declares that he is the resurrection and the life promptly demonstrates this by raising Lazarus from the dead. In addition, the correspondence between Jesus' predictions and their fulfillment is also noted throughout the narrative (cf., e.g., 2:19, 22; 6:70–71; 12:32–33; 13:18–19).

This truth of the effectiveness of God's word in the world in Jesus and of Jesus' word in the world needs witnesses. Even the witness of John the Baptist functions in this context of correspondence between word and fulfillment. The last reference to him in the narrative highlights this aspect. His testimony about Jesus is viewed as matching what is taking place in Jesus' mission and leads to the assertion of many who had heard it that "everything John said about this man was true" and to their belief in Jesus (10:41–42). But the disciples, since they have been with Jesus from the beginning, are in a special position to be witnesses to this truth (15:27). The beloved disciple is witness to the water coming from Jesus' side, which is a fulfillment of Jesus' words in 7:38 (19:34). And the beloved disciple, in causing the narrative about the truth of Jesus as the Logos to be written down, is testifying to this truth (21:24). But the beloved disciple represents a community ("we") to which the actual narrator belongs, and this community also bears witness. This is seen in both the prologue and the epilogue. The community's testimony in 1:14, 16–17 is that "we have seen his glory," that this glory was "full of grace and truth," and that indeed grace and truth came into being through Jesus. The narrative begins with their testimony to the truth of Jesus and ends with their testimony to the truth of the beloved disciple's testimony about Jesus—"and we know that his testimony is true" (21:24). The truth of the cause on which righteous judgment has been given depends on, and is transmitted through, this chain of witnesses, guided, to be sure, by the continuing witness of the Spirit. The final links in this chain are the written testimony and its endorsement by a community testifying to its truth. The truth of the trial is embodied in the Logos but also becomes inscripturated as the beloved disciple's testimony. The witness of the Word becomes the written witness of his followers' words about the Word. The written witness is partial, provisional, and incomplete (21:25), yet the claim can still be made that it is true, that it constitutes reliable testimony to the true judgment in the lawsuit.

Just as Jesus' witness to the truth is self-authenticating, so the community's witness to Jesus in its written testimony is self-authenticating. In an inevitable circularity, the community claims that its own witness is true. In the end, in knowing where truth lies in the cosmic lawsuit, there can be no going behind the witness. This would be to assume that there is some superior vantage point from which to make a judgment; if, as the narrative claims, the truth of the lawsuit is about God, then by definition there can be no such vantage point. In line with such a perspective, the response the narrative calls for is acceptance of its witness or belief. The only way to discover its truth for oneself, to align oneself with true judgment in the world, is to participate in it by believing. Hence Jesus' words to Pilate, "Everyone who belongs to the truth listens to my voice" (18:37). The attitude that correlates to this narrative's notion of truth is faith seeking understanding, or as Jesus puts it earlier: "Anyone who resolves to do the will of God will know whether the teaching is from God or whether I am speaking on my own" (7:17) and "believe . . . so that you may know and understand that the Father is in me and I am in the Father" (10:38).

Thus, if truth is approached from the angle of the cosmic lawsuit, it is seen as embracing the entire issue at stake in the lawsuit. It is the true judgment about God's acting in Jesus in a salvific trial that intends life for the world. Truth, then, entails the reality of God's existence and of this particular God's existence as the God whose self-expression is in Jesus. It is theological and it is christological—truth is embodied in Jesus. It is also soteriological. Truth is the divine reality as it comes to expression in the whole of Jesus' mission, including his death, and it is the establishment of the divine verdict of life through that death. Insofar as truth is about the establishment of the relationship between God and Jesus and about the provision of life for the world, it can also be said that the truth is about love.[33] After all, the relation between God and Jesus is depicted as one of love. Jesus is the one who is in the bosom of the Father, close to the Father's heart (1:18); he is the one to whom in his love the Father has given all things (3:35; cf. also 10:17). Jesus speaks of the outcome of his mission in the lawsuit in terms of the world knowing

---

[33] Cf. also Söding, "Die Macht der Wahrheit," 49.

"that I love the Father" (14:31; cf. also 17:23). In his prayer he talks of his sovereign reputation having been secured because of the Father's love for him before the foundation of the world (17:24). The mutual indwelling of Father and Son (cf., e.g., 10:38) is a reciprocal relationship based in love. The divine reality that has been established by the lawsuit is therefore a reality of love between the Father and the Son. The verdict of life that has been pronounced arises out of the self-giving nature of the divine love—"God so loved the world that he gave his only Son" (3:16)—and those who experience this verdict are thereby invited into the experience of the love between God and Jesus (cf. 14:21, 23; 17:23, 26). We have also seen that the truth at issue in the lawsuit requires witnesses. Witnessing to the truth of love entails demonstrating that love. Jesus' mission of witness has been one of love, and it culminates in a particular demonstration of this in "his hour": "Having loved his own who were in the world, he loved them to the end" (13:1b). He washes his disciples' feet in an act of loving service that foreshadows the giving of his life that completes his witness. His disciples' witness to the truth is to include washing one another's feet (13:14–15), for "by this everyone will know that you are my disciples, if you have love for one another" (13:35).

E. The Opposition and Its Case

The narrative also presents a point of view that does not prevail in the judgment in the lawsuit—that of those who oppose Jesus and his followers.[34] Inevitably we do not have the case that the opposition itself would have made but only the implied author's view of it. From this vantage point, what is essentially wrong with the opposition's case is the criteria it employs for judging. Jesus admonishes the crowd in 7:24, "Do not judge by appearances, but judge with right judgment," and indicts the Pharisees in 8:15 for judging "according to the flesh," or on the basis of merely human standards.

In both cases, what earned the evaluation of a false judgment according to appearances or simply at a human level was a judgment based on an interpretation of the Torah. In the first case, Jesus' healing of a man on the Sabbath has been interpreted as a violation of Sabbath law, and in the second case, his testifying about himself has been seen as an infringement of the law about the necessity of two or three witnesses.

---

[34] The full-scale study of Pancaro, *The Law*, remains important for an understanding of the presentation of the opposition's case.

Jesus is held to be a lawbreaker or sinner in four main ways.[35] His healing constitutes work on the Sabbath (cf. 5:16; 7:23; 9:16, 20). He blasphemes, particularly in the way he talks of God as his Father, making himself equal to God (cf. 5:17–18; 8:58–59; 10:30–39; 19:7). In terms of Deut 13:1–5 and 18:21–22, the signs he performs and the claims he makes show him to be a false prophet who is leading the people astray, and therefore an enemy of the nation (cf. 7:12b; 11:47–50). When put under interrogation on such charges, he can only witness to himself (cf. 8:13, 17; cf. also 5:31). On all these counts, there is no reason that Jesus should escape the law's sentence of death.

At the heart of the trial, then, there is a clash between Jesus' witness and what appears to be a straightforward interpretation of the Mosaic law. This is indeed surprising in a Jewish context. Is not the opposition right in expecting that true judgment in a lawsuit about claims for God will be determined by the law that God has given? Yet from the implied author's perspective, Jesus' witness is now the criterion of true judgment, and this requires a totally new assessment of the law. This perspective is apparent from the start. In the prologue, not only are the grace and truth previously associated with the glory of Yahweh in the covenant with Moses (cf. Exod 34:6) now associated with the glory of the incarnate Logos (1:14), but the prologue also then makes an explicit contrast: "The law indeed was given through Moses, grace and truth came through Jesus Christ" (1:17). This is not a denial that, before the coming of the Logos, the law was previously an expression of Yahweh's grace and truth. It is, rather, an assertion by the community, which has seen the fullness of grace and truth in the Logos's glory, that these qualities are not now to be found in the law.[36] The contrast with Moses continues into 1:18. The declaration that no one has seen God at any time denies any claims that might be made for Moses. Since God is inaccessible, only God can make God known. And this is where Christ is superior to Moses. He is "only God," always in the most intimate relationship possible with God, and this qualifies him to make God known. This way of knowing God becomes the criterion by which the previous way through the law is to be judged, and not vice versa.

This theme is developed in ways too numerous and too well known for detailed discussion. They include the depiction of what were previously symbols of the law, such as water, bread, and light, as having their true realization in Jesus; of the festivals prescribed in the law as having

---

[35] See ibid., 9–125.
[36] Cf. ibid., 537–40.

their significance fulfilled in Jesus; and of terminology associated with obeying the law as now being appropriate for use in connection with believing in Jesus.[37] In the very first sign (2:1–11), the water jars employed for purification under the law are now filled with the wine that represents the life and joy of the new order. The following episode, the temple incident of 2:13–22, is recounted in such a way as to make clear that the temple, whose regulations were based on the law, is to be replaced as the locus of God's presence by the body of the risen Jesus. That this is the issue creating the divide between the two sides in the lawsuit emerges clearly in the account of the giving of sight to the man born blind. When the man goes on the offensive and mischievously asks his interrogators whether the fact that they want him to tell them again what exactly happened means that they, too, wish to become Jesus' disciples, he receives the reply, "You are his disciple, but we are disciples of Moses" (9:28). And what is the reason for their preferred allegiance to Moses? "We know that God has spoken to Moses, but as for this man, we do not know where he comes from" (9:29). Their point of certainty, and therefore their criterion for judgment, is the law as the divine revelation to Moses.

But as is clear all along from the attempts of the opposition to stone Jesus, the law, in their view, calls for Jesus' death. The attempts to stone Jesus come after his words have been construed as blasphemous, and Lev 24:16 requires the death penalty for blasphemers. This stance emerges for a final time in the trial before Pilate. Since the Jewish authorities have no legal power to execute the death sentence themselves, they hand him over to Pilate on a different charge, that of being a messianic king. Before the end of the trial, however, the implied author allows what he believes to be the real charge to emerge. After Pilate has, for the third time, declared that he finds no case against Jesus, "the Jews answered him, 'We have a law, and according to that law he ought to die because he has claimed to be the Son of God'" (19:7). If, in the overall pattern of thought, the Mosaic law leads to the sentence of death on Jesus and yet the overall judgment in the lawsuit is a vindication of the one who was sentenced to death, then this positive divine verdict is also a negative verdict on the law.

This last point might be challenged. It could be argued that since the death of Jesus is clearly part of God's sovereign plan in this narrative, the law, as a means to this end, is simply the necessary vehicle for achieving this purpose and no negative judgment on the law need be implied. But

---

[37] See esp. ibid., 368–487.

the same argument does not apply to the humans who are a means to that end. There can be no question that Judas, the Jewish religious leaders, and Pilate are all judged negatively. Like them and like the ruler of this world behind them, the law also has a negative verdict placed on it, and what we see elsewhere in the narrative discourse about the law simply reinforces such an interpretation.

Significantly, the implied author is, for the most part, not particularly interested in attempting to show that the Jewish opposition has misinterpreted or misread the law on its own terms. In two places there are arguments of the latter sort, pointing to an ambiguity in the law that can be exploited for Jesus' cause. In 7:19–24, in what will be a discussion about the Sabbath, Jesus first accuses the Jewish opposition of not keeping the law. Some interpreters, pointing to the opposition's desire to kill Jesus, which he mentions in his next question, think that their breaking of the law refers to the intent to kill the one whom God has sent.[38] But the assertion that "none of you keeps the law" may well be wider in its reference and best explained by the point about circumcision that follows. This seems to be that since it is the normal practice to circumcise on the Sabbath so that the law about circumcision might not be broken, in fact another law, the Sabbath law, is broken in the process. This perspective then allows Jesus to argue from the lesser to the greater and ask, "are you angry with me because I healed a man's whole body on the sabbath?" (7:23). In 10:33–38 a similar approach is taken in Jesus' reply to the accusation that he is making himself God. There he appeals to the law in its broadest sense to point out that in it (in fact, in Ps 82:6), "I say, 'You are gods'" is addressed to those who received the law at Sinai, so that the term *god* could be employed appropriately of human beings. Again this allows Jesus to argue from the lesser to the greater. If this is the case, "can you say that the one whom the Father has sanctified and sent into the world is blaspheming because I said, 'I am God's Son'?" (10:36).

But the dominant way of presenting the clash between Jesus and the law is not to dispute that the law is being rightly interpreted but to see Jesus as an exception to the law. Thus in 5:17 Jesus simply admits that he is working on the Sabbath, but appealing to the notion that God never ceases creative activity, he claims to be in unity with God in this. Similarly, there is acknowledgment of the law's need for two or three witnesses, but Jesus is seen to be an exception because of who he claims to be in relationship with God (8:14). And when the blasphemy issue sur-

---

[38] Cf., e.g., ibid., 137.

faces elsewhere (cf. 5:18–30), the law about making oneself equal to God is not debated. This would hold for other humans, but Jesus' point is that he is different. In his case it is not a question of making himself equal to God; this equality in judging and giving life has been bestowed on him by God.

This narrative's point of view is that, because of who he is, Jesus is not subject to the law but instead fulfills all that the law previously stood for. The law, then, is to be judged in the light of Jesus and his mission and not the other way round. Both of the previously mentioned strategies—exploiting aspects of the law itself and seeing Jesus as an exception—are compatible with this perspective. Once Jesus' unique identity is accepted by faith, then various parts of the law can be seen to be fulfilled by him, but his unique identity also means that he fulfills the law by transcending it. A number of other features in the presentation of the law flow from this stance. Moses is now seen as having written about Jesus, so those who refuse to believe Jesus can be indicted for in fact not believing Moses. Moses, whom they are employing to accuse Jesus, will therefore turn out to be the one who accuses them in the overall trial (5:45–47). At the same time, the law, interpreted without faith in Jesus, can be depicted as becoming a hindrance to true judgment. A notable instance is in 18:28–29, where the narrator comments on "the Jews" being so concerned about avoiding ritual defilement that they will not enter Pilate's headquarters. This is meant to convey ironically that while they adhere to the law's regulations about the necessity for purity in order to eat the Passover lamb, they are completely unable to make the true judgment about the one who is in reality the Passover lamb. Also, because of this overall perspective on the relation between Jesus and the law, the discourse puts a distance between them. In two places Jesus the Jew talks not about "our law" or "the law" but "your law" (8:17; 10:34), and similarly in 7:19, 22 he speaks of Moses giving "you" the law and circumcision. In 12:48–50 Jesus' summary of his mission recalls what is said of the prophet like Moses. Because he is the prophet like Moses, his word, which is the Father's commandment of eternal life, will serve as the ultimate criterion of judgment. Previously the Mosaic law was seen as giving life and as the standard of judgment, but now these qualities belong to the witness of Jesus. The teachings Jesus gives to his disciples can therefore be called commandments that they are to keep (cf. 13:34; 14:15, 21; 15:10, 12).

What becomes clear, then, in this lawsuit is that Jesus' self-authenticating witness cannot simply be accommodated to a judgment, even a theological judgment, that has its starting point elsewhere, even if that elsewhere is the Mosaic law. Although it does not say so explicitly, in this sense, for the Fourth Gospel, the law as used by Jesus' opponents has become an idol that needs to be judged. The reason for this radical evaluation of the law is not that, as in Pauline thought, the law is seen as encouraging "works," whether these are understood as the boundary markers that give Israel a sense of ethnic elitism or, more traditionally, as the need to perform successfully to satisfy the requirements of the covenant. It is, rather, that the law is seen as providing the wrong categories for judging. This radical attitude might have been expected to emerge in a context, like Paul's, where Gentile admission into the believing community was the issue. But here, although Gentiles are among the implied readers, there is no hint that a discussion about their inclusion has been the catalyst for this new evaluation of the law. Instead it appears to have come about in the context of an intra-Jewish debate and been seen as the consequence of one group of Jewish Christians' developed understanding of the significance of Jesus' messiahship and of his relationship to God as Son.[39] For the Fourth Gospel, the way unbelieving Jews are using the law shows that it is no longer being connected rightly with its source— God, a God who cannot be boxed in by its categories.[40] On the basis of these categories, it can only be concluded that Jesus is a blasphemer who deserves to die. What is needed is a transformation of judgment that sees that God is continuing to act in judgment for the world and accepts Jesus' claim to be God's unique representative in this judgment and therefore the lens through which the law is to be viewed. Through this lens it can be seen in its rightful place in the lawsuit, not as an independent criterion of judgment but as part of Scripture's witness to Jesus as the Christ, the Son of God.

While there is distancing from, and judgment of, the law in the discourse, there is no similar treatment (as "your Scripture") of the Jewish Scripture as a whole.[41] Nevertheless, there is an indictment of the opposition's misuse of Scripture. In 5:39–40 Jesus acknowledges that his opponents search the Scriptures, but what is wrong with the search is that "you think that in them you have eternal life." This accusation *is* similar to the perspective on the law. Just as the law in itself is not to be seen as

---

[39] For Paul also there is evidence that his view of the law was not simply a result of the debate about his Gentile mission but was related to the realization that his zeal for the law was what had led him into a head-on collision with the cause of Jesus and his followers (cf. Gal 1:13–14).

[40] As Rensberger, *Johannine Faith,* 45, puts it regarding the discussion in John 9, "The blind man's God does not live in a book, not even in the book of the law itself, but in the act of mercy that has been done to him."

[41] Cf. Pancaro, *The Law,* 327, 521.

the sufficient criterion for judging, so the Scriptures in themselves are not to be seen as sufficient for experiencing the positive verdict of eternal life. From the perspective represented by Jesus, only when the Scriptures are seen as a witness to him as the one who gives life do they play their proper part in the lawsuit. Then Moses, as part of Scripture, can also function in this way and be seen as writing about Jesus (5:46). The bread-of-life discourse that follows in 6:25–59 serves as a model for how such a perspective works. At the end this discourse/dispute is described as a piece of synagogue teaching by Jesus (6:59). This gives the clue to its form, which combines a midrashic commentary on the saying of Jesus in 6:27 with a midrashic commentary on the scriptural text from Moses (Exod 16:4, 15) cited in 6:31. Both the form and the content of the passage show Jesus as the giver of life who is the hermeneutical key to Scripture.

The opposition's use of Scripture for its case can be seen in the discussion of whether the Messiah or a prophet is to come from Galilee (7:42, 52). In 7:42 some in the crowd say that the Messiah does not come from Galilee and that Scripture states the Messiah is descended from David and comes from Bethlehem. This interpretation is not disputed. But the crowd's use of it is shown to be mistaken in two ways. First, the implied reader is, in all probability, expected to know of the traditions that Jesus was in fact born in Bethlehem, and the narrator has already indicated that Jesus' own country is not Galilee in 4:43–44.[42] So, ironically, the crowd has adduced a scriptural proof that in fact witnesses to Jesus, but they are unable to see this themselves. Second, the implied reader knows that, in any case, to focus on Jesus' geographical origins is to employ the wrong categories because the narrative constantly makes clear that the answer to the question about where Jesus is from is that he is from God, from above, or from heaven. When Nicodemus suggests that "our law" does not judge people without first hearing them (7:51), the religious authorities, who despise the crowd as not knowing the law (v. 49), are depicted as saying, "Search and you will see that no prophet is to arise from Galilee" (v. 52). Here is a prime example of what has been alleged in 5:39 to be wrong with the searching of Scripture. The authorities have an interpretation of Scripture that excludes the possibility of their listening to Jesus. The irony is heightened as the narrative makes plain that, without the hermeneutical key provided by Jesus, such a search not only is a dead end but also leads to error. The authorities show themselves in fact to be more ignorant than the despised crowd,

---

[42] Cf., e.g., Barrett, *Gospel according to St. John*, 246.

because Scripture does talk of prophets who come from Galilee. The implied reader not only knows this but, again, also knows that Jesus is not in fact from Galilee and that, as the Son who has come from the Father, he is more than a prophet.

In contrast to the opposition's use of Scripture, Scripture functions for the implied author as a major witness to Jesus in the lawsuit, whether it is through the citation of particular passages that find their fulfillment in Jesus' mission or through the use of scriptural symbols that have their referent in Jesus. In the case of Isa 40–55, a whole section of Scripture is taken up and reworked in the light of what is believed to have taken place in Jesus. In addition, scriptural figures are called upon within the overall scriptural witness, so that Abraham is portrayed as having rejoiced to see Jesus' day (8:56) and Isaiah as having seen Jesus' glory (12:41). The response to Jesus deemed appropriate is that of Philip's witness early in the narrative, "We have found him about whom Moses in the law and also the prophets wrote" (1:45).

But who are the opposition within Israel who employ both the law and Scripture to judge in a way that the narrative depicts as mistaken and therefore as false witness in the lawsuit? Sometimes it is part of the crowd, sometimes it is the religious authorities, who can be called Pharisees, or chief priests, or chief priests and Pharisees, sometimes a mixture of the crowd and such authorities. As already discussed, all these groups can characteristically be designated simply as "the Jews." The term is not simply an ethnic one; the narrative discourse makes clear that its reference is to unbelieving Jews as opposed to believing Jews. What is the theological dimension of the role of these unbelieving Jews in the cosmic trial? The trial is between God and the world. The goal of its judgment is salvation, but there are those in the world who come under condemnation because of their unbelief. This is the reason "the Jews" are frequently said by interpreters of this Gospel to be representatives of the unbelieving world.[43] But just as *Jews* can have a neutral or a negative connotation, so in this narrative discourse *world* can also have a neutral or a negative connotation. The Jewish nation as a whole can be seen as the representative of the world in its neutral sense also. After all, there is a particular part of the world, a particular nation, into which God's agent is sent for the main phase of this trial with the world.

---

[43] Cf. Bultmann, *Theology of the New Testament,* 2:5: "For John 'the Jews' are representatives of 'the world' in general which refuses to respond to Jesus with faith."

This relation between Israel and the world is made clear in the prologue. The Logos was in the world that came into being through him, yet the world did not know him (1:10). The last part of this assertion indicates that the world of humanity is particularly in view. But then v. 11 focuses this perspective more narrowly in its parallel statement. He came to his own property, to his own home within the world, and in this setting his own people did not accept him. Not to be accepted by Israel as a whole is the functional equivalent of not being known by the world. The coming of the Logos as light into the world effects a judgment that cuts two ways. On the negative side, his own people as a whole do not accept him, but on the positive side, there are those who do receive him and who through believing are born of God, while others remain on the merely human level in regard to life, remain born of the flesh (v. 13).

When this preview of the plot is developed in the main narrative, the initial correlations are reinforced. The Pharisee, Nicodemus, a ruler of the Jews, remains at the level of being born of the flesh rather than being born from above (3:6). The Pharisees who accuse Jesus in 8:13 are said to judge according to the flesh (8:15). In 3:17–21 the major category is again the world of humanity, and through the judgment that is meant for salvation, the world divides up into believers who come to the light and are not condemned and unbelievers who prefer the darkness and are condemned. Later, in line with the divisions that have already been set out, "the Jews" are told that they are from below, of this world, while Jesus claims his origin is not of this world but from above (8:23), and they come under Jesus' condemnation (8:26). The man born blind receives his sight and believes, but the Pharisees, who claim to see, are truly blind and remain in the dark (9:40–41). Elsewhere, when the talk is of the world in a negative context, it is clear that unbelieving Jews have to be the primary referent. This is the case when Jesus tells his brothers, "The world cannot hate you, but it hates me because I testify against it that its works are evil" (7:7). The same holds for Jesus' words to his disciples in 15:18–19: "If the world hates you, be aware that it hated me before it hated you. If you belonged to the world, the world would love you as its own. Because you do not belong to the world, but I have chosen you out of the world—therefore the world hates you." The term *the world* may well take on the broader connotations of humanity as a whole in unbelieving hostility to Jesus and God, especially when the mission of Jesus' followers takes them beyond the Jewish people. But the particularities of the narrative's setting require that, in the first place, the world that hated Jesus be the unbelieving religious authorities and other Jews and that the world out of which the disciples were chosen be unbelieving Israel as a whole.

Israel as a whole is seen as remaining in unbelief. Hence, it becomes appropriate, in the view of the implied author, to use the term *the Jews* for unbelieving Israel and to see them as representative of the world that does not know the Logos through whom it came into being, even though he comes to bring judgment for it. When, therefore, Pilate, the chief representative of the Gentile world in this narrative, asks, "I am not a Jew, am I?" (18:35), the previous discourse, with its correlation between the Jews and the world, enables the implied readers to appreciate the irony and to realize that although the answer expected by Pilate is negative, the answer to be supplied by them is affirmative. Pilate is a Jew in the special negative sense of the term, as a member of that part of the world whose response to the judgment is an unbelieving one.

All this allows us to see clearly again how the pattern of the cosmic lawsuit from Deutero-Isaiah has been reworked. Although there are accusations against Israel and mention of condemnation in Deutero-Isaiah, the latter has already been effected in the exile, and the predominant emphasis is on Israel's salvation and homecoming. It regarding the nations and their idols that the lawsuit stresses negative judgment, although even here there is still the offer of salvation to those who will turn to Yahweh (cf. Isa 45:22). In general, however, Israel as a whole, represented by the servant-witness in particular, is to have the role of witnessing to the world of the nations. In the Fourth Gospel, because Israel as a whole is unbelieving, it is now aligned with the nations in coming under condemnation. It is ironic when Jews under Roman occupation appeal to their Abrahamic descent as meaning that they have never been enslaved to anyone (8:33). The irony becomes more biting when this subjection is graphically depicted at the end of the Roman trial scene. When Pilate presents Jesus as their king and asks, "Shall I crucify your King?" the chief priests respond, "We have no king but the emperor" (19:15). Not only do they put the Jewish people alongside the other nations as loyal subjects in the Roman world; in doing so, they also renounce their allegiance to God as their one king and therefore replace God with an idol.

The accusations and condemnations brought against the unbelieving Jewish opposition earlier in the narrative are also serious. Nicodemus, who is sympathetic to the cause of Jesus, is a teacher of Israel and yet does not understand (3:10; cf. 8:43). Those who accuse Jesus do not honor the Father (5:23). They have never heard the Father's voice nor seen his form, and they do not have his word abiding in them (5:38). They do not seek God's glory but are far more concerned about their own reputation with others (5:44; cf. 12:43). They are slaves to sin

(8:34). God is not their Father (8:42). They do not hear (8:43, 47; cf. also 9:27). Even though they invoke God as their God, they do not know God (8:54–55; cf. also 7:28; 8:19). They are blind (9:39–41). Those who violently persecute Jesus' followers think they are offering worship to God in doing so, but they do not know this God (16:2; 15:21). It is important to remember that such charges against unbelieving Jews are leveled by other Jews, primarily in the person of the Jew Jesus, in terms of the narrative depiction. Against the scriptural background, they would not have been heard as something new, and similar charges are leveled in a number of the prophets. In particular, our discussion of 8:12–59 has already noted that nearly all these charges are in fact leveled by Yahweh against Israel in Isa 40–55. In addition, because some of them overlap with the charges made against the nations and their idolatry in Isaiah, in this new context they now again serve to associate unbelieving Jews with the unbelieving world.

It is also important to underline that, in contrast to the opposition, there are Jews who do take up the role that Israel was meant to serve in Deutero-Isaiah. In the end, the opposition of unbelieving Jews does not prevent Israel from being depicted as playing its intended positive part. Both Jesus as the servant-witness and his Jewish followers who witness to the one who now uses the divine self-identification of "I am" are depicted in this part. These believing followers are now seen as "his own [people]" (13:1) in contrast to those with this designation who were said not to have accepted him (1:11). Salvation in the cosmic lawsuit can therefore still be claimed to be "from the Jews" (4:22), although the terms *Israel* and *Israelite* are generally preferred in a positive context. Nathanael can be called "truly an Israelite in whom there is no deceit" (1:47) and responds by confessing that Jesus is the king of Israel (1:49). This title is used to acclaim Jesus as he enters Jerusalem later (12:13). It also raises questions about how to view the title "the King of the Jews," which predominates in the trial and crucifixion. Clearly the traditions about the charge against Jesus and the inscription on the cross have been determinative for the narrative depiction. But at the same time, this designation for Jesus is developed extensively in his presentation as king and judge in the trial narrative, whose blatant irony dictates that the implied reader see the designation as in fact a statement of the true state of affairs. The irony is underscored in the crucifixion scene by having the chief priests protest the wording of the superscription (19:21). The narrator also points out that the inscription "Jesus of Nazareth, the King of the Jews" was in three languages—Aramaic, the vernacular; Latin, the language of the Roman goverment; and Greek, the language of trade and commerce (19:20). No doubt these are meant to suggest the universality of the reign of the one who is lifted up (cf. 12:32). Despite the unbelieving opposition's lack of acknowledgment, in the judgment of the lawsuit Jesus is to be seen as truly their king precisely at the point at which the sentence they demanded is carried out. Salvation is thereby portrayed as indeed from the Jews, in such a way that the king of the Jews is also the Savior of the world (cf. 4:22; 4:42).[44]

F. The Witness of Jesus' Followers and the Spirit as Another Advocate

What distinguishes the group the narrator calls Jesus' "own" (cf. 13:1) from those who were supposed to be the Logos's own (cf. 1:11) is that the latter did not accept the Logos but the former are those who did accept him by believing in his name, thereby becoming children of God (1:11–12). In the context of the lawsuit, accepting Jesus means accepting his witness or the witness about him. Believing is therefore the equivalent to accepting witness.[45] Again this is established in the prologue, where the purpose of John the Baptist's testimony to the light is to produce belief in the light (1:7), and reinforced later, in the discourse with Nicodemus, where not receiving testimony (3:11) is the equivalent of not believing (3:12). In the narrative's trial setting, believing also entails a choice between testimonies. A decision or judgment has to be made between true and false witness, between the one who speaks the truth and the liar, between light and darkness. In more concrete terms, this choice manifests itself in whether to judge Jesus on the basis of his own categories or on the basis of the categories employed by the opposition—the law and their interpretation of Scripture. Sometimes the narrator comments on people who appear to be unable to follow through on the choice. Thus we are told that there were some even among the authorities who actually believed Jesus but who were unwilling to confess this or testify to it because they feared the Pharisees would put them out of the synagogue (12:43), and that Joseph of Arimathea was a secret disciple "because of his fear of the Jews" (19:38). Pilate holds Jesus not

---

[44] In light of the significance of the inscription on the cross, it is difficult to see how Pancaro, *The Law,* 300, can maintain that Jesus "was not the King of the Jews at all, but the King of Israel."

[45] Cf. also G. E. Ladd, *A Theology of the New Testament* (rev. ed.; Grand Rapids: Eerdmans, 1993), 307: "This simple sense of believing and accepting the truthfulness of the witnesses to the person and mission of Jesus is basic to the Johannine idea of faith."

to be guilty of the charge brought against him but fails to follow through on this judgment, so that eventually his attempt not to become involved reveals itself to be actually a judgment against Jesus.

Those who accept testimony align themselves with the true judgment in the lawsuit; they ratify the truth of God's cause (3:33). They also secure the right verdict—life instead of condemnation and death (cf. 3:16–18, 36). They are now also in a position to play their part as witnesses in the trial. In doing so, they join a whole chain of witnesses. This notion of witnesses as links in a chain is developed in the last part of John 1. In response to John the Baptist's witness, "Look, here is the Lamb of God!" two of his disciples follow Jesus, who issues the invitation to them to come and see. One of these two, Andrew, then witnesses through his confession to his brother, Simon, "We have found the Messiah," and brings Simon to Jesus (cf. 1:35–42). A similar chain is started by Jesus when he calls Philip to follow him. Philip witnesses through his confession to Nathanael and offers the invitation to come and see. This then results in Nathanael's own confession (cf. 1:43–51). Later the Samaritan woman's testimony, with its invitation to come and see, leads to many other Samaritans believing (cf. 4:29, 39). In the light of the subsequent narrative discourse, where coming (cf. 6:35; 7:37–38) and seeing (cf. 6:40; 12:44–46) are paralleled with believing, the invitation to come and see turns out to be the functional equivalent of an invitation to believe.

Like all witnesses, the followers of Jesus in this narrative testify to what they have seen and heard. But what we have just observed about the discourse cautions us not to expect that this will always have the straightforward sense of visual and aural witness. Since seeing and hearing are both equivalents of believing, testifying to what one has seen and heard is frequently testifying to one's belief. When in the prologue the community testifies that "we have seen his glory" (1:14), this is testimony to what it believes about Jesus' status.[46] When John the Baptist testifies, "I saw the Spirit descending from heaven like a dove, and it remained on him" (1:32), this may be based on a visionary experience but

---

[46] It is extremely difficult to see how Boice, *Witness and Revelation*, 130, can claim, "The natural meaning of this verse is that the fourth evangelist claims at the beginning of the gospel to be an eyewitness of the events he is about to narrate." He also assumes that this eyewitness evangelist is the apostle John (p. 124). Bultmann, *Theology of the New Testament*, 2:72, is quite right that this verse "does not mean that 'we' were 'eyewitnesses' in the sense that is meant in historical enquiry."

is scarcely to be taken in a straightforward eyewitness sense. Its force is as a statement of belief about Jesus' relation to the Spirit. Again, when Jesus as representative of the community declares, "we speak of what we know and testify to what we have seen" (3:11), it turns out that this is a reference to heavenly things (v. 12), realities not accessible to normal human sight and requiring the sort of spiritual sight that only comes with being born from above (v. 3). In the same way, testifying to what one has heard is not what it might seem, because it turns out that the sort of hearing that counts is hearing that has to be given to one by God (cf. 8:47).

The episode of Thomas' encounter with the risen Jesus drives home both these previous points—the necessity that the true judgment in the lawsuit be transmitted through witnesses, and the notion that after Jesus' immediate first followers have seen the risen Lord (cf. 20:18, 25), the seeing involved in both believing and witnessing is that of faith, not physical sight. Thomas is absent from the first appearance of the risen Jesus to the disciples as a group, but they tell him, "We have seen the Lord." His response is that unless he sees the mark of the nails in Jesus' hands and puts his finger in the mark and his hand in Jesus' side, he will not believe (v. 25). Eight days later, Jesus again appears and this time tells Thomas, "Do not doubt but believe" (v. 27c). Why does he need this exhortation? After all, by asking to see Jesus' hands and feet, he is requesting no more that was given to the other disciples (cf. v. 20). Adding to the wish to see the wish to touch simply makes his request more graphic. The real problem is that this wish to see and touch is part of an adamant disbelief of the other disciples' testimony, a setting of his own conditions for accepting testimony. The force of Jesus' final words to Thomas in v. 29 is, then, "Have you believed their testimony because you have physically seen me? Blessed are those who have not physically seen and yet have come to believe their testimony." Such persons have the sort of seeing that the earlier discourse has defined as believing. The narrator then underlines the significance of this saying. Faith in the risen Jesus is not limited to Jesus' immediate followers; it is the chain of testimony, which should have been sufficient for Thomas, that makes this possible. The narrative itself has been written as the testimony (cf. 21:24) through which "you"—the readers—may have appropriate belief in Jesus and thereby enjoy the life made available on the basis of his death and resurrection (20:31).

After the vindication and departure of the chief witness, Jesus, his immediate followers become the key link in the chain of witnesses that is still needed in the ongoing lawsuit. In John 13–17 it emerges that the disciples are to be Jesus' successors in the trial, and the grounding is provided for their future role. Much of what Jesus tells the disciples in preparation for his departure is about their relation to him and to the Father and their relation to one another. In the context of talking about their relation to a hostile world, Jesus speaks first about the Advocate as witness and then about the disciples' task as that of witness: "You also are to testify because you have been with me from the beginning" (15:27). There has already been the clear implication that Jesus considers the disciples those whom he sends (13:16, 20), but now the nature of their mission becomes explicit. When Jesus later prays to the Father, "As you have sent me into the world, so I have sent them into the world" (17:18), the implied reader understands that they have been sent to witness. After all, the major reason that Jesus was sent in the first place was to be the Father's representative in the lawsuit as witness and judge (cf. esp. 18:37). The disciples are actually commissioned for their task when the risen Jesus appears to them and says, "As the Father has sent me, so I send you" (20:21). The buildup of the discourse has made clear by this point that the disciples are being sent primarily to witness, that as they perform this task, they are the authorized agents of Jesus and fully represent him, and that, because of the relationships in the chain of commissioning, they are also the authorized agents who represent the Father.

Two other elements of Jesus' instruction in John 13–17 particularly inform the nature of their task as witnesses. The early language about sending in 13:16, 20 occurred in the context of Jesus washing the disciples' feet and explaining that "servants are not greater than their master, nor are messengers greater than the one who sent them." Just as Jesus fulfilled the role of the servant-witness, so his disciples' witness is also to include the element of service, demonstrated in their willingness to wash one another's feet (v. 14). Later such loving service of one another is seen as contributing to their witness to the world: "By this everyone will know that you are my disciples, if you have love for one another" (v. 35).

It is noticeable that when Jesus is speaking to the disciples in the Farewell Discourse, the language of love also replaces that of eternal life. Love, it seems, is therefore also the primary manifestation of the present experience of the positive verdict of eternal life. Just as in Paul love is the characteristic power of the new age, so in John love is the distinctive feature of the new life. For love to be displayed, a community of disciples is required. A community that enacts the pattern of life of *the* witness in loving service is essential for the credibility of the continuing witness in the world. The literary shape of the narrative, too, suggests that witness has to be embodied in a community. The community's witness comes to expression in the "we" language of the prologue and again in the epilogue, with its closing witness to the truth of the beloved disciple's testimony. In this way it provides a frame for the written testimony. Jesus' prayer for his disciples and for those who will believe through their witness makes clear that the community of loving service in which the witness is embodied is to be a united one and that the issues at stake in the trial hinge on this: "that they may become completely one, so that the world may know that you have sent me" (17:23). Since the truth established in the trial is the oneness between Jesus and God, it is not surprising that the testimony to that truth is displayed by the oneness of the witnesses. But the link between these two aspects of the trial motif is an especially strong one. It is not simply that the unity of the witnesses mirrors the union between the Father and the Son. Rather, the unity of the believing community even participates in the unity that defines the relation between Jesus and God (cf. 17:21). In this way, in the ongoing trial, the life of the community is meant to be an embodied witness to the right verdict about Jesus.

A second major aspect of these chapters helps to define the disciples' witness. Immediately after telling them they are to witness, Jesus speaks of the persecution that will follow, which will include being put out of the synagogue and being killed. Again, just as Jesus' witness entails humiliation and a martyr's death, so social humiliation and martyrdom are part and parcel of his followers' witness. Where these occur, they are simply the ultimate consequence of the teaching on discipleship that Jesus gave earlier, in the context of facing the hour of death, which was also to be his hour of glory. In 12:25–26 he asserted, "Those who love their life lose it, and those who hate their life in this world will keep it for eternal life. Whoever serves me must follow me, and where I am, there will my servant be also. Whoever serves me, the Father will honor." If servant-witness entails following Jesus and following him to death, then just as the Father glorified Jesus in his death, so will the Father honor Jesus' follower.

In the lawsuits of Deutero-Isaiah, Israel qualified as a witness when, perceiving the truth of Yahweh's word of prediction as it comes to fulfillment, Israel came to know and believe Yahweh and to understand that Yahweh is "I am," the only God (cf. esp. Isa 43:9–10). In the Fourth Gospel, the disciples qualify as witnesses who are able to see the fulfillment of the words of Jesus, God's representative, because they have been with him from the beginning (John 15:27). The narrator takes pains to point out, when Jesus makes a prediction about his resurrection, that later his disciples remembered this and believed (2:22). Another narratorial aside comes at the end of the public trial before Israel. This time it is stated that the disciples understood later, after Jesus was glorified, when "they remembered that these things had been written of him and had been done to him" (12:16). Here they are witnesses of the correspondence between God's prophetic word in Scripture and its fulfillment in Jesus. It is particularly significant that when Jesus predicts his betrayal by one of the disciples, he says, "I tell you this now, before it occurs, so that when it does occur, you may believe that I am" (13:19). Thus, an element of witnessing the truth of Jesus' word, and of God's word through him, is taking place within the time period of Jesus' mission, although it is mainly a qualification that is only achieved after Jesus' death and resurrection.

Are the disciples qualified to be witnesses because, during his mission, they already know and believe Jesus and understand his identity as the "I am" who is one with God? The concentration on Jesus' public trial before Israel means that there is only sporadic mention of the disciples in the early part of the narrative. Certainly, the initial belief and confessions of some of them are mentioned in John 1, and the disciples as a group are said to believe after the first sign (2:11). After the bread-of-life discourse, when others defect because they are offended at Jesus' words, Peter, representing the twelve (cf. 6:70), confesses that Jesus is the holy one of God and that his words are the words of eternal life (6:68–69).

When we are given a closer look at these disciples in John 13–17, however, it becomes clear that their early faith needs reinforcing, nurturing, and maturing before they are ready to perform as witnesses. Their lack of insight becomes woefully apparent. This emerges first in Peter's response to the foot washing, when he has to be told that he does not know now what Jesus is doing but will only understand later (13:7), and then in his lack of understanding about where Jesus is going and in his protestation about laying down his life, his unpreparedness for which is underscored by Jesus' response predicting that instead he will deny Jesus three times (13:36–38). Thomas and Philip both reveal their ignorance about basic aspects of Jesus' teaching (14:5, 8), and Philip earns the rebuke "Have I been with you all this time, Philip, and you still do not know me?" (14:9).

In 16:18 the disciples as a group confess that they do not know what Jesus is talking about when he speaks of his departure and return. But by the end of the chapter, they are saying that now they know and believe (16:30). What is the content of this knowledge and belief? They know about Jesus' knowledge of all things and therefore believe that he came from God. We are left wondering about how much content to give this expression of faith. After all, it does not differ formally from that of Nicodemus, who also believes Jesus has come from God (3:2) but who goes on to reveal the inadequacy of his initial declaration. Jesus himself at this point responds in a way that seems to call their belief into question: "Do you now believe?" (16:31). Strangely, shortly after this, we are encouraged to treat their belief positively by the prayer of Jesus, in which he tells the Father that the disciples have received his words "and know in truth that I came from you; and they have believed that you sent me" (17:8); but we cannot help noting that the prayer as a whole is offered from the later vantage point of the completion of Jesus' mission.

Even if we give the benefit of the doubt to the disciples' belief that Jesus came from God, it is clear that they still do not have much of a clue about the equally important second part of Jesus' identity, namely, that he is going to God. Our perception of their lack of insight into this aspect of Jesus' mission and identity is reinforced by Jesus' prediction that they will be scattered and leave him alone (16:32). The events that follow illustrate the inadequacy of their faith and their unpreparedness for any role as witness. Peter is again the focus of the depiction. Jesus has to rebuke his attempt to prevent Jesus' arrest through the use of the sword (18:10–11), and this is followed by his threefold denial of Jesus (18:15–18, 25–27). With the exception of the beloved disciple, Jesus' mother and her sister, and Mary Magdalene, the other disciples are all absent at the crucifixion and are next depicted as a group behind locked doors "for fear of the Jews" (20:19). Yet it is now that they are deemed ready to be commissioned as witnesses. What makes the difference? Primarily the appearance of the risen Jesus, which produces joy to replace the fear. It also confirms the witness they have received from Mary Magdalene, with its announcement from Jesus that he was ascending to his Father and their Father. The other transforming factor is that, in commissioning the disciples, the risen Jesus at the same time imparts the Spirit. Because of all the earlier hints in the narrative discourse, it can now be assumed that, after Jesus' glorification in his death and resurrection and with the giving of the Spirit, the disciples will be adequately equipped in belief, knowledge, and understanding to be witnesses to the truth about Jesus in the lawsuit.

Yet even after the resurrection, if the disciples are to be sent by Jesus just as he was sent by the Father, they will need to show the same total dependence on Jesus for their witness as he showed in relation to the Father. There is a reminder of this in the epilogue of John 21. Here the disciples who have been sent on mission are, without any explanation, now found fishing back in Galilee. At the first sign in Cana of Galilee, the reader was told that Jesus manifested his glory (2:11). That this fishing episode is to be considered a final sign is indicated when the narrator states twice, in the form of an *inclusio* (cf. 21:1, 14), that Jesus manifested himself. The activity of fishing is now treated as a sign of the task for which the disciples have been commissioned. To recognize its symbolism clearly, the implied reader needs to be familiar with the synoptic Jesus' words about making the disciples those who fish for people (cf. Mark 1:17; Matt 4:19; Luke 5:10). Behind these words lie also the traditions from the Jewish Scriptures that picture God's eschatological judgment in terms of fishing or catching people in nets (cf. Jer 16:16; Ezek 29:4–5; Amos 4:2; Hab 1:14–17). A saving as well as a judging function now attaches to God's eschatological mission, of which Jesus and the disciples are agents.

At this symbolic level of the narrative, the disciples' catching nothing during the night suggests the failures and frustrations of mission. The implied reader is reminded of Jesus' words in the Farewell Discourse that where fruitfulness is concerned, "apart from me you can do nothing" (15:5). The sovereignty and supernatural knowledge that have been seen frequently in the earlier narrative reappear in the risen Jesus' command to cast the net on the right side of the boat. The disciples' compliance results in the miracle of the great haul of fish. When, according to LXX Ezek 47:10, the life-giving waters flow from the eschatological temple in Jerusalem, one of the consequences is that the fish will be like the fish of the great sea; there will be an exceedingly great number. As the disciples obey the word of the risen Jesus, who is the new temple from which life-giving waters flow, they are unable to haul in the net because of the great number of fish. When Peter later responds to Jesus' invitation to bring some of the fish he has supplied, he hauls from the boat 153 fish in a net that remains untorn. The stress on the number of fish and the condition of the net not only attests to the magnitude of the miracle but also, at the level of the symbolism of the sign, suggests the completeness and the unity of those drawn in by the disciples' mission of witness.

If the disciples are the characters with whom the implied readers are most likely to identify, then the phenomenon of their struggle to come to full belief and understanding may also shed light on the statement of purpose in 20:31, where it is said that the narrative has been written so that the readers may believe that Jesus is the Christ, the Son of God. Here, too, believing may be the reinforcing, nurturing, and maturing of faith that will enable the readers also to play their part as witnesses. For such readers the narrative supplies further models of witnessing, primarily through the characters who face interrogation. Of these, Jesus, in his relationship to the one who sent him and in his willingness to submit to death, is the paradigm. Earlier John the Baptist maintained a faithful testimony under interrogation, and his basic stance towards Jesus—"He must increase, but I must decrease" (3:30)—remains suggestive for future witnesses. Many of the elements of witness under interrogation are brought out in the narrative of the man born blind. After his move from darkness to light, like a good witness he testifies to what he knows and sees: "One thing I do know, that though I was blind, now I see" (9:25). He grows in boldness and, through the clash of claims that his witness provokes, has an increasing appreciation of the identity of the one who healed him; this witness leads to his expulsion from the synagogue. At the same time, although he is the center of attention in the episode, it is made apparent that, through the man's trial, Jesus is in fact being tried in his absence and that, in the verdict made on this new disciple, a verdict is being made about Jesus. In addition, Peter provides encouragement as the failed witness who is rehabilitated and finally considered ready to make good on his early rash promise to lay down his life for Jesus in dying a martyr's death. And the beloved disciple, though not shown under interrogation in the narrative, indicates clearly, through his part in the written witness, that witness ending in martyrdom is not the only significant form of witness.

Just as Yahweh's witness in the scriptural lawsuit and Jesus' witness in this narrative testimony take on prosecuting and judging functions, so does the witness of Jesus' followers. The man born blind, as noted, is a witness who goes on to the offensive and indicts his interrogators (cf. 9:27–34). What is described in 16:8–11 as the Spirit's prosecuting work in fact takes place through the human witness of the disciples. And in the commissioning of the disciples by the risen Jesus, they are told, "If you forgive the sins of any, they are forgiven them; if you retain the sins of any, they are retained" (20:23). This formulation suggests a continuity between their mission and that of Jesus, which, as John the Baptist testified, was to take away the sin of the world (1:29). Their task of witness, like John's, entails pointing to Jesus as the Lamb of God. It also includes pressing home the verdict about sin that has already been given in the death and resurrection of Jesus. It is worth pointing out again that the passive forms of the verbs in this depiction of their mission are to be taken as divine passives. This underlines the chain of commissioning in the lawsuit. The Father has sent Jesus, and Jesus in turn sends his disciples. This means that these disciples are not only authorized agents of Jesus but also authorized agents of the Father. Thus God's authority stands behind their witness, so that forgiveness or retention of sins by them is forgiveness or retention by God.

The form of the divine presence that accompanies the disciples' witness is the Spirit, who has the same task as theirs: "When the Advocate comes, whom I will send to you from the Father, the Spirit of truth who comes from the Father, he will testify on my behalf" (15:26). It is clear from this saying that the Spirit's coming is for the sake of the disciples. Jesus will send the Spirit to them so that there will be two witnesses in the next stage of the lawsuit. Just as Jesus was accompanied by the divine witness of the Father, so now his followers are accompanied by the divine witness of the Spirit. As John 20:22, where Jesus sends out the disciples and imparts the Spirit to them, underlines, the Spirit is Jesus' link with them so that they can play the same role as Jesus has done in the lawsuit. The depiction of this commissioning also makes clear that just as the Father's witness has primarily been through Jesus, so the Spirit's witness is not to be thought of as totally independent of that of the disciples but as taking place through their witness. Elsewhere the Spirit is described as abiding with the disciples and being in them (14:17). Jesus states that his departure is advantageous for the disciples because it means that the Spirit will come to them (16:7a). In fact, for their effective witness, the presence of the Spirit is not only advantageous but essential. They do not embark on their mission of witness as Jesus' successors until they experience the presence of his other successor, the Spirit.

Chapter 3, above, has already discussed the significance of the designation of the Spirit as Paraclete or Advocate. The influential patron who takes on the role of advocacy is a divine agent. The advocacy is both for the cause of the lawsuit as a whole—that is, God's judgment of the world that is summed up in the mission and person of Jesus—and, therefore, on behalf of Jesus' followers who are now promoting this cause. As Advocate, the Spirit has a relation to all the major aspects of the trial.

Like Jesus, the Advocate has been sent by the initiator of the lawsuit, God, as God's authorized representative (14:26), and so, like Jesus, the Spirit comes from the Father (15:26). But because of Jesus' relationship to the Father, it can also be said that the Spirit has been sent by Jesus as his fully authorized agent (15:26; 16:7). In relation to Jesus, the Spirit can also be called "another Advocate" (14:16), indicating that the Spirit will carry on the functions that Jesus has already been performing.

Indeed, just as Jesus has acted in his Father's name (5:43; 10:25), so the Spirit will act in Jesus' name, bearing his reputation that is at stake in the trial (14:26). It will be a primary task of the Spirit to secure Jesus' reputation and honor—to glorify him (16:14). Again, in doing so, the Spirit will have a relation of dependence to Jesus similar to that which Jesus had to God. The Spirit will not be speaking on his own but passing on what he hears, taking what belongs to Jesus and therefore also what belongs to God and declaring it to the disciples (16:13–15; cf. 12:49–50). Insofar, then, as the Spirit's advocacy involves witness, the Spirit not only witnesses *through* the disciples but also witnesses *to* them. In both cases the content of this testimony is Jesus and his witness. According to 15:26, the Spirit will testify about Jesus, and according to 16:13–15, the Spirit will take the words of witness Jesus continues to speak and be the transmitter of these to the disciples. Earlier this is formulated in terms of Jesus' past witness. In teaching the disciples, the Spirit will remind them of all that Jesus has said (14:26).

This mediating between past and present witness—between what Jesus said in the past and what he is saying now, and between Jesus' words in his earthly mission and the disciples' present situation—is a highly significant activity. For the implied author, it functions as an explanation for the interpretive activity of Jesus' followers. The Spirit enables them to make connections between the traditions about Jesus' ministry and their own situation, to perceive the correspondence between Jesus' earlier witness and the events that have unfolded in the lives of his followers. According to the reworking of the scriptural lawsuit motif, such perception is necessary for witness. And attributing these connections—between the setting of the past witness of Jesus and the setting of his followers' own witness in the present—not just to the Spirit but to the Spirit passing on Jesus' present witness has affected the very form of this narrative testimony. Not only does it explain why the implied author intermingles so thoroughly the two different temporal perspectives of the time of Jesus and the time of his followers; it also accounts for why Jesus himself is presented in this narrative as speaking to the issues of a later time. Although he sets them in the context of a story about the past, the implied author views these discourses as the present witness of the risen Jesus, transmitted by the Spirit to his followers. This attribution of the interpretive activity of Jesus' followers both to the Spirit and, through the Spirit, to the risen Jesus also serves to give that activity authority.

The Spirit enables Jesus' followers to combine the two temporal perspectives. But when it comes to the Spirit's own role in the story line, it looks at first sight as if there is a fairly clear temporal differentiation between pre- and post-resurrection periods in the Spirit's relation to the disciples. In 7:39 the narrator makes clear that Jesus' saying about the rivers of living water that will flow from his belly is "about the Spirit, which believers in him were to receive; for as yet there was no Spirit, because Jesus was not yet glorified." Clearly, the Spirit is not yet part of the believers' experience. Similarly, in 16:7 Jesus explains that his going away is the condition for the Spirit's coming to his followers, and this perspective is reinforced both by the reference to the water flowing from Jesus' side at his death in fulfillment of the saying of 7:38 and by the imparting of the Spirit after the resurrection.

Despite these clear markers in the narrative discourse, three passages in particular complicate the picture. In Jesus' discourse with Nicodemus, he speaks about the necessity of being born of the Spirit (3:5–6); this appears to be an option for Nicodemus to experience in the present. Also, the prologue states that those who received Jesus and believed in his name were born of God (1:12–13); since being born of the Spirit appears to be a functional equivalent of being born of God, one wonders about Jesus' disciples during the ministry. They are said to have believed. Did they not, then, experience birth from above and through the Spirit? In the second passage, Jesus, conversing with the Samaritan woman about worship, says, "The hour is coming, *and is now here*, when the true worshipers will worship the Father in spirit and truth" (4:23; cf. also v. 24). The majority of commentators rightly take the passage as referring to the divine Spirit rather than the human spirit.[47] In this case, the experience of worshiping God in the Spirit is said to have been already inaugurated. In the third passage (6:63), in the bread-of-life discourse, Jesus makes plain that he is promising life: "The words that I have spoken to you are spirit and life." The implication is equally plain: anyone who accepts these words thereby receives the Spirit and life that they mediate. It appears, then, that even in the case of human experience of the Spirit, there is a mixing of perspectives, that what was in fact experienced only after the resurrection, as reflected in the dominant story line, is retrojected into the time of Jesus in these instances. What remains clear for our motif is the important point that, regarding witnessing, only Jesus is said to have the Spirit during the pre-resurrection stage of the lawsuit. The Spirit descends and remains on him as he starts the earthly phase of his mission (1:33), enables him in his witness to speak the words of God (3:34), and makes these words life-giving in their effect as

---

[47] Cf. Burge, *Anointed Community,* 192–93.

they pronounce the lawsuit's positive verdict (6:63). Only after the decisive moment of verdict in Jesus' death and resurrection does Jesus pass on the Spirit to the disciples to enable them to be his successors as witnesses in the next stage of the lawsuit (20:22).

The Spirit is clearly an advocate for the truth of the cause that is on trial. Hence the appropriateness of the other major title he is given—the Spirit of truth (14:17; 15:26; 16:13). Since the truth of the cause at issue is the truth of God and Jesus, this title also underlines that the Spirit is the Spirit of both God and Jesus. All the Spirit's activities contribute to promoting the true judgment that has been made at the decisive point in the trial and to enabling the truth of its issues to prevail and be experienced as the further stage of the trial unfolds. Not only does the Spirit, as already noted, enable Jesus' followers to see the correspondence between God's or Jesus' words and particular events, which provides evidence of the truth of their cause; the Spirit also provides the disciples with deeper understanding of, and conviction about, all aspects of its truth (16:13). Because the Spirit is aligned squarely with the truth of the cause of God and Jesus, by definition the Spirit is on the opposite side to the world, in its negative sense of the unbelieving opposition. As was true of Jesus in his advocacy, the Spirit as Advocate is one "whom the world cannot receive, because it neither sees him nor knows him" (14:17a). In relation to such opposition, the Spirit's advocacy moves from witnessing to accusing and judging, as was again the case with Jesus. The Advocate becomes the prosecutor as the Spirit presses home the divine verdict of the lawsuit, confronting the world with the negative judgment that has been passed on it and convicting it of its guilt in the issues that are contested in the trial (16:8–11). In this way, "the Spirit . . . places the world in the position which it will occupy at the last judgment."[48]

The diverse verdict promoted by the Spirit overturns the world's values and criteria of judgment in three ways. First, it is sin that causes the plight of death from which the trial is intended to rescue the world. The prosecuting work of the Spirit includes showing the world that it is culpable in its sin and that the chief manifestation of this sin and its culpability is the world's very refusal to believe in the one who has brought the salvific judgment it needs. Second, in convicting the world of its sin, the Spirit convicts it also of the rightness or justice of Jesus' cause, since without such a conviction there would be no conviction that it was guilty in its refusal to believe. Third, the other corollary of the truth or

---

[48] Barrett, *Gospel according to St. John,* 90.

right judgment of Jesus' cause is that the same verdict that vindicated Jesus condemned the world. The Spirit convicts the world that it is the recipient of this negative verdict, just as the world's ruler has been.

The Spirit is more characteristically associated, however, with the positive verdict in the lawsuit, that of life. It is because Jesus has experienced the positive verdict of the resurrection that he can pass on the life-giving Spirit to the disciples when he commissions them (20:21–22). It is not enough for the disciples to know they are to be witnesses in the cosmic trial; they also need the new power that has been released through the trial's decisive verdict to enable them to accomplish their task. Just as the Spirit empowered Jesus' witness, mediating life through it (6:63), so the Spirit will do the same for the witness of Jesus' followers. Easter and Pentecost come together in this narrative as the risen Jesus breathes on the disciples and says to them, "Receive the Holy Spirit" (20:22). Jesus' conferral of the Spirit by breathing on the disciples links the Spirit with the life breathed by God into humanity (cf. Gen 2:7). Ezekiel's vision of Israel's end-time renewal had also contained the new life of resurrection breathed into dry bones (Ezek 37:5; cf. also 37:9–10). The disciples' reception of the Spirit can therefore be viewed as the inauguration of the eschatological new creation, as they experience the first part of the verdict, the life of the Spirit, that will eventually culminate in the full participation in resurrection.

The disciples' reception of the Spirit is also the sign that Jesus has been glorified (cf. 7:39). But the narrative does not allow its readers to forget that this glorification also has Jesus' death at its heart. The Spirit is linked with both parts of the verdict—Jesus' death and resurrection. The power of the new life in the Spirit in no way bypasses the weakness of the cross. The promise of the life-giving waters of the Spirit flowing from the belly of Jesus (7:38) is informed by the scriptural background of the wilderness rock on which Yahweh as judge submitted to judgment in order to give life. It also anticipates the crucifixion scene, in which water flows from the wounded side of Jesus the judge, who has submitted to the sentence of death in order to make possible this positive verdict of life (cf. 19:34). In the Spirit's role in the cosmic lawsuit, not only Easter Sunday and Pentecost come together; so also do Good Friday and Pentecost.

G. The Trial's Cosmic Setting

This study has referred throughout to the cosmic-lawsuit motif. In what sense is it cosmic? Again the features of the lawsuit in Deutero-Isaiah can set the initial agenda for our discussion. There the lawsuit can be described as cosmic because it is not confined to the relationship between God and Israel but concerns God and the whole world, as the rest of that world is represented by the nations. After all, the claim is that Yahweh is the Creator God as well as the God of the covenant with Israel; this means that the whole world, and not simply Israel, owes Yahweh acknowledgment: "The LORD is the everlasting God, the Creator of the ends of the earth" (40:28; cf. also 45:12, 18). Yahweh's judgment and its salvific verdict embrace the whole world (cf. 40:5; 51:4, 5; 52:10). And as part of Yahweh's purposes in this judgment of Yahweh's world, Israel as the servant-witness has a role to play among the Gentile nations: "he will bring forth justice to the nations. . . . He will not grow faint or be crushed until he has established justice in the earth" (42:1, 4; cf. also 42:5–6; 49:6). In this setting the cosmic dimension of the lawsuit is also emphasized by the references to the created cosmos of heaven and earth, which provides the theater where the trial takes place and which is affected by its proceedings (cf. 40:22–23; 44:23–24; 45:18; 48:13; 51:6; 55:9–11).

The Fourth Gospel retains these cosmic features of the trial. Again this is not simply a lawsuit between God and Israel. Although the trial of Jesus' public ministry clearly focuses on the relationship with Israel, the nations are represented through the Samaritans who confess that Jesus "is truly the Savior of the world" (4:42) and the Greeks who wish to see Jesus (12:20–22). The climactic trial before Pilate, however, sets the lawsuit squarely on the world stage and in the context of the nations. And as an influence on the proceedings, the emperor himself stands behind Pilate. In this narrative, God, through Jesus as God's authorized representative, is seen as judging the nations, represented by the official of the ruling Roman Empire.

The cosmic scope of the narrative's trial has already been made clear in the prologue. Again there is reference to the creation, which establishes the context of what will take place. Absolutely everything came into existence through the Logos as God's immanent presence (1:3). The life of the Logos is then depicted in terms of light that shines into the darkness (vv. 4–5), recalling the first creative act of Yahweh (cf. Gen 1:3–4) and anticipating that, in the later narrative, light will be an image for the coming of judgment into the world (cf. esp. John 3:19–21; 12:46–47). This light, it is said, shines for humanity as a whole (1:4). It could not be clearer, then, that when the Logos comes into the world, he comes to establish the sovereign rights of the Creator as well as those of Israel's covenant Lord. This is spelled out in vv. 10–11: the Logos was in the world that came into being through him, and so, in coming to the world, he was coming to his own property, what was his rightful possession; in particular, he was coming to his own people, Israel as the covenant people. Given this introduction, the incarnation of the Logos (v. 14) is not some totally anomalous event. In becoming flesh, the Logos takes on what has been created through him in the first place. The Logos is at home, and rightfully so, in his own created world. The anomaly, examined further below, is that the world refused to know him and his own people refused to accept him. The point here is simply to establish the cosmic setting and its presuppositions, within which the lawsuit takes place. The spatial elements in the setting—heaven and earth, above and below—need to be seen in this light. They are the two parts of the created universe, where the upper part also functions to point beyond itself to the abode of God. Thus, as the witness and the judge, Jesus comes from above, from heaven, and will return there. He is the descending and ascending Son of Man. But this should not be taken to mean that the earth, the flesh, the world in which Jesus carries out his mission are in themselves alien territory.

Throughout the narrative, the cosmic claims set out in the prologue recur in connection with both Jesus' sovereignty and the extent of the salvific judgment he brings. The reference to John the Baptist's witness in the prologue also paves the way. His witness to the light has not just Israel but the world as its stage; it is "so that *all* might believe through him" (1:7). His later witness contains a similar emphasis: Jesus is "the Lamb of God who takes away the sin of the world" (1:29). The narrator explains that God has sent the Son into the world to save the world (3:17), that the one who comes from above is above all—the supreme ruler of this world (3:31)—and that God has placed all things in his hands (3:35; cf. also 13:3). In witnessing to himself as the bread from heaven, Jesus claims to give life for the world (6:33, 51). He depicts himself as the light of the world (8:12; 9:5; cf. 12:46). He sees his being "lifted up from the earth" as the event that will draw all to himself (12:32; cf. also 11:52, where, although the language of the Jewish Diaspora is employed, the universal effects of Jesus' death are in view). Indeed, the depiction of the crucifixion, with the narrator's comment that the superscription, "Jesus of Nazareth, the King of the Jews," was in the world's three major languages, stresses Jesus' universal reign from the cross (19:19–20). Jesus' sovereignty and the universal scope of his salvific judgment are brought together in his prayer, where the former is the precondition for the latter: "you have given him authority over all people, to give eternal life to all whom you have given him" (17:2).

To the question "Whose world is it?" the answer of this narrative is unequivocal. It is not the world of the powers of evil and their ruler. In the trial's verdict, "the ruler of this world" is driven out (12:31), has no power over Jesus (14:30), and has been condemned (16:11). It is not the world of the Jewish religious authorities, who are depicted as impotent to carry out their own law and dependent on and confessing their allegiance to Rome (cf. 18:31; 19:15). It is not the world of Rome, whether represented by Pilate or the emperor, since the former is reminded that whatever power he has is from above (19:11). No, the world rightly belongs to the one who has come into it from above to bring salvific judgment. The nature of the positive verdict in the trial is also significant here. Since the experience of eternal life includes a resurrection body for Jesus and will include this for his followers, the verdict is one that reclaims created life. Eternal life is not the abandonment of creation but the establishment of God's claim through the renewal of the created world.

We have primarily being talking about the world in the neutral sense of the term. But the picture is more complicated because the narrative discourse also uses the term *world* in a negative sense, the world of humanity that rejects the claims of the judgment that is taking place.[49] It makes for confusion when interpreters fail to distinguish adequately these two senses. Bultmann, although he will later talk of the world as the creation of God and of the perversion of this creation into "the world,"[50] begins his discussion by asserting that "the essence of the kosmos . . . is darkness."[51] This is true only of the negative sense of the term, and it can skew the entire discussion to make this one's starting point for depicting the perspective of the Gospel.

Where the truth is contested, judgment is inevitably divisive. The world of the Logos into which he comes is divided in two by his coming. There are those within humanity who do not receive him, the world that did not know him (1:10), and another group within humanity who do receive him, the children of God who believed in his name (1:12). This determines the use of *world* in the negative sense in the rest of the narrative. Such a world has a totally different value system from the incarnate Logos and those who believe in his witness. Neither Jesus nor his followers belong to the world in this sense. He and his kingdom are

---

[49] On the use of the term κόσμος in the Fourth Gospel, see Blank, *Krisis*, 186–98.

[50] Bultmann, *Theology of the New Testament*, 2:26–27.

[51] Ibid., 15.

not of this world (cf. 8:23; 18:36). Instead their origins are from above, from God. His followers do not belong to the world, but have been chosen out of it or have been given to him out of it (cf. 15:19; 17:6, 9, 14, 16). It is also made clear, however, that they are not taken out of the world in its neutral sense (17:15), since this is the territory that rightly belongs to Jesus and his followers.

The very first reference to the world in an unfavorable sense—"the world did not know him" (1:10)—makes clear that the dualism in the narrative is an ethical and epistemological one. This unbelieving world has become alienated from its source of life, and this results in an inability to know and recognize the true state of affairs in the world. The cosmic contrast between light and darkness in the prologue becomes a clearly ethical contrast when it recurs in 3:19–20, where people are said to love darkness because their deeds are evil. In his definition of the negative sense of the world, Rensberger rightly underlines this ethical dimension: "What is meant by 'the world' is not something essential (matter or human nature) but something willed and wilful."[52] Later the epistemological aspects of this contrast are to the fore: those in the darkness do not know where they are going (12:35), whereas the light enables people to see and believe (cf. 9:39; 12:44–45). The world in the negative sense represents a different system of values that leads to different criteria for judging and knowing. The much discussed Johannine dualism should be seen, then, as referring to this division within a world that remains God's world, where humanity is answerable to its Creator.[53] It has become clear that, in the lawsuit between God and the world, the truth at issue involves not simply God but God in relation to God's world. The clash of claims in the trial about the identity of God and Jesus also involves a clash of claims about the world, about who is sovereign in the world and defines its values. There is an obvious link here with the synoptic presentation of the kingdom of God invading that of Satan and with Paul's notion of the two dominions, where Christ and the Spirit are set over against the forces of sin, the flesh, the law, and death.

Witness to the world that is hostile to God can result in people believing and coming out of that world, or it can have the effect of arousing its hatred. Jesus discovered this—"The world . . . hates me because I testify against it that its works are evil" (7:7; cf. also 15:24–25)—and he

---

[52] Rensberger, *Johannine Faith,* 146.
[53] Cf. ibid., 146: "For John, evil does not lie in creation but in the human response to creation and to the Creator."

promises that it will be no different for his followers (15:18–19). Again, those who evidence a hostile response to the witness do so "because they do not know him who sent me" (15:21). The world may claim that its criteria of judgment are God-given, but these criteria need to be overturned and the world convicted of its guilt, as 16:8–11 indicates. The world resists the judgment that would restore it to life, because it does not want the status quo threatened. In the world's system of values, Jesus' Jewish opponents operate as judges of themselves and others on the basis primarily of their interpretation of the law. But as 18:36–37 indicates, the values of Jesus' kingdom also clash with those who run their and others' lives on the basis of the political power that requires violent means to achieve its ends. Those who are content with a system of judging and honoring one another with its rewards of status, and with a system of manipulating one another with its rewards of power, resent the claims of the divine judge to be given supreme honor. This is so especially when this honor is displayed in self-giving that entails humiliation and death and thereby calls for the restructuring of human relationships in conformity with this new perspective. Their resistance to the witness to the establishment of this type of divine reputation is seen as leading Jesus' opponents to attempt embracing more firmly this world's system of values, with its alienating forces that mean death.

The opposition may be in the majority and it may be hostile, but according to the perspective of the Fourth Gospel, this does not mean that it is in charge in the cosmic court. Instead the narrative presents the world as the place where true judgment has been and is being given, even in the midst of the victimization and violence that can characterize the opposition's system of justice. Despite the hostility of the opposition, Jesus' followers have a mission in the world: to make clear the nature of the verdict in the true judgment that has been given. Israel's role as the servant-witness to the nations was taken up by Jesus and is now continued in his followers' witness to the world. In Jesus' prayer of John 17, the neutral and the negative senses of *world* are frequently juxtaposed. Jesus is not praying on behalf of the opposing world but on behalf of the people God has given him (v. 9). Even though, in the narrative, Jesus is speaking the words of the prayer in the world that is the theater of the lawsuit (v. 13), he can be said to be no longer in the world because he is returning to the Father. His followers are, however, still in that world (v. 11). Just as it was the appropriate place for his life and mission, so it is the appropriate setting for theirs. They do not belong to the world in the negative sense, just as Jesus does not, and for this reason that world hates them (v. 14; cf. also v. 16). But the world's hatred does not at all mean that the world in the neutral sense is an alien place from which they need to be removed (v. 15a). What they need instead is divine protection from the evil one, who, although he has been condemned, is still lashing out at those who witness to the verdict (cf. v. 15b). Therefore, just as Jesus was sent into the world that was his by rights, so his followers are being sent into the world that remains his and has been reclaimed by him in the lawsuit (v. 18). The purpose of their presence in the world is that the rest of the world might come to its senses, recognize God as the rightful instigator of the lawsuit and Jesus as the divine agent, and, through the unity of the agent's agents, perceive the love that has been the motivation for the process of salvific judgment (v. 21, 23). That this vocation of Jesus' followers in the world is expected to have positive results is indicated by the fact that Jesus prays not only for them but also for those who will believe in him through their witness (v. 20).

The Farewell Discourses that precede the prayer and prepare the disciples for this role in the world emphasize not withdrawal and fear but the positive qualities of peace, joy, and love, despite persecution by the hostile world. When in 20:19–23 the time comes for the disciples to be commissioned for their role in the cosmic lawsuit, their withdrawal behind locked doors for fear of "the Jews" is transformed, there is peace and rejoicing, and then they are sent out into the world, empowered by the Spirit, to pass on the lawsuit's verdict. As noted, the last scene of Jesus with the disciples as a group, in the epilogue, makes the miraculous catch of fish a sign of the success of their universal mission (21:1–14). "The function of the Fourth Gospel, then, is to enable the community to step back from its situation of rejection, reflect upon it in the light of the fate of Jesus, and to be *sent out again with its faith renewed.*"[54]

This narrative, then, invites its readers to see their world as a cosmic courtroom, to see history as the locus of God's judicial process, and to see the created cosmos of heaven and earth as the setting in which God conducts this lawsuit. It invites them to see the purpose of this cosmic trial as a setting of the world to rights, a reversing of the alienation of death that blights it, and a restoring of it to the Creator God's purposes for life. It invites them to see the story of the protagonist, Jesus, not as that of a witness and judge who is a stranger in the world but as that of a witness and judge who took on the flesh created through him, who claimed the world as his rightful possession, who experienced judgment from an alienated humanity, and who, in embracing their judgment, turned death into the source of life for the world. If this summary points

---

[54] Ibid., 144.

in the right direction, it provides a rather different picture of the stance of the Christian community toward the world from that painted by those who suggest the Fourth Gospel has a dualistic attitude that has written off the world and a sectarian ethos that simply looks inward and treats salvation as an experience of the individual in some spiritual sphere.[55] We may still want to ask whether this more optimistic stance is to be explained in terms of attempted compensation for the marginalized role played in its society by the community from which this Gospel emerged. But in the terms of the narrative the community endorsed, the dualism between the two value systems within the world is one that is meant to be temporary. The entire point of instigating the lawsuit is to overcome the sinful alienation that produces this dualism. After all, in one of this Gospel's most striking and most well known formulations, God is said to love even a hostile world that is in antithesis to the divine values and to save it by the divine self-giving in the Son, who absorbs its alienation and death and establishes the truth that is life-giving (cf. 3:16). As he goes to his death, Jesus himself can see that his mission in the lawsuit as it affects the world is already accomplished: "In the world you face persecution. But take courage; I have conquered the world!" (16:33). This is a ringing announcement that he has emerged triumphant in the lawsuit with the world, having reclaimed what was rightfully his, and that this makes all the difference for his followers, who are to live in that world and carry out their mission there, willing to accept persecution and pain because they are confident in their knowledge of whose world it is.

---

[55] Bultmann, *Theology of the New Testament*, 2:11–14, with his talk of John's "dualistic-Gnostic thinking," has remained highly influential despite the rejection by most scholars of his notion of the specifically Gnostic background of the Fourth Gospel. Rensberger, *Johannine Faith*, 137, provides a much needed corrective when he points out that "the Johannine dualism between spirit and flesh, the world above and the world below, is not a dualism between interior and exterior, personal and social," but one that cuts right across these categories.

chapter six

THE FOURTH GOSPEL'S
LAWSUIT *in* HISTORICAL
and SOCIAL PERSPECTIVE

The point of view of this narrative and its theological discourse are not simply abstract formulations but closely related to the lived realities of its author and readers. Accordingly, our focus in this chapter shifts to what might be discovered about such realities. Up to this point, we have worked primarily with the categories that arise from the encounter between the implied author and the implied reader, that is, intratextual factors. We have also noted that the narrative's self-depiction is that of a testimony in a lawsuit. But when it comes to extratextual historical issues, the testimony needs to be interrogated, both by asking about the historical information it purports to provide and its accuracy and by asking to what factors it may witness despite itself. Even when we have noted that accounts of history themselves are narratival in form and have their own emplotment, there still remain the question of the relation between a Gospel narrative and a historical narrative and the issue of how the former represents historical reality.[1] To put matters even in this way is to oversimplify because there is the further question of how a historical narrative represents historical reality.[2]

If we ask why the literary device of this extended metaphor is so dominant in the Fourth Gospel, then it makes sense to investigate

---

[1] These matters will be explored further in ch. 8, sec. B.
[2] See, e.g., Ricoeur, *Time and Narrative,* 1:95–225; 3:104–26, 142–56, 180–92.

whether it might have had special connotations for the community associated with the Gospel, connotations that came not only from the Jewish Scriptures but also from the traditions about Jesus it had inherited and, even more immediately, from its own experience.[3] Investigation of such factors will also illumine issues of the function of the motif and the conditions under which its truth claims were deemed to be plausible.

The testimony of the Fourth Gospel is a trace left from the past. If we want to reconstruct the past from this trace, then we need to follow the trace back. The first link in the chain backward is provided when we inquire into the circumstances that produced this testimony. This is not to deny that the narrator also intends a reference to the time of Jesus. It is, rather, an attempt to be clear about where our historical investigation has its most appropriate starting point. The need to start at this point rather than with the events the narrative ostensibly relates is reinforced by the nature of the narrative. It clearly provides a blending of two temporal perspectives: the narrative is a witness to the significance of certain past events in the history of Jesus; but this witness is shaped by the events and experiences of the recent and immediate past of the implied author and readers, and therefore the narrative is also a witness to these latter events.

This two-level nature of the witness means that the written text is closer to the latter history. This history of the author and readers is, then, its most immediate extratextual referent. Unfortunately, we have no name for the author and no identity for him outside the text's characterization of him. We need, then, to look at the community that endorses his testimony and for which he speaks as the implied author. Here the major clue to this influential setting lies in the references to the experience of being put out of the synagogue.

Before we pursue this clue, our talk about the community behind the Gospel and our understanding of its hermeneutical significance needs clarification in the light of recent criticism of such an approach.[4] Clearly, one should not simply assume that writers of the Gospels either represent or write for a particular community. This has to be argued regarding each Gospel. In the case of John, this study has already suggested that the "we" language in significant places of John's discourse

---

[3] Beutler, *Martyria,* 339–61, already concluded that the "witness" theme in the Fourth Gospel reflected a setting in life in which the conflict between Johannine Christians and the synagogue played a major role.

[4] Cf. esp. R. Bauckham, ed., *The Gospels for All Christians: Rethinking the Gospel Audiences* (Grand Rapids: Eerdmans, 1998).

most plausibly indicates a group that stands behind, is represented by, and endorses the narrative's point of view. The phenomenon of the Johannine Epistles also attests to the existence of a specific community of Johannine Christians with a distinctive tradition and theological language. In what has been said and in what follows, this study takes care to distinguish between this group, from which the Gospel emerged, and either the implied readers or intended audience that it addresses. The former group may well be included in, but certainly does not exhaust, the latter. In other words, in the view posited here, although the narrative is shaped by and addresses the needs of the group from which it emerged, it also gives clear indications in its final form that its perspective transcends any particular experiences of this group and is addressed to a wider audience. It is possible to agree, then, that early Christian groups were not totally isolated conventicles whose teachings and writings were meant only for their own internal consumption. We do not, however, need to banish all discussion of communities behind particular Gospels and any consideration of the hermeneutical significance that the enquiries behind such a discussion might have.

For our topic, therefore, it will be significant to explore the narrative's clues about the experiences of the Jewish Christians that lie behind it. At the same time, however, the perspectives about God, Christ, and Christian existence in the world that emerged from such experiences in the recent past were deemed to be of wider appeal to an audience that now included Gentiles and other Jews. Although they had not had these precise experiences, they might face analogous conflicts and trials within their particular setting in the Greco-Roman world if they made, as they should, the same confession about Jesus as the Christ, the Son of God.

A. A Community under Trial

To ensure that the necessary detail does not obscure the goals of this section's enquiry, it is worth stating some of the key questions that will be pursued. (1) Do the references in the narrative to the expulsion from the synagogue of those who professed allegiance to Jesus—references that are anachronistic as far as the mission of Jesus himself is concerned—reflect actual experience, or are they, as some scholars hold, part of a reworking of the synoptic tradition to provide a literary legitimation of this community's distancing from official Judaism? (2) If, as part of the response to this first question, we discover there is evidence of Christians being excluded by the synagogue elsewhere, how does this activity reflected in this narrative relate to such evidence? In particular, how does it relate to the Twelfth Benediction, promulgated at Jamnia, which has often been linked with the setting of the Fourth Gospel? (3) How close to the time of writing is any such experience of trials likely to have been? (4) On the basis of our findings in response to these questions, what impact did trials in connection with persecution have on the social status and corresponding values of the writer and the community he represents, as these are reflected in the narrative? (5) Should the search be exclusively for evidence of Jewish persecution of Jewish Christians, or should it be broadened to see whether the narrative's concern with trials also reflects Roman persecution of Christians?

1. *Historical Enquiry and the Twelfth Benediction*

Strictly speaking, all that is necessary for the presentation of our case is to show the strong historical probability that a number of the community's members underwent interrogation or trial on account of their belief in Jesus. Such interrogation does not need to have been connected with excommunication itself, nor does the historical situation behind the reference to excommunication need to be pinpointed precisely for the case to hold. Nevertheless, the latter issues, which have loomed large in recent discussion of the Gospel's setting, are worth reviewing to see whether they enable us to fill out any details of the community's experience of trials that would correspond to the dominance of the metaphor of trial in the narrative.

There is widespread evidence within the NT that Jewish Christians experienced synagogue discipline, which is likely to have involved some form of trial followed by punishment. The synoptic tradition knows of such encounters with synagogues. There is the prediction of Mark 13:9: "for they will hand you over to councils [συνέδρια]; and you will be beaten in synagogues [συναγωγαί]; and you will stand before governors and kings because of me, as a testimony to them." In Matthew this becomes, "for they will hand you over to councils and flog you in their synagogues; and you will be dragged before governors and kings because of me, as a testimony to them and the Gentiles" (10:17–18). Matthew has an additional saying in the woes to the scribes and Pharisees: "Therefore I send you prophets, sages, and scribes, some of whom you will kill and crucify, and some you will flog in your synagogues and pursue from town to town" (23:34). The Lukan version of the Markan prediction is, "they will arrest you and persecute you; they will hand you over to synagogues and prisons, and you will be brought before kings and governors because of my name. This will give you an opportunity to testify" (21:12–13). Luke also adds in this context, "and they will put some of you to death" (21:16b). This synoptic tradition suggests that early Christians experienced punishment by the synagogue, involving physical beating, and connects the experience with an opportunity for witness. This indicates the likelihood of some form of interrogation or trial preceding the punishment. What other evidence is there for the subjection of early Jewish Christians to such treatment by the synagogue?

Acts 9:2 depicts Saul requesting authority from the high priest to extricate followers of the Way from synagogues in Damascus in order to take them as prisoners to Jerusalem, presumably for trial before the Sanhedrin (cf. also 22:4–5). According to Acts, Saul also participated in the decision that the punishment of believers in Jesus should be death (cf. 26:10; also 22:20). He is further portrayed as attempting to make Jewish Christians "blaspheme" when he took part in local synagogues' punishment of them, both in Jerusalem and elsewhere: "By punishing them often in all the synagogues I tried to force them to blaspheme; and since I was so furiously enraged at them, I pursued them even to foreign cities" (26:11; cf. also 22:19). After his conversion, as 2 Cor 11:24 ("Five times I have received from the Jews the forty lashes minus one") indicates, Paul himself appears to have submitted to synagogue discipline. What is not evident from such accounts is that the trials resulted in Christians becoming excommunicates. According to the Acts account, when there is a break between Paul and various synagogues on his travels, it is at his own initiative rather than as a result of a synagogue ruling against him (cf., e.g., 18:6–7; 19:9).

None of the evidence above, then, indicates anything like the official excommunication of Jewish Christians reflected in John 9:22: "for the Jews had already agreed that anyone who confessed Jesus to be the Messiah would be put out of the synagogue." Only the Fourth Gospel speaks of being put out of the synagogue, being made ἀποσυνάγωγος. The only functional equivalent of this sort of language elsewhere in the NT is in Luke 6:22: "Blessed are you when people hate you, and when they exclude [ἀφορίσωσιν] you, revile you, and cast out your name as evil [ἐκβάλωσιν τὸ ὄνομα ὑμῶν ὡς πονηρόν] on account of the Son of Man." Some commentators have indeed seen in the Lukan beatitude a reference to the sort of excommunication associated with the twelfth synagogue benediction. Others, however, argue that what is more likely in view is informal ostracism involving verbal abuse.[5]

---

[5] Cf. D. Hare, *The Theme of Jewish Persecution of Christians in the Gospel according to St Matthew* (Cambridge: Cambridge University Press, 1967), 53: "A more

Has John's Gospel simply elaborated on this tradition as part of a wholesale reworking of the synoptic tradition for primarily literary purposes, or does its extensive reworking suggest that experiential factors in the group that this Gospel represents prompted its intense interest in this tradition? Margaret Davies doubts that there is sufficient first-century evidence for any general practice of excluding members from synagogue communities, and has indeed argued that the Fourth Evangelist extrapolated from Scripture and from the Lukan beatitude to produce the formulation of 9:22. In her view, this reference does not therefore reflect any specific historical situation in the community's life but is simply meant to justify the fact that the Christian community has nothing to do with the Jewish community.[6] Even on this supposition, however, one would still have to ask whether the formulation of Luke 6:22 does not itself have a historical referent in encounters between Christians and the synagogue and therefore function as counterevidence.

Kimelman suggests similarly that the references in John might have been concocted to persuade Christians to stay away from the synagogue or to convince Jewish Christians that there was no turning back.[7] But this persuasive device would surely only be effective if the readers knew it had some basis in reality, and Hebrews shows that there were quite different ways of arguing that Jewish Christians should not turn back. Hare asserts, "John's peculiar hostility toward the Jews makes it difficult for us to know whether these passages represent historical facts or unfulfilled predictions on the part of the author."[8] It seems to me, however, that the nature and intensity of the controversies with "the Jews" in the narrative make a real dispute between Christians and the synagogue more plausible than these explanations.[9] To remove any historical reference for the passages on excommunication from the synagogue would at the same time remove any explanation for "John's peculiar hostility to-

---

likely frame of reference for Luke 6:22 is the informal ban employed by every community, ancient and modern, towards individuals it despises. Social ostracism is a kind of excommunication which could well inspire the words of the Lukan beatitude."

[6] Davies, *Rhetoric and Reference*, 293–301.

[7] R. Kimelman, "Birkat Ha-Minim and the Lack of Evidence for an Anti-Christian Jewish Prayer in Late Antiquity," in *Jewish and Christian Self-Definition* (3 vols.; ed. E. P. Sanders et al.; Philadelphia: Fortress, 1981), 2:226–44, here 234–35.

[8] Hare, *Jewish Persecution*, 55.

[9] Cf. also, e.g., C. Setzer, *Jewish Responses to Early Christians* (Minneapolis: Fortress, 1994), 92.

ward the Jews." In further response to Hare, the fulfillment of Jesus' predictions, as we have seen, is a very important aspect of the Fourth Gospel's portrayal of Jesus' witness; but if predictions about excommunication remained unfulfilled, it would undermine the depiction of this witness for the readers. On the more likely assumption that his narrative reflects a real dispute, it may still be allowed that, from one specific situation involving his community and a number of local synagogues, the Fourth Evangelist has formulated a general exclusion.

But what of the widely held view that the author's formulation accurately reflects awareness of a more widespread break between synagogues and Christians? Martyn maintains this position, claiming also that the Jamnia conference of the second-last decade of the first century C.E. and the twelfth of the Eighteen Benedictions, the *birkat ha-minim,* lie behind the Johannine formulation about a decision reached by some authoritative Jewish group.[10] Martyn accepts the tradition that the reformulation of the Twelfth Benediction was undertaken by Samuel the Small under the instigation of Gamaliel II (cf. *b. Ber.* 28b–29a), early in the period between 80 and 115 C.E., and renders it as follows:

1. For the apostates let there be no hope

2. And let the arrogant government

3. be speedily uprooted in our days.

4. Let the Nazarenes [Christians] and the *Minim* [heretics] be destroyed in a moment

5. And let them be blotted out of the Book of Life and not be inscribed with the righteous.

6. Blessed art thou, O Lord, who humblest the proud![11]

Lines 4 and 5 appear to have been added to make an old benediction, which called for the overthrow of Israel's oppressors, relevant to a new situation by associating the *minim* with such enemies of Israel. It is worth noting that the Lukan formulation "cast out your name as evil" has a conceptual link with line 5 and could reflect an earlier, more localized version of an anathema on Jewish Christians. In Martyn's view, the Twelfth Benediction served to bring to light a person's faith in Jesus because Christians would not want to utter a curse on themselves. Any adult male could be asked to be the delegate of the congregation and lead

---

[10] Martyn, *History and Theology;* cf. also, e.g., Pancaro, *The Law,* 249.
[11] Martyn, *History and Theology,* 53–60.

in the recitation of the benedictions. If someone's beliefs aroused suspicion, this person would be asked to lead the recitation, and if he faltered on the Twelfth Benediction, he would be removed and excommunication procedures would follow.

Two main elements of Martyn's hypothesis have been disputed: (1) the specific link he draws between the Twelfth Benediction and the setting of the Fourth Gospel and (2) his interpretation of the significance of the benediction itself. On the latter point, it is generally agreed that Martyn has overestimated the importance of the benediction for Jewish-Christian relations in general. In opposition to Martyn, Kimelman in particular[12] argued that the *birkat ha-minim* was not a watershed in the early history of relations between Jews and Christians, since it was not directed against Gentile Christians but against Jewish sectarians, and the reference to *notsrim* was a much later gloss in the Genizah version, probably dating from the fourth century and specifying the *minim* of that time as the Jewish Christian sect of the Nazoreans (cf. Epiphanius, *Pan.* 29.9.1; Jerome, *Epist.* 112.13 to Augustine).[13] He held that only at this later stage in the fourth century is there reference to cursing during the prayers thrice daily and that before this time there is no unambiguous evidence in writers such as Justin or Origen for the cursing of Christians during Jewish prayers. He also observed that instead there is evidence pointing in a different direction—in patristic passages that presuppose that Christians were sometimes welcomed in synagogues.[14] Thus, Kimelman can assert in regard to the Fourth Gospel that there is no evidence that the excommunication John mentions was prevalent anywhere else (Luke 6:22 is dismissed as irrelevant)[15] and that John "makes no reference to the prayers of the Jews nor to any curse and thus is not helpful for establishing any part of the formulation of *birkat ha-minim.*"[16]

Regarding the dating of the tradition, on which Martyn relies, it should be observed that the connection of the *birkat ha-minim* with Samuel the Small is found only in *b. Ber.* 28a–29b, that its connection with Jamnia is mentioned elsewhere only in *y. Ber.* IV, 3 (8a), and that both are rather late strands within rabbinic literature. Nevertheless, the existence of a *birkat ha-minim*, whatever its relation to Jamnia and whatever its precise original wording, can in all probability be claimed for the first part of

---

[12] Kimelman, *"Birkat Ha-Minim,"* in Sanders et al., *Self-Definition*, 2:226–44.
[13] Ibid., 237–38.
[14] Ibid., 234–40.
[15] Ibid., 234; 396, n. 54.
[16] Ibid., 235.

the second century because of the evidence for its use found in the references in Justin, *Dial.* 16, 96, to Jews cursing Christians in the synagogue.[17] Kimelman is in all probability right that in the original wording *notsrim* did not appear before *minim* and is a later addition. If this were not the case, then this twelfth *berakah* would have been called *birkat ha-notsrim*. Instead both patristic and rabbinic writings refer to it as *birkat ha-minim*. But even if the original wording in the Palestinian recension of the benediction only referred to *minim,* Jewish Christians would have been prime candidates for this category. As Alexander notes, from the perspective of the rabbis, "a *min* was basically a Jew who did not accept the authority of the Rabbis and who rejected Rabbinic halakhah," and the term was used in order to discriminate among those who still assembled in the synagogue and thought of themselves as loyal to Israel.[18] Of the Jews about whom we know at the end of the first and beginning of the second century, this would most clearly, though not exclusively, apply to Jewish Christians.

Kimelman is, however, not to be followed on the later development of the benediction and the inclusion of *notsrim* in its wording. Schiffman argues that after 70 C.E. the Tannaim saw the need to close ranks and to urge greater unity among Jews.[19] He agrees that the Twelfth Benediction was aimed at Jewish Christians and sees its specific function as "to ensure that those who were *minim* would not serve as precentors in the synagogue. After all, no one would be willing to pray for his own destruction."[20] Katz, too, sees the benediction as having for its intended effect the gradual withdrawal of Jewish Christians from the synagogue.[21] He is strictly accurate but slightly disingenuous when he adds, "But this was the result of their, namely, the heretics' choice." It was not much of a choice for any genuine Christian believers to deny that belief by praying for their own destruction!

Schiffman stresses, "While the benediction against the *minim* sought to exclude Jewish Christians from active participation in the synagogue

---

[17] Cf. also P. S. Alexander, "'The Parting of the Ways' from the Perspective of Rabbinic Judaism," in *Jews and Christians* (ed. J. D. G. Dunn; Tübingen: J. C. B. Mohr, 1992), 1–25, here 7.

[18] Ibid., 9.

[19] L. H. Schiffman, *Who Was a Jew? Rabbinic and Halakhic Perspectives on the Jewish-Christian Schism* (Hoboken, N.J.: Ktav, 1985).

[20] Ibid., 152.

[21] S. T. Katz, "Issues in the Separation of Judaism and Christianity after 70 C.E.: A Reconsideration," *JBL* 103 (1984): 43–76, here 51.

service, it in no way implied expulsion from the Jewish people."[22] A *min* was misguided but nevertheless remained a Jew. He holds that after the separation of Jewish Christians from the synagogue was accomplished, at a later date, "perhaps by 150 C.E. but definitely by 350 C.E., as the fate of Christianity as a Gentile religion was sealed, the mention of Gentile Christians was added as well to the prayer."[23] This was when the term *notsrim* was added; the new term was necessary because Gentile Christians could not be called *minim*.[24] Against Kimelman, he holds that *notsrim* must be taken not as a reference to the Jewish Christian sect of the Nazoreans but to Christians in general or Gentile Christians. Epiphanius (c. 315–403 C.E.) mentions the Jews cursing Christians three times daily in their prayers and links *notsrim* to the sect of the Nazoreans, but Jerome (c. 340–420 C.E.), who also knows of the curse and gives *notsrim* the more general sense of Nazarenes, is to be relied on as much better informed than Epiphanius. Indeed, Jerome, *Epist.* 112, shows that Jerome was well able to distinguish between Nazoreans, whom he mentions only in this passage, and Nazarenes, whom he mentions in all his other references.[25] The term *notsrim,* then, is to be taken as a reference not to the Jewish Christian sect of the Nazoreans but to Nazarenes, Christians in general.

Horbury is one of the few recent scholars to dispute the view that the original benediction does not contain a curse against all Christians, including Gentiles.[26] He does so primarily on the basis of the evidence from Justin in the middle of the second century but appeals, for more general support, to the widespread references in the first two centuries C.E. to Jewish persecution of Christians. In addition to the remarks in Justin about Christians being cursed in the synagogues, Horbury also brings into play the more general references where Trypho and his companions are told that "you," the Jews, curse believers in Christ (*Dial.* 93, 95, 108, 123, 133) and the claims that Jews have been forbidden to converse with Christians (*Dial.* 38, 112). To corroborate the view that Justin

---

[22] L. H. Schiffman, "At the Crossroads: Tannaitic Perspectives on the Jewish-Christian Schism," in *Jewish and Christian Self-Definition* (ed. Sanders et al.), 2:115–56, here 152.

[23] Ibid., 152.

[24] Cf. Katz, "Separation of Judaism and Christianity," 72.

[25] Cf. also P. W. van der Horst, "The *Birkat Ha-minim* in Recent Research," *ExpTim* 105 (1994): 363–68, here 367.

[26] W. Horbury, "The Benediction of the *Minim* and Early Jewish-Christian Controversy," *JTS* 33 (1982): 19–61.

accurately reflects the historical circumstances surrounding the Twelfth Benediction, he suggests that Justin's remarks fit the other available evidence. He argues that the self-definition of the Christian community as a *single* group of both Jews and Gentiles was accepted in Jewish and pagan sources from the beginning of the second century.[27] Horbury further claims that "the direction of the imprecation against Christians in general would be consonant with its inclusion in a section of the Tefillah invoking universal judgment upon the Jew first, but also the Gentile."[28] In addition, that the benediction was aimed against all Christians would be consonant with the condemnation, in the synagogue, of heretics in the presence "of the non-Jews for whose allegiance church and synagogue were vying."[29]

Horbury also believes that his interpretation of the benediction is compatible with, on the one hand, the NT and patristic accounts of Christians being excluded from the synagogue and, on the other, the patristic references to Christians attending synagogue, to which Kimelman drew attention. The former evidence indicates "the Christian loss of right to synagogue membership, in the late first century," and the latter reflects the missionary rivalry of the early patristic period when Christian visitors, "like other interested Gentiles, could be regarded as potential proselytes. The malediction on Christians in the Prayer . . . is one expression of those exclusive and universal claims of Judaism which form the presupposition under which such visits can be encouraged."[30] The Tefillah was gaining importance as a bond of Jewish unity and "expressed, for the benefit of both Jews and Gentiles, the sole rights of Judaism in the biblical inheritance and its promise to the nations."[31] According to Horbury, Justin's references to prohibition of converse indicate a measure designed, on the one hand, to reinforce loss of synagogue membership for Jewish Christians and, on the other, to prevent Jews listening to Christian preachers or entering ill-advisedly into discussions where they could be subjected to Christian propaganda, although the measure is compatible with some forms of contact between Jews and Christians.[32]

---

[27] Ibid., 28.
[28] Ibid., 48.
[29] Ibid., 51.
[30] Ibid., 53.
[31] Ibid., 59.
[32] Ibid., 52–53, 58.

Horbury has made as good a case as can be made that the original benediction was aimed not simply against Jewish Christians but against all Christians. The linchpin of his argument, however, is a reading of Justin that takes his comments at their face value. As Horbury is fully aware in his review of scholarship,[33] numerous scholars from the mid–nineteenth century onward have questioned Justin's accuracy on this point. He himself is agnostic about the original wording of the benediction and, since Justin fails to mention the name by which Christians were cursed, has to guess that this is likely to have been "Nazarenes." But if, as we have seen, *notsrim* is probably a later addition to the benediction and *minim* always referred to Jews, then there appears to be little basis in the benediction itself for a term that refers to Christians in general. Two options, then, are available for explaining the data in Justin. The first, as suggested by most scholars, is that, in the polemical situation in which he found himself, Justin misunderstood or exaggerated a curse that included Jewish Christians, and treated it as referring to all Christians.[34] The second option is that *notsrim* was added early on and understood correctly by Justin as a reference to all Christians.[35] Wilson suggests more specifically that the term may in fact have been added after the Bar Kokhba revolt, which exacerbated relations between Jews and Jewish Christians. The second option would mean that Justin need not be discredited—there was in his time a reference to Gentile Christians in the Twelfth Benediction—but that Horbury should not be followed in using Justin as evidence for the original formulation.[36]

The importance of any link between the *birkat ha-minim* and Jamnia should not be overstated, since the rabbis at Jamnia were in no position to enforce their formulations in the synagogues of Palestine, let alone in those of the Diaspora.[37] Only regarding the third century can one speak in any meaningful way of the triumph of the rabbinic party. It is much more likely that the *birkat ha-minim* was introduced into the synagogue liturgy piecemeal and over an extended period of time as followers of the rabbinic party either were asked to act as precentors in particular syna-

---

[33] Ibid., 20–22.

[34] Cf., e.g., van der Horst, "The *Birkat Ha-minim*," 367.

[35] See J. T. Sanders, *Schismatics, Sectarians, Dissidents, Deviants* (London: SCM, 1993), 53.

[36] S. G. Wilson, *Related Strangers: Jews and Christians, 70–170* C.E. (Minneapolis: Fortress, 1995), 182–83.

[37] Cf. Alexander, "The Parting of the Ways," 10, 21.

gogues or interrupted services in them from the body of the congregation and insisted on this benediction being recited. This was not the only or necessarily the most effective means of excluding *minim* and therefore Jewish Christians. As *t. Ḥul.* 2:20–21 indicates, rabbinic Jews were forbidden not only to eat with *minim* but also to have virtually any form of social contact with them. As the rabbis grew in influence, this would have had the effect of ostracizing Jewish Christians from the rest of the community.[38]

In a later article, however, Horbury provides an important modification of this picture.[39] On the basis of references in Justin, he argues that, by the middle of the second century, there had developed a network of communication among rulers of synagogues and teachers that reached into the Diaspora. The sort of measures designed to ensure Jewish solidarity and reflected in the Eighteen Benedictions are likely therefore to have been carried out by groups of synagogues and communities, partly through the authority of officeholders and teachers and partly through the watchfulness of those more zealous for the law.[40] One need not believe that the Jamnian measures were immediately and universally enforceable to find it likely that the cursing of Jewish Christians and the prohibition of converse, of which Justin speaks, were in operation by his time and that they built on earlier measures evidenced in the NT.

We can now return to Martyn's original hypothesis. Even if the earliest form of the Twelfth Benediction did not include Gentile Christians, this in itself would by no means undermine Martyn's argument. Neither the Fourth Gospel nor Martyn, in his attempt to link the Gospel's narrative with Jamnia, appear to have had Gentiles in view. Expulsion from the synagogue would primarily have affected Jews. Any Gentile Christians who had at one time been sympathetic to Judaism and attended the synagogue but had not become proselytes would have been unlikely to attempt to stay once Jewish Christians had been ousted. But the Fourth Gospel does not mention cursing in the synagogue prayers. It speaks of exclusion from the synagogue, and this is not quite the same as weeding out some of those called on to lead in prayer. This

---

[38] Cf. ibid., 15–16.

[39] W. Horbury, "Jewish-Christian Relations in Barnabas and Justin Martyr," in *Jews and Christians* (ed. Dunn), 315–45, here 344–45.

[40] Cf. also Katz, "Separation of Judaism and Christianity," 45: "Most likely, the decisions of the Yavneh circle on many matters, decisions that would have the most far-reaching consequences for all subsequent Judaism, were transmitted internationally to Jewish communities."

again is not necessarily decisive against Martyn's view. It could simply mean that the Fourth Gospel's writer has focused on the primary cause—confession about Jesus—rather than on the means of expulsion.

Other factors, however, also cast doubt on whether the Twelfth Benediction is likely to have been directly behind the Fourth Gospel's references. There are questions whether an original formulation simply against *minim* would have been precise enough to have caused Jewish Christians problems. They are more likely to have thought of themselves as true Jews rather than as heretics.[41] And if only adult males who were not slaves were eligible to pray aloud on behalf of the congregation, this would mean that a sizable group of Jewish Christians might have remained unaffected by such a test.[42] These observations, however, need to be balanced against the exclusionary effect that would have been felt by Jewish Christians present at a service in which they knew the majority present were directing this malediction against them.[43] Nevertheless, it is safest to conclude that this synagogue prayer was not likely to have been the main means of expulsion experienced by Johannine Christians.[44] In drawing attention to the Twelfth Benediction, then, Martyn may have illuminated some possible aspects of the experience of expulsion reflected in the narrative of the Fourth Gospel, but he cannot be followed when he makes the formulation of that benediction at Jamnia the precise cause of the expulsion of Johannine Christians.

Nevertheless, Matsunaga, in response to the recent debate, asserts, "The burden of proof lies on those who claim that the *Birkat Ha-Minim* was not the decision referred to in John 9:22. It is up to them to show what other kind of Jewish decision could have given rise to an effect of this magnitude."[45] The effect to which he refers is a separation of Christians from the synagogue, characterized by the finality reflected in the Fourth Gospel. His assertion clearly goes much too far. What can be said

---

[41] Cf. Kimelman, "*Birkat Ha-Minim*," in Sanders et al., *Self-Definition*, 2:227; Katz, "Separation of Judaism and Christianity," 74–75; Setzer, *Jewish Responses*, 90–91.

[42] Cf. Setzer, *Jewish Responses*, 91.

[43] Cf. Sanders, *Schismatics, Sectarians*, 88.

[44] Sanders, ibid., 60, however, is still prepared to assert cautiously, "It is at least possible that the promulgation of the *birkat-ha-minim* led precisely to the separation, hostility, and name-calling that we see in the Gospel of John, and perhaps to similar situations elsewhere."

[45] K. Matsunaga, "Christian Self-Identification and the Twelfth Benediction," in *Eusebius, Christianity, and Judaism* (ed. H. W. Attridge and G. Hata; Leiden: E. J. Brill, 1992), 355–71, here 367, n. 1.

is that the evidence of the Fourth Gospel seems to require that a decision similar in intent to that which has been associated with Jamnia be carried out at least in the particular locality of the Johannine community. Schiffman is willing to entertain the notion that the expulsion could have been the end result of the institution of the benediction against the *minim*.[46] Katz is willing to concede that John may be reflecting the social, if not the legal, reality of his own milieu, seeing the effect of the benediction from a Christian perspective, as enforced exclusion of Jewish Christians, when this was not necessarily its specific intent.[47]

It may be more accurate, however, to reverse this chronology and see John 9:22, and even earlier Luke 6:22, as evidence of the initial stages of the conflict between the synagogue and Jewish Christians. The fierce debate between the leaders of particular synagogues and some of their Jewish Christian members resulted in the expulsion of the latter. As this conflict developed and became more widespread and as the rabbis gained in influence, the specific mechanism of the *birkat ha-minim* became increasingly one of the means employed to root out Jewish Christians; in later rabbinic tradition, its formulation for this purpose was attributed to the conference at Jamnia. Horbury, via his different route, reaches a similar conclusion: "The Johannine evidence . . . reflects the impact of measures more drastic than such a benediction alone. The Jamnian ordinance belongs to this more systematized opposition of the late first century, and probably reinforces an earlier exclusion attested in John, although uncertainties of dating leave open the possibility that these two measures may be contemporaneous."[48] The official-sounding assertion of John 9:22 that "the Jews had already agreed that anyone who confessed Jesus to be the Messiah would be put out of the synagogue" probably does not have the Twelfth Benediction in view. But the latter at least provides general corroboration that, at around the same time that the Fourth Gospel indicates that Christian Jews in its locale were being excluded from the synagogue, leading Jewish authorities were formulating more general measures designed to achieve the same aim of reinforcing Jewish identity although they would have taken time to be effectively enforced on a wide scale.[49]

Again, even if John 9:22 has to be seen as stating in general terms what was a particular experience in the history of those for whom the

---

[46] Schiffman, "At the Crossroads," in Sanders, et al., *Self-Definition*, 2:151.
[47] Katz, "Separation of Judaism and Christianity," 51, 74.
[48] Horbury, "Benediction of the *Minim*," 60.
[49] Cf. M. Casey, *Is John's Gospel True?* (New York: Routledge, 1996), 104.

evangelist writes, our discussion of the Twelfth Benediction suggests that some public test of faith, leading to removal from the synagogue, may well have been involved in the excommunication to which the narrative refers here and in 12:42 and 16:2. Interrogation is likely to have both preceded and followed such a test. Later Tannaitic evidence makes explicit the element of trial if one was suspected of being a *min:* "It happened that R. Eliezer was arrested for words of minut and they brought him to the tribunal for judgment" (*t. Ḥul.* 2.24). Initial questioning by the authorities would lead to clear suspicion of a person; then failure to pass the test satisfactorily could result in a further interrogation or trial before a sentence of excommunication.

2. Excommunication and Its Consequences

It appears, then, that some of the Johannine community's Jewish members had found themselves examined, tried, and then excommunicated by the synagogue for the apostasy and blasphemy of their confession about Jesus (cf. John 9:22; 12:42; 16:1–4). They had discovered painfully that testifying is a speech-act with public dimensions and consequences and that not only their notion of God but also their roots in a tradition, their relationship to the social structures, and their sense of identity were at stake in their confession. A profound religious dislocation had been experienced. "The synagogue meetings, the public liturgy, the festivals and observances were all now denied them, and the authoritative interpretation of the sacred scripture itself was in the hands of their opponents. What was threatened was thus the entire universe of shared perceptions, assumptions, beliefs, ideals, and hopes that had given meaning to their world within Judaism."[50] Both unofficially and officially, these Jewish Christians had been put on trial, and they needed to remain faithful in their witness to Jesus as the Christ, the Son of God. In particular, the experience of the man born blind in John 9 would have resonated with their own. They appreciated what it meant to be interrogated or tried (cf. 9:13–34a), to be driven out or expelled (ἐκβάλλω ἔξω—v. 34b), and to know that Jesus comes to those who are driven out (v. 35). They would also have found reassurance in his earlier promise, "anyone who comes to me I will never drive away [ἐκβάλλω ἔξω]" (6:37). They might even in retrospect have been able to see Jesus as the one who was behind their being driven out and who now goes before them: "When he has driven [NRSV: 'brought'] out [ἐκβάλῃ] all his own,

---

50 Rensberger, *Johannine Faith,* 27.

he goes ahead of them" (10:4).[51] It is not surprising, then, that the evangelist perceived through such experiences that belief in Jesus affected the whole of life, and that he found this scriptural metaphor of a trial of truth on a cosmic scale to be an appropriate vehicle for expressing such a conviction.

Do we have any other evidence of how excommunication would have been perceived and what its consequences are likely to have been? To gain a clearer idea, it helps to examine what is known about Jewish forms of discipline, particularly the practice of the ban. Martyn has argued, however, that neither the *herem* nor the less severe *niddui*, mentioned in rabbinic sources, appear to fit the bill.[52] The latter was a form of inner-synagogue discipline, not a means of excluding a person from the community. It was "intended as a temporary, revocable ban, usually of at least thirty days, which was leveled against those who threatened the Pharisaic halakic process as much as against those who threatened halakic decisions."[53] There is no reference to the former, the *herem*, with the meaning of "excommunication" or permanent exclusion from the community before the third century C.E.[54]

Horbury makes clear that he would find such a conclusion about the *herem* simplistic and overdrawn.[55] He believes that, despite the paucity of evidence, a consistency in disciplinary measures can be traced in postexilic and prerabbinic Judaism. This would mean that the later rabbinic evidence for the *herem* as involving excommunication from the synagogue should be seen as referring to a practice that was in basic continuity with earlier exclusion measures. Horbury sees these earlier measures as principally associated with two overlapping concerns—admission to the temple congregation and loyalty to the covenant. In relation to the latter, exclusion from the community would have served as a surrogate

---

[51] Cf. Sanders, *Schismatics, Sectarians,* 45, 60.

[52] Martyn, *History and Theology,* 43–44, 156–57.

[53] Katz, "Separation of Judaism and Christianity," 48.

[54] Katz, ibid., 50, stresses that even then such excommunication did not annul completely a person's status as a Jew: "*Herem* made one an excommunicant, but an excommunicant Jew." But as Alexander, "The Parting of the Ways," 5, points outs regarding heretics: "A heretic *(min),* if not strictly outside the Community *de jure,* is certainly outside it *de facto.* He not only loses the blessings of the Covenant in this life, but runs the risk of losing his portion in the world to come. . . . It is as if he had never belonged to *Kelal Yisra'el.*" Sanders, *Schismatics, Sectarians,* 88, makes the same point about the de facto situation of those Christians labeled "heretics."

[55] W. Horbury, "Extirpation and Excommunication," *VT* 35 (1985): 13–38.

for, or a preliminary to, the death penalty.[56] On the basis of Deut 23:1–8, the exclusion of the uncircumcised, the unclean, and the alien was emphasized after the exile, but moral factors also played a role (cf. Ezek 44:6–8). Philo (*Spec.* 1.324–45) and Josephus (*Ant.* 4.290–91) also take Deut 23 to exclude Jews who are defective not only physically but also ethically. The Deuteronomic laws were thus understood in the Second Temple period as entailing exclusion from the community.

In addition, the covenantal curses had, as their sanction for those who broke the covenant, exclusion from the land and destruction, and were influential in the disciplinary actions of the Qumran community and Mattathias (cf. CD XIX, 4–35; 1 Macc 2:23–27). In the covenantal context, verbal forms of חרם referred to the imposition of the death penalty, while the noun "*herem* comes to describe a communal vow, guarded by curse and exclusion or death."[57] The action of expelling from the whole community is attributed to Ezra in Ezra 10:8, and the same root, בדל, found there is used of exclusion from the congregation in Neh 13:3 and Isa 56:3. The LXX Isa 56:3 has ἀφορίζω, which is the same verb employed in Luke 6:22 alongside ἐκβάλλω for what may be a reference to exclusion from the synagogue. Ezekiel 13:9 speaks of exclusion from enrollment among the house of Israel, and Ps 69:18 of exclusion from enrollment among the righteous; the latter is the terminology found in the curse on the *minim* in the Twelfth Benediction—"let them not be written with the righteous." Josephus, *Ant.* 11.340, 346–7, speaks of the expulsion of allegedly apostate Jews who were fugitives from Jerusalem; here the verb is ἐκβάλλω, the same verb employed in John 9:34–35 for the expulsion of the man born blind. In 3 Macc 7:12 some Alexandrian Jews are said to have obtained permission to destroy and punish with death others who had lapsed; the verb used for destruction (ἐξολοθρεύω) is one of the Septuagintal renderings of חרם. Horbury holds that these last two references should be interpreted as linked with the covenantal penalty of death for apostasy. The Josephus reference, then, would be an instance of exclusion as a substitute for the death penalty, since Josephus (*Ant.* 4.309–10) interprets Deut 13 as requiring execution or a surrogate.[58] Philo, *Spec.* 1.60, and CD XII, 4–6 also interpret exclusion as a substitute for the death penalty.

Horbury argues that the NT's evidence for Jewish disciplinary measures should not be ignored. In addition to Luke 6:22 and the Johannine

---

[56] Ibid., 16.

[57] Ibid., 18.

[58] Cf. ibid., 27–28.

references, he points to 1 Cor 5:5 as containing a reference to an excommunication from the Corinthian church that involves "the destruction of the flesh" (ὄλεθρον τῆς σαρκός), language that recalls the LXX rendering of the חרם tradition. That this procedure is assumed without discussion suggests that existing Jewish disciplinary measures are presupposed. Horbury argues that this variety of evidence, taken together, indicates that excommunication from the community was practiced in Second Temple Judaism and was appropriate to the context of "the common post-exilic inheritance of intense corporate loyalty to the covenant."[59] In addition, according to Horbury, the references for חרם in a covenantal context referring to the death penalty and to a curse and penalty in a communal vow mean that it was understood as a covenantal curse, effecting exclusion and expected to issue in death. The Septuagintal renderings of the term with ἀνάθεμα and cognates and Paul's use of this term (cf. Rom 9:3, 1 Cor 16:22; Gal 1:8–9) would continue the association of *herem* with a curse; and all this would have prepared the way for the later employment of *herem* to refer to the synagogue ban.[60]

Horbury has made a good case that concern about exclusionary measures continued throughout the Second Temple period, in which a cluster of the same notions and similar terminology reappear. In the nature of things, this evidence only provides a broader context for the debate about disciplinary measures in the synagogue. His evidence draws primarily on the thinking behind exclusion from the temple, and it is not necessarily the case that a passage such as 1 Cor 5 draws on already existing synagogue practices rather than the scriptural notions of discipline associated with the temple.[61] What has been demonstrated, however, is that whenever synagogues, either separately or in concert, began practicing excommunication, this set of ideas would have been operative in justifying the practice. Since we have already concluded that the Johannine community experienced the effects of this synagogue practice, these findings about how such sanctions were viewed are of more than passing significance.

The Jewish Christians who had been excommunicated from the synagogue were under a ban that was associated with curse and death. It is not surprising, therefore, that the prediction of Jesus in John 16:1–2 that his followers would be put out of the synagogue also speaks of some

---

[59] Ibid., 30.
[60] Ibid., 34–35.
[61] See Davies, *Rhetoric and Reference*, 296.

being put to death. Those who will carry out the death sentence are from the same group of authorities who will exclude from the synagogues, and they "will think that by doing so they are offering worship to God."[62] For them the death sentence would be simply an extension of what was already entailed in the act of excommunication. It is also little wonder that Johannine Christians would therefore fasten on to the notion of life as the chief benefit of belief in Jesus as the Christ, the Son of God. In confessing their allegiance to Jesus, they stress that this confession, far from leading to a sentence in which they pass from the realm of life to that of destruction and death, in fact entails the opposite. The cosmic lawsuit allows the verdict to be reversed. The synagogue judged them and condemned them to a form of death. But in their telling of the story of Jesus in the light of their experience, those who believe in Jesus will not perish or be destroyed in death but have eternal life (cf. 3:16; 10:28). Indeed, they have already passed from death to life (cf. 5:24). It is those who reject Jesus who will not see life but experience death and condemnation (e.g., 3:18, 36; 8:24).

The later rabbinic evidence of *t. Ḥul.* 20–21 suggests other factors that would have been involved in the process of exclusion. There rabbinic Jews are prohibited from eating with *minim,* from reading their books, which are deemed to be those of witchcraft or magic, and from having any business dealings with them, including taking on their sons as apprentices. Children of *minim* are classified as *mamzerim (bastards),* marriage to whom would have been forbidden for other Jews. The fairly complete social ostracism envisaged by such rulings could not have been enforced by any central authority until at least the third century. But it is likely that they represent a heightening of measures that were already in practice earlier on a more piecemeal basis.[63] Jewish Christians in the Johannine community who had been excommunicated from the synagogue would have experienced the force of a number of such concrete marks of disapproval and means of social alienation.

But if this was not enough, two further elements in their experience brought pain and anguish. The threat and actuality of excommunication

---

[62] On the basis of John 10:31–32, Sanders, *Schismatics, Sectarians,* 47–48, envisages that the impromptu throwing of rocks or the stoning of Johannine Christians by fellow Jews may occasionally have resulted in death. Brown, *Beloved Disciple,* 42–43, however, hypothesizes that the killing might have been carried out by the Romans after Jews denounced Christians to them.

[63] For further discussion of this material, see Alexander, "The Parting of the Ways," 15–16; Sanders, *Schismatics, Sectarians,* 63–64.

from the synagogue would have had its impact on family life and allegiances, and different responses to the threat among those who had professed faith in Jesus would have brought about mutual recriminations. Both elements are reflected in the narrative.

The ostracism resulting from excommunication came not only from the Jewish community as a whole in the area where the Johannine Christians were located; in some cases it would also have resulted in conflict and alienation from members of their families. The interplay between the parents of the man born blind and their son in John 9 shows some of this. The parents fear the consequences of any acknowledgment of Jesus as the healer, knowing that these will include expulsion, yet they are prepared to put their son on the spot (cf. 9:23) and see him experience these consequences.

It also appears that members of the community who experienced trials and excommunication felt a keen sense of betrayal by those who had remained within the synagogue despite initially professing faith in Jesus as Messiah. In the narrative, "fear," an unwillingness to accept the consequences of making the full testimony about Jesus as Son of God, is attributed to them as the motivation for such a stance. As noted, the fiercest invective appears to have been saved for this group in the trial scene of 8:31–59, where the primary referent is "the Jews who had believed in him" (v. 31). Those who initially believed but failed to remain in Jesus' word (v. 31), to hold on to his word (v. 51), and therefore who ultimately showed they were unable to accept this word (v. 43) are seen as more reprehensible than those who had not believed in the first place; they are therefore called children of the devil, who is a murderer and the father of lies (v. 44). In terms of social dynamics, it is not at all surprising that this passage reflects the community's stance toward those whom it regarded as lapsed or apostatized believers. It is also easy to imagine that those depicted as onetime believers might even have approved of the authorities' measures against those they considered more extreme in their views, and would have been in a position to inform on and betray such Jewish Christians. These actions would have earned the antagonism of those who could now impute to them the motive of wanting to kill Jesus and his followers.[64]

The warnings of 15:1–17 may provide support from elsewhere within the narrative for the interpretation that, in the setting of the Gospel's writing, those who were not willing to take the consequences of

---

[64] Cf. Rensberger, *Johannine Faith,* 125; Brown, *Beloved Disciple,* 78.

their confession of Jesus were viewed as apostates. As in 8:31, so here in 15:4–7, 9–10, remaining or abiding (μένειν) is what characterizes true followers of Jesus. Again the strongest language is used about those who do not abide in Jesus—they are thrown away like a branch and wither. Indeed, "such branches are gathered, thrown into the fire, and burned" (15:6b). Significantly, those who abide, who keep Jesus' commandments, are called "friends," not "slaves," while those who failed to continue in Jesus' word in John 8 were designated slaves (cf. 8:34–35). In both contexts, what characterizes slaves is lack of knowledge (compare 15:15a with 8:55, also 8:43). Again it is in the context of the exhortation to abide and the warning about the consequences of not abiding that the disciples are told to love one another and that love is described in terms of laying down one's life for one's friends (15:12–13).

Given that 16:1–2 indicates that the possibility of excommunication from the synagogue and death is a likely reason that believers fall away from the faith, it is probable that, in the background in John 15, the fear of such persecution and its social dislocation caused some to be tempted not to remain or abide. Failure to abide in Jesus would be seen as realigning oneself either implicitly or explicitly with the persecuting majority group and as equivalent to abandoning one's former friends to their fate, that is, failing to love them and to show the solidarity that is willing to lay down one's life for them. The sort of language used of those who, primarily under external pressure, fail to continue in the faith is similar to that in other passages about apostates. Hebrews 6:6, 8 has a not dissimilar setting, where coming out from official Judaism holds too many negative consequences and so there is the temptation to return under its umbrella. Any who have done so are held to "have fallen away, since on their own they are crucifying again the Son of God and are holding him up to contempt," and to be like ground that "produces thorns and thistles, it is worthless and on the verge of being cursed; its end is to be burned over."

The Twelfth Benediction, as noted, contained a curse against both *minim,* (heretics) and *meshummadim* (apostates), and in rabbinic Judaism lists of sinners invariably link both groups (cf. *Exod. Rab.* 19.4; *t. Sanh.* 13.5; *ʾAbot R. Nat.* 16; *t. B. Meṣiʿa* 2.33). Now Johannine Christians followed a similar pattern and, in order to ensure the solidarity of the community, reacted with harsh language about their own apostates and heretics. The attitude they took toward lapsed believers who may have remained in, or returned to, the synagogue when the going got too tough is similar to that which the Johannine Epistles take toward the secessionists who were former members of the community. They, too, are branded as liars, deceivers, antichrists, children of the devil (cf. 1 Jn 2:4, 18–22; 3:8–10; 4:3; 2 Jn 7, 10). Within the Gospel's narrative, the other figure who is linked with the devil is Judas; he, too, had become a prime example of someone who initially believed but then apostatized in an act of betrayal.

The evidence examined here raises a further question: how much time elapsed between these experiences, associated with exclusion from the synagogue, and the final form of the Gospel? Although it cannot be pursued at any length here,[65] suffice it to say that enough time must have elapsed for Johannine Jewish Christians to become a separate community with an identity clearly differentiated from that of the synagogue and for some Gentiles to join them, as is suggested by the Gospel's universal perspective on salvation. The explanation of basic Jewish terms and customs demonstrates the clear inclusion of Gentiles among the intended readers of the Gospel, but that the narrative has been made accessible for such readers need not mean that Gentiles now predominated in the community from which it emerged. Obviously, not enough time had elapsed to heal the scars from such experiences and for the Johannine community to view their impact as in the distant past. The extent and nature of the narrative's depiction of the confrontation between Jesus and "the Jews" are such that its issues still appear to be alive.

3. Social Honor, Shaming, and the Lawsuit

Although the social consequences, for Johannine Christians, of their belief in Jesus as Son of God can be described in a number of ways, they can also be summed up in one word—shame. Students of the NT are indebted in particular to Bruce Malina for underlining the importance of the honor/shame value system in the patron-client society of the Mediterranean world in the first century C.E.[66] This is especially relevant for the discourse of the Fourth Gospel's narrative and for consideration of the social realities that may lie behind it.[67] Here we are interested in both these aspects and in their interaction. The way the values of honor and

---

[65] Nor is this the place to explore whether the "high Christology" of this Gospel was the cause of the expulsion, was the result of it, or—more likely in my opinion—not only contributed to the expulsion but also was shaped by it.

[66] B. J. Malina, *The New Testament World* (Atlanta: John Knox, 1981).

[67] J. H. Neyrey, " 'Despising the Shame of the Cross': Honor and Shame in the Johannine Passion Narrative," *Semeia* 68 (1994): 113–37, has provided a reading of the passion narrative in the light of these categories. See also Malina and Rohrbaugh, *Social-Science Commentary*.

shame function in the narrative discourse may reflect the social realities of the group from which the narrative emerged. The viability of a reading from the perspective of a group of Christians who have been marginalized within their society would reinforce the conclusions we have arrived at by other means.

One aspect of the notion of glory that is stressed in the narrative discourse is honor. From the Jewish Scriptures, glory has connotations of the splendor and radiance of the divine presence and also of the honor or reputation of the divine name; God's people were thought of as participating in such divine glory. Significantly, the notion of divine glory or honor is frequently juxtaposed in the Fourth Gospel with that of human honor or reputation: "How can you believe when you accept glory from one another and do not seek the glory that comes from the one who alone is God?" (5:44); "Those who speak on their own seek their own glory; but the one who seeks the glory of him who sent him is true" (7:18). How pressing an issue for the community is this contrast of two value systems is shown in 12:42–43, where the narrator speaks of those who believed but were not willing to confess their belief for fear that the Pharisees would put them out of the synagogue, "for they loved human glory more than the glory that comes from God."

"Honor might be described as socially proper attitudes and behavior in the areas where the three lines of power, sexual status, and religion intersect."[68] To honor a person is to judge that his or her attitudes or behavior conform to what society expects in these areas and to make public acknowledgment of this. Honor involves both one's own sense of worth and its public recognition, or as Malina puts it, "Honor is a claim to worth along with the social acknowledgement of worth."[69] Honor is therefore clearly bound up with identity, and in first-century Mediterranean societies, identity was a matter of both social identity and social recognition. On the individual level, identity was closely associated with one's name, which represented one's public persona, one's reputation. But honor was important for both individuals and groups, and it was what was vied for and gained at the expense of other individuals and groups.

Shame in such a society was positive because it meant sensitivity to one's reputation and to questions of honor in human interaction. The negative aspects of the system were to be shameless, that is, to be lacking

---

[68] Malina, *New Testament World,* 27.
[69] Ibid.

in respect for such social issues, and to be shamed, that is, to be denied honorable status by public opinion.[70] The most intense shaming was experienced in being rejected by one's own group or society, where expectations of acceptance and honorable recognition were highest. But one could also be shamed when the group to which one belonged was despised or dishonored by some other individual or group. Social groups possessed a collective or corporate honor in which individuals shared, so that if a person's family or patron or god was affronted, this person's honor would be seen to be at stake and the attempt would need to be made to restore that honor. Of course, celebrating the honor of one's own group could provide the temptation to despise other groups, particularly if they were seen as a threat in any way. It should be clear, then, that honor and shame were not simply social symbols but represented social realities that were experienced at every level of social interaction and were intimately bound up with individuals' and groups' sense of identity.

In this light, in the trial of the Fourth Gospel, not only truth but also honor are being contested, and the two are intertwined. If being shamed included being denied status and recognition of worth, if it included social humiliation, then Johannine Christians had experienced a double dose of shaming. First, as a group, they confessed allegiance to a head who acted shamelessly in not observing proper social boundaries in his behavior and who had been disgraced by being judged by the Jewish religious authorities as lawless and a blasphemer and then by being ignominiously executed by the Romans. Crucifixion was the most shameful way to meet one's end, and the Letter to the Hebrews explicitly speaks of shame in connection with the cross (cf. Heb 12:2).[71] To show honor to a shameless and disgraced person was to share in this person's disgrace, to show oneself to be contemptible and foolish, unworthy of honor. Then, in being put out of the synagogue and socially ostracized, Johannine Christians had felt the full force of being shamed.[72] Individually, they had been rejected by their own society, and then corporately, their new minority group was looked down upon and scorned by the majority. It is little wonder that the narrative discourse of the Gospel, which reflects their experience, should be so preoccupied with this value of glory or

---

[70] Cf. ibid., 44–46.

[71] On the progressive humiliation of the process of crucifixion, see Neyrey, "Despising the Shame of the Cross," 113–15.

[72] Sanders, *Schismatics, Sectarians,* 142: "Being singled out as a heretic is not punishment. It is shaming pure and simple."

honor. If public opinion had failed to ascribe the correct honor and worth to Jesus, then appeal needed to be made to a higher court of opinion, that of God, and the story of Jesus needed to be told in such a way as to safeguard and make clear his true honor. As Neyrey explains in relation to the passion narrative: "The issue might be rephrased: Who gets to judge whether the crucifixion is honor or shame? If the public verdict lies with the Judeans, then Jesus is shamed. But if the community of believers renders the verdict on the basis of God's riposte or Jesus' demonstration of power in death, then the verdict is of honor."[73]

It is highly significant for our motif that taking someone to court was not a way to restore honor. A lawsuit was a means by which the powerful were able to establish their superiority, and the public embarrassment of this was to be avoided at all cost.

> Satisfaction in court, legal satisfaction, does not restore one's honor because (1) to go to court is to demonstrate inequality, vulnerability, and puts one's own honor in jeopardy; (2) court procedure allows those who deprived you of honor to gloat over your predicament; and (3) to have the court obtain recompense or ask for an apology from another is dishonoring in itself, implying that one cannot deal with one's equals. . . . In the first century world, normal legal procedures are used to dishonor someone or some group perceived to be of higher, more powerful status, and recourse to them is an admission of inequality.[74]

On the one hand, this adds to the irony of Jesus and his followers being put on trial. Implicitly the opponents were conceding the very thing at stake in the trial proceedings—the honor or glory of Jesus. On the other hand, it reinforces what was the only recourse for the evangelist and his community. There was no possibility of their attempting to reverse their experience and to take their opponents to any human court. The Jewish majority was in charge of any such legal proceedings, and in any case, even if it had been possible, it would have been counterproductive and simply an admission of loss of honor. Far more effective, then, is the recourse to the motif of the divine lawsuit. In the only law court worth recognizing, the divine patron serves as judge and establishes where true honor lies in the contest for honor; at the same time, this divine lawsuit puts society's legal proceedings in a quite different light.

In the Fourth Gospel's trial story, Jesus has honor throughout his life, and what seemed to his opponents the moment of his most obvious

---

[73] Neyrey, "Despising the Shame of the Cross," 119.
[74] Malina, *New Testament World,* 39.

disgrace and humiliation, his crucifixion, is narrated instead as the supreme point of his being honored by God, the ultimate Judge. Not only judgment but also witness, linked with the process of judgment, are essential for establishing honor. "Again, publicity, witnesses, are crucial for the acquisition and bestowal of honor. Representatives of public opinion must be present, since honor is all about the tribunal or court of public opinion and the reputation that court bestows."[75] Thus the Fourth Gospel's narrative of the lawsuit provides a whole chain of witnesses to Jesus' honor so that others can also reach the appropriate verdict about what constitutes genuine honor and where it is to be found.

As noted in chapter 2, above, Deutero-Isaiah provided the major scriptural source for the Gospel's framework of a lawsuit. It is now possible to see a further reason why this section of Scripture would have been so appealing. It, too, speaks of the shaming and disgrace of Yahweh's people being reversed and provides assurances of Yahweh's glory and love to heal Israel's shame. Its lawsuits are part of a message designed to overcome the exiles' feelings of fear, of being shamed, and of having been forgotten by Yahweh. The oppressor nation is called to trial for its humiliation of Yahweh's people, who are depicted as victimized, wounded, tormented, insulted, spat upon, and walked upon (cf. Isa 42:22; 50:6; 51:21–23). The servant, Israel, is portrayed as deeply despised, abhorred by the nations, the slave of rulers (49:7), without glory (δόξα—LXX 52:2), suffering, dishonored (ἠτιμάσθη), and of no account (LXX 53:3). Yahweh's people are tempted to feel that, in their humiliation and shaming by others, Yahweh has also forsaken and forgotten them (49:14). They are in constant fear: "You fear continually all day long because of the fury of the oppressor, who is bent on destruction" (51:13).

The cosmic-lawsuit imagery comes as a reminder that in this setting they do have a recourse. Their cause (κρίσις) is with the Lord (LXX 49:4), and in fact Yahweh is the one who judges (ὁ κρίνων) Yahweh's own people (LXX 51:22), pleading their cause and vindicating them. This brings the ringing assurance of 50:7–9: "I have not been disgraced; . . . I shall not be put to shame; he who vindicates me is near. Who will contend with me? Let us stand up together. Who are my adversaries? Let them confront me. It is the Lord GOD who helps me; who will declare me guilty?" Yahweh's promises bring the same message: "Do not fear, for you will not be ashamed; do not be discouraged, for you will not suffer disgrace; for you will forget the shame of your youth, and the disgrace of

---

[75] Ibid., 36.

your widowhood you will remember no more" (54:4; cf. also 45:17; 49:23); "you shall confute every tongue that rises against you in judgment. This is the heritage of the servants of the LORD and their vindication from me, says the LORD" (54:17). There is thus no need for fear, and again and again the command comes, "Do not fear" (cf. 41:10, 13–14; 43:1, 5; 44:2, 8; 54:14). Since God is with them throughout their ordeal (43:2), they are to be his witnesses without fear (44:8). There is no reason to fear the reproach or reviling of others (51:7): "I am he who comforts you; why then are you afraid of a mere mortal who must die?" (51:12). The situation will be reversed, and it will be Israel's enemies who experience being shamed: "All who are incensed against you shall be ashamed and disgraced" (41:11; cf. 45:24). They will be put to shame (44:9, 11; 45:16), and Babylon's shame will be seen (47:3). Israel will never be forgotten by God (44:21; 49:15). Quite the reverse: "you are precious in my sight, and honored, and I love you" (43:4). There is the constant reminder that Yahweh's glory is bound up with Israel and that, whatever the status of Yahweh's people in the eyes of the nations, in Yahweh's own eyes they are glorious and will be glorified. They have been created for Yahweh's glory (43:7); the Lord will be glorified in Israel (44:23; cf. 49:3). "In the LORD all the offspring of Israel shall triumph and glory" (45:25); Israel will be glorified before the Lord (LXX 49:5), and the servant will be exalted and lifted up (52:13). Indeed, Israel is Yahweh's glory (46:13) and has been glorified by Yahweh (55:5)

Immediately, in its prologue, the Fourth Gospel reflects these issues of honor and shaming. The Logos experienced the shaming of being rejected by his own people: "He came to what was his own [or 'to his own home'], and his own people did not accept him" (1:11). John 4:44 will make the same point, employing the term τιμή, *honor*. Jesus' witness acknowledges his lack of human honor, as he makes use of the proverb that a prophet has no honor in his own country. Since the narrator immediately goes on to report a positive reception in Galilee, Jesus' own country here is probably to be understood as Judea.[76] But the first corporate witness of his community of followers makes the opposite evaluation of the Logos in terms of his glory or honor: "we have seen his glory, the glory as of a father's only son, full of grace and truth" (1:14).

There were different ways of being granted honor. Ascribed honor was the honor people gained simply by virtue of who they were rather

---

[76] Cf., e.g., Barrett, *Gospel according to St. John*, 246; W. A. Meeks, "Galilee and Judea in the Fourth Gospel," *JBL* 85 (1966): 159–69, here 164–65.

than by virtue of what they had done. Lineage played an important role here; people could be granted honor because of the family into which they were born. It was by knowing whose children they were that others knew who they were and what honor to ascribe them. Since who people were perceived to be depended on the reputation of their father, sometimes a fictive father or family of origin could supply what was missing in terms of the actual circumstances of birth. Often patrons supplied this for their clients in a fictive kinship relationship.

This is all relevant to the prologue's claim about the honor of the incarnate Logos. Whatever might be thought about his human family and descent, Jesus' glory is described "as of the unique one from the Father [NRSV: 'as of a father's only son']" (1:14). His lineage is impeccable, and he has an incomparably privileged status in the family. He is in the bosom of the Father, "close to the Father's heart" (1:18). Later in the narrative (17:5), Jesus will reflect on this sharing in the Father's glory before the foundation of the world. Little wonder, then, that to honor the Son is to honor the Father (5:23). This is reflected throughout the narrative in its key title for Jesus—"Son of God" or "the Son"—and in its focus on questions about Jesus' birth and origin. The implied readers are repeatedly told that Jesus is, comes, or has been sent from God, the Father, heaven, or above. They can appreciate the irony of Nathanael's reaction to being told that Jesus is the son of Joseph from Nazareth: he finds no honor in such origins—"Can anything good come out of Nazareth?"—but then himself comes to the quite different and more appropriate appreciation of Jesus' origin: "Rabbi, you are the Son of God!" (1:45–49). They can appreciate the irony of "the Jews" later having difficulty over the same issue—how the one who is the son of Joseph, the one whose parents they know, can have come from heaven (6:42); of the play on the two levels of meaning for the "whence" of Jesus (7:27–28); of the discussion about whether the Messiah can come from Galilee (7:41, 52); of the exchange between the man born blind and the Jews about where Jesus is from (9:29–33); and of Pilate's question (19:9), to which Jesus gives no answer and readers now need no answer, "Where are you from?"[77]

Believers also share in Jesus' ascribed family glory, as is again made clear in the prologue (1:12–13). Here the Logos takes over the role of patron and is said to grant those who receive him or believe in him the right to become children of God, and in this fictive family, their birth is

---

[77] See Neyrey, "Despising the Shame of the Cross," 127–28, on how this question touches Jesus' honor.

seen not as a human, physical birth but as a divine birth. As the rest of the narrative makes clear, their origin also can be said to be from above, since they are born from above, from the Spirit (3:3, 5). Jesus calls his followers "little children" (13:33) and promises that he will not leave them as orphans (14:18). His words from the cross (19:26–27) to his mother and the beloved disciple and the subsequent action of the beloved disciple mark the beginnings of the new family. It is natural, then, that Jesus' words to Mary Magdalene in 20:17 reflect the disciples' full membership of the new family and participation in its glory: "But go to my brothers and say to them, 'I am ascending to my Father and your Father, to my God and your God.'"

Family lineage, however, was by no means the only factor in the ascription of honor. The ideal patron was also an ideal father figure who provided favors and intervened on one's behalf and protected one's honor. A person of power could ascribe honor to another and compel public acknowledgment of such honor. Significantly, Malina sees this view articulated most clearly in John's Gospel, since "Jesus, as an utterly shamed and disgraced crucified person, is ascribed honor from God. . . . Jesus' death is an exaltation, a glorification."[78] Throughout the Gospel God as patron is concerned about and safeguards his Son's honor, and in turn, promoting his Father's honor is the motivation in Jesus' mission. As the supreme Judge, God is seeking to establish Jesus' honor in the lawsuit (8:50; cf. 8:54), and one means of doing so is to give Jesus also the authority to judge: "The Father . . . has given all judgment to the Son, so that all may honor the Son just as they honor the Father" (5:22–23). Thus, the role Jesus has been granted as judge in the lawsuit is precisely to establish his honor. And it is because Jesus as Son is so closely related to the Father that the issue of the glory of each is inseparable and Jesus can be characterized as "the one who seeks the glory of him who sent him" (7:18; cf. also 8:49—"I honor my Father"). Jesus' anticipatory declaration after Judas has left to betray him in 13:31–32, with its mouthful of glory, underlines this reciprocal honor: "Now the Son of Man has been glorified, and God has been glorified in him. If God has been glorified in him, God will also glorify him in himself and will glorify him at once" (cf. also 17:1).

Since a person's name stood for his or her public persona, reputation, or honor, the stress on "the name" in the Fourth Gospel can be viewed in this same context. Jesus is described as sharing his Father's

---

[78] Malina, *New Testament World*, 29.

name or reputation and as coming in that name, and the reason that his opponents nevertheless do not accept him is that they are bound to human evaluations of honor and "do not seek the glory that comes from the one who alone is God" (5:43–44). Jesus' mission entails making God's name known (17:6, 26); this is the same as glorifying God's name, which God acknowledges as taking place in Jesus' completion of his task (12:28). God's reputation and honor have been enhanced and seen in their true light in Jesus' mission, especially as this culminates in his death.

Jesus also acts as patron regarding his followers' honor, granting them favors and protecting their reputation. Again this is reflected in the prologue (1:14, 16), where the community confesses that from the fullness of the incarnate Word's glory believers have all received glory, "grace upon grace" or an abundance of favor. Jesus repeats this thought in his prayer in John 17: "The glory that you have given me I have given them" (17:22). In addition, Jesus' followers and servants will be honored by the Father himself (12:26). Those who have staked their all on Jesus' reputation and honor despite appearances, who have believed in his name (cf. 1:12; 3:18), will be hated by the world because of this name (15:21) but will experience life through this same name (20:31). They are assured that Jesus protects their honor through his own name: "I protected them in your name that you have given me" (17:12; cf. v. 11).

People could also acquire honor through their actions and the public recognition of these actions. Clearly, Jesus' signs function in this way. After the first of these, the changing of water into wine, the narrator comments that Jesus "revealed his glory; and his disciples believed in him" (2:11). The latter clause, with its stress on the recognition of the glory, is important. Similarly, the second sign results in the belief of the royal official and all his household (cf. 4:53b), and after the fourth sign, the feeding of the five thousand, the crowd who have seen it say, "This is indeed the prophet who is to come into the world," and want to make Jesus king (6:14–15). All the signs function to reveal Jesus' glory or honor, but the issue is not made explicit each time. It surfaces again ironically in the giving of sight to the man born blind as the authorities enjoin him to give glory to God (9:24). The implied readers know that the way to honor God in response to the signs is to recognize that in them Jesus is the revealer of God's glory! The last sign of Jesus' public career, like the first, makes the matter of the honor of both God and Jesus explicit. Jesus claims, as soon as he hears of Lazarus's illness, that "it is for God's glory, so that the Son of God may be glorified through it" (11:4; cf. also 11:40). Again the public recognition of this sign is underlined, and this factor becomes crucial for the development of the plot, leading to the decision to put Jesus to death. "Many of the Jews therefore, who . . . had seen what Jesus did, believed in him" (11:45), and the Sanhedrin's response was, "If we let him go on like this, everyone will believe in him" (11:48). The aftermath of the sign continues in Jerusalem with further public witness: "The crowd that had been with him when he called Lazarus out of the tomb and raised him from the dead continued to testify" (12:17). This draws further crowds and results in the Pharisees' frustrated exclamation, "Look, the world has gone after him!" (12:18–19).

Not only the signs but also Jesus' teaching contribute to the acquisition of honor and recognition. A teacher was honored if his followers accepted his teaching, believed and affirmed its truth, and acknowledged his authority, but was dishonored if they disagreed with it, refused to accept his authority, and abandoned him. The narrative of the Fourth Gospel shows Jesus at the beginning of his career acquiring followers and honor rapidly and on the basis of a minimal interchange. John the Baptist ascribes honor to Jesus by speaking of him as "a man who ranks ahead of me because he was before me" (1:30), and calls him Lamb of God and Son of God. Two of John's disciples, one of whom is Andrew, then become disciples of Jesus and introduce other disciples; they respond to Jesus with ascriptions of honor through the titles "Messiah," "Son of God," and "King of Israel" (1:41, 49). Jesus' teaching then leaves Nicodemus, "a teacher of Israel" (3:10), respectful but uncomprehending (cf. 3:1–21). In 4:1–2 the narrator endorses but corrects the report that Jesus was making and baptizing more disciples than John. Many Samaritans believe because of Jesus' teaching (4:39, 41), and the importance of witnesses to this teaching is stressed (5:31–39). By the time many of Jesus' followers abandon him because they find his teaching too difficult (6:60, 66), and thereby dishonor him, it has been made clear that such unbelief derives from a perverted perception of honor that makes human honor more important than divine honor: "How can you believe when you accept glory from one another and do not seek the glory that comes from the one who alone is God?" (5:44). And even in terms of human honor, Jesus' honor as a teacher is salvaged both by the narrator's comment that Jesus knew from the first who were going to disbelieve (6:64) and by the response of the twelve disciples, formulated by Peter: "You have the words of eternal life. We have come to believe and know that you are the Holy One of God" (6:68–69).

It might have been expected that, from this point on in the narrative, Jesus' teaching would be honored only by the Twelve, but in fact the narrator continues to highlight Jesus' teaching activity and to show that it receives public recognition and acceptance. It is not that all refuse his teaching. Far from this being the case, there is, rather, a division within the audiences. In 7:14–15 "the Jews" are said to be astonished at Jesus' teaching and the learning it displays, and in response Jesus emphasizes that his teaching comes from God and is true because in it he is not seeking to promote his own honor but God's (7:16–18). There is a divided response but many believe (7:30–31, 40–44), and there is even public recognition from the temple police: "Never has anyone spoken like this!" (7:46). Again, in John 8, as a result of Jesus' teaching in Jerusalem, "many believed in him" (8:30), although this belief apparently soon turns to hostility. Later, when Jesus teaches in the region across the Jordan, "many believed in him there" (10:42). By this time it has been made abundantly clear to the reader that the reason some do not accept Jesus' teaching is that they are "not from God" (8:47). John 13–16 goes on to portray Jesus as a teacher among his own group of followers, who rightly honor him by calling him Teacher and Lord (13:13) and by responding appropriately at the end of their instruction, "Now we know that you know all things, and do not need to have anyone question you; by this we believe that you came from God" (16:30). In his own prayer in 17:6–8, Jesus can therefore look back on the teaching he has done and see it as successful. From the point of view of the implied author, Jesus' teaching, just as his mission as a whole, has brought him honor.

It is not only Jesus' honor that the narrative attempts to establish. Frequently Jesus' teaching gives rise to interchange and debate, and here in particular we see reflected the dynamics of honoring and shaming between groups. The minority group of Johannine Christians had been perceived as a threat to stability and to purity by the majority of Jews in the synagogue and had been made outsiders by expulsion. They remained sensitive to the shaming by the religious establishment that this entailed, and in the attempt to establish their own community identity, they indulged in rhetoric designed to demonstrate their own honor and at the same time shame their perceived oppressors. This situation is transparent in the narrative of the confrontation between the man who had been blind and the religious authorities: "They reviled him, saying, 'You are his disciple, but we are disciples of Moses'" (9:28). Here are the two major groupings—those who claim to be the true representatives of Judaism and guardians of the law and those who are disciples of Jesus. Reviling consists in the use of language to shame by alienating or excluding from one's own group and by putting down the claims of the other. It is a challenge to the honor of those on the receiving end.[79] Significantly, in this case the disciple of Jesus responds as an equal, defending his honor and using sarcasm to shame his challengers as he gives the Pharisees a lesson in theology and tries to show how Jesus must obviously be from God (9:30–33). They can only heighten the level of insult—"You were born entirely in sins, and are you trying to teach us?"—before expelling him (9:34).

At other places in the narrative, the opposition has attempted to dishonor the claims of Johannine Christians about Jesus by casting aspersions on his reputation and attempting to cut him down to size. He cannot be from heaven; he is only the son of Joseph (6:42). He is not equal to God; he is only a human blasphemer and therefore one who dishonors God (5:18; 10:33). Some of the strongest invective, as already seen, takes place in the context of the rival claims to be the true inheritors of Judaism. The Jews who believed in Jesus but then failed to continue as full disciples claim, "We are descendants of Abraham" (8:33). Jesus' response is to challenge their family honor by disputing that they have either Abraham or God for a father and then claiming that their father is the devil (vv. 39–44). Not surprisingly, "the Jews" respond in kind with the accusation that Jesus is a Samaritan, an outsider to the covenant, and that he in fact has a demon (vv. 48, 52; cf. also 7:20; 10:20). At this point, in his denial of the latter accusation, Jesus spells out the issue of honor that is involved—"I honor my Father, and you dishonor me" (8:49)—and claims that the divine judge is settling where true honor lies (v. 50).

In this interchange, as well as elsewhere in the narrative, questions of truth and falsehood arise. To claim to be telling the truth is to give one's word of honor, and repeatedly Jesus makes just such a claim (cf. vv. 14, 16, 26, 32, 40, 45–46). To eliminate ambiguity about whether a person's honor was at stake in a given interchange, swearing or oath taking, as a means of giving one's word of honor, could be resorted to; for Malina, "Jesus' characteristic 'truly, I say to you' seems to function like a word of honor."[80] The stronger version of this in the Fourth Gospel, with the double Amen at the beginning of the assertion, functions, as already suggested, as the oath taking of the witness, and this certainly makes the assertion a word of honor. In the interchange in John 8, the formula occurs three times (vv. 34, 51, 58). "On the other hand, to be called a liar by anyone is a great public dishonor. The reason for this is

---

[79] Cf. ibid., 30–32.
[80] Ibid., 37.

that truth belongs only to one who has a right to it. To lie is to deny the truth to one who has a right to it . . . to deprive the other of respect, to refuse to show him honor, to humiliate him."[81] The Pharisees began (v. 13) by declaring Jesus' witness to be false, thereby calling him a liar. By calling their father, the devil, a liar and the father of lies in v. 44, Jesus implicitly calls his opponents liars. He then makes this explicit in v. 55 by stating that if he were to say he did not know God, he would be a liar like them. There is no mistaking that, in this first-century intra-Jewish religious debate, group honor is at stake and that Jesus represents the honor of the Johannine Christians.

Within the system of collective honor, "the *head* of the group is responsible for the honor of the group with reference to outsiders, and symbolizes the group's honor as well."[82] Ultimately the Johannine community derives its honor from Jesus, who in turn derives his honor from God. But after Jesus' departure two other figures play a role in the community's defense of its honor. One is the Spirit, who is another Advocate in place of Jesus (14:16) and whose task is both to honor Jesus (16:14) and to prove the world wrong in its dishonoring of Jesus (16:8–11). The other is the beloved disciple. In voluntary groups or associations, honor was invested in posts or offices within the group. "Sacred persons or posts have power over all the dimensions of honor in their respective groups. They arbitrate questions of value; they delimit what can be done or maintained without sacrilege; they define the unconditional allegiance of their members."[83] The beloved disciple functions in this way. The Gospel's narrative about Jesus is attributed to the beloved disciple, and he has a particular place of honor because of his intimate relationship with Jesus. From his own position of being lifted up in honor on the cross, Jesus gives the beloved disciple a unique role in the new community of his followers (19:26–27), and the beloved disciple is present as the decisive witness to the significance of Jesus' death and resurrection (19:35; 20:8). In addition, he has the same honored position in relation to Jesus as Jesus has to the Father—reclining in his lap (13:23, 25; cf. 1:18). As the ideal witness and as the disciple who believed before seeing the risen Jesus (cf. 20:29), he defines the allegiance of the members of the Johannine community.

Although many aspects of the honor/shame value system are reflected in the Fourth Gospel, its narrative discourse presents a new perspective

---

[81] Ibid., 38.
[82] Ibid., 40.
[83] Ibid., 41.

on these matters for those who are dishonored according to their society's evaluation. Not only is Jesus vindicated by the resurrection, as in the other Gospel narratives; in this narrative Jesus' whole career is depicted in terms of glory. There is no place for the anticipated glory of the transfiguration depicted in the Synoptics. In a mission suffused with glory, the transfiguration would simply not stand out. And the suffering and death in which the mission results are no detraction from Jesus' honor but, rather, its climactic moment. In the equivalent to the Synoptics' Gethsemane account, the one note of suffering—"Now is my soul troubled" (12:27a)—is immediately turned into a recognition of its glory: "'it is for this reason that I have come to this hour. Father, glorify your name.' Then a voice came from heaven, 'I have glorified it, and I will glorify it again'" (12:27b–28). And the completion of Jesus' mission in his death on the cross (19:30; cf. 17:4) is the lifting up, the hour of glory, the point at which the honor of both God and Jesus is most clearly seen. The lawsuit motif is vital in this presentation. It allows for an appeal to a higher court than the synagogue or public opinion about where truth and glory or honor are really to be found. What God the Judge determines to be honorable and this God's ascription of glory are what count. The words of Jesus in 8:50 sum up this perspective: "I do not seek my own glory; there is one who seeks it and he is the judge." And the divine judge gives the positive verdict at the point when the human trial of Jesus reaches its outcome, as he undergoes the sentence of death.

This is not simply a reversal of values regarding Jesus' honor. The narrative discourse enables its implied readers to view their own experience of shaming in a quite different light. As they reflect on Jesus as the repository of God's honor, they will become more fully aware that this honor of the one to whom they owe allegiance becomes theirs, that, as members of his group of followers, they share in the true reputation of their leader. Instead of fearing society's opinion and seeking its approval, they have a different perspective on their role in the world. Honor for them will lie in following and serving Jesus—"Whoever serves me, the Father will honor" (12:26)—and in being disciples who bear fruit in works of love: "My Father is glorified by this, that you bear much fruit" (15:8; cf. 13:34–35). Indeed, the purpose of the community's sharing the honor that God the Father has given to the Son is the promotion of its unity, which will in turn be a witness to the world (17:22–23). The most effective way of defending the group's honor and displaying it to others is therefore to concentrate on the mutual love that will ensure unity. The disunity that appears to have occurred by the time of 1 John (cf. 1 Jn

2:19) is viewed here as not only bringing further dishonor in the eyes of the world but also as dishonoring the Father and the Son. Mutual love is a means of witness, and honor for the Johannine Christians lies in completing the task of witness that they have been given, just as Jesus glorified his Father by completing his task (17:4). As they continue to testify, "we have seen his glory" (1:14), they will also be emulating the honored founder of their community, the beloved disciple. And if their witness should result in martyrdom, then they know clearly that this will be no humiliation but glory, since Jesus has already set this pattern for ascertaining where true honor lies. The narrator's comments specifically underline that Peter's death as a martyr, foretold by Jesus, is to be his way of glorifying God (21:18–19).

Clearly, the aim of the Fourth Gospel's implied author is to turn the stigma of social shaming into an honor. His point of view is exemplified remarkably in Jesus' washing of the disciples' feet, an incident that occurs only in this narrative and that serves as a preparation not only for the cross but also for the disciples' mission in the world. Foot washing was normally the work of a slave, and slaves as a group were shamed by the rest of society. After compiling the most extensive catalogue of citations about foot washing in Jewish and Greco-Roman antiquity, J. C. Thomas claims that "Jesus' action is unparalleled in ancient evidence, for no other person of superior status is described as voluntarily washing the feet of a subordinate."[84] What is more, the details of the narration—Jesus divests himself of his robe, ties a towel around himself, takes a basin, and pours water into it, and Peter initially adamantly refuses to take part in such an incongruous act—are designed to ensure that the implied readers understand that Jesus is taking the role of the slave.

The reversal of the roles of honor and humiliation is driven home to the disciples in the narrative by Jesus' painstaking explanation of the significance of his action. The one who is rightly called Teacher and Lord is the one who has just washed the disciples' feet (13:12–14). This unique example of a superior deliberately taking a position of shame is, for the narrator, also evidence of Jesus' love: "Having loved his own who were in the world, he loved them to the end" (v. 1b). This extraordinary reevaluation of values, acted out by Jesus, is to be the paradigm for life in the community. The Gospel makes this clear twice. The disciples are explicitly told that they ought to wash one another's feet in accordance

---

[84] J. C. Thomas, *Footwashing in John 13 and the Johannine Community* (Sheffield: JSOT Press, 1991), 59.

with Jesus' example, since slaves are not greater then their master (vv. 14–16). And a little later they are given the new commandment to love one another (vv. 34–35), implicit in which is that if Jesus' love for them could bring him to take the position of the slave and wash their feet, then their love for one another will include such acts.

The implied readers are thus given a new perception of glory or honor, one that locates honor in acts that would normally have been considered shaming. Above all, however, those who have been shamed need not simply to find ways to have honor restored; they need to have experiences that heal the deep wounds such shaming has produced. Significantly, those pursuing the current psychological interest in shame in our own society suggest that the dynamic behind shame is the fear of abandonment or disgrace or rejection and that therefore the most effective healing comes from discovering the security of accepting love. Whether in ancient or in modern society, the most basic human need is to be accepted by significant others, and the most basic remedy for those who have been shamed is to experience that, in spite of everything, they are accepted by the love of those they most need to accept them.

It is no accident that, in this narrative of the Fourth Gospel, fear is so frequently the motive behind failing to believe properly or failing to act properly as Jesus' followers. Fear of "the Jews" and fear of being put out of the synagogue are explicitly mentioned by the narrator in 7:13, 9:22, and 12:42; it is implicit in Peter's denials in 18:15–27; and on the day of the resurrection, "the doors of the house where the disciples had met were locked for fear of the Jews" (20:19). In addition, the Farewell Discourses are designed to deal with the disciples' (and the implied readers') fear. The fear reflected here is twofold—not only fear because of the hatred and accompanying rejection by the world (cf. 15:18–20) but also fear that Jesus' departure and absence mean separation from, and abandonment by, him.

Bultmann suggests that the key questions that activate this section of the Gospel are: "Can the disciples still love him, when he is gone? Can the next generation love him, without having had a personal relationship with him?"[85] But the more pressing questions may well have been: "Can he still love us when he is gone? Can the next generation still experience his love when he is absent?" Again and again reassurance is provided: "Do not let your hearts be troubled" (14:1); "I will ask the Father, and he will give you another Advocate, to be with you

---

[85] Bultmann, *Gospel of John*, 613.

for ever" (14:16; cf. 16:7); "I will not leave you orphaned; I am coming to you" (14:18); "those who love me will be loved by my Father, and I will love them and reveal myself to them" (14:21b); "Those who love me will keep my word, and my Father will love them, and we will come to them and make our home with them" (14:23); "abide in my love. If you keep my commandments, you will abide in my love" (15:9b–10a); "the Father himself loves you, because you have loved me and have believed that I came from God" (16:27); "I have said this to you, so that in me you may have peace. In the world you face persecution. But take courage; I have conquered the world!"(16:33); "I made your name known to them, and I will make it known, so that the love with which you have loved me may be in them, and I in them" (17:26). The clear purpose of Jesus' commands, promises, assertions, and prayers in this section is to replace his followers' fear both by assurance of love and by joy as the deep gratitude that savors such love (cf. 15:11; 17:13). After his departure and in his absence, they can still experience the continuing love of both Jesus and the Father and will know, with and in them, the loving presence of both. This major aspect of the message of the Farewell Discourses is summed up admirably in 1 Jn 4:18: "There is no fear in love, but perfect love casts out fear."

It is not only God and Jesus, however, who are the sources of love. Other believers are also to provide loving acceptance. The rejection experienced from the religious authorities is to be replaced by the love offered by the other members of the Johannine community. Again it is not surprising, given its history, that the norm for behavior in this community is the love for one another that is prepared to wash another's feet (13:14–15) and to lay down one's life for another (15:13). This is the new commandment that Jesus leaves his followers—"that you love one another as I have loved you" (15:12; cf. 13:34–35; 15:17)—and it is precisely through demonstrating such love that they will give effective witness to the world (13:35; 17:23). There should be no reason for the followers of Jesus to feel that they are unloved or unlovable. In the face of the world's hatred and rejection, they can know the divine Judge whose love for the world entailed giving the only Son in order to provide the verdict of life rather than condemnation; they can know the witness to the truth who will never cast out those who come to him, who will not leave his followers abandoned as orphans, and who retains the scars of love in his hands and side; and they can know the community of accepting love constituted by all those called to witness to the love of the Father and the Son.

4. Trials and a Roman Context?

It is highly likely, as we have seen, that the experience of expulsion from the synagogue, with its interrogations and trials, was a major factor in the choice of the trial motif, with its distinctive perspectives, to shape the Fourth Gospel's narrative. But this is a narrative written in Greek in a setting somewhere in the Roman Empire. Its writer and readers would also have known the realities of responding to imperial power and claims. Would they have understood the trial motif with reference to experiences of trials under Roman state officials?

Cassidy has claimed that John was concerned in his Gospel to present elements and themes of special significance to Christians facing Roman imperial claims and Roman persecution.[86] Elsewhere in his study, he makes the somewhat weaker claim that some of John's audience would have heard the narrative "within a situation in which denunciations, Roman trials and sentences of death were immediate realities."[87] Cassidy admits that there is no way in which this hypothesis can be confirmed from external evidence, but hopes to show a high degree of correlation between elements and themes in the text and the circumstances of first-century Christians under Roman rule. He points to three Roman realities that he wishes to correlate with the Fourth Gospel—the Jewish tax; the imperial cult;[88] and the situation of persecution of Christians in Bithynia et Pontus, reflected in the correspondence between Pliny and Trajan.

Regarding the *fiscus Judaicus,* Roman officials had to decide who was Jewish and therefore liable to the tax, and Jewish Christians would have had to determine whether their belief in Jesus meant that they no longer belonged to the Jewish religion and could therefore evade the tax. Suetonius records that the tax was "levied with the utmost rigour and those were prosecuted who without publicly acknowledging that faith yet lived as Jews as well as those who concealed their origin and did not pay the tribute levied upon their people."[89] Since failure to pay led to prosecution and trial, Cassidy holds that the tax "was a practice that had the potential for engendering the denunciation of both Christians and

---

[86] R. J. Cassidy, *John's Gospel in New Perspective* (New York: Orbis, 1992), esp. 1, 28.

[87] Ibid., 62.

[88] This is treated below in the discussion of the titles applied to Jesus.

[89] Suetonius, *Dom.* 12.2; cf. Cassidy, *John's Gospel,* 6–10.

Jews."[90] Goodman suggests that Jewish Christians would have faced a serious dilemma about paying the tax. On the one hand, payment would have enabled Jewish Christians to continue affirming their Jewishness; on the other, payment could be considered a sin because the taxes went to the upkeep of the temple of Jupiter in Rome.[91]

There is no doubt that the tax was a major factor in the relationship between Rome and Jews, and therefore also between Rome and Jewish Christians. It is highly likely that it was a factor contributing to the parting of the ways between Jews and Christians. But relating these general realities of life under Roman rule to the specific situation of Johannine Christians is another matter. There is no evidence from elsewhere that would allow us to determine with any certainty what the attitudes on both sides of the divide would have been. Would Jewish Christians have wanted to pay the tax as a sign that they were still true Jews, whatever the synagogue leaders might say? Or would they have treated their excommunication as casting doubt on their public identification with Judaism and therefore have seen it as a way of avoiding what was, in any case, a hated tax? Or would some have taken one view, and others the opposite? Similarly, would the synagogue officials have held that they did not want these apostate Jewish Christians paying the tax as Jews, and therefore have done their best to isolate them from the synagogue; or would they have taken the view that if they themselves had to pay the despised tax, then there was no reason why these Jewish believers in Jesus should not also be made to pay? It must, in any case, be concluded that there is no evidence at all in the Fourth Gospel itself either that the tax played any role in the dispute between the synagogue and followers of Jesus or that it led to any persecution of Christians by Rome.

The correspondence between Pliny and Trajan in 110 C.E. is of no greater help for indicating the situation of the Johannine Christians. This correspondence is some ten to twenty years after the probable date of the writing of the Fourth Gospel. Cassidy rightly observes that the correspondence indicates that there had been previous trials of Christians, probably under Domitian.[92] Pliny (*Ep.* 10.96) makes clear that the line he is taking for the moment is simply to ascertain whether a person professes to be a Christian, that it is on such a charge that people are being brought before him, and that the charges are becoming more

---

[90] Cassidy, *John's Gospel,* 27.
[91] M. Goodman, "Diaspora Reactions to the Destruction of the Temple," in *Jews and Christians* (ed. Dunn), 27–38, here 33–34.
[92] Cassidy, *John's Gospel,* 19.

widespread and a considerable number of people are involved. Although Pliny knows of earlier trials of Christians, he indicates that he does not know of the grounds for the investigations that led to such trials. The very fact that he asks for a rescript, a legally binding reply, from Trajan about his present practice suggests that there is no precedent for the prosecution of Christians simply for being Christians, and the lack of precedent in turn suggests that trials of Christians were previously not frequent enough to have needed any standardized procedure.

Although Pliny speaks here of "persons brought before me on the charge of being Christians," there is some evidence from the correspondence that earlier charges may have been more specifically about Christians acting as a benefit society, a type of organization that had been forbidden by Pliny on Trajan's advice (cf. *Ep.* 10.91, 92). In *Ep.* 10.96 itself, Pliny mentions Christians who had given up their practice of assembling together "since my edict, issued on your instructions, which banned all political societies." It appears that it was only after Pliny's investigations through torture had discovered that Christians were in fact involved in no more than "a degenerate and immoderate cult" that he asked for Trajan's advice on "whether it is the mere name of Christian which is punishable." It is difficult, then, to believe that the original readers of John's Gospel were already being persecuted by the Roman state simply for being Christians. In addition, the correspondence between Pliny and Trajan deals with circumstances that, as far as we know, were peculiar to the province of Bithynia-Pontus. Even if it is held that these readers were located at Ephesus and therefore in an eastern province adjacent to Bithynia-Pontus, "the available evidence indicates that a rescript directed to a particular province did not have the force of an empire-wide law," as Cassidy himself concedes.[93]

Cassidy makes a stronger case when he is content simply to point to elements in the Gospel itself that lend themselves to correlation with the more general realities of a Roman setting. In my view, three elements in particular are worth noting. The first relates to two of the titles employed in confessions about Jesus. In John 4:42 the Samaritans acclaim Jesus as "the Savior of the world." "Savior" was a common title for emperors, but "Savior of the world" was applied specifically to Nero and then later to Hadrian.[94] Thomas's climactic confession, "My Lord and my God!" (20:28), may also reflect the imperial claims made about

---

[93] Ibid., 26.
[94] Cf. ibid., 13.

Domitian in terms of "our Lord and our God," *dominus et deus noster* (cf., e.g., Suetonius, *Dom.* 13.2). Whatever its roots in the debate with the synagogue, John's Christology also makes clear that it is Jesus, and not the emperor, who is to be confessed in terms of universal lordship.

Second, we have already seen that the extensive elaboration of the trial before Pilate in the Fourth Gospel explicitly sets the cosmic lawsuit in the context not simply of Israel but of the Roman world, makes the issue of allegiance to Caesar critical, and contrasts Jesus' power in weakness with that of the imperial claims represented by Pilate. Rensberger's treatment of the Roman trial shows that "if it is correct to suppose that the general inclination of early Christianity . . . is toward an apologetic aimed at improving relations with the Roman government, then John at least does not share in that inclination."[95] He can also assert, "Jesus' interviews with Pilate very likely represent a model for the Johannine community's dealings with Roman officials."[96] Our study has already indicated that Jesus' own witness at his Roman trial provides a paradigm for his followers' witness when they are on trial. All the clear evidence from the narrative indicates that the primary context for the original readers' trials would be the confrontation with Judaism. But the themes of trial and persecution lend themselves to application beyond that original context, and any later readers who found themselves facing persecution from the Roman state because of their beliefs might well have discovered a valuable resource in the Gospel's message. Certainly, as with Pilate in the Roman trial, they would also face in some way the issue of whether Jesus or Caesar is king.

The third element, suggesting that the readers of the Gospel in its final form would be aware of Roman trials and persecution, is the allusion to Peter's martyr death in 21:18–19.[97] After Jesus' threefold commissioning of Peter to shepherd the flock, in a saying introduced by the double Amen formula, he predicts that Peter will later follow in the footsteps of the good shepherd himself by laying down his life. The content of the prediction is vague. It contrasts a younger Peter, who has been able to gird himself and go where he wants, with an older Peter, who will stretch out his hands, be girded by another, and be taken where he does not wish to go. The emphasis on stretching out the hands by the older Peter need signify no more than stretching out the hands to be bound as part of being girded and taken away to death. On the other

---

[95] Rensberger, *Johannine Faith*, 91.
[96] Ibid., 96; cf. Cassidy, *John's Gospel*, 40.
[97] Cf. Cassidy, *John's Gospel*, 74, 78.

hand, early Christian writers often viewed the stretching out of the hands a reference to crucifixion. For example, both *Barn.* 12 and Justin, *Dial.* 90–91, see Moses' stretching out his hands in Exod 17:12 as a type of Christ on the cross. The fact that stretching out the hands is mentioned before being girded and led away need not be considered an insuperable problem, since the victim of crucifixion would have had outstretched hands secured to the crossbeam, or *patibulum,* that he then carried as he was led away to death.[98] Whatever the precise manner of his death, the narrator's comment in John 21:19a makes explicit that the reference is to Peter's martyrdom.

The earliest evidence about Peter's death outside the canonical writings is in *1 Clem.* 5. There, in a warning about the sin of jealousy, Peter and Paul are adduced as examples of those who suffered because of jealousy and envy. Of the former it is simply said that "it was by sinful jealousy that Peter was subjected to tribulation, not once or twice but many times; it was in that way that he bore his witness, ere he left us for his well-earned place in glory" (5:4). Despite the tradition that Peter was martyred in Rome, there is no direct reference in *Clement* either to the place or to the manner of Peter's death. This tradition is probably first evidenced in *Acts Pet.* 36–41, from around the end of the second century, where a dramatic depiction of the apostle's death situates it in Rome during the persecution under Nero and has Peter crucified upside down. Tertullian, at the beginning of the third century, also refers to Peter being crucified upside down.[99] Eusebius, too, citing a letter of Dionysius of Corinth, written around 170 C.E., records the tradition that the death occurred under Nero in Rome.[100] The consistency of the basic tradition about crucifixion in Rome makes it likely that the readers of John 21 would also have understood Peter's martyrdom to have taken place in that city during the Neronian persecution. Since Peter at this point functions as a model for the witness of Jesus' followers, the fact that he met his martyr's death at the hands of Roman officials would not be insignificant, suggesting a context in which they might be faced with the consequences of their own witness.

It may well be, then, that, after going through the experience of some of its members being expelled from the synagogue and after becoming a group that now included Gentiles among its members, the

---

[98] For a fuller argument for this interpretation, see esp. G. R. Beasley-Murray, *John* (Waco: Word, 1987), 408–9.

[99] Tertullian, *Scorp.* 15.3.

[100] Cf. Eusebius, *Hist. eccl.* 2.25.8; 3.1.2.

Johannine community had to face in a new way the question of its stance toward the Roman Empire. Johannine Christians would no longer simply have been able to go along with the stance of the local Jewish community in their locale and increasingly would have been no longer protected by Jewish rights of assembly and exemption from imperial worship. The Gospel contains some elements that reflect the reality of this new situation. The cosmic lawsuit as a whole lent itself not only to an explanation of the past and present relationship to the synagogue but also to any interrogations and trials that might have arisen for those readers of the Gospel who found themselves forced to make a public christological confession in confrontation with the state's claims for Caesar. But we have only to turn to Revelation if we want to see what Johannine themes would look like when deliberately and extensively adapted for a situation of believers facing Roman imperial claims and possible persecution. There witnessing and martyrdom in the context of the imperial cult are dominant features, suggesting also some contact between the author of Revelation and the tradition behind the Gospel of John.

B. The Reworking of Gospel Traditions

Although the issue of John's relationship to the Synoptics cannot be fully treated here, our discussion will have a bearing on this much debated topic. Up to this point, we have treated the narrative in literary terms, dwelt on its relationship to earlier scriptural texts, and attempted to look at the experience of the community out of which it arose. This does not necessarily mean that the use of the lawsuit motif to shape the narrative discourse is a complete invention of the author in order to buttress claims about Jesus. On the other hand, we are not treating the narrative as if it were meant to be simply a retrial of Jesus in terms of the issues that surrounded his own historical ministry. Harvey, although he recognizes that the trial framework "in part . . . may be seen as a literary device,"[101] treats it primarily as the writer's attempt to answer the question "Given that Jesus was (as a matter of history) condemned to death by men competent in the law of Moses, who was right, he or they?"[102] This may, however, put the emphasis in the wrong place and not do enough justice to the two levels at which the narrative works.

---

[101] Harvey, *Jesus on Trial*, 17.
[102] Ibid., 14–15.

The concern of the implied author is not so much whether Jesus was right some sixty years previously as whether Christians have been right in making their claims about him since. To take the cosmic-lawsuit motif seriously as a literary device yields a perspective different from viewing the narrative primarily as a retrial of the issues of Jesus' ministry according to the procedures of a Jewish court. Also, speaking about the use of historical traditions that may lie behind this lawsuit motif is not necessarily the same as speaking about its historicity. Harvey is fairly cautious about the implications of his study for historicity yet neverthe- less still appears to suggest that he has achieved a narrowing of the gap between John and the Synoptics and that such a narrowing supports the general historicity of John.[103] He goes so far as to suggest that the Johannine account of an extended Jewish trial throughout the ministry is more plausible than the Jewish trial in the Synoptics.[104] Harvey's argu- ment is that the former is more plausible because of its conformity to Jewish legal procedures. But the evidence for our knowledge of these procedures is from a much later date, and we have already had cause to question how far what the narrative says about legal procedures during Jesus' public ministry portrays him as in conformity to them. We shall also note below the problems that the Fourth Gospel's depiction of the ministry in terms of trial scenes creates for the story line and the some- what artificial solution that appears to be required. It is more likely that John knows of the general synoptic tradition of some form of Jewish in- terrogation, which he retains in very brief form in the interrogation be- fore Annas, but that he has chosen to rework the tradition to suit his own emplotment in terms of the lawsuit motif.

According to Harvey, "there is no reason to doubt that Jesus was in fact involved in legal disputes of this kind,"[105] that is, of the kind John re- counts. The issue here revolves around the phrase "of this kind." In all probability, Jesus was involved in legal disputes about the Sabbath and about purity regulations, although even this would be contested by some. But it is highly improbable that the historical Jesus was involved in legal disputes of the kind John characteristically narrates, namely, dis- putes concerning his explicit claims about his own identity and his rela- tionship as the unique Son to the Father who sent him. Chapter 8, below, will discuss some general issues surrounding the mix of histori- cal tradition and creative storytelling that constitutes the narrative and

---

[103] Cf. ibid., 125.
[104] Cf. ibid., 126–27.
[105] Ibid., 127.

how these bear on its truth. The purpose here, however, is to explore which elements in the traditions likely to have been available to the author would have suggested themselves as particularly appropriate for employment in developing the imaginative construal of Jesus' entire mission in terms of a lawsuit. A further question—one not pursued here—is how far such traditions reflect the ministry of the historical Jesus. We are simply asking (a) which traditions in the Synoptics provide parallels to the main aspects of John's lawsuit schema and (b) whether these are likely to have been independent parallels or were known, taken up, and reworked by the Fourth Evangelist for his own purposes. This study, however, can set out only the broad contours of a response to these questions. There can be no detailed interaction here with the mass of literature on the relationship of John to the Synoptics or to other earlier sources, and no fully discussed justification for the stance taken.

1. The Jewish and Roman Trials

The obvious place from which to start is the matter of the Jewish and the Roman trials and their place in the overall shaping of John's plot in comparison with earlier traditions. A combination of Jewish and Roman elements in Jesus' trial and death is found in both the Synoptics and John. Two bedrock features of the tradition were that Jesus was crucified by the Romans and that the charge on the cross read, "the King of the Jews." The Synoptic accounts explain the connection between the trials in the following way. Jesus was found guilty by the Sanhedrin of claiming to be a figure who could be described as the Messiah or the Son of God. The Jewish religious authorities interpreted this as blasphemy, which, under Jewish law, was punishable by death. Unable to carry out such a sentence themselves, they needed to obtain a verdict from the Roman governor. They therefore made much of the popular description of this messianic figure as king; such a claim on Jesus' part could be seen as providing a political threat that a Roman governor would likely take seriously. The same features reappear in the Fourth Gospel. The Jewish religious authorities deem Jesus guilty of blasphemy, but this occurs during his public mission. In John's depiction, when it comes to the trial before Pilate, which is now made the centerpiece of the passion narrative, the Jewish authorities, unable to carry out themselves the legal penalty for this offense, make much of Jesus as king to Pilate, who eventually carries out their wishes. The narrator heavily underscores the connection in 18:31–32.

Thus, the two major obvious differences are that John has chosen to spread the Jewish trial over the public mission of Jesus and that, in the passion narrative, he simply has an interrogation before Annas rather than a trial before the Sanhedrin. It is sometimes suggested that the latter element in John's narrative is to be explained by his possession of a more historical tradition and that the Sanhedrin trial in the Synoptics, with all its illegal procedures according to later Mishnaic tradition, is in any case implausible historically. Yet it may well be that John has arrived at what appears to be greater historical plausibility not because of his traditions but because of his literary structuring. He does appear to be aware of the tradition that the Sanhedrin trial took place in the house of the high priest (cf. Mark 14:53; Luke 22:54), who is named as Caiaphas in Matt 26:57. John's use of this is rather awkward in his own narrative. It has Jesus being sent to Caiaphas in 18:24 (the wording πρὸς Καϊάφαν τὸν ἀρχιερέα, "to Caiaphas the high priest," is the same as in Matt 26:57) and then being taken from the house of Caiaphas to the praetorium in 18:28, but nothing happens in this halfway house between Annas and Pilate. Instead the second and third of Peter's denials are recounted. It as if, in constructing his own plot, John has left a gap where the Sanhedrin trial originally stood in the tradition. It is clear that he knew of the issues at stake in the Sanhedrin trial but, as we shall see, has moved these back into the earlier mission of Jesus. In any case, even if it were thought that this emplotment creates greater plausibility for the end of Jesus' mission, it does so at the expense of plausibility for the public ministry. The Synoptics suggest there are implications about Jesus' identity that begin to get aired explicitly in the Sanhedrin trial. In John these elements become, in the midst of his mission, explicit and extensive announcements by Jesus about his identity. Not only is this intensive christological debate about Jesus as Son of God implausible for the time of Jesus' mission; the shaping of this mission in terms of interrogation and trial scenes creates further implausibilities for the plot.

By having Jesus on trial throughout the ministry and not before the Sanhedrin at the end, the Fourth Gospel's narrative creates a problem for itself. A number of the trials and interrogations condemn Jesus, and his opponents take steps to put him to death by stoning. Yet the narrative has to proceed to the Roman trial, which in fact brought about his crucifixion. The question that this distinctive emplotment raises is, How did Jesus manage to survive that long? The answer provided by the narrative discourse is the stress on Jesus' "hour" and the explanation to readers that, in the divine plan for Jesus, this hour had not yet come. In the narrative's action, this is accomplished in two ways. At the decisive moments when it appears that Jesus will meet his end prematurely, he is given a strange elusiveness that enables him to escape the opponents' clutches, or quite mysteriously, the opposition are thwarted in the attempt to arrest him or carry out the death sentence.

In 5:18 the narrator tells us of the attempt to kill Jesus because of his infringement of the Sabbath and the claim to be equal with God, but simply remains silent about what happened and moves instead to Jesus' defense speech. In John 7 the temple police are sent to arrest Jesus (v. 32) but mysteriously fail to do so. The reason they give in v. 46 is, "Never has anyone spoken like this!" Yet when we ask what is the amazing teaching they must have heard, we are left somewhat mystified. The only teaching the narrator reports is that which the opponents fail to understand (cf. vv. 35–36). It is that Jesus is searched for but not found because he is going where they cannot come, to the one who sent him, and there then follows an invitation for those who are thirsty to come to him and drink. Was this enough to stun those who were about to arrest him? In 8:20 it is sufficient for the narrator to report that "no one arrested him, because his hour had not yet come." At the end of the same chapter, after the opposition has gone so far as to have the stones in their hands to kill him for blasphemy, Jesus somehow manages to hide himself and leave the temple. Finally, again in 10:31 "the Jews" have stones in hand but are delayed by Jesus' debating the interpretation of the law with them; after this, without explanation, their intent changes from stoning him to arresting him, "but he escaped from their hands." How he was able to do so, the narrator neglects to tell us.

At one level the narrative device of the protagonist who appears to be able to outwit those who are pursuing him at the crucial moments may have a certain appeal.[106] It also serves to build up an element of suspense in the plot. But at another level these escapes appear rather contrived and suggest that the narrator has had to make frequent use of them because his entire treatment of the public ministry as a trial with a number of minitrials has entailed a complete reworking of any traditions and consequently left him with a problem to which this appears to him to be the best solution. There is a precedent in the tradition for this mysterious elusiveness on the part of Jesus. In Luke 4, after Jesus' synagogue sermon in Nazareth, his audience drive him out of town and are about to throw him off a cliff when "he passed through the midst of them and went on his way" (4:30). But what Luke records as a singular miraculous escape, the Fourth Gospel resorts to far more frequently as a consequence of its distinctive plot.

---

[106] For a study of this aspect of the narrative, see M. W. G. Stibbe, "The Elusive Christ: A New Reading of the Fourth Gospel," *JSNT* 44 (1991): 20–39.

The Fourth Gospel, in having the Jewish trial during the public mission of Jesus, clearly shows its awareness of the synoptic tradition of a Sanhedrin trial, dealing with all the key issues of this trial at an earlier stage. Instead of the false witnesses in Mark 14:58 who make the accusation that Jesus threatened to destroy the temple and build another in three days, Jesus makes a similar assertion himself in John 2:19, in the account of the temple incident.[107] John 10:24-38 takes up the question and answer about Jesus as Messiah and Son of God and the issue of blasphemy found in the trial before the Sanhedrin in Mark 14:61-64 and its parallels in Luke 22:67-71 and Matt 26:63-66. John's account has, "If you are the Christ" (10:24), the claim to be "God's Son" (10:36), and the issue of "blasphemy" (10:31-33, 36). The opening of the dialogue in John 10:24-25—" 'If you are the Christ, tell us plainly.' Jesus answered, 'I have told you, and you do not believe' "—in fact has the closest verbal links with Luke 22:67-68: " 'If you are the Christ, tell us.' He replied, 'If I tell you, you will not believe.' " In John 10:36 Jesus asks, "can you say . . . [I am] blaspheming, because I said, 'I am God's Son'?" In the synoptic Sanhedrin trial, Mark has, "Are you . . . the Son of the Blessed One?" with Jesus replying, "I am" (14:61-62), while Luke formulates this as, "Are you, then, the Son of God?" with Jesus replying, "You say that I am" (22:70). Just as in Mark 14:63-64 the high priest accuses Jesus of blasphemy and then all condemn him as deserving death, so in John 10:31-33 "the Jews" accuse Jesus of blasphemy and attempt to stone him to death. And the role of the high priest, Caiaphas (according to Matthew), in securing the agreement of the Sanhedrin to calling for Jesus' death in the synoptic Jewish trial has already been set out in John after the raising of Lazarus, in 11:47-53 (cf. 18:14).

Predictably, Dodd again concludes that John obtained the same material found in Mark and Luke from an independent tradition.[108] The appeal to an unknown source is always possible but, in the nature of the case, is not susceptible to verification, and it is not the most obvious explanation. The simpler conclusion is that John knows of the Markan and Lukan traditions and has reworked them by placing them in a different

---

[107] C. H. Dodd, *Historical Tradition in the Fourth Gospel* (Cambridge: Cambridge University Press, 1963), 90–91, asserts, but without providing any substantial evidence to justify his level of certainty, "That John's version is derived from either [Matthew or Mark] is in no way probable," and, "His rendering of the saying itself almost certainly depends on a tradition different from that which lies behind the Synoptic Gospels."

[108] Cf. ibid., 92.

setting. Dodd's objection is that John would have no theological reason for doing this.[109] Yet there is a very clear reason from the theological point of view of the narrative's emplotment. Whereas in the Synoptics the trial before the Sanhedrin adds something new to the explicit claims of Jesus in his public mission and provides the christological climax that leads to his sentencing, this is not the perspective of the Fourth Gospel. In the latter Jesus has been open in his self-revelation and claims in the public mission before Israel, and therefore the trial has been taking place throughout. John's account of the hearing before Annas in 18:19–24 explicitly reinforces this point: "I have spoken openly to the world. . . . I have said nothing in secret" (18:20). There is nothing new about Jesus' identity to be revealed to the Jewish religious leaders and therefore no need for a further official trial before them.[110]

There are further points of contact between Mark's Sanhedrin trial and John's earlier narrative. In Mark 14:62 Jesus responds to the question "Are you the Christ, the Son of the Blessed One?" with the words "I am." It appears that the seed in the synoptic material for John's frequent depiction of Jesus' witness to himself in terms of "I am" is Mark's narrative. In Mark this self-identification first occurs in the episode of the walking on the water in 6:50. That the Markan usage has influenced John is signaled by John's taking over the Markan sequence of the feeding followed by the walking on the water and by the fact that the first use of "I am" in John is also in the episode of walking on the water in 6:20. But because Mark, and Mark alone, also uses the straightforward response "I am" in the trial before the Sanhedrin in 14:62, this may well be the catalyst from the Gospel tradition that, together with the scriptural background in Isa 40–55, produces John's extensive and distinctive development of this self-identification in a forensic setting in 8:24, 28, 58. Mark 14:62 continues, "and 'you will see the Son of Man seated at the right hand of the Power,' and 'coming with the clouds of heaven.' " This sounds the note that, although it is at present Jesus who is on trial, the future will see a reversal of roles, with Jesus as the Son of Man in the position of the judge of his present judges. John not only has the Son of Man as a future judge (cf. 5:27), but also, as we have seen, in both the Jewish trial of the public ministry and the Roman trial before Pilate, portrays Jesus as already acting as judge of his would-be judges.

---

[109] Cf. ibid..

[110] Cf. Pancaro, *The Law*, 70–71.

Whereas John's passion narrative has no Sanhedrin trial, the trial before Pilate is an episode held in common by John and the Synoptics. Is there evidence in the latter episode that John was familiar with any of the Synoptics in producing his account?[111] Although the Fourth Gospel has made this trial the central section of its passion triptych, that the trial has the same basic outline as in the synoptic Gospels suggests John's knowledge of these accounts although he has made extensive additions and changes in sequence for theological and dramatic reasons, highlighting especially the themes of witness and judgment. The response of "the Jews" to Pilate in the opening scene of the Johannine account reflects knowledge of Mark in both its parts. "If this man were not a criminal" (John 18:30a) picks up on Pilate's question "Why, what evil has he done?" in Mark 15:14, while "we would not have handed him over to you" (18:30b) makes use of the notion of the handing over of Jesus by the Jewish leaders in Mark 15:1b. Pilate's question "Are you the King of the Jews?" is the same in John 18:33 as in Mark 15:2 and parallels, and John expands the synoptic reply, "You say (so)," with, "that I am a king," and then adds the statement of Jesus' mission in terms of witnessing to the truth (18:37). John's threefold attestation by Pilate of Jesus' innocence in 18:38; 19:4, 6 follows that of Luke in 23:4, 14, 22, and the wording in both Luke and John is very similar: "I find no basis for an accusation against this man" (Luke 23:4, cf. 23:22) and "I find no case against him" (John 18:38; 19:4, 6).

John 18:39–40 reproduces, in a much more succinct form, the dialogue between Pilate and the Jewish leaders, found in Mark 15:6–15 and parallels, about the custom of releasing one person at the feast of Passover and about whether it should be Jesus or Barabbas. Pilate's question about releasing Jesus has the same wording in John 18:39b as in Mark 15:9: ἀπολύσω ὑμῖν τὸν βασιλέα τῶν Ἰουδαίων, "[Do you want] me to release for you the King of the Jews?" Luke has already shortened the account, and John makes it even shorter. John employs the same contrast between τοῦτον, "this man," and τὸν Βαραββᾶν, "Barabbas" (cf. Luke 23:18; John 18:40) and, like Luke but more briefly, provides a description of Barabbas after the mention of his name. He appears to assume, without narrating it, the outcome that is related in the Synoptics (cf. Mark 15:15; Matt 27:26; Luke 23:24–25), namely, that Pilate released Barabbas. The scene of the soldiers' scourging and mocking of Jesus,

---

[111] For a review and evaluation of some detailed studies of the issue, see M. Sabbe, "The Trial of Jesus before Pilate in John and Its Relation to the Synoptic Gospels," in *John and the Synoptics* (ed. Denaux), 341–85.

which Mark 15:16–20a and Matt 27:27–31a have after the trial, has been moved up for dramatic effect in John's sequence to the central scene (John 19:1–3) of the seven in his narrative. The wording πλέξαντες στέφανον ἐξ ἀκανθῶν ἐπέθηκαν, "wove a crown of thorns and put it," is shared by John and Matthew. Luke has a mockery scene earlier in his narrative, with Herod and his soldiers the mockers (cf. Luke 23:11); John 19:2 employs the same verb, περιβάλλειν, *to array,* for the dressing up of Jesus as does Luke's account.

Toward the end of John's Roman trial, Jesus refuses to give an answer (John 19:9) just as he had refused in Mark 15:5 and Matt 27:14, and Pilate is depicted as wanting to release Jesus (John 19:12) just as in Luke 23:20. Then John 19:13 mentions Pilate's judgment seat, which is found elsewhere only in Matt 27:19. The issue of Jesus' claim to kingship pitting him over against Caesar, which John uses to such effect at the conclusion in 19:13, 15, had already been introduced by Luke right at the beginning of his account, in 23:2, where the accusation was that Jesus was "forbidding us to pay taxes to the emperor, and saying that he himself is the Messiah, a king." The final wording of John 19:16— παρέδωκεν . . . ἵνα σταυρωθῇ, "he handed him over . . . to be crucified"—repeats the formulation found in Mark 15:15 and Matt 27:26. Some explain all these similarities with the synoptic accounts of the Roman trial in terms of John's employing an independent passion narrative source that had points of contact with the synoptic tradition.[112] But again, rather than attempting to reconstruct presumed sources, the simpler solution appears to be that the Fourth Evangelist was a creative author who himself knew the synoptic versions of the Roman trial and appropriated and recast elements from them to suit his own distinctive purposes.

2. The Public Mission of Jesus

John has moved elements from the synoptic Sanhedrin trial back into the mission of Jesus and elaborated on the Roman trial. But is this framing of the public mission in terms of a trial a complete imposition on the synoptic tradition, or is there anything in the synoptic tradition of Jesus' ministry that has some correspondence to such a perspective? When we examine the beginnings of the Fourth Gospel's account with John the Baptist as the first major witness to Jesus, the evidence does not look promising for finding any close correspondence with the earlier

---

[112] Cf., e.g., R. T. Fortna, *The Fourth Gospel and Its Predecessor* (Philadelphia: Fortress, 1988), 163–76.

tradition. There is a major reshaping of the synoptic traditions about John the Baptist.[113] Harvey attempts to show an affinity with Mark 11:31 and its parallels, which present the Jewish religious leaders, in the dispute about Jesus' authority, caught in the trap of having to say whether they believed John.[114] But it is a long stretch from these texts, which require an answer to the question about the divine origin of John's baptism, to characterizing John as a witness whose testimony about Jesus as the light or as the preexistent Son of God is to be believed. Closer is the synoptic characterization of John as the messenger who, pointing to a coming one who is more powerful than himself, prepares the way of the Lord (cf. Mark 1:2, 7; Matt 3:3, 11; Luke 3:4–6, 16). The Fourth Gospel has placed the citation of Isa 40:3, employed by the synoptic narrators, in the mouth of the Baptist himself. At the beginning of the Q material (Luke 3:7–9, 15–18; Matt 3:7–12), John the Baptist is portrayed as preaching a coming judgment and so is associated in the tradition with the judgment aspect of the motif. The Fourth Gospel takes the herald of the Lord and of this Lord's coming judgment and makes him a witness to the coming of the light in judgment into the world, and to Jesus as the embodiment of this light and therefore in a unique relation to God. Whereas in the Synoptics Jesus' divine sonship is attested by a voice from heaven at his baptism by John, in the Fourth Gospel John himself is the witness to Jesus as Son of God. Elements of the synoptic depiction of the Baptist have lent themselves to John's distinctive account, shaped by the lawsuit motif, but have become transformed in the process.

Regarding Jesus' own mission, Jesus is indeed embroiled in disputes with the religious authorities in the synoptic accounts, where these disputes primarily take the form of controversy stories. It is from such stories that, in all probability, the Johannine interrogations and minitrials have been developed. Significantly, in Mark's collection of controversy stories in 2:1–3:6, the debate over Jesus' words and actions, particularly his Sabbath activities, leads to the first reference in Mark's narrative to a decision that the threat posed by Jesus merits his death: "The Pharisees went out and immediately conspired with the Herodians against him, how to destroy him" (3:6). The first reference to such a decision in the Fourth Gospel is in the context of Jesus' defense in the trial scene of

---

[113] See Casey, *Is John's Gospel True?* 63–79, for a succinct and clear discussion of the secondary nature of John's account in relation to the Synoptics and for a convincing rebuttal of the earlier arguments to the contrary by Dodd, *Historical Tradition,* 248–312.

[114] Harvey, *Jesus on Trial,* 31–32.

John 5: "For this reason the Jews were seeking all the more to kill him" (5:18); this account shows clear points of contact with Mark's collection of controversies. The first of Mark's stories in 2:1–12 recounts the healing of a paralyzed man; in it Jesus' forgiveness of his sins provokes in some scribes the unspoken charge of blasphemy. The first part of John 5, in a quite different setting (Jerusalem rather than Capernaum), also recounts a healing of a paralyzed man that leads to a charge of blasphemy. In both cases Jesus says to the paralyzed man, "Stand up, take your mat and walk." In John 5:8 the wording is Ἔγειρε ἆρον τὸν κράββατον σου καὶ περιπάτει, while Mark 2:9 has καί, "and," between "stand up" and "take," and the repetition in Mark 2:11 omits the καί between the first two imperatives, as in John 5:8. The Matthean and Lukan variations on the Markan wording indicate that this is likely to be more than coincidence. Both John and Mark link the healing with the issue of forgiveness of sins (cf. John 5:14; Mark 2:5, 9–11). John appears to be familiar with the Markan controversy stories and has combined the healing of a paralytic with the Sabbath controversies by placing the healing on a Sabbath. He has also included a charge of blasphemy arising from a saying of Jesus and the decision to try to kill Jesus. All these features have been reworked in distinctive Johannine fashion to lead into the forensic discourse of John 5:19–47.

The synoptic tradition had some controversy stories in its sources, but the transmitters of the tradition also took some sayings of Jesus and developed them into controversy stories by introducing opponents as adversaries.[115] The synoptic stories in this form have, for subjects of controversy, such issues as Jesus' authority and his implied claim that it is from heaven (Mark 11:27–33; Matt 21:23–27; Luke 20:1–8), paying taxes to Caesar (Mark 12:13–17; Matt 22:15–22; Luke 20:20–26), and fasting (Mark 2:18–20; Matt 9:14–15; Luke 5:33–35). John takes this development further and, on the basis of such stories in the tradition, forms extended interrogations and trial scenes. Controversies provoked with the religious establishment by Jesus' teaching on matters of the law and by his table fellowship with sinners now have, as their equivalent in John, issues provoked with "the Jews" about the person of Jesus and his identity in relation to God. Synoptic disputes about the Sabbath (cf. Mark 2:23–28; 3:1–6; Matt 12:1–8; 12:9–14; Luke 6:1–5; 6:6–11; 13:10–17; 14:1–6), about purity and the law (cf. Mark 7:1–16; Matt 15:1–20; Luke 11:37–54), and about divorce (Mark 10:1–12; Matt 19:1–12) have disappeared from John's narrative. Only the discussion of

---

[115] See, e.g., A. Hultgren, *Jesus and His Adversaries* (Minneapolis: Augsburg, 1979), esp. 50–53, 100–148.

John 7:22–23 resembles the synoptic disputes about the interpretation of Sabbath law. Purity issues appear to be no longer urgent matters. Jesus has replaced the water of purification with the wine of the new age at the beginning of the narrative (cf. 2:1–11); after this discussion purity is confined to a dispute between the disciples of John the Baptist and another Jew in 3:25 and is only of concern for Jesus' opponents who will not enter the praetorium for fear of defilement. Thus, controversy with opponents carries over from the Synoptics to John, but the nature of the controversy is drastically changed. What is now contested is Jesus' witness to his relationship as Son to the Father and all that this entails.

Even though the controversy stories of the Synoptics have been transformed into longer disputes and discourses with a different subject matter in John, one might still ask whether other elements in the Synoptics' portrayal of Jesus bear some correspondence to John's portrayal of Jesus as God's agent in a cosmic trial. Once the question is put this way, we can respond that in broad terms the central assumption of the trial motif—namely, God's claim on the world—is a Johannine replaying of the synoptic notion of God's kingdom or rule, whereby God's claim on the world is established. God as judge and God as king are closely related images in Jewish thought. To look no further than Deutero-Isaiah, Yahweh as king is the judge who calls for the lawsuit—"Set forth your case, says the LORD; bring your proofs, says the King of Jacob" (Isa 41:21)—and Yahweh's justice going out for a light to the nations is the equivalent to Yahweh's arms ruling the peoples (Isa 51:4–5). Similarly, Jesus as God's agent is both judge and king in John's account of the Roman trial. The lawsuit motif is John's preferred way of viewing God's activity in the world in the pursuance of God's sovereign rights.

Already in the Synoptic Gospels Jesus is the unique agent of God in the establishment of God's rule. Jesus identifies himself so closely with his mission that what happens to him is linked with what happens to the kingdom whose rule he announces. For example, in the Beelzebul controversy the issue is whether Jesus should be seen as the agent of God or of Satan, and the kingdom of God is deemed to have come to the extent that Jesus drives out demons (Matt 12:28; Luke 11:20). In the same context Jesus is said to claim that whoever is not for him is against him—with consequences for the relation of such a person to the kingdom (Matt 12:30; Luke 11:23). That Jesus is the unique agent of God's purposes and claims is evidenced more widely in the synoptic material. His person and deeds signify the presence of eschatological salvation (cf. Matt 11:4–6; Luke 7:22–23). His words have crucial consequences for the salvation or judgment of his hearers (cf. Matt 7:24, 26; Luke 6:47,

49). Both deeds and words represent what prophets and the righteous longed to see (cf. Matt 13:16–17; Luke 10:23–24). A person's attitude to Jesus in the present serves as the criterion for future judgment, since confessing or denying Jesus before humans on earth will have corresponding consequences in Jesus' advocacy with his Father in heaven (cf. Mark 8:38; Matt 16:27; Luke 9:26; Matt 10:32–33; Luke 12:8–9). Gaining or losing one's life is related to one's attitude to Jesus (cf. Matt 10:38–39; 16:24–25). A characteristic feature of Jesus' teaching in the synoptic tradition is the prefacing of some of his sayings with the term "Amen" [NRSV "Truly"], underlining the special significance of his own words. The Fourth Gospel takes up and doubles the prefatory "Amen," which, as we have seen, can now serve as equivalent to the solemn swearing of an oath for the reliability of his witness. It is not surprising, then, that the synoptic tradition's depiction of Jesus as the unique agent of God's rule, with its consequences of salvation or judgment, can become the Fourth Gospel's depiction of Jesus as the unique agent of God's lawsuit.

In the Synoptics Jesus' role as agent of God's judgment is closely linked to the use of the Son of Man title. Here also is a precedent for the Johannine conception of Jesus as the agent of God's lawsuit. Although there are references to the Son of Man in the present and to the Son of Man's coming suffering, particularly in passion predictions, this earlier usage in the Synoptics has the Son of Man both judging and acting as advocate before God as judge in the future. In Matt 16:27 the coming of the Son of Man in glory is explicitly linked with judging: "For the Son of Man is to come with his angels in the glory of his Father, and then he will repay everyone for what has been done" (cf. Mark 8:38; Luke 9:26). The Fourth Gospel retains the reference to the Son of Man in the context of future judgment (John 5:27), but in general, in line with the present prosecution of the lawsuit, there has been a moving back of future references into the present. Thus, in John 9:35–39 the Son of Man occurs in a present context with reference to judging. As already noted, the most striking aspect of this moving back is that the references to glory have now been linked to the references to suffering in the passion predictions. Indeed, in the Fourth Gospel's equivalent to the three Markan passion predictions (Mark 8:31; 9:31; 10:33–34), suffering and glory have been collapsed together in the expression *to lift up,* a double entendre that has in view both the lifting up on the cross in Roman execution and the lifting up in glory and exaltation (cf. John 3:14; 8:28; 12:32–34). In addition, in John's reworking of the synoptic Son of Man traditions, the Son of Man who will come from heaven in the future is now the one who has already come from heaven and will return there: the descending and ascending Son of Man, the one who provides the link between the two key places in the lawsuit—heaven, from where it is set in motion, and earth, the place where it works itself out (cf. 3:13; 6:62). Taken as a whole, the synoptic references already suggest the notion of a future judge who is first judged by undergoing suffering and death, a judge who is also a victim (cf., e.g., Mark 9:12; Matt 17:12). The way has been prepared for the shift in the Fourth Gospel whereby the one who is judged has already been shown to be God's agent in witness and judgment.

When we look at material other than the Son of Man title itself, we can see that even this shift is not as great as might first appear, since in the Synoptics the proclamation of judgment is bound up with proclamation of God's rule and there is a present as well as future aspect to this judgment. Jesus' parables frequently have judgment as a theme or an element, whether it is the parable of the Unjust Steward in Luke 16:1–8, the Talents in Matt 25:14–30 and Luke 19:11–27, the Invitation to the Dinner Feast in Matt 22:2–14 and Luke 14:16–24, the Unmerciful Judge in Luke 18:1–8, or the Unforgiving Servant in Matt 18:23–35. The parables themselves both invite and exclude, both open up the possibility of life in God's rule and carry the possibility of judgment. One consequence of not responding appropriately is the judgment of being confirmed in one's deafness and blindness (cf. Mark 4:10–12, 23–25; Matt 13:12–15). The element of judgment heightened the note of urgency in Jesus' proclamation, with threats and warnings serving to underscore the summons to repent and align oneself with God's rule. Those addressed by God's rule mediated through Jesus find themselves in a situation with ultimate consequences. To refuse the rule is to judge themselves. But there are also places in the Synoptics where it is Jesus who announces that judgment, oracles in which Jesus pronounces woes on the cities of Galilee (Matt 11:20–24; Luke 10:12–15), on the rich (Luke 6:24–26), on the scribes and Pharisees (Matt 23:15–36), or, in Luke's equivalent passage, the Pharisees and lawyers. (Luke 11:42–52), declaring the end-time judgment ahead of time. Jesus also declares that, in the courtroom setting of the last judgment, the queen of the South and the Ninevites will stand up as prosecuting witnesses who will condemn the present unbelieving generation of Israelites. Again, this judgment is being decided in the present through the stance adopted by people toward Jesus' words and deeds, the "something greater" that is among them (Matt 12:41–42; Luke 11:31–32). In another saying, which casts Gentiles in a favorable light over against Israel, Jesus proclaims that at the eschatological banquet many will come from east and west to eat with Israel's ancestors but that the present descendants of these ancestors will be thrown out into the place of punishment with its darkness, weeping, and gnashing of teeth (Matt 8:11–12; cf. Luke 13:28–29).

If the Synoptics contain aspects of present judgment in the negative sense of condemnation, they also give expression to the positive judgment in a fashion similar to John, namely, in terms of life. In some passages the eschatological destiny of humans is depicted through the alternatives of life or destruction (Matt 7:14) and life or eternal fire, and "to enter life" stands in parallel to "to enter the kingdom of God" (Mark 9:43–47; cf. also Matt 18:3–9). Elsewhere "to inherit eternal life" is the equivalent of "to enter the kingdom of God," and the salvation of the age to come is formulated in terms of what becomes the characteristic Johannine phrase—"eternal life" (Mark 10:17–30; cf. also Matt 19:16–30; Luke 18:18–30). Matthew's parable of the Sheep and the Goats makes inheriting the kingdom and eternal life functional equivalents (Matt 25:34, 46), and Luke speaks of inheriting eternal life in 10:25 (cf. also 10:28: "do this, and you will live").

The opposition in John's lawsuit is depicted as both supernatural and human. On the one hand, behind the unbelieving world stands the ruler of the world, the devil, who has to be defeated in the lawsuit (cf. 8:44; 12:31; 13:2, 27; 16:11; 17:15). On the other hand, the main human representatives of the unbelieving world who engage in disputes with Jesus are designated "the Jews." Again there are comparable features in the Synoptics that the Fourth Gospel has developed in its own distinctive way. In the synoptic tradition Jesus' mission entails a clash between God's rule and Satan's (Mark 3:23–27; Matt 12:25–29; Luke 11:17–22). Jesus is tempted by Satan or the devil (Mark 1:13; Matt 4:1–11; Luke 4:1–13). Satan opposes Jesus' mission in a number of ways (Mark 4:13; Matt 13:18; Luke 8:12; Mark 8:33; Matt 16:23; Luke 13:16; Matt 6:13; 13:39; Luke 22:3, 31) but is seen as a defeated enemy (Luke 10:18). What is often overlooked is that John's depiction of "the Jews" as the human opponents of Jesus has its functional equivalent in the Synoptics with the depiction of "this generation" and that in the Synoptics pejorative rhetoric is used against this group far more frequently than in John. *This generation*, the generation of Jesus' contemporaries, in the synoptic tradition most frequently stands for unbelieving Israel as a whole, just as *the Jews* does in John's Gospel.

It is worth setting out the synoptic polemic against contemporary Jews characterized in this way. In Mark 8:11–12 the Pharisees are addressed, but the answer given them indicts "this generation" as a whole:

"Why does this generation ask for a sign? Truly I tell you, no sign will be given to this generation." Matthew and Luke take up the discussion about "this generation" and a sign in a number of places. In Matt 12:38–39, after Jesus has just addressed the Pharisees as "brood of vipers" (cf. v. 34), he addresses some scribes and Pharisees, but the indictment that follows extends to "this generation" as a whole: "An evil and adulterous generation asks for a sign, but no sign will be given to it except the sign of the prophet Jonah." This statement is repeated in Matt 16:4 for an audience of Pharisees and Sadducees. Luke's version is formulated differently. Speaking to the crowds, Jesus says, "This generation is an evil generation. . . . For just as Jonah became a sign to the people of Nineveh, so the Son of Man will be to this generation" (Luke 11:29–30). By requesting a sign, therefore, "this generation" attempts to judge Jesus rather than submit to his judging presence. That the one in its midst provides the criterion of judgment is made clear in Mark 8:38: "Those who are ashamed of me and of my words in this adulterous and sinful generation, of them the Son of Man will also be ashamed when he comes in the glory of his Father with the holy angels." "This generation" proves itself to be faithless (Mark 9:19), or faithless and perverse (Matt 17:17; Luke 9:41), failing to respond to either John the Baptist or Jesus and their different messages (Matt 11:16–19; Luke 7:31–35), and must reject the Son of Man (Luke 17:25). "This evil generation" shows itself to be like someone who has been left by an unclean spirit but to whom this spirit returns with seven other more evil spirits and whose last state is therefore worse than the first (Matt 12:45). This is a generation ripe for judgment. In Matt 23:36, a passage addressed to those who have again just been called snakes and a brood of vipers (v. 33), "all this" that will come on "this generation" refers to its blood guilt for the prophets and the righteous it has murdered (cf. also Luke 11:49–51: "the blood of all the prophets . . . will be charged against this generation"). Indeed, at the final judgment even the Gentile Ninevites and the Gentile queen of the South will condemn "this generation" because something greater than Jonah or Solomon has been in its midst without proper recognition (Matt 12:41–42; cf. also Luke 11:31–32).

The issue of signs and the characterization of "this generation" as murderers are both aspects of John's depiction of "the Jews" as the opponents in the lawsuit. In the Fourth Gospel, Jesus provides a number of striking signs, but these produce a division among "the Jews" (9:16). The witness of Jesus' signs or works encounters unbelief and hostility from "the Jews" (10:25–26, 32–33, 37–38; 12:37–40). Indeed, his signs lead to the opposition's decision to put him to death (11:46–53). But from Jesus' perspective, his works serve a judging function, leaving his opponents no excuse for their sin and hatred (15:24). In the polemic of John 8:44, the charge that because "the Jews" are trying to kill him, they are doing the desires of their father, the devil, who was a murderer from the beginning can be seen as a variation on the sort of indictment of "this generation" found in Matt 23:29–36: "You testify against yourselves that you are descendants of those who murdered the prophets" (cf. Luke 11:47–51). With both *this generation* in the synoptic tradition and *the Jews* in John, the reference is not to the Jewish people as such but to the un-believing contemporaries of Jesus and of his disciples in the former case, and to these and the unbelieving Jewish opposition of John's time in the latter case. John has presumably found the appellation "this generation" inappropriate for his purposes. A reference such as Mark 13:30—"this generation will not pass away until all these things have taken place"—(cf. also Matt 24:34; Luke 21:32) ties the term too closely to the first gen-eration, in which the Parousia and its accompanying judgment were ex-pected. John writes from a later setting and in his two-level narrative frequently collapses the time of Jesus with the time of his own readers. The designation *this generation* does not fit such a perspective, while *the Jews* both takes up the issues John's community has faced in terms of its identity and, given that a comprehensive term for the opposition needed to be employed, is better adapted to his purposes in the narrative.

This sketch of judgment in the mission of the synoptic Jesus is by no means exhaustive, yet it is sufficient to indicate that Jesus as the agent of God's judgment is a major feature of the tradition. For John to use the cosmic-lawsuit motif to shape his narrative of the mission of Jesus was by no means to distort this element of the traditions with which he was likely to have been familiar. The present and future aspects of eschato-logical judgment are also present in the Fourth Gospel, but subsuming them under the lawsuit theme, which was employed in Scripture in terms of Yahweh's present relationship with Israel, enables this Gospel to give greater prominence to the present aspect of Jesus' role as witness and judge in the trial.

3. The Witness of the Disciples and of the Spirit

This section turns to the ongoing aspect of John's cosmic trial: the disciples continue the cause of Jesus in their witness, aided by the wit-ness of the Paraclete, or Advocate. Does this aspect, too, have its roots in the synoptic tradition? The answer is in the affirmative. What is strik-ing is that some of these roots already have a trial setting as their con-text. In John this aspect of the trial is primarily set out in the Farewell

Discourses, which are the equivalent to the so-called apocalyptic discourses in the Synoptics, where Jesus warns and instructs the disciples about impending events and their own future role. In Mark 13:9–13 the disciples are told that, because of their allegiance to Jesus, they will find themselves handed over to councils, beaten in synagogues, and standing before governors and kings to bear witness (εἰς μαρτύριον) to them. When they are brought to trial, however, they are not to be concerned about what to say but to utter whatever is given to them at the time, because it will not be they who speak but the Holy Spirit. This will also be a period when they experience betrayal and death through the opposition of other family members and "will be hated by all because of my name." The Matthean (Matt 24:9–14) and Lukan (Luke 21:12–19) parallels paint pictures similar to Mark of this witness in the midst of persecution, although at this point Matthew omits any mention of the Spirit and of the concern about what to say and Luke omits the mention of the Spirit and instead has the disciples being given "a mouth and a wisdom that none of your opponents will be able to withstand or contradict" (21:15). But Matthew and Luke do mention the Spirit in similar material earlier in their narratives. What Matthew says in connection with the mission of the Twelve in 10:17–23 is in fact closer in wording to Mark 13:9–13 than the later sequential parallel in Matt 24:9–13. Luke's mention of the Spirit's part in the disciples' trials is located in the teaching contained in Luke 12:11–12 and connected with the need to acknowledge Jesus before others: "When they bring you before the synagogues, the rulers, and the authorities, do not worry about how you are to defend yourselves or what you are to say; for the Holy Spirit will teach you at that very hour what you ought to say." From these passages, then, John has developed the material in 15:18–16:4 about the disciples being hated by the world on account of Jesus' name, the joint witness of the disciples and the Paraclete, and the warnings about being persecuted, put out of the synagogue, and killed. In addition, the role of the Spirit as a teacher of the disciples picks up on Luke 12:12. Although nothing in the Synoptics compares explicitly to the notion of the Spirit also acting as prosecutor of the world, as in John 16:8–11, according to Luke 21:15 their opponents will not be able to withstand or refute what the disciples are given.

There are further thematic links between John's lawsuit motif and the synoptic tradition. In one place Luke broadens the notion of the disciples as witnesses beyond any trial setting (Luke 24:48), and this is taken up more frequently in his second volume, Acts. The disciples are to be judges in the future, at the end of history (Matt 19:28; Luke 22:30), but in the mission on which they are sent out by Jesus, there is also an element of realized judgment; for example, they shake the dust off their feet as a witness against those who refuse to accept them or their message (Mark 6:11; Luke 9:5; cf. also Matt 10:14–15, where the reference to witness is omitted). We have seen that in John's narrative the disciples' witness also has an element of realized judgment; in John 20:23 they are to press home the divine verdict regarding the forgiveness or retention of sins. The Johannine formulation has conceptual associations with that of Matt 18:18—"whatever you bind on earth will be bound in heaven, and whatever you loose on earth will be loosed in heaven"—but the latter has now been transferred to a mission context. Also, in the cosmic-trial scene in the parable of Matt 25:31–46, with the Son of Man as judge and all the nations assembled for judgment, the verdict is given on the basis of how the nations have treated the Son of Man in the person of his followers, "the least of these who are members of my family." The trial therefore has already been taking place in history although its participants have been unaware of it.

This discussion on points of contact between the Fourth Gospel's use of the lawsuit motif and aspects of the synoptic tradition suggests strongly that John was familiar with this tradition. This is not the place to debate the nature of the relationship in any detail. It is not the same sort of literary relationship as that among the Synoptics themselves. If we do not resort to talk of hypothetical earlier editions of the Synoptics, such as proto-Mark, the main options are that John knew the Synoptics (whether by hearing them read or reading them at some point); that John used oral traditions or written sources that had been influenced by the Synoptics, especially Mark; or that the traditions and sources John used had in fact influenced Mark and the other synoptic evangelists.[116] What appears most likely is this: the links we have seen come primarily from John's prior knowledge of the Synoptic Gospels, though he did not have them before him as he wrote; but his use of some oral traditions influenced by the Synoptics should not be ruled out, since such traditions

---

[116] This third option is the view consistently espoused by Dodd. On the links we have pointed out between John's and the Synoptics' depictions of the disciples and the Spirit as witnesses in a trial setting, for example, he writes (*Historical Tradition*, 409), "Various permutations and combinations would be consistent with the view that the Fourth Evangelist was working upon recollections of the Synoptic Gospels, but it would more naturally suggest that they belong to a nucleus of tradition common to all, worked up by each according to his particular tendency." Why this is a more natural explanation is by no means apparent from the evidence.

did not simply disappear with the publication of the written Gospels. Clearly, some major elements of the synoptic tradition have been woven into his own creative composition. But John's large-scale reshaping of the story of Jesus in terms of the cosmic trial is not simply an imaginative invention. Most of its main features and episodes are an elaboration, from his own perspective, of what was already in the traditions known to him and, for that matter, to many of his readers.

C. The Functions of the Lawsuit in Its Historical and Social Setting

This study has suggested that the community behind this Gospel had experienced the trauma of official and unofficial trials and excommunication from the synagogue; that the relationship with Judaism, with questions of identity and honor and shame associated with it, remained a pressing issue for its members; and that among the potential readers of the Gospel would be those who might well face trials in the setting of their relation to the Roman state. Such concrete factors in the setting point to a correlation with the Gospel narrative's most pervasive motif. The features of this cosmic-lawsuit motif did not have to be invented ex nihilo. They were already present in the community's Scriptures, and major elements of the traditions about Jesus, with which the Gospel's author and readers were already familiar, lent themselves to a reshaping of the story of Jesus in terms of a cosmic trial.

By highlighting such features, the evangelist is able to help his readers make sense of their own experiences by setting them in the context of a larger picture. Their witness to Jesus, in a setting of persecution that could lead and had led to trials and punishment, is seen as part of a cosmic trial in which the criteria of judgment are quite different from those of their historical trials and in which their stance is vindicated. Their stance is vindicated because in this larger trial the one to whom they bear witness is God's unique witness and agent of judgment, in whom the divine verdict in the trial is embodied.

What, then, is the question to which this narrative testimony is the answer? On one level the answer appears fairly obvious from the statement of purpose in John 20:31. The question is, Who is Jesus? And the answer is that he is the Christ, the Son of God. But if we ask why this answer takes the form it does in the narrative, then the readers' question to which it is responding is more like, Are we justified in staking our identity, our security, and our lives on belief in Jesus? The narrative testimony can thus be seen to serve as a means both of pointing to the decisive significance of what God has done in Christ and of persuading people to continue in their belief about this. The lawsuit motif, of which the Gospel's testimony is a part, makes the point that this belief is the right judgment in line with the divine verdict. At the same time, this motif takes full account of the fact that the truth to which the members of the community confess allegiance has been disputed in a contest of claims. In Deutero-Isaiah the trial motif functioned as "a type of legal procedure which is adapted to ascertain publicly the truth of certain assertions."[117] In the Fourth Gospel, where the truth of the claims about Jesus are in dispute, it is therefore a natural vehicle for displaying the perspective of Johannine Christians. In telling the story of trial and recounting its verdict, the narrative both legitimates their side in the dispute and provides the basis for persuading people to become fully settled in their judgment about the disputed claims.

Given the setting that influenced the shaping of the Fourth Gospel's narrative, it is easy to see why Isa 40–55 would have been found to be such a helpful resource. Its lawsuit speeches had been addressed to Israelites in exile, assuring them of Yahweh's purposes of judgment and salvation and their role in these purposes, giving them a new perspective on their situation and on Babylon as their oppressor, and encouraging them to take up Yahweh's offer of freedom, homecoming, and well-being. Many of the members of the Johannine community would also have seen their situation as one of exile, in that excommunication and ostracism had put them outside the majority group to which they had previously belonged. The underlying question for Israel's exile was, Is Yahweh reliable if, despite our covenant relationship with Yahweh, we find ourselves in exile? Now the community of Johannine Christians asks, Is the God we believe to be revealed decisively in Christ reliable if, despite our belief, we now find ourselves put outside the structures of the religion that professes allegiance to God but refuses allegiance to Christ? And just as Deutero-Isaiah gave exiles a vision of well-being beyond despair, including peace, freedom, and being at home in the land, John offers exiled Jewish Christians a vision of well-being or life, including peace, freedom, and being at home that are all now to be found in their relationship with Jesus. This Gospel's use of the lawsuit motif reinforces new plausibility structures in which life, identity, and security come from Jesus rather than any other source in official Judaism. It enables the Johannine community to construe its life in a fresh setting

---

[117] Nielsen, *Yahweh as Prosecutor and Judge*, 72.

where the criteria of the dominant society no longer define the community and where these criteria have been exposed and no longer pertain.

In Deutero-Isaiah the lawsuit with the nations had proved itself highly suited for apologetic purposes. It was "not the gods who must be convinced, but Israel. . . . In reality, then, this is a case between Yahweh and Israel, in which the legal proceedings between Yahweh and the foreign gods function as Yahweh's deposition as well as his defense against Israel's accusations."[118] Similarly, in the Fourth Gospel, the rehearsal of God's dispute with Israel, now representing the nations or the world, functions as an apologetic for the community that has believed in Jesus, reassuring it of the rightness of God's actions regarding Jesus. The reworking of traditions in terms of the cosmic lawsuit in effect takes the form of a retrial. Harvey makes this point well.[119] But as mentioned earlier, the issues are not simply those of the time of Jesus. Jesus' cause is now seen in terms of the beliefs about him that have developed over time in this community, some of them through the very process of debate and antagonism with the synagogue that led to the excommunication of the community's Jewish Christians from the synagogue. This Gospel's narrative testimony does not engage directly with the opposition but addresses readers in the light of the issues raised by the opposition. The disputes with opponents in Jesus' public mission provide a perspective on the clash of ultimate commitments that strengthens Johannine Christians' own allegiance, so that they can press home the verdict of the cosmic trial with confidence, exposing the allegiance and accompanying values of "the world" (cf. John 16:8–11).

In order to reconstrue its life, the community in which the Fourth Gospel's traditions were developed needed to come to terms with, and make sense of, its history. Fastening on to the lawsuit motif was a prime help in doing so. It provided the framework for the overall story of Jesus, into which the community was able to fuse its key traditions and memories. A major function of testimony in any community is to keep the past and its traditions alive and to transmit knowledge of them to future generations. The beloved disciple's testimony served this purpose for the community that looked to him as its founding figure. With the death of the beloved disciple (cf. 21:23), the writing down of this witness became all the more important for the preservation of the community's memories. As we have seen, the implied author and his narrator speak for a

---

[118] Ibid., 68.
[119] Harvey, *Jesus on Trial,* 104.

"we" in this narrative. The written testimony, therefore, acts as a means of retrieving the past in a communal memory.

Memory is also an important factor for Jesus' followers within the narrative (cf. 2:22; 12:16; 14:26; 15:20; 16:4). It is linked to the notion of testimony in that these followers are to testify because they have been with Jesus from the beginning and are therefore in a position to recall his words and deeds (cf. 14:27). Their witnessing traditions provided the early stories from which members of the Johannine community reproduced the past. The traditioning process entailed the retelling of narratives about Jesus with the incorporation of new material and the reconfiguring of earlier traditions in a way that would speak to new circumstances. The chain of testimony did not allow memory to become simply an inventory of past events. Instead, memory made a claim about the significance of those events that shaped the narration of them. As it functioned as community memory, it made that claim by means of a framework of shared understanding and thereby produced a particular narrative of selected events and elaborated sayings that were basic for the survival and identity of the community. The resulting narrative attributes this interpretive activity to the guidance and work of the Spirit-Paraclete. It is this Advocate who is witnessing on behalf of Jesus through the testimony of Jesus' followers (15:26), leading them into all the truth (16:13), as he teaches them and reminds them of the significance of all that Jesus said (14:26).

The interpretive device of the lawsuit motif gave continuity to the past by connecting Jesus' story with that of the community and established coherence by setting both within a larger overall perspective. The events that had been traumatic for the community could now serve to reinforce its identity. As discussed earlier, the telling of a story such as that of the man born blind, with his healing, interrogation, and excommunication, in John 9 is a particularly clear instance. It fused the community's past with the traditions about Jesus and allowed that past to continue to shape the present. It preserved the memories of members of the community in a typical narrative but now sets them within a larger perspective that enables Johannine Christians to face the future with a renewed sense of purpose. The experience of trial retains its stamp but is also transformed.

Clearly, there was an issue of justice for those whose belief in Jesus as Son of God had had the consequences we have suggested. Many Johannine Christians would have considered themselves wronged, and perceived both the trial of Jesus and their own treatment by the synagogue a betrayal of human justice. The lawsuit spoke to such feelings.

ll, as noted earlier, the appeal to God as judge, the invoking of the it on the part of Israel, had been an appeal to God's justice in the expectation that wrongs would be righted, that life and well-being would replace the alienation and deprivation that is a form of death. For Johannine Christians, too, the lawsuit would have functioned as a call to God to show God's self to be on the side of the marginalized and oppressed. God as judge would have been a positive image, one that sustained hope as part of an appeal to the court of last resort in the face of perceived misjudgments and injustice. As discussed, even if it had been possible, further appeal to a human court would only have reinforced the group's lack of honor. But to be fully persuaded that God is judge and that this judge has given a quite different verdict about Christ and Christian claims about him would help to draw the sting from the opponents' power to indict, condemn, and punish and from the consequences of such human judgment. In their situation power had been in the hands of the synagogue and its leaders and in the court of public opinion, but to be reinforced in their perspective and reminded that, despite appearances, they had an honorable status and a significant role in God's purposes would have empowered these Christians to continue their witness in the face of persecution.

The value system of Johannine Christians' everyday world is reversed in the narrative world. The stigma of being cast out into the sphere of death is overturned by the positive judgment of life, which can be enjoyed in the present by those who believe in Jesus. The extreme shaming of their treatment is overturned by their sharing in the honor or glory that attaches to God and Jesus. The discourse of the narrative undermines any temptation to futile acts of retaliatory violence and instead functions as a powerful means of resisting the viewpoint of the dominant society. In reinforcing different values and reestablishing coherence, it also allows for the gaining of some redemptive and healing perspective on earlier traumas. For individuals and communities, trauma can be the catalyst either for introverted withdrawal and self-destruction or for a creative move toward a new integration and sense of identity. It depends on how the traumatic experience is handled, whether there is ability to embrace its pain, and what meaning is given to it. Rather than simply erect a fortress around the wounds of the traumas, this narrative with its lawsuit motif encourages healing by dealing with the experience of shaming. As we have seen, the narrative not only projects a quite different honor system by which its readers can live; to replace the deep sense of rejection, it also witnesses to the reality of a love that accepts. Those who confess allegiance to Jesus are continually reassured of the love of both God the judge and of Jesus, God's unique witness, and are exhorted to display the same quality of accepting love to other members of the witnessing community.

Thus, for the community in which the major elements of this narrative took shape, the trial motif served a number of functions appropriate to the experiences of its members. It provided the framework that made sense of the community's witness to the identity of Jesus and of the memory of the consequences this entailed. It thereby performed teaching and apologetic functions. At the same time, it offered consolation and healing, assurance and encouragement in the face of hurt, humiliation, and fear. In addition, it informed the narrative's elements of exhortation and admonition, for it summoned community members to continued right belief in line with God's verdict and to appropriate conduct as witnesses called to continue Jesus' witness in the face of a hostile world.

The scope of the lawsuit motif allows for a larger purpose than simply dealing with the group's past, legitimating its claims and strengthening its identity. Does this narrative serve the interests of Johannine Christians? Yes. It is a testimony that embraces the pain of exclusion, as God and Jesus are depicted in solidarity with those who have been cast out. It deals with exclusion by a reversal of the competing groups' roles. Those cast out are now the privileged people in God's purposes, and those who cast them out are depicted as under the judgment of condemnation. In the narrative world of the Gospel, the confession of Johannine Christians is neither a lie nor blasphemy but the truth, and they experience not the death of excommunication but life, not the shame of ostracism but glory. These elements of compensation by reversal appear in the story because of these Christians' need to be bolstered in their identity in the marginalized situation in which they found themselves. They needed the legitimation of their viewpoint in the conflict over who had the right to the traditional symbols of God's relationship with God's people. But does the lawsuit motif serve only such needs? No. It would be too simple to read this narrative as merely a means of compensation. It was only because of the consequences of their attempt to explain the impact of Jesus and his mission that Johannine Christians found themselves needing this sort of reverse legitimation.

The genre of this narrative testimony—a life of Jesus—indicates that its original raison d'être has not been forgotten in the need to come to terms with subsequent experiences. These experiences color but do not constitute the witness the evangelist, as representative of this community, is now prepared to pass on to a wider audience. The cosmic dimensions of the trial motif, which enable the narrative to transcend the particular circumstances out of which it was developed, also come into play here. God's concern for the world serves to counteract any self-serving tendencies within this narrative witness. The trial's positive verdict of life is meant to be for all, not to remain as the exclusive possession of this particular group of early Christians. On the basis of the verdict depicted in the narrative, its readers' task is to witness to the divine purposes of life and well-being for the world at large, whatever hostility they may encounter in the process. Particularly in the face of hostility from the dominant forces in society, a community can become preoccupied with its own identity and survival. But these followers of Jesus are also summoned out of any self-absorption by being shown that the quality of their life together is indeed a highly significant component of the witness that has to be borne in a wider world. A reductionist claim that the narrative's values are projections of the community's own concerns, aimed at giving them divine sanction, would misread the narrative. In it the legitimation of Jesus' followers and their claims not only carries them out in mission to the world but also militates against self-congratulation and arrogance. Their own honor is entirely subordinate to the emphasis throughout on God's establishment of God's own honor and reputation in Jesus and on giving glory to this God. The very fact that the final form of the Fourth Gospel's narrative has in view a broad readership, including some Gentiles who need basic Hebrew terms explained to them, indicates that the evangelist saw the potential for the trial motif because it is on a cosmic scale, speaking to a variety of settings and not just compensating for the particular individual and social needs of the group of Christians whose experiences he had shared. Such settings would include not only those of Christians faced by the claims of the Roman state and its imperial cult, as we have seen, but also—far beyond the literal trials that may have originally led to the adoption of the motif in the first place—those of any believers who found their confession about the identity of Jesus in dispute.

chapter seven

THE LAWSUIT METAPHOR
in CONTEMPORARY
FOCUS

The Fourth Gospel portrays Jesus' mission as part of a lawsuit, as a witness to which all must respond. In their response lies the Judge's verdict. The readers are shown, through the prologue in particular, that the division within Israel and within humanity resulting from Jesus' coming is part of a larger struggle between light and darkness that has been taking place in history. The response to Jesus, whether in Jesus' time or in that of the readers, is a response to God's claim on God's world. The controversy in which the community associated with this Gospel has been, and continues to be, embroiled is therefore not simply a local but a cosmic one. In this way the narrative transcends the particular situation in which it was formed.

A. The Endurance of the Metaphor

The bare assertion of the previous sentence leaves many questions unresolved. The writer of the Gospel may well have seen particular and local issues in the light of a more embracing metaphor that transcends his own setting, but does this in itself give his narrative universal or enduring significance? Certainly, its status as part of the canon of the NT indicates that this document was felt to continue to speak to a variety of continuing needs of churches and to give authentic witness to the significance of the life, death and resurrection of Christ. The experience of readers of the NT with this Gospel down through the centuries is also

evidence that it has continued to transcend the circumstances of its original production. But such observations are not really to the point. What
we are asking about is specifically the power of this Gospel's cosmic-
lawsuit metaphor to transcend its original setting, where its audience
was far more familiar with its scriptural foundation and where the audience's own experiences helped to give such a metaphor its particular
force. Simply pointing to the Church's continuing experience with the
Fourth Gospel, then, does not in itself provide an answer because a variety of the Gospel's aspects have appealed to Christians at particular times
and in particular places. And one would be hard pressed to show either
that Christians over the centuries in fact recognized the cosmic-lawsuit
motif sufficiently for them to have given it serious attention or that if it
was recognized, this is what gave this Gospel its appeal for them. Although it would be interesting to explore the subject, it is beyond the
scope of this study whether, even in later settings analogous to those reflected in the narrative, where the persecution of Christians included
and includes their being put on trial, its cosmic-lawsuit motif has stood
out and become alive for such readers or whether they were attracted to
other documents more overtly and more familiarly associated with persecution, such as Revelation and 1 Peter.

For those who have been persuaded of the dominance and pervasive
shaping power of this motif in the Fourth Gospel and have an interest in
appropriating the Gospel read in this light, how much imaginative effort
needs to be expended before finding its cosmic trial an appropriate
metaphor by which to live? To clarify the issue again, this is not simply a
question about the language of witness or testimony. Use of such language is common in a variety of settings, from religious services to business meetings to political rallies to self-help groups. When people are
called on, or volunteer to talk about, their experiences or convictions in
such settings, it is frequently called testifying. But unless competing
claims are present, such language is usually divorced, at least consciously, from any association with an overarching trial in which the testifying plays a part. Our question has to do, then, with the motif as a
whole, not just with this one aspect. Unlike the intended first readers,
we may well not be immersed in the scriptural use of the trial metaphor
as part of our cultural heritage. Some NT metaphors about the mission
of Christ, such as atonement, that have a major scriptural background
and have been perpetuated in the Church's liturgy have nevertheless lost
much of their force in our general culture. The cosmic-lawsuit motif itself, and not just the extended use of testimony language, is not one of
these. Whatever its currency in Christian imagination, it is still alive and

well in Western culture. This is partly due to the universality of the legal process in some form or other in human society, a phenomenon that lends itself to the extension of its language to other aspects of human life, and partly due to an adaptation of, and reaction to, the general scriptural—and therefore both Jewish and Christian—notions of a divine judgment.

The resonances of the trial metaphor can be heard at various levels. Literal trials still have the power to evoke issues of meaning and value on a broad scale and to become metaphors for life. To take a recent example, the O. J. Simpson trials attracted so much attention not simply because it was a sports and media celebrity on trial for murder. What became clear was that in the trial not only the guilt or innocence of this one well-known individual was at stake but also an entire set of surrounding issues. The notion of justice itself and society's values in the areas of racism and sexism were being put on trial.

The trial metaphor also remains pervasive in the Western literary tradition. Some of the past century's great writers have utilized it. On the European scene, the classic instance is Franz Kafka's disturbing novel *The Trial*, with its probing of the human dilemma as the sense of being on trial, of being judged in some way that one ambivalently rejects yet at the same time goes along with, because to be born may be to be guilty. Its hero, Joseph K., is engaged in the task of ascertaining the charges against him, a task that by its very nature is impossible to conclude satisfactorily because his alleged guilt is never explained and the charge against him never described. The narrative has its irony because some revelation of the case against the protagonist always appears imminent and yet is indefinitely deferred. This is a quite different sort of irony from the stable irony entailed in the Fourth Gospel's lawsuit. It is a cosmic irony that undermines the notion of access to any ultimate source or criterion of judgment. In the setting of Kafka's cosmic trial, "any authoritative or transcendent revelation would be philosophically suspect."[1] In Kafka's vision of life on trial, if there is an ultimate reality, it is inaccessible; this easily becomes the secular vision replacing the biblical tradition—in which the world was on trial before God—with a world that is simply on trial.

---

[1] Leitch, *What Stories Are*, 71. Some interpreters of *The Trial* dispute this reading. R. Gray, *Franz Kafka* (Cambridge: Cambridge University Press, 1973), 125, for example, simply asserts, "The universal applicability some readers find was not put there by Kafka. That most men undergo a trial is not a sufficiently close parallel to justify seeing in his novel a parable of the human condition."

Each of the major novels of Albert Camus, *The Outsider, The Plague,* and *The Fall*, exploit in different ways this notion of humanity on trial and its issues of guilt and judgment against the backdrop of an indifferent universe.[2] When, at the end of *The Plague*, the narrator reveals himself as the doctor, Bernard Rieux, he writes, "Dr. Rieux resolved to write this chronicle, so that he should not be one of those who hold their peace but should bear witness in favor of those plague-stricken people, so that some memorial of the injustice and outrage done them might endure."[3]

On the American scene, Arthur Miller captured something of this mood in his play *After the Fall*, where one of the characters says,

> When you're young, you prove how brave you are, or smart; then what a good lover; then a good father; finally how wise or powerful or what-the-hell-ever. But underlying it all, I see now, there was a presumption. That I was moving on an upward path toward some elevation, where—God knows what—I would be justified, or even condemned—a verdict anyway. I think now that my disaster really began when I looked up one day—and the bench was empty. No judge in sight. And all that remained was the endless argument with oneself—this pointless litigation of existence before an empty bench.[4]

Richard Fenn, a sociologist of religion, also claims that the biblical tradition in which the world was on trial before God has become secularized and that in this process the trial theme has become institutionalized in all areas of social life, including education, politics, and science, where individuals, ideas, and policies are under constant quasi-judicial review: "The individual is perpetually facing judgment by abstract and impersonal criteria that are only partially revealed while always calling into question the individual's own sense of worthiness. . . . the theme of the 'last judgment' loses its theological framework, and the process of adjudication becomes as endless as it is inescapable."[5] Part of his thesis, which is in many ways a sociological application of Kafka's vision, is that secularization of the heavenly trial lends a seriousness to human life and speech[6] but that the negative aspect of this is that, while in religion or the liturgy there is a resolution of the trial, the secular trial of life produces

---

[2] For readings of *The Plague* and *The Fall* as testimonies to the Holocaust, see S. Felman and D. Laub, *Testimony* (New York: Routledge, Chapman & Hall, 1992), 93–119; 165–203.

[3] A. Camus, *The Plague* (New York: Random House, 1972), 287.

[4] A. Miller, *Plays: Two* (London: Methuen, 1991), 127.

[5] R. K. Fenn, *Liturgies and Trials* (Oxford: Basil Blackwell, 1982), 1.

[6] Ibid., 50–51.

no final verdicts. Indeed, he claims, "It is in the absence of religious guarantees to secular speech . . . that the trial never ends."[7] The secular trial even invades the family. "One is less frequently on trial in the family than in the classroom, although the secularization of the family makes standards of performance and the conditional giving of love increasingly acceptable. . . . Divorce makes all marriages 'trials' in which the parties may be found wanting."[8] Being on continuous trial is difficult to bear. "The secularization of the divine lawsuit against mankind leads to desperate measures, strenuous achievements, quiet despair, and occasionally to renewals of religious fervor to obtain divine forgiveness."[9]

Finally, there is a major exception to the notion, stated above, that the use of testimony language has usually lost connection with any sense of life as a trial: the body of literature, produced by those who have written on the Holocaust, where testimony has become a dominant category.[10] In the Fourth Gospel, the role of witness is seen as being taken over from Israel as a whole and given to Jesus and his first Jewish followers in a setting of persecution. Yet now we have the phenomenon of the use of witness language by a group of twentieth-century Jews, survivors of the Holocaust and others, to refer to the uniquely horrific extermination of five to six million Jews by Nazi Germany, in which Christians—and in some measure the history of their interpretation of this same Gospel—are implicated. The metaphor of testimony in a context of trial has been kept alive in Jewish usage, and in recent times this has occurred precisely in the context of the Shoah. Elie Wiesel can go so far as to claim, "If the Greeks invented tragedy, the Romans the epistle and the Renaissance the sonnet, our generation invented a new literature, that of testimony."[11]

Such literature has taken various forms—scraps of paper that recorded events at the time, diaries, memoirs, poems, novels—and testimony

---

[7] Ibid., 77.

[8] Ibid., 7.

[9] Ibid., 2.

[10] For reflections on Holocaust testimonies, see, e.g., Felman and Laub, *Testimony;* G. H. Hartman, ed., *Holocaust Remembrance* (Oxford: Blackwell, 1994); L. L. Langer, *Holocaust Testimony: The Ruins of Memory* (New Haven: Yale University Press, 1991).

[11] E. Wiesel, *Dimensions of the Holocaust* (Evanston, Ill.: Northwestern University Press, 1977), 9. Hartman, *Holocaust Remembrance,* 18, talks of "a body of works 'between history and literature.' "

has also moved to archived interviews with survivors, to art, and to film. The literature that reflects on such testimony also inevitably reflects on the role of memory and the interrelation between witness and memory. What needs to be emphasized here, however, is that this witness frequently explicitly, but also implicitly, sees itself as performing a role in a larger trial. It wants to witness and accuse in the larger tribunal of human history, to state the truth passionately in the midst of conflicting claims and denials, to put humanity on trial for the evil of which it is capable, and to cry out for justice in this world. And when justice has not been seen to be done, when the oppressors have refused to admit to the moral enormity of their atrocities, and when even family and friends who did not have the same experience have thought the testimony unbelievable, these witnesses have continued to testify for the sake of their own grasp on reality, in the cause of truth and in the hope that somewhere, somehow this will contribute to a reckoning. One such witness, Jean Améry, wrote his testimony in 1966 and in the preface expressed the hope that it would help Germans to recognize better their recent past and would reach "all those who wish to live together as fellow human beings."[12] When he reissued the book in 1977, one year before he took his own life, such hopes had vanished from the preface. Instead he wrote, "Nothing is resolved. . . . Nothing has healed, and what was perhaps on the point of healing in 1964 is bursting open again as an infected wound. . . . I can do no more than give testimony."[13]

The poignancy of this testimony literature and the dreadful irony of its emergence from the fate of Jews at the hands of a so-called Christian civilization should give pause to any call for a reappropriation of the Fourth Gospel's use of the motif. Nevertheless, given the endurance of the lawsuit metaphor in a variety of forms and given the haunting and desperate visions of life presented by those employing it as a depiction of the human condition where there is no transcendent referent, some might hold that, for the Fourth Gospel's perspective to be found compelling, it only need be reasserted in its full theological form. There is certainly a place for positive exposition and sensitive preaching of the Fourth Gospel's message from the perspective of the cosmic lawsuit and for allowing the motif to do its own work. For it situates believing hearers in relation to God and the world, gives them a perspective on the

---

[12] J. Améry, *At the Mind's Edge* (New York: Shocken, 1990).
[13] On Améry's testimony, see A. Rosenfeld, "Jean Améry as Witness," in *Holocaust Remembrance* (ed. Hartman), 59–69.

Church's task, and thereby makes connections with whatever imaginative construals of the trial metaphor for life they already entertain.

For a number of reasons, however, a critical appropriation of the Fourth Gospel read in the light of this motif will want to reflect further. Five of these reasons, some of them closely related, are given here without providing justifications for them: (1) The Christian gospel may well have intrinsic power, but the same does not necessarily hold for the formulations in which it was couched in the first century. Even if one, accepting the perspective of this study that the lawsuit motif was used in the Fourth Gospel to reassure and confirm Christians in their faith, wishes to appropriate it for the same purpose, simply to repeat the language of this Gospel in a quite different temporal, spatial, and cultural setting may well be not faithfulness but faithlessness, however well intentioned. (2) Wishing to appropriate the biblical witness is not therefore the same as being a biblicist. Contemporary Christians who treat the NT as authoritative need to be aware that they do not do so outside the stream of an ongoing Christian tradition and outside Christian theologizing that is also informed by hermeneutical and philosophical reflection. (3) Even if one is persuaded that the Gospel employed this motif for the benefit of Christians, it clearly did so in order not simply to make a claim about Christian existence but to convince its readers that its view of God and the world, its perspective on all of life, was true. Its message for Christians therefore entailed a universal claim. Contemporary Christians, then, need to reflect not simply on the power of this metaphor for Christian living but on its public status. Does it still work as a way for Christians to explain not only to themselves but also to others how to make sense of life, how to construe reality? (4) Christians do not simply inhabit the world of the text of Scripture and the language of Christian theology. They also inevitably inhabit the world of their society and its culture. This means that at the same time they endeavor to read the latter world in the light of scriptural construals of reality, they are also reading these scriptural construals in the light of the cultural assumptions that shape them as readers. This interaction calls for critical reflection. (5) Both the history of Christian interpretation of the Fourth Gospel—including therefore, to some extent, the lawsuit motif, whether this has been consciously exploited or not—and Western culture's adaptation of, and reaction to, the motif shape responses to it; this puts in doubt the viability of simply restating it without addressing the context of reception. The issues include the history of interpretation of the role of "the Jews" in the cosmic lawsuit, how the God who would initiate such a lawsuit with the world has been perceived, why some would rather have a cosmic lawsuit without a divine Judge, whether, on such a vital matter, believing on the basis of someone else's say-so is a responsible act, and whether the universal claims of a metanarrative about a cosmic lawsuit are not dangerously imperialistic.

We shall return to a number of these observations and issues in the next chapter. But since Paul Ricoeur has already reflected on some of the broader theological and philosophical issues surrounding the metaphor of the lawsuit and its use in the Fourth Gospel, it would be foolish simply to ignore his contribution. Since his essay "The Hermeneutics of Testimony" is still not sufficiently known by readers of the Fourth Gospel, the following section will discuss his study.

B. Ricoeur and the Hermeneutics of Testimony

Ricoeur is interested in the lawsuit motif's potential for illuminating both human existence in the world and the interpretation of this existence. "The Hermeneutics of Testimony," then, can be seen as related to his overall reflections on hermeneutical theory[14] and is in line with his work on symbols[15] and metaphors[16] and on narratives[17] as an extension of these, all of which he holds to be forms of discourse that have the power to provide new insights into reality and to orientate our living in the world. For Ricoeur the most fundamental aspect of human existence is the passion to be, a saying "yes" to life in the world, and this he calls "original affirmation." But he also holds that human existence is finite and fallible. This has two consequences. On the one hand, the human subject does not grasp its basic consciousness through immediate intuition; it has the task of reflection. Since he was convinced by his earlier work on Freud that fallibility involved a false consciousness—"The subject is never the subject one thinks it is"[18]—here Ricoeur speaks of the need for "divestment," including the renunciation of "all the object-

---

[14] Cf. esp. P. Ricoeur, *The Conflict of Interpretations: Essays in Hermeneutics* (ed. D. Ihde; Evanston, Ill.: Northwestern University Press, 1974); and *Interpretation Theory: Discourse and the Surplus of Meaning* (Fort Worth: Texas Christian University Press, 1976).

[15] Cf. esp. P. Ricoeur, *The Symbolism of Evil* (Boston: Beacon, 1969).

[16] Cf. esp. Ricoeur, *Rule of Metaphor.*

[17] Cf. esp. Ricoeur, *Time and Narrative.*

[18] P. Ricoeur, *Freud and Philosophy: An Essay on Interpretation* (New Haven: Yale University Press, 1970), 420.

ifications that understanding imposes."[19] On the other hand, it means that authentic existence can only be achieved in relation to, and in response to, the claim of the absolute. Human experience of the absolute is through external contingent historical events or acts, and divestment disposes human consciousness to receive the meaning of such events or acts. But what is it that mediates these external manifestations of the absolute to the internal consciousness of the absolute in "original affirmation"? This question provides the context of Ricoeur's essay, and his answer is that it is the hermeneutics of testimony.[20] These initial categories may be unfamiliar to the reader of the current study. In any case, in the context of this study, they move us into a new realm of discourse and remind us that Ricoeur comes to the biblical text and its language primarily as a philosopher and not as a theologian.[21]

In keeping with his belief that attention to language and its use will provide a better understanding of human existence, Ricoeur's essay proceeds first to examine various dimensions of the meaning of *testimony* in ordinary language. To testify is to relate what one has seen or heard.[22] Ricoeur rightly calls this dimension of meaning quasi-empirical because testifying is not the seeing or hearing itself but the report or story of what has been seen or heard. Immediately one becomes aware of the link between testimony and Ricoeur's interest in narrative. In this dimension testimony is part of a process of communication. The person who receives the testimony has not seen or heard the original event to which testimony is given, and can believe in its reality only on the basis of hearing and believing the report of the witness. In this way "testimony is at the service of judgment." It becomes essential to forming an opinion about the meaning of what has happened; testimony seeks to provide a reliable basis for another's judging. This is the reason the eyewitness aspect of testimony cannot be sufficient in itself to show the meaning of testimony. What counts as testimony is a report of what has been seen that is used to support a judgment about its truth or meaning.

This brings Ricoeur to move from the quasi-empirical to the quasi-juridical dimension of meaning.[23] He underlines that the primary context for the characteristic discourse of testimony is the trial with its social

---

[19] Ricoeur, "Hermeneutics of Testimony," 120.

[20] Ibid., 119–23.

[21] This is also the conclusion of K. J. Vanhoozer, *Biblical Narrative in the Philosophy of Paul Ricoeur* (Cambridge: Cambridge University Press, 1990), 275–88.

[22] Ricoeur, "Hermeneutics of Testimony," 123–24.

[23] Ibid., 124–28.

and institutional conventions. "Testimony is one of the proofs that the prosecution or the defense advances with a view to influencing the decision of the judge." It includes the particular ritual of swearing, which qualifies what is said by the witness as testimony. But this dimension of meaning is quasi-juridical because a number of its aspects spill over, by analogy, into the use of the terms *witness* and *testimony* in ordinary language; in such use the fundamental characteristics of a trial are still recognizable. Testimony is not confined to the courtroom but can occur in any dispute between two parties with conflicting claims and in which a decision or judgment must be made. In historical science, for instance, a document takes on the status of testimony when there is a dispute about events and their significance. And just as in a juridical context testimony arises in respect to a contestable claim, so in ordinary language testimony is never simply descriptive but serves to support or invalidate some claim. In this way, both in juridical and in other discourse, testimony constitutes a proof that takes place between the dispute and the judgment. It forms part of an argument, part of the rhetoric of persuasion. Here Ricoeur has recourse to Aristotle's discussion of proof and testimony in *Rhetorica* (as does ch. 4, above). The orator who undertakes to persuade the listeners or the judge must anticipate the argument of the adversary in order to refute it. Such argumentation involves logical proof of the probable, rather than the necessary, kind, but it also has to keep in mind the audience whose dispositions need to be aroused. Ricoeur notes that for Aristotle, however, witness, whether it is the witness of an ancient authority to which appeal is made or the witness of someone to recent events, belongs to nontechnical proofs and is inferior to the arguments the orator invents himself, because it makes judgment dependent on something external.

A third dimension of testimony becomes apparent when attention is paid to the act of witnessing and the character of the witness that it reveals.[24] Here Ricoeur begins with the notion of false testimony. This is not simply making an error in the account one gives. Rather, "false testimony is a lie in the heart of the witness. This perverse intention is so fatal to the exercise of justice and to the entire order of discourse that all codes of morality place it very high in the scale of vices." Similarly, then, a true or faithful witness is something other than an exact or scrupulous narrator. Ricoeur does not use the terminology of speech-act, but it is appropriate here. Testimony is a speech-act by which a witness professes

---

[24] Ibid., 128–30.

publicly a conviction, indicates devotion to a cause. Ricoeur makes use of the play on the Greek term μάρτυς to evoke the notion of the witness as one who is so identified with a cause that he or she is willing to stake his or her life on it. Ricoeur holds that with this notion one has moved from the juridical dimension because in a trial it is the person who is accused, rather than the witness, whose life may be at stake. This may be the case in most legal conventions and therefore in ordinary language usage, but it ignores ancient Jewish legal conventions reflected in the biblical lawsuit. In the latter, as we have seen, when two parties are pressing their claims against one another, the witness for one party can at the same time be the one who is accused by the other side in the dispute.[25] At any rate, this dimension emphasizes that testimony goes beyond mere narration. It is the sort of narration that implicates the witness, that signifies the engagement of the witness with that to which testimony is borne, an engagement in which life itself may be risked. As such, "testimony is the action itself as it attests outside of himself, to the interior man, to his conviction, to his faith."

Clearly, this is where the religious dimension of testimony becomes most apparent. In the third part of his essay, Ricoeur turns to biblical interpretation and points to what he calls the "irruption of the prophetic and kerygmatic dimension."[26] This process of analysis is part and parcel of Ricoeur's broader approach to symbol and metaphor and what he speaks of as their "double meaning." So far he has observed a variety of functions of testimony language with its juridical connotations in ordinary language. Now he moves to look at its second level—to the way it functions in religious discourse—and to explore the relation between the two levels. In other words, we are looking at metaphor with its ability to produce new possibilities for viewing human life in the world.

Not surprisingly in the light of our discussion of the Jewish Scriptures in chapter 2, above, he turns first to Isa 43:8–13.[27] He points to four elements in this passage. First, the witness does not simply volunteer but is sent, and so "originally, testimony comes from somewhere

---

[25] In an essay originally written later but appearing earlier in the same volume as "Hermeneutics of Testimony," Ricoeur appears to have recognized this point: "But a witness can become the accused and the righteous may die. Then a great historical archetype arises: the suffering servant, the persecuted righteous, Socrates, Jesus . . ." ("Toward a Hermeneutic of the Idea of Revelation," in Ricoeur, *Essays on Biblical Interpretation,* 113).

[26] Ricoeur, "Hermeneutics of Testimony," 130–42.

[27] Ibid., 131–34.

else." Second, because it is Yahweh to whom testimony is borne, "the witness does not testify about isolated and contingent fact but about the radical, global meaning of human experience." Third, the testimony to be given by Israel has as its aim proclamation to all nations. And fourth, it entails "a total engagement not only of words but of acts and, in the extreme, in the sacrifice of a life." The last point is not evident from this passage itself, and so it is strange that Ricoeur is reluctant to make any connection between the notion of the witness and that of the suffering servant,[28] which might have provided some justification for this interpretation.

Nevertheless, the overall implications Ricoeur goes on to draw about the significance of testimony in the prophetic context are well grounded. He particularly wishes to underscore that "what separates this new meaning of testimony from all its uses in ordinary language is that the testimony does not belong to the witness. It proceeds from an absolute initiative as to its origin and content." At the same time, he underlines that this religious dimension takes up elements from the everyday, and particularly the juridical, dimensions. Regarding the latter, testimony is made in the context of a trial, in which "the right of Yahweh to be and to be the only real God" is at stake, and this trial between Yahweh and the nations and their idols calls for a decision between their claims. Ricoeur also stresses that the religious dimension can include the quasi-empirical. He does this by making the general point that Israel's faith included a confession of Yahweh through a narrative of Yahweh's acts of deliverance in history, as in Deut 26:5–9. As we have seen, this point could have been made from Isa 40–55 itself, with its concern about the relation of Yahweh's word of prediction and its fulfillment in history. Ricoeur is, in any case, at pains to clarify that a theology of testimony is not simply a theology of confession of faith. Although a judgment has to be made by one who has not seen on the basis of the witness of one who has, "there is no witness of the absolute who is not a witness of historic signs, no confessor of absolute meaning who is not a narrator of the acts of deliverance."

Within the NT the confessional aspect of testimony is central—witness to Jesus as the Christ—but Ricoeur employs the Acts account to show that this includes eyewitness testimony, especially about resurrection appearances (cf. Acts 2:32; 3:15; 5:32; 13:30–31), so that confession and narration are inseparable in this testimony in a way that only "a

---

[28] Ibid., 132.

modern mind, formed by historical criticism," finds problematic.[29] He notes, however, that there remains a tension between the two, since later witnesses, particularly Paul, "will be less and less eyewitness to the extent that faith will be transmitted by the hearing of preaching." In an interesting comparison, Ricoeur places Luke more at the narrational pole and John more at the confessional pole of testimony. His statistics about John's use of testimony language appear strange[30] until we realize that, here and in what follows, when he speaks of John or even of the Fourth Evangelist, Ricoeur in fact draws his evidence from the Gospel, the Johannine Epistles, and Revelation. In his view, because Revelation calls Christ "the faithful and true witness" (Rev 3:14; cf. 1:5) and the testimony of Jesus Christ is a synonym for the revelation of Jesus Christ (1:1–2), the Johannine writings move toward a testimony of manifestation. By this he means that Jesus' witness to God entails the Son's manifestation of the Father and that, in the Gospel, testimony is borne to this manifestation; for example, John the Baptist is designated a witness to the light (cf. John 1:7). Although John the Baptist's testimony appears to be that of an eyewitness (v. 34), Ricoeur points out that what he has seen depends on his reception of an interior word from God for any significance (v. 33).

For Ricoeur the two notions of faithful witness and a theological content to the testimony are linked by Jesus' declaration that he has come to bear witness to the truth (18:37). That Jesus bears witness to himself and that God also bears witness to him (cf. 8:14; 5:37) is seen as an "internalization of testimony." The thought of 1 Jn 5:9–10 ("If we receive human testimony, the testimony of God is greater; for this is the testimony of God that he has testified to his Son. Those who believe in the Son of God have the testimony in their hearts") and the notion of the testimony of the Spirit found in John 15:26–27 provide Ricoeur with further evidence of this internalization. Despite this emphasis, Ricoeur claims that the eyewitness element of testimony is not totally neglected. In the Gospel the witness of Jesus' works (cf. 5:36; 10:25) and the fact that witness is "not testimony to an idea, to an atemporal *logos*, but to an incarnate person" indicate the external aspect of testimony and allow Ricoeur to assert that "testimony-confession cannot be separated from testimony-narration without the risk of turning toward gnosticism."

---

[29] Ibid., 134–42.
[30] Cf. ibid., 136.

Ricoeur does not fail to observe that John takes up the juridical dimension and to stress that the juridical is the key link between the ordinary usage and the religious. His brief observations here have already been covered in the earlier more detailed analysis of our study. Indicating his indebtedness to the essay by Preiss,[31] Ricoeur sees the ministry of Jesus and his trial as episodes in the "cosmic trial," the contest between God and the prince of the world. The faithful witness of Christ therefore takes place "in the framework of a suit over rights," a setting of confrontation and accusation, in which he is the emissary who evokes the judgment on the world. So Christ is both witness and judge. "By a strange reversal, the defendant of the earthly trial is also the judge of the eschatological trial. For the Christ, to be witness is to join these two roles of the earthly accused and the heavenly judge." For Ricoeur it is also this juridical dimension that proves determinative for the Johannine perspective on the Spirit and on suffering. The internal testimony of the Spirit (cf. 1 Jn 5:5–8; John 15:26–27) derives its meaning from the eschatological trial, as does the act of martyrdom (cf. Rev 12:11). In closing his sketch of this biblical material, Ricoeur makes an important suggestion that has been emerging implicitly from his discussion: "Could we not say, then, that it is the juridical moment which ties together the two moments which had appeared to us to be at the point of being dissociated: testimony as confession (of faith) and testimony as narration (of facts)?"[32]

With this suggestion the essay finally returns to the philosophical issues with which it began.[33] The main issue is posed this time in terms of how to bridge the gap between "the interiority of original affirmation and the exteriority of acts and of existence which would claim to give testimony of the absolute." This also entails the question "Do we have the right to invest a moment of history with an absolute character?" The likely contours of the response will already have become apparent. Ricoeur claims that what is needed is a philosophy of interpretation, and this philosophy has to be, he suggests, "an ellipse with two foci"—the historical and the reflexive, which can come together but never be reduced to a unity. Testimony provides the point of convergence because involved in the interpretation of testimony are both "an act of historical understanding based on the signs that the absolute gives of itself" and "an act of consciousness of itself." Indeed, "the signs of the absolute's

---

[31] Cf. Preiss, "Justification in Johannine Thought," 9–31.
[32] Ricoeur, "Hermeneutics of Testimony," 142.
[33] Ibid., 142–53.

self-disclosure are at the same time signs in which consciousness recognizes itself." Precisely what is meant by consciousness recognizing itself will be clarified later. Ricoeur begins to demonstrate the convergence of the historical and the reflexive, however, by stressing that testimony both gives a content to be interpreted and calls for an interpretation. In the giving of content, we return to the notion of manifestation of the absolute, seen at its clearest in John's Gospel. Here Ricoeur is unapologetic. "In testimony there is an immediacy of the absolute" that makes interpretation "the endless mediation of this immediacy." Yet without testimony to the absolute, "interpretation will forever be only an interpretation of interpretation . . . condemned to an infinite regress in a perspectivism with neither beginning nor end."[34]

Discussing the interpretation that testimony demands, Ricoeur draws on the three dimensions of the ordinary use of testimony, which, in his discussion of the NT material, he has claimed are taken up in the religious dimension. First, testimony calls for interpretation because of its internal dialectic of meaning and event, confession and narration. In the NT there is a unity of the two, "there is no separation between the Jesus of History and the Christ of Faith." Yet there remains a tension because the relation of the two still calls for interpretation and the event to which testimony is borne is both apparent and hidden. This is to allude to an idea that looms large in Ricoeur's writings, that, like symbols and metaphor, revelation both reveals and conceals, discloses and hides.[35] In the early church, Ricoeur points out, the process of interpretation was one in which the manifestation of the absolute in the person of Jesus was indefinitely mediated by means of available meanings taken primarily from Jewish tradition, in the form of such concepts as Christ, Son of Man, high priest, or Logos. Second, the juridical dimension of testimony also indicates that testimony requires interpretation, since what is given evokes a crisis of decision between false and true witness. There is "no manifestation of the absolute without the crisis of false testimony, without the decision which distinguishes between sign and idol," because "the works and signs that the revealer 'gives' are so many bits of evidence and means of proof in the grand trial of the absolute." Third, Ricoeur refers back to his point about the involvement of the witness in his or her testimony to the point of suffering. It is not entirely clear from Ricoeur's own discussion how this shows that testimony requires interpretation, but the thought appears to be that although martyrdom may

---

[34] Ibid., 144.

[35] Cf. esp. Ricoeur, "Toward a Hermeneutic."

prove nothing, a testimony that produces such a sacrifice does demand to be accounted for in some way.

Ricoeur is now ready to elaborate on the reflexive pole and to show the relation between original affirmation and testimony. The key lies in the link he makes between original affirmation and the "criteriology of the divine," terminology drawn from the philosophical theology of Jean Nabert,[36] who had already linked interpretation of the absolute with the notion of testimony. Human consciousness, says Ricoeur, as we observed at the beginning of this exposition of his essay, has to become aware of the affirmation of life that constitutes it, and it has to do so in a critical act. This act involves negation before affirmation, since consciousness must first divest itself of all impediments to affirmation, all illusory attempts to justify itself by means of anything finite, in order to come to an awareness of affirmation freed from limitations, which is at the same time an awareness of the absolute. In this way original affirmation corresponds to the criteriology of the divine because inherent in it is an act of judgment that distinguishes between the absolute and idols, that "sifts the predicates of the divine." The judgment called for by testimony and the judgment in which self-consciousness is laid bare prove to be part of the same trial. The dialectical nature of the alliance between the external and the internal judgments, claims Ricoeur, is precisely what one should expect when dealing "with the perception of the divine by and in a finite consciousness. It is, in effect, a fact of finitude that original affirmation cannot appropriate itself in a totally intuitive reflection but that it must make a detour through an interpretation of the contingent signs that the absolute gives of itself in history."[37] Thus, finite humans cannot know themselves directly; they can only come to knowledge of themselves indirectly by taking a detour that entails interpretation of the signs of the absolute, and in this essay that means interpretation of testimony.[38] To believe otherwise, Ricoeur asserts, would be to follow Hegel down the illusory path of absolute knowledge. Absolute knowledge makes the mistakes of attempting to fix "the criteriology of the divine in a closed system" instead of allowing for an advance in self-consciousness; of attempting to bring all the signs of the absolute to-

---

[36] Cf. J. Nabert, *Le désir de Dieu* (Paris: Aubier, 1966), 265.

[37] Ricoeur, "Hermeneutics of Testimony," 148–49.

[38] In his introductory essay to Ricoeur, *Essays on Biblical Interpretation,* Mudge formulates Ricoeur's own work in these terms: in contrast to Heidegger, "Ricoeur takes the long route. He proceeds by way of the hermeneutical 'detour'" (p. 13).

gether in a coherent whole instead of allowing for the uniqueness and newness of such signs demanded by their temporality; and of trying to identify reflection and testimony instead of permitting them a reciprocal relationship. Absolute knowledge of the absolute either in internal or external judgment is impossible for the finite human consciousness.

We see in the above reflections not only Ricoeur's critique of Hegel's idealism but also the immense importance, for the notion of "the criteriology of the divine," of the trial between God and the idols of the nations in Isaiah and of the judgment between true and false testimony in John. This act of judgment necessary for original affirmation is also illumined by setting it within the broad sweep of Ricoeur's work, with its two well-known moments of a hermeneutics of suspicion and a hermeneutics of retrieval. The former involves an exposing and judging of idols that are projections of human false consciousness. This allows a listening with openness to symbols and metaphors. "*The idols must die—so that symbol may live.*"[39] Testimony and the judgment about it allow both to take place.

What remains is the hermeneutics of testimony, with its double judgment and therefore double trial. This again underlines Ricoeur's general dictum that "to interpret is to understand a double meaning."[40] In comparison with the scientific ideal of absolute knowledge, such a hermeneutics will always appear to be relative. And "there is no apodictic form of a response to the recurring question: how do we assure ourselves that the affirmation is not arbitrary, that God is not constructed, almost picked, from certain testimonies that other consciousnesses could contest, since there indeed is no fact which can be dissociated from the idea which gives meaning to it, a meaning that transcends the fact itself."[41] The juridical dimension of testimony means that it is always contestable, its interpretation only probable. Whether at the reflexive or the historical pole, interpretation will always be different from verification in the sense of logical empiricism "because the manifestation of that which reveals itself is inseparable from an adherence which implies a choice and because this choice is produced in a trial akin to the criteriology by which the reflexive act gives account of itself." Yet Ricoeur wants also to say that something of the absolute is retained in interpretation, both at the internal and at the external poles. The self-manifestation of the absolute "confers on a finite revocable act of recognition

---

[39] Ricoeur, *Freud and Philosophy*, 531. See esp. A. C. Thiselton, *New Horizons in Hermeneutics* (London: HarperCollins, 1992), 344–78.

[40] Ricoeur, *Freud and Philosophy*, 8.

[41] Ricoeur, "Hermeneutics of Testimony," 149–50.

the seal of its own absolute. This is why one can indeed say paradoxically that the hermeneutics of testimony is *absolute—relative."* The judgments in this hermeneutics rest on two acts—the act of self-consciousness in divesting itself of limitations so as to proceed toward original affirmation, and the act of testifying mediated by the story of the witness and through which the absolute is revealed in its signs. The two remain distinguishable but are in a reciprocal relation. In other words, one could say that what remain discrete but in a circular relation in the double trial that constitutes the hermeneutics of testimony are philosophy and religion, reason and faith.

The emphasis on the probability rather than absolute knowledge of interpretation and on the necessity of choice between conflicting testimonies recalls Ricoeur's discussion elsewhere on the need to wager that one set of symbols will give more meaning than some other set. "How shall we get beyond the 'circle of hermeneutics'? By transforming it into a *wager.* I wager that I shall have a better understanding of man and all beings if I follow the *indication* of symbolic thought. That wager then becomes the task of *verifying* my wager and saturating it, so to speak, with intelligibility."[42] In terms of the circular relation of philosophy and religion, reason and faith, this puts the onus on the latter term in each pair. The commitment of faith is always necessary. Believing is needed in order to understand, and then understanding is needed in order to believe.

Ricoeur's essay attempts to weave together philosophy of religion, semantics, and biblical interpretation into a coherent hermeneutics of testimony. The first section of this chapter suggested that there is a general cultural space in which the Gospel's lawsuit motif can be experienced as effective. Ricoeur's analysis shows that there is also a philosophical space. Indeed, his essay is a stunning tour de force that helps to clear this space so that the lawsuit motif and testimony may be heard again.[43] It indicates that, despite the use—prevalent in twentieth-century literature—of the motif to depict a view of the universe as ultimately meaningless, the motif still has the power to evoke a view of human existence that is full of meaning. Still, the essay raises questions, some of which others have also posed about Ricoeur's work as a whole.[44] Is the function of the extended trial metaphor in Scripture *only*

---

[42] Ricoeur, *Symbolism of Evil,* 355.

[43] Cf. also Vanhoozer, *Biblical Narrative,* 288: "Ricoeur is not principally a Proclaimer. His is the more humble task of 'making space' for this proclamation."

[44] E.g., Vanhoozer, ibid., 119–47, who asks whether Ricoeur reduces the Christian kerygma to philosophy, and concludes that in the end "the goal of

to illumine human existence and its task of interpretation? The reader might well be left with this impression. For all its talk of testimony to the self-disclosure of the absolute in signs in history, the essay provides very little on the way testimony reveals God and illumines the divine perspective on human existence. And if we start with a phenomenology of human existence, even one that includes the absolute, does not this dictate that we will also end up with such a phenomenology? In the quotation in the last paragraph above, admittedly not from "Hermeneutics of Testimony," the wager of belief is about having a better understanding of human existence. Regarding testimony to signs in history, we are given little help in discerning which particular signs in history are essential for the testimony of, say, the Fourth Gospel with its confessional stance.[45] But expressing these reservations may be asking Ricoeur to become what he does not claim to be, namely, a theologian rather than a philosopher of religion. The insights of Ricoeur's analysis of the function of testimony are valuable, as is the suggestiveness of its correlation of the lawsuit motif with reflection on human existence and issues of interpretation. Still, a critical theological appropriation of the motif, especially one that does not wish to depend on any one general theory about the religious dimension of human experience, will need to take matters further.

It will need to do so in two ways. It will have to give the analysis of the motif more specific theological content, provide some reflection on this content, and clear away any misperceptions that surround it. It will also have to reflect on issues of historicity and ideology that are not explored by Ricoeur. Regarding the former, a theological appropriation can move relatively easily from Ricoeur's discussion of human consciousness in relation to the absolute to the Judeo-Christian language of humans created in the image of God with an innate sense of deity. It can develop his notion of human fallibility and tendency to idolatry in terms of the theological category of sin and explore further the way in which the Christian gospel, in its witness to God's revelation in Christ, claims that this truth can set humans free for authentic living. In so doing, it will want, among other issues, to make clear what is being asserted about judgment and the nature of God as judge in the context of such a claim.

Ricoeur's hermeneutics, of the Bible or anything else, is self-understanding" (138).

[45] Vanhoozer, ibid., 257–66, is particularly critical of Ricoeur on this score, holding that his notion of testimony in the end is more about the reader's historicity than past events.

After all, Ricoeur himself asserts elsewhere that the religion that calls for suspicion is one "grounded in the fear of punishment and the desire for protection" and that one of the idols that needs to be abandoned is the notion of God as the Father who punishes.[46] A theological appropriation may also want to say more than Ricoeur's essay does on what we have claimed about testimony as the Fourth Gospel's own mode of discourse. It has been alleged that, in his overall views, Ricoeur does not sufficiently emphasize revelation as proclamation and that instead this tends to be overshadowed by revelation as manifestation.[47] It is not clear that this is the case in this essay. He does stress that Jesus' witness takes the form of the manifestation of the absolute, the manifestation of the Father by the Son, and he might have done more with the proclamatory aspects of Jesus' witness. But he also speaks of John's confessional testimony, and confession certainly involves proclamation. We can, however, attempt to take further the notion of the Gospel's witness to the manifestation as proclamation. It is a proclamation in narrative form that takes the shape of an inscripturated testimony.

As stated, a critical theological appropriation of the motif will also have to reflect on issues of historicity and ideology that are not explored by Ricoeur. In reaction to the dominance of historical-critical readings and because of his own views on the self-reference of a text, his interpretation of the text places all its emphasis on listening to the symbol and so tends to focus on the surface level of the narrative discourse. On a relatively trivial matter, one can see the neglect of historical criticism operative in his talk about John instead of the Gospel, the Epistles, and Revelation. But this becomes more noticeable when, despite his helpful remarks on the relation between witness to history and confessional witness, Ricoeur is content simply to leave these observations at the level of generality, so that there remains an ambiguity about the historical referentiality of narrative—and, in this case, testimony in the Fourth Gospel as part of the juridical motif. Yet in principle, his hermeneutical approach, with its distinctive talk of both suspicion and retrieval, allows, indeed calls for, historical criticism.[48] One may be sympathetic to Ricoeur's views about the difference between oral and written proclamation, and that it is the text and not what has taken place behind the text that is to be appropriated, but still hold that historical and other in-

---

[46] Ricoeur, *Conflict of Interpretations,* 441, 467.
[47] Cf. Vanhoozer, *Biblical Narrative,* 169–70.
[48] Cf. Thiselton, *New Horizons,* 361, 365.

vestigations may have some role in distinguishing between true and false testimony. Indeed, we may think that such investigations are indispensable if, as contemporary interpreters, we are to proceed to what Ricoeur in his famous formulation has called a "second naïveté."[49]

Particularly someone who comes to theological appropriation of the motif as a NT specialist will want to analyze further the particular combination of historical report and narrative refiguration that constitutes the use of the lawsuit motif in the Fourth Gospel. Chapter 6, above, has already engaged, to some extent, this question, and we shall return to the question of the truth of the narrative in the next chapter. And someone engaged in theological appropriation may well want to engage in ideological as well as historical criticism and ask about the legitimating purposes this juridical motif served and has continued to serve. We will likewise return to this issue, which also has been discussed in chapter 6. Since he acknowledges the real possibility of projecting one's own consciousness and its interests onto texts, Ricoeur ought to find these moves conducive to his program of both destroying the idols and listening to the symbols. The intent here is precisely that—to analyze the motif in such a way that, despite its historical and cultural conditionedness, its limitations and potential for abuse, we can return to it at the level of its narrative power and hear its claims afresh.

---

[49] Ricoeur, *Symbolism of Evil*, 351. Elsewhere Ricoeur, *Essays on Biblical Interpretation*, 44, admits, "The question of the referential claim of these stories remains unavoidable."

chapter eight

APPROPRIATING
the FOURTH GOSPEL'S
LAWSUIT: *Four Objections*

As a lead into a fuller exploration and appropriation of some of the theological implications of the claims of the Fourth Gospel's narrative, four major issues need to be briefly addressed. The first two are primarily issues that arise from typically modern approaches to knowledge; the third is an ethical issue of concern from both a modern and a postmodern stance, but it leads into a fourth that takes its force from a typically postmodern way of thinking.

A. Accepting Testimony and Exercising Critical Judgment

Our approach so far has included analysis of the Fourth Gospel's testimony from historical and sociological angles, but this has been part of a larger project that not only describes the witness of this Gospel's narrative but, from within a Christian perspective, holds that its testimony is to be accepted. We have referred to such an approach as critical appropriation. Is this a contradiction in terms for a Christian reading of a canonical text? What is the relation between accepting testimony and exercising critical judgment?

The issue can be put in a slightly different way. The Fourth Gospel leaves its readers in no doubt about the necessity of accepting its testimony to Jesus Christ. This clashes with the critical ethos and its frequent insistence that nothing be taken at face value and that valid knowledge is only knowledge discovered by people for themselves. Is there an irreducible conflict therefore between acceptance of testimony and critical scholarship? Does anyone who wishes to accept this text's testimony to Jesus Christ as the truth about God and about life in the world thereby forfeit the right to be considered critical?

The stance to be taken here can be stated simply. Both acceptance of the Gospel's testimony and critical judgment are required. Indeed, the initial act of acceptance entails the exercise of critical judgment. Talk of an initial act of acceptance need not be thought to mean that such acceptance takes place, for most readers, in direct encounter with the text of this particular Gospel. For many it will have taken place in relation to more general Christian witness to Jesus Christ and will have provided a predisposition to read this Gospel's witness with a trust in its basic truth and an expectation of finding this trust confirmed and deepened. Whether the disposition to trust is already present or is established through the reading of this Gospel narrative, it is itself a judgment—a radical one, to be sure, that by its very nature is willing to allow the testimony to Jesus to transform and reconfigure one's previous categories. In other words, it is the sort of judgment that is willing to be judged in the process of opening itself to the testimony. It is therefore also a judgment that does not suppose that it already has some indisputable criteria to which the testimony must conform if it is to be persuasive. But since, as Ricoeur puts it, "testimony is at the service of judgment,"[1] the belief this disposition entails—that the Gospel's witness to Jesus is in some sense true—is nevertheless a judgment. In Christian theological terms, this positive judgment about testimony is itself a result of grace and given by God. In specifically Johannine terms: "No one can come to me unless drawn by the Father who sent me" (6:44).

Further acts of critical enquiry and evaluation, then, take place from within a perspective shaped by this prior acceptance; they become part of the way in which faith seeks understanding. As seen in our discussion of Ricoeur, one makes a judgment that is a wager of faith in accepting testimony, and "that wager then becomes the task of *verifying* my wager and saturating it, so to speak, with intelligibility."[2] In practice, faith seeks understanding by learning to see both the connections and distinctions between the gospel of the death and resurrection of Jesus Christ as God's witness and the various inscripturated human witnesses to this basic witness. It is not, then, an acceptance of witness providing security

---

[1] Ricoeur, "Hermeneutics of Testimony," 124.
[2] Ricoeur, *Symbolism of Evil*, 355.

independent of our judgment of its truth. The process is similar to the way we grow in knowledge in any discipline. We start off by relying on the testimony of teachers and experts, and therefore this testimony has an authoritative role; but the function of this authoritative testimony is to lead us to judge for ourselves that what we have been taught is true. Christians enter into an authoritative tradition of understanding based on foundational testimony and, from within this tradition, come to judgments that both make its understanding their own and help to modify the continuing tradition.

In the context of the Church's tradition and experience and of a discriminating assessment of more general human knowledge and experience, such critical faith learns how the scriptural witness mediates the truth about Jesus Christ, where it challenges unbelief and nourishes faith, and where it may become necessary to judge particular formulations and expressions within the scriptural witness by the gospel to which it witnesses. Such judgments cannot be our initial attitude to testimony. In fact, "tradition binds us to things already said and to their truth claim before we submit them to research."[3] Our criticism is inevitably shaped by that which we criticize. Whether it makes this explicit or not, Christian theology has always recognized such a principle in its practice of reading and interpreting Scripture in the light of what it deems to lie at its center—God's self-disclosure in the death and resurrection of Jesus Christ. Indeed, all living traditions engage in just such debate and judgment about what constitutes their center. What is called for is a combination of acceptance of the Gospel's witness and the readiness to risk our own critical judgment on how this witness is to be appropriated and brought to bear on our own different circumstances. This is part of being a member of a particular witnessing tradition that, as it meets new situations, inevitably changes and develops.

This is quite different from any notion of a supposed autonomous critical reason. In fact, the acceptance of testimony about a matter of such fundamental significance constitutes an offense to our sense of the autonomy of the self.[4] But as Ricoeur has underlined, a hermeneutics of testimony will renounce any pretension that consciousness is able to constitute itself and will entail the acknowledgment of a sense of de-

---

[3] Ricoeur, *Time and Narrative*, 3:223.

[4] Ricoeur, "Toward a Hermeneutic," 109, claims that testimony "throws itself therefore against one fundamental characteristic of the idea of autonomy; namely, not making the inner itinerary of consciousness depend on external events."

pendence on the absolute. Such a hermeneutics also reminds us that historical and ideological judgments are themselves never free of interests and prejudices, that they are not carried out from a position of neutrality or autonomy. Since all critical reasoning operates within particular linguistic and cultural traditions, it functions within a worldview embodied in such traditions. Criticism that rejects the theological claims of the text is also, in its own way, just as much accepting of some other overall truth claim, whether it be that of Enlightenment positivism, with its ideal of autonomous reason, or of postmodern suspicion of all truth claims, which is in itself a truth claim. Thus, casting aspersions about a naive willingness to accept some particular truth claim is hardly to the point. Champions of the autonomy of critical reason in interpreting biblical texts are, in this sense, no less fideistic than those they accuse of being uncritical. But the abandonment of belief in the autonomy of critical judgment does not mean the abandonment of critical judgment. The latter now takes place within a perspective that is open to trusting the claims of testimony.

Witness to the broad basic significance of testimony can be drawn from what might seem to some a surprising quarter—the thought of Jacques Derrida. Derrida has given increasing consideration to the matter of testimony. Contrary to the popular misconception that deconstruction entails a nihilistic skepticism, he insists on the primacy and undeconstructibility of faith and testimony. While particular religions and beliefs can be deconstructed, "you cannot address the other, speak to the other, without an act of faith, without testimony. What are you doing when you attest to something? You address the other and ask, 'believe me.' Even if you are lying, even in a perjury, you are addressing the other and asking the other to trust you."[5] Derrida developed this thought earlier in an essay on faith and knowledge. He claims that testimony is a marvel, a miracle, that walks on the water or air of interpersonal space, in which I promise and you believe, and that without it everything would come crashing down.[6] Talk of crashing down evokes stock markets, and Derrida indeed takes the world of finance as an example of the credit built up by testimony. Even calculating economists and financiers believe what they are being told about the movement of

---

[5] In J. D. Caputo, ed., *Deconstruction in a Nutshell: A Conversation with Jacques Derrida* (New York: Fordham University Press, 1997), 22.

[6] Cf. J. Derrida, "Foi et savoir: Les deux sources de la 'religion' aux limites de la simple raison," in *La religion* (ed. J. Derrida and G. Vattimo; Paris: Seuil, 1996), 9–86, esp. 83–85.

money that takes place mainly through electronic signals. When one of the big players starts to lose confidence and belief in the testimony of the system evaporates, then the market, which has been held in midair by faith, does indeed crash.[7] Testimony highlights the universal structure of the promise: "When I speak to you, I am telling you that I promise to tell you something, to tell you the truth. Even if I lie, the condition of my lie is that I promise to tell you the truth. So the promise is not one speech act among others; every speech act is fundamentally a promise."[8] Deconstruction of particular speech-acts is dependent on faith in the promise that is testimony. In the end, however, Derrida's view remains unsatisfactory because of his inability to allow it to have any decisive impact in the area of knowledge. Everyday life, science, and philosophy all depend on faith and testimony, but this testimony is to what cannot be seen, to what there can never be any question of knowing.[9] As Caputo explains, "Witnessing takes place in the element of faith and justice, not in the order of knowledge and truth."[10] The value of testimony as a universal structure is indispensable, but actual testimonies are something else—they can be deconstructed.

The next chapter will return to Derrida, but here it is simply noted that his perspective on specific testimonies fits in with what remains a persistent idea: that accepting testimony cannot be part of the critical pursuit of knowledge and indeed violates one's right to pursue life according to one's own knowledge of what authentic living is about. Part of the reason is that neither modernity nor postmodernity is tolerant of the suggestion that there might be anyone who has the right to tell us what authentic life is and how to live it. But this general prejudice against accepting testimony is in fact belied by the way in which we live. The work of Coady is helpful here, with its persuasive argument that "our trust in the word of others is fundamental to the very idea of serious cognitive activity."[11] Austin made a similar point about testimony as part of communication: "It seems, rather, that believing in other persons, in authority and testimony, is an essential part of the act of com-

---

[7] Cf. J. Derrida, *Given Time: I. Counterfeit Money* (Chicago: University of Chicago Press, 1991), 92–96.

[8] Derrida, in Caputo, *Deconstruction in a Nutshell*, 23.

[9] Cf. J. Derrida, *Points-: Interviews, 1974–94* (ed. E. Weber; Stanford: Stanford University Press, 1995), 201.

[10] Caputo, *Deconstruction in a Nutshell*, 168.

[11] C. A. J. Coady, *Testimony: A Philosophical Study* (Oxford: Clarendon, 1992), vii.

municating, an act which we all constantly perform. It is as much an irreducible part of our experience as, say, giving promises, or playing competitive games, or even sensing coloured patches."[12]

The epistemological issue is, Can beliefs based upon testimony be considered part of knowledge? The gist of Coady's response is, "When we inquire into the basis of some claim by asking: 'Why do you believe that?' or 'How do you know that?' the answer 'Jones told me' can be just as appropriate as 'I saw it' or 'I remember it,' 'It follows from this' or 'It usually happens like that.' "[13] He claims that reliance on testimony is pervasive in what we regard as reasonable belief and knowledge in everyday and practical life as well as in all forms of scientific enquiry and theory and that its neglect and supposed unimportance have come about through the rise of an ideology that stresses the powers, rights, dignities, and autonomy of the individual person. Augustine and Aquinas both saw the role of testimony as providing true and highly advantageous belief but, because of a notion of knowledge as synoptic or scientific understanding—derived from Plato and Aristotle—hesitated to give it the status of knowledge. The tension is most acute in Augustine, who on a number of occasions does describe what has been learned from the testimony of others as knowledge.[14] In his work as a whole, Coady argues against the view of those who, holding to an ideal of "autonomous knowledge," will accept testimony only if it can be shown that reliance on it gives rational support to their beliefs because they can check observationally on the fact that testimony is truth-preserving. Instead he demonstrates that belief on the basis of testimony is in fact a form of knowledge and that reliance on testimony is as fundamental to the justification of belief as perception, memory, and inference are.

Frequently the acceptance of testimony is seen as a lack of integrity on the part of critical historians. One of the influential proponents of this view regarding historical criticism of biblical material has been Harvey. He explicitly makes what he calls "the radical autonomy of the historian" one of the premises of his methodology.[15] By this he means that historians accept no authority. Rather, it is critical historians who

---

[12] J. L. Austin, "Other Minds," in J. L. Austin, *Philosophical Papers* (Oxford: Clarendon, 1961), 82.

[13] Coady, *Testimony*, 6.

[14] Ibid., 3–23.

[15] Van A. Harvey, *The Historian and the Believer* (New York: Macmillan, 1966), 39–42.

confer authority on their sources.[16] Here he builds on and cites the critique of R. G. Collingwood about the role of testimony in historical investigation: "In so far as an historian accepts the testimony of an authority and treats it as historical truth, he obviously forfeits the name of historian."[17] The accounts of witnesses from the past cannot simply be trusted because they reflect and are shaped by particular cultural judgments and biases. But whether this last, more moderate statement about issues in judging testimony necessitates the earlier assertions of principle is another matter. It is not a matter of dispute that historical enquiry requires, among other procedures, an assessment of whether sources are trustworthy, a recognition of a witness's biases, a judgment about whether these biases discredit the witness, and a search for appropriate evidence to help one make such judgments. Nor is it a matter of dispute that historians would be unwise to treat any one witness or source as having unquestionable historical authority. The problem is the move from such observations to a conclusion about the value of testimony per se and the critical integrity of a historian who accepts any testimony.

Coady distinguishes two types of the latter conclusion.[18] The first, exemplified by Collingwood, he calls "the puritan response" to the issue of testimony. Collingwood's view is that acceptance of testimony "can never be historical knowledge, because it can never be scientific knowledge."[19] Instead scientific historical knowledge is the result of the inferential and systematic enquiry that is part of the autonomous historian's imaginative reenactment of the past. The second type of view of the autonomy of the historian regarding testimony Coady labels "the reductive response." This allows for some dependence on testimony in practice but holds that it must always be justified by the more basic evidence provided by the historian's own observations and inferences from those observations. Here the autonomous historian can accept testimony only if it gives support to knowledge arrived at by more reliable empirical and observational means. Hume's discussion of testimony falls into this category, and although Harvey sometimes relies on Collingwood for his views, as a whole they take the less radical form of asserting that a historian can accept no witness without the sort of critical examination of this

---

[16] Ibid., 42.

[17] R. G. Collingwood, *The Idea of History* (Oxford: Oxford University Press, 1970), 256.

[18] Coady, *Testimony*, 21–23.

[19] Collingwood, *Idea of History*, 257.

witness that determines, on other grounds than the witness itself, that the witness is to be treated as reliable. He provides an extended discussion about the necessity of appropriate warrants being in place for the evaluation of any testimony.[20]

Coady has no difficulty in showing that both forms of this autonomous stance toward testimony are untenable.[21] The thrust of his argument is this: Historical knowledge is no different from other forms of knowledge in its reliance on testimony. Clearly, the experience of an individual is insufficient to provide a check on the trustworthiness of most witnesses, especially ancient ones. In fact, therefore, the requirement for an empirical warrant becomes a communal one. But as soon as this is conceded, it is obvious that the individual historian has to rely on the observational and empirical experience of many other people, and this entails accepting their testimony at numerous points. To be skeptical of all testimony on principle, if the principle were carried through consistently, would make the task of the historian impossible. The rejection of the "puritan" and "reductive" approaches does not mean the acceptance of all testimonies in what Collingwood has caricatured as a "scissors and paste" approach to history, in which the historian simply constructs an account by piecing together and harmonizing the available witnesses. What it does mean is that in practice there will often be reasons to think particular witnesses are untrustworthy in certain respects but their cross-examination and sometimes rejection will take place within a framework that recognizes the vital nature of testimony for historical knowledge and is initially positive, rather than skeptical, toward its value.

This puts Coady's perspective on testimony in basic agreement with Donald Davidson's "principle of charity" in issues of interpretation and truth. Although Coady has some points of disagreement with the specifics of Davidson's truth-conditional theory of meaning and finds it excessively charitable, he holds its core idea to be defensible and confirmatory of the conclusions about the pervasiveness and status of testimony that he has reached by other means. This core idea is that, in order to interpret the speech of others, agreement must be optimized between us and them, so that we take their expressed beliefs to be largely correct. Only against a background of shared belief can differences and disagreements make sense.[22] Coady's version of this is that we must begin not with the

---

[20] Harvey, *Historian and Believer*, 49–64.

[21] On the reductive response, see Coady, *Testimony*, 79–100; on Collingwood, see ibid., 233–48.

[22] Cf., e.g., ibid., 199–200.

assumption of having to prove that testimony is true but "with an inevitable commitment to some degree of its reliability. . . . Cultural values and physical circumstances will play their part in determining just how reliable local testimony will be and, once we abandon illusory justificatory endeavours which allow no rationality to any prior trust in any testimony, we can investigate the facts of such matters."[23] For Coady, once testimony is not isolated from certain broad facts of cohesion and coherence, there is epistemic legitimacy to "the strong commitment to trusting the word of others that is embodied in our actual cognitive procedures."[24]

Acceptance of the religious aspects of a text on the basis of its own testimony is no different in principle, therefore, from what we have observed about acceptance of testimony in other spheres of knowledge. This is corroborated from a quite different angle of approach in Daniel Patte's explication of Greimas's structural semiotics.[25] Patte also acknowledges the aversion in our culture to accepting anything as true on the basis of testimony and points to the fact that, despite this, people are constantly accepting the word of so-called specialists or experts. He proposes that when one accepts the word of someone credited with religious authority, this is no different and one is entitled to hold that when one believes what such an authority says, one has a "true" belief. He shows how, for Greimas, this aspect of belief is central to the entire process of communication and that communication only takes place effectively when there is a "fiduciary contract" between the speaker and the receiver of a message.[26] It is not the case, he argues, that one believes a message to be true only when one has been able to pass a judgment on its validity. Rather, in many instances, one posits a fiduciary relationship with a speaker whom one regards as trustworthy, and views as true what one has accepted on this speaker's authority. There are other instances where one has doubts about or mistrusts a speaker and therefore does not accept his or her utterances as true. But these instances only underline the fiduciary contract entailed in coming to truth through the process of communication.[27] Biblical texts, because of their canonical status, are a prime example of religious discourses that are believed as true on

---

[23] Coady, *Testimony*, 173. For Coady on Davidson, see ibid., 152–76.

[24] Ibid., 176.

[25] Cf. D. Patte, *The Religious Dimensions of Biblical Texts* (Atlanta: Scholars Press, 1990).

[26] Ibid., 130.

[27] Cf. ibid., 131.

the basis of their authority.[28] Through the authority structure of this particular fiduciary contract, the texts bring about a transformation in the figurative world of the receiver of their message that defines the identity of this person.[29] Because this sort of believing is part of a discursive process, the text's message will frequently be mediated through a chain of belief whereby one receiver of the message will have come to belief through a prior receiver, and the chain can be traced back to an original revelation. Precisely this pattern of belief in testimony is characteristic of the Fourth Gospel's perspective. What is brought about through this process is in fact a set of convictions that now operate at the level of being self-evidently true.

Patte's analysis makes room for another sort of belief, namely, that arrived at as a result of reasoning or study. But significantly, Patte makes clear that this sort of belief in fact depends on the system of convictions a person already has through believing on the basis of testimony. "And since, as we well know, studying and reasoning cannot take place without presuppositions and preunderstandings (self-evident truths), it appears that this definition of believing refers to a dimension of faith in which the convictional character of believing is occulted."[30] What this aspect of belief really amounts to is the assumption of personal responsibility for one's system of convictions by self-consciously reflecting on these convictions and evaluating them. Again, but this time via Patte's exposition of Greimas's generative trajectory of semiotic systems, we see that the exercise of critical theological and ethical reflection already presupposes belief based on acceptance of testimony.

In his magisterial *Theology of the Old Testament,* Brueggemann makes extensive and helpful use of the category of testimony, rightly pointing out that an appeal to testimony requires a break with positivistic epistemology and a different attitude to certitude. In the course of his discussion, however, he employs, in a way that raises some questions, the analogy with general courtroom procedures to make a point about the acceptance of testimony and revelation.[31] It might seem pedantic to quibble with an analogy, but since it is one that takes on considerable importance for Brueggemann's theological claims, it is worth exploring in the hope of clarifying our own perspective. Brueggemann rightly states, "In any trial situation the evidence given by witnesses is a mixed

---

[28] Cf. ibid., 132.

[29] Cf. ibid., 137.

[30] Ibid., 174.

[31] Brueggemann, *Theology of the Old Testament,* 120–22.

matter of memory, reconstruction, imagination and wish."[32] He might then be expected to say that it is the task of a jury to sift this testimony and come to their own reconstruction of whether it is true. Instead he continues, "The court must then determine, *with no other data except testimony*, which version is reality [my emphasis]. It is on the basis of *testimony* that the court reaches what is *real* [his emphasis]."

Two observations may be made about this construction. First, although he will go on to say that there are competing versions of what the reality under dispute is, Brueggemann predominantly focuses on the situation where the court has to decide about reality on the basis of one testimony, and indeed argues that when the court decides to accept such a testimony as true, it becomes true; the court's verdict establishes it as legal reality. This appears to ignore that in most cases a court does not hear just one testimony. If, for example, a defendant testifies in a road accident case, the jury will have to take into account the testimony of a surviving victim of the accident, of others who may have seen the accident, of police about the defendant's alcohol level, of medical experts about whether the defendant or the victim had a physical condition that precipitated the accident, and so on. The court may well decide on the basis of testimony but will have to do so by exercising independent judgment and deciding from the conflicting evidence what is likely to have happened. It is doubtful, then, whether Brueggemann's further point will hold, that the court "cannot go behind the testimony to the event, but must take the testimony as the 'real portrayal.' Indeed it is futile for the court to speculate behind the testimony."[33] For as soon as there are conflicting testimonies, this is precisely what the court has to endeavor to do—to make its own reconstruction of the event by sifting the conflicting testimonies or to accept one testimony rather than others on the basis of its more likely correspondence to what happened as the court perceives it.

The second observation is related. The jury will not come to its judgment with no other data except testimony. Extralinguistic factors come into play. The jury also have the data of their own experience, perhaps of driving or being a pedestrian at the same site, but certainly of similar situations, of people's actions and motives, of how people tell their stories, including their body language; all these, not simply the testimony of the defendant, will be influential in coming to a verdict. One

---

[32] Ibid., 120.
[33] Ibid., 121.

could choose to call such data testimony because, in recalling such relevant data, jurors will implicitly be constructing their own versions of reality against which they test the testimony of the defendant and others, but Brueggemann does not take this tack and ignores at this point the factors that go into the jury's weighing of testimony.[34] How true is it, then, to claim that "the utterance leads reality in the courtroom, so that the reality to which testimony is made depends completely on the utterance"?[35] The utterance of the witness is only one factor on which the contested reality depends. The final point Brueggemann makes, namely, that by the verdict of the court the testimony is turned into reality, also suffers from oversimplifying the courtroom analogy. The verdict of a court does not necessarily establish any witness's testimony as reality. More frequently the verdict is a decision whether the defendant is to be acquitted or to be found guilty. As already seen, such a decision is not simply made on the basis of the defendant's testimony. It is a verdict about the defendant's status in regard to the law on the basis of the jury's construal of the evidence. The verdict does constitute a new reality, but it is the verdict and not simply a testimony that does so. And it is not any testimony as such that now becomes reality but the legal status of the defendant through the pronouncement of guilt or innocence.

It appears, then, that Brueggemann's analogy may be too problematic to help his case; some of his points might have been better supported if he had remained with the biblical trial metaphor instead of appealing to general court procedures. But it also prompts further thought about the main theological claim he is attempting to make, that when human testimony about God in the Bible is accepted by the faithful, it becomes revelation, a disclosure of the reality of God, and that therefore "the utterance is everything,"[36] the formulation of the witness establishes the truth about God. Even this formulation contains the seeds of its own deconstruction through the notion of the acceptance of the faithful. One might be sympathetic to such a theological account, and certainly a divine witness's utterance or even a human claim for the divine witness might be expected to be constitutive of reality. But not only does this scarcely follow from the general courtroom analogy; it

---

[34] Elsewhere he does speak about the need for interpreters to construe Yahweh's character from Israel's testimonies (e.g., ibid., 267), about the court's cross-examination (p. 317), and about the court's decision changing the shape of the world (p. 750).

[35] Ibid., 121.

[36] Ibid., 122.

also leads one to suspect that just as in the analogy Brueggemann's depiction left out factors other than the one witness, so here his discussion ignores similar factors affecting the reader or the recipient of revelation. Once these come into play, then the logical emphasis that follows is that the recipients have to make a judgment concerning the testimony about God, and it is their judgment—on the basis of the testimony, to be sure, but including other factors—that determines whether the testimony is revelation. It is no longer the utterance that is everything; the recipients' judgment about the utterance becomes just as significant, if not more so.

One could pursue the theological question of whether revelation only becomes revelation when it is received or perceived as such. But the main purpose of this interaction with Brueggemann's discussion is to suggest that although it may not be helpful to his particular theological claim at this point, a more nuanced view of the general status of testimony in the courtroom indeed holds true regarding the question of appropriating the witness of the Fourth Gospel. Contrary to a pure theology of the word that calls for a straightforward acceptance of testimony, we cannot afford to ignore that, as the jury of real readers, we inescapably are involved in judging the testimony and evaluating it in relation to our experience of the world, experience that may indeed have been partially formed by the testimony in the first place. The call for an unqualified acceptance of the testimony as divine testimony also allows no distinction between the disclosure that takes place in Jesus as the divine witness and the human testimony to this witness that constitutes the Fourth Gospel. In other words, the critical moment is critical. At the same time, it is a moment and not the whole of the interpretive enterprise. Hence the heading for this section of the chapter—critical appropriation of the Fourth Gospel's testimony. We cannot dismiss this testimony just because it is testimony; on the other hand, it is not the case that we have no alternative but simple and total acceptance of it because it is testimony.

The position espoused here, then, is that a hermeneutics of testimony involves a hermeneutics of trust. Brueggemann says it well: "At some important level, faith consists in a willingness to live in the world of this utterance, and to accept as reliable its speech as testimony."[37] Basic trust is the willingness to look for life where God tells us to look for it. Yet this does not mean that there is no room for suspicion. Indeed, a hermeneutics of suspicion is at times essential for our well-being, and

---

[37] Ibid., 722.

in relation to the Fourth Gospel, in a number of places we have seen that suspicions about the ideology behind the narrative's testimony to the lawsuit motif can be raised and need to be faced. But it does mean that, for any relationship and communication, trust is more basic than suspicion. If we rigorously and systematically suspected every statement, we would not be able to proceed. This also entails that we must have the presumption that a testimony and the witness who gives the testimony are worthy of trust.

In the Fourth Gospel's own terms, acceptance of witness may involve dispensing with false notions of human autonomy, but it does not lead to some abject intellectual servitude. Instead its claim is that, through the witness of Jesus' word, one knows the truth and the truth sets one free (8:31). This is a freedom from sin and its slavery and therefore from the illusion of autonomy over against God, which always manifests itself in enslavement to some other power. For the Fourth Gospel the root of slavery lies in alienation from God and the alienation from others that is a consequence. Acceptance of Jesus' witness and the Gospel's witness about him entails therefore giving up the notion of self-sufficiency in order to discover the true freedom in dependence that results in the power to love and in the promotion of life rather than death. "If the Son makes you free, you will be free indeed" (8:36) is, as we have seen, addressed in its context to those whose slavery to sin takes a religious form—closing oneself to God's activity in Jesus while invoking God in the process (cf. 8:41–42). Such refusal to accept the witness of the living God is to condemn oneself to remain in the alienation of autonomy that is death (cf. 8:24), to be captive to the lie and to be unable to hear the truth (cf. 8:43–47). The lawsuit with the world has been instigated in order to reverse the situation of death, and because its judgment and cause are summed up in Jesus, it can be said that either the truth or the Son will accomplish the liberation of the verdict that brings life. So it is not that people need to claim or assert their freedom as the only way to the truth. Rather, real freedom only comes from knowing the truth.

Part of the continuing offense of this narrative's message is its view that people are not simply free inquirers after truth from a position of neutrality. We are alienated from the truth, indeed hostile to it, so that, as in this section of the Gospel, our typical reaction, when we are confronted with it, is to attempt to do away with it. Whether the purported autonomy that appears so precious is that of the individual or of a religious or a political system, its end is slavery in all its varieties, whether to one's self-image, tradition, consumerism, or state tyranny. The claim of this testimony in the trial of truth is that the willingness to accept its witness is not to give up one's freedom—such freedom does not in any case really exist—but is to experience the truth of the judgment that is able to liberate one from the system of death, with its illusions and lies, in order to be truly human in the world.

If, in the debate in John 8, slavery to sin takes the form of clinging to one's religious tradition instead of opening oneself to what God is now doing in Jesus, this slavery to the system of sin and death is seen in its political dimensions in the trial before Pilate. In both contexts Jesus embodies the truth of God's salvific judgment, which brings freedom. Jesus' witness to the truth before Pilate relativizes this world's structures of power. The claims of God in the cosmic lawsuit are brought to bear on Pilate as the representative of the empire, and because they are brought to bear through a vulnerable witness and a crucified judge, they function to judge and subvert any claim to ultimacy on the part of imperial power. Pilate discovers there is a choice to be made between Jesus and the emperor. Followers of Jesus again discover that their acceptance of his witness is not an abandonment of freedom but, rather, the prerequisite for a liberation from the tyranny of Caesar's hold on power and from every oppressive system or ideology that plays a similar role.[38]

Since this witness takes the form of a narrative, there is a sense in which any acceptance of it can never be other than a critically engaged acceptance. The Gospel narrative discloses a world into which it invites its readers, and this narrative world becomes the context that is able to shape readers' beliefs and actions. Yet this world is not simply read off the text and accepted. Readers are involved in construing the text and constructing the world in the first place. It emerges only as a result of their critical engagement with the text. The authority of such a world lies not in its ability to compel acceptance but in its ability to persuade of its basic trustworthiness in the course of engagement with it.

In our most important human interactions, a relationship of basic trust is also a relationship of love with all its risks. The Fourth Gospel claims that, in choosing to accept its testimony, one is opening oneself to vulnerable love. In its lawsuit God does not force or manipulate; rather, testimony is the divine means of urging and persuading. Distinctive to this Gospel is its talk of mutual love between Father and Son and be-

---

[38] Cf. Rensberger, *Johannine Faith*, 118: "By giving allegiance . . . to Jesus as King, it [Johannine Christianity] lays the groundwork for an ongoing nonviolent resistance to every nationalism, every oppression, and every ideology that would play the role of Caesar."

tween Jesus and his followers. Jesus' witness has its origin in, and testifies to, his relationship of love with the Father (cf. 5:20; 10:17), and his followers' witness stems from, and points to, their relationship of love with him. Not only is it those whom Jesus loves (13:1) who are called to be witnesses, but also the ideal witness is precisely the *beloved disciple* or, as the Gospel itself formulates it, "the disciple whom Jesus loved."[39] The beloved disciple and Peter once again provide complementary models here. If the beloved disciple's insightful witness is the result of being loved, Peter's role, which will culminate in his laying down his life as a martyr, is characterized by his love for Jesus. "Do you love me?" he is asked three times, and three times he repeats his avowal of love in his rehabilitation (John 21:15–19). In accepting witness, one enters this relationship of love. Experiencing this same relationship will give insight to be a witness. The relationship of love makes exacting demands on its witnesses, including assumption of the varied risks of critical engagement with the subject matter of their testimony and of self-sacrifice, yet such witnesses trust that this relationship will sustain their witness.

B. The Truth of the Narrative of the Trial of Truth

What is the truth of this narrative about truth? Does it affect its claims to be a true witness if it is not a strictly historical record or if it is in fact historically inaccurate? If the creative artistry apparent in its narrative world makes it more of a work of narrative fiction rather like a historical novel, what claim to truth is involved? These are large questions that inevitably arise from discussions about the narrative world of the Gospels but are frequently not directly addressed.[40] Particularly where, as in the case of the Fourth Gospel, that world itself is dominated by claims about truth and testimony, such questions demand some reflection, however inadequate. Before presenting general observations, we shall address two more specific main angles of approach. The first is to briefly set our discussion where it belongs—within the conventions of ancient biography, of which the Fourth Gospel is a part by virtue of its taking up the genre of gospel. The second is to remind ourselves of the

---

[39] For some profound reflections on the significance of this epithet for the narrator and his narrative, see P. W. Gooch, *Reflections on Jesus and Socrates: Word and Silence* (New Haven: Yale University Press, 1996), esp. 232–33, 254–71, 285–88, 296–301.

[40] Tovey, *Narrative Art and Act,* 170–228, does have an extended discussion of these issues from a somewhat different angle, where he treats them under the category of the Fourth Gospel as a "display text."

way in which the language of witness functions in the Fourth Gospel and to explore further its implications.

1. The Gospel as Ancient Biography

What were the conventions of the subgenre of gospel within the broader genre of ancient biography? Ancient biographers operated on a continuum that stretched from history writing on one end through the encomium to the ancient novel or romance on the other. Indeed, the genre of *bios* was a flexible one, able to overlap with some of these other forms of literature.[41] Biographers were interested in the impact of their subjects, their significance for ethical and philosophical questions, and employed a mixture of techniques to elicit this impact and significance. Burridge uses the example of Tacitus's *Agricola* to point out that although a quarter of this biography is devoted to the final battle between the Romans and the Britons somewhere in Scotland, Tacitus gives none of the basic details about location or time but simply concentrates on the speeches of the two opposing generals before battle. Agricola, who was Tacitus's father-in-law, could have reminisced with him about his speech, but the speech by Calgacus, the Caledonian general, is clearly made up by Tacitus.

> It is extremely unlikely that an ancient Briton would have known about half of the Roman behaviour mentioned, let alone be able to denounce it in beautifully balanced Latin rhetoric—but neither Tacitus nor his audience would have dreamt of applying the modern connotations of "fabrication" to his work. The force of terse, pithy comments like "solitudinem faciunt, pacem appellant" ("they [the Romans] create a wilderness and call it peace," 30.5) is true, and an ethical challenge to Tacitus' audience, even if Calgacus could never have said it.[42]

The convention of presenting something that could have been said but, historically speaking, was not or that could have taken place but did not is described by later rhetoricians as myth. "The process of 'mythologizing' a man's life by using fiction to convey truth became one of the enduring features of biography."[43]

In her study of biography in late antiquity, which pays special attention to biographers such as Eusebius and Porphyry, Cox reflects further on the mix of what we would call "historical" and "fictional" elements in

---

[41] Cf. Burridge, *What Are the Gospels?* 61–69.

[42] R. A. Burridge, *Four Gospels, One Jesus?* (Grand Rapids: Eerdmans, 1994), 167–68.

[43] Cox, *Biography in Late Antiquity,* 8.

ancient biography, arguing that biographies of holy men, in continuity with earlier Greco-Roman biographies, were not so much representations as revelations, evoking the inner significance of their character's lives.[44] This could well be a description of the Fourth Gospel's biography of Jesus, with its emphasis on the significance of Jesus' life as the revelation of God. "In antiquity biography was not simply a subgenre of history. It had its own unique characteristics and sustained historical veracity was not one of them. To impugn the integrity of a Greco-Roman biography on the basis of factual discrepancy is to misconceive the literary tradition of the genre to which it belongs."[45] Momigliano also claimed that "the borderline between fiction and reality was thinner in biography than in ordinary historiography."[46] This might be taken to imply that "ordinary historiography" did have a clear borderline between fiction and reality, but this implication would be a highly disputed judgment.[47] In any case, it clearly means that it is an error to judge John's biography as witness by the canons even of ancient historiography, let alone of modern historical study.

Because of the flexibility of the genre of biography, however, there can be no absolute distinction between history writing and biography. Some biographies stayed closer to the conventions of historiography, and some did not. Plutarch in his *Lives* is an example of a biographer who can work quite closely to the conventions of historiography. But even here the individual *Lives* can vary considerably in the concern their author shows for history.[48] Pelling argues that, in Plutarch's biographies, as in ancient history writing, invention or free composition was a central feature but that there remained limits, even if these limits are surprising ones to us, to how far Plutarch would go in fabricating anecdotes. Frequently he tacitly rewrote any sources, elaborating and changing emphases and details, but in doing so, he may well have thought that he was creatively reconstructing history, retrospectively setting out what he perceived to have been the case regarding his subject's life, either on the basis of other incidents or from his own view of the subject's character.

---

[44] Cf. ibid., xii.

[45] Ibid., 5.

[46] A. Momigliano, *The Development of Greek Biography* (Cambridge: Harvard University Press, 1971), 56.

[47] See A. J. Woodman, *Rhetoric in Classical Historiography: Four Studies* (London: Croom Helm, 1988), esp. 197–215.

[48] See C. B. R. Pelling, "Truth and Fiction in Plutarch's *Lives*," in *Antonine Literature* (ed. D. A. Russell; Oxford: Clarendon, 1990), 19–52.

In this light Pelling claims, "It is simply that the boundary between truth and falsehood was less important than that between acceptable and unacceptable fabrication."[49] What counted was the plausibility of the portrait, and to achieve this, Plutarch was willing "to help the truth along."[50] Pelling suggests that, like Tacitus, one of the more scrupulous historians with a concern for history as enquiry, Plutarch would have had to admit that on occasions what he wrote was imagination rather than fact, but would have been surprised to be pressed on this, because he thought it was perfectly acceptable to use license to draw out the significance of history and to divert his audience in order to deepen their insight into his subjects. As Pelling puts it, for Plutarch, as a biographer with a historical bent, what we view as fabrications would fall into the category not of true or false but of "true enough."[51] This is not dissimilar to the view of the later biographer Eusebius, who declared himself ready to accept as having "the air of truth" imaginative reconstructions, "highly colored" statements, if they appeared likely.[52] What counted as historical truth was not, then, what could be authenticated by evidence but what was agreed in prevailing convention to be adequately plausible. This is the reason the term *history-like,* thought by some to be a weasel word avoiding hard questions of historical truth, is in fact entirely appropriate when used of ancient biographical narratives such as the Gospels.

Whereas lives of politicians and military leaders, such as those produced by Plutarch, naturally tended to stay closer to history writing, lives of philosophers and religious leaders or holy men were more idealized and were often used by adherents of a philosophy or a religious tradition as propaganda against competitors. In such biographies the writers' overall convictions are even more in play in their portraits of their subjects. From early on, writers such as Xenophon and Aristoxenus used legendary traditions, invented characteristic traits, and fabricated anecdotes, which they employed in a mix with more historical material to produce portraits of philosophers that functioned as claim and counter-

---

[49] Ibid., 43.

[50] Cf. also J. L. Moles, "Truth and Untruth in Herodotus and Thucydides," in *Lies and Fiction in the Ancient World* (ed. C. Gill and T. P. Wiseman; Exeter, England: University of Exeter Press, 1993), 120: "No serious ancient historian was so tied to specific factual truth that he would not sometimes help general truths along by manipulating, even inventing, 'facts.'"

[51] Pelling, "Truth and Fiction," 43, 49.

[52] Eusebius, *Hier.* 12. On this and on the way the creative license of myth can be regarded as true, see Cox, *Biography in Late Antiquity,* 74.

claim between rival philosophical schools.[53] Similarly, the later religious biographies were written in order to influence belief, and their subjects molded to fit and convey their biographers' visions of life or religious ideals. "Biographies of holy philosophers were creative historical works, promoting models of philosophical divinity and imposing them on historical figures thought to be worthy of such idealization."[54] In such biographies anecdotes were told if they were plausible rather than because the writers were concerned about their value as hard evidence; they were the vehicle for the biographers' ideals to take concrete form within a historically framed narrative, thereby creating verisimilitude. Similarly, the discourses attributed to their subjects were meant to be received as ones the subjects could have spoken; they therefore functioned as literary vehicles for conveying ideals through the historical subjects.[55] Their aim was not so much to reconstruct their historical subjects as to create convincing portrayals that captured the ideals they saw represented in these subjects. "Biographies were personal statements, statements which, though couched in religious and philosophical terms, addressed sociopolitical and cultural concerns as well. . . . If these works functioned not only to recall the significance of the life of a hero of the past but also to make sense of contemporary life, we must attempt to describe the historical context of the authors in order to discover situations that may have prompted their literary activity."[56]

Scholarly discussions of both history writing and fiction in the ancient world recognize that what some contemporary theorists are saying about the similarities between history and fiction was also the case, though for rather different reasons, in Greco-Roman writings. "We have long grown accustomed to hearing of late that history itself is a fiction, or rhetoric, or whatever. The ancients would not have found that a particularly surprising doctrine, inasmuch as they drew only a faint line between myth and history and, as Cicero put it, considered the writing of history an *opus oratorium*—a rhetorical work."[57] The combination of rhetorical and dramatic elaboration with the concern for seeking out the events of the past makes it extremely difficult to categorize ancient history writing as either fact or fiction. "Rewriting the past—the intrusion of fiction into what was

---

[53] Cf., e.g., Cox, *Biography in Late Antiquity*, 7–12.
[54] Ibid., 45.
[55] Ibid., 60–63.
[56] Ibid., 135.
[57] G. W. Bowersock, *Fiction as History* (Berkeley: University of California Press, 1994), 12, citing Cicero, *Leg.* 1.5.

taken to be history—becomes from this period of Lucillius and Martial an increasingly conspicuous feature of the Graeco-Roman world."[58]

What was said earlier about the role of speeches in biography obviously also holds for speeches in history writing and helps to make clear the role of what we would call fiction. Thucydides, often considered one of the more scrupulous ancient historians, in his famous passage about his historical method (*Hist.* 1.22.1), discusses reconstructing what a speaker would say about "what was necessary," indicating that his "conception of truth is becoming something much more complex than mere factual truth. His speech material is a mixture of factual truth and imaginative truth, specific truth and general truth."[59] And this license was extended to the fact of a speech as well as to its content. When it comes to deeds in the Peloponnesian War, Thucydides claims to have evaluated these as accurately as possible and to aim to establish clarity, but this allows also for deducing general truths about human nature (*Hist.* 1.22.2–4). The result is again a mixture of more factual reporting and "less solid generalizing material."[60]

Woodman goes further and shows that, despite his claims, Thucydides' narrative is not nearly as accurate as is usually thought and that instead what he has done is create "an impression of complete accuracy, in order to enhance the credibility of a narrative which is intended to demonstrate that the Peloponnesian War is the greatest of all."[61] In this light Woodman has even argued that "classical historiography is different from its modern namesake because it is primarily a rhetorical genre and is to be classified (in modern terms) as literature rather than as history."[62] Thucydides and Tacitus, as much as any others, were prepared to manipulate factual data for rhetorical purposes and therefore to include in their narratives events that might or could have happened. Still, historians required that there be a hard core of factual material and that the elaboration of it be plausible. They saw no contradiction in mixing what we would regard as true and false. Indeed, they were expected to use their considerable rhetorical skills to build the superstructure of their narrative around such a core.[63]

---

[58] Bowersock, *Fiction as History*, 9.

[59] Moles, "Truth and Untruth," 105–6.

[60] Cf. ibid., 109.

[61] Woodman, *Rhetoric*, 23. For his analysis of the relevant materials in Thucydides, see ibid., 1–69.

[62] Ibid., 197.

[63] Cf. ibid., 90–94.

Ancient theorizing about the novel did not have a clear-cut category called "fiction" or contrast the novel with truth but, rather, conceptualized the techniques of the novel by relating them to the historian's license to expand narrative with illustrative discourse and events and to aim for rhetorical verisimilitude.[64] Indeed, what was said of fiction by Sextus—that it must represent what would be plausible or credible for its readers—was precisely what was said by others of history.[65] Given the rhetorical dimension of history writing, invention was part and parcel of a writer's technique. *Inventio* was defined in the rhetorical handbooks as "the devising of matter true or probable which will make a case appear convincing."[66] The *narratio* of a forensic speech was where the facts of the case were meant to be set out, and historiography was seen as an extension of the *narratio*.[67]

The aim was persuasion, and here plausibility was more important than factual accuracy. Thus Cicero remarks, "The narrative will be plausible if in it there seem to be those things which are accustomed to appear in reality . . . if the event fits with the nature of those who do it, with general custom and with the belief of the audience."[68] Modern historians stress the quality of evidence, but in rhetorical writing *evidentia* meant vivid illustration.[69] The ancient historian "would see himself in the role of advocate and would know in advance, as it were, the case which he would have to make."[70] Convinced that a certain matter was true, the ancient historian would aim to relate whatever it was reasonable to imagine must have occurred. "The invention of circumstantial detail was a way to reach the truth."[71] Bowersock has suggested that parallels in both form and content may well indicate that the massive proliferation of fiction that began in the time of Nero, in the middle of the first century, was influenced by, rather than was an influence on, the fictional elements in the Gospel narratives or the oral versions that preceded these.[72]

---

[64] Cf.Gill and Wiseman, *Lies and Fiction*, esp. 88–146, 175–229.

[65] Cf. Bowersock, *Fiction as History*, 10–11, 51.

[66] Cicero, *Inv.* 1.9.

[67] See Woodman, *Rhetoric*, 84–88, 96–98.

[68] Cicero, *Inv.* 1.29.

[69] Quintilian, *Inst.* 4.2.63; 8.3.61.

[70] Woodman, *Rhetoric*, 87–88.

[71] T. P. Wiseman, "Lying Historians: Seven Types of Mendacity," in *Lies and Fiction* (ed. Gill and Wiseman), 146.

[72] Cf. Bowersock, *Fiction as History*, 121–43, although he too easily defines the Gospels as narrative fictions, neglecting the likely mix of history and fiction in their biographical genre (p. 123).

Such conclusions about ancient biography and ancient historiography make clear that it is not possible, even in the case of the writers most explicit about their concern for factual truth, for modern interpreters to distinguish clearly between what is rhetorical or imaginative and what is historically reliable. Both historians and literary critics are bound to try, but as Moles puts it:

> Can the literary aspect of ancient historiography be sliced off like icing from the Christmas cake? Emphatically, no. You can try to extract factual material from an ancient historiographical text, but (to change the metaphor) it is like cutting a vital organ from the body. You may or may not succeed (that depends on your surgical skill and the constitution of the individual body), but it will always be a messy business: you may take out more than you bargained for, and you cannot always be sure even which organ you should be pulling out.[73]

It is interesting to juxtapose Moles's perspective with that of a recent NT critic of the Fourth Gospel. In *Is John's Gospel True?* Casey brings together in a lucid and rigorous way historical data and arguments that he believes the majority of NT scholars would, for the most part, accept but whose necessary implications, as he sees them, they have been hesitant to draw because they know they have Christian believers among their readers. But truth is not simply scholarly honesty for Casey. He clearly holds that there is such an entity as historical truth, to which the Fourth Gospel fails woefully to conform. His answer to the question his title poses is a resounding no. This Gospel fails on two counts—historically and ethically (because of its anti-Judaism, which has fostered anti-Semitism). On the first count Casey claims that, using the tools of historical criticism and measuring John's account particularly against Mark's (about whose basic historicity he may well be too sanguine), it can be shown that John's Gospel is historically inaccurate and a distortion. He concludes that the rewriting of history in this Gospel is "the large scale preaching of falsehood. . . . It consists to a large extent of inaccurate stories and words wrongly attributed to people."[74]

The purpose here is not to quibble with Casey's detailed historical judgments, many of which are highly probable, or with his criticisms of more conservative scholars, most of which are extremely telling, but to point to the questionable premise he appears to share with many historical critics: that we can have this sort of confidence in establishing the facts about the historical Jesus and his mission from ancient biographical texts. This confidence is based on the premises of modern historiogra-

---

[73] Moles, "Truth and Untruth," 114.
[74] Casey, *Is John's Gospel True?* 197, 229.

phy, with its ideals of detached scholarship and objective knowledge. At one point Casey concedes that John's Gospel may well be within the range of what passed for historical writing in both the Jewish and Greco-Roman contexts of its time. Then, because it is now read from a different cultural perspective, he strangely rejects it for failing to do what it could never have done—that is, accord with the modern era's standards of historical accuracy—and therefore concludes it purveys falsehood.[75] One is left wondering whether he would also see this as the necessary verdict of modern readers about the rest of ancient historiography and biography.

Thus, not only is there Moles's question about the degree of success that modern historiographical tools can claim when dealing with the type of ancient literary evidence that texts such as the Gospels constitute; there is also the questioning of the very premises of modern historiography by more postmodern critics who point out the impossibility of discarding one's own perspective and interests. "The notion of a single neutral nonpartisan history is one more illusion engendered by the academic standpoint of the encyclopaedist; it is the illusion that there is a past waiting to be discovered, *wie es eigentlich gewesen* [*sic*], independent of characterization from some particular standpoint."[76] That our limited knowledge and tools are shaped by the interests that we pursue and are filtered through the cultures and traditions we inhabit means that we can only know in part, that there is no access to "pure facts," and that we are unable to reconstruct strictly objective accounts of what happened. To presume otherwise may not only exhibit overconfidence but also have hazardous consequences, because the claim to universal truth that is presupposed often serves to give legitimacy to very particular interests. Modern historical inquiry will continue to want to ascertain what is likely to have happened, but it will need to make clear the necessary qualifications that are attached to this quest in terms of probabilities and to be aware that, in seeking what happened, it is serving certain limited and specific interests that have no imperial claims on truth.

We see, then, the wide range of connotations of truth that need to be in play when an attempt is made to evaluate the Fourth Gospel's claims in terms of its genre, and therefore the mutual expectations of author and readers about such claims. Even some of the most sophisticated treatments of the Fourth Gospel neglect this context and proceed as if

---

[75] Ibid., 222–23.

[76] MacIntyre, *Three Rival Versions of Moral Enquiry* (Notre Dame: University of Notre Dame Press, 1990), 51.

contemporary notions of historical truth were in play at the time of the Gospel. In ancient readers' expectations, verisimilitude and plausibility were what counted if the narrative's message was to be persuasive, and we should not assume that they had the same notions about what rings true as do we. We can expect that, in line with ancient historians and biographers, the evangelist believed himself to be working with a core of factual data from the tradition—how extensive or minimal remains to be investigated—and composed a narrative that was an interpretive superstructure built around the core events.[77] We should also expect that if ancient readers were both disinclined and usually unable to disentangle the two, it will be much more difficult than is often thought by NT scholars to distinguish these elements with any certainty, especially from our distance in time. But by now it should also be clear that, in regard to the truth of the narrative in its own terms, such an attempt at disentanglement is unnecessary and inappropriate.[78]

2. The Gospel as Witness

From this perspective we can turn to a closer look at the Fourth Gospel and particularly assumptions that are regularly made about the Gospel's language of witness. Not infrequently the Fourth Gospel's language of seeing and testifying is held to be incontrovertible proof that its author is giving, or at least appealing to, eyewitness tradition and that this is meant to underline the historicity of his account. Sometimes the argument is framed in such a way as to appear to be recognizing the difference between the author's notion and modern notions of what might count as reliable history. For instance, it is asserted that these elements in the narrative make clear that whatever the modern critic might make of it, John's Gospel claims to be a reliable historical account.[79] The student of the Gospel is then left with the choice between its own claims and the findings of historical critics, and when conservative Christian interpreters carry on this discussion, good Christians are left in little

---

[77] Cf. Tovey, *Narrative Art and Act*, 226–27, 255, whose conclusion is that the Gospel is theologized history, "a theological elaboration upon an historical substratum." On the spectrum between history and fiction, however, he places it between "natural narrative" and "eyewitness account" (221–23). On the problems associated with the Gospel as eyewitness account, see below.

[78] Cf. ibid., 186: "A sharp distinction between 'fact' and 'fiction,' history and non-history, is to some extent misconceived. The question ought not to be put in those terms to the Fourth Gospel."

[79] Cf., e.g., Maccini, *Her Testimony Is True*, 245–46.

doubt where their choice should lie. On the other hand, as already seen, those who place a premium on critical scholarship can be just as forthright. Since the Fourth Gospel's historical assertions are demonstrably untrue, it is argued, this Gospel is to be rejected as a source of truth.[80]

Clearly, a much more wide-ranging discussion of the relation of scriptural authority to issues of historicity is possible. Here, however, our focus is narrower and is directed particularly on the notion of testimony. Both sides in the debate sketched above often ignore the fact that the use of eyewitnesses in a narrative can have functions other than to claim historicity. The device can be part of more inventive or fictional material, where, along with the related perspective of an omniscient narrator, it gives the writer's point of view authority by lending verisimilitude to what is being narrated. It is therefore by no means as clear as is often assumed that the Gospel's language of witness means that it is making claims to be a more or less straightforward historical account. This issue has already been raised earlier in this study when commenting on particular references and most recently has received our attention in the discussion of Ricoeur's work. We should recall Ricoeur's suggestive comparison of two poles within testimony—narrational and confessional—and his claim that while elements of both are found in Luke and John, Luke's use of the notion of testimony, with its stress on eyewitnesses to the resurrection, is more narrational but John's is more confessional and that John comes closest to Luke in the formulation of John 19:35.[81]

Ricoeur's observation is worth further examination. It is frequently argued that there are two stages to John's appeal to witness. The first is meant to convince readers that the narrative is true in the sense of a historically trustworthy account of Jesus' words and deeds. The second is then to persuade them to embrace the truth of the evangelist's claim about Jesus' identity.[82] But it is extremely doubtful whether this is how the appeal to witness functions. The witness is to the significance of the

---

[80] Cf., e.g., Casey, *Is John's Gospel True?* 217. For him, it is particularly the link between the historical inaccuracies and anti-Jewishness that makes the Gospel even more profoundly and disastrously untrue; cf. 2–3, 222–23.

[81] Cf. Ricoeur, "Hermeneutics of Testimony," 134–39.

[82] Maccini, *Her Testimony Is True,* 19. Boice, *Witness and Revelation,* 118–20, 135, and Trites, *Concept of Witness,* 114–15, work with a similar distinction. Tovey, *Narrative Art and Act,* provides a far more sophisticated account, but the distinction still appears to inform it at a number of points, e.g., 128, 143, 161, and 163, as the implied author's claim to be a witness is taken by Tovey to be based upon the real author's status as an eyewitness.

person of Jesus, and the narrative of Jesus' words and deeds is shaped and formulated in terms of this significance and to support the claims that are made for it. In any case, for the issues at the heart of the lawsuit, the basic "facts" are not in dispute. As the narrative presents it, Jesus' deeds and teaching were controversial and could be construed as blasphemous and lawbreaking; he antagonized the Jewish religious authorities, who had him arrested and then handed him over to Pilate on a charge of political sedition; he was executed by the Roman governor for his alleged claim to be the king of the Jews. Both sides agree on these data. They disagree on the slant that should be put on them. The witness of the Gospel is to its own slant, which it claims to be the true one. In Ricoeur's terms, the Gospel's witness is primarily confessional. To hold that its language of witness refers to a prior independent witness to historicity is to impose a modern concern on the narrative. Furthermore, to begin with a literary analysis, which we have argued earlier is appropriate, is to recognize first of all that the narrative is history-like, without determining at this stage whether this history-likeness is the result of accurate reporting, is a mix of historical tradition and fictional elements for the sake of making theological points, or is simply a piece of fiction aiming for verisimilitude.

Our claim has been that this history-like narrative is deliberately shaped in terms of a cosmic lawsuit that presents God's claims on the world and in which Jesus is portrayed as the divine agent in the lawsuit. This means that even if one believes in the reality of this God, the historical existence of Jesus, and the historicity of a controversial mission within Israel and of a trial before Pilate, the theme that dominates the narrative—the relationship between God and the world—is represented by a metaphor. The narrative's point of view is that God's relationship with the world is *like* a lawsuit. The language of witness, therefore, has to be seen first and foremost as functioning within this metaphorical framework. Those who witness are testifying to key aspects of disputed claims about the relationship, in particular to the identity and role of the one who purports to be God's agent. To attempt to make the witness language function first regarding the historical accuracy of the narrative's discourse is to lose sight of the reason such language was originally chosen—as part of the lawsuit metaphor. To employ Ricoeur's categories, the quasi-empirical aspect of testimony is taken up in a quasi-juridical extended metaphor that is in turn part of a religious discourse where testimony is not about isolated "facts" but about the whole meaning of human existence as disclosed through the historical person of Jesus.

Three major related questions need to be pursued here: How does the Fourth Gospel's language of witness function, and how does this function bear on readers' understanding of the eyewitness elements? What truth claims are being made by the narrator's linking of his account to the witness of the beloved disciple? Does the Fourth Gospel claim to be an eyewitness narrative, and if so, how does it do this? The last question will in turn provoke further reflection on the nature of the narrative's claims.

Assumptions that all witness terminology in the Fourth Gospel concerns eyewitness claims to historical facts are so prevalent that it pays to remind ourselves of how the language of seeing and witnessing actually functions. In this matter, as in others, the prologue sets the tone and guides readers' expectations. In 1:7–8 John the Baptist's mission is depicted as having witness as its purpose, and this witness is then spelled out as testifying to the light so that all might believe. Clearly, the aim of this first use of the witness terminology is to point to the significance of Jesus' identity as the embodiment of the divine light and all that it symbolizes. It presupposes John's acquaintance with Jesus, but it does not refer to a physical seeing of a light or to the reporting of a historical fact. Precisely the same holds for the force of the verb *to testify* when it is used again of John in v. 15. John's testifying about the incarnate Logos has continuing force (the present tense of the verb is employed) and is to the effect that the one who appeared on the scene since he began his own mission ranks before him because he indeed existed before him—a theological evaluation of Jesus' status, based on belief in his preexistence. Again there is no reference here to what John has seen with his eyes. But immediately before and after this second mention of John the Baptist's witness, there is a confession or testimony, by a group among whom the narrator is to be numbered, that uses a verb of seeing: "we have seen his glory, . . . full of grace and truth. . . . From his fullness we have all received, grace upon grace" (vv. 14, 16). Still, our conclusion can be no different. This is not the everyday language of physical seeing. Petersen underlines this point: " 'Beholding' is not 'observing,' because only some people 'beheld' the 'glory' of 'the Word' in Jesus. Jesus did not have something like a halo that all could observe."[83] Instead this

---

[83] N. R. Petersen, *The Gospel of John and the Sociology of Light* (Valley Forge, Penn.: Trinity Press International, 1993), 20. Petersen studies the way this Gospel's special use of language transforms its ordinary, everyday usage. He claims that it thereby becomes an antilanguage. Here he is taking up the terminology of M. Halliday in *Language as Social Semiotic: The Social Interpretation of Language and*

seeing is connected with the other verbs in the context—receiving (vv. 11–12, 16), knowing (v. 10), and believing (vv. 7, 12)—with which it is virtually synonymous.

Seeing is again associated with receiving and knowing when it refers to the Spirit of truth in 14:17. Seeing the glory of the incarnate Logos, then, is a response of faith on the part of the community the narrator represents. And since it is a response of faith to witness about Jesus (cf. 1:7), the "we" for whom the narrator speaks includes the original believing disciples but should not be limited to apostolic eyewitnesses.[84] It is a mistake to claim that the evangelist never attributes this sort of seeing to the believing community.[85] In 3:3 to be born from above is to be enabled to see the kingdom of God, and in 3:36 to believe is to be enabled to see life; both of these statements are explicitly formulated in the most general terms. The clause "Whoever believes in me" parallels "Whoever sees me" in 12:44–45. In addition, the narrative about the man born blind, as we have seen, is told as a paradigm for the witness of believers, and his confession—"though I was blind, now I see"—is explicitly related to the response of believing in Jesus (9:35–41; cf. especially v. 39: "I came into this world for judgment so that those who do not see may see, and those who do see may become blind"). The communal testimony to what has been seen is the witness of faith in Jesus as the incarnate Logos. In Ricoeur's terms, it is the language of confession.

If the prologue sets expectations about the force of the language of seeing and testifying, the early part of the ensuing narrative confirms them. The declarations of John the Baptist in 1:19–34 are described as his witness (vv. 19, 34), and the Baptist becomes the mouthpiece of the implied author's belief that Jesus is the Lamb of God, the baptizer with the Spirit, and the Son of God. Again the language of seeing is employed alongside that of witnessing. In vv. 32–33 John testifies to seeing the Spirit descend from heaven like a dove and remain on Jesus. Whatever is to be understood by this, and if the reader is meant to think of a vision-

---

Meaning (Baltimore: University Park Press, 1978, 164–82) to describe the language of an antisocial group set up within a larger society as a conscious alternative to it. B. J. Malina, *The Gospel of John in Sociolinguistic Perspective* (Berkeley: Center for Hermeneutical Studies, 1985), 43, earlier saw the relevance of this approach for the notion of witnessing. See also Malina and Rohrbaugh, *Social-Science Commentary,* 7–11.

[84] *Pace* F. Mussner, *Historical Jesus,* 71, although he allows that others can later place themselves in this "we" circle.

[85] As does Mussner, ibid., 23; 106, n. 15.

ary experience that was granted to the Baptist, this is still scarcely the everyday use of eyewitness language. The point is reinforced in v. 34 when John attests, "And I myself have seen and have testified that this is the Son of God." For its force in the narrative, this presupposes that John had a special experience in connection with Jesus, but the reference of the seeing and testifying language in this statement is not to an observable fact but to a belief about Jesus' identity. The use of such language by Jesus is no different. The language of witness is first found on his lips in 3:11, in what is also a "we" statement: "we . . . testify to what we have seen; yet you do not receive our testimony." Here Jesus is the mouthpiece for the implied author and his community. What is it that he has seen and to which he testifies? He represents those who, unlike Nicodemus (v. 3), have seen the kingdom of God, who have seen through the earthly things of which Jesus speaks to the heavenly realities (v. 12) because they are born from above (v. 3). The community sees and testifies by faith. Jesus sees and testifies (vv. 31–32) from the vantage point of his unique relationship to God, which means that he has come from above, has had experience of heavenly realities (v. 31). In neither case therefore—whether of Jesus or of the believing community—do seeing and witnessing have eyewitness experience of historical events as their reference.

There is no need to review further mention of witnessing regarding Jesus speaking about himself, or God's witness to Jesus in the Scripture's witness, or the Spirit's witness, and so on. But it is possible to grant the case for the overall usage of witness language as confessional yet still argue that there are significant exceptions, particularly regarding the disciples and the beloved disciple. This is, however, different from simply assuming that witness language should be taken as referring to eyewitness testimony. There might be exceptions to the overwhelmingly dominant metaphorical and confessional usage. Does the reference to the witness of the disciples in 15:27 constitute such an exception? After all, having spoken of the witness of the Spirit on his behalf, Jesus tells them, "You also are to testify because you have been with me from the beginning." It is important to be clear about the precise nature of the enquiry. There can be no denying that, according to the narrator, the disciples saw the mission of Jesus and that this experience would therefore lie behind their witness. The question is whether the use of the narrative's distinctive language about testifying has in view here the factual reporting of such experience. What 15:27 makes clear, in the light of the previous use of the language of witnessing, is that the disciples, by virtue of having been with Jesus from the beginning, are in a position to testify to the significance of his mission as a whole, not that their testifying will itself amount to, or be limited by, reporting what they saw with their eyes. Their testimony will be an interpretative representation of the mission, seen now in the light of their resurrection beliefs about Jesus and elaborated under the guidance of the Spirit to draw out its significance (cf. v. 26).

What is said about the witness of the beloved disciple complicates the picture we have given, and it does so in an interesting fashion. This study has already given reasons for taking the majority view that 19:35 refers to the beloved disciple.[86] The use of witness terminology here includes a reference to what could have been seen and is accompanied by a strong claim to truth. As in the later episodes of the beloved disciple seeing and believing at the empty tomb (20:8) and of other disciples seeing the risen Lord (20:18, 20, 25, 29), the verb for seeing in 19:35 appears to have an object that could be seen with one's eyes. The passage reads literally, "But one of the soldiers pierced his side with a spear, and at once blood and water came out. And the one who saw has testified, and his testimony is true, and that one knows that he tells the truth, so that you also may believe" (19:34–35). The difference from the use of a verb of seeing in the resurrection accounts is twofold. First, there is no explicit object for the verb here, although most likely the object to be supplied is the antecedent clause—"at once blood and water came out." Second— and the reason the passage is important for our discussion—seeing is here explicitly linked to testifying. Ricoeur is right, then, to claim that here, in an exception to the confessional notion of witness, John comes closest to Luke's eyewitness narrational testimony. The implied author has not left the confessional mode but incorporates the notion of eyewitnessing. At the level of the narrative, the beloved disciple is an eyewitness to the flow of blood and water, yet clearly the witness based on what has been seen is not given simply to enable the readers to believe that blood and water flowed from Jesus' side but to believe in the significance of this phenomenon. This witness bearing takes place not within the story line itself but in the addressing of the readers ("you"), that is, in the writing of the Gospel.[87]

This ordinary use of seeing as part of confessional testimony in connection with the beloved disciple colors the way the reader will take what is said about his testimony in 21:24, when, at the end of the narra-

---

[86] See ch. 4, sec. D, above.

[87] Cf. Bauckham, "Beloved Disciple," 40–41.

tive, it is revealed that the narrator, although distinguishing himself from the beloved disciple ("we know that his testimony is true"), links his account intimately with this disciple's witness ("This is the disciple who is testifying to these things and has written them [or 'caused them to be written']"). Nothing is said explicitly about having seen that to which testimony is being given, and taken by itself, there is no reason to think that testimony involves anything different from the predominant confessional usage or that it is being asserted that the beloved disciple is providing eyewitness reporting of each of the events and speeches in the narrative as a straightforward historical account. Certainly the narrator is claiming the beloved disciple as the source for his narrative and therefore as the authority for the distinctive perspective on the identity of Jesus that shapes and pervades it. But in the light of 19:35 and what has been said about the beloved disciple's seeing and believing at the empty tomb and about his presence at other key events in the narrative from John 13 onwards, the likelihood that he is also being claimed as an eyewitness increases. Once it emerges that the narrative as a whole is being attributed to the beloved disciple's witness, readers have only to think back to realize that the narrative has indeed been told from the perspective of an omniscient narrator, one who saw and heard all that was going on. They are now in a position to identify this omniscient narrator as the beloved disciple.

We are faced, then, with an intriguing phenomenon—a narrative that turns out implicitly to be meant to be understood as the eyewitness account of the beloved disciple and yet in which, from the very start, the notion of witness and even of seeing is clearly metaphorical and part of the extended metaphor of the cosmic trial. Where does this leave us regarding the truth of the narrative? Are readers meant to take the eyewitness claim to be a straightforward claim to factual reporting? Are they to see it as a narrative convention? After all, they would know that eyewitness claims could be part of a variety of types of literature in which there was a need to give verisimilitude to one's narrative. They would also know that legends and romances could employ omniscient narrators (although they would not have used such categories), as could historiographies. Are there any clues to how straightforwardly the device of narrator as eyewitness is being used?

How consistently is the device used? How far does the role of the beloved disciple go back? Is he to be identified with the unnamed disciple who accompanies Andrew in 1:35–40, or does he only play a role in the last part of the narrative, from 13:23? In favor of the former alternative, not only would this give consistency to the notion of the author as eyewitness; also, once readers have encountered the later functioning, in anonymity, of the disciple whom Jesus loved, they would have little difficulty in retrospectively making the connection with an anonymous disciple at the beginning of Jesus' mission, in a context where he could not yet appropriately be described as the disciple whom Jesus loved because he was there encountering Jesus for the first time. This would make the beloved disciple a witness both to the beginning of Jesus' mission and to the important prelude to that mission in the witness of John the Baptist, since Andrew and the anonymous other disciple began as disciples of John. The beloved disciple would therefore be in a position to be the author of the entire scope of the narrative from 1:19 to 21:23. It is also not without significance that the one who witnessed John the Baptist's testimony about Jesus being the Lamb of God that takes away the sins of the world (cf. 1:34) also witnesses the fulfillment of these words in the death of Jesus as the Passover lamb (cf. 19:35, 36).[88] Thus, regarding the overall extent of the narrative, it can be read consistently in terms of an authorship tied to the witness of the beloved disciple. On the other hand, the narration is not given by the beloved disciple in the first person but by an omniscient narrator who generally uses the third person[89] and always talks of the beloved disciple in the third person; also, the ending of the narrative shows distance between the narrator and the beloved disciple as well as identification. It seems as though the final author, who writes after the death of the beloved disciple as a known figure in the community and who does the narrating, has chosen to present the beloved disciple as the author but at the same time has left a necessary gap between himself and the beloved disciple.

The omniscient narrator's use of the beloved disciple in the narrative does make the latter's role as eyewitness less than straightforward. On the one hand, the beloved disciple as implied omniscient author is given insight into Jesus' and other characters' motivations and into events that goes far beyond eyewitness knowledge. On the other hand, there are places where the knowledge of the beloved disciple as a character in the narrative fails to be a significant factor in the action. The first time this character is introduced as the disciple whom Jesus loved is a prime example. Peter asks him to discover the identity of Jesus' betrayer (13:24). Although he learns this from Jesus' subsequent action, he does not tell Peter nor do anything to prevent Judas from carrying out the be-

---

[88] Cf. ibid., 37.

[89] The first-person plural is employed in 1:14; 21:24, and the first-person singular in 21:25.

trayal. To add to the strangeness, the narrator's own comments in 13:28 about Jesus' words to Judas ignore what the beloved disciple has just found out: "Now no one at the table knew why he said this to him." This adds to the impression that the beloved disciple is at the same time both inside and outside the story line. As Kurz explains, "It is as though the beloved disciple joins the narrator and implied readers as omniscient observers outside the plot rather than being a participant in the plot."[90] This surely underscores that the beloved disciple's role in the narrative constitutes a particular literary device. He enables the omniscient narrator's retrospective knowledge to be communicated to the readers within the story line and gives it the authority of a character who was present during the time being narrated. This is part of the perspective to be brought to bear on 19:35. Here the reference to the eyewitness is parenthetical. The narrative flows smoothly without it, so that "these things" that are said to be the fulfillment of Scripture in v. 36 are a reference to the events of vv. 31–34. Readers are also left to fill in the gap and assume that the eyewitness who addresses them is in fact the beloved disciple who was present near the cross in vv. 26–27. Again he is there in v. 35 without really being a participant in the action. His seeing and testifying are not for the benefit of other characters but for the readers. As a literary device, the role of the beloved disciple once more allows the narrator to draw the implied readers into the story line, underlining for them the significance of the blood and water that flowed from Jesus' side and inviting them to share the perspective of this witness and to believe that Jesus' death was a sacrifice that brought life.

Two major factors therefore bear on the way the truth claim of 19:35 should be taken. The first is the realization that the eyewitness status of the beloved disciple is meant to lend verisimilitude and to give authority to the distinctive overall perspective on the significance of Jesus in this biography. The second is that the way seeing and testimony are used regarding all the other characters provides an essential clue to how the eyewitnessing of the beloved disciple is also meant to be taken. It is to be interpreted as part of the overall metaphor of the trial. The narrative device of literal eyewitnessing is itself incorporated into this cosmic trial motif.

Does the truth claim of 19:35, then, depend on whether blood and water actually flowed from Jesus' body and whether there was an actual disciple present who is more than the ideal figure the beloved disciple is

---

[90] W. Kurz, "The Beloved Disciple and Implied Readers," *BTB* 19 (1989): 103.

often held to be and who saw this with his own eyes? The truth claim must be seen as related to what is implied by these statements within the universe of discourse of the Gospel's narrative world as a whole. In this light, the truth being asserted is that the condemnation of death that Jesus experienced results in the positive verdict of life. Just as Jesus' witness to the truth (18:37) is to true judgment in the lawsuit that is not observable to ordinary human sight, so the beloved disciple's witness is to this same divine judgment. And since, in the discourse of the Fourth Gospel, seeing can be the equivalent of believing (cf. 9:39–41; 12:39–40, 46), what is claimed as true is the beloved disciple's witness to his belief about the significance of Jesus' death.[91] If it is claimed that, to the contrary, the beloved disciple's witness is to the fact of Jesus' death,[92] it must be replied that this is not how the narrative reads. The death of Jesus is recounted in 19:30 and confirmed by what is said about the soldiers in 19:33. If the beloved disciple's witness were for this purpose, one would have expected it earlier, at one of these points. Instead it is specifically in relation to the flow of blood and water and immediately before the citation of two scriptural passages that highlight the significance of Jesus' death (19:36–37). If it is objected that unless there were blood and water that flowed from Jesus' side, the beloved disciple could not have seen the significance of Jesus' death, then it must be replied that this is still only so within the narrative. Blood and water are the narrative means for conveying this significance. Whether Jesus' side was actually pierced and with these consequences is a separate issue. And to take just two examples, Matthew and Paul are well able to make a similar theological point without any awareness of this particular occurrence. What Paul simply asserts theologically, namely, that the death of Jesus issues in life for believers (1 Thess 5:10), Matthew depicts in narrative symbolism with the bodies of the saints resurrected at the point of Jesus' death (Matt 27:51–52), and John portrays here in terms of blood and water flowing from Jesus' side.[93] The distinction being made here is one that Frei has made familiar—that between sense and reference. The plain sense is that the beloved disciple saw the blood and water. But this is not simply to be identified with the narrative's reference. We may agree with Ricoeur's assertion that "it is not possible to testify *for* a meaning without

---

[91] Cf. also Davies, *Rhetoric and Reference*, 63–64.

[92] Cf., e.g., Barrett, *Gospel according to St. John*, 556: "John intended to provide evidence that Jesus was a real man, and that he really died." The first edition of Barrett's commentary is followed by Trites, *Concept of Witness*, 85.

[93] Cf. also 1 Pet 2:24.

testifying *that* something has happened which signifies this meaning."[94] The question is, What is the "that"? The suggestion being made here is that, for the implied author's testimony to satisfy such conditions, the death of Jesus itself is sufficient as the something that has happened and that its meaning as life is testified to through the details of the narrative and its symbolism.

When in 21:24 the narrator adds, "and we know that his testimony is true," he is asserting that he and his community find the beloved disciple's witness persuasive. Why do they find it persuasive? Unraveled a little more in the light of our entire discussion, such a statement is affirming that this testimony about Jesus and its vision of life in the world are convincing to the community because it trusts and agrees with the perspective of the beloved disciple, because it finds it plausible and in line with what it already knows about the traditions of Jesus' life and death, and because this version of the significance of that life and death matches its experience of the state of affairs in the world as it affects the community as a particular group of Christian believers.

3. The Gospel as History-like Narrative

The truth claims of the Fourth Gospel's narrative, then, are not at the level of particular narrative assertions but at the level of its overall interpretation of Jesus and his mission. Since it is a history-like narrative, its events, characters, and actions have to be plausible, in relation to their setting, for readers familiar with traditions about Jesus; its truth claim, however, is not to its circumstantial accuracy but to the explanation of God's purposes for human existence implied by its narrative discourse.[95] By seeing the links between the traditions about Jesus' conflicts and trial, Scripture's cosmic lawsuit, and the experience of his community, the narrator does not testify to Jesus' original words and deeds but projects his vision onto the traditions available to him and thereby bears faithful witness in his narrative to their overall significance for his readers in the present.

For a text to reflect the conviction that the Logos was incarnate in history and that the core events in its story about Jesus happened is not

---

[94] Ricoeur, "Hermeneutics of Testimony," 133.

[95] Regarding narrative fiction, Leitch, *What Stories Are,* 166–83, makes a convincing case that the truth to which such works are committed is not at the level of the propositions they advance but at the level of the implications of these propositions within the conventions of particular genres.

the same thing as to tell this story with historical accuracy.[96] The narrative both relates to history and refigures. It relates to history because its refiguring is of events that have taken place, but the very form of narrative means that these past events are only present through their refiguration in emplotment. There is no referring separate from this. This still leaves the question of whether everything in the refiguration has some correspondence to what happened or whether some elements are there as artistic and creative features of the refiguration in order to elaborate on the meaning of any events that have been reconfigured. Just as the events to which the narrative is related are already changed creatively by being placed in a particular plot sequence, so the recounting of these events within this sequence could introduce creative changes, such as additions to these events or new events.

Thus, our rigid distinctions between history and fiction employ a false dichotomy. The Fourth Gospel as ancient biography contains elements of both. This is part of its taking the form of narrative. Ricoeur has shown that historical narrative contains elements of fictionalization and fictional narrative contains elements of historicization.[97] He argues that both artist and historian have comparable constraints in their emplotment of narratives. The artist's debt is to a particular vision of the world, while the historian's debt is to the dead.[98] Both factors appear to be at work in the Fourth Gospel—the constraining power of its vision of the world in terms of the cosmic lawsuit, and the constraining power of its debt to the past in terms of traditions about Jesus' life, death, and resurrection. For Ricoeur, fiction recounts something as if it were past: its past tenses are a quasi-past. So fiction is quasi-historical just as much as history writing is quasi-fictional.[99] The fictional elements of the Fourth Gospel's narrative come from its account of the ministry of Jesus in terms of a retrial about the issues of its own day; it is narrating what might have been. Yet in so doing, it also illumines and releases the potentialities of the "real" past.

We have seen that the modern fact-fiction dualism is being deconstructed in reflection on ancient biography. Ricoeur shows the fragility

---

[96] Boice, *Witness and Revelation,* 135, in his study of our motif is unable to make this distinction: "It is hard to see . . . how the historical interest could be genuine without an equal concern for verified historical material." Again this is to impose a modern historical concern on an ancient text that operates within quite different conventions.

[97] See Ricoeur, *Time and Narrative,* vol. 3, esp. 180–92.

[98] Ibid., 177.

[99] Ibid., 188–89.

of this dualism in regard to more recent narrative theory. The work of Frei has shown well the problems with imposing this dualism on the biblical narratives and especially on the Gospels' passion and resurrection narratives. Indeed, Frei can claim, "We are actually in a fortunate position that so much of what we know about Jesus . . . is more nearly fictional than historical in narration."[100] The reason is that one fictional element is the provision of direct or inside knowledge of the subject of the narrative. Whereas Ricoeur speaks in terms of quasi-historical and quasi-fictional aspects of narrative, Frei conceives of the Gospel narratives as both history-like and fictionlike. For him, they are "at once intensely serious and historical in intent and fictional in form."[101] As Green puts it in his assessment of Frei, "We are compelled . . . to take an apparently fictional story as the gospel truth."[102] Green helpfully suggests four implications that emerge from such a view of the Gospel narratives. First, historical criticism can be employed on the narratives, and this will show that, in terms of historical reference, they contain what we would call fiction as well as fact. It is appropriate therefore to talk of fictive or fictionlike aspects of the narratives, "with the proviso that the question of their truth is not thereby prejudged."[103] Second, "the meaning of the texts is the story they tell—'fictive' elements and all!"[104] Critical awareness of the fictionlike qualities of a Gospel need not be an obstacle to affirming its truth. Third, this stance need not entail fideism. Although it includes a fiduciary element—a commitment to viewing the narrative in this way—this way of viewing is open to being changed in the light of a more persuasive paradigm.[105] Finally, this view treats the Gospel narratives as inviting readers to see the world "as something different from the kind of world that it otherwise appears to be," and Christians are those who "imagining the world in terms of the biblical story, . . . find themselves persuaded that the story is true."[106] In terms of our specific example, then, the beloved disciple's witnessing of the blood and water coming

---

[100] H. W. Frei, *The Identity of Jesus Christ: The Hermeneutical Bases of Dogmatic Theology* (Philadelphia: Fortress, 1975), 144.

[101] Ibid., 15.

[102] G. Green, " 'The Bible as . . .': Fictional Narrative and Scriptural Truth," in *Scriptural Authority and Narrative Interpretation* (ed. G. Green; Philadelphia: Fortress, 1987), 83.

[103] Ibid., 91.

[104] Ibid.

[105] Cf. ibid., 91–92.

[106] Ibid., 92, 93.

from the side of Jesus may well be a fictive element in the Fourth Gospel's narrative, but readers who have been persuaded by the symbolic world of this narrative are still able to find themselves compelled to see this part of its alternative world as true. They will want to confess that the death of Jesus is not what it appeared to be—simply the demise of a false prophet rejected by the religious authorities of his day—but is truly the means by which the one God has chosen to bring about life for the world.

One of Frei's major contributions in The Eclipse of Biblical Narrative was to show that the significance of realistic narrative had been eclipsed by the modern tendency to think that a text of this sort has to be interpreted through a description of its subject matter that is logically independent of the narrative. What he finds wrong with this is that "meaning . . . is not illustrated (as though it were an intellectually presubsisting or preconceived archetype or ideal essence) but constituted through the mutual, specific determination of agents, speech, social context, and circumstances that form the indispensable narrative web."[107] Marshall has related Frei's view of meaning to the notion of truth by underlining that the late-eighteenth- and nineteenth-century interpreters studied by Frei made a mistake about the truth of the Gospel narratives: "They interpreted the narratives which identify Jesus as a particular person without ascribing primacy or centrality to those narratives in deciding about truth."[108] They did not usually give up on the truth of these narratives altogether but instead interpreted them in conformity to other standards of truth, historical or religious, to which they gave priority. These other notions of truth were not necessarily false. The problem was in giving them primacy over the meaning of the Gospel narratives. For Marshall, therefore, the theological corollary of Frei's claim about the unity of narrative sense and subject matter is that understanding the Gospel narratives about the identity of Jesus is to know their truth. "If this is the case then there are no further criteria of truth to which one need to appeal to decide the truth of this narrative and in terms of which one might interpret it; and so it is eo ipso the primary criterion of truth, in terms of which all else must be interpreted." It is "logically basic to and decisive for all of our talk about God and ourselves."[109]

---

[107] H. Frei, *The Eclipse of Biblical Narrative* (New Haven: Yale University Press, 1974), 280.

[108] B. D. Marshall, "Meaning and Truth in Narrative Interpretation: A Reply to George Schner," *Modern Theology* 8 (1992): 177.

[109] Ibid., 178–79.

What, then, is the difference between fiction as false witness ("the defendant's testimony was a tissue of fictions") and fiction as part of true witness? It is the conventions of the literary genre of which the fiction is a part that make the difference. Regarding contemporary fiction, Searle makes the point that its conventions mean that the writer is not committed seriously to the truth of particular assertions:

> What distinguishes fiction from lies is the existence of a separate set of conventions which enables the author to go through the motions of making statements which he knows to be not true even though he has no intention to deceive. . . . In the case of realistic or naturalistic fiction, the author will refer to real places and events intermingling these references with the fictional references, thus making it possible to treat the fictional story as an extension of our existing knowledge. The author will establish with the reader a set of understandings about how far the horizontal conventions of fiction break the vertical connections of serious speech. . . . What counts as coherence will be in part a function of the contract between author and reader about the horizontal conventions.[110]

As already seen from our earlier discussion, what counted in whether the fictive elements in the Fourth Gospel would have been regarded as truth or lies are the conventions of ancient biography about plausibility. The contract between ancient author and ancient readers on the basis of shared knowledge and judgment would have been that the Fourth Gospel's story world relate persuasively to readers' experience and convictions and be plausible in terms of other stories about Jesus they may have heard.

In probing this contract between author and readers, we can also ask whether this narrative as testimony presupposes any extralinguistic states of affairs. In its testifying, this Gospel also specifies identity because its testimony is to Jesus as the Christ, the Son of God. And it also calls to believe this particular identification, because the testimony is offered for acceptance. At the same time, this narrative witness also promises because believing is said to have life as its result. As an act of promise, it appears to have as a condition of its meaning and truth that Jesus as Son of God is indeed able to give life. But now our probing becomes more complicated. In the narrative Jesus gives life in various forms in the course of his public ministry. Does he do this by virtue of his unity with God, or does his being given new life through the resurrection provide the presupposition for this portrayal of him earlier in the narrative? A strong argument can be made for the latter being the

---

[110] J. R. Searle, *Expression and Meaning* (Cambridge: Cambridge University Press, 1979), 67, 73.

case.[111] If so, the readers' belief that they will receive the promise of life implies the belief that Jesus has been raised to new life and that the risen Jesus is the source of this new life conveyed by the Spirit. Thus, the promissory nature of this testimony appears to imply, in addition to the belief in a God who reveals God's self, at least the belief in a resurrected Christ and in the reality of the Spirit. These beliefs logically imply others about the extralinguistic world of the text. If Jesus has been raised, he has to have actually existed and died in the first place. Further, the plausibility of the trial motif depends on Jesus' meeting his death through a trial that resulted in judgment on him in the form of crucifixion. Again, the plausibility of the trial motif for his public ministry depends on his involvement in controversy with the Jewish religious leaders, controversy that led to his coming to actual trial in the first place. To pursue the chain further, his actions and words must have been such as to imply claims that provoked the controversy.

All of this confirms by a different route what has been suggested about the shared knowledge that would be necessary for the implied readers to appreciate the narrative—the basic components of the synoptic tradition. If we are right that author and readers shared a knowledge of the major events in the synoptic tradition, then certainly the author did not expect to have the truth claims of the narrative questioned by his placement of the temple incident at the beginning of the narrative rather than at the end, by his omission of a formal trial before the Sanhedrin, and by having its elements already played out in the public ministry. Readers could be expected to be accustomed to this type of creativity. What our probing of the contract between author and readers does not do is get us any closer to knowing whether the readers would have believed that every event recounted actually happened in some form. Would they have believed, for instance, as part of their commitment to the truth of the narrative identification of Jesus, that Jesus actually turned water into wine? Here we can only return to the conventions of ancient history-like narrative and say that they would have had to find such an event plausible, given their beliefs about Jesus and the stories they had heard.

But to reiterate, the Fourth Gospel's own truth claims are in terms of its narrative presentation. What the Gospel as testimony offers is a literary retrial of Jesus under the overarching schema of the cosmic lawsuit and from the perspective of the belief that Jesus had been vindicated as

---

[111] Cf. Lincoln, "I Am the Resurrection and the Life," 122–44.

God's unique agent. An assessment of its truth on its own terms, then, will depend on whether one is persuaded by such a point of view. Can its readers join with the narrator and declare about the narrative of the beloved disciple, "we know that his testimony is true" (21:24)? Thus, part of this testimony's truth claim is the entire issue of the correspondence between the world of the narrative and the world of the readers.

How does testimony function in this context? Here the categories of speech act theory may be helpful. Searle has shown that whereas in assertions the point is to make words match the reality of the world, in promises (and their fulfillment) the point is to make the world of reality match the word.[112] In a normal courtroom, testimony has the function of asserting the truth about what happened; that is, it matches its words to the world. But as we have seen, testimony does not have this straightforward function in the Fourth Gospel, and Ricoeur has complicated the notion of testimony by showing that in a religious context testimony is quasi-testimony with different dimensions from ordinary eyewitness testimony. Thus, testimony as confessional may well have a different function. It points primarily to an alternative world by providing a different construal on reality in the light of a conviction on which one is willing to stake one's life.[113] In this way, the Fourth Gospel matches the words of its testimony to an alternative world, but precisely because that world is alternative and not simply the world of everyday reality, the Fourth Gospel's testimony can at the same time be said to be proclaiming that world and transforming the present one. It is aiming at a world-to-word fit. And as we have seen, in the relation between word and world that is a key part of the lawsuit motif—in both Isaiah's trial scenes and the Fourth Gospel's narrative—the one true God is known through the correspondence between this God's predictive word and its fulfillment in history. Israel and Christian believers are witnesses to this. Their testimony looks back and points out that the word of God, or of God in Christ, matches a certain event or state of affairs in the world that this transformative word brought about in the first place. And so in this way the testimony also constitutes a word-to-world fit. The two movements come together in this Gospel because its testimony's claim that there *has been* a word-to-world fit is part of the way it reinforces its other claim that there *will be* a world-to-word fit, in which the readers' world can be brought into line with God's purposes for reality, to which the alternative

---

[112] Searle, *Expression and Meaning*, 3.

[113] See also the view of Brueggemann, *Theology of the Old Testament*, 722–23, that the utterance of Israel's testimonies constitutes a world.

world of the narrative testimony witnesses. Both past and present aspects of the readers' world can be transformed in this way. The past world known to the readers through the traditions about Jesus with which they and the author were familiar and the experiences they have been through in relation to the synagogue are now transformed and seen to be capable of an interpretation that matches the purposes of the God of the lawsuit. Their present world is also transformed as they now see this world as the site of the cosmic lawsuit and their role in this world as that of participants in the ongoing trial to which the narrative witnesses.

The Fourth Gospel's testimony aims at drawing its readers into its narrative world in such a way that they will be convinced of its witness to the realities of such a world and return to their own world to believe and live in their light. As Thiselton shows in his comprehensive and illuminating discussion,[114] this observation bears on a crucial question in contemporary hermeneutical debate: Can texts challenge or transform readers and their communities from outside? Put differently, can the Bible's symbols affect and produce changes in the life worlds of its readers? For Thiselton, the claim arising from the Bible is that "divine promise transforms the world-as-it-is in accordance with the word of promise."[115] The truth claim of the witness of the Fourth Gospel's narrative functions as a claim to transform the world as its readers know it. The judgment of such a claim is not therefore on the basis of whether its world matches precisely what happened in the life of Jesus. It is assumed that the readers would have found a sufficient match for its narrative to be plausible. Instead readers will reach a verdict on its truth by discovering whether the testimony's reconfiguration of that past world now has power in their present world.

The relation of the word of the narrative to the world of the readers reflects its depiction of the relation of its chief witness, Jesus, to the world. As we have seen earlier, according to the prologue God's word has found its precise correspondence in history in Jesus as the incarnate Logos. The testimony of the narrative declares that in Jesus' witness in word and deed there is the fit between God's word and the world. At the same time, the Logos became flesh, entered this world, in order that his witness to the truth might transform this world and bring it into line with God's purposes for its well-being. Jesus' witness was intended to produce a fit between the world and God's word. His witness—"I am

---

[114] Thiselton, *New Horizons*, esp. 515–620.
[115] Ibid., 618.

the truth"—can be seen as attesting to both these functions of testimony as truth.

The Fourth Gospel underlines the inevitable circularity of claims to truth. Jesus' witness to truth is self-authenticating ("even if I testify on my own behalf, my testimony is valid" [8:14, cf. also 14:6]), and the witness of the Gospel to this witness is self-authenticating ("we know that his testimony is true," assert the narrator and his community about the beloved disciple's witness [21:24]). In the end, whatever our probing and questioning, there can be no going behind such witness. Our historical investigations will continue, but they will not be the determinative criteria of truth by which we judge the Gospel.[116] The truth of this witness can only be discovered by participating in it. We are back to faith seeking understanding as the only appropriate stance toward this sort of truth. In the words of Jesus' witness in the narrative—"Anyone who resolves to do the will of God will know whether the teaching is from God or whether I am speaking on my own" (7:17)—and in this Gospel's narrative discourse, doing the will of God is the equivalent to having faith (cf. 6:29). Those who have this faith seeking understanding affirm the truth of the Gospel's testimony by participation in its story, by telling it and living it as part of the community that is willing to risk following the witness of Jesus' suffering love.

C. The Trial Motif and Anti-Judaism

Earlier generations of Johannine scholars were more or less blind to the problem of the Gospel's alleged anti-Judaism. But post-Holocaust awareness and Jewish-Christian dialogue have brought it to the top of the agenda. Its seriousness can perhaps be judged from the response of two recent writers. Casey's claim that this Gospel is not true does not simply depend on his view of its historicity but also, and more heavily, on his indictment of its moral deficiency. For him, it attributes false views both to Jesus, which as a Jew he could never have held, and to his opponents, labeled "the Jews." In this way John's Gospel is anti-Jewish and has fostered anti-Semitism, and he claims that this feature is so pervasive as to make the Gospel irredeemable.[117] Hays, who, in contrast to Casey, approaches the NT from an explicitly Christian perspective,

---

[116] Cf. Brueggemann, *Theology of the Old Testament,* 714: "What 'happened' (whatever it may mean) depends on testimony and tradition that will not submit to any other warrant."

[117] Casey, *Is John's Gospel True?* esp. 3, 223–29.

concludes, in his large volume on NT ethics, that in its view of Judaism the Fourth Gospel distorts the Christian gospel and is a "theologically misconceived development."[118]

There is no denying the difficulty, complexity, and sensitivity of the issue. Much has been written on it, and the literature cannot be reviewed here. In addressing the topic here, this volume will draw on some of the findings of its earlier literary, exegetical, and theological studies. The earlier investigation (ch. 6) of the excommunication of Jewish Christians from the synagogue, the final part of this present chapter, and "Faithful Witness and the Dialogue with Judaism" (ch. 9, sec. D) are also all relevant as part of a response. The gist of our argument here, however, will be that if we accept the widely held definition of anti-Semitism as hatred of the Jewish people as a group because they are Jewish, then this Gospel itself is certainly not anti-Semitic. Instead we need to understand in what sense it contains phenomena that are labeled anti-Jewish and to distinguish these from their misappropriation by Christians who have sought legitimation for their hostility toward Jews as Jews. In elaborating this position, we can take up only some of the salient phenomena in the Fourth Gospel; no claim is made to provide a detailed discussion of them.

a) First, this Gospel's notorious use of the term *the Jews*. Some have suggested that its negative use only refers to the Judeans or to the Judean religious authorities. But this does not work. It is also employed of Galileans or the crowds. The sense of the term is the broad one of Jews in contrast to members of other religious or ethnic groups, but its referent can vary, sometimes having particularly the authorities in view and frequently, like the depiction of nearly all the characters in the narrative, having a representative function. The Jewish opposition to Jesus in the narrative is the vehicle for the views, attitudes, and actions of the Jews in the author's locale who have rejected the testimony of Johannine Christians about Jesus as Son of God, who have put them out of the synagogue for their beliefs, and who may have killed some of their number (cf. 9:22; 12:42; 16:2). But in the narrative such Jews are also representatives of the unbelieving world as a whole. The term *the Jews* clearly has an ethnic sense, but its referent transcends ethnic categories. It is worth repeating that this representative and not purely ethnic function can be seen on the surface of the narrative (see ch. 1, above), as the following three examples demonstrate. In 9:22 the parents of the man born blind,

---

[118] R. B. Hays, *The Moral Vision of the New Testament* (San Francisco: HarperCollins, 1996), 434.

obviously Jews themselves, are said to fear "the Jews." A similarly strange usage occurs in 13:33 when Jesus, a Jew, says to his disciples, themselves Jews, "as I said to the Jews so now I say to you." In the first example, "the Jews" feared by other Jews are the unbelieving religious authorities; in the second, one group of Jews, Jesus and his disciples, are distinguished from another group composed of unbelieving authorities, who include Pharisees, chief priests, and temple police who have been sent to arrest Jesus (cf. 7:32–36). But then, in 18:35, Pilate, the Roman governor, asks the ironic question "I am not a Jew, am I?" He expects the answer to be in the negative, but the answer the implied reader is supposed to supply is in the affirmative. In his response to Jesus, Pilate proves himself to be a Jew in the special sense of this narrative's discourse, namely, one who belongs to the unbelieving world.

Those who put Johannine Christians out of the synagogue clearly held that these Jewish Christians were in some sense no longer true Jews, particularly in the status they assigned to Christ in relation to God. It is a fair inference that, in the light of such a dispute, the evangelist decided to allow the unbelieving opposition to retain the disputed name, which was now given a primarily negative twist to mean unbelieving, as opposed to believing, Jews. At the same time, he shows that what matters is not so much the name as the substance: in his narrative, Jesus embodies all that is significant about the community's Jewish heritage, and his believing followers experience the fulfillment of the salvation that is of the Jews.[119]

For John, the Logos was incarnated as a Jew, and the response to him, both believing and unbelieving, was primarily by Jews. The unbelieving response is identified with "the Jews" because this was the majority response. Particularly for those cut off from the synagogue and from their previous relationship to official Judaism because of their believing response, such labeling becomes understandable. But it is worth thinking about what might have been the alternatives. The opposition might have been labeled simply "the unbelievers" or "the sinners." Yet these terms would not have expressed the particularities of their situation in the same way. The specific opposition Johannine Christians had faced was from unbelieving Jews who were concerned about who had

---

[119] J. D. G. Dunn, *The Partings of the Ways* (Philadelphia: Trinity Press International, 1991), 158, makes a similar point: "John may have been willing to yield the self-understanding of Judaism which largely comes to expression in the distinction of 'Jew' from 'Gentile,' while continuing to claim that the 'true Israelite' recognizes Jesus to be 'king of Israel' (1.47, 49)."

the right to be thought of as Jews. This is what gives the situation its poignancy. To assert that the writer could then have talked of "the unbelieving Jews" is to return to precisely the force that we have claimed his negative use of the term actually has. He has made it clear, from the way the term has been used in his narrative, that this is what is in view, and he would have expected his contemporary readers to understand this. Unfortunately and tragically, the shorthand nature of the labeling has been the stumbling block, and later readers have frequently demonstrated all too clearly that they have not understood what it entailed.

Although the point does not alter the objection being pressed, John's Gospel is by no means completely distinctive regarding this phenomenon. As already seen, virtually all the same issues are present in the Synoptics' depiction of the Jewish opposition to Jesus with the blanket term "this generation," and upon "this generation" are heaped condemnations far more elaborate than those in John.[120] While the term can occasionally have neutral connotations and retains temporal and ethnic force in this synoptic labeling, its predominant use contains clearly negative ethical overtones. In addition, although sometimes the immediate addressees are the Jewish religious leaders, the employment of "this generation" broadens the object of the polemic to the entire generation that they represent by what is deemed to be their inappropriate response to Jesus' words and deeds. And so, while "this generation" might be taken to mean all Jews of Jesus' and, by extension, the writers' time, in fact its referent is the unbelieving majority of Jews at the time. To the extent that its anti-Judaism is a problem, it is a problem that John shares with the Synoptics.

b) What is probably most offensive to modern sensibilities is the fierceness of the Fourth Gospel's polemic against the opponents in the trial. In John 8, a passage that is often considered the *locus classicus* of Christian anti-Semitism, Jesus accuses his opposition of trying to kill him and on this basis asserts, "You are from your father the devil, and you choose to do your father's desires. He was a murderer from the beginning" (8:44). First we need to try to hear such rhetoric in its first-century context. Our earlier exegetical study of this passage noted that the accusations would not have sounded any different, to Jews, from some of the fierce indictments of them in their own Scriptures. Indeed, nearly all of the accusations Jesus makes in John 8 were made by Yahweh against Israel in Isaiah. Their lack of knowledge (8:14, 19, 55; cf. Isa

---

[120] See ch. 6, sec. B.

48:8), their being from below (8:23; cf. Isa 55:9), their being slaves because of sin (8:33, 34; cf. Isa 50:1), and their not hearing (8:43, 47; cf. Isa 42:18, 20) are indicted in both places. In addition, in Isaiah Yahweh told Israel that its ancestor was a transgressor (Isa 43:27), that from birth it, too, had been a rebel (48:8), that it was involved in idolatry (44:9), and that such idolatry was participation with the devil (cf. LXX Isa 65:11: "you are those who have left me, and forget my holy mountain, and prepare a table for the devil [τῷ δαίμονι]"). Intra-Jewish polemics continued in this vein. In *T. Dan* 5.6, "your prince is Satan" is an accusation of Dan against his children, who, he believes, are abandoning the Lord; and in *Yebam.* 16a, one rabbi calls his brother "the first born of Satan" for giving a ruling with which he disagrees. This was typical of ancient debate in general, where terms of abuse were expected and functioned as ways of labeling one's opponents as opponents.[121] This is also reflected elsewhere in early Christian argumentation, where Jesus tells Peter, "Get behind me, Satan!" (Mark 8:33), and Paul calls other Jewish Christian missionaries false apostles, deceitful workers, and servants of Satan (2 Cor 11:13–15). This sort of language could thus be employed for those who would have considered themselves Christian believers but whose stance other believers found objectionable. Precisely this is the case with the fiercest rhetoric of John 8. As we have seen, "You are from your father the devil" is addressed to Jews who have believed in Jesus (8:44; cf. 8:31–32) but have not continued in their belief in a way the Johannine Christians find satisfactory. When the test came, and persecution and death became real options, they appear to have remained in the synagogue instead of identifying with those who made the full Johannine confession. It is easy to see that they would have been thought of as betraying both Johannine Christians and Jesus by their stance. Nevertheless, even in this reading of 8:44, lapsed believers, because of their failure to continue, are seen as ultimately no different from unbelievers and so can simply be designated as "the Jews" from 8:48 onward. Although the most abusive language in this later section is

---

[121] See L. T. Johnson, "The New Testament's Anti-Jewish Slander and the Conventions of Ancient Polemic," *JBL* 108 (1989): 419–41, esp. 440–41, where, regarding the polemical language in the Fourth Gospel, Johnson asks, "If Socrates was suspect because of his 'demon' and sophists are 'evil-spirited' and the brothers of Joseph are driven by evil spirits and the sons of the pit are children of Belial, should we be surprised to find that Samaritans have demons, or that Jesus has a demon, or that his opponents have the devil as their father, or that when he betrays Jesus, Judas is said to have Satan enter his heart?"

the implication in 8:55 that the addressees are liars, it is inevitable that, whatever its primary referent, because of this shift in designation, some of the earlier language about lapsed Jewish believers rubs off on the Jewish opposition as a whole in the narrative discourse.

Dunn puts well the necessary point about the fierceness of the rhetoric. It "has the character and intensity of sibling rivalry—able to be so hurtful, because the weak points are so well known; having to be dismissive, in order to establish their own identity in distinction from the other." This is quite different from our contemporary sensitivities, and Dunn goes on to draw the lesson that "we should certainly be slow to let our own sensitivities dictate a verdict of anti-Judaism or anti-semitism on those whose world of discourse was so very different from our own."[122] It is not even clear that we should take the language of 8:44 as entailing a final writing off of those to whom it is addressed. The fierce polemic of the prophets and the accusation in the *Testament of Dan* about having Satan as one's prince are judgments aimed at producing repentance.[123]

c) The dualism of this Gospel, in which "the Jews" are associated with this world, the below, the flesh, or the devil, while believers are not of this world and are linked with the above, the Spirit, and God, is not an ontological dualism.[124] The rhetoric in which the dualism is couched is not about a person's essential nature or the origin of his or her being. Instead this dualism is an epistemological and ethical one. In addition, it is clear that the negative side of such a dualism, according to John's Gospel, applies to all unbelievers, whether they are Jews, Samaritans, or Greeks. It is this distinction between belief and unbelief that determines on which side of the dualism a person is found in John's narrative. The very first reference to the world in an unfavorable sense makes clear the nature of the dualism. The coming of the Logos into the world created through him produces a division, whereby some believe but "the world did not know him" and "his own people did not accept him" (1:10–12).

---

[122] J. D. G. Dunn, "The Question of Anti-Semitism in the New Testament Writings of the Period," in *Jews and Christians* (ed. Dunn), 177–211, here 210–11.

[123] Motyer, *Your Father the Devil?* 148–49, claims that John 8:44 is in the tradition of the prophetic language and "a judgment out of which restoration may be born."

[124] Cf. Dunn, *Partings of the Ways,* 159, who makes a similar point: "But it is not an ontological dualism, far less a dualism dividing Jews from others (*all* are 'from below,' 'of the flesh,' 1.13; 3.6; 8.15), rather a *rhetorical* dualism which intensifies the alternative in order to provoke a decision (3.19–21)." This is where Hays, *Moral Vision,* 427, 433, among others, goes astray in his reading.

Not knowing and not accepting are clearly both volitional and part of the unbelieving world's alienation from its source of life. The prologue's dualism between light and darkness becomes a clearly ethical one when it recurs in 3:19–20, where people are said to love darkness because their deeds are evil. Elsewhere the epistemological aspects of this contrast are to the fore: those in the darkness do not know where they are going (12:35), whereas the light enables people to see and believe (cf. 9:39; 12:44–45). The world in the negative sense represents a different system of values that leads to different criteria for judging and knowing. The narrative's dualism concerns this division within a created world on which God and Jesus lay rightful claim in the lawsuit. It is meant to be temporary, since the entire point of instigating the lawsuit is to overcome the sinful alienation that produces such a dualism. Accordingly, in reading this Gospel's polemic, we need to remember that the similarly fierce indictments by the prophets or by the *Testament of Dan* were also not ontological statements but judgments aimed at producing repentance. The stated purpose of this Gospel remains that of attempting to persuade all to believe that Jesus is the sort of Messiah who is Son of God, so that in believing they might find life (20:31). The note of condemnation that is certainly present is always a secondary consequence that, from the evangelist's point of view, comes through choosing to exclude oneself from the life-giving purposes of the God of Israel for humanity. For the Fourth Gospel, it is perfectly compatible to see a division taking place within Judaism and humanity over the claims of Jesus and still hold that the God of Jesus loves the world. After all, in one of this Gospel's most striking and best-known formulations, God is said to love even the hostile world that is in antithesis to the divine values and includes unbelieving Jews and Gentiles, and is said to desire to save it by the divine self-giving in the Son (cf. 3:16).

d) These observations indicate that the narrative's labeling and rhetoric have a totally different purpose from condemnation of Jews as Jews. But once the text was employed beyond the sibling rivalry of this specific Jewish family context, there could never be the same warrant for the debate about the significance of Jesus to take this particular form. Such an explanation of the narrative's discourse underlines the particularity of its witness, showing the danger of treating Scripture as truth that is timeless. In the light of the reception history of this Gospel, any talk of its plain meaning or literal sense has to be in the context of consistent teaching about its cultural conditions and conventions. This teaching needs to make absolutely clear that what is said about "the Jews" in the narrative reflects the setting of the debate between Johannine Jewish Christians and the unbelieving Jewish majority in their locality and was never meant to be taken as referring to all Jews then or since. Given how the characterization has been taken, this may sound like too little too late. But clarifying the object of our indictment—the Fourth Gospel in its original context or its later Christian use—and suggesting that its later use was not the inevitable result of this Gospel becoming Christian Scripture remains significant. Understandably, some who erase such a distinction have also wanted to expunge all references to Jewish unbelief from public readings of the narrative. Nevertheless, it seems clear that holding to the truth of John's Gospel in any meaningful sense demands a willingness to bear some of the scandal of particularity and to maintain that, with the mission and person of Jesus in the midst of Israel and with the proclamation of his followers, something decisive occurred that brought about and continues to bring about a division between belief and unbelief. The unbelieving Jews at the time of the evangelist represent the unbelieving world in its response to Christian claims about Jesus. Unless one regards the entire move from viewing Jesus as a Jewish prophet to acknowledging him as one with God as a horrendous mistake,[125] the central debate, no longer restricted to its particular ethnic makeup at the end of the first century in the evangelist's location, will remain the same. It seems highly questionable whether Christians can be true to their tradition and its roots in the NT, particularly the Gospel of John, if they are willing to give up on its distinctive truth claim about God's decisive and definitive revelation in Jesus Christ.

D. The Trial Metanarrative, Violence, and Exclusion

A fourth objection to any notion of appropriating the truth of the Fourth Gospel, although it overlaps at some points with the concern about anti-Judaism or anti-Semitism, derives from a different concern. This narrative of a cosmic trial of truth is a metanarrative, and as noted in the introduction to this volume, all metanarratives are suspect in a postmodern context. They are seen as master stories seeking mastery, as making false claims to totality that induce marginalization, oppression, and violence. A metanarrative that has truth as its explicit content must be doubly suspect! From such a perspective, this Gospel can be no more or less true than any other grand claims to truth because they are all a lie. All claims to truth are simply a disguise of the will to power. Following Nietzsche, such a view sees all claims to truth as ways of asserting one's

---

[125] This is the implication of the view taken by Casey, *Is John's Gospel True?* e.g., 61–62, 219, 229.

place in the world and as inevitably leading to manipulation and violence. Nietzsche himself refers to John's Gospel to expound his view:

> Need I add that in the whole New Testament there is only a *single* figure who commands respect? Pilate, the Roman governor. To take a Jewish affair seriously—he does not persuade himself to do that. One Jew more or less—what does it matter? The noble scorn of a Roman, confronted with an impudent abuse of the word "truth," has enriched the New Testament with the only saying *that has value*—one which is its criticism, even its *annihilation:* "What is truth?"[126]

For Nietzsche's postmodern heirs, the bigger the claim to truth, the worse the consequences. John's Gospel provides a prime example. It started out as the claims of an oppressed religious minority, the Johannine Christians, who had been excommunicated from the synagogue because of their distinctive belief in Jesus. The only means of power it had left was to assert that the one to whom it professed allegiance surpassed all the claims that had been made by its parent religion turned oppressor, about Moses and the law and its major festivals. Such counterclaims escalated to include Jesus even sharing the divine name, "I am," and being one with God, an extraordinary assertion in the context of a monotheistic religion. But the stakes were high for a group dispossessed of their religious heritage and therefore, in a setting where religion and society were so closely interwoven, dispossessed also of their social identity and status. This is a claim to truth with a vengeance from a marginalized group. "With a vengeance" is literally true, it is held, if we pay attention to the rhetoric of this Gospel, placed in the mouth of Jesus, which calls its opponents murderers and liars and children of the devil. The truth claims of this Gospel, then, are part of a power conflict and indeed could be nothing other. This is reinforced by the tragic irony of what later happened to this Gospel. With the Christian movement's expansion and rise in power and the acceptance of this document into its canon, its truth claims changed from those of an oppressed minority to those of the dominant religion and became weapons to use against the now marginalized religion of Judaism. Its characterization of the group's compatriots who declined to believe its claims simply as "the Jews" was exploited in an anti-Semitism that took this to refer to all ethnic Jews, who could now be written off. Indeed, a ghastly line can be traced from this Gospel's portrayal of "the Jews" through the anti-Semitic statements of Cyril of Alexandria and of Chrysostom, the medieval proliferation

---

[126] F. Nietzsche, *The Antichrist,* in *The Portable Nietzsche* (ed. W. Kaufmann; New York: Viking, 1968), 626–27.

of anti-Semitic tracts illustrated with woodcuts of "the Jews and their father, the devil," and the inflammatory outbursts of Luther up to the Nazi propaganda that employed the slogan *Der Vater der Juden ist der Teufel.*[127]

Does not such an account of the Gospel and its influence suggest that our earlier discussion of the probable setting out of which the Gospel developed and our exploration of its intra-Jewish polemic in its first-century C.E. context are part of a perhaps well-intentioned but misguided salvage attempt? Does not a narrative such as the Fourth Gospel, with its story about God's lawsuit with the world that has truth as a dominant concern, simply have to be just another master narrative inducing marginalization, exclusion, and oppression? We should not, however, accept such charges too quickly. Those who repeat them have their own dilemmas. Two major associated premises lie behind their charges. The first concerns metanarratives and truth claims, and the second moves on from the first to replace the notion of truth with that of power. It is asserted that there are no timeless truths of universal reason, that there are only metanarratives that are the products of particular histories and cultures. All such metanarratives are embodied in specific languages that have in turn been developed in particular communities. But the problem comes when the further step is taken and it is assumed that because this is the case, none of them can be true or all are equally true or false. But this does not necessarily follow. In fact, such a deduction still rests on the typically modern view that, in order to be true, a claim must be "objective" or "universal," not embodied in the assertions of particular people employing particular linguistic symbols. Once this myth is seen for what is, there is no reason to deny that culturally embodied truth claims can make contact with a reality that exists beyond them. This is what Christians claim about their metanarrative, including its version in the Fourth Gospel's cosmic lawsuit—that, in and through such culturally conditioned stories, there is a true interpretation of human life in the world before God. It would be rash to think that all metanarratives must simply be jettisoned. And since metanarratives turn out in fact to be constitutive in the formation of human culture, the issue is, rather, which or whose metanarrative we live by.

Not only is the claim that all metanarratives are equally true or false inevitably part of its own broader metanarrative; its accompanying claim that they are therefore simply functions of the exercise of power leaves

---

[127] Cf., e.g., R. Lowry, "The Rejected-Suitor Syndrome: Human Sources of the New Testament 'Antisemitism,' " *JES* 14 (1977): 229.

us to the competing stories of rival groups with their own smaller truths or lies, which themselves still produce violence.[128] Foucault has stated as clearly as anyone the case for truth as power: "Truth is a thing of this world: it is produced only by virtue of multiple forms of constraints. And it induces regular effects of power. Each society has its regime of truth, its 'general politics' of truth: that is, the types of discourse which it accepts and makes function as true."[129] His language of "multiple forms of constraint" and of a "regime of truth" indicates the relation between truth and power. Power produces what passes for truth, and this truth then becomes the means by which the powerful wield more power. But once this is accepted as the explanation of truth, not only are any supposed criteria for judging between truth claims undermined because they, too, are socially produced; in addition, the truth claim that wins out is simply the one that has most power. If truth is the manifestation of power, this inevitably enthrones violence. If some larger truth "ceases to matter more than our individual or communal interests, violence will reign and those with stammering tongues and feeble hands will fall prey to those with smooth words and sharp swords."[130] The earlier quotation from Nietzsche reveals that there is a cost to leaving open the question of truth, a cost to its victims. The person who treats the question about truth with contempt has no compelling reason not to treat human life with contempt and say, "One Jew more or less—what does it matter?" We need to be alert not only to the dangers but also to the potential for human well-being bound up with the claim to truth that the Fourth Gospel sees embodied in Jesus.[131] What is needed, then, in the face of postmodern suspicion of metanarratives is not the discarding of all such grand stories but instead a metanarrative that witnesses to a transcendent truth from its own inevitably particular perspective, recognizing the relation of its truth claim to issues of power but at the same time decisively subverting violence.

---

[128] Volf, *Exclusion and Embrace,* 272, puts it well: "If we do not relinquish violence, the many little truths that we like to enthrone in place of the one big Truth will lead to as many little wars—wars that are as deadly as any war waged in the name of the one big Truth."

[129] M. Foucault, *Power/Knowledge: Selected Interviews and Other Writings, 1972–1977* (New York: Pantheon, 1980), 131.

[130] Volf, *Exclusion and Embrace,* 272. For a discussion of regimes of truth, see ibid., 244–50.

[131] T. Söding, "Die Macht der Wahrheit," 36; cf. also Volf, *Exclusion and Embrace,* 270–71

Like the Synoptics, John's Gospel is about a victim of violence. Yet one of the features that distinguishes this Gospel is that it so explicitly makes the death of the victim the criterion for truth. Rehearsing some of our earlier discussion will remind us how this works itself out. In the context of a lawsuit, truth is specifically the judgment about an issue at stake, and its content is determined by this issue. What is the issue in John's narrative? According to 20:31, at its heart is whether the crucified Jesus is the Messiah, the Son of God, and—from the rest of the narrative discourse we can add—therefore one with God. The discourse's depiction of the relation between Jesus and God also justifies putting the issue the other way around. As it concerns God, it is also whether God is the God who is now known in the crucified Jesus. Truth is the affirmative judgment on these interrelated issues as this judgment develops into a culminating verdict. The verdict is given in Jesus' "hour," the hour of his arrest, trial, and death, which is also the hour of his glorification. Two features of the narrative's account of this hour are particularly pertinent.

The passage to which Nietzsche referred in the citation above is Jesus' trial before Pilate. In this trial Pilate asks Jesus about his kingship. This is a question about power, and Jesus' response, subordinating his kingship to his witness to the truth, produces the exchange about truth. Jesus' strongest statement about his mission—"For this I was born, and for this I came into the world, to testify to the truth" (18:37)—is uttered by one who knows he is about to be sentenced to death, and it comes in a setting that involves a struggle for power.[132] The entire Roman trial, just like the scriptural cosmic lawsuit, revolves around what is true judgment and who speaks truly and has sovereign power. In addition, this version of the lawsuit in the Fourth Gospel highlights the issues of how true judgment is made, how the truth is witnessed to, and how sovereign power is exercised. There can be no denying that power is involved in truth claims, but this passage makes clear that the more important issue is the nature of such power. Jesus has just said that his kingship or power is not of this world (v. 36). It is exercised and displayed in this world, but it has its source elsewhere. It is therefore not to be categorized from within Pilate's this-worldly value system, where power refers to political dominance, diplomatic maneuvering, and strategic treaties and where, if Jesus is a king, it means he is claiming to overthrow Rome's rule. The consequence of Jesus' claim is that there can be a radical reevaluation of

---

[132] See esp. Söding, "Die Macht der Wahrheit," and the development of Söding's insights by Volf, *Exclusion and Embrace,* esp. 264–71.

human power. And so, when Jesus says that if his kingdom were of this world, his followers would be fighting to keep him from being handed over to "the Jews" (v. 36), he is saying that its power is not such as to be coopted by the destructive forces of this world's cycle of violence. Both the programmatic use of force by an insurrectionist such as Barabbas against an oppressive system (cf. v. 40) and the attempt by a follower such as Peter to use force in self-defense in order to resist injustice are ruled out as part of Jesus' kingdom program.[133] Peter's attempt to use the sword (cf. v. 10) is to be viewed not as in line with Jesus' kingship but as part of Peter's own misguided perspective on Jesus' cause: he does not yet realize that drinking the cup of suffering, rather than wielding worldly power, lies at the heart of Jesus' mission (cf. v. 11).

To talk of Jesus' kingdom as being not "of this world" is the same as saying it is "from above" (cf. 8:23; 19:11), and this is simply another way of saying it is "of God"—the kingdom of God. The narrative has consistently presented Jesus' claim that his words and deeds are in total dependence on God, so it is no surprise that it also equates Jesus' kingdom and God's kingdom. In focusing on Jesus, the Fourth Gospel's cosmic lawsuit—and this part of it—also raises the issue of who is the true God and how this God exercises sovereignty. Its linking of God's kingdom and Jesus' kingdom means that the way God exercises kingdom power is represented here in the figure of Jesus in his apparent weakness over against the apparent strength of Rome's political system. Jesus now makes clear that this way of exercising power is in fact dependent on his role within a different frame of reference, his role as witness to the truth. Indeed, everything about his life and mission is to be seen as bearing witness to God's just judgment in God's lawsuit with the world and to the truth of God's cause that is at stake in it. Both Jesus' kingship and the truth of this cause are therefore "from above" and not "of this world." As Volf points out, this notion of truth is making a claim quite different from Foucault's notion that "truth is a thing of this world."[134] Thus, the issue of truth and of Jesus' embodiment of it becomes the arbiter of the nature, purpose, and use of power. "In the exchange with Pilate, Jesus argues against 'the truth of power' and for 'the power of truth.'"[135] For this narrative, it is not that power is the arbiter of truth, with Jesus' kingdom power battling it out against the religious establishment and Roman imperial power with an inevitable result. "No," says Jesus, "you

---

[133] Cf. Rensberger, *Johannine Faith*, 148.
[134] Volf, *Exclusion and Embrace*, 267.
[135] Ibid., 266.

say that I am a king but I tell you that my whole mission is to testify to the truth." The trial on the earthly level before this representative of Rome is explicitly placed in the context of a larger and more ultimate trial that is taking place, one whose true judgment calls into question the values and the power play at work in the earthly trial. In the confrontation between Jesus' witness to the truth and this world's religious and political power, the forced recourse by the representatives of the world's power to crucifying the truth will demonstrate the weakness of power.[136] Jesus' willingness to give his life will demonstrate that the power of truth is a quite different sort of power. It is not "produced only by virtue of multiple forms of constraints" (Foucault) but is the power of weakness. Jesus "would rather have the truth carry a victory while he himself suffers a defeat than trample truth underfoot and emerge a 'hero.' "[137] The cosmic lawsuit demonstrates that Israel does have a sovereign over the world and its powers—"Jesus of Nazareth, the King of the Jews" is proclaimed in the major languages of the first-century world (19:19–22)— but it also makes clear that this sovereign is enthroned on, and rules from, a cross.

Chapter 5, above, noted that because the truth of the trial is about the relationship between God and Jesus and about their salvific judgment, it is also rooted in love. And so, when here the power terminology of kingship is set in the framework of the truth terminology, it is redefined further. It is not simply that Jesus' claim to kingship is through weakness; because his mission is witness to the truth, the weakness of his witness becomes the vehicle for the power of love. In contrast to the power play of this world's way of judging, Jesus stands as witness to a judgment motivated by, accomplished through, and experienced in self-giving love. Because of his unique relation to God, Jesus, in the witness of his life, death, and resurrection, embodies the truth of this loving judgment. It could not be clearer that in this narrative love and the refusal of violence are essential to its notion of truth.

The fulfillment of Jesus' task of witnessing to the truth is signaled by his final words on the cross: "It is finished" (19:30). The truth is established, true judgment in the lawsuit is given, in and through Jesus' death. By absorbing the violence of the negative verdict of death, Jesus

---

[136] Cf. P. Lehmann, *The Transfiguration of Politics* (New York: Harper & Row, 1975), 59: "The weakness of power is that when power is confronted by the authority of truth, it is no match for the power of weakness that bears the mark of truth."

[137] Volf, *Exclusion and Embrace*, 268.

becomes the source of the positive verdict of life as blood and water flow from his side (19:34). As already noted, the narrator stresses the importance of this verdict through the beloved disciple's witness and the double underlining of its truth. The symbols of the blood and the water have been explained earlier in the narrative in 6:53–54 and 7:38–39. They point unmistakably to the positive verdict of life for humanity through the death of the victim.

The Fourth Gospel is here reinforcing a pattern found earlier in the larger scriptural narrative's use of the lawsuit motif. There are echoes of the remarkable Exod 17 account of the Meribah incident (see ch. 2, above). The place-name picks up on the use of the Hebrew term *rîb, lawsuit,* which features in Exod 17:2, where the people are said to bring a suit or file a complaint against Moses. Their accusation against Moses is that he has betrayed them by bringing them to their present plight, and they are prepared to sentence him to death by stoning (vv. 3–4). Moses, however, perceives that, in accusing him, it is in fact Yahweh whom the people are testing and putting on trial (v. 2b), and the narrator underlines that what is at issue is not so much Moses' leadership as whether Yahweh is present among the people (v. 7). In this setting Yahweh instructs Moses to go on ahead of the people and to take with him the rod of judgment with which he struck the Nile. But instead of Moses having to stand before Yahweh to be judged, Yahweh promises to stand before Moses. Yahweh will stand trial and will stand on the rock to receive the sentence of judgment the people wished to carry out on Moses (vv. 5–6). Under these circumstances, Moses' striking of the rock signifies that Yahweh as the true judge takes the penalty the rebellious people in fact deserved, and through this action provision is made for them and a stream of life-giving water gushes out from the rock. The Fourth Gospel depicts, in the person of the incarnate Logos, this God taking the final consequences of being willing to be tried and judged. When Jesus, as witness and judge, absorbs the violent judgment of humans in this world, he, instead of passing on its destructive consequences, opens up the possibilities of new life. The power of the ultimate arbiter of truth is exhibited in the weakness of suffering and death. Jesus embodies the truth of divine judgment while subverting the notion that truth is simply power. The suffering and death of this Jesus as *the* witness is to be the paradigm for his followers in bearing their own witness to the truth.

Any treatment of victims and violence in the Gospels can hardly avoid some reference to the work of René Girard on violence and the sacred.[138] As we have argued, this narrative with its trial motif reflects the perspective of the persecuted rather than the persecutors. How does its handling of this motif match up to Girard's claims that the Gospels present Jesus in his death as the scapegoat who breaks the cycle of driving out violence by violence and takes the place of all victims and that these texts provide what is needed for humans to be liberated from the mimetic and violent mechanisms in which they are imprisoned? Much of Girard's discussion reinforces the point that John's Gospel portrays Jesus as the innocent victim.[139] He draws attention to the application of Ps 35:19 to Jesus by John 15:18–25—"They hated me without a cause"—and to Pilate's threefold declaration of Jesus' innocence in the Roman trial (18:38; 19:4, 6), so that, for all their differences, both Pilate and the Jewish leaders are ultimately united in their irrational persecution of this victim. And for Girard, making explicit the absence of any cause is able to expose the illusion on which persecution and violence are based. Girard also observes that this Gospel contains a passage that encapsulates the scapegoat mechanism.[140] It is found in the words of Caiaphas: "it is better for you to have one man die for the people than to have the whole nation destroyed" (11:50). "Caiaphas is the perfect sacrificer who puts victims to death to save those who live. . . . Not only do Caiaphas and his listeners not know what they are doing, they do not know what they are saying. They must therefore be forgiven."[141] The Fourth Gospel makes clear what other texts about persecution hide, namely, the knowledge that the victim is a scapegoat. It does not use this term but substitutes the image of the Lamb of God (1:29; cf. 19:36), which, in comparison with a scapegoat, "indicates more clearly the innocence of this victim, the injustice of the condemnation, and the causelessness of the hatred of which it is the object."[142] Since 16:2 says that those who make martyrs of Jesus' followers "will think that by doing so they are offering worship to God," they are presented as displaying the collective persecution that gives birth to religious illusions but also as showing themselves to be those who do not know what they do and who must therefore be forgiven. Girard goes further and sees what is said about the Paraclete as summing up his own perspective.

---

[138] Cf. esp. R. Girard, *The Scapegoat* (Baltimore: Johns Hopkins University Press, 1986).

[139] Ibid., 100–11.

[140] Ibid., 112–24.

[141] Ibid., 114.

[142] Ibid., 117.

Whereas Satan is the representation of persecution, the principle of violent expulsion, the accuser, who deceives humans "by making them believe that innocent victims are guilty," "the Paraclete is the universal advocate, the chief defender of all innocent victims, the destroyer of every representation of persecution."[143] Thus, the Paraclete's work in history is to reveal the meaning not only of Jesus' innocent death but of every innocent death.

One can question whether the texts from John will bear the weight of Girard's particular theologizing, and in the case of the Paraclete passages, they probably will not. One may also suspect that, for all its insights, there is a tendency in Girard's views to reduce the spectrum of sin and evil to violence, and the salvation Christ brings to the exposure of that violence. But more to the point here is the question of whether in fact the Fourth Gospel undermines what Girard sees as the heart of the Christian message. Does the Fourth Gospel and its framework of a cosmic lawsuit end up reinstituting the very patterns of violence that are meant to be decisively broken by the event it recounts as central to its plot? Girard himself appears to think that there is a danger that its notion of a trial may have this effect. Discussing the Paraclete, he asserts,

> It is a question neither of individual trials nor of some transcendental trial in which the Father plays the role of *Accuser*. This sort of thinking, even with the best of intentions—hell is paved with them—constantly makes the Father into a satanic figure. There can only be a question of an intermediary process between heaven and earth, the trial of "heavenly" or "worldly" powers, and of Satan himself, the trial of the representation of persecution in its entirety. Because the Gospel writers are not always able to define the place of trial they make it sometimes too transcendent or too immanent."[144]

This is in line with Girard's view that there is a "distance separating Jesus and his spirit from those who were the first to receive his message and transmit it to us" and that "the writing of the Gospels was influenced by the very same mimeticism that was the subject of Jesus' endless reproaches to his disciples."[145] It is difficult to see, however, how the Fourth Gospel could be accused of making the trial too transcendent or too immanent. Whether it is the trial of Jesus before "the Jews" in his mission, or his trial before Pilate, or the trials of his followers in the world, they are all in history, yet at the same time they are given a cosmic context because, in and through them, the lawsuit between God and the

---

[143] Ibid., 207.
[144] Ibid., 209.
[145] Ibid., 161.

world is taking place. The trial motif therefore operates on both the immanent and the transcendent level and at the same time takes in what Girard calls the intermediary process through the roles given to the Paraclete and Satan. Nor, on the transcendent level, can the primary role of the Father in the narrative be said to be as accuser but, rather, as judge. It is true that, as in Deutero-Isaiah, the judge can sometimes take on a prosecuting role through agents, Jesus and the Paraclete, but this hardly turns God as judge into a permanent accuser who can be compared to Satan. Instead the prosecuting role is a means to achieving the desired verdict, and it is continually emphasized that such a verdict is the positive verdict of life, which is the primary aim of the divine agent's mission.

The fact that the world represented by "the Jews" is judged by God unless it accepts the claims of Jesus' witness might suggest that the group represented by the evangelist has projected onto God its hatred of its persecutors. But this would be a superficial observation because the attitude God has to the world is one of love, not hatred (3:16), and it is a self-giving love demonstrated in Jesus' victimization. In any case, the trial motif suggests a community looking not for vengeance but for justice. It makes God not a God of violent hatred but a God who judges justly, and the wrath of God (3:36) is not God's angry vengeance but the negative aspect of God's just judgment. In fact, this God puts judgment into the hands of the witness-martyr (5:22, 27), so that it is the lifted up Son of Man, the crucified and exalted victim, who is the judge, and the world is judged in terms of its relationship to this victim. And judgment, at least, is left to the God who is known through the victim; it is not something Jesus' followers see themselves carrying out. Their task is simply to witness to the truth, and a substantial part of this truth is that, in the victim of the world's hatred and miscarriage of justice, God is truly made known. This is a truth that sets people free, free to imitate this self-giving love and free from rivalry. The pattern of believers' witness in the unbelieving world, as we have seen, is to be the pattern of Jesus himself, including a willingness to be martyrs, to be the victims of the world's uncomprehending hatred.

But there still remains the question of whether the community consistently lives up to this ideal. Do the persecuted in any way become the persecutors? In terms of the original setting of the Gospel, there was, in any case, little or no opportunity for this to happen. All the language of persecution and hatred in the narrative discourse concerns the attitude of the world toward Jesus and his followers, and the only follower who tries to strike back in any way, Peter in 18:10–11, receives a clear rebuke.

At most, what could be argued is that the polemic against Jesus' opposition in the narrative betrays hatred and the wish to persecute. The only passage that is a real candidate for such suspicion is 8:31–59. Presumably it is on the basis of this passage that some speak of "the Johannine church's hatred and rejection of Jews who had rejected it."[146] It is undoubtedly true that its language contained a potentially poisonous deposit that would later, under very different circumstances, feed into persecution of Jews by Christians. But if we were right in our earlier reading of this section, then in the Gospel itself it is not unbelieving Jews per se who receive the indictment that links them with the devil as a murderer and the father of lies but those who had believed but did not continue in the faith, those who had abandoned any solidarity with Johannine Christians. These were not people whom the Johannine Christians had driven out but those who had removed themselves and aligned themselves again with established Judaism. No doubt it could no longer be said of such people that they did not know what they were doing, in the same sense that this might be said of unbelievers. Yet while the language in which they are indicted appears to leave little room for any sympathetic understanding of their stance and to write them off, this may well, as we have seen, be importing contemporary sensitivities into the text. Similar and just as strong accusations and indictments of unbelieving Israel are found in the prophetic literature. It is easy to forget that, just as in the prophets, particularly Isaiah, who influenced John, and just as in the words of the Jesus of the synoptic tradition, so here fierce polemic and harsh judgment are meant to reinforce the call to repentance and belief. Jesus begins the discussion of 8:31–59 with a group of Jews who had believed in him with an invitation to them to continue in his word (v. 31) and, after the harshest part of the exchange, reiterates his salvific mission: "whoever keeps my word will never see death" (v. 51). Those who loosely characterize Johannine Christians in terms of hatred and violence must be asked whether there is any real evidence for the view that this community desired to succumb to vengeance in mimetic repetition of its persecutors' actions.

The Fourth Gospel's narrative of truth on trial undermines the ideological use of its story to bring about marginalization and violence, for it embraces pain in making the suffering servant-witness and the

---

[146] E.g., W. Wink, *Engaging the Powers* (Minneapolis: Fortress, 1992), 148. D. Boyarin, *A Radical Jew: Paul and the Politics of Identity* (Berkeley: University of California Press, 1994), 203, goes so far as to speak of the "violence of a community such as the one that later would produce John's gospel."

crucified God the criterion of truth. By setting its depiction within God's overarching universal purposes for the world, it also counters the tendency of any one group to justify itself with reference to this story in a way that lays exclusive claim to it. Inevitably Johannine Christianity defined itself over against the Judaism from which many of its Jewish Christian members had been excluded, and undoubtedly it employs clear-cut formulations about, on the one hand, believers in Jesus and, on the other, the world that opposes them. It is also true that victims hardly ever see themselves as former victims. The scars remain and such victims always have to deal with resentful memories. But the narrative, with its emphasis on accepting love, indicates the resources for healing (see ch. 6, above). Out of the assurance of love, rather than fear, emerged a vision that was shaped but not preoccupied by the experience of exclusion.

> The gospel of John presents a solution greater than the problems with which it was faced. Written in a situation of conflict and oppression, and with all the limitations imposed by adherence to one party in a hard-fought and many-sided struggle, the gospel of John refuses to restrict that struggle to its own terms of time, place and society but connects it instead to the deepest issues of God's relation to the world and the human race, and of the human response to God and to one another.[147]

It is precisely the universal scope of the cosmic lawsuit that enables this to happen. The interrogations and trials of Johannine Christians are presented as a microcosm of the lawsuit between God and the world that is unfolding and will unfold until the public ratification of the verdict that was made in the mission of Jesus. The two aspects of the verdict in the cosmic trial are not evenly balanced. Repeatedly it is made clear that the purpose of the trial is the positive verdict of life as God reclaims the world for God's purposes of human well-being. The negative side of judgment, even though the story is told from the experience of a marginalized group, always remains a secondary consequence and not God's original intent. In Isaiah, where the template for the lawsuit motif had been provided, there is both particularity and universalism as God reaches out to the nations through God's dealings in Zion. And in Isa 40–55 the word of judgment is, surprisingly, not the last word in the trial of nations; rather, there is the offer of salvation if they will turn to the true God. In John also there is no denying the scandal of particularity in the necessity of belief in Jesus, but again its benefit of eternal life remains on offer to all and is not seen as the exclusive possession of one community. The scope of Jesus' authority in giving eternal life is "all

---

[147] Rensberger, *Johannine Faith*, 137.

flesh" (17:2), and the mission of the believing community has as its goal that the world may believe and know (17:21, 23). The purpose of the cosmic trial, then, is not the perpetuation but the overcoming of the present hostility between the world and Jesus' followers. But given the history of misuse of this Gospel's discourse, readers who find themselves in very different circumstances from those reflected in its narrative have no option other than continual vigilance lest its clear-cut categories of "believers" over against "the world," instead of making sense of an exclusion by others, now become employed to write off others as excluded from God's offer of well-being and life.

This Gospel speaks of God's love for the hostile world, a love that discloses itself in the divine self-giving in the Son as the victim of the world's violence. It witnesses to a God whose justice is not only directed toward life but contains within it the grounds and motivation for remaining open toward the hostile other. With this as its founding narrative, the community from which the Fourth Gospel originated, whatever its temptation to reciprocate the hostility of the world, was continually reminded that the cross of Jesus is the radical openness of God toward that world. Its members could now also never forget that they themselves were part of the antagonistic world for which God has given God's self. Those who understand Jesus' role in this lawsuit know that in his death God provides life for those who do not deserve this positive verdict. This means that God's love is greater than the sin of unbelief, including the community members' own sin, and so, in the nature of the lawsuit, believers in Jesus are not free to view themselves as a totally innocent "us" against an evil "them"; they are reminded of their own status as needing the Judge's positive verdict. Johannine Christians could be involved in intense and fierce debate precisely because they were concerned for the truth that was on trial and took seriously their differences with others. But there could be no question of perpetuating the destructive cycle of violence through manipulation, intimidation, and hatred of those with whom they disagreed. This would be to succumb to the notion of truth as self-serving power. "Jesus, who claimed to be the Truth, refused to use violence to 'persuade' those who did not recognize his truth."[148] The whole thrust of the Gospel narrative that his followers acknowledge as true renounces the values of regimes of truth, with their "multiple forms of constraint," for an entirely different set of values based on the weakness of a love that is prepared to risk following this Jesus.

---

[148] Volf, *Exclusion and Embrace,* 272.

chapter nine

APPROPRIATING
the FOURTH GOSPEL'S
LAWSUIT: *Four Reflections*

The task of human witnesses is to point beyond themselves, by their words and deeds, to that to which they are testifying. The witness of the Gospel of John points away from itself to the only self-authenticating witness, the one it claims is the disclosure of God, the Word of God. Its particular, partial, and fallible human words constitute its witness to the God revealed in Christ. If this is the case, then any interpretation of this Gospel that remains content with setting it in its historical and social context, elucidating its syntax, or analyzing its plot would not be doing justice to the human words with which such an interpretation is concerned. These words claim to be a testimony. And to take testimony seriously is to pay attention to that to which it testifies. Therefore, any adequate interpretation of the Fourth Gospel has to be theological interpretation.[1]

This is not to suggest that only at this late stage will we begin to approach the theological subject matter. There are a variety of ways to undertake theological interpretation, and we have already engaged in some of them. Inevitably, for example, the discussion of the theological perspective of the Fourth Gospel from the vantage point of the trial motif (see ch. 5, above) was shaped not only by analysis of the text as a docu-

---

[1] See Barth, *Church Dogmatics* (Edinburgh: T&T Clark, 1956), 1.1.466–69, for the more general development of this point in relation to Scripture.

ment from the past but also by the present theological horizons of the interpreter. That discussion is presupposed here, where the present theological concerns become more explicit. In addition, the interaction with some of the objections to the appropriation of our chosen motif in the previous chapter has obviously entailed theological interpretation. Its treatment of issues has made clear that the scope for, and implications of, such reflection are far-reaching. This final chapter can offer reflections in only four broad areas, with the understanding that these merit even more extensive and profound theological treatment and that further areas could have been treated.

Our basic assumption is that just as the Fourth Gospel has taken up a scriptural metaphor and interpreted it for its own setting, so Christian theological interpretation of this Gospel is engaged in a similar enterprise. In Deutero-Isaiah the metaphor encompassed the varying roles of Yahweh, Israel (particularly as represented in its community of exiles), and the nations and their gods (particularly in the form of Babylon). In the Fourth Gospel, the main actors become God in Christ, the community of Christ's believing followers, and the unbelieving world, now represented particularly by unbelieving Judaism but also by the power of Rome in the form of Pilate. For contemporary Christians, the parties in the lawsuit are God in Christ, the church, and the unbelieving world, with the dominant representatives of this world now being construed as its religious, economic, political, and philosophical ideologies. God is still to be seen as having established the divine verdict in Christ, and John's witness is part of the tradition that urges Christian believers to trust their lives to this verdict rather than to the competing ideologies.

A. Christ and the Truth about God

It has become clear that the Fourth Gospel's trial of truth is not the story of the human quest for truth, even for the truth of God. The cosmic trial is the story of God's loving encounter with rebellious creatures whom God desires to persuade of the truth—the truth about their Creator, the truth about the world, and the truth about their place in the world. Its distinctive claim is that, in carrying out the lawsuit, this God has become part of the world's story through Jesus Christ. All of these truths are therefore centered around the protagonist, Jesus, who is himself the truth and promises to lead his followers into all the truth through the Spirit of truth. And since this truth will not be completely known until the completion of the trial at the end of history, each generation has the responsibility of receiving it and working out its implications for that generation's own time and circumstances on the basis of the witness supplied by the Fourth Gospel. If truth is tied to God and God's cause in the trial, then it is not simply that which resides in the world. Truth is that which comes to humans rather than that which they can possess and manipulate. So God's witness in Christ offers a new starting point for viewing truth and a different notion of certitude about truth. Such certitude is based neither on some irrefutable proof of the truth of the witness nor on its conformity to some universal criterion. This would be to hold that there are more reliable grounds than what is offered in the witness of Christ and to accommodate this witness to the reigning plausibility structures of our time. Instead the certitude associated with this witness is trust in the faithful persuasion of a loving God who is not under human control but who identifies with the human situation to the point of undergoing death.

John's version of the trial of truth makes the identity of Jesus a matter of ultimate significance for human beings. This is a basic observation but one which Christians can sometimes either take for granted without continuing to be amazed and challenged by it or be tempted to downplay out of embarrassment in a pluralistic religious context. There would be only one justification for giving another human such decisive and definitive significance for human existence as a whole, especially within the context of Second Temple Judaism, where God alone could legitimately lay claim to ultimate allegiance from humans: if it could somehow be maintained that this human, in distinction from others, had a relationship to the one God of Israel that uniquely identified him with this God. This is the central issue in John's story of the divine lawsuit—the relation of Jesus to God. God's judicial action on behalf of the world takes place within the sphere of human and cosmic history and is identified with the witness of the life and death of Jesus of Nazareth. This is the reason John's trial motif and the Gospel as a whole posit absolute significance for Jesus Christ. The truth is held to be that Jesus does indeed have an identity that can be said to be one with that of God and that God is the God who is now known in Jesus. This theological assertion is reinforced by the results of literary probes into the characterization of God in this Gospel's narrative discourse: "God is characterized by Jesus and . . . having understood the gospel's characterization of Jesus one has grasped its characterization of God,"[2] and "God is characterized as *the God who is known through*

---

[2] Culpepper, *Anatomy,* 113.

Jesus."[3] The return to literary categories here is not inappropriate. It serves as a reminder that a primary means of identifying God throughout Scripture is narrative. God's identity is disclosed through the establishment of character and the execution of purposes that are presented in particular narratives. In the case of the Fourth Gospel's narrative, God's identity is disclosed in the role played by the person and mission of Jesus in the cosmic trial, and its plot and discourse explicitly make Jesus' person and mission intrinsic to the divine identity.

To align oneself with the divine judgment on Jesus' person and mission is to experience the trial's positive verdict of eternal life. The words of Jesus' farewell prayer in 17:3—"And this is eternal life, that they may know you, the only true God, and Jesus Christ whom you have sent"— summarize the entire narrative's perspective on what is entailed. The gift of eternal life depends on knowing the one God and this God's uniquely authorized representative, Jesus Christ. It is striking that although Jesus, as God's unique agent, is clearly presented in the narrative as one with God, the relationship does not entail, in this formulation, any abrogation of monotheism for the evangelist. The formulation about the only true God is reminiscent of the exclusive claims for Yahweh that can be found in the Jewish Scriptures. Among these claims in Deutero-Isaiah is this assertion by Yahweh: "I am the LORD, that is my name; my glory I give to no other" (Isa 42:8). But if there is one true God, how can this God share the divine glory with Jesus, as the prayer of John 17 makes clear he does, without Jesus being a second god? Since for John there remains only one true God, Jesus, in his relationship as Son to the Father, must be intrinsic to this one God's identity. As Jesus' petition in 17:5 makes clear, he was always included in the identity and glory of the one God, even before the foundation of the world. It is not the case, then, that in glorifying Jesus God shares the divine glory with some lesser being. Rather, the glorification and exaltation of Jesus display the glory of the one God. The truth of the trial is that in Jesus the one God of Israel is encountered. This also has a historical theological implication. Given the persistence of views to the contrary, it bears underlining that the divinity of Jesus, in the sense of his full inclusion in the identity of the one God of Israel, is not a later invention of, or even development within, patristic debate and Greek thought forms but is already the clear witness of the Fourth Gospel.

---

[3] M. M. Thompson, " 'God's Voice You Have Never Heard, God's Form You Have Never Seen': The Characterization of God in the Gospel of John," *Semeia* 63 (1993): 201.

Since this is the case, and particularly since the one God's glorification is now seen as taking place supremely in the crucifixion of the one who is sent, the Fourth Gospel's perspective on the truth of the trial requires a transformation in the definition of God. It becomes appropriate to speak of "the radical changes in the content of the word *God* that were made necessary by the death of Jesus."[4] These changes are made necessary both by Jesus' death and by his humanity, which is the presupposition for his death. Essential to the new content of the word *God* is the claim that God is uniquely present in the witness and judgment that constitute the mission of Jesus. Indeed, God has so identified God's self with Jesus that Jesus in his humanity embodies God. The God to whom Jesus witnesses is the God who chooses to include humanity, the particular humanity of Jesus of Nazareth, in God's own identity. "The Word became flesh," and thus Jesus can say, "Whoever has seen me has seen the Father" (1:14; 14:9). And because the mission of Jesus in the trial is presented as culminating in his death by execution, which is equated with his glorification, the radicality of the change in the definition of God goes further. In Jesus' death it is especially the case that "whoever has seen me has seen the Father." God is identified as the God who not only takes humanity into God's self but also takes suffering humanity into God's self. This God is a God who is vulnerable to the point of death, the crucified God. In experiencing death, such a God identifies with humanity in the consequences of its hostility to God and its judgment by God. God therefore takes into God's self that which is the antithesis to God, so that God's glory is now to be seen in the shame and degradation in the death of Jesus as the victim of the world's injustice. This is also the force of the declaration that God so loved the world—the world of humanity in its opposition to God and in its resulting state of death—that God gave God's only Son (cf. 3:16). The God disclosed in the Fourth Gospel's narrative embraces that which contradicts God—alienated and hostile humanity and its condemnation.

These changes inevitably also transform the notion of God as judge. The vision, generated by the general cosmic-trial metaphor, of God as judge and lawgiver and of history as a vast tribunal could in itself convey the idea that the whole of existence is based on moral accounting.[5] In

---

[4] Minear, *John: The Martyr's Gospel*, 29.

[5] Cf. Ricoeur, *Symbolism of Evil*, 314, who reflects on this problem in relation to Job. For extensive discussion of issues of retribution and judgment in the biblical material, cf. also S. H. Travis, *Christ and the Judgment of God* (London: Marshall Morgan & Scott, 1986).

such a view, God is the God of retribution, and suffering is punishment. Undeserved suffering remains at best an accusation against such a God. Already the covenantal lawsuit in the Jewish Scriptures had qualified this perception; it placed the issue of the divine response to obedience or disobedience within the context of a relationship of trust between Yahweh and Israel, and it showed that Yahweh's judgment often entailed undeserved rescue of Israel from its plight. The Fourth Gospel's use of the lawsuit motif, however, clearly subverts the general moral view of a cosmic trial. Interestingly, such a moral view rears its head at the beginning of the passage that turns out to be the interrogation of the man born blind. There the disciples' question assumes that the man's blindness must be punishment for sin, either his own or his parents (cf. 9:2). But the assumption is immediately dismissed by Jesus, who focuses instead on the works of God that constitute his mission. The disciples "see suffering as an occasion for moralizing about the victim. Jesus sees it as an occasion for doing the works of God, that is, for relieving the suffering. . . . The 'work of God,' it turns out, is not punishing sinners with suffering but overcoming the suffering."[6] What the overall lawsuit makes clear is that the overcoming of suffering and the giving of light and life ultimately derive from Jesus' identity and the divine verdict on that identity displayed in Jesus' own suffering and death. Since the truth of the trial is the unity between God and Jesus, the suffering and death of Jesus is at the same time the suffering and death of the judge. In this way, far from merely reinforcing notions of retribution, the Fourth Gospel's use of the lawsuit motif, with its depiction of the suffering of the judge, breaks the schema of strict ethical accounting. The suffering of this victim is not deserved, and precisely because it is not, it is able to deal with the sin of the world and offer life in place of death, disrupting the cycle of moral retribution with a gift. Ricoeur claims that it is only this sort of Christology, in which suffering is taken up into the divine life, that can transcend the problems of an ethical monotheism.[7] The God uniquely disclosed in Jesus is not simply, then, a sovereign judge who remains aloof but the judge who is judged and undergoes the sentence of death. Suffering and death are not alien to this God. God's freedom to be both the judge and the accused, the exalted and the lowly one, is not divine caprice but essential to the identity of the God who has initiated the trial, commissioned Christ to be the divine agent, and accomplished a saving verdict.

---

[6] Rensberger, *Johannine Faith*, 44.
[7] Ricoeur, *Symbolism of Evil*, 327–28.

Given these changes in the content of the word *God,* is the God of Jesus still recognizable as the God of Israel? For John, as already seen, it is vital that the God of this narrative is indeed the one God of Israel. The continuities between the God of Jesus and the God of the Jewish Scriptures are evident, and only the most salient are rehearsed here. The entire background of the lawsuits between God and Israel and between God and the nations that shapes and informs the narrative presupposes that it is only Israel's God who has the exclusive right to put the world on trial. The identification of this God has already been made in the Jewish Scriptures by showing that divine judgment includes specific acts in the world, such as the exodus and the bringing back from exile, that arise from God's identification of God's cause with that of a particular people, Israel. Within the covenant relationship, God has allowed God's self to be put on trial and accused. In the remarkable account of the Meribah incident, Exod 17 presents God as prepared to undergo judgment for the sake of the people, a judgment that produces life, symbolized by the water that flows from the rock. The identification of the God of Jesus in John's Gospel is both completely in line with such characteristics and yet radically new. Israel's sovereign God retains the right to surprise. The God willing to be identified as Israel's God now chooses to be identified as the God of one particular Israelite, Jesus. The God who acted in the world on behalf of humans now takes on human form. The God willing to experience judgment for the sake of the life of God's people now undergoes the judgment of death in the death of Jesus for the sake of the life of all humanity. The identification of God through Jesus, for all its newness, is still discernibly an identification of Israel's God.

For the Fourth Gospel, the nature and identity of God as judge is seen in God's saving activity and the manner in which it is accomplished. Since not only God but also Jesus have the role of judge in John's version of the lawsuit, the notion of the judge who is judged applies to both. This formulation has emerged naturally from the Johannine discourse, but it is significant that Barth independently made "The Judge Judged in our Place" a key category in his treatment of the doctrine of reconciliation.[8] He applies it particularly to the work of Christ: "If He were not the Judge, He would not be the Saviour. He is the Saviour of the world in so far as in a very definite (and most astonishing) way He is also its judge."[9] Barth rightly draws attention to the

---

[8] Cf. K. Barth, *Church Dogmatics* 4:1.211–83.
[9] Ibid., 217.

point that, in the OT, judging includes helping and rescuing as well as pardoning and condemning. He also stresses that when Jesus comes to exercise this role as judge, he comes to execute the divine judgment, so that it is God, the divine judge, who is also in the person of Jesus pursuing judgment in the world. For this reason, there can be no appeal beyond Jesus to some higher court; this Judge is the criterion of all justice. For this reason also, the coming of Jesus as the judge reveals the full seriousness of the human situation. The Judge comes into a setting in which humans have given a different account of themselves and made themselves the measure of judgment. Indeed, this is the essence of sin—that humans set themselves up as their own judges. In so doing, they give themselves to a world set in conflict with the true judge and to the consequences of such alienation in suffering and destruction. A world looking for justification from itself is a world hostile to the God from whom alone justification can come. Because of this setting of the world into which he comes, the coming of Jesus as judge would inevitably entail the condemnation of a hostile world to perishing. Yet God chooses to execute this sentence in a strange way. Without mitigating its condemnation, God carries out the sentence in such a way that it produces the pardon that humanity could never secure for itself. What results is a serious judgment of the world that achieves "love out of wrath, life out of death."[10] This is what took place in God's judgment in Christ, who fulfilled the righteous judgment on humans by becoming human and "in our place undergoing the judgment under which we had passed." God "judged, and it was the Judge who was judged, who let Himself be judged."[11] Because of his humanity, Jesus was able to be judged like us. Because of his identity with God, he had the power to allow this to happen to him and, in doing so, to exercise a saving judgment that freed us from accusation and condemnation.

Lest anyone accuse this account, in rehearsing the Barthian discussion, of straying far from John and of imposing a Pauline or an Anselmian view (or a Pauline view read through the lenses of Anselm!) of the atonement on the Gospel, that person is urged simply to return to the discussion of the Gospel's perspective on God, Jesus, and the outcome of the trial (ch. 5, secs. A–C, above), especially the treatment of the death of Jesus as the death of the judge. This should serve as a reminder that these theological categories are all there *in nuce* when the Gospel is

---

[10] Ibid., 221.
[11] Ibid., 222.

seen from the perspective of the cosmic-lawsuit motif. If, then, Barth will be of further assistance here in his development of the discussion of "The Judge Judged in our Place," it is in the service of elaborating on the witness of the Fourth Gospel itself.

Grasping the truth about God as judge makes all the difference to the way humans live their lives, and Barth will take up the significance of God's strange judgment by returning to the notion of sin as the arrogance in which humans want to be both their own and their neighbors' judges, an arrogance that in practice means wanting to pronounce ourselves righteous and others more or less guilty.[12] Since *The Fall*, a novel by Camus, provides penetrating insights into precisely this aspect of the human predicament, it will serve here as a backdrop to Barth's exposition. Its protagonist, Jean-Baptiste Clemence, whose name evokes both John the Baptist's preaching of judgment and the notion of clemency or mercy, was formerly a highly successful lawyer in Paris who has made judging an art, a philosophy, a way of life, a vocation. He ends up frequenting Amsterdam's waterfront, where he relates his "fall" to a chance acquaintance, having introduced himself as a "judge-penitent." Before the fall Jean-Baptiste had been in an Eden-like state of harmony where he took pleasure in his own superiority and moral excellence with no sense of self-condemnation. "Even in the details of daily life, I needed to feel *above*. . . . My profession . . . set me above the judge whom I judged in turn, above the defendant whom I forced to gratitude."[13] His fall can be dated to the evening when a young woman in black jumped into the Seine just after he had passed her. He heard her drowning cries but did not turn back to help. His initial sense of moral weakness and failure is reactivated two or three years later when, at the height of his self-satisfaction, he hears bursting out behind him a laugh whose source he is unable to discover. The laughter of scorn and condemnation at his hypocritical posturing, whether it comes from an unknown quasi-cosmic source, from himself, or from others, punctuates his gradual disintegration. He cannot maintain the picture of himself as one who "has a vocation for justice and is the predestined defender of the widow and orphan" when he becomes aware that "when I was threatened, I became not only a judge in turn but even more: an irascible master who wanted, regardless of all laws, to strike down the offender and get him on his knees."[14] While Jean-Baptiste regretted his failings, his love for

---

[12] Cf. ibid., 231.

[13] A. Camus, *The Fall* (Harmondsworth, England: Penguin, 1963), 19, 21.

[14] Ibid., 42.

himself enabled him to forget them. "The prosecution of others, on the contrary, went on constantly in my heart." This might not be logical. "But the question is not how to remain logical . . . yes, above all, the question is how to elude judgement." But this is by no means an easy matter. "Today we are always as ready to judge as we are to fornicate."[15] Indeed, he discovers that "the circle of which I was the centre broke and they lined up in a row as on the judges' bench. The moment I grasped that there was something to judge me, I realized that, in fact, they had an irresistible vocation for judgement. Yes, they were there as before, but they were laughing. Or rather it seemed to me that every one of them that I met was looking at me with a hidden smile."[16] Since the sense of being judged by others is intolerable, "people hasten to judge in order not to be judged themselves. . . . Each of us insists on being innocent at all costs, even if he has to accuse the whole human race and heaven itself."[17]

In the attempt to drown out the laughter of judgment, Clemence drifts into simply playing a role with total scornful indifference toward others. But "wasn't it this, after all, for which, on top of my blunders, I could not forgive myself, which made me revolt most violently against the judgement I felt forming, in me and around me, and that forced me to seek an escape?"[18] Alcohol and debauchery offered some solace. "Because I longed for eternal life, I went to bed with harlots and drank for nights on end."[19] But they ultimately provide no escape and have their consequences. "One plays at being immortal and after a few weeks one doesn't know whether or not one can hang on till the next day."[20] Eventually the solution dawns. In a world without God, he cannot wait for the last judgment that was in any case taking place every day.[21] Instead "I was obliged to make myself a judge-penitent."[22] He discovers that, in accusing himself and confessing his failures in a particular way, he can disarm the judgment of others and at the same time draw them into judging and condemning themselves. "The portrait I hold out to my contemporaries becomes a mirror. . . . The more I accuse myself, the

---

[15] Ibid., 57.
[16] Ibid., 58.
[17] Ibid., 60.
[18] Ibid., 65.
[19] Ibid., 76.
[20] Ibid., 77.
[21] Cf. ibid., 98, 82, 62.
[22] Ibid., 62.

more I have a right to judge you. Even better, I provoke you into judging yourself, and this relieves me of that much of the burden."[23] This stance allows him to confess his guilt while all the time remaining in the judgment seat. "Inasmuch as one couldn't condemn others without immediately judging oneself, one had to overwhelm oneself to have the right to judge others. Inasmuch as every judge some day ends up as a penitent, one had to travel the road in the opposite direction and practise the profession of penitent to be able to end up as judge."[24] "Once more I have found a height to which I am the only one to climb and from which I can judge everybody."[25]

In the course of his confession, Clemence reveals that he is harboring a stolen painting in a cupboard. It turns out to be *The Just Judges*, a panel from the Van Eyck altarpiece *The Adoration of the Lamb*, where the judges on horseback are on their way to meet the lamb. In Clemence's world the Christian linking of human justice to the divine judgment of mercy is severed—"justice being separated once and for all from innocence—the latter on the cross and the former in the cupboard."[26] Instead he can operate in "the closed little universe of which I am the king, the Pope, and the judge."[27] Here, as he treats everyone as guilty, he is "an enlightened advocate of slavery." Since freedom is too heavy to bear and "at the end of freedom is a court-sentence,"[28] he announces his own law—in place of heaven's law—which consigns all to a collective slavery of guilt and of judgment that has no escape.[29] "How intoxicating to feel like God the Father and to hand out definitive testimonials of bad character and habits. . . . I pity without absolving, I understand without forgiving and, above all, I feel at last that I am being adored!"[30]

Here indeed, with its reversal of Christian values, is a profound depiction of the complex plight to which the insistence on being one's own judge can lead. As we have seen, the Fourth Gospel describes the human judging that resists the judgment of Jesus as a judging by appearances or according to the flesh (7:24; 8:15), and it holds that such judging arises from, and results in, the sin of refusal to be the creature who is

---

[23] Ibid., 102–3.
[24] Ibid., 101.
[25] Ibid., 104.
[26] Ibid., 96.
[27] Ibid., 94.
[28] Ibid., 97.
[29] Cf. ibid., 87, 100.
[30] Ibid., 105.

accountable before the Creator and Judge. The Gospel elaborates on this plight in terms of both slavery (8:34) and death (cf., e.g., 8:21, 24). Clemence ends up attempting to usurp and, in the process, aping the role of the divine judge, while still hopelessly caught up in the slavery and death of guilt and condemnation. He pronounces the verdict on others while undergoing it himself, and the world's judgment on him is turned into his judgment of the world. In John, Jesus pronounces the divine verdict that he undergoes himself, and the world's judgment on Jesus is in reality his judgment of the world. But a merely guilty judge can only make others complicit in his slavery. It requires a divine and therefore truly innocent judge and victim for such a role to be liberating and life-giving. Only when the destructive judgment of humans is absorbed by such a judge is there opened up the possibility of real life instead of the passing on of the slavish and deathly consequences of human judgment. Rowan Williams captures the human dilemma well: Since "judging exposes me to judgment . . . I am my own victim, no less than the one I judge, and that is why I need salvation, rescue from the trap of the judge-victim relationship, the gift of a relationship which is not of this kind."[31]

As Barth points out, when we perversely want to be judge, "we enjoy ourselves in this craft and dignity. We find our consolation and refuge and strength in exercising it."[32] But Jesus Christ as judge claims this role as his own right, reestablishing the function of God as judge. In doing for us what we wanted to do for ourselves, his action removes us from the judge's seat. This is threatening, since he as judge will also judge me and I shall not be able to stand, and he and not I will judge others. But at the same time, Jesus Christ's judging in our place brings liberation and hope, since it lifts an intolerable burden we have placed on ourselves. Indeed, "we are in the process of dying from this office of judge which we have arrogated to ourselves."[33] But now it is no longer necessary to find ways to pronounce myself innocent and see others as more or less guilty. "I am not the Judge. Jesus Christ is judge. The matter is taken out of my hands. And that means liberation."[34] People can turn to other more fruitful pursuits, knowing that their own and others' cases are in safe hands—those of the judge who is *for* us.

---

[31] R. Williams, *Resurrection* (London: Darton, Longman & Todd, 1982), 12.
[32] Barth, *Church Dogmatics*, 4:1.231–32.
[33] Ibid., 234.
[34] Ibid., 234.

By taking our place as judge, Jesus does not do what humans have been doing but accepts the responsibility for, and consequences of, our usurpation of the judgment seat. He exposes himself to the charges and the sentence that result from such judging. He becomes "the one rejected man, the Lamb which bears the sin of the world that the world should no longer be able to bear it, that it should be radically and totally taken away from it."[35] In this way God has in Christ made our sin God's own, thereby judging it and judging those who committed it. What makes the passion and crucifixion of Jesus a unique occurrence in comparison with other human suffering is precisely the person and mission of the one who suffered and died. It is because the one who died is one with God, it is because the Judge is judged in the place of those who ought to be judged, that the crucifixion is the decisive event for the history of the world. In the cosmic trial it needed nothing less than God the Judge to intervene if there was to be a positive verdict. There was nothing humans could do themselves to achieve such an outcome. Despite all their ingenuity and subtlety, their state remains one of condemnation and death. By initiating the cosmic trial, God intends to do for the world what the world cannot do for itself—pronounce a positive verdict about its own state. In being judged in their place, in experiencing death, Christ has provided the solution to the all-important question of how to elude judgment and has rescued them from death and its destructive powers. When human judgment submits itself in adoration to the divine judgment in the lamb that takes away the sin of the world (1:29), the burden of having to become a judge-penitent, with its despairing cynicism, is removed. Instead the human vocation becomes that of the forgiven and forgiving witness, the servant who, having had his or her feet washed, is able to wash the feet of others (cf. 13:10, 14–15). Rather than being the arrogant judge or the enslaved victim or some combination of the two, the witness, freed from the need to remain in the judgment seat at all costs, simply points to and communicates the divine verdict that has already been pronounced (20:23). This is a vocation that is full of hope because it is accompanied by the divine Spirit, who promotes the trial's verdict, which overturns the usual criteria of human judgment, by pointing to the root problem—sin—and to its solution in the justice of Jesus' cause (16:8–11) and by communicating the positive verdict of life (7:38–39). Belief in the God disclosed in Jesus, the judge who is judged, means that human life need no longer be

---

[35] Ibid., 237.

haunted by the hollow laughter of condemnation but can be surprised and filled by the joy that is the fruit of the positive verdict of life (cf. 15:11; 17:13).

B. Christ and the Truth about Justice and Life

Eternal life in the Fourth Gospel, then, depends on knowing the God who is disclosed in Christ, and in the context of the lawsuit, restoration to the relationship constituted by such knowledge is what makes eternal life the trial's positive verdict for humanity. There is, however, a widespread tradition of reading the Fourth Gospel as dealing with the individual Christian's relationship to Christ and interpreting this relationship in purely spiritual terms. *Justice* would then be reduced to the individual believer's experience of God's verdict on his or her life, and *life* to the subjective inner experience of communion with God through Christ. Such a reading may also have been encouraged by Clement of Alexandria's labeling of this Gospel as a "spiritual gospel," although he primarily has in view a comparison between John's approach to the Jesus tradition and that of the Synoptic Gospels.[36] To read the Fourth Gospel in the light of the lawsuit motif, however, allows one to place these emphases in a broader context, where they take on a more than merely individual and spiritual connotation.

The purpose of the scriptural lawsuit was the bringing of justice and life to God's people. Justice was indeed seen as the condition for life. In many instances the setting for the lawsuit was Israel's experience of concrete injustices and its crying out for Yahweh to intervene in such a way as to deal with oppression and restore what was necessary for Israel's well-being. Jewish eschatological hopes also followed this pattern. There would be a last judgment in which wrongs would be righted and at which the resurrection of the righteous would be followed by their enjoyment of the life of the age to come. The Fourth Gospel depicts how in Jesus the God of Israel, the one true God, is bringing to the world the justice for which it longs and the fullness of life that accompanies such justice. In its narrative Jesus functions as the witness to this purpose—justice and life for all, for the world—and as the judge who has authority to accomplish it. The truth of the divine verdict in the lawsuit is therefore not only about theological claims for Jesus but also about the relation of his followers and the relation of human existence as a whole to the divine purpose.

---

[36] Cf. the citation of Clement in Eusebius, *Hist. eccl.* 14.7.

It is not only the scriptural framework of the lawsuit that prompts a reading in which justice and life are not simply reduced to spiritual notions. Chapter 6, above, suggested that another catalyst for the evangelist's employment of the motif was the specific setting in the life of the community from which the Gospel emerged. The trial's themes addressed the concrete issues of what Johannine Christians considered the injustice of Jesus' treatment at the hands of Jewish religious and Roman political authorities and of their own treatment at the hands of the Jewish authorities in their area, whereby their expulsion from the synagogue was accompanied by social deprivation and shaming and could be considered a form of death. The matter of justice had real religio-political and social dimensions. To be assured, therefore, that God's just verdict for believers in Jesus entailed life rather than death was to have confidence not only that they had been placed in the right relationship to the Creator and Judge but that this relationship had similarly concrete consequences for the whole of their lives in society. The positive verdict of life in the cosmic trial was an assurance that in Jesus God was at work in this world against all that threatened created life, including injustice, violence, and death, and was restoring the conditions that make for human well-being, even though these would be experienced at present in the midst of continuing hostility and death. When the cosmic trial is played out in John's narrative, we should assume, then, that its purpose remains that of setting the created world to rights. It achieves this purpose by dealing with the world's fundamental problem, humanity's relation to its Creator and Judge. This means that although the overcoming of human sin and death is indeed an essential part of the story as people are restored to communion with God, it serves the goal of establishing God's just claim on the creation and of experiencing created life as God intended it to be.

That this is the goal of the trial is clear from the narrative itself.. The Logos became flesh and did not discard this flesh on completing his task. The Logos who shares in the divine creative life (1:3) has the task, in the cosmic trial, of mediating this life to humanity, of putting created life back in relation with its source. Through the trial's verdict, those who already have created human life will be given new life from the same origin as the Logos; they will be "born . . . of God" (1:13). There will be a new beginning for life among humans because the divine life of the Logos itself undergoes something decisively new; it becomes identified with human bodily life in its temporality and weakness and susceptibility to death. The flesh taken on by the Logos is not abandoned on the cross or in the tomb but embraced anew by the divine life in resurrection form. The climax of Jesus' mission in the lawsuit is neither his death itself nor his resurrection itself but the return of the crucified Jesus in a resurrected body to the Father. In the two Jerusalem appearances in 20:20 and 20:25, 27, the risen and ascended Jesus shows his hands and side, demonstrating that the transformed body of the risen Jesus is that of the crucified one. What has happened in the divine verdict on Jesus indicates what is involved in the divine verdict for humans. Its notion of eternal life takes up the notion of the life of the age to come inaugurated by the resurrection. The present experience of this positive verdict of life is thus an anticipation of, but not a substitute for, physical resurrection. Eternal life for humans, while at present not simply the same as creaturely existence, cannot be viewed as divorced from physical life, existing on some totally separate "spiritual" level. The Logos mediates divine life to a world that, alienated from its Creator, is under the domination of death both spiritually and physically (cf. 5:21, 24–25, 28), and so the experience of the renewal of life as a restored relationship to the Creator will also include the body in this relationship. The climactic sign in Jesus' public mission, the raising of Lazarus, drives home this point. His temporary restoration to normal human life points beyond itself to the full resurrection and the eschatological life Jesus provides. In doing so, it makes clear that human bodily life is significant and that eternal life will not finally entail an escape from the body but physical resurrection. Since God's promise of eternal life includes the body, then it also includes both society (because the body provides one's connectedness with others) and the cosmos (because the body is intimately linked to the rest of the creation).

In taking in the transformation of the body, the verdict of life therefore also takes in the transformation of society and the cosmos. The divine life itself is lived in trinitarian communion, and the gift of participation in this life through the trial's verdict entails not only communion with God but also communion with other humans. The transformation of society is taking place primarily in the new community that already displays the relationships appropriate to the life of the age to come. The physical and tactile practice of washing one another's feet is a prime indication of the way in which the body already plays an essential part in the new communal relationships that characterize the present experience of eternal life.

As a metaphor by which to live, then, this Gospel's narrative of the cosmic lawsuit bears on life in all its dimensions, not just some inner spiritual realm. With most narratives one cannot be sure about the purpose of the story being told until one reaches the end. How can those who live in the midst of the cosmic story know how it is going to turn out, and how can they orientate themselves to its purpose? The only way is for the author to disclose this ahead of time. This is precisely the force of John's cosmic-trial narrative. The verdict of the Creator and Judge that would reveal its significance no longer only awaits the end. It has been rendered in the life and death of Jesus and therefore already supplies the decisive clue to the whole of history from within its midst. The realized aspect of the trial does not render the rest of history meaningless because all has already been decided. Rather, it enables there to be the basic trust about a justice that has in view human well-being, a trust without which human activity is in danger of being undermined by despair or cynicism. The Fourth Gospel claims that, in the divine verdict given in Jesus, not only has the purpose of human existence been made known; the power to experience it has been released. A new quality of life is now available within history through the death of Jesus as witness and judge. It also claims that knowledge of this transforming verdict has been entrusted to chosen witnesses for the sake of all humanity. When witness to the verdict is given, it provides men and women with the opportunity to know the truth about who they are because they can have a sense of the whole of which their lives are a part. In doing so, it also presents them with the necessity of making their own verdict about the human story, a verdict that does not simply leave them, from then on, in the same situation.

Being faced with making this judgment on the witness of the Gospel's narrative is at least a consciousness-raising exercise, for it makes people aware that if this witness is not accepted, some other rival verdict about justice and life is endorsed. One pervasive rival modern verdict, reinforced by the advertising industry, includes the claim that individual persons, seen as autonomous units, have the right to whatever well-being and happiness they choose and that these can be found through the gaining and consuming of a variety of material goods. Along with this conviction goes a notion of justice that considers that having a disproportionate amount of whatever it takes to gain happiness and security is justified and that indeed the exploitation of others by various means, including the use of force and violence, may also be justified in the competition to gain or maintain this disproportion.

But there are also more sophisticated postmodern alternative verdicts about justice and life. Some recent aspects of the thought of Derrida may in fact help us to explore the significance of the themes of justice and life from the Fourth Gospel's cosmic trial. To appreciate the ironies of such a move, we need to remind ourselves that Derrida is the father of deconstruction. And so, when this deconstructionist speaks of the structure of promise or when his leading North American exponent, Caputo, characterizes his thought in terms of prayer, such terms do not have their usual force. There is no stable structure and no transcendental signified to whom prayer can be addressed. For Derrida there remains no way to get beyond the text, no way to relate language to the world. And as will be seen, his notion that nothing is or can ever be fully present continues as a constant throughout his recent thought. What is beyond language with its perpetual play of signs, what is beyond the text, is unknowable, and yet the unknowable (including the world, reality, values) still has to be spoken about. Deconstruction still inhabits the space between the unknowable, the impossible, and the existing actualities, the programmable possibilities, that it deconstructs. And when it speaks of the former, as it must, it is inevitably parasitic on the notions, many of them biblical, that have always been employed to talk of the transcendent. The difference is that it must now talk of these in a new way, a way that ensures that they remain indeterminate. So our brief encounter with Derrida will be an encounter with themes associated with justice and life in the biblical tradition and transposed into a postmodern key. What is the point of such a detour if we simply end up putting such themes back into their Johannine and Christian context? Two considerations immediately suggest themselves. The first has already been intimated. The centrality of these themes in Derrida reminds us of their continuing significance. The second is that in this case, as in others, it sometimes takes the discussion of ideas in a quite different context to enable us to discover them afresh in a familiar text and tradition. And so, without falling into the trap of thinking that the only alternative to indeterminate meanings is determinate meanings,[37] we shall travel through some aspects of Derrida's thought in order to explore, through comparison and contrast, something of their force when they can be given Johannine content.

The previous chapter showed that testimony is a major element in Derrida's view that life is structured by promise and calls forth faith, not faith as conditioned by a particular religion but the act of faith as universal. For Derrida the structure of promise holds together faith without religion, justice without law, and messianicity without messianisms. "This universal structure of the promise, of the expectation for the future, for the coming, and the fact that this expectation of the coming has

---

[37] Cf. S. E. Fowl, *Engaging Scripture* (Oxford: Blackwell, 1998), 32–61.

to do with justice—that is what I call the messianic structure."[38] Derrida distinguishes justice itself from law, with its legal systems and specific laws that can be and have to be deconstructed, particularly by keeping an eye open for the other to which the law is blind. Justice, however, is what provides the drive to deconstruct the law. "The condition of possibility of deconstruction is a call for justice."[39] Agreeing with Levinas, Derrida sees this justice as the relation to the other. Such justice is incalculable, and it shares this condition with the gift. As an indestructible, justice, like gift, is also "im-possible." A gift is im-possible because, for Derrida, once it appears as a gift to either giver or receiver, it is caught in a circle of reappropriation, where knowing one is giving a gift rewards one with the knowledge one is a giver, or being grateful for it puts one in a situation of obligation and contract, both thereby canceling it out as a pure gift.[40] In similar fashion, as Caputo explains, "justice does not exist, is nothing present, no thing, is not found somewhere either here, in present actuality, nor up ahead as a foreseeable ideal, a future-present." Instead "justice solicits us from afar, from the future, from and as future always structurally to come, calls 'come' to us, preventing the walls of the present from enclosing us in the possible."[41] And it is this that gives deconstruction its passion. "Justice is the welcome *given* to the other in which I do not, as far as I know, have anything up my sleeve; it is the hospitality that I extend to the other, the expenditure without return, given without a desire for reappropriation. . . . The passion for justice and the passion for the gift come together in and as the passion for the impossible."[42]

Justice as hospitality, mentioned in this last citation, is another major element in Derrida's reflections. For him the traditional concept of politics has to be deconstructed in order to "to think of another way of interpreting politics, that is, . . . the place for hospitality."[43] Hospitality is the welcome of the other, and Derrida draws out its significance by playing with the term's etymology. He proposes that it derives from the Latin *hospes* and that this is formed from *hostis*, the stranger, the enemy, the hostile stranger, and *pets* (linked with *potis, potes*), to have

---

[38] Derrida, *Deconstruction in a Nutshell,* 23.

[39] Ibid., 16.

[40] Cf. ibid., 18–19, and for a fuller exposition, see Derrida, *Given Time,* 1991.

[41] Caputo, *Deconstruction in a Nutshell,* 134–35.

[42] Ibid., 149.

[43] Derrida, *Deconstruction in a Nutshell,* 18.

power. Hospitality, in such an account, can be seen as the receiving of strangers while remaining in control, remaining the owner of one's own property. Neither the otherness of the stranger nor the power of the host are annulled in hospitality. Indeed, both are essential to the concept. But can the stranger feel truly welcome and at home as long as the home remains my home? This returns us to the im-possibility, like that of the other concepts we have noted, of "hostil-pitality"! With Derrida, for hospitality to occur, for the guest to really feel at home, there would need to be an act of excess beyond hospitality, in which the host made an absolute gift of his or her property, and this is impossible. So hospitality is also always to come, as something demanded of me that I am never able to achieve. Yet, as with the other im-possibles of justice and the gift, this is not meant to justify inertia. Humans have to act hospitably even though they know it is im-possible.[44]

Acts that affirm what is to come, and the questions that deconstruct the present for the sake of what is to come, are a responsive "yes." For Derrida "deconstruction is 'yes,' is linked to the 'yes,' is an affirmation."[45] His view of life as this sort of affirmation is linked to his work on Joyce, whose *Ulysses* has Molly's "yes" as its last word. Derrida explains it in this way:

> Nothing precedes the "yes." The "yes" is the moment of institution, of the origin; it is absolutely originary. But when you say "yes," you imply that in the next moment you will have to confirm the "yes" by a second "yes." When I say "yes," I immediately say "yes, yes." I commit myself to confirm my commitment in the next second, and then tomorrow, and then the day after tomorrow. . . . I promise to keep the memory of the first "yes."[46]

But built into the second "yes," haunting and threatening it from inside, is the fact "that the second 'yes' may be simply a parody, a record, or a mechanical repetition."[47] The second "yes," therefore, can be either a lifeless repetition or a living, constant response.

In his *Ulysse gramophone*,[48] Derrida's two words for and from Joyce are *oui, oui*. For him all language presupposes a primal "yes" that, like a vast "Amen," accompanies every word and gesture.[49] So my "yes" is always

---

[44] For an account of Derrida's unpublished lectures on hospitality, see Caputo, *Deconstruction in a Nutshell,* 109–13.

[45] Derrida, *Deconstruction in a Nutshell,* 27.

[46] Ibid., 27.

[47] Ibid., 28.

[48] J. Derrida, *Ulysse gramophone: Deux mots pour Joyce* (Paris: Galilée, 1987).

[49] Cf. Ibid., 122.

a responsive "yes" to the other, to the call of justice, of the gift, of hospitality. Derrida sees "yes" as the signature, the distinctive idiom of Joyce's text, and it belongs to the structure of the signature to call for a counter-signature, a way of repeating the text. The question that concerns him is whether everything has been said in *Ulysses* or whether there are new ways of saying "yes" to the text.[50] Playing with the link between *oui dire* ("saying yes") and *oui rire* ("yes-laughter"), Derrida makes laughter that which relates the signature and the "yes." There are two sorts of laughter, corresponding to the two ways of repeating "yes." One is bitter and sarcastic, wanting to circumvent everything by its signature; the other is joyous, like the gift, surrendering its desire for control.[51] The latter invites numerous new and unexpected countersignatures, "lets itself be joyfully dispersed in a multiplicity of unique yet numberless sendings, then the other yes laughs, the other, yes, laughs."[52] In Caputo's words, "the 'yes' in this second, more affirmative sense is to be taken as itself a response to what has already been *sent* our way."[53] Faith, then, has the structure of the signature, the second "yes" that must countersign the first. At the same time as it responds to the "yes" by which we are called, it binds us to the future, to the confirmation of the promise in a second "yes."

Derrida's other major way of formulating the structure of the promise is in terms of messianicity. The passion for the im-possible that informs the gift, justice, and hospitality also informs the messianic structure. "This messianic structure is not limited to what one calls messianisms, that is Jewish, Christian, or Islamic messianism, to these determinate figures and forms of the Messiah."[54] These are all deconstructible. Derrida concedes, however, that it remains an enigma for him whether the messianisms are simply specific examples of the general structure of messianicity or whether there have been absolute, irreducible events in the Jewish, Christian, and Islamic traditions that have unveiled this structure of messianicity, so that we would not know the latter without the former. Either way, what remains most important, even if the singularity of the traditions is maintained, is the structure of messianicity.[55] For Derrida the catastrophe of messianisms that believe

---

[50] Cf. ibid., 98–101.

[51] Cf. ibid., 116–20.

[52] Ibid., 195.

[53] Caputo, *Deconstruction in a Nutshell,* 195.

[54] Derrida, *Deconstruction in a Nutshell,* 23.

[55] Cf. ibid., 23–24.

the Messiah has already shown up is that they unfailingly provoke war, and "holy war," as Caputo puts it, "means, alas, killing the children of God in the name of God, who too often really are children, killing the innocent in the name of peace and justice, killing in the name of the promise."[56] An actual Messiah who was present would also destroy the structure of messianicity, of hope, expectation, and the future. Caputo explains, "The Messiah is a very special promise, namely, a promise that would be broken were it kept, whose possibility is sustained by its impossibility."[57] The Messiah always has to be imminent. We have no alternative but to say "come," but the Messiah must always be to come. Thus, for Caputo "deconstruction is a way of hanging on by a prayer." The prayer? An old Jewish prayer, "Amen," or in its postmodern translation, *Viens, oui, oui*.[58]

There is, however, a particularly revealing moment in Derrida's discussion of the Messiah when he allows,

> But the Messiah might also be the one I expect even while I do not want him to come. There is the possibility that my relation to the Messiah is this: I would like him to come, I hope that he will come, that the other will come, as other, for that would be justice, peace, and revolution—because in the concept of messianicity there is revolution—and at the same time, I am scared. I do not want what I want and I would like the coming of the Messiah to be infinitely postponed, and there is this desire in me.[59]

Caputo interprets this positively, as a recognition that the coming of the Messiah asks something of us that we would rather not have to give yet that we must give. So undecidability and *différance* do not mean indecision. Rather, "the messianic commands us not to wait—to bring about justice today, to change our lives today—even as it puts us also under the obligation to wait—to concede, to insist that justice is never here."[60] But another, more deconstructive, reading is possible. The confession that we want the coming of the Messiah to be infinitely postponed because of what it might entail raises the suspicion that this could be precisely why this particular structure of promise is being posited in the first place.[61]

---

[56] Caputo, *Deconstruction in a Nutshell*, 161.

[57] Ibid., 163.

[58] Ibid., 201–2.

[59] Derrida, *Deconstruction in a Nutshell*, 24–25.

[60] Caputo, *Deconstruction in a Nutshell*, 180.

[61] Cf. also B. J. Walsh, "Derrida and the Messiah," *re:generation quarterly* 5 (1999): 29–33.

Derrida continues, "So there is some ambiguity in the messianic structure. We wait for something we would not like to wait for. That is another name for death."[62] Again this last sentence could be construed simply: waiting for something we would not like to wait for is like waiting for death. But as it stands, it is also susceptible to a stronger reading: waiting for something we would not like to wait for *is* death. This stronger interpretation brings us back to the Fourth Gospel. Here a postponement of decision about the Messiah is in fact a decision, a decision to remain in the state of death. Only a decision to align oneself with God's verdict on the Messiah effects a transfer from death to life. The postmodern alternative to John's view of a Messiah who has come and who has acted as judge turns out to be a promise that cannot be kept, a Messiah who cannot come, an infinitely deferred justice. Each term is in danger of becoming a formal and contentless universal, however much passion it may engender. The passion for justice, the invocation of the Messiah, must drive us on, but without an instantiated justice, an actual Messiah, the reign of violence and victimization will know no end. Yet a Messiah who really comes, even one with peace, not war, makes us scared. It would call into question our own acts of judgment in a determinate fashion. It would mean not only peace and justice but that our own notions of what they entail might need to be transformed. It would mean, as the Fourth Gospel insists so clearly, a decision, a risk of specific, not vague, faith, even if this also includes vulnerability to its deconstruction.

For the Fourth Gospel, then, there is obviously more than simply the play of its signifiers. Its claim is that its words point beyond themselves to the reality of God's presence in Christ. In this sense its witness represents what Derrida would designate as "logocentrism"—not the logocentrism of reason but that of revelation—with God in Christ as the stable reality beyond the text and to which the text refers. At its center is the Logos, God's Word, the one God's immanent presence, now enfleshed in the world in the person of Jesus of Nazareth. There is no clearer claim to presence than Jesus' self-attestation—so prominent in the trial—that reiterates the divine self-designation: "I am." Yet this presence does not eradicate all traces in a desire to deny death, as Derrida claims is the case in the role of presence in metaphysics, since the Fourth Gospel's Logos has a mission that culminates in death. Nor does this Gospel's logocentrism lead to the privileging of oral over written lan-

---

[62] Derrida, *Deconstruction in a Nutshell,* 25.

guage, a privileging that Derrida resolutely opposes. The Logos, the embodiment of the divine presence, is in fact now known through the inscripturated witness of the Gospel (21:24–25). "These are written so that you may come to believe that Jesus is the Messiah, the Son of God" (20:31). Here there is a dialectic of text and presence. Because the text functions as witness, it testifies to what is beyond the text. But what is beyond the text can only be known by means of the text. There is presence, but access to this presence is textually mediated. The Word not only became flesh; the enfleshed Word has also been entrusted to the neither wholly determinate nor wholly indeterminate medium of human written words.

In this world of the Fourth Gospel, there is a very different structure of promise. Here promise is not simply that which is always to come and can never actually be kept. The narrative tells of a promising God who always keeps the divine promises. Derrida can say, "So the promise is not just one speech act among others; every speech act is fundamentally a promise."[63] But in Derrida's thought, making promise into a universal structure robs it of its usual illocutionary force as a speech act that commits a speaker to a future action. The language of promise is in fact always language that points beyond itself to the world. In Searle's terms, its logic is *"to get the world to match the words."*[64] The scriptural cosmic lawsuit has its own structure of promise. The divine partner in the covenantal relationship promises to judge the world in a way that will have saving consequences for Israel, rescuing the nation from its plight and restoring it to well-being. The Fourth Gospel claims to be a testimony to the definitive fulfillment of this promise. Its version of the lawsuit holds that God has kept God's promise to judge and that the world is therefore at present undergoing a process of transformation that will be demonstrated for all to see at the end of time. As already observed, there are four stages in the fulfillment of the promise. In the mission of the uniquely authorized agent, Jesus, God was already exercising a saving judgment of the world, but one that would also have condemnatory consequences for those who refused its offer of life (cf., e.g., 3:17–21; 5:21–24, 30). This mission would culminate in the death and exaltation of Jesus, which provided the supreme occasion for the divine verdict. In the light of this verdict, the judgment would continue through the mission of Jesus' witnessing followers and would take its final form at the

---

[63] Ibid., 23.
[64] Searle, *Expression and Meaning,* 3.

end of history, when justice would be seen to have been done. This is the reason the formulation "the hour is coming, and is now here" can sum up the structure of the promise of judgment (cf. 5:25). There is already fulfillment, and yet this fulfillment itself serves as the promise and pledge of further fulfillment. The inscripturated testimony to this promise of judgment thus directs attention beyond the text to the present and future transformation of the world, a transformation that conforms the world to the divine words and claims in the cosmic trial.

This structure of promise not only informs the framework of the cosmic trial but is also pervasive in the narrative's depiction of the outworking of the trial. Essential to the claim of Yahweh to be the one true God in the lawsuits of Isa 40–55 had been the demonstrable correspondence between Yahweh's predictive word and what had taken place in history. In the Fourth Gospel, the very title, Logos, for Jesus signals the same issue. Jesus is to be seen as the point at which—and, in this case, as the person in whom—God's word has its exact correspondence within history. This is reinforced by the numerous instances where it is pointed out how God's previous words in Scripture have their correspondence in what is taking place in Jesus' mission. Whether it is Philip's confession, "We have found him about whom Moses in the law and also the prophets wrote" (1:45), or the disciples' remembrance of Scripture at the temple incident or upon Jesus' entry into Jerusalem on a young donkey (2:17, 22; 12:15, 16), or Jesus' own claims that the Scriptures testify on his behalf and that Moses wrote about him (5:39, 46), or the narrator's use of specific scriptural citations to demonstrate their fulfillment (cf., e.g., 12:38–41; 19:24, 28, 36–37), Jesus is depicted as the actualization of God's word of promise. Indeed, God's dealings with Israel in its history, its institutions, and its festivals take on the pattern of promise of which Jesus is seen as the fulfillment. Since Jesus is one with God, it is also important to show the reliability of his own predictions and promises. To recall only a few examples, his words about the raising up of his body (2:19), his being lifted up (3:14; 8:28; 12:32), the restoration of the royal official's son (4:50, 53), the betrayal by Judas (13:18–19), the denial by Peter (13:38), and his being seen by the disciples in a little while (16:16) all come to pass within the narrative. Other predictive sayings in the narrative—for instance, those about believers' experience of the Spirit, or their expulsion by the synagogue, or their encounter with hostility and persecution, or Peter's death by martyrdom—readers know to have been reliable. All this gives confidence that Jesus' many other words of promise, including those about the completion of the positive verdict of life in the raising up of believers at the last day, will also find their certain fulfillment. This text's promises are meant to guarantee change in the world beyond the text.

Naturally, the Fourth Gospel's perspective on Jesus as the Messiah is related to its structure of promise. It presents Jesus as the anointed one of Jewish expectation (cf. 7:27, 31, 42). John the Baptist denies that he is the Messiah (1:20) and instead points to one who is still to come after him but whose coming is imminent (1:27, 30; 3:28). It is not long before it becomes clear that the Messiah has indeed arrived. Andrew, following John the Baptist's lead, announces to his brother, Peter, "We have found the Messiah" (1:41). The Samaritan woman expresses the messianic expectation ("I know that Messiah is coming"), and Jesus' "I am" announcement following this has the Messiah as its implied predicate (4:25–26). The woman then witnesses to Jesus' messiahship, and through her testimony many Samaritans come to believe that he is the Messiah who has come to bring salvific judgment to the world (cf. 4:29, 42). But this is a Messiah who does not exercise his kingly role by means of force (cf. 6:14–15; 18:38). His respect for the other means that he invites trust rather than compels belief and that his messiahship therefore remains contested (cf. 7:26–27, 41–43). But for those with eyes to see, there is certainly enough evidence in Jesus' public mission to warrant belief in his messiahship. The signs Jesus performs are the signs of the messianic age. The many in the crowd who believe rightly ask, "When the Messiah comes, will he do more signs than this man has done?" (7:31), and Jesus himself, when asked to state clearly whether he is the Messiah, says that he has already done so and that his works testify to who he is (10:24–25). He is the supplier of the wine of the messianic banquet and the bread of the messianic feast; he is the healer of the lame, the giver of sight to the blind; he demonstrates his power over nature; and he is the one who raises the dead to life. Readers are therefore expected to echo Martha's confession: "Yes, Lord, I believe that you are the Messiah, the Son of God, the one coming into the world" (11:27).

So the Messiah has come, but this does not yet mean the end of history. The messianic age has arrived, but it has not fully arrived. Its expected judgment and the accompanying verdict of life or condemnation have already begun within history, but though decisive, these remain to be worked out and completed. The coming of this Messiah does not mean the end of promise. As Thiemann has also argued, promise in the biblical witness has "a complex narrative structure. It evokes the remembrance of God's promises to Israel, the fulfilment of those promises in Messiah's coming, the bestowing of the promised blessing and the renewal of the promise in forgiveness and justification, and the further promise of a final consummation in eternal life."[65] What is most unexpected about the fulfillment of the messianic promise, as it is presented in the Fourth Gospel, however, is that this Messiah can be rejected and even killed. Indeed, this is the way that the Messiah brings the justice and life of the age to come. This Messiah judges for the poor and decides with equity for the meek, not by striking the earth with the rod of his mouth nor by killing the wicked with the breath of his lips (cf. Isa 11:3–4) but by being judged as the innocent victim and by absorbing death. The Fourth Gospel is adamant, however, that the expected glory of the messianic age has not simply been deferred to the end of history. Instead messianic glory has to be interpreted in the light of what has happened to Jesus as the Messiah. The divine glory and reputation are seen as manifested throughout his mission, and his ignominious death, far from negating this, is the supreme hour of glory. The coming of the Messiah brings a transformation of human notions of glory and power. This Gospel could not be clearer that Jesus is the Messiah, but it is more concerned about establishing what sort of Messiah he is—the Son of Man whose suffering is his glory and the Christ who is not simply an anointed divine agent but the Son who has a unique relationship of unity with God as Father. Its readers are invited to believe in this sort of Messiah (20:31). To appeal to such a Messiah to justify the waging of holy war would be a total travesty of all that he stands for as the crucified one, the innocent victim of this world's injustice. And in this Messiah the divine is fully present, but the structure of expectation is not thereby destroyed. The narrative's focus is on the Messiah having come, but this same Messiah promises to come again (14:3; 21:22–23).

The advantage to this messianic structure is that when believers say, "Come," they say it not to an im-possible ideal but to a person and they say it to a person whose identity is already known and whose promise is trustworthy. In longing and praying for the Messiah and justice to come, we are dealing neither with an unknown entity nor with a vengeful, vindictive judge. The one who will fulfill his promise, the one who will be encountered at the end, is the one who has already come. The judge will be the same Messiah who was crucified, the judge who was judged, the victim of humanity's violence who remains the Lamb of God who takes away the sin of the world. Why should the coming of such a Messiah make one feel scared, or be something one does not want? Much of the appeal of therapy in our culture springs from a desire for someone from

---

[65] R. Thiemann, *Revelation and Theology* (Notre Dame: University of Notre Dame Press, 1985), 105.

outside our situation but sympathetic with it to take a look at the whole, to understand and reveal to us the truth. There is a longing that our lives and the injustices of our history be evaluated, a longing for a safe place to be judged in the context of mercy and forgiveness. Such judgment is essential to hope. There can be no enduring hope if the ambiguities and ambivalences of our present, the continuing interplay between power and victimization without resolution, are all there is. Indeed, our very ability to recognize ambiguity in the present and to be torn apart by injustice is parasitic on a sense of ultimate justice. Since, at the Last Judgment, the crucified one is the judge, the justice that will be displayed is his merciful and life-giving judgment. But just as therapy can become threatening when it asks us to change our behavior, so the only reason for not wanting this messianic justice is that we have become too comfortable with the status quo, that we deep down resist giving up the role we have assumed as judges and resist having it subverted by the one whose judgment is truly in the service of life.

Derrida's major concern regarding justice is the other whom he holds to be marginalized by logocentric thinking. Views of universal justice based on reason or the consensus of all reasonable people are deemed to be inherently oppressive because they are blind to both large and small differences between people. Deconstruction is justice because it values uncontrollable plurality, the maximization of differences, and because, in order to maximize differences, the other has to be respected.

The Fourth Gospel's use of the cosmic-lawsuit motif does, however, immediately suggest the notion of universal justice. At its heart is a just God who exercises a primarily saving judgment, one that is for human well-being. The positive verdict of the trial as it affects humans is summed up in terms of life, the quality of life of the age to come that begins now. The narrative also depicts this salvific judgment as the bread and the water of life, as the light that enables humans to see, as freedom from slavery to sin, as assurance and peace rather than fear, as glory instead of shame, and as joy to replace weeping and mourning. But does such judgment operate for some at the expense of others? The goal of the judgment is the benefit of all—life for the world (cf. 3:17; 6:33; 12:32). No one need be excluded. But the narrative discourse makes clear that there are those who are excluded and who find themselves under the judgment of condemnation. More properly, they exclude themselves by their unwillingness to receive the divine judgment. The result is, however, a division between believers and the unbelieving world. Yet deconstructive ethics also has its own exclusion and division. The other is to be respected, but not all others. The other who disrespects others is not to be respected. The issues of who defines the other and how an excluded other is to be treated cannot be avoided.

If there is no ultimate judge in the cosmic trial and if, as with Derrida, justice tends to remain an abstract noun, it continues to mask the particular interests of those who use the term. Justice is in the end defined by whoever has power, and rival claims for justice, including deconstructionist claims, are conflicts of interest that still threaten to destroy any hope of peace in this world. The Fourth Gospel tells a story in which justice is embodied in specific ways that provide a criterion for evaluating other claims about justice. At the center of its readers' imagination will now be the figure of a servant-witness for justice and life. Jesus' witness refuses the modes of power taken for granted in the world, with its systems of domination. The God of the trial pronounces a verdict on the basis of the death of the servant-witness as victim. To judge rival claims in this way is inevitably to take sides. But because this God takes sides, oppressed and marginalized people can have hope. At the same time, because the judgment has absorbed the hostility of the victimizers, it is not one in which their violence is now turned back on them. Instead the judgment's positive verdict is held out to all who will avail themselves of it.

For Derrida justice can be said to take the form of hospitality. Yet because hospitality is a gift, like the gift, true justice and hospitality are impossible. As Milbank has argued, however, Derrida is working with a conception of pure gift, and such a conception is not, as has sometimes been supposed, part of Christian theology.[66] Gift is never completely pure but is always part of a relationship involving exchange. Christian love entails not pure gift but a purified gift exchange.[67] Indeed, love within the Trinity "is relation and exchange as much as it is gift."[68] When set firmly in a relationship between persons, gift can be distinguished from contract to the extent that there is a delay in any return and any return gift is different. Without some delay the return gift would imply the necessity of discharging a debt as soon as possible, and to give the same gift back would amount to an insult.[69] In a relational setting, giving is not some totally free random act but a creative expression of the

---

[66] J. Milbank, "Can a Gift Be Given? Prolegomena to a Future Trinitarian Metaphysic," in *Rethinking Metaphysics* (ed. L. G. Jones and S. E. Fowl; Oxford: Blackwell, 1995), 119–61.

[67] Cf. ibid., 131.

[68] Ibid., 136.

[69] Cf. ibid., 125.

giver that takes into account and respects the other by being a suitable gift, and wanting "to receive back (in some fashion) may be a recognition of ineradicable connection with others and a desire for its furtherance."[70] This giving entails the commitment of the giver to the gift and an expectation of some nonidentical return as part of a reciprocal relationship. This is precisely what is seen in the covenantal relationship between God and Israel, and because God's gifts are always appropriate to Israel's situation, justice, with its focus on respect for the other, is intimately related to gift. Both God's giving and God's justice are suited to their recipients. God acts in accordance with the specific character of each person. This is the reason God's justice is a justice of love. "God treats different people differently so that all will be treated justly."[71]

Within the framework of the covenantal lawsuit of Isa 40–55, the agent of God's justice is the servant who will establish justice for all; he is given as a covenant to the people and also as a light to the nations (Isa 42:6; 49:6, 8). In the Fourth Gospel's cosmic lawsuit, God gives saving judgment for all humanity in the person of the servant-witness, Jesus. Jesus, the Son, becomes God's gift of love to the hostile world (3:16). The return expected is the appropriation of the divine verdict in trust and an equivalent but nonidentical life of loving witness to the truth of the divine verdict. And so, in order to provide the trial's saving verdict, the gift par excellence, the gift of the self of the divine giver has been given. From this gift flow the accompanying gifts, such as life and the peace necessary for its sustenance. Jesus gives the water of life as the gift of God (4:10–14) and the bread of life (6:51); he gives eternal life (10:28; 17:2); and he gives peace (14:27a). The gift of peace that was at the center of Israel's eschatological hopes is now available in Jesus. And his giving is not as the world gives (14:27b). Commentators on this last reference usually focus on its context and make the contrast one between the world's peace and that offered by Jesus. This is no doubt a secondary connotation, but the primary contrast is between the manner of Jesus' giving and the manner of the world's giving. In Derrida's terms, one might say that Jesus' giving is incalculable, not in the sense that it is allegedly uncontaminated by notions of exchange but in the sense that it cannot be simply measured from within some contractual agreement. In his giving peace through the giving up of his life in a violent death, Jesus' giving has an excess about it. The narrative has also earlier claimed that the giving of the Spirit, the agent of the justice and life of the age to

---

[70] Ibid., 132.
[71] Volf, *Exclusion and Embrace*, 222.

come, by God has the same quality of incalculability and immeasurability about it: "for he gives the Spirit without measure" (3:34b).

In the Fourth Gospel, God's giving and God's positive judgment are expressed as hospitality toward the other, and this hospitality becomes the model for human attitudes and actions toward others. God's hospitality is all the more striking because it takes place in the face of human inhospitality toward God. In pursuing God's rightful claims in the trial, God as the Logos enters the created environment that is God's own property and is refused a welcome even by the people God had chosen as God's own possession (1:10–11). Yet God extends a welcome to just such inhospitable humans, a welcome into the home that is the divine presence itself. Those who respond by receiving or welcoming the Logos, a reception that is held to be the equivalent of believing in him, are themselves received into the family of God as God's children (1:12). In Jesus' mission his supplying of wine, water, and bread are signs of his hospitable giving of the life of the age to come, and at the end of the narrative, he is again the host supplying bread and fish at breakfast. He issues an invitation to a reciprocal relationship of hospitality whereby he opens himself to men and women and they open themselves to him— they abide in him and he abides in them (6:56). His welcome is genuine and dependable; he will never cast out or drive away those who come to him (6:37). A hospitable response to Jesus is the signal of belief, while an inhospitable one reflects unbelief. The Samaritans ask Jesus to stay with them (4:40), and Galileans welcome him (4:45). Jesus is welcomed in the home of Lazarus and given a dinner at which Martha serves and Mary anoints his feet (12:1–3). But there are those who do not receive Jesus (5:43), and their refusal of him is depicted as a lack of hospitality in 8:39–40, where, despite their claim to be Abraham's children, they are indicted for not doing what Abraham did in providing hospitality for the divine messengers (cf. Gen 18:1–8). They have become closed in on themselves and will not accommodate Jesus, allowing no place or space within themselves for Jesus' word (8:37).

The theme of mutual indwelling or abiding is taken up in the farewell section of the narrative (14:20; 15:4–5; 17:21, 23). In the present, God and Jesus make believers their dwelling place (14:23), and in the future, believers will be with Jesus in the divine dwelling place (14:2–3; 17:24). It is in this section that Jesus performs his memorable act of hospitality by washing the disciple's feet. A good host would ensure that guests had their feet washed by the servants. But in unprecedented fashion, Jesus breaks the conventions of hospitality and, in an act of excess, washes his disciples feet himself. The one into whose hands all things have been given exercises his sovereign authority by taking on the role of servant (13:3–4). Accepting this gesture of hospitality is said to be necessary for having a share in him (13:8b). Jesus' act is one of welcoming the other into himself. This hospitality makes space for the other within oneself without entailing the dissolution of the self. Jesus' identity is dynamic, capable of readjusting in order to make room for others within himself. His act becomes the paradigm for the outworking of justice among humans. Followers of Jesus are themselves to take the same vulnerable stance in relation to others by washing their feet (13:14–17). Jesus knows that among those whose feet he is prepared to wash is a betrayer, an enemy, and he later continues to extend his hospitality to Judas in the special gesture of offering him the dipped piece of food (13:26). The self-giving in the washing of the disciples' feet points forward to Jesus' ultimate self-giving in his death. Here the hostile world's unjust trial of Jesus, its final act of inhospitality and violence, and God's generous hospitality in the cosmic trial meet. God's welcoming love is such that, in the self-giving of the Son, God suffers humanity's violence in order to make space within God's self for this hostile other and to share the divine life (cf. 3:16).

What the Fourth Gospel says about the mutual hospitality between God and humanity made possible in Christ is grounded in its view of the divine life itself. Father and Son can be spoken of as distinct Persons who are open to the other in a dynamic relationship that molds their identities: "the Father is in me and I am in the Father" (10:38). By extension, the Spirit, who is sent by the Father and glorifies the Son (15:26; 16:14), is also a distinct Person but shaped by these relations to the other two Persons. The divine Persons, who in their self-giving make space for one another without abandoning their own identities, also open up their divine life to provide the space that is the ultimate home for humanity. Jesus can pray, "As you, Father, are in me and I am in you, may they also be in us" (17:21). Trinitarian hospitality is the model for the regard for the other that constitutes human justice, and the community life of believers is to be the model for what justice is to look like in the world. At the cross Jesus delegates to the beloved disciple the task of hospitality. The beloved disciple is given the responsibility for Jesus' mother, "and from that hour the disciple took her into his own home" (19:27b). Through its founder and authority figure, the Johannine community receives the commission to welcome into its home those represented by the mother of Jesus, namely, all believers or perhaps, more specifically, Jewish believers.[72]

---

[72] Cf. Schnackenburg, *Gospel according to Saint John*, 3:278–79.

But the hospitality for which the community is responsible reaches out beyond those who are already believers. Although Jesus' prayer of John 17 strongly demarcates the identity of those who belong to the community from that of those who belong to the world, the boundaries are clearly permeable, since the prayer speaks of the disciples' mission in the world and offers petition also for "those who will believe in me through their word" (17:20). The identity of the community is also to remain open and to be flexible regarding those who are welcomed into its own space, including former enemies. The extension of loving justice to the hostile other by God and Jesus, especially in the verdict rendered at the cross, shows that the responsibility of believers to show hospitality by loving the other and washing his or her feet is not restricted only to the other in the community. In the cosmic trial of the Fourth Gospel, the Logos becomes incarnate in order to embody the justice of the divine judgment and to enable humans to share with God and with one another the hospitality that characterizes the divine life that the trial's verdict opens up to all.

This model of hospitality operates on a quite different basis, however, from that which informs Derrida's thinking. Hospitality does not have to be an absolute gift in which the identity and power of the host are given up, but is part of an exchange that, in its self-giving, decisively shapes the identity of the host without annulling it. Similarly, the identity of the other, the stranger, is extended in the reception of hospitality without being swallowed up by the one who offers it. The gift of hospitality need not succumb to an economy of exchange in which the difference between the self and the other inevitably leads to violence to one or the other; this gift can be one in which both giver and receiver are enlarged and enriched rather than diminished and impoverished. There are problems with deconstruction's own ethic of hospitality because, in the end, it has no stable other whom it might respect or on whose behalf it might struggle for justice; it has only an other whose presence is always deferred, whose identity is permanently decentered and always being constructed, whose words of self-identification are always undecidable. A theological reading of hospitality in John's Gospel refuses the choice between identity as an unchanging essence and identity as a constantly changing construction and opts for the centered self that can be radically open to the other in self-giving or receiving and thereby be recentered without being dissolved in the process.

If a Christian perspective on justice is shaped by this Gospel's narrative of the cosmic trial, it recognizes that, for such hospitality to be operative, humans need to be liberated by the divine verdict from sinful patterns of inhospitality. This is what John's Jesus promises: "you will know the truth, and the truth will make you free" (8:32), and "If the Son makes you free, you will be free indeed" (v. 36). In the context, this is freedom from the sinful system that does not practice hospitality (cf. vv. 39–40) and that, when push comes to shove, will do violence to what is different, will be prepared to kill the other (vv. 40, 44). Knowing the truth of the divine verdict in Jesus ought therefore to be a hospitable knowledge, which, in responding to the divine Other, also makes room for the differences of gender, race, and culture that have traditionally been ignored in the dominant Western perspective on knowledge and which takes the risks involved in mutual recognition, empowerment, and transformation. This freedom to receive the other is not, however, a relativism that simply accepts all difference as equally valid. The notion of freedom occurs in a chapter of John (John 8) containing the strongest judgment of those who are seen as manipulating the truth for violent ends. There is deceit and there are enemies. Such differentiating judgments have to be made without their becoming exclusionary. When they are made by human witnesses rather than the divine judge, there always also has to be the recognition that such necessary judgments are provisional and fallible. But beyond this, there has to be the willingness, which has now been made possible, to show hospitality, with all its attendant risks, to those whom we feel compelled to acknowledge as enemies of the truth. The very tradition of truth and justice within which Christians stand and from which they operate requires and gives the freedom for constant openness to the other and precludes it from becoming a closed system. Christians inhabit not only their own tradition but also the overlapping and changing social and cultural worlds of their own time. Their constant coming up against the other requires, as Volf puts it, the art of "enlarged thinking."[73] Christians witness to the one God of the cosmic trial and this God's saving justice in Jesus, but their understanding and practice of this justice remain imperfect. These are always in need of correction and enrichment, and one of the major ways of accomplishing this is to allow the perspectives of those with whom Christians are in conflict to resonate within themselves and, where necessary, to readjust their own understanding. In this way, "true justice will always be on the way to embrace—to a place where we will belong together with our personal and cultural identities both preserved and transformed, but certainly enriched by the other."[74]

---

[73] Volf, *Exclusion and Embrace*, 213. His entire discussion of justice (193–231) provides a fuller and illuminating perspective on this stance.
[74] Ibid., 225.

Derrida insists that ultimately deconstruction's stance is a positive one. It is a way of affirming an originary affirmation, a responsive "yes" to the primal "yes" in its call for justice and with its claim of the other. In the Fourth Gospel, the primal "yes" comes from the Creator God. In the cosmic trial, God's loving "yes" to humanity is a second "yes." God as Creator has already made a preoriginary affirmation in bringing creation and humanity into being (1:3). In the trial God reaffirms the divine intention for life in the face of humanity's alienation and death. The positive verdict of life through Jesus' death, confirmed also in his resurrection, becomes God's "yes, yes" to humanity. Jesus' mission is depicted as embodying this "yes, yes." Indeed, the introductory formulation that accompanies many of his sayings is precisely "Amen, amen." His words express the divine intention for humanity and are given the strongest form of affirmation. He is the reliable and self-authenticating witness to the truth of God's verdict of life. Indeed, he is the truth and the life (14:6). His entire mission participates in God's affirmative verdict: "I came that they may have life, and have it abundantly" (10:10). But Jesus' witness demonstrates that the trial's "yes" to life is no facile one. Its positive verdict is only possible through the witness's death. God's "yes" has in Jesus encountered the negation of death and, in absorbing it, overcome it.

As we have already underscored, in Deutero-Isaiah the correspondence between Yahweh's word and deed is evidence of Yahweh's credibility, but this also requires the response of human witnesses, their confirming Amen—"Yes, it is true" (NRSV: "He is right"; "It is true") (cf. Isa 41:26; 43:9). In the Fourth Gospel, the beloved disciple is the witness par excellence whose testimony is the "yes" to Jesus' witness. In particular, he testifies to the truth of the divine verdict in Jesus' death with a testimony for whose truth he vouches (19:35). If, as we have asserted throughout, witness is one of the most characteristic features of the Fourth Gospel, then the "yes, yes" of its witness to life can lay claim to providing the Gospel's signature. There are indeed a number of signatures in this vein. God provides a signature, setting the divine signatory seal on Jesus as the Son of Man who gives eternal life (6:27). The distinctive idiom, the signature, of Jesus' own witness to the truth is its pervasive introductory "Amen, amen." The Gospel carries no actual signature but is attributed to the beloved disciple. His signature is provided by the testimony that he, as the perceptive witness, has caused to be written—his inscripturated "yes" to Jesus' "yes" (21:24a; cf. 19:35). But the written testimony has a second "yes" in its signature to correspond to Jesus' double Amen. To the attribution to the beloved disciple is added the narrator's countersignature on behalf of the community, its "yes" to the beloved disciple's "yes": "and we know that his testimony is true" (21:24b). The community's confirmation of the witness in its experience and living out of the positive verdict of life constitutes its countersignature. The narrative's pattern—of response to witness that in turn becomes a further witness that invites response—is that of the "yes" that continues to find its echo in a second "yes."

This is the type of signature that, rather than simply closing off the narrative world in a totalizing gesture, leads to new possibilities for imagining and living and invites a multiplicity of further countersignatures in an ongoing "yes, yes." It is, in Derrida's terms, the signature of joyous laughter, releasing into unique yet numberless future sendings of witnesses the written witness to the one who has been sent. In the narrative the response to the divine "yes" in Jesus' death and resurrection is indeed joyous affirmation: "I will see you again, and your hearts will rejoice, and no one will take your joy from you" (16:22; cf. also 15:11). This profound and exuberant joy in reaction to the verdict of life is what Moltmann has called "Easter laughter."[75] What the Gospel's written testimony explicitly invites is continued belief (20:31). Belief is the equivalent to the acceptance of testimony, saying "yes" to the witness, and such belief itself entails a signature. The person who has accepted Jesus' testimony "has set a seal to this, that God is true" (3:33). Here we are also back to the divine "yes" in Jesus, which is the issue of the cosmic trial. Belief is the affirming "yes" to the divine "yes." And the "yes" of belief is repeated in a second "yes" in the life of witness to which all believing followers of Jesus are called. This second "yes" cannot be merely a mechanical repetition. The work of the Spirit of truth helps to ensure that it is a living, creative repetition. In accompanying human witness, the Spirit keeps the memory of the first "yes," and the Spirit's "yes" to Jesus' witness recalls, interprets, and applies the words of Jesus for changing circumstances (cf. 15:26; 14:26; 16:13–14). The witness of Jesus' followers is thus one that is constantly working out in word and deed the implications of the first "yes" for its own time and place. An authentic second "yes" of witness will be as unique as the witness who enacts it and as the situation in which it is enacted. It involves constant risk and is a testimony to which the witness is continually committed, since it remains disputed and the witness has to be prepared to die for it. In this way the second "yes" also provides a countersignature to, an equivalent

---

[75] J. Moltmann, *The Coming of God* (London: SCM, 1996), 339.

but nonidentical repetition of, the "yes, yes" of Jesus' own witness. Its "yes" to the loving offer of life from the divine Other entails a "yes" to the human other as witness takes the form of the hospitality of a life of love and justice.

If Derrida's recent thought can be summed up in a nutshell by Caputo in the prayer *Viens, oui, oui,* then perhaps the Fourth Gospel's perspective on the trial's verdict for humans has its own corresponding nutshell—"Yes, yes [NRSV: 'Very truly'], . . . I came that they may have life" (10:7a, 10b). Less succinctly, its claim is that the coming Judge has come and, as the crucified victim, pronounced the costly "yes, yes" of the divine verdict. "Amen, amen [NRSV: 'Very truly'], I tell you, anyone who hears my word and believes him who sent me has eternal life, and does not come under judgment, but has passed from death to life" (5:24). "Yes" says the believer, and "again yes" says the believing witness in commitment to the truth of justice and life, while waiting not in fear but in joyful anticipation for that future coming of the crucified and risen one that will be the full revelation of the "yes, yes" of the God who sets to rights and restores to life all that was once created and affirmed.

C. Christian Witness and Advocacy

To advocate is to speak or act in favor of a person or a cause. Not only in the case of the Paraclete or Advocate does witness take this form (cf. 15:26); advocacy also captures much of what is included in the task of human witnesses in the Fourth Gospel's lawsuit. Followers of Jesus are to be his advocates, witnessing by their words and deeds to who he is. In so doing, they also serve as advocates of the entire cause represented in the lawsuit, since its verdict on Jesus is at the same time a verdict about God and about human existence. Of course, any adequate discussion of Christian existence as advocacy would need reflections from different Christians engaged in various aspects of life and coming from various cultures. How individuals see the implications of taking up their part in the cosmic lawsuit by bearing witness will differ according to their own concerns and the contexts in which they find themselves. First, this section will consider some general features of the form this advocacy is meant to take in the life of the Christian community; then it will treat the more specific activity of verbal advocacy and, all too briefly, its particular manifestations in preaching and biblical and theological scholarship.

Both the justice and the life that lie at the heart of the divine verdict are, as already seen, expressed in the hospitality that is open in love to the other. In this way the existence of Jesus' witnessing followers embodies, in advance of their final demonstration, these elements of the trial's verdict. Indeed, the sort of advocacy that is most closely tied to the truth of the trial is not so much that of the individual witness as that of the community as a whole.[76] This emerges most clearly in the prayer of Jesus that provides the climax of the farewell section. Toward the end of the prayer, Jesus intercedes not only for his immediate followers but for all those who will believe as a result of their witness. His petition is "that they may all be one . . . so that the world may believe that you have sent me" (17:21), and this notion is repeated in what follows: "so that they may be one, as we are one" (v. 22), and "that they may become completely one, so that the world may know that you have sent me" (v. 23). The community in which believers' witness is embodied is to be a united one, and the issues at stake in Jesus' mission hinge on this. Since the truth established in the cosmic trial is the unity between the one who is sent and the one who has sent him, it is not surprising that the continuing advocacy of this truth is to be displayed in the oneness of the witnesses.

It is not simply that the unity of the witnesses mirrors the union between the Father and the Son. Rather, the unity of the believing community participates in the unity that defines the relation between Jesus and God (cf. v. 21). The goal of its mission is not only that the world come to know Jesus' identity as the one sent by God but also that it come to know that his followers are loved by God just as Jesus is loved by God (v. 23c). How does the world come to know that the God of the trial is uniquely disclosed in Jesus and that this God is love? Not only through hearing the witness that Jesus and the Father are one and that Jesus' death was God's loving gift to the world but also through seeing and experiencing the advocacy of a community united in loving acceptance of one another. When the grounds for Jesus' petition are given in vv. 25–26, the address is to God as "righteous Father." The adjective *righteous* and the noun *righteousness* occur earlier in forensic contexts (cf. 5:30; 7:24; 16:8, 10). The Father to whom Jesus prays, then, is also the righteous judge of the cosmic trial, and 17:26 goes on to summarize the mission of Jesus in the trial: "I made your name known to them." At the same time, the assertion "I will make it known" points to the ongoing trial that is carried forward through the witness of the Paraclete-Advocate

---

[76] Cf. J.-P. Jossua, *The Condition of the Witness* (London: SCM, 1985), 43: "Witnessing comes about in a community and has its roots there; in turn, it points back there."

and the community of Jesus' followers (cf. 15:26–27). God's name is made known in the relationship of love between God and Jesus, and it continues to be made known as this relationship of love shapes the life of the community of Jesus' witnessing followers and as, through this relationship, Jesus, who embodies God's name, is present in the community.

Speaking of a relationship of love provides the reminder that the oneness at issue in the trial is a oneness that respects difference. The one who sends and the one who is sent have an identity in difference. The Father and the Son can be said to be one, but they also remain distinct Persons; the Father is not the Son. In this way the God of the trial is the one God who embodies harmony in difference as Father, Son, and Spirit. Similarly, the witness of the community to this God entails a unity in diversity. The injunctions to wash one another's feet and to love one another (13:12, 34–35) by no means assume that the others encountered in such actions will be congenial; rather, these injunctions require a self-giving regard for those who may well be radically different in many ways. The very fact that this behavior is commanded tells us that it is not simply about the mutuality expected between like-minded people but that it will be costly and demanding. Both the trinitarian grounds and the community practice mean that difference need not be interpreted as inevitably leading to violence. Christian community is to be both a witness to the prior ground of unity in our world and an anticipation of the full revelation of the just and merciful judgment in which all differences will be embraced.

The truth to which the Fourth Gospel's narrative bears witness is known and experienced to be true when it is encountered in a community that lives by the narrative's metaphor of a trial and all that this entails. It is here that the notion that the truth of the trial involves a match between the word and the world strikes home for Christians. Just as that truth was embodied in the Logos becoming flesh, so the truth about the achievement of God's verdict of life for the world has to be enfleshed in a community whose witness takes the form not only of proclamation but also of love: "By this everyone will know that you are my disciples, if you have love for one another" (13:35). To be a follower of the sent one—who was in a relation of loving intimacy with the one who sent him and through whose sacrificial love the trial's verdict was obtained—is to produce evidence that substantiates the truth of the sent one's cause by displaying unity in love. As a French Dominican puts it, "Despite the centuries of clericalism, of abbatial paternalism, of masculine tutelage, and so on, the essence of the witnessing relationship in the church remains the mutual help given by one believer to another, in complete equality and reciprocity."[77] And just as Jesus' witness had a confrontational function in its relation to the world, so should that of the community of his followers. "Jesus, coming into the world to bring it life, confronts its infatuation with death and with death-dealing systems. Johannine Christianity does no less, and can do no more, than to repeat again and again that confrontation." In being what it is meant to be, "the community of love is itself a part of the gospel."[78]

If Christian believers are witnesses to the truth of the cosmic trial, then their primary group allegiance is to this community shaped by its witness to the truth of the trial and by the witness of the Christian tradition as a whole. They hold this allegiance together with a variety of secondary allegiances and ties to other social, cultural, political, ethnic, and national groupings. The question they therefore continually face is how to be effective advocates for the truth to which the community bears witness in the midst of these other relationships. One vital answer that has already emerged is that they need to pay attention to their relationships within their primary community of allegiance because the state of these relationships is not an optional extra concern nor an ecumenical luxury to be pursued after individuals have achieved some other satisfactory approach to truth and advocacy. Failure to display a unified witness undermines drastically the credibility of all other attempts at advocacy.

The particular challenge of the Fourth Gospel is to the witness of service that helps to bond the believing community, but clearly, within the light of the NT as a whole, such witness will also extend to the neighbor, as an expression of solidarity with whoever is needy, distressed, or oppressed. Gooch's observations about the language of love in John's Gospel are worth noting. He argues that "John's paradigm of intimacy is Father/Son, who are so close as to collapse spatial differences. And his word for this intimacy is love." This determines the dominant use of the term in the narrative discourse and makes it difficult for such vocabulary to function appropriately in the context of strangers or enemies. "It does not follow that, for John, treatment of nonintimates or the hostile must be radically different than that prescribed by the synoptics' Jesus. It's just that . . . for John, . . . love is among friends, shared in the family."[79] To this can be added that the family is an open one and that the presupposition of Jesus' followers' witness in the world is that all others are to be invited into the family.

---

[77] Ibid., 85.

[78] Rensberger, *Johannine Faith*, 147.

[79] Gooch, *Reflections*, 260.

The perspective of the Gospel is that just as the familial love between Father and Son is extended to Jesus' disciples, so through the mission of these disciples the world should know of God's loving intention that it become an integral part of the extended family. The only exception to the pattern of the Fourth Gospel's language of love is highly significant and underscores what has been suggested about the potential scope of the family. It is found in 3:16, which asserts that God's love for the hostile world is so great that God gave God's only Son in order to enable this world to share in the divine life.

The mutual service that characterizes the life of the Christian community is grounded in both the servant-witness of Jesus and the cruciform nature of the truth that is on trial. The previous section, on justice and life, already had cause to discuss this in terms of hospitality. Here it will be sufficient to underline the link between service and witness. Jesus' commission to the disciples is, "As the Father has sent me, so I send you" (20:21b). In what manner did the Father send the Son to witness to the truth? In the form of a servant who was willing to give his life. As already seen, the narrative of John 13 has the only account, in the whole of ancient literature, of a superior performing the service of foot washing for those who would have been seen as subordinates. Jesus, as the slave down on his knees with the basin and towel, prepares the reader for the culmination of the story with Jesus as the one lowered in order to be lifted up on the cross. The way of *the* witness is to be the pattern for his witnessing followers. The basin, the towel, and the cross are to characterize their advocacy—in the sphere of personal relationships and in the wider social and political spheres.

Jesus' model of servant-witness remains deeply subversive of the normal cultural values of autonomy and self-preservation. In the sphere of relationships, the paradoxical truth that Christ's cross was his glory, that his death meant life, is to be lived out in the humdrum daily choices that present themselves. All too frequently our society's assumption is that the only way to secure happiness is to insist on one's own rights, come what may, and that what matters is fulfilling one's own potential. Other people then tend to become obstacles in the way, standing between a person and the fulfillment of his or her potential, ambition, or even vocation. Advocates for the truth are willing to hang loose about their own private quests for fulfillment and, by giving a hand to this person over here and that person over there, discover unawares fulfillment coming over them gloriously from behind. To be on one's knees, with a basin and towel, in front of someone else is to put the other person in a position of power and oneself in a position of vulnerability. Followers of

Jesus are called to risk such vulnerability even when—and particularly when—there are deep differences of opinion among them.

In the broader social and political sphere, the Christian community's advocacy of the truth also follows the pattern of glory through vulnerability, power through weakness. This kind of servant witness does not mean passive submission to evil but an uncompromising witness against all its manifestations—whether these be the violation of others' rights, racism, sexism, elitism, economic injustice, or exploitation of the environment—and a willingness to pay the price of this witness in suffering, if this is the consequence. Witness to the truth that has its focus in the cross becomes a challenge to any assumption that peace is to be secured either by the strength of humanity's inherent goodness or through violent means. Instead, recognizing that cycles of domination and violence cannot be broken by further assertions of power that only escalate the hostilities, it attempts to embody, through nonviolent resistance, the peace that is not of this world but that has its source in the one who has overcome the world through his death.

This is an advocacy that can call into question the world's values because it comes from a community that is not afraid to lose its status in the world for the sake of its witness and is realistic about the consequences of this witness. It is aware that witness to the new life provided by the trial's verdict will also entail a confrontation with the powers of death still at work in the old order, with all its impediments to the well-being God intends for humans, whether these are traditional religious categories that prevent people from recognizing God's disclosure in Jesus or acts of oppression that marginalize and victimize other human beings. We can recognize the purposes the lawsuit motif served in its original setting for legitimating the claims of a group of believers that was itself marginalized, but as we have seen, there is no reason to limit the significance of the narrative to such a setting. The narrative discourse places Jesus' death on the cross in a universal and cosmic context, seeing it as the divine verdict that establishes new criteria for judgment. Just as the Fourth Gospel's interpretation of this verdict originally necessitated a rethinking of categories derived from the law and a rethinking of social categories of honor and shame, so now, as a foundational document of the Christian community, it can continue to judge the quality of witness as well as model the cost of witness. There always remain a variety of traditional and social values that affect the lives of those in the Christian community, because such a community continues to be linked through a variety of networks to its surrounding world. Values are sifted both as Christians find that the turning upside down of ordinary human assessments by the cross meets with resistance in themselves and as they arouse fierce resistance from others.

The witnessing community will not be surprised, then, that it encounters hostility from the idolatrous and destructive attitudes of a world that is resistant to the overtures of its Creator and Judge. It is no accident that those who received the commission "As the Father has sent me, so I send you" had just been shown Jesus' hands and side. This can be seen as a reinforcement of Jesus' earlier warning: "Remember the word that I said to you, 'Servants are not greater than their master.' If they persecuted me, they will persecute you" (15:20). There should therefore be no illusion about what it means to be sent as a witness. Witnessing in the Fourth Gospel, we are reminded, is a self-involving speech-act in which the lives of witnesses serve as a pledge of the truth of their testimony. They have to be prepared not only to shape their lives by this testimony but also to give their lives for it. They do not become μάρτυρες because they are killed, but they may be killed because they are μάρτυρες.

As Ricoeur puts it, "Testimony is . . . the commitment of a pure heart and a commitment unto death. It thus belongs to the tragic destiny of truth."[80] He sees this as the logical consequence of the movement of reflection that abandons the autonomous consciousness, the "letting go wherein we affirm an order exempt from that servitude from which finite existence cannot deliver itself."[81] In Johannine terms, if the witness's stance is, "He must increase, but I must decrease," as exemplified by John the Baptist (3:30), then martyrdom can be seen as a decreasing to the point of death so that Jesus and his cause might be honored by one's advocacy. Thus, testimony to Jesus can lead through persecution, suffering, imprisonment, and torture to death. To be a witness is not to indulge in a religious hobby. The Fourth Gospel's trial narrative, which speaks not only of Jesus but also of his disciples facing death for their advocacy of the truth, should provide a constant reminder of the many who are oppressed and killed precisely because of their Christian witness. Martyrdom is not simply a phenomenon of previous periods in the history of the church, as is sometimes supposed in the West, whose media generally turn a blind eye to this form of oppression. Whereas at some earlier stages the individual martyr's heroic witness was a major focus of attention, we now need to be aware of the more anonymous

---

[80] Ricoeur, "Toward a Hermeneutic," 113.
[81] Ibid., 116.

martyrdoms that occur around the world when sometimes whole groups of Christians are massacred because of their faith.[82] Such witness through the persecution of millions and through the death of tens of thousands of Christians every year most clearly bears testimony to the destiny of Jesus in the narrative of the cosmic trial. It is evidence also that as the trial continues in the lives of his followers, its conflict has equal intensity and remains a struggle to the death. "The act of following Jesus in his sufferings has been written into the 'texture' of the tormented victim and can be read there. At the same time, this texture represents a testimony for the prosecution against the persecutors."[83] Persecutors and executioners are thereby given a further chance either to perpetuate the cycle of violence and destruction, with its erosion of their own humanity, or to be persuaded of a different set of values rooted in the mission of Jesus, in which power is not to be identified with truth. As already discussed, when the cause of Jesus is seen as intimately related to God's intentions for justice and human well-being, then the martyrdom to which advocacy can lead may be on account of not only an explicit confession of faith in Jesus but also resistance to injustice or solidarity with those who are oppressed. In a superficial, apathetic, and often dehumanized culture, the willingness to risk suffering and death in advocating the truth should be seen not, as it frequently is seen, as a sign of irrational fanaticism but as a mark of spiritual health.

The narrative of the cosmic trial is realistic, however, in recognizing that fear can be a major obstacle to witnessing. In Deutero-Isaiah "Do not fear" was Yahweh's constant message to exiled Israel in the face of the intimidating threat of Babylon. In Isa 44:8 this exhortation precedes the assertion that Israel is to witness. Fear of Babylon is replaced, in the Fourth Gospel's replaying of the lawsuit, by "fear of the Jews" (cf. 7:13; 19:28; 20:19). Exhortations within the Farewell Discourse not to be troubled or afraid but to take courage (cf. 14:1, 27; 16:33) serve as an invitation to Jesus' witnessing followers not to be uncertain about survival or the future in the face of persecution but confidently to risk all in view of the verdict and its accompanying resources, which God has provided in Christ. The summons not to fear is necessary because being a witness to Christ in the hostile environment of the world is, as noted, a dangerous enterprise. The task can engender fear of unpopularity, of being

---

[82] For a recent well-documented account of the worldwide persecution and martyrdom of millions of contemporary Christians, see P. Marshall, *Their Blood Cries Out* (Dallas: Word, 1997); cf. also Arens, *Christopraxis,* 132.

[83] Arens, *Christopraxis,* 132.

marginalized, of losing a promotion or a job, of alienating family, of physical threat, or of death itself. When the stakes are high in the dispute about truth, the witness becomes an endangered figure. Yet anxious testifying should be a contradiction in terms. The story to which advocates bear witness is not their possession. They are part of a larger purpose that they do not control, and are responsible only to be faithful advocates in their words and deeds. The outcome can be, indeed has to be, entrusted to God. In Jesus' prayer of John 17, he requests that the Father sanctify the disciples in the truth, setting them apart for the role of witnessing to the verdict established in the trial (17:17a). At the same time, he prays that they may be kept in God's name and protected from the evil one (17:11b, 15b). His prayer places them and their mission in the hands of the loving Father, who is also the righteous Judge (17:25a). Believers can be reassured that not only has any hostile setting into which their mission leads them been foreseen and prayed about by Jesus; it is also part of the outworking of God's purposes for the world in the ongoing trial. Just as God has given Jesus what it took to complete his task in the death that constitutes his glorification, so now Jesus summons God to give believers what it will take to accomplish their mission. The ultimate source of both Jesus' and their confidence is that the trial remains God's cause and God can be entrusted with it. The peace that is promised and given also acts as the antidote to fear (cf. 14:27; 16:33). It is the precondition for witness. Before the risen Jesus commissions the disciples for witness, he twice says, "Peace be with you" (20:19, 21). This is not the bestowal of a security that comes from removal from conflict but the gift of the centeredness that comes from knowing who is in control and whose judgment really counts in the trial of truth.

A second gift accompanies the commission as its major resource: "Receive the Holy Spirit" (20:22). Advocates know they are not alone in the continuation of the trial but have *the* Advocate accompanying them. In the Fourth Gospel, it is not so much that disciples must ask for the help of the Spirit. Since it is assumed that the Spirit has already been sent or given to believers and is at work, it is more that the Spirit enables believers to speak and act as faithful witnesses and makes their testimony the vehicle of the Spirit's own witness (cf. 15:26–27). The Spirit has been given to assist believers to bear witness to Jesus by recalling the traditions about Jesus and updating them for new situations, by fostering the conviction, in the midst of a world of illusory values, that truth and justice and life are rooted in the glory of God disclosed in the crucified Jesus. The Spirit has been given to guide believers into all truth. The trial's truth about God, humanity, and the world contains inexhaustible riches. Its advocates will never stop exploring and learning, and the Spirit-Advocate nourishes a growing confidence that as they discover more and more, they will eventually find that it is related to what they have already been shown of its source in the crucified and exalted Jesus. The Spirit has been given to help them find connections, to improvise, and to take risks as they testify to the truth that embraces all of life, in ways that fit their particular setting and their particular time. It is the Spirit working in and through human advocates who produces the effective witness that results in men and women seeing existence not as some pointless litigation before an empty bench;[84] rather, they are led to see that all their personal and social concerns have significance because on the bench is the crucified and exalted Jesus, the one who takes away the sin of the world and invites them to receive and enjoy the positive verdict of life.

Ideally, the need for verbal advocacy should arise as an explanation for the new reality seen in the relationships within the community of Jesus' followers. "I do not see the witness as someone who takes the initiative in speaking to others. I see the witness, rather, as a man or woman living in such a way—and looking at the world and everything in it in such a way—as to make other people ask themselves, and ask those who are witnesses, what gives them their unique character."[85] The words of the witnessing community would, then, reinforce its deeds. But clearly this sequence has no monopoly. The claims of the truth that the community advocates may well first be encountered by others through its proclamation. In this case its actions would reinforce its words, giving substance to their claims. The verbal activity of witnessing is often thought of as the attempt to share one's faith with others. Is there more that can be said? What difference is made by placing the notion in the explicit and larger context of the cosmic lawsuit? For a start, it helps to clarify the nature and purpose of any such witness. It cannot be simply reduced to the rehearsal of one's own story of faith or spiritual journey. This certainly may be a part, but only as it points to the one God revealed in the life, death, and resurrection of Jesus, to the just claims of this God on the world, and to this God's accomplishment of a verdict that entails life in its fullness. This underlines that although witness is to a reality that has cosmic significance, it can only be a particular perspective on, and a limited linguistic expression of, this reality.

---

[84] See the citation from Arthur Miller's *After the Fall* near the beginning of ch. 7, above.

[85] Jossua, *Condition of the Witness,* 1.

But why is the partisan, provisional, fallible, and therefore often mistaken verbal advocacy of human beings still needed in the cosmic trial? This question reminds us that advocacy is all of a piece with the notion of the trial and its truth. This is a cosmic lawsuit that has taken place in history and whose truth is tied up with this history. Just as a scandal of particularity about this truth and its embodiment in the witness of Jesus makes it disputed, so there is a scandal of particularity about the witness that continues to be borne to this truth and about its verbal communication. The truth of the trial is not the sort of truth that is accessible to all through the operation of some universal notion of reason or of some general religious experience. Since it is a particular truth, it becomes accessible through particular channels—the inscripturated witness of this Gospel and the testimonies of those who constitute the community of Jesus' followers and who, in the continuation of the lawsuit in history in their time and place, attempt to articulate the significance of the decisive verdict of God in Jesus' death and resurrection. It could not be otherwise. A witness that was not embodied in a particular cultural tradition and in a specific place and time would not be able to influence human activity in history. The claim of the Fourth Gospel that this is not the work of human witnesses alone but of the divine witness of the Spirit does not change this situation. The Spirit is able to mediate between past and present, not only bringing the events of the past to remembrance but also drawing out their significance for the future. The Spirit's witness therefore transcends history, but it is still inextricably linked to the historical process and does not proceed independently of the human witness that is mediated within socially embodied traditions.

Thus, the necessity of verbal advocacy is a reminder that there is no pure or abstract form of knowledge capable of judging the truth claims of particular traditions. The truth at stake in the cosmic trial is not found by stripping away the accidents of history to reveal some essence that gives the meaning of life. At every point our access to it depends on others who bear witness, and their witness is embodied in, and expressed through, the language of a tradition and community. The trial is on a cosmic scale, but its verdict is made known through specific people in concrete relationships employing particular language, and it is in this way that this verdict of life reaches out to achieve God's purposes for the entire world. It is as members of a particular community that witnesses in the trial have a universal mission. While advocacy is part of the Christian community's universal mission and can be said to have a universal intent in that it makes its claims public and invites all to examine and accept them,[86] it does not aim at some universal theory or total construal of the truth. It also refuses the rationalistic split between objective and subjective knowledge because the very structure of testimony values both a reality beyond oneself, to which one testifies, and, at the same time, the perspectival and fragmentary perception of this reality that one's testifying entails.

Verbal advocacy is required not only because the truth of the trial involves a particular claim but also because such truth claims are always disputed. The witnessing community will therefore constantly be engaged in the endeavor to persuade others of the truth of its claims. Again, such witnessing is not an activity that proceeds from having established a complete knowledge or agreed foundation on the basis of which it then seeks to persuade. Advocates can only start where they are, speaking in the midst of incomplete knowledge, uncertainties, arguments, and conflicts. It is in the process of these verbal exchanges that further knowledge is gained.[87] As has been indicated earlier in this study, it is highly likely that the community behind the Fourth Gospel developed some of its crucial insights into the significance of Jesus' identity and the relevance of the trial metaphor itself in the process of its disputes with the synagogue. Witnessing to the truth is not therefore simply an activity directed at outsiders but also an essential means for Christian believers themselves to grow in their knowledge and articulation of that to which they bear witness. They are learners who are discovering as they go what is entailed in relating the truth found in Jesus to the rest of life and to the truths of such spheres as science, politics, and the arts. And their discovery is itself a further witness to that truth, enabling it to be disputed as public truth.[88] Such advocacy is also always open to revision and correction, remaining accountable to the truth to which it attempts to point. This holds for the Fourth Gospel's own witness. By depicting his narrative as a testimony, its narrator reminds us that it is still part of the continuing lawsuit. Because of its canonical status and its stress that the

---

[86] Cf. L. Newbigin, *The Gospel in a Pluralist Society* (Grand Rapids: Eerdmans, 1989), 126.

[87] Cf. Jossua, *Condition of the Witness,* 63: "The need for me to prepare to bear witness or actually to testify clarifies and refines my perception. . . . It can happen that in trying to express our faith to someone else, we discover in ourselves an understanding that we did not think we had; we find a power of expression so unexpected that in this way more than one person overcomes the doubts he or she thought they had."

[88] On the notion of the gospel as public truth, see L. Newbigin, *Truth to Tell: The Gospel as Public Truth* (Grand Rapids: Eerdmans, 1991).

verdict in the trial has already taken place, there is a temptation to read this testimony simply as one that brings closure to the trial of Jesus by reinforcing the divine verdict. Yet the ending of the narrative not only indicates that its testimony is incomplete but, by the very self-description of testimony, indicates that it, too, is still on trial. There will be no closure on its own witness until the trial has run its course. To be sure, this testimony also makes claims to the testimony of the Spirit, but it remains human testimony and as such, even in its positive and foundational role in the trial of truth, remains accountable to the truth to which it gives witness and to the divine verdict it narrates. Despite the subject matter of this testimony, it continues to be a particular speech-act in written form. Such a linguistic act does not itself constitute the final verdict. There is a difference between Jesus as the embodiment of the truth of the trial and the Fourth Gospel's witness to this. Like all other acts of verbal advocacy, its witness commits itself to the truth it perceives, and does so in trust that this truth will be finally and publicly vindicated.

But what happens to testimony deriving from religious convictions when it encounters the larger pluralistic society, in which it has no privileged position in discourse? Fenn has put forward the thesis that secularization has produced a clash between the rules for witness or testimony in the religious sphere and the rules of discourse in other areas of life, such as the courtroom or the academic seminar.[89] The liturgy, where the verdict of the ultimate trial is celebrated, is his paradigm for the effectiveness of speech-acts in the religious community, and he shows how religious testimony that takes its force from such a context is undermined or disallowed by the criteria for credible witness that prevail in other contexts. If in the liturgy the primary direction of the speech-act is that of the world conforming to the word, in other contexts this is reversed, and it is primarily a matter of the word conforming to the world. Fenn draws a contrast between, on the one hand, religious testimony and religious language in general, where the connection between word and event remains indispensable and is epitomized in the incarnation, and, on the other, the "prison-house" of secular language, "which prevents the individual from fully encountering the reality of which language speaks."[90] The danger, he claims, is that where speech makes nothing happen, deeds, power, and violence are seen as substitutes. If liturgical language is "eventful" and if testimony requires response, Fenn

---

[89] Fenn, *Liturgies and Trials.*

[90] Ibid., 79.

analyzes "seminar talk" for a contrasting example of talk that may be interesting but in which nothing happens.[91] Such talk is characterized by negotiating personal statements of opinion, and speakers "self-consciously work at freeing language in general, and particularly their own speech, from contextual or personal constraints."[92] Authority and credibility are gained by speaking "without apparent effort to be taken too seriously,"[93] and there is a tacit agreement that no one really has the kind of authority that can bring the trial of opinions to closure.

To illustrate further his claim that "the polarity between the liturgy and the trial creates the dynamic tension between the sacred and secular authority in modern societies,"[94] Fenn analyzes three striking instances, from court cases in the United States in the 1960s and 1970s, where religious testimony itself was put on trial and found wanting by the norms of the secular court.[95] In each instance attempts at religious testimony were in the end redefined by the constraints of the court in terms of merely personal convictions, sincere but idiosyncratic, or their meaning was reduced to a metaphor for some dimension of social reality, such as ethnic loyalty. "In the same courtroom in which oaths on the Bible must be taken before individuals will be considered as authentic and credible witnesses to their experience, the same individuals will find that their testimony to their religious faith is restricted by strict standards of reliability and relevance: standards set by secular professions that derive their authority from the state."[96] Indeed, "the situation is rather that, in order to be taken seriously, the individual does well not to take religion or the sacred itself too seriously in secular contexts."[97]

In Fenn's view, despite this dominant effect of the secular context, its authority, when it is interrupted by religious testimony, can be temporarily challenged and gaps in the letter of the law can be exposed, so that, again at least temporarily, room is made for the things of the spirit.

---

[91] Ibid., 101–17.

[92] Ibid., 103.

[93] Ibid., 108.

[94] Ibid., 6.

[95] The three are the Catonsville Nine trial, in which the testimony of the Berrigan brothers attempted to put the court itself and the state on trial before God (ibid., esp. 184–98), the Karen Ann Quinlan case (esp. 118–39), and the trial of Maria Cueto and Raisa Nemikin, members of the Episcopal Church's Commission on Hispanic Affairs (esp. 140–62).

[96] Ibid., 64.

[97] Ibid., 62.

Fenn's observation is reinforced by the experience of Christians outside democratic Western societies. Faced with repressive governments ruling by military and police power, they have found time and again that court-rooms that are little more than puppets of state power can become places of Christian testimony that paradoxically creates, for just a while, space for truth and freedom in the midst of a world of propaganda and coercion. At the end of Fenn's study, he ventures the guess that this disruptive effect of testimony may be an increasing occurrence: "Secular contexts may well find their rules for discourse broken more frequently in the future than in the past as individuals demand the right to testify to their religious convictions in the classroom, in the court, on the political campaign trail, and even in the hospital where matters of life and death have been the prerogative of only one profession to decide."[98] What he envisages and clearly endorses is something like a culture of advocacy, and since he wrote, the influence of postmodern thinking has further loosened the hold of a supposedly monolithic secular society.

Christians need little reminder that the truth to which they testify is still on trial before the world, competing for allegiance among a plurality of beliefs and values. In the light of Fenn's thesis and our study of the Fourth Gospel, two questions confront Christians in this connection. The first is whether they have succumbed to the judgment of society as a whole that concern for the truth about Christ is at best a personal and private affair, only marginal to the real concerns of life, or whether they are still convinced that the truth that is on trial and the often feeble witness to it that they bear are about a reality ultimate enough to put all on trial and to act as the final criterion of judgment. If they are convinced of the latter, the second question is how the witness to this truth within the community of faith relates to testifying to it in pluralistic contexts. Using Fenn's categories, we shall look briefly at the latter issue. Taking preaching as an example of advocacy in the liturgical or ecclesiastical context and biblical and theological scholarship as an example of advocacy in a pluralistic academic context, we will consider the relationship between the two.

Christian worship can be seen as the celebration of the divine verdict in the cosmic trial, and preaching as the prime form of verbal advocacy of this verdict within worship. Witness has long been seen as one of the biblical images that illuminate the role of the preacher. Indeed, some would argue that it is the most appropriate and adequate image.[99]

---

[98] Ibid., 197.

[99] Cf. esp. T. G. Long, *The Witness of Preaching* (Louisville: Westminster John Knox, 1989), 23–47.

Preachers who turn to the Scriptures on behalf of the believing community in order to hear a word of God that they then address to the community enact key features of witnessing. The move from text to sermon, which conscientious preachers negotiate week by week, incorporates the two major elements that make witnessing what it is. "The witness has seen something, and the witness is willing to tell the truth about it."[100] To move from analysis of, and reflection on, a biblical text to preaching on it is to move from the perceptive seeing and hearing of something to its truthful communication—elements essential for the role of a witness. What the preacher has experienced and then advocates can be described in a variety of ways. Faithful preaching does not simply repeat or paraphrase what is in a text but aims at discerning the text's claim, as the word of God, on a particular community—its potential for shaping and changing the identities and actions of the members of that community—and at articulating in an appropriate and effective fashion what has been discerned.

But further dimensions of what we have seen to be involved in witnessing in the lawsuit are bound up with preaching. Preaching is not simply the delivering of insights into the human condition, derived from preachers' own experiences of life. Instead preachers point beyond themselves to the God revealed in Christ and to what this God has accomplished in Christ for human well-being. Aware both that there is no incontrovertible proof of the realities to which they point and that they and their tradition have frequently distorted these realities, they nevertheless continue to point to such realities as the truth. At the same time, these realities are already mediated through prior witnesses in the chain of testimony and foundationally in the inscripturated witnesses of the texts on which they preach. In addition, preachers' discerning perception of the claims of God in promise and judgment in these texts is not an objective, disinterested enterprise. Their own training and skills, their spiritual awareness, their cultural and social embeddedness in particular traditions, their ethical commitments, their imagination, and their pastoral sensitivies mold not only the way they communicate but their very perception of what is to be communicated. The entire life of the preacher is bound up in her or his advocacy in preaching.

Again, as in witnessing, preaching does not aim at general truths or a comprehensive grasp of texts but attempts to convey a particular word for a particular context. In this it depends on the accompaniment of the

---

[100] Ibid., 43.

Advocate, who conveys the presence of Christ, gives life to the words, brings conviction, and leads the community into the truth by making the appropriate connections between the past history of the trial and its present context. Preaching is done in the name of Christ, and so, like witnesses, preachers are authorized agents of Christ and God (cf. 13:20). But as a form of witnessing, preaching is not simply an individual activity; it is carried out as an integral aspect of the life of the witnessing community as a whole. It is a particular expression of the self-giving service that enables the community to be an embodiment of the verdict in the cosmic trial. The preacher is an advocate for the word of God on behalf of the community and so must be open to the needs and concerns of the community if these are to be brought to the text. Increasingly, the practice of preaching is incorporating this theological principle as representatives of congregations not only are involved in planning the worship but also meet with preachers as part of the process of preparation for the sermon. But this does not mean that preachers only communicate what the community wants to hear. They are to be truthful witnesses who may well find that their exposure to the Scripture means that some cherished assumptions or concerns of their communities need to be called into question. They therefore must have the courage not to be afraid of the unpopularity and suffering that witness can entail.

As an act of witness, preaching aims to persuade others to accept its testimony and to experience the truth of the divine verdict as it bears on their lives. Preaching that is in line with the function of witness in the Fourth Gospel will be clear that it arises from the confession of faith. It will attempt to engender and deepen faith in the significance of the person and mission of Jesus Christ for the particular situations of its addressees in the ongoing trial of truth. It cannot compel belief yet will use its persuasive skills to insist that such a response is necessary. At the same time, both the regard for the other that is demanded in the service and hospitality of witnessing and the very content of the testimony, with its refusal on the part of Jesus to use this world's means of domination in the pursuit of his cause, mean that manipulation and bludgeoning have no part in preaching. In witnessing to the truth of the cosmic trial, preaching has in view God's interaction with the whole creation. It is not restricted to taking place within the worship of the community but can occur in any public setting. Yet even within an ecclesiastical context, preaching has a universal intent in its witness, with all of life and all of humanity in its scope. Believers do not, of course, live only in the community of faith but inhabit a variety of other worlds; faithful preaching will point to God's claims on all these spheres, drawing connections, including confrontational ones, between, on the one hand, the definitive verdict of the trial that displays in Jesus God's purposes of justice and life and, on the other, particular present manifestations of injustice and death in the world. In making such public claims, preaching, as much as witness, will be a disputed activity, necessitating provisional judgments and being open to revision and correction from other perspectives..

It is one thing for members of the witnessing community to engage in preaching. But what happens when its members wish to be advocates for the cause of Christ as they carry out their occupations in the spheres of life in which they are engaged outside the ecclesiastical context? Here are presented brief reflections on one of these spheres, one that was singled out by Fenn, namely, the academic world, in particular that aspect of it most closely related to the subject matter of this study—biblical and theological scholarship. Is talk of advocacy in such academic scholarship appropriate? If so, does this not take a form quite different from the advocacy of preaching?

Contrary to the misconception of some, both outside and inside the academy, who have imagined that biblical studies and theology could only be pursued as some sort of propaganda exercise, the situation until recently has generally been the reverse. To paint the picture with a broad brush and therefore inevitably fail to do justice to particular settings and individuals: in most universities and liberal-arts colleges of the English-speaking world, it has been assumed, where these disciplines have been taught, that those who engage in them would do so in terms of the dominant paradigm of critical objective scholarship and that whatever beliefs teachers and students had about the subject matter would be left aside in the academic enterprise. Indeed, in many traditional introductory courses, much time and effort were expended in attempting to ensure that students rid themselves of all presuppositions and beliefs deriving from a confessional or ecclesiastical context and learn to take a detached, critical, neutral stance to the Bible or to claims about the existence of God. Biblical studies have therefore been seen as part of the historical study of ancient texts, and theology as part of the phenomenology of religion, with its language treated as one expression of universal religious experience. Engagement with the Bible and Christian doctrine from the perspective of faith, if appropriate at all for a thinking person, was seen as a private matter or held to be an activity that ought to be restricted to church groups and ecclesiastical educational institutions such as theological colleges and seminaries. Under the influence of this ethos, in their study, teaching, and writings, Christian biblical scholars and theologians predominantly limited themselves to descriptions of the thought of the biblical writers and of later Christian thinkers, analyzing such aspects as the background, context, literary composition, form, and structure of such thought. Expressing explicitly any commitment to the same beliefs, let alone advocating such beliefs and allowing them to inform one's critical approach, would have been to step outside the rules of the academy and no longer be taken seriously as a scholar by one's colleagues.

The tacit agreement to keep Christian witness out of the academic enterprise, other than its expression in personal relationships and ethical behavior, produced a variety of anomalies. For example, in contrast to the strictly nonconfessional arrangements for the meetings of the predominantly North American Society of Biblical Literature, some European academic biblical societies at their annual conferences have offered worship or prayers at the start of the day for those who desire such activities. This might be thought to encourage a confessional approach, but for the most part, it was considered quite inappropriate to bring the Christian realities celebrated earlier to bear, in any direct fashion, on the seminar sessions that followed. Instead the academic sessions operated under a different ethos, in which it was assumed that Christians and non-Christians shared the same scholarly worldview of detached, objective knowledge. In fact, Christian scholars in the academic world often found it difficult to play by the rules, and whether they were aware of it or not, interpretations and conclusions that they claimed to have arrived at on purely critical and historical grounds were often clearly influenced not only by personal, social, and cultural factors but also by unstated theological convictions and assumptions. To salve their conscience about failing to allow their basic Christian commitment to the subject matter to be fully operative in their study, Christian biblical scholars frequently appealed to a strict division within the theological disciplines and held that it would be improper for them to engage in anything like theological advocacy and that, if this were to be done, it would in any case be the task of the systematic theologian.

It was precisely in the context of discussing witness or martyrdom that the theologian Nicholas Lash pointed out the unsatisfactoriness of any model of interpretation in which exegetes are seen as doing their purely descriptive work first and then passing on their results to the systematic theologian, who is supposed to produce their meaning for the contemporary situation. He rightly insisted that the question "What might 'witness' or 'martyrdom' mean, today?" should be restated as "What form might contemporary fidelity to 'the testimony of Jesus' appropriately take?"[101] In this context he suggested that the function of the NT scholar is one aspect of "the broader task of Christian interpretative practice, of the attempt to bear witness faithfully and effectively to God's transformative purpose and meaning for mankind."[102] In Lash's view, for the exegete to deal only with meaning and not also with truth is "to refrain from giving, or to refuse to give—not to a 'meaning,' but to a man—the kind of trust that the authors of the New Testament gave, and in giving it, exhibited their intention to maintain 'the testimony of Jesus.'"[103] Although phrased carefully, it is a strong charge against Christian NT scholars who would claim to be simply descriptive exegetes. It indicts their efforts as a failure to believe and to bear witness. For a Christian biblical scholar or theologian, the determinative question is not how someone can be considered a critical scholar if he or she holds to the values of the subject matter of his or her study. The crucial issues are, rather, (a) how someone who has come to believe, let us say, the key claims of the Fourth Gospel could not be an advocate for its truth in his or her scholarship and (b) why someone who holds that God has a claim on this world and that the Gospel's trial of truth reveals the nature of this claim would be willing to carry out his or her daily work in conformity with a completely contrary claim about truth. Lash's indictment of a certain form of biblical scholarship might even be seen as analogous to the Fourth Gospel's indictment of secret believers, who, in conformity to the religious and social constraints of the synagogue, failed to provide a full witness (cf. 12:42–43; 19:38).

Since Lash wrote, the situation in academic study of the Bible and theology has changed dramatically, with increasing emphasis placed on (a) the demand that scholars be explicit about the interests they bring to their reading of texts or to theological argumentation as members of particular socially located interpretive communities and (b) on the role such interests play in the construal of meanings of texts and in the theological task. Liberation and feminist concerns have contributed significantly to this shift of perspective, but so also have more general hermeneutical discussion, reader response approaches, attention to the rhetorical dimensions of discourse, cultural criticism, and postmodern

---

[101] N. Lash, "What Might Martyrdom Mean?" in *Theology on the Way to Emmaus* (London: SCM, 1986), 91. (His essay first appeared in *Suffering and Martyrdom in the New Testament* [eds. W. Horbury and B. McNeil; Cambridge: Cambridge University Press, 1981].)

[102] Ibid., 92.

[103] Ibid., 89.

epistemology. It has been recognized that all scholarship is in fact some sort of advocacy and that its practitioners need to come clean about their particular brand. This new state of affairs could be illustrated in numerous ways. D. S. Cunningham, a theologian, writes,

> Composed neither of propositions, nor of directives, nor even primarily of narratives, exhortations, or prophecies, Christian theology is instead—and above all—a form of persuasive argument. . . . Theologians are not neutral observers, abstracted from the real world of Christianity. Rather they are rhetors, attempting to persuade an audience that *their* vision of the Christian faith is a vision *worthy* of that faith.[104]

If theology is to be effective persuasion, it has to take account of the situation of both speaker and audience in dealing with its subject matter. Such theology is therefore always contextual and always attentive to praxis—to the thought and action to which a particular audience is being persuaded to move. Brueggemann, an OT scholar states, "We now recognize that there is no interest-free interpretation, no interpretation that is not in the service of some interest and in some sense advocacy."[105] And in a presidential address to the Society of Biblical Literature, Schüssler Fiorenza, a NT scholar, insisted, "Not detached value-neutrality but an explicit articulation of one's rhetorical strategies, interested perspectives, ethical criteria, theoretical frameworks, religious presuppositions, and sociopolitical locations for critical public discussion are appropriate in such a rhetorical paradigm of biblical scholarship."[106]

Clearly, the recognition of the role of advocacy in scholarship and of a plurality of possible advocacy stances ought to mean that there is now room for Christians to do what they ought always to have done and to attempt to bring their own Christian witness explicitly to bear on their work. But the situation is not as simple as our description of the shifting ethos has implied. On the one hand, the newer paradigm has not yet won the day, and there are still conflicts and tensions within university departments and academic societies between representatives of modern and postmodern approaches. On the other hand, even where the latter predominate, it is not at all clear whether they lead to a genuine plural-

---

[104] D. S. Cunningham, *Faithful Persuasion: In Aid of a Rhetoric of Christian Theology* (Notre Dame: University of Notre Dame Press, 1991), xv, 81. Cunningham's work provides a thorough discussion of the entire enterprise of theology as advocacy.

[105] Brueggemann, *Theology of the Old Testament,* 63.

[106] E. Schüssler Fiorenza, "The Ethics of Interpretation: Decentering Biblical Scholarship," *JBL* 107 (1988): 13–14.

ism of perspectives. Inevitably issues of power arise, and certain interpretive voices prevail over others. In the world of biblical scholarship, the exposure of the myths of neutrality and of objective scientific knowledge has meant the reappearance of some explicitly Christian theological readings of texts. Others in the profession, however, continue to see such efforts as an affront to critical autonomy and have deemed them to be out of place in publicly funded, secular institutions of learning.

Given the desirability of, and opportunity for, Christians to remain advocates or witnesses in their scholarship, how might this best take place, and how does it differ from the sort of advocacy we have seen to be involved in preaching? There are a variety of ways in which Christian notions of what is true impinge on the disciplines of biblical and theological study, informing views of history, of language, and of hermeneutics, for example, and influencing how particular methods are employed. But if Christian theological inquiry is seen as an interpretation of Christian texts and traditions that are the Christian community's witness of having experienced the reality of God in Christ, then a prime area, though by no means the only one, in which witness is borne and that provides an area of overlap for biblical studies and theology is the theological interpretation of the Bible. Our focus in the remainder of this section will be on this form of witness, remembering Lash's indictment of those who remain content with exegetical description and his exhortation that they bear witness to God's transformative purpose and meaning for humanity. To insist that, whatever else it does, no Christian approach to the interpretation of the Bible is adequate unless it includes theological interpretation is to argue that it needs to engage with the subject matter of the biblical texts in such a way as to advocate its continuing significance for life in this world. The renewed interest in this topic is reflected in the increasing amount of recent literature devoted to it. This is not the place to interact with the different approaches that are being proposed. But what are needed are more attempts to risk this sort of advocacy in actually providing theological readings. To point out the obvious, this is the motivation behind the project of this book, particularly the discussion of its last three chapters. Some broad features of theological interpretation will be outlined here that relate to what we have discovered about the function of witness or advocacy in the lawsuit.

A witness is always situated somewhere, and this shapes the person's advocacy. This holds true also for theological interpretation. In my own case, my Christian advocacy comes from being a male non-ordained Anglican who has been most influenced by the evangelical tradition and who has worked as a NT specialist both in theological colleges and in universities, and at times in both settings at once. These factors are inevitably part of the perspective that shapes my research and writing. Since the stance of a witness is particular, limited, and provisional, such factors operate, I hope, in an open-ended way that has by no means settled all interpretive issues in advance and that expects my own perspective to be changed, modified, and enriched in conversation with the scholarship of those from other perspectives. The dangers of advocacy in research and teaching are well known—such as taking a blinkered and narrow approach, or manipulating evidence, or not exposing oneself or one's students fully to the variety of views in the discipline. But in my view, being aware of these dangers should not be allowed to stifle attempts to find legitimate ways of enthusiastically advancing one's own perspective even while fairly presenting rival viewpoints and demonstrating a willingness to revise or expand that perspective in the light of weighty objections or new interpretations and evidence. This type of approach would have some right to be considered an advocacy appropriate to the discipline. It would take in the two main aspects of witness we have considered: It points beyond itself to the subject matter of the biblical texts, the claims of God in Christ, while attempting to do justice to the issues that arise from their particular literary form and historical and social conditionedness. And it recognizes that the construal, communication, and advocacy of these theological claims is always shaped by the perception, imagination, character, setting, and relation to particular audiences of the witnessing interpreter.

These two interrelated aspects of witnessing—the requirement of attesting to a reality that is beyond oneself but also the ability to do this only in terms of one's own contextually conditioned perspective—are a reminder of the dialectical nature of theological interpretation. In the case of the Fourth Gospel, what the interpreter points to as the subject matter of the text is its overall message about God's claim on human existence that is disclosed in Christ. Discernment of this subject matter will include, but is not reducible to, discovering as much as possible about what the Fourth Gospel meant to an original audience toward the end of the first century C.E. But the overall goal of the task will be a construal of the Fourth Gospel's words as a word of God for the present. To employ Barth's famous dictum, theological interpretation "does not ask what the apostles and prophets said, but what we ought to say on the basis of the apostles and prophets."[107] To say that the witness of theo-

---

[107] Barth, *Church Dogmatics* 1.1.16.

logical interpretation is based on the words of the apostles and prophets, however, raises questions about the relationship between our theological construal and what we can discover of the earlier witness of the apostles and prophets. This does not mean that we have to have some definitive criterion for establishing the meaning of the scriptural witnesses in their original setting, so that this can then serve to judge the adequacy of our theological interpretation. After all, what we are after in theological interpretation is God's word for us in our setting through the human words of the texts. Aquinas, who had already thought about this issue, at the beginning of the *Summa Theologica* responds to the objection that "Holy Writ ought to be able to state the truth without any fallacy. Therefore there cannot be several senses to a word in Holy Writ." In his reply he argues, "Since the literal sense is that which the author intends, and since the author of Holy Writ is God, Who by one act comprehends all things by His intellect, it is not unfitting, as Augustine says if, even according to the literal sense, one word in Holy Writ should have several senses."[108] And so, although he talks about the literal sense and the author's intention, "it turns out that Thomas' reflection on the literal sense leaves matters surprisingly underdetermined and that the author's intention functions in his hands more to promote diversity than to contain it."[109] The reason is that, for Thomas, God is the author of Scripture. Rogers claims that Thomas' account of the literal sense, of what God intends through Scripture, is in the end that which commands communal assent.[110] This is not dissimilar to the postliberal view of Frei, who treats the literal sense as that meaning established within the community of those who take the Bible to be their Scripture.[111]

If, then, the Christian advocate's theological interpretation of Scripture is aware of the two-sided nature of witness, it will endeavor to point to God's word through the words of Scripture but, instead of looking for

---

[108] Thomas Aquinas, *Summa Theologica* I, q. 1, art. 10 (Chicago: Encyclopaedia Britannica, 1952), 9–10.

[109] E. Rogers, "How the Virtues of the Interpreter Presuppose and Perfect Hermeneutics: The Case of Thomas Aquinas," *JR* 76 (1996): 65. Cf. also the use of Rogers' article by Fowl, *Engaging Scripture,* 32–61, in setting the notion of underdetermined over against determinate or antideterminate interpretations.

[110] Rogers, "Virtues of the Interpreter," 68.

[111] See H. W. Frei, "The 'Literal Reading' of Biblical Narrative in the Christian Tradition: Does It Stretch or Will It Break?" in *The Bible and the Narrative Tradition* (ed. F. McConnell; New York: Oxford University Press, 1986), 36–77.

one meaning, will also recognize the witness's own role in the construal and formulation of that word. Here the variety of interpretive aims with which Christians approach Scripture comes into play, and this means that there can be no specifying in advance of any one method or any particular combination or sequence of methods by which a successful interaction with Scripture will take place. Witnesses know that their own theological convictions, ecclesial practices, and social concerns both shape and are shaped by their reading of Scripture. They will therefore treat theological interpretation as a complex process of interaction between the scriptural text and the variety of interests brought to it, in an attempt to hear from it a word that will enable them and their audiences to live faithfully before God. This suggests a flexible advocacy, in which awareness of the theological subject matter of the texts and of one's own theological interests is clearly essential but also in which a knowledge of the probable original theological impact of these texts, of how the texts have been interpreted theologically, and of the theological traditions and the present needs of the communities for which one is interpreting them is highly desirable. Such advocacy is not a license for any reading so long as it can claim to be Christian. There are certain things a faithful witness cannot plausibly make the marks in the text say, but the same marks can say a variety of things to different witnesses at various times and in various places.

The various critical methods provide the competencies for reading in our time, and advocates need to be competent contemporary readers if they are to be persuasive theological interpreters. Competence in theological interpretation is not reducible to, but cannot exclude competence in, other modes of interpretation. One who wishes to be a Christian witness through theological interpretation will also acquire, for example, literary, historical, and hermeneutical skills and learn to discern how and when these can enhance a theological reading. The issue is not whether critical methods are any good but what they are good for. What place a particular method, such as tradition or redaction or cultural criticism, has in practice will be determined on an ad hoc basis, in case-by-case application. This relativizing of critical methods means that theological interpretation, like preaching, is more an art than a science. Its essential presupposition is sensitivity to, and sympathy with, its subject matter—the theological implications of the content of Scripture. Its effective practice depends on a discernment of what information and what methods are most appropriate for a fruitful conversation between the theological concerns of the text and those of contemporary interpretive communities.

Since notions of canon and scriptural authority play a vital role for Christian advocates, the theological conversation they pursue will be primarily with the final form of the text, and literary methods will be particularly appropriate for hearing its witness. This explains the place given to such methods at the beginning of this project in preparation for theological appropriation of a testimony that takes narrative form. Advocacy through theological interpretation will be most concerned with the Fourth Gospel's narrative as we now have it rather than with whatever part this Gospel may or may not be able to play in the reconstruction of the historical Jesus or of the Johannine community behind the narrative. The latter issues are not, of course, completely irrelevant. Knowledge of historical-Jesus questions will, for example, remind interpreters that they are dealing with the history-like narrative of ancient biography, not with modern conceptions of historical accounts; and knowledge of the likely concerns of the evangelist and his community may, as suggested, shed some light on the shaping of themes in the narrative and on particular issues within it. But in theological interpretation, what determines the use of insights gained from these other areas will be the interpreter's discernment of the help they can give in understanding the end product, the narrative testimony through which the word of God is heard.

At the same time, Christian advocates engaged in academic scholarship will be aware that one of the constant dangers of theological interpretation is that the dominant theological tradition or the present theological concerns of their communities may simply become determinative in their reading of Scripture. There is a need therefore both to assert and to learn to live with the freedom of the word of God to which the words of Scripture witness. Just as theological interpretation can loosen the straitjacket of historical-critical categories, so historical, literary, social, and cultural readings can be means to prevent the theological categories that are inevitably brought to the text from becoming a straitjacket; to change the metaphor, they can help to bring about a change of prescription for the lenses through which the advocate reads. They are, however, not the only means. Awareness and understanding of others' differing readings can likewise keep Christian advocates self-critical. Continual spiritual and moral vigilance is also necessary on the part of interpreters and their communities lest Scripture be interpreted in ways that reinforce their sinful attitudes and practices.

A recognition is also required that the attitude of needing to have the Bible on one's side at all costs may well be detrimental to faithful witness. Instead of attempting a revisionist exegesis, it seems far better to admit, on some occasions, that John or Paul, for example, said one thing but now contemporary advocates need to say something different in different circumstances, with different questions to address, as they strive to be faithful to the same gospel to which John or Paul bore witness—whether on obvious ethical issues such as the role of women, slavery, or homosexuality, or on Jew-Gentile concerns, or on soteriological formulations—and that they need to be open to debate whether and in what ways they are being faithful to the same gospel. In practice, faith seeks understanding by learning to see both the connections and the distinctions between the gospel of the death and resurrection of Jesus Christ and the various inscripturated human witnesses to this gospel (see ch. 8, above). Christian theological interpreters inevitably work within a tradition of understanding based on foundational testimony and then, within this same tradition, come to judgments that both make its understanding their own and help to modify and develop it. They are engaged in discerning what constitutes the center of Scripture's subject matter and how this center is to be appropriated in their own witness in a different setting. Perhaps we can say that a valid theological interpretation, like an effective sermon, is one that, in the consensus judgment of one's primary interpretive community, enables people to think and live faithfully in relation to the triune God in their present situation in the world. It is always provisional, always disputed, always open to correction. Indeed, one mark of a valid theological reading is its willingness to engage in continued discussion and disagreement with other perspectives.

Another obvious danger of theological interpretation is that it can be, and has often been, employed in a controlling fashion, both by individuals and by ecclesiastical authorities, in an attempt to set strict norms for reading Scripture, to impose uniformity, and to suppress disturbing minority voices. Any renewed enthusiasm for advocacy through theological interpretation will therefore need to be alert to such temptations and suspicious of those who welcome it simply as a way of coping with the fragmentation of the discipline or with what they see as a myriad of strange and threatening interpretations. Again, attention to the characteristics of testimony will be essential. The witnessing community does not possess the truth but points to it from its own perspective. The provisionality, cultural embeddedness and fallibility of a particular witness mean that theological interpretation needs and will welcome different perspectives as correctives to its own understanding because frequently other witnesses point not only to aspects of the truth one has not seen but also to those one does not want to see. And if witness is inevitably associated with suffering, theological interpretation ought to value, in particular, readings of Scripture that come from those who have experienced the pain of marginalization and oppression, not least those who have experienced such pain from oppressive theological interpretations.

Theological advocates who reflect the hospitality and love required of witnesses will not be undiscerning but will, first of all, display not fear of, but openness to learn from, interpretations arising from circumstances very different from their own.

In these ways, like other forms of witness, theological interpretation will attempt to do justice to the other—to the inscripturated witness as other, to challenging or new interpretations as other, and to the recipients of one's witness as other. The task of asking what was being communicated by the text in its original context, while not a final criterion of validity, can play an important role in enabling interpreters to respect the text as other. In this way, the text becomes a real partner in a conversation in which contemporary advocates refrain from putting into the mouth of the other what they would like this other to say, and instead attempt to listen to the other so that its strangeness can surprise them and challenge their assumptions. In a pluralistic context, the initial strangeness of the interpretations of others can perform a similar function if interpreters practice a sympathetic listening to the different judgments they embody and if they make space for the variety of such stances in appreciation of diversity and in the hope of a fuller realization of the possibilities of the text. Regarding the stance toward the recipients of one's witness, there need be no incompatibility between witnessing to the truth and respecting the other. Rather, if a witness respects the other, he or she will want to tell the other the truth, to put the other in the picture about the real situation in God's world that is on trial, and will, at the same time, be convinced that an essential part of witnessing to this truth is demonstrating the self-giving love that refuses to impose one's own viewpoint, values difference, and allows the other to remain other.

So far it has been claimed that both preaching and the sort of academic work that entails theological interpretation of Scripture are forms of verbal advocacy or witness. But it should also have become clear that the two are not simply unrelated forms of this activity. Any serious preaching from Scripture is itself theological interpretation. Indeed, for many Christians, preaching provides their principal exposure to theological interpretation, supplying, in the context of the Christian community's worship, mission, and social action, the resources from Scripture for what they should believe and how they should lead their lives. Preaching is the performance of theological interpretation in and for the life of the Church, with each new sermon a new event in the history of theological interpretation of the text. And academic theological interpretation of Scripture can feed into the process of reflection that leads to the sermon. Indeed, a number of new commentaries are inviting professional biblical scholars and theologians to rethink commentating as aiming at purely descriptive exegesis and to provide not sermons as such but the sort of theological interpretation that bridges between the world of the text and the world of the contemporary reader in ways that will aid preachers in their distinctive task. Preachers then take the process one step further in risking the word of witness that can become the word of God addressed to a particular group of people in a particular local setting. Christians engaged in theological interpretation in the academy have a responsibility to the academy and to the wider intellectual life of society. But they can work as interpreters whose primary community is the Christian church and who hope thereby to serve and benefit the believing community in a variety of ways. One of these ways is to help preachers in their own task of theological interpretation.

The stress here on witness and the links between preaching and theological interpretation may already have horrified some colleagues for whom the secular ethos of all public institutions of learning is a given. One biblical scholar has written that scholarship should endeavor "to ensure as far as possible that exegesis is studied in such a way that it does not issue in proclamation."[112] Have we ended up reinforcing the offending view that Christian theological interpretation of Scripture in the academy is preaching in disguise or, if not simply another form of preaching, has preaching in view as its ultimate goal? Service of the Church's mission of proclamation is indeed one of the legitimate tasks and benefits of such activity, but this does not mean that academic theological interpretation should be seen only as subservient to preaching. It has its own distinctive role to play in the task of witness, a role that includes providing constructive theological readings of Scripture; self-conscious and systematic reflection on what is involved in this task; rigorous analysis and testing of the theological claims it produces; and constant dialogue with, and adjudication of, the findings of related disciplines. This activity is part of Christian witness to the truth in its own right, and part of the discipline of theology as a whole, seen as seeking to understand God truly.[113] The attempt to understand God does not take place in some supposedly neutral context but within the context of commitment to the Christian God within a particular tradition in the church and within the concrete settings of particular congregations within this tradition. Theological interpretation includes reflective and critical second-

---

[112] C. F. Evans, *Explorations in Theology 2* (London: SCM, 1977), 83.

[113] See D. Kelsey, *To Understand God Truly: What's Theological about a Theological School* (Louisville: Westminster John Knox, 1992).

order activity; this is not carried out, however, before the bar of some neutral rationality but through the use of criteria internal to Christian faith and practice. It will not seek norms from beyond; rather, presupposing the first-order language of the Christian community's witness, it will strive, through its critical reflection, to understand this witness more fully. It will explore its internal structure and its external connections with other disciplines and will ask how its interpretation of Scripture bears on an overall view of Christian theology; what types of response in speech or action, doctrine, or ethics are appropriate to this view; and whether and how some particular view of its subject matter is true.

This combination of tasks will ensure that, despite its analogies with preaching, advocacy through academic theological interpretation of Scripture will not be the same as preaching. Because of its essentially pluralistic context, even the positive and constructive side of theological interpretation will not take the same form as preaching in either its teaching or its evangelistic mode. Whereas the latter makes direct appeals to its hearers in the names of God and Christ, summoning them to belief, advocacy in the academic context will seek a more indirect form of address that explores the claims and implications of its subject matter for its audience without explicitly pressing these home. While saying of a sermon, "That was interesting," is certainly preferable to an expression of boredom, preachers will know that such a reaction falls short of their aim of confronting their hearers with a word of God that demands a personal or communal response. Christian academic interpretation of Scripture in a pluralistic context, however, will attempt to engage its audience in a variety of ways that do not have this explicit goal. To say, "I am a Christian who takes seriously the status of the Fourth Gospel as Scripture, and here, as I see them, are some of the implications, problems, and possibilities for humanity, for the church, and for society that arise for a contemporary believing engagement with its subject matter," is to be an advocate without being a preacher and to invite discussion of the significance of this subject matter from a variety of perspectives, including radically opposing ones. On the other hand, unlike Fenn's depiction of academic-seminar talk, this does not mean that theological interpreters need to take the stance that their own view is simply one opinion that is no better than others and can be detached from their own ultimate commitments. Christians believe they are witnessing to what is true, not simply what is true for them, and so engage in pluralistic conversation and dispute with others in order to invite them to see whether the truth of the Christian narrative to which witness is borne also makes sense of their lives in the world. One can—without confusing the witness of one's own interpretation with the ultimacy of the subject matter itself—seek to be persuasive as an advocate in the belief that the subject matter under discussion makes public claims of universal significance. Such advocacy will not forget what has been underlined here so many times: a witness is always situated somewhere and is never disinterested. If they are aware, as far as possible, of the interests that are operative because of their setting, advocates through theological interpretation will be willing to engage in the constant and sometimes difficult process of listening, negotiating, and modifying their interpretations because these can only be provisional judgments.

Theological interpretation as witness shares all the general features of Christian witness sketched earlier, including its cost. How this effects its practitioners will differ in different settings, with their varied distributions of power. As they do their work and give an account of their interpretation to various audiences in the academy and in society, they will not be hankering for a state of affairs in which their own beliefs rule the day and are somehow imposed on everyone engaged in biblical and theological scholarship, even though they obviously hope to be effective in their persuasion,. The very subject matter with which they are dealing, with its God who in Christ rejects this sort of use of power and is characterized by suffering love, makes such a state of affairs—and any other attempts to manipulate what are the remnants of a Christian culture and society in favor of the imperialism of Christian perspectives in this discipline, as in any other—a contradiction in terms. Yet in a pluralistic society, to allow the Christian voice to be ruled out of academic conversations, particularly conversations about the Bible, should be equally unthinkable. If, for example, teaching literary criticism from a neo-Marxist perspective is deemed perfectly acceptable, it seems extremely strange that teaching biblical studies or theology from a Christian perspective is thought to be so controversial. What may be required is, on the one hand, the insistence that, in what is supposed to be a pluralistic context, one has a right to be heard and to attempt to persuade and, on the other, the willingness to experience various forms of marginalization if this is the consequence of a Christian scholarly advocacy sometimes clashing with the values and power structures that surround rational inquiry in the academic world.

D. Faithful Witness and the Dialogue with Judaism

It is one thing to discuss the nature of the alleged anti-Judaism of the original Gospel of John. It is another to discuss here contemporary reading of the Gospel in the light of some of the effects of its history of interpretation, although some of what was said in the previous chapter will be relevant for this topic also. This final reflective section proved difficult to write, and some might wish it had been omitted. It might be argued that while, for the Fourth Gospel, Israel was a primary representative of the hostile world, this is no longer the case in our own setting, where Judaism should be seen as the closest ally to the church, and so there is little more to be said except to urge greater understanding and cooperation between the two faiths. Certainly it can also be argued that after the Shoah the clear task of Christians in relation to Judaism is repentance and that even to raise the question of Christian witness to Jews is to betray a lack of sensitivity and Christian love. Yet dialogue between Jews and Christians is a major part of our contemporary setting, and in such dialogue churches and other Christian groups are issuing theological declarations, about the appropriateness or otherwise of Christian witness, that affect the core of traditional christological claims. The Gospel of John is a major contributor to such claims, and at least on the surface, it appears that the way the Gospel relates them to the Judaism of its own day needs to be taken into account when we are thinking seriously about the issues in our time. To evade this topic in reflecting on the appropriation of the Fourth Gospel would be to take the easy way out.

Nevertheless, I am well aware that what follows represents preliminary thinking and goes against the trend of what is being written on the topic. Much more Christian theological work is needed that attempts to do justice to the entire scope of the Christian canon.[114] Theological interpretation both points to the subject matter of the scriptural witness and construes this subject matter for contemporary witness. But the discussion here asks whether, in the relation between the two, the former is not too often and too quickly submerged by the properly urgent concerns of the latter. However one reacts to what follows, it can at least be taken as a plea to those who work with Scripture to show in their formulations that they are taking seriously the data of the NT witness and to make clear the hermeneutical strategy they are adopting toward this witness.

Here a major dialogue partner is David Tracy, primarily because he has discussed this issue in terms of Christian witness[115] and has also

---

[114] R. K. Soulen, *The God of Israel and Christian Theology* (Minneapolis: Fortress, 1996), represents one such attempt to struggle with the issue of supersessionism without denying either God's fidelity to Israel or the relevance of the Christian gospel for Jews.

[115] D. Tracy, "Christian Witness and the Shoah," in *Holocaust Remembrance* (ed. Hartman), 81–89.

been influenced by the essay by Ricoeur, a former colleague of his, that we treated in an earlier chapter (ch. 7, sec. B). Tracy is rightly and deeply concerned lest Christian witness, especially after the Shoah, become "false witness against the Jewish neighbour."[116] He gives examples of two such instances—the wish to establish a Carmelite convent, with its symbol of the cross, at Auschwitz and the declaration of Edith Stein as a Christian martyr after her murder by the Nazis at Auschwitz. The first is seen by him as a facile inclusiveness that carelessly assumes the cross as a symbol for Jewish suffering, and both are seen as forgetting the particularity of the Shoah as a Jewish experience. Edith Stein was killed because she was a Jew, not because she was a Christian.[117] We may well share Tracy's evaluation of such misguided attempts on the part of the Catholic Church to bear witness. As always with Tracy's work, however, he reaches such an evaluation on the basis of broader hermeneutical concerns.

He reminds us that "the pre-understanding interpreters bring to the text, as well as the text's authorized claim, are constantly changing realities. Insofar as we understand the Scriptures at all, we understand them differently than the original authors did."[118] He distinguishes between scriptural texts as authoritative witnesses and the revelatory event to which they bear witness. This and our knowledge of the circumstances that shaped the writings of the NT witnesses mean that we have to be engaged in a critical conversation with such texts. Clearly, then, the preunderstanding of contemporary interpreters must be informed by a historical consciousness, and above all, this consciousness must include the specific history of the Jewish people and especially the Shoah. With Ricoeur, Tracy advocates a hermeneutics of suspicion as well as a hermeneutics of retrieval. He stresses that particularly where self-understanding has been infected by a systemic distortion, such as that disclosed by the Shoah, a thoroughgoing hermeneutics of suspicion has to be operative.[119] Minimally, Tracy claims, a post-Shoah Christian hermeneutics "must be one that cannot forget the Shoah and therefore can no longer remember anything—even the central Christian confession, even the gospel as confessing narrative, even the grounding passion narrative—in the same way ever again."[120] Our own earlier discussion both

---

[116] Ibid., 83.
[117] Ibid., 82–83.
[118] Ibid., 86.
[119] Cf. ibid., 84–85.
[120] Ibid., 84.

of anti-Judaism and of broader hermeneutical issues suggests our sympathy with such an assertion and with a later forceful repetition of it: "The witness of the Shoah smashes against and demands new reflection on the original Christian scriptural witnesses of Matthew, John and Paul."[121]

But when Tracy spells out what he means by not remembering in the same way and by new reflection, some concerns arise. He believes not simply that the language and conceptuality of such witnesses about the opposition of their unbelieving Jewish compatriots need to be scrutinized and reinterpreted but that the central revelatory event to which they witness needs reinterpretation. What "is forced upon us by the nature of Christian hermeneutics and the light—that is, the darkness, of the Shoah" is a different understanding of the Christ event.[122] By this he means that Christian theologians can no longer speak of new-covenant fulfillment themes that are always in danger of becoming supersessionist, and instead he holds out the hope that Christian theology will embrace the concept of two covenants, one for Jews and one for Christians, and thereby join with Jews in mutual witness.[123] While affirming Tracy's aims to avoid false witness and to have a hermeneutic that is historically rooted, I find his resolution problematic for a number of reasons. It seems that his reinterpretation of the revelatory event is such as to necessitate not simply a new interpretation but a different event. The discontinuity it creates not only means a complete unraveling of the authoritative witnesses, in which, of course, no such notion of two equal covenants can be found,[124] but a rewriting of the historical circumstances in which the event to which they witness was disclosed. This is to move away from the particularity of history, precisely the move that Tracy himself indicts when he speaks of the present hermeneutical situation. Earlier he said that logically the Christian tradition "would best honor its own witnesses . . . by fidelity to the crucified Christ, Himself true witness to God and humankind. But once history intervenes—as it always will—the logic of Christian witness yields something far more complex: a troubling hermeneutics."[125] Yet now he appears to want to solve a troubling hermeneutics by removing an earlier troubling history.

---

[121] Ibid., 89.

[122] Ibid., 86.

[123] Cf. ibid., 84, 89.

[124] One or two scholars have attempted (unsuccessfully) to read Paul in this way.

[125] Tracy, "Christian Witness," 82.

If one indeed believes that divine revelation took place in the Jew Jesus, there can surely be no avoidance of the recognition that inherent in this revelation was an implication about the status of previous revelation and that it was this that precipitated a division among his own people. The logic of the two-covenant view is that this revelation should not have taken place in the midst of the Jewish people but should have been a revelation purely for Gentiles, compatible with Jewish covenantal religion and in no way a challenge to it. Unfortunately, taking the NT witnesses seriously shows us that history was a much messier affair. Although in a short essay one cannot say everything that might be wished, Tracy also makes no attempt to show how his two-covenant view relates to his definition of Christian faith: "To believe 'in Jesus Christ' means, for Christians, to find in the ministry, message, fate, death and resurrection of this particular Jew, Jesus of Nazareth, the decisive witness to God."[126] In this statement Jesus is not only "true witness" but also "the decisive witness." If we ask, "Decisive in respect to what?" the answer must be in comparison with other witnesses, and they must include the Torah and other witnesses within Jewish Scripture. The two-covenant view has Jesus as the decisive witness for the rest of humankind but not for the people to whom he came to be such a witness.

Tracy criticizes what he sees as a post-Enlightenment Christian retreat from living history, with its liberal optimism and theologies of universalist and inclusivist reconciliation. But does not his two-covenant solution not only retreat from history but also have its own version of the dangers of an optimistic and universalist reconciliation? After the Shoah, it is claimed, we can hope that Jews and Christians can henceforth live together in mutual witness because of the recognition that both groups have an equally valid way to the same God. Does not such a hope suggest a premature and inclusivist Christian response to the Shoah? Elsewhere in the volume in which Tracy's essay appears, Friedlander discusses the fact that Jewish writers on the Shoah have not been able to give it some sense of redemptive resolution and that indeed the temptation to provide closure needs to be resisted. He calls instead for keeping watch over absent meaning.[127] Tracy, however, appears to want to find a resolution regarding relations between Christians and Jews, a resolution that appears damaging in its implications for

---

[126] Ibid., 81.

[127] S. Friedlander, in G. H. Hartman (ed.), *Holocaust Remembrance*, 252–63, citing M. Blanchot's formulation "to keep watch over absent meaning" in *The Writing of the Disaster* (Lincoln: University of Nebraska Press, 1986), 42.

Christian witness to the decisiveness, let alone uniqueness, of God's revelation in Jesus.

A further observation indicates the problems of any simple "theory of the two covenants where the Christian follows and learns from the Jewish [sic] a return to history."[128] In their reflections on the Fourth Gospel in this context, Gentile Christians are apt to ignore an entire group of believers who are in a much closer relation than themselves to the original setting of this Gospel, namely, Jewish Christians, including messianic Jews. It would be exceedingly strange and a false witness to such believers if, under the logic of the two-covenant theology, Gentile Christians ended up endorsing a view that not only meant, to all intents and purposes, forgetting the history of early Jewish Christianity but also rejected as an anomaly the existence and experience of Jewish Christians in the present. Even Jewish Christians, when their existence is recognized, are told by proponents of the theology of the two covenants that their witness to their own people is illegitimate.

A rather different solution is sketched by Lindbeck, who talks not of two covenants but of one unified canonical narrative, of which both Christians and Jews are a part.[129] In an exploratory essay that is not always as clear as it might be, Lindbeck holds that the church as portrayed in the NT looks "more like Israel, including Israel *post Christum*, than Christians have customarily supposed."[130] He claims that while the Gospel narratives identify Jesus as the summation, fulfillment, and transformation of Israel's history, the church and Christian believers are not identified as the fulfillment of this history or as antitype to its type. "Rather, the kingdom already present in Christ alone is the antitype, and both Israel and the church are types."[131] The church is to be seen as sharing rather than fulfilling the story of Israel, and in some of the NT, it can be seen as sharing the parts in which Israel was unfaithful, as admonitions are offered on this basis (cf., e.g., 1 Cor 10:5–11). But Lindbeck's argument is scarcely self-evident. Even in his example from 1 Cor 10, although the church is to learn from Israel's history, it is actually in a very different position from Israel, sharing in the fulfillment of history as those "on whom the ends of the ages have come" (v. 11). There are only

---

[128] Tracy, "Christian Witness," 89.

[129] Cf. G. Lindbeck, "The Story-Shaped Church: Critical Exegesis and Theological Interpretation," in *Scriptural Authority and Narrative Interpretation* (ed. G. Green; Philadelphia: Fortress, 1987), 161–78.

[130] Ibid., 162.

[131] Ibid., 166.

two uses of the term *antitype* in the NT, and in the one that corresponds to this pattern, 1 Pet 3:21, it is a church practice, Christian baptism, that is the antitype of which Noah's salvation in the ark is a type. Contrary to Lindbeck, it can be argued persuasively that the usual NT pattern is that Christians or the church are in Christ and therefore share with Christ the notion of fulfillment and the situation of antitype. To take just one example from John's Gospel, Jesus is the true vine that is the fulfillment and replacement of Israel as the vine and believers united to Christ are the branches, sharing in his role if they abide in him.

But what does Lindbeck's alleged pattern suggest about members of Israel who have not believed in Jesus? This is where his proposal is not entirely clear. He says that Israel and the church continued to be one people for the early Christians and, even after the coming of Christ, Israel remained Israel as the people of God. He holds that narrative interpretation "presses the exegete toward finding the same basic understanding of the church in all the New Testament literature,"[132] and he makes Rom 11 the pattern to which everything else is to conform. This assumption is itself problematic. In dealing with his key passage, he acknowledges that Paul asserts that unbelieving Jews have been cut off from the olive tree, but claims that this does not differentiate them from Christians because Paul says the latter, too, can be cut off from the root and that "unbelieving Jewry will ultimately be restored."[133] The "sense of uninterrupted peoplehood" Lindbeck finds here, however, seriously downplays the discontinuity that has caused Paul to address the issue of Rom 9–11 in the first place (cf. Rom 9:2–3). There is also a difference between having already been cut off and the warning that those who have been grafted in could be cut off. The fact that for Paul the restoration of unbelieving Israel awaits the eschaton, however imminent he may have thought this would be, in itself underlines the present disruption.[134]

Lindbeck then refers to Ephesians, with its discussion of the inclusion of the Gentiles—"where there were two, there is now one, the new man in Christ (2:11–3:11)"—but then almost immediately seems to forget his own words by stating that "the inclusion through Christ of the

---

[132] Ibid., 168.

[133] Ibid., 167.

[134] It also means, *contra* Lindbeck, ibid., 168, that 1 Thess 2 need not be thought of as contradictory to what Paul says about unbelieving Jews in Romans, for there he states that at present "as regards the gospel they are enemies for your sake" (Rom 11:28).

uncircumcised in the one eternal covenant constituted . . . not the formation of a new people but the enlargement of the old."[135] Yet Ephesians could not be clearer that Gentiles have not simply been brought into Israel's election but, out of the two previous entities of Israel and the Gentiles, a *new* humanity has been *created* that transcends these previous categories.[136] Lindbeck recognizes that there are variations from his suggested narrative about the church and Israel within the NT itself, but treats these as modifications of the same story for new circumstances.

The key hermeneutical move that follows from his dubious version of the story is this:[137] Faithful Israel before Christ can be more the people of God, even more Spirit-filled, than the faithless church. The same (he claims) can be true of the synagogue after Christ. The latter statement is given two warrants. The first is that those who have not heard the gospel message "live theologically in the time before Christ," and the second is "that Jews for the most part do not and cannot hear because of Christian persecution." From this it follows that Judaism after Christ is actually living theologically before Christ and, to revert to his earlier formulation, is therefore just as much a type of Christ as the church.

This is an interesting proposal and one that avoids traditional supersessionism. For Tracy the Shoah is a decisive hermeneutical factor, and for Lindbeck Christian persecution of Jews has the equivalent function. But unlike Tracy's view, Lindbeck's still defines present Judaism in relation to Jesus and so, while it may have some appeal to Christians, is hardly likely to be acceptable to Jews. His presentation of it is, however, not without difficulties of coherence for Christians. He states clearly that what the Bible meant is not necessarily what God is now saying and that theology is not tied to historical exegesis. Nevertheless, in this case he still wants to argue that his theological proposal is in line with what he calls "the canonically unified and authorized narrative pattern."[138] Presumably, such a pattern needs to be exegetically demonstrated. As already seen, even in the case of the Pauline literature, this is not easy to do, and although this is not the place to make the case, it would not be difficult to show that this pattern, as formulated by Lindbeck, is not

---

[135] Ibid., 167.

[136] On Ephesians, see A. T. Lincoln, "The Church and Israel in Ephesians 2," *CBQ* 49 (1987): 605–24.

[137] I dispute Lindbeck's assertion that his exegeses "are for the most part commonplaces of New Testament scholarship" ("Story-Shaped Church," 169).

[138] Ibid., 171.

found in Matthew, John, Luke–Acts, or Hebrews.[139] The so-called unified pattern may well exist only in one possible reading of Rom 11. It might have been less confusing to admit that the NT itself depicts a relation between the church and Israel different from what now appears theologically desirable. But this, too, would leave him in difficulties because he also holds that proper present theological interpretation has to be scripturally faithful. He makes the narrative meaning of the stories of Jesus his control within Scripture. But this does not move us any further forward because it is precisely the implications of these stories for the status of unbelieving Jews that is in dispute, and in the case of the Gospel story that is our concern in this study, the implications appear to be all too clear. The other major difficulty is that while this proposal appears to take history seriously by giving recognition to what has happened in later relations between Christians and Jews, it does so through a theology that denies Israel a real history in relation to the Christ and the Christian gospel because it defines Israel theologically as "before Christ." The well-thought-out reasons that many Jews have for not believing in Jesus as their Messiah are simply set aside by the view that because Christians have persecuted Jews, this means the latter have never really heard about Jesus. This borders on an idealism that is not prepared to live with the sometimes tragic ambiguities of the historical process. It also fails to take account of the fact that some Jews have claimed to have heard the gospel, despite the history of Christian persecution, and have come to believe in Jesus as their Messiah.

Significantly, it is often Jewish writers who, even after the Shoah, are willing to face in all its starkness, rather than find ways to ameliorate, the fact of an unbelieving response to Jesus on the part of the majority of Jews. George Steiner isolates as determinative of "the tragic destiny of the Jew over these past two thousand years . . . the moment in which the core of Judaism rejects the messianic claim and promises put forward by Jesus of Nazareth and his immediate adherents." He considers our lack of precise knowledge about this moment "a black hole near the actual centre of Jewish history and fate,"[140] but asserts that "what we do know is this: however motivated, this abstention, this tenacious dissent has marked to their very depths, the histories of Judaism and Christianity. The identifying destiny of the Jew, but also in a more oblique sense, that

---

[139] Lindbeck himself appears to sense this difficulty in his footnote observations (ibid., 176–77, nn. 9, 12).

[140] G. Steiner, *No Passion Spent* (New Haven: Yale University Press, 1996), 328.

of the Christian, is that of the ineradicable scars left by that hour of denial, by the veto of the Jew."[141] Steiner himself sees the genesis of the
Shoah in the Christian response, from the very beginning, to this unbelieving denial. For him this response takes the form of Jew hatred, and
within the NT, although many would consider his a less-than-adequate
reading of Paul, he finds this response particularly in Paul's reaction to his
perception that unbelieving Jews have prevented the coming of the messianic realm, a reaction on the part of early Jewish Christians that was at the
same time a Jewish self-hatred.[142] Steiner does not therefore let Christians
off the hook. Their attempts to eradicate the Jew have, he claims, been attempts to eradicate this constant reminder, indeed their own remembrance, of failure, and they should be appalled that this failure generated
the Shoah.[143] Nevertheless, he is ultimately dismissive of well-meaning
post-Holocaust Christian attempts to revise Christian theology in a way
that would make Jewish unbelief fit with Christian belief: "These cannot
be pressed too far, if Christianity is not to efface or trivialize the basic ten-
ets of its revelation. How can there be authentic truth and salvation outside Christ?"[144] Steiner is equally clear that "the Jew cannot negotiate his
rejection of a messianic Jesus. . . . Precisely to the extent that Jews remain
Jews, these denials must stand and must, by the existential fact of continued Jewish life and history be constantly affirmed."[145] His conclusion: "So
what is there 'really,' taking reality to be of the essence, to be talked
about? . . . On both sides might it not be salutary if words now failed
us?"[146] This parallels Friedlander's call to Jews, regarding the Shoah, to
"keep watch over absent meaning." Concerning the theological divide between Jews and Christians because of Christian claims and Jewish rejection of these claims, Steiner, too, for all his attempts to penetrate the
relationship between Golgotha and the Shoah, has to admit an absence of
coherent meaning. "All too plainly, the issues defy the ordering of common
sense. . . . They are extraterrestrial to analytic debate."[147] This admission
of an ultimate incoherence is refreshing and appears to be a more incisive
and realistic insight than the attempts at coherence in well-intentioned
Christian theologies that appear flawed by inconsistencies.

---

[141] Ibid., 335.
[142] Cf. ibid., 336–37.
[143] Cf. ibid., 342, 344.
[144] Ibid., 344.
[145] Ibid., 344.
[146] Ibid., 344, 347.
[147] Ibid., 346.

Many recent Christian approaches to dialogue with Jews in fact end up with a strange contradiction. On the one hand, Christians are rightly urged to recover the Jewishness of Jesus and of the NT writers, but then, on the other, they are urged to treat the Christian faith as an entirely Gentile phenomenon quite unrelated to Judaism, which is to be seen as a separate but equal way to God. For all the appeals to Rom 11, this is to treat Jews very differently than Paul does. Paul, the Jewish Christian apostle to the Gentiles, while refusing to deny God's election of Israel, sees both Jews and Gentiles as part of one humanity. As part of this humanity, they are one and equal in their plight before God, one and equal in their access to the salvation that God has provided in Christ and that is available to faith, and one and equal in the new humanity that is being formed in Christ. For the Fourth Gospel also, for all its depiction of unbelieving Jews as representatives of the alienated world, the verdict of life is available to all, both Jews and Gentiles equally, through believing that Jesus is the Jewish Messiah, the Son of God (cf. 20:31). Rather than in any way undermining the Jewishness of Jesus, the Gospel's "high" Son of God Christology reinforces it. The human flesh taken on by the Logos is Jewish, the human face in which God is now disclosed is a Jewish face. Jesus is the Savior of all the world, but because *Jesus* is Savior, salvation is of the Jews. In the light of God's disclosure in Jesus, the symbols of Jewish history are reinterpreted, but it is Jewish symbols that receive this treatment. The judgment that takes place and that produces a division within Israel means that it is Jewish believers who originally constitute the believing community, and it is into this community that Gentile believers then enter on the basis of the same faith. The Fourth Gospel could not be clearer that there is now a continuing dispute over all the basic aspects of their tradition between this community and the Jews who continue in unbelief. The dispute is not just about Jesus' messiahship; this is now seen to involve the identity of God. Both Jewish and Gentile Johannine Christians' understanding of their own witness and therefore also their self-understanding depend on this relationship to Israel in all its complexity and contentiousness. The contemporary Christian community makes it too easy on itself if it attempts to live as if this dispute no longer existed, either by glossing over its own essential Jewish roots, or by attempting to ignore the continuing existence of Judaism, or by refusing to come to terms with its past history of persecution of Jews, or by being so concerned to make amends for past hostile relationships that it is willing to suppress the basic disagreements that led to the original division within Judaism.

The view that Jesus Christ is for Gentiles and not for Jews rests ultimately on a relativizing of NT claims for Jesus. In such a view, Jesus is no longer the decisive revelation of God for human beings, there should be no witness to Jews based on such a claim, and even dialogue with Jews is to avoid the crucial question of the identity of Jesus. This raises the further question of whether Jews are the only people to be deprived of what has traditionally been deemed to be the good news of the Christian faith. There are historical and theological reasons for treating Judaism as a special case, but is not the logic of such a reduced Christology a universalism in which the faiths of Islam and Buddhism or even of Marxism and humanism can all be seen as supplying their own route to God and in which it is arrogance for Christians to wish to see any further converts to Jesus Christ? Is there no significance to the difference between belief in Christ and unbelief in Christ? In his fine monograph on the Fourth Gospel, Rensberger, somewhat surprisingly, writes, "We must frankly declare that the gospel of John is of no use in attempting to establish, or reestablish, Christian-Jewish relationships today."[148] It depends on what he means by this, but it is difficult to see how the Gospel's issues of whether Jesus is the Messiah, Son of God, and whether God was acting definitively in him have become irrelevant to any honest dialogue between Christians and Jews.

So, what stance is possible for Christian readers of the Fourth Gospel who do not want to bear false witness after the Shoah? I can only suggest that we have to live with an unresolved and agonizing tension. On the one hand, it would be false witness to give up on the truth claims of the Jesus to whom we bear witness and to exclude in principle his own people from hearing such claims; on the other, it would be false witness ever to forget the radical evil of the Shoah and to think we can read the NT or offer witness to Jewish people in the same way after the Shoah as before it. There can only be shame for the way in which the language of the Fourth Gospel, taken out of its original context, has contributed to the mentality that either encouraged or tolerated the events that led to the Shoah. At the same time, Christians are not free to abandon the scandal of particularity that has always been at the heart of their witness or the particularly poignant part of it that affects the Jewish people. This means that they will engage in dialogue with Jews both with repentance for the sins of the past and with something substantial about which to dialogue. Like the Paul of Romans in relation to his

---

[148] Rensberger, *Johannine Faith*, 139.

compatriots, they will believe that God has by no means abandoned the Jewish people, and will certainly hold that the eschaton will provide the resolution that is not yet apparent. In the meantime, however, they will not presume to know or suggest how the Shoah might fit with such beliefs, offering closure for themselves or others, but will instead attempt a chastened retrieval, for their own lives, of the suffering witness of Christ to the love of God. In the light of the witness of the entire NT, they will see themselves as continuing to be in a relationship with the Jewish people that at present entails dispute and contradiction but that is on its way to what they believe will be the disclosure, in the Messiah, of God's merciful judgment that will embrace the Jewish people.

Why some recognize the truth of Jesus' witness that "the Father and I are one" and some do not remains a mystery. But this witness, in its context of John 10:22–39, does two things. It has the secondary effect of producing a division within humanity whose causes not we, but only the ultimate Judge, can fathom, but primarily it is meant to motivate those who do believe, by giving them assurance. It is not the business of Christian believers to unravel the mystery of unbelief but to make their own witness to Christ's witness. Instead of engaging in inadequate theological attempts to overcome the difference between belief and unbelief in Christ, might it not be more salutary for both Christians and Jews to own their differences? Facing and exploring the difference between us may be the best means we have at present to remove the threat this difference frequently presents and to discover enrichment and the possibilities and limitations of mutuality.

If the universal reconciliation for which Christians hope is eschatological, then until that final reconciliation, there will always be the believing church and the unbelieving world. It would be naive to think that this difference will always be exhibited in mutuality and not involve an excluding other. The reception history of the Fourth Gospel shows that its Christian readers certainly and frequently failed the key test of any revolution—how will the liberated oppressed treat their former oppressors when the liberated now have control?—and became the excluding other. Yet we need to remember that a text that played a role in power struggles, as all texts do in some form or other, is not thereby robbed of the right to be treated as authoritative or normative. "Normative statements are characteristically and inescapably statements wrought in conflict, which serve power interests and which continue to be endlessly in dispute."[149] John's Gospel is testimony, and testimony consti-

---

[149] Brueggemann, *Theology of the Old Testament,* 53

tutes just such a text. By definition it includes a context of dispute and conflict. To view this Gospel as authoritative or true is not thereby to ignore what we may be able to discover of its original ideological function, nor is it to imagine that our own confession of its truth can be removed from inevitable disputes of interpretation with their own interests of power. Any critical appropriation of the Fourth Gospel by those who find themselves in very different circumstances from the experience of victimization that influenced the writing of this Gospel will therefore, for example, always need to reexamine how its clear-cut categories of believers over against the world are now operating. Are they having the effect of encouraging believers to exclude others instead of, as in the Gospel's original setting, being the way in which believers make sense of their exclusion by others? Are those categories shaping an identity that is defined more by being over against the unbelieving world than by the self-giving love of the one who promised that whoever came to him he would not cast out?

So-called supersessionist claims about the uniqueness and finality of Jesus' witness to God need not, as such, lead to violence. The only solution to hatred and violence against Jews on the part of Christians is not to rewrite the claims of apostolic Christianity for Jesus but to follow Jesus and the apostolic witness to him in renouncing all violence, any attempt to force one's beliefs on others. It bears repeating that the witness of the Fourth Gospel that transcends the setting that produced it is in the form of a narrative that has at its center a marginalized victim of the injustice of both Jewish and Roman trials and of the self-protective ideologies of both the Jewish religious authorities and Pilate. The narrative claims that this particular sentenced and executed Jewish witness embodies the loving purpose of the Creator and Judge in bringing an alienated and hostile world to trial. This purpose was to render the positive verdict of life that entails a restoration of humanity to the relationship with the Creator it was meant to have. The resolution of this trial's plot and of the conflict provoked by the sin and violence of humanity is brought about precisely by the protagonist embracing in his own body the pain and suffering produced by this world's evil. In the narrative's own discourse, from the pierced side of the crucified one flow blood and water. Any authentic witness to this verdict will be characterized by a similar forswearing of this world's means of power for the sake of a truth that is not to be identified with power but is exhibited in self-giving. The way of *the* witness is to be the way of his witnessing followers, whether in their special continuing conversation with Judaism or in their existence in the world as a whole.

BIBLIOGRAPHY

Abrams, M. H. *A Glossary of Literary Terms*. 4th ed. New York: Holt, Rhinehart & Winston, 1981.

Alexander, P. S. "'The Parting of the Ways' from the Perspective of Rabbinic Judaism." Pages 1–25 in *Jews and Christians*. Edited by J. D. G. Dunn. Tübingen: J. C. B. Mohr, 1992.

Améry, J. *At the Mind's Edge*. New York: Shocken, 1990.

Amsler, S. "Le thème du procès chez les prophètes d'Israel." *Revue de Théologie et de Philosophie* 111 (1974): 116–31.

Arens, E. *Christopraxis: A Theology of Action*. Minneapolis: Fortress, 1995.

Ashton, J. *Understanding the Fourth Gospel*. Oxford: Clarendon, 1991.

Austin, J. L. *Philosophical Papers*. Oxford: Clarendon, 1961.

Ball, D. M. *"I Am" in John's Gospel*. Sheffield: Sheffield Academic Press, 1996.

Barrett, C. K. *The Gospel according to St. John*. 2d ed. Philadelphia: Westminster, 1978.

Barth, K. *Church Dogmatics*. Edinburgh: T&T Clark, 1956.

Bartlett, D. L. "Story and History: Narratives and Claims." *Interpretation* 45 (1991): 229–40.

Bauckham, R. J. "The Beloved Disciple as Ideal Author." *Journal for the Study of the New Testament* 49 (1993): 21–44.

———, ed. *The Gospels for All Christians: Rethinking the Gospel Audiences*. Grand Rapids: Eerdmans, 1998.

Beasley-Murray, G. R. *John*. Waco: Word, 1987.

Beck, D. R. "The Narrative Function of Anonymity in Fourth Gospel Characterization." *Semeia* 63 (1993): 143–58.

Betz, O. *Der Paraklet*. Leiden: E. J. Brill, 1963.

Beutler, J. *Martyria*. Frankfurt: J. Knecht, 1972.

Bittner, W. *Jesu Zeichen im Johannesevangelium*. Tübingen: J. C. B. Mohr, 1987.

Blank, J. *Krisis. Untersuchungen zur johanneischen Christologie und Eschatologie*. Freiburg: Lambertus, 1964.

————. "Die Verhandlung vor Pilatus: Joh 18,28–19,16 im Lichte johanneischer Theologie." *Biblische Zeitschrift* 3 (1959): 60–81.

Boice, J. M. *Witness and Revelation in the Gospel of John.* Grand Rapids: Zondervan, 1970.

Bond, H. K. *Pontius Pilate in History and Interpretation.* Cambridge: Cambridge University Press, 1998.

Booth, W. C. *The Company We Keep: An Ethics of Fiction.* Berkeley: University of California Press, 1988.

Borgen, P. "God's Agent in the Fourth Gospel." Pages 137–48 in *Religions in Antiquity.* Edited by J. Neusner. Leiden: E. J. Brill, 1968.

Bowersock, G. W. *Fiction as History.* Berkeley: University of California Press, 1994.

Brodie, T. L. *The Gospel according to John: A Literary and Theological Commentary.* Oxford: Oxford University Press, 1993.

————. *The Quest for the Origin of John's Gospel.* Oxford: Oxford University Press, 1993.

Brooks, P. *Reading for the Plot.* Oxford: Clarendon, 1984.

Brown, R. E. *The Community of the Beloved Disciple.* New York: Paulist, 1979.

————. *Death of the Messiah.* 2 vols. New York: Doubleday, 1994.

————. *The Gospel according to John.* 2 vols. New York: Doubleday, 1966–1970.

Brox, N. *Der Glaube als Zeuge.* Munich: Kösel, 1966.

————. *Zeuge und Märtyrer. Untersuchungen zur frühchristlichen Zeugnis-Terminologie.* Munich: Kösel, 1961.

Brueggemann, W. *Theology of the Old Testament.* Minneapolis: Fortress, 1997.

Bultmann, R. *The Gospel of John.* Oxford: Blackwell, 1971.

————. *Theology of the New Testament.* 2 vols. New York: Scribners, 1955.

Burge, G. M. *The Anointed Community: The Holy Spirit in the Johannine Tradition.* Grand Rapids: Eerdmans, 1987.

Burridge, R. A. *Four Gospels, One Jesus?* Grand Rapids: Eerdmans, 1994.

————. *What Are the Gospels? A Comparison with Graeco-Roman Biography.* Cambridge: Cambridge University Press, 1992.

Caird, G. B. *The Language and Imagery of the Bible.* London: Duckworth, 1980.

Campbell, R. *Truth and Historicity.* Oxford: Clarendon, 1992.

Camus, A. *The Fall.* Harmondsworth, England: Penguin, 1963.

————. *The Plague.* New York: Random House, 1972.

Caputo, J. D., ed. *Deconstruction in a Nutshell: A Conversation with Jacques Derrida.* New York: Fordham University Press, 1997.

Carroll, J. T. "Present and Future in Fourth Gospel 'Eschatology.'" *Biblical Theology Bulletin* 19 (1989): 63–68.

Carson, D. A. "The Function of the Paraclete in John 16:7–11." *Journal of Biblical Literature* 98 (1979): 547–66.

————. *The Gospel according to John.* Grand Rapids: Eerdmans, 1991.

————. "The Purpose of the Fourth Gospel: John 20:31 Reconsidered." *Journal of Biblical Literature* 106 (1987): 639–51.

Casey, M. *Is John's Gospel True?* New York: Routledge, 1996.

Cassidy, R. J. *John's Gospel in New Perspective*. New York: Orbis, 1992.

Castelli, E., ed. *La testimonianza*. Rome: Istituto di Studi Filosofici, 1972.

Charles, J. D. "'Will the Court Please Call In the Prime Witness?' John 1:29–34 and the Witness Motif." *Trinity Journal* 10 (1989): 71–83.

Charlier, J. P. "L'exégèse johannique d'un précepte légal: Jean viii 17." *Revue biblique* 67 (1960): 503–15.

Chatman, S. *Story and Discourse: Narrative Structure in Fiction and Film*. Ithaca, N.Y.: Cornell University Press, 1978.

Coady, C. A. J. *Testimony: A Philosophical Study*. Oxford: Clarendon, 1992.

Collingwood, R. G. *The Idea of History*. Oxford: Oxford University Press, 1970.

Cox, P. *Biography in Late Antiquity: A Quest for the Holy Man*. Berkeley: University of California Press, 1983.

Culpepper, R. A. *Anatomy of the Fourth Gospel*. Philadelphia: Fortress, 1983.

———. "The Plot of John's Story of Jesus." *Interpretation* 49 (1995): 347–58.

Cunningham, D. S. *Faithful Persuasion: In Aid of a Rhetoric of Christian Theology*. Notre Dame: University of Notre Dame Press, 1991.

Dahl, N. A. "Anamnesis." Pages 11–29 in *Jesus in the Memory of the Early Church*. Edited by N. A. Dahl. Minneapolis: Augsburg, 1976.

———. "The Johannine Church and History." Pages 124–42 in *Current Issues in New Testament Interpretation*. Edited by W. Klassen and G. F. Snyder. London: SCM, 1962. Repr. pages 122–40 in *The Interpretation of John*. Edited by J. Ashton. London: SPCK, 1986.

Davidson, D. *Inquiries into Truth and Interpretation*. Oxford: Oxford University Press, 1984.

Davies, M. *Rhetoric and Reference in the Fourth Gospel*. Sheffield: JSOT Press, 1992.

Derrida, J. "Foi et savoir: Les deux sources de la 'religion' aux limites de la simple raison." Pages 9–86 in *La religion*. Edited by J. Derrida and G. Vattimo. Paris: Seuil, 1996.

———. *Given Time: I. Counterfeit Money*. Chicago: University of Chicago Press, 1991.

———. *Points— : Interviews, 1974–1994*. Edited by E. Weber. Stanford: Stanford University Press. 1995.

———. *Ulysse gramophone: Deux mots pour Joyce*. Paris: Galilée, 1987.

Dewey, J. "*Paroimiai* in the Gospel of John." *Semeia* 17 (1980): 81–100.

Dietrich, S. de. "'You Are My Witnesses'—a Study of the Church's Witness." *Interpretation* 8 (1954): 173–79.

Dodd, C. H. "A Hidden Parable in the Fourth Gospel." Pages 30–40 in *More New Testament Studies* (Manchester: Manchester University Press, 1968).

———. *Historical Tradition in the Fourth Gospel*. Cambridge: Cambridge University Press, 1963.

———. *The Interpretation of the Fourth Gospel*. Cambridge: Cambridge University Press, 1953.

Duke, P. *Irony in the Fourth Gospel*. Atlanta: John Knox, 1985.

Dunn, J. D. G. *The Partings of the Ways*. Philadelphia: Trinity Press International, 1991.

————. "The Question of Anti-Semitism in the New Testament Writings of the Period." Pages 177–211 in *Jews and Christians.* Edited by J. D. G. Dunn. Tübingen: J. C. B. Mohr, 1992.

Evans, C. F. *Explorations in Theology* 2. London: SCM, 1977.

Fee, G. D. "On the Text and Meaning of John 20,30–31." Pages 2193–2205 in vol. 3 of *The Four Gospels, 1992.* 3 vols. Edited by F. van Segbroek et al. Leuven: Leuven University Press, 1992.

Felman, S., and D. Laub. *Testimony.* New York: Routledge, Chapman & Hall, 1992.

Fenn, R. K. *Liturgies and Trials.* Oxford: Blackwell, 1982.

Fish, S. *Is There a Text in This Class?* Cambridge: Harvard University Press, 1980.

Fortna, R. T. *The Fourth Gospel and Its Predecessor.* Philadelphia: Fortress, 1988.

Fowl, S. E. *Engaging Scripture.* Oxford: Blackwell, 1998.

Franck, E. *Revelation Taught: The Paraclete in the Gospel of John.* Lund: Gleerup, 1985.

Frei, H. W. *The Eclipse of Biblical Narrative: A Study in Eighteenth and Nineteenth Century Hermeneutics.* New Haven: Yale University Press, 1974.

————. *The Identity of Jesus Christ: The Hermeneutical Bases of Dogmatic Theology.* Philadelphia: Fortress, 1975.

————. "The 'Literal Reading' of Biblical Narrative in the Christian Tradition: Does It Stretch or Will It Break?" Pages 36–77 in *The Bible and the Narrative Tradition.* Edited by F. McConnell. New York: Oxford University Press, 1986.

Gaventa, B. R. "The Archive of Excess: John 21 and the Problem of Narrative Closure." Pages 240–52 in *Exploring the Gospel of John.* Edited by R. A. Culpepper and C. C. Black. Louisville: Westminster John Knox, 1996.

Gemser, B. "The Rib- or Controversy-Pattern in Hebrew Mentality." Pages 120–37 in *Wisdom in Israel and the Ancient Near East.* Edited by M. Noth and D. Winton Thomas. Leiden: E. J. Brill, 1955.

Giblin, C. H. "Confrontations in John 18, 1–27." *Biblica* 65 (1984): 210–32.

————. "John's Narration of the Hearing before Pilate (John 18,28–19,16a)." *Biblica* 67 (1986): 221–39.

Gill, C., and T. P. Wiseman, eds. *Lies and Fiction in the Ancient World.* Exeter, England: University of Exeter Press, 1993.

Girard, R. *The Scapegoat.* Baltimore: Johns Hopkins University Press, 1986.

Gooch, P. W. *Reflections on Jesus and Socrates: Word and Silence.* New Haven: Yale University Press, 1996.

Goodman, M. "Diaspora Reactions to the Destruction of the Temple." Pages 27–38 in *Jews and Christians.* Edited by J. D. G. Dunn. Tübingen: J. C. B. Mohr, 1992.

Gray, R. *Franz Kafka.* Cambridge: Cambridge University Press, 1973.

Green, G. "'The Bible as . . .': Fictional Narrative and Scriptural Truth." Pages 79–96 in *Scriptural Authority and Narrative Interpretation.* Edited by G. Green. Philadelphia: Fortress, 1987.

Greimas, A. J. *Sémantique structurale*. Paris: Larousse, 1966.

Griffiths, D. R. "Deutero-Isaiah and the Fourth Gospel." *Expository Times* 65 (1953–1954): 355–60.

Griffiths, J. G. *The Divine Verdict: A Study of Divine Judgement in the Ancient Religions*. Leiden: E. J. Brill, 1991.

Grundmann, W. *Der Zeuge der Wahrheit*. Berlin: Evangelische Verlagsanstalt, 1985.

Hare, D. *The Theme of Jewish Persecution of Christians in the Gospel according to St. Matthew*. Cambridge: Cambridge University Press, 1967.

Harner, P. B. *The "I AM" of the Fourth Gospel*. Philadelphia: Fortress, 1970.

Hartman, G. H., ed. *Holocaust Remembrance*. Oxford: Blackwell, 1994.

Hartman, L., and B. Olsson, eds. *Aspects on the Johannine Literature*. Uppsala: Uppsala University Press, 1987.

Harvey, A. E. *Jesus on Trial*. London: SPCK, 1976.

Harvey, J. *Le plaidoyer prophétique contre Israel après la rupture de l'alliance*. Bruges: Desclée de Brouwer, 1967.

Harvey, Van A. *The Historian and the Believer*. New York: Macmillan, 1966.

Hays, R. B. *The Moral Vision of the New Testament*. San Francisco: Harper-Collins, 1996.

Hemmerle, K. "Wahrheit und Zeugnis." Pages 54–72 in *Theologie als Wissenschaft*. Edited by K. Hemmerle. Freiburg: Herder, 1970.

Hengel, M. "Die Schriftauslegung des 4. Evangeliums auf dem Hintergrund der urchristlichen Exegese." *Jahrbuch für biblische Theologie* 4 (1989): 249–89.

Hengel, M. "The Old Testament in the Fourth Gospel." *Horizons in Biblical Theology* 12 (1990): 19–41.

Hindley, J. C. "Witness in the Fourth Gospel." *Scottish Journal of Theology* 18 (1965): 319–37.

Horbury, W. "The Benediction of the *Minim* and Early Jewish-Christian Controversy." *Journal of Theological Studies* 33 (1982): 19–61.

———. "Extirpation and Excommunication." *Vetus Testamentum* 35 (1985): 13–38.

———. "Jewish-Christian Relations in Barnabas and Justin Martyr." Pages 315–45 in *Jews and Christians*. Edited by J. D. G. Dunn. Tübingen: J. C. B. Mohr, 1992.

Horbury, W., and B. McNeil, eds. *Suffering and Martyrdom in the New Testament*. Cambridge: Cambridge University Press, 1981.

Horst, P. W. van der. "The *Birkat Ha-minim* in Recent Research." *Expository Times* 105 (1994): 363–68.

Huffmon, H. B. "The Covenant Lawsuit in the Prophets." *Journal of Biblical Literature* 78 (1959): 285–95.

Hultgren, A. *Jesus and His Adversaries*. Minneapolis: Augsburg, 1979.

Ibuki, Y. *Die Wahrheit im Johannesevangelium*. Bonn: Peter Hanstein, 1972.

Johns, L. L., and D. B. Miller. "The Signs as Witnesses in the Fourth Gospel: Re-examining the Evidence." *Catholic Biblical Quarterly* 56 (1994): 519–35.

Johnson, L. T. "The New Testament's Anti-Jewish Slander and the Conventions of Ancient Polemic." *Journal of Biblical Literature* 108 (1989): 419–41.

Jonge, M. de. *Jesus: Stranger from Heaven and Son of God.* Missoula, Mont.: Scholars Press, 1977.

Jossua, J.-P. *The Condition of the Witness.* London: SCM, 1985.

Joubert, S. J. "A Bone of Contention in Recent Scholarship: The *'Birkat Haminim'* and the Separation of Church and Synagogue in the First Century A. D." *Neotestamentica* 27 (1993): 351–63.

Käsemann, E. *The Testament of Jesus.* Philadelphia: Fortress, 1968.

Katz, S. T. "Issues in the Separation of Judaism and Christianity after 70 C.E.: A Reconsideration." *Journal of Biblical Literature* 103 (1984): 43–76.

Kelsey, D. *To Understand God Truly: What's Theological about a Theological School.* Louisville: Westminster John Knox, 1992.

Kimelman, R. *"Birkat Ha-Minim* and the Lack of Evidence for an Anti-Christian Jewish Prayer in Late Antiquity." Pages 226–44 in vol. 2 of *Jewish and Christian Self-Definition.* 3 vols. Edited by E. P. Sanders et al. Philadelphia: Fortress, 1980–1982.

Kinman, B. "Pilate's Assize and the Timing of Jesus' Trial." *TB* 42 (1991): 282–95.

Klaus, M. B. *Gemeinde zwischen Integration und Abgrenzung.* Frankfurt: Peter Lang, 1992.

Koester, C. "The Spectrum of Johannine Readers." Pages 5–19 in *"What Is John?": Readers and Readings of the Fourth Gospel.* Edited by F. F. Segovia. Atlanta: Scholars Press, 1996.

Korting, G. *Die esoterische Struktur des Johannesevangeliums.* 2 vols. Regensburg: Pustet, 1994.

Kurz, W. "The Beloved Disciple and Implied Readers." *Biblical Theology Bulletin* 19 (1989): 100–107.

Ladd, G. E. *A Theology of the New Testament.* Rev. ed. Grand Rapids: Eerdmans, 1993.

Lakoff, G., and M. Johnson. *Metaphors We Live By.* Chicago: University of Chicago Press, 1980.

Langer, L. L. *Holocaust Testimony: The Ruins of Memory.* New Haven: Yale University Press, 1991.

Lash, N. "What Might Martyrdom Mean?" Pages 181–98 in *Suffering and Martyrdom in the New Testament.* Edited by W. Horbury and B. McNeil. Cambridge: Cambridge University Press, 1981. Repr. pages 75–92 in N. Lash, *Theology on the Way to Emmaus.* London: SCM, 1986.

Lee, D. A. *The Symbolic Narratives of the Fourth Gospel.* Sheffield: JSOT Press, 1994.

Lehmann, P. *The Transfiguration of Politics.* New York: Harper & Row, 1975.

Leitch, T. M. *What Stories Are.* London: Pennsylvania State University Press, 1986.

Limburg, J. "The Root *rib* and the Prophetic Lawsuit Speeches." *Journal of Biblical Literature* 88 (1969): 291–304.

Lincoln, A. T. "The Church and Israel in Ephesians 2." *Catholic Biblical Quarterly* 49 (1987): 605–24.

———. "From Wrath to Justification: Tradition, Gospel, and Audience in the Theology of Romans 1:18–4:25." Pages 130–59 in *Romans*. Vol. 3 of *Pauline Theology*. Edited by D. M. Hay and E. E. Johnson. Minneapolis: Fortress, 1995.

———. " 'I Am the Resurrection and the Life': The Resurrection Message of the Fourth Gospel." Pages 122–44 in *Life in the Face of Death: The Resurrection Message of the New Testament*. Edited by R. N. Longenecker. Grand Rapids: Eerdmans, 1998.

———. *Paradise Now and Not Yet*. Cambridge: Cambridge University Press, 1981.

Lindars, B. *The Gospel of John*. London: Oliphants, 1972.

———. "The Persecution of Christians in John 15:18–16:4a." Pages 48–69 in *Suffering and Martyrdom in the New Testament*. Edited by W. Horbury and B. McNeil. Cambridge: Cambridge University Press, 1981.

Lindbeck, G. "The Story-Shaped Church: Critical Exegesis and Theological Interpretation." Pages 161–78 in *Scriptural Authority and Narrative Interpretation*. Edited by G. Green. Philadelphia: Fortress, 1987.

Lindsay, D. R. "What is truth? Ἀλήθεια in the Gospel of John." *Restoration Quarterly* 35 (1993): 129–45.

Long, T. G. *The Witness of Preaching*. Louisville: Westminster John Knox, 1989.

Lowry, R. "The Rejected-Suitor Syndrome: Human Sources of the New Testament 'Antisemitism.' " *Journal of Ecumenical Studies* 14 (1977): 219–32.

Lundin, R. *The Culture of Interpretation*. Grand Rapids: Eerdmans, 1993.

Lyotard, J.-F., *The Postmodern Condition: A Report on Knowledge*. Translated by G. Bennington and B. Massumi. Minneapolis: University of Minnesota Press, 1984.

Maccini, R. G. *Her Testimony Is True: Women as Witnesses according to John*. Sheffield: Sheffield Academic Press, 1996.

MacIntyre, A. *Three Rival Versions of Moral Enquiry*. Notre Dame: University of Notre Dame Press, 1990.

———. *Whose Justice? Which Rationality?* Notre Dame: University of Notre Dame Press, 1988.

Malina, B. J. *The Gospel of John in Sociolinguistic Perspective*. Berkeley: Center for Hermeneutical Studies, 1985.

———. *The New Testament World*. Atlanta: John Knox, 1981.

Malina, B. J., and R. Rohrbaugh. *Social-Science Commentary on the Gospel of John*. Minneapolis: Fortress, 1998.

Marsh, J. *Saint John*. Harmondsworth, England: Penguin, 1968.

Marshall, B. D. "Meaning and Truth in Narrative Interpretation: A Reply to George Schner." *Modern Theology* 8 (1992): 173–79.

Marshall, P. *Their Blood Cries Out*. Dallas: Word, 1997.

Martyn, J. L. *History and Theology in the Fourth Gospel*. 2d ed. Nashville: Abingdon, 1979.

Matera, F. J. "Jesus before Annas: John 18, 13–14, 19–24." *Ephemerides theologicae lovanienses* 66 (1990): 38–55.

Matsunaga, K. "Christian Self-Identification and the Twelfth Benediction." Pages 355–71 in *Eusebius, Christianity, and Judaism.* Edited by H. W. Attridge and G. Hata. Leiden: E. J. Brill, 1992.

May, J. M. *Trials of Character: The Eloquence of Ciceronian Ethos.* Chapel Hill: University of North Carolina Press, 1988.

Meeks, W. A. "Galilee and Judea in the Fourth Gospel." *Journal of Biblical Literature* 85 (1966): 159–69.

———. "The Man from Heaven in Johannine Sectarianism." *Journal of Biblical Literature* 91 (1972): 44–72. Repr. pages 141–73 in *The Interpretation of John.* Edited by J. Ashton. London: SPCK, 1986.

———. *The Prophet-King: Moses Traditions and the Johannine Christology.* Leiden: E. J. Brill, 1967.

Melugin, R. F. *The Formation of Isaiah 40–55.* Berlin: de Gruyter, 1976.

Michel, O. "Zeuge und Zeugnis." Pages 15–31 in *Neues Testament und Geschichte.* FS O. Cullmann. Edited by H. Baltensweiler and B. Reicke. Zurich: Theologischer Verlag, 1972.

Middleton, J. R., and B. J. Walsh. *Truth Is Stranger Than It Used to Be: Biblical Faith in a Postmodern Age.* Downers Grove, Ill.: InterVarsity, 1995.

Milbank, J. "Can a Gift Be Given? Prolegomena to a Future Trinitarian Metaphysic." Pages 119–61 in *Rethinking Metaphysics.* Edited by L. G. Jones and S. E. Fowl. Oxford: Blackwell, 1995.

Miller, A. *Plays: Two.* London: Methuen, 1991.

Minear, P. *John: The Martyr's Gospel.* New York: Pilgrim, 1984.

Moltmann, J. *The Coming of God.* London: SCM, 1996.

Momigliano, A. *The Development of Greek Biography.* Cambridge: Harvard University Press, 1971.

Motyer, S. "Method in Fourth Gospel Studies: A Way out of the Impasse?" *Journal for the Study of the New Testament* 66 (1997): 27–44.

———. *Your Father the Devil? A New Approach to John and "the Jews."* Carlisle, England: Paternoster, 1997.

Moule, C. F. D. "From Defendant to Judge—and Deliverer: An Enquiry into the Use and Limitations of the Theme of Vindication in the New Testament." *SNTS Bulletin* 3 (1952): 40–52.

Mussner, F. *The Historical Jesus in the Gospel of St. John.* Translated by W. J. O'Hara. London: Burns & Oates, 1967.

Nabert, J. *Le désir de Dieu.* Paris: Aubier, 1966.

Newbigin, L. *The Gospel in a Pluralist Society.* Grand Rapids: Eerdmans, 1989.

———. *Truth to Tell: The Gospel as Public Truth.* Grand Rapids: Eerdmans, 1991.

Neyrey, J. H. " 'Despising the Shame of the Cross': Honor and Shame in the Johannine Passion Narrative." *Semeia* 68 (1994): 113–37.

———. "The Forensic Defense Speech and Paul's Trial Speeches in Acts 22–26: Form and Function." Pages 210–24 in *Luke–Acts: New Perspectives from the SBL Seminar.* Edited by C. H. Talbert. New York: Crossroad, 1984.

————. *An Ideology of Revolt: John's Christology in Social-Science Perspective.* Philadelphia: Fortress, 1988.

————. "Jesus the Judge: Forensic Process in John 8,21–59." *Biblica* 68 (1987): 509–42.

Nicholson, G. C. *Death as Departure: The Johannine Descent-Ascent Schema.* Chico, Calif.: Scholars Press, 1983.

Nielsen, K. *Yahweh as Prosecutor and Judge.* Sheffield: JSOT Press, 1978.

Nietzsche, F. *The Antichrist.* Pages 626–27 in *The Portable Nietzsche.* Edited by W. Kaufmann. New York: Viking, 1968.

O'Day, G. R. "The Gospel of John." Pages 493–865 in vol. 9 of *The New Interpreter's Bible.* 12 vols. Ed. L. E. Keck. Nashville: Abingdon, 1995.

Painter, J. "John 9 and the Interpretation of the Fourth Gospel." *Journal for the Study of the New Testament* 28 (1986): 31–61.

————. *John: Witness and Theologian.* London: SPCK, 1975.

Pancaro, S. *The Law in the Fourth Gospel.* Leiden: E. J. Brill, 1975.

Parsons, M. C. "Reading a Beginning/Beginning a Reading: Tracing Literary Theory on Narrative Openings." *Semeia* 52 (1990): 11–31.

Patte, D. *The Religious Dimensions of Biblical Texts.* Atlanta: Scholars Press, 1990.

Pelling, C. B. R. "Truth and Fiction in Plutarch's *Lives."* Pages 19–52 in *Antonine Literature.* Edited by D. A. Russell. Oxford: Clarendon, 1990.

Petersen, N. R. *The Gospel of John and the Sociology of Light.* Valley Forge, Penn.: Trinity Press International, 1993.

Phelan, J. *Reading People, Reading Plots.* Chicago: University of Chicago Press, 1989.

Placher, W. C. *Unapologetic Theology.* Louisville: Westminster John Knox, 1989.

Porsch, F. *Anwalt der Glaubenden: Das Wirken des Geistes nach dem Zeugnis Johannesevangeliums.* Stuttgart: Katholisches Bibelwerk, 1978.

————. *Pneuma und Wort: Ein exegetischer Beitrag zur Pneumatologie des Johannesevangeliums.* Frankfurt: Knecht, 1974.

Potterie, I. de la. "Jean-Baptiste et Jésus, témoins de la vérité d'après le IVe Evangile." Pages 317–29 in *La testimonianza.* Edited by E. Castelli. Rome: Istituto di Studi Filosofici, 1972.

————. "Jesus King and Judge according to John 19:13." *Scripture* 13 (1961): 97–111.

————. "Jésus roi et juge d'après Jn 19, 13, Ἐκάθισεν ἐπὶ βήματος." *Biblica* 41 (1960): 217–47.

————. "La notion de témoignage dans Saint Jean." Pages 193–208 in *Sacra Pagina II.* 2 vols. Edited by J. Coppens, A. Descamps, and E. Massaux. Paris: Gabalda, 1959.

————. "Le témoin qui demeure: Le disciple que Jésus aimait." *Biblica* 67 (1986): 343–59.

————. *La vérité dans S. Jean.* 2 vols. Rome: Biblical Institute Press, 1977.

Preiss, T. "Justification in Johannine Thought." Pages 100–118 in *Hommage et reconnaissance à K. Barth.* Neuchâtel: Delachaux & Niestlé, 1946. Repr. pages 9–31 in T. Preiss, *Life in Christ.* London: SCM, 1957.

Rahner, K. "Interprétation théologique du témoignage." Pages 173–87 in *La testimonianza*. Edited by E. Castelli. Rome: Istituto di Studi Filosofici, 1972.

Rebell, W. *Gemeinde als Gegenwelt: Zur soziologischen und didaktischen Funktion des Johannesevangeliums.* Frankfurt: Peter Lang, 1987.

Reim, G. *Studien zum alttestamentlichen Hintergrund des Johannesevangeliums.* Cambridge: Cambridge University Press, 1974.

Reinhartz, A. "Jesus as Prophet: Predictive Prolepses in the Fourth Gospel." *Journal for the Study of the New Testament* 36 (1989): 3–16.

———. *The Word in the World: The Cosmological Tale in the Fourth Gospel.* Atlanta: Scholars Press, 1992.

Rensberger, D. *Johannine Faith and Liberating Community.* Philadelphia: Westminster, 1988.

Resseguie, J. L. "John 9: A Literary-Critical Analysis." Pages 295–303 in vol. 2 of *Literary Interpretations of Biblical Narratives.* 2 vols. Edited by K. R. Gros Louis. Nashville: Abingdon, 1982.

Ricoeur, P. *The Conflict of Interpretations: Essays in Hermeneutics.* Edited by D. Ihde. Evanston, Ill.: Northwestern University Press, 1974.

———. *Freud and Philosophy: An Essay on Interpretation.* New Haven: Yale University Press, 1970.

———. "The Hermeneutics of Testimony." Pages 119–54 in P. Ricoeur, *Essays on Biblical Interpretation.* Philadelphia: Fortress, 1980.

———. *Interpretation Theory: Discourse and the Surplus of Meaning.* Fort Worth: Texas Christian University Press, 1976.

———. *The Rule of Metaphor.* Toronto: University of Toronto Press, 1977.

———. *The Symbolism of Evil.* Boston: Beacon, 1969.

———. *Time and Narrative.* 3 vols. Chicago: University of Chicago Press, 1984–1988.

———. "Toward a Hermeneutic of the Idea of Revelation." Pages 73–118 in P. Ricoeur, *Essays on Biblical Interpretation.* Philadelphia: Fortress, 1980.

Rogers, E. F. "How the Virtues of the Interpreter Presuppose and Perfect Hermeneutics: The Case of Thomas Aquinas." *JR* 76 (1996): 64–81.

Sabbe, M. "The Trial of Jesus before Pilate in John and Its Relation to the Synoptic Gospels." Pages 341–85 in *John and the Synoptics.* Edited by A. Denaux. Leuven: Leuven University Press, 1992.

Sanders, J. N. *The Gospel according to St. John.* Edited by B. A. Mastin. London: A. & C. Black, 1968.

Sanders, J. T. *Schismatics, Sectarians, Dissidents, Deviants.* London: SCM, 1993.

Schiffman, L. H. "At the Crossroads: Tannaitic Perspectives on the Jewish-Christian Schism." Pages 115–56 in vol. 2 of *Jewish and Christian Self-Definition.* 3 vols. Edited by E. P. Sanders et al. Philadelphia: Fortress, 1981.

———. *Who Was a Jew? Rabbinic and Halakhic Perspectives on the Jewish-Christian Schism.* Hoboken, N.J.: Ktav, 1985.

Schnackenburg, R. *The Gospel according to St. John.* 3 vols. Vols. 1–2. New York: Seabury, 1980. Vol. 3. New York: Crossroad, 1982.

Scholes, R. *Semiotics and Interpretation*. New Haven: Yale University Press, 1982.

Scholes, R., and R. Kellogg. *The Nature of Narrative*. Oxford: Oxford University Press, 1966.

Schoors, A. *I Am God Your Saviour: A Form-Critical Study of the Main Genres in Is. XL–LV*. Leiden: E. J. Brill, 1973.

Schüssler Fiorenza, E. "The Ethics of Interpretation: Decentering Biblical Scholarship." *Journal of Biblical Literature* 107 (1988): 3–17.

Schweizer, E. "Jesus der Zeuge Gottes: Zum Problem des Doketismus in Johannesevangeliums." Pages 161–68 in *Studies in John Presented to Professor Dr. J. N. Sevenster on the Occasion of His Seventieth Birthday*. Leiden: E. J. Brill, 1970.

Searle, J. R. *Expression and Meaning: Studies in the Theory of Speech Acts*. Cambridge: Cambridge University Press, 1979.

Segovia, F. F. *The Farewell of the Word: The Johannine Call to Abide*. Minneapolis: Fortress, 1991.

———. "The Journey(s) of the Word of God: A Reading of the Plot of the Fourth Gospel." *Semeia* 53 (1991): 23–54.

Setzer, C. *Jewish Responses to Early Christians*. Minneapolis: Fortress, 1994.

Smiga, G. M. *Pain and Polemic: Anti-Judaism in the Gospels*. New York: Paulist, 1992.

Söding, T. "Die Macht der Wahrheit und das Reich der Freiheit: Zur johanneischen Deutung des Pilatus-Prozesses (Joh 18,28–19,16)." *Zeitschrift für Theologie und Kirche* 93 (1996): 35–58.

———. "Die Schrift als Medium des Glaubens: Zur hermeneutischen Bedeutung von Joh 20,30f." Pages 343–71 in *Schrift und Tradition*. FS J. Ernst. Edited by K. Backhaus and F. G. Untergassmair. Paderborn: F. Schöningh, 1996.

Soulen, K. *The God of Israel and Christian Theology*. Minneapolis: Fortress, 1996.

Staley, J. L. *Reading with a Passion*. New York: Continuum, 1995.

———. "Stumbling in the Dark, Reaching for the Light: Reading Character in John 5 and 9." *Semeia* 53 (1991): 55–80.

Steiner, G. *No Passion Spent*. New Haven: Yale University Press, 1996.

Stibbe, M. W. G. "The Elusive Christ: A New Reading of the Fourth Gospel." *Journal for the Study of the New Testament* 44 (1991): 20–39.

———. *John*. Sheffield: JSOT Press, 1993.

———. *John as Storyteller*. Cambridge: Cambridge University Press, 1992.

———. *John's Gospel*. London: Routledge, 1994.

———. " 'Return to Sender': A Structuralist Approach to John's Gospel." *Biblical Interpretation* 1 (1993): 189–206.

Strathmann, H. "μάρτυς, κτλ," *TDNT* (1967): 4:474–508.

Talbert, C. H. *Reading John: A Literary and Theological Commentary on the Fourth Gospel and Johannine Epistles*. New York: Crossroad, 1992.

Tenney, M. C. "The Meaning of 'Witness' in John." *Bibliotheca sacra* 132 (1975): 229–41.

Thielman, F. "The Style of the Fourth Gospel and Ancient Literary Critical Concepts of Discourse." Pages 169–183 in *Persuasive Artistry*. Edited by D. F. Watson. Sheffield: JSOT Press, 1991.

Thiemann, R. *Revelation and Theology*. Notre Dame: University of Notre Dame Press, 1985.

Thiselton, A. C. *New Horizons in Hermeneutics*. London: HarperCollins, 1992.

Thomas Aquinas. *Summa theologica*. Chicago: Encyclopaedia Britannica, 1952.

Thomas, J. C. *Footwashing in John 13 and the Johannine Community*. Sheffield: JSOT Press, 1991.

Thompson, M. M. "'God's Voice You Have Never Heard, God's Form You Have Never Seen': The Characterization of God in the Gospel of John." *Semeia* 63 (1993): 177–204.

———. *The Humanity of Jesus in the Fourth Gospel*. Philadelphia: Fortress, 1988.

Thyen, H. "Johannes und die Synoptiker." Pages 81–107 in *John and the Synoptics*. Edited by A. Denaux. Leuven: Leuven University Press, 1992.

Todorov, T. *The Poetics of Prose*. Ithaca, N.Y.: Cornell University Press, 1977.

Tolmie, D. F. *Jesus' Farewell to the Disciples: John 13:1–17:26 in Narratological Perspective*. Leiden: E. J. Brill, 1995.

Tovey, D. *Narrative Art and Act in the Fourth Gospel*. Sheffield: Sheffield Academic Press, 1997.

Tracy, D. "Christian Witness and the Shoah." Pages 81–89 in *Holocaust Remembrance*. Edited by G. H. Hartman, Oxford: Blackwell, 1994.

Travis, S. H. *Christ and the Judgment of God*. London: Marshall Morgan & Scott, 1986.

Trites, A. A. *The New Testament Concept of Witness*. Cambridge: Cambridge University Press, 1977.

Uspensky, B. *A Poetics of Composition*. Translated by C. Zavarin and S. Wittig. Berkeley: University of California Press, 1973.

Vanhoozer, K. J. *Biblical Narrative in the Philosophy of Paul Ricoeur*. Cambridge: Cambridge University Press, 1990.

Volf, M. *Exclusion and Embrace*. Nashville: Abingdon, 1996.

Wahlde, U. C. von. "The Witnesses to Jesus in John 5:31–40 and Belief in the Fourth Gospel." *Catholic Biblical Quarterly* 43 (1981): 385–404.

Walsh, B. J. "Derrida and the Messiah." *re:generation quarterly* 5 (1999): 29–33.

Warner, M. "The Fourth Gospel's Art of Rational Persuasion." Pages 153–77 in *The Bible as Rhetoric*. Edited by M. Warner. London: Routledge, 1990.

Watson, F. *Text, Church, and World*. Grand Rapids: Eerdmans, 1994.

———. *Text and Truth*. Grand Rapids: Eerdmans, 1997.

Wengst, K. *Bedrängte Gemeinde und verherrlichter Christus*. Neukirchen-Vluyn: Neukirchener Verlag, 1981.

Westermann, C. *Basic Forms of Prophetic Speech*. London: Lutterworth, 1967.

———. *Isaiah 40–66*. London: SCM, 1969.

———. *Das Johannesevangelium aus der Sicht des Alten Testaments*. Stuttgart: Calwer, 1994.

———. "Sprache und Struktur der Prophetie Deuterojesajas." Pages 92–170 in C. Westermann, *Forschung am Alten Testament: Gesammelte Studien*. Munich: C. Kaiser, 1964.

White, H. "The Value of Narrativity in the Representation of Reality." *Critical Inquiry* 7 (1980): 5–27.

Whybray, R. N. *Isaiah 40–66*. London: Oliphants, 1975.

Wiesel, E. *Dimensions of the Holocaust*. Evanston, Ill.: Northwestern University Press, 1977.

Williams, R. *Resurrection*. London: Darton, Longman & Todd, 1982.

Wilson, S. G. *Related Strangers: Jews and Christians, 70–170 C.E.* Minneapolis: Fortress, 1995.

Wink, W. *Engaging the Powers*. Minneapolis: Fortress, 1992.

Woodman, A. J. *Rhetoric in Classical Historiography: Four Studies*. London: Croom Helm, 1988.

Young, F. W. "A Study of the Relation of Isaiah to the Fourth Gospel." *Zeitschrift für die neutestamentliche Wissenschaft und die Kunde der älteren Kirche* 46 (1955): 215–33.

INDEX OF MODERN AUTHORS

INDEX OF ANCIENT SOURCES

PSEUDEPIGRAPHA